PICTORIAL PRICE GUIDE TO AMERICAN ANTIQUES

SECOND EDITION

PICTORIAL PRICE GUIDE TO AMERICAN ANTIQUES

and Objects Made for the American Market

ALMOST 6000 OBJECTS IN 300 CATEGORIES ILLUSTRATED AND PRICED

BY

Dorothy Hammond

A Dutton  *Paperback*

E. P. DUTTON / NEW YORK

For information contact: E.P. Dutton, 2 Park Avenue,
New York, N.Y. 10016
Library of Congress Catalog Card Number: 78-74223

ISBN: 0-525-47517-6

Published simultaneously in Canada by Clarke, Irwin & Company
Limited, Toronto and Vancouver

10 9 8 7 6 5 4 3 2 1

First Edition

CONTENTS

KEY TO ABBREVIATIONS

Every item listed within this volume is keyed to either a dealer price, or an auction value. The letter "D" denotes "Dealer," whereas the letter "A" denotes an "Auction" price. The two letters that follow indicate the state, and the numbers indicate the year.

Abbreviations for the states included are:

Alabama ....AL	Maine ....ME	Ohio ....OH
Arizona ....AZ	Maryland ....MD	Oklahoma ....OK
Arkansas ....AR	Massachusetts ....MA	Oregon ....OR
California ....CA	Michigan ....MI	Pennsylvana ....PA
Colorado ....CO	Minnesota ....MN	Rhode Island ....RI
Connecticut ....CT	Mississippi ....MS	South Carolina ......SC
Delaware ....DE	Missouri ....MO	South Dakota ....SD
Florida ....FL	Montana ....MT	Tennessee ....TN
Georgia ....GA	Nebraska ....NE	Texas ....TX
Idaho ....ID	Nevada ....NV	Utah ....UT
Illinois IL	New Hampshire ....NH	Vermont ....VT
Indiana ....IN	New Jersey ....NJ	Virginia ....VA
Iowa ....IA	New Mexico ....NM	Washington ....WA
Kansas ....KS	New York ....NY	West Virginia ....WV
Kentucky ....KY	North Carolina ......NC	Wisconsin ....WI
Louisiana ....LA	North Dakota ....ND	Wyoming ....WY

ACKNOWLEDGEMENTS

This book would not have been possible without the assistance of many people. I am especially indebted to the many auction companies who have so generously provided photograph illustrations. I would like to express my deepest appreciation to: Richard A. Bourne, Company, Inc., Hyannis Port, MA; Garth Auctions, Inc., Delaware, OH; Gene Harris Antique Center, Marshalltown, IA; C.B. Charles' Galleries, Pontiac, MI; Laws Auctions & Antiques, Manassas, VA; Stratford Auction Center, Delaware, OH; Robert C. Eldred Company, Inc., East Dennis, MA; Brown Brothers, Buckingham, PA; Julia's Auction Barn, Fairfield, ME; and Pennypacker Auction Centre, Kenhorst, Reading, PA. I am also indebted to the following persons who have given me assistance in the compilation of photos: Melton's Antiques, Cheasapeake, VA; William S. Taylor, Old Town Farm Antiques, Peterborough, NH; Lee Vines, Hewlett, NY; G. Levine, photography, Hewlett, NY; Fred & Harriet Schuster, Platte Purchase Antiques, Gower, MO; Mona Smith, Cranberry Cottage, Payson, AZ; Eula Fraser, Fairfax, MO; Homestead Antiques, Harper, KS; Crazy Horse Antiques, Lenox, MA; Fisher's Antiques, Eldorado, KS; Garner Settle, The Old House, Richmond, MO; Hope Farm Antiques, Hope, ME; and Jim & Jane Apuzzo, Round Mountain Country Antiques, Hopewell Jct., NY.

To Gail Hendry go my deepest thanks for her invaluable assistance in organizing the thousands of entries, and to Linda Kice and Carey Witham for assisting. I am also very grateful to Cynthia Worl and Barbara Hart for their assistance in compiling entries.

INTRODUCTION

The second edition of PICTORIAL PRICE GUIDE TO AMERICAN ANTIQUES includes approximately 6,000 items within 12 sections: Ceramics, Clocks, Dolls, Furniture, Glass, Kitchenwares and Metals, Lighting, Paintings, Pictures and Prints, Textiles, Toys, Weapons and Miscellaneous. The latter includes photos of multiple items, in addition to many singular items, when there were not enough photos available in a particular field to structure a complete section. The majority of the items included here date from the nineteenth or early twentieth century, with information necessary to make accurate identification.

Each entry is keyed to an auction price or a dealer's price. A state abbreviation has been included for the readers' convenience, since prices vary in different locations across the country. Additionally, the year each item was either noted in an antiques shop, shown or sold in an auction, has been indicated. This unique method of pricing objects makes this price guide extremely helpful to the antiques dealer or collector.

As people everywhere are becoming more and more aware auctions constitute really the best method for both buying and selling objects of value, the majority of the entries were taken from auctions. Every effort has been made not to include an item that has sold for an unrealistic figure — because, on occasion a group of acquisitive, auction-loving buyers with money to spend, can send prices up to ridiculous levels.

Furniture — especially fine period pieces along with quality pieces of country furniture continue to set record prices. Twentieth-century golden oak pieces are very much in demand throughout the country, and several New England antiques dealers have begun to stock their shops with choice pieces. American art pottery, toys, art, clocks, lamps of all types, weapons, kitchenwares from all periods, art glass, and American glassware from the 1930-60 period, are especially in demand and increasing steadily in value. And the nostalgia craze for advertising items has again sent prices soaring — especially for choice items.

Every attempt has been made to record accurate and correct information. However, the writer cannot be responsible in the event of clerical or typographical errors that may have occurred.

Dorothy Hammond

ABC PLATES - Alphabet plates were made especially for children as teaching aids. They date from the late 1700s, and were made of various material including porcelain, pottery, glass, pewter, tin and ironstone.

AMPHORA ART POTTERY was made at the Amphora Porcelain Works in the Teplitz-Turn area of Bohemia during the late 19th and early 20th centuries. Numerous potteries were located here.

BATTERSEA ENAMELS - The name "Battersea" is a general term for those metal objects decorated with enamels, such as pill, patch, and snuff boxes, door knobs, etc. The process of fusing enamel onto metal — usually copper — began about 1750 in the Battersea District of London. Today, the name has become a generic term for similar objects — mistakenly called "Battersea."

BELLEEK porcelain was first made at Fermanaugh, Ireland in 1857. Today, this ware is still being made in buildings within walking distance of the original clay pits according to the skills and traditions of the original artisans. Irish Belleek is famous for its thinness and delicacy. Similar type wares were also produced in other European countries as well as the United States.

BENNINGTON POTTERY - The first pottery works in Bennington, Vermont was established by Captain John Norton in 1793; and, for 101 years, it was owned and operated by succeeding generations of Nortons. Today, the term "Bennington" is synonymous with the finest in American ceramics because the town was the home of several pottery operations during the last century — each producing under different labels. Today, items produced at Bennington are now conveniently, if inaccurately, dubbed "Bennington." One of the popular types of pottery produced here is known as "Rockingham." The term denotes the rich, solid brown glazed pottery from which many household items were made. The ware was first produced by the Marquis of Rockingham in Swinton, England — hence the name.

BISQUE - The term applies to pieces of porcelain or pottery which have been fired, but left in an unglazed state.

BLOOR DERBY - "Derby" porcelain dates from about 1755 when William Duesbury began the production of porcelain at Derby. In 1769, he purchased the famous Chelsea Works and operated both factories. During this Chelsea-Derby period, some of the finest examples of English porcelains were made. Because of their fine quality, in 1773 King George III gave Duesbury the patent to mark his porcelain wares "Crown Derby." Duesbury died in 1796. In 1810, the factory was purchased by Robert Bloor, a senior clerk. Bloor revived the Imari styles which had been so popular. After his death in 1845, former workmen continued to produce fine porcelains using the traditional Derby patterns. The firm was reorganized in 1876 and in 1878, a new factory was built. In 1890, Queen Victoria appointed the company "Manufacturers to Her Majesty," with the right to be known as Royal Crown Derby.

BUFFALO POTTERY - The Buffalo Pottery of Buffalo, New York, was organized in 1901. The firm was an adjunct of the Larkin Soap Company, which was established to produce china and pottery premiums for that company. Of the many different types produced, the Buffalo Pottery is most famous for their "Deldare" line which was developed in 1905.

CANARY LUSTRE earthenware dates to the early 1800s, and was produced by potters in the Staffordshire District of England. The body of this ware is a golden yellow and decorated with transfer printing, usually in black.

CANTON porcelain is a blue-and-white decorated ware produced near Canton, China from the late 1700s through the last century. Its hand-decorated Chinese scenes have historical as well as mythological significance.

CAPO-di-MONTE, originally a soft paste porcelain, is Italian in origin. The first ware was made during the 1700s near Naples. Although numerous marks were used, the most familiar to us is the crown over the letter "N". Mythological subjects, executed in either high or low relief and tinted in bright colors on a light ground, were a favorite decoration. The earlier ware has a peculiar greyish color as compared to later examples which have a whiter body.

CARLSBAD porcelain was made by several factories in the area from the late 1800s and exported to the United States. When Carlsbad became a part of Czechoslovakia after World War I, wares were frequently marked "Karlsbad." Items marked "Victoria" were made for Lazarus & Rosenfeldt, Importers.

CASTLEFORD earthenware was produced in England from the late 1700s until around 1820. Its molded decoration is similar to Pratt Wares.

CHINESE EXPORT PORCELAIN was made in quantity in China during the 1700s and early 1800s. The term identifies a variety of porcelain wares made for export to Europe and the United States. Since many thought the product to be of joint Chinese and English manufacture, it has also been known as "Oriental or Chinese Lowestoft."

As much of this ware was made to order for the American and European market, it was frequently adorned with seals of states or the coats of arms of individuals, in addition to eagles, sailing scenes, flowers, religious and mythological scenes.

CLEWS POTTERY - see also, Historical Staffordshire - was made by George Clews & Co., of Brownhill Pottery, Tunstall, England from 1806-1861.

CLIFTON POTTERY was founded by William Long in Clifton, New Jersey, in 1905.

COALPORT porcelain has been made by the Coalport Porcelain Works in England since 1795. The ware is still being produced at Stroke-on-Trent.

COPELAND-SPODE - The firm was founded by Josiah Spode in 1770 in Staffordshire, England. From 1847 W. T. Copeland & Sons, Ltd., succeeded Spode, using the designation "Late Spode" to their wares. The firm is still in operation.

COPPER LUSTRE - See Lustre Wares

CROWN DUCAL - English porcelain made by the A.G. Richardson & Co., Ltd., since 1916.

CUP PLATES were used where cups were handleless and saucers were deep. During the early 1800s, it was very fashionable to drink from a saucer. Thus, a variety of fancy small plates were produced for the cup to rest in. The lacy Sandwich examples are very collectible.

DAVENPORT pottery and porcelain were made at the Davenport Factory in Longport, Staffordshire, England by John Davenport — from 1793 until 1887 when the pottery closed. Most of the wares produced here — porcelains, creamwares, ironstone, earthenwares and other products — were marked.

DEDHAM - (Chelsea Art Works) - The firm was founded in 1872 at Chelsea, Massachusetts by James Robertson & Sons, and closed in 1889. In 1891, the pottery was reopened under the name of The Chelsea Pottery, U.S. The first and most popular blue underglaze decoration for the desirable "Cracque Ware" was the rabbit motif — designed by Joseph L. Smith. In 1893, construction was started on the new pottery in Dedham, Massachusetts and production began in 1895. The name of the pottery was then changed to "Dedham Pottery," to eliminate confusion with the English Chelsea Ware. The famed crackleware finish became synonymous with the name. Because of its popularity, over fifty patterns of tableware were made.

DELFT - Holland is famous for its fine examples of tin-glazed pottery dating from the 16th century. Although blue and white is the most popular color, other colors were also made. The majority of the ware found today is from the late Victorian period and, when the name Holland appears with the Deflt factory mark, this indicates that the item was made after 1891.

DORCHESTER POTTERY was established by George Henderson in Dorchester, a part of Boston, in 1895. Production included stonewares, industrial wares, and later some decorated tablewares. The pottery is still in production.

DOULTON - The Pottery was established in Lambeth in 1815 by John Doulton and John Watts. When Watts retired in 1854, the firm became known as Doulton & Company. In 1901, King Edward VII conferred a double honor on the company by presentation of the Royal Warrant, authorizing their chairman to use the word "Royal" in describing products. A variety of wares has been made over the years for the American market. The firm is still in production.

DRESDEN, See Meissen

FLOWING BLUE ironstone is a highly glazed dinnerware made at Staffordshire by a variety of potters. It became popular about 1825. Items were printed with the patterns (oriental), and the color flowed from the design over the white body so that the finished product appeared smeared. Although purple and brown colors were also made, the deep cobalt blue shades were the most popular. Later wares were less blurred, having more white ground.

GAUDY DUTCH is the most spectacular of the Gaudy wares. It was made for the Pennsylvania Dutch market from about 1785 until the 1820s. This soft paste tableware is lightweight and frail in appearance. Its rich cobalt blue decoration was applied to the biscuit, glazed and fired — then other colors were applied over the first glaze — and the object was fired again. No lustre is included in its decoration.

GAUDY IRONSTONE was made in Staffordshire from the early 1850s until around 1865. This ware is heavier than Gaudy Welsh or Gaudy Dutch, as its texture is a mixture of pottery and porcelain clay.

GAUDY WELSH, produced in England from about 1830, resembles Gaudy Dutch in decoration, but the workmanship is not as fine and its texture is more comparable to that of spatterware. Lustre is usually included with the decoration.

HISTORICAL STAFFORDSHIRE - The term refers to a particular blue-on-white, transfer- printed earthenware produced in quantity during the early 1800s by many potters in the Staffordshire District. The central decoration was usually an American city scene or landscape, frequently showing some mode of transportation in the foreground. Other designs included portraits and patriotic emblems. Each potter had a characteristic border which is helpful to identify a particular ware, as many pieces are unmarked. Later transfer-printed wares were made in sepia, pink, green and black, but the early cobalt blue examples are the most desirable.

IRONSTONE is a heavy, durable, utilitarian ware made from the slag of iron furnaces, ground and mixed with clay. Charles Mason of Lane Delft, Staffordshire, patented the formula in 1813. Much of the early ware was decorated in imitation of Imari, in addition to transfer-printed blue ware, flowing blues and browns. During the mid-nineteenth century, the plain white enlivened only by embossed designs became fashionable. Literally hundreds of patterns were made for export.

JACKFIELD POTTERY is English in origin. It was first produced during the 17th century, however most items available today date from the last century. It is a red-bodied pottery, oftentimes decorated with scrolls and flowers in relief, then covered with a black glaze.

JUGTOWN POTTERY - This North Carolina pottery has been made since the 18th century. In 1915, Jacques Busbee organized what is to become the Jugtown Pottery in 1921. Production was discontinued in 1958.

KING'S ROSE is a decorated creamware produced in the Staffordshire district of England during the 1820-1840 period. The rose decorations are usually in red, green, yellow and pink. This ware is often referred to as "Queen's Rose."

LEEDS POTTERY was established by Charles Green in 1758 at Leed, Yorkshire, England. Early wares are unmarked. From 1775, the impressed mark, "Leeds Pottery" was used. After 1800, the name "Hartly, Green & Co." was added, and the impressed or incised letters "L P" were also used to identify the ware.

LIMOGES - The name identifies fine porcelain wares produced by many factories at Limoges, France since the mid-1900s. A variety of different marks identify wares made here including Haviland china.

LIVERPOOL POTTERY - The term applies to wares produced by many potters located in Liverpool, England from the early 1700s, for American trade. Their print-decorated pitchers - referred to as "jugs" in England - have been especially popular. These featured patriotic emblems, prominent men, ships, etc., and can be easily identified as nearly all are melon-shaped with a very pointed lip, strap handle and graceful curved body.

LUSTRE WARES - John Hancock of Hanley, England invented this type of decoration on earthenwares during the early 1800s. The copper, bronze, ruby, gold, purple, yellow, pink and mottled pink lustre finishes were made from gold - painted on the glazed objects, then fired. The latter type is often referred to as "Sunderland Lustre." Its pinkish tones vary in color and pattern. The silver lustres were made from platinum.

McCOY POTTERY - The J.W. McCoy Pottery was established in 1899. Production of art pottery did not begin until after 1926, when the name was changed to Brush McCoy.

METTLACH, Germany, located in the Zoar Basin, was the location of the famous Villeroy & Boch factories from 1836 until 1921 when the factory was destroyed by fire. Steins (dating from about 1842) and other stonewares with bas relief decoration were their specialty.

MOCHA WARE - This banded creamware was first produced in England during the late 1700s. The early ware was lightweight and thin, having colorful bands of bright colors decorating its cream-colored to very light brown body. After 1840, the ware became heavier in body and the color was oftentimes quite light - almost white. Mocha Ware can easily be identified by its colorful banded decorations - on and between the bands, including feathery ferns, lacy trees, seaweeds, squiggly designs and lowly earthworms.

NILOAK POTTERY with its prominent swirled, marbleized designs, is a 20th century pottery first produced at Benton, Arkansas in 1911 by the Niloak Pottery Company. Production ceased in 1946.

NIPPON porcelain has been produced in quantity for the American market since the late 19th century. After 1891, when it became obligatory to include the country of origin on all imports, the Japanese trademark "Nippon" was used. Numerous other marks appear on this ware identifying the manufacturer, artist or importer. The hand painted Nippon examples are extremely popular today and prices are on the rise.

OWENS POTTERY was made from 1891 to 1928 at Zanesville, Ohio. The first art pottery was produced after 1896. Their different lines included Utopian Ware, Navarre, Feroza, Cyrano and Henri Deux. Art pottery was discontinued about 1907.

PISGAH FOREST POTTERY - The pottery was founded near Mt. Pisgah in North Carolina in 1914 by Walter B. Stephen. The pottery remains in operation.

REDWARE is one of our most popular forms of country pottery. It has a soft, porous body and its color varies from reddish-brown tones to deep wine or light orange. It was produced in mostly utilitarian forms by potters in small factories or by potters working on their farms, to fill their everyday needs. Glazes were used to intensify the color. The most desirable examples are the slip-decorated pieces, or the rare and expensive "sgraffito" examples which have scratched or incised line decoration. This type of decoration was for ornamentation, since examples were rarely used for ordinary utilitarian purposes, but were given as gifts. Hence, these highly prized pieces rarely show wear, indicating that they were treasured as ornaments only. Slip decoration was made by tracing the design on the redware shape with a clay having a creamy consistency in contrasting colors. When dried, the design was slightly raised above the surface. Because these pieces were made for practical usage, the potter then pressed or beat the slip decoration into the surface of the object.

RED WING POTTERY of Red Wing, MN was founded in 1878. The firm began producing art pottery during the 1920s. The pottery closed in 1967.

ROCKINGHAM, See Bennington Pottery.

ROOKWOOD POTTERY - The Rookwood Pottery began production at Cincinnati, Ohio in 1880 under the direction of Maria Longworth Nichols Storer, and operated until 1960. The name was derived from the family estate, "Rookwood," because of the "rooks" or "crows" which inhabited the wooded areas. All pieces of this art pottery are marked, usually bearing the famous flame.

RORSTRAND FAIENCE - The firm was founded in 1726 near Stockholm, Sweden. Items dating from the early 1900's and having an "art nouveau" influence are very much in demand these days and expensive.

ROSE MEDALLION ware dates from the eighteenth century. It was decorated and exported from Canton, China in quantity. The name generally applied to those pieces having medallions with figures of people alternating with panels of flowers, birds and butterflies. When all the medallions were filled with flowers, the ware was differentiated as Rose Canton.

ROSEVILLE POTTERY - The Roseville Pottery was organized in 1890 in Roseville, Ohio. The firm produced utilitarian stoneware in the plant formerly owned by the Owens Pottery. In 1898, the firm acquired the Midland Pottery of Roseville, also producers of stoneware, and the Linden Avenue Plant at Zanesville, Ohio, originally built by the Clark Stoneware Company. In 1900, an art line of pottery was created to compete with Owens and Weller lines. The new ware was named "Rozane," and it was produced at the Zanesville location. Following its success, other prestige lines were created. The Azurine line was introduced about 1902.

ROYAL BAYREUTH manufactory began in Tettau in 1794 at the first porcelain factory in Bavaria. Wares made here were on the same par with Meissen. Fire destroyed the original factory during the late 1800s. Much of the wares available today were made at the new factory which began production in 1897. These include Rose Tapestry, Sunbonnet Baby novelties and the Devil and Card items. The Royal Bayreuth blue mark has the 1794 founding date incorporated with the mark.

From 1946 to 1949, the firm reproduced some Tapestry and Devil and Card items, using the Royal Bayreuth crest, but the color of the mark was changed to light green.

ROYAL BONN - The trade name identifies a vareity of porcelain items made during the 19th century by the Bonn China Manufactory, established in 1755 by Clemers August. Most of the ware found today is from the Victorian period.

ROYAL DOULTON wares have been made from 1901, when King Edward VII conferred a double honor on the Doulton Pottery by the presentation of the Royal Warrant, authorizing their chairman to use the word "Royal" in describing products. A variety of wares have been produced for the American market. The firm is still in production.

ROYAL DUX was produced in Bohemia during the late 1800s. Large quantities of this decorative porcelain ware were exported to the United States. Royal Dux figurines are especially popular.

ROYAL WORCESTER - The Worcester factory was established in 1751 in England. This is a tastefully decorated porcelain noted for its creamy white lustreless surface. Serious collectors prefer items from the Dr. Wall (the activator of the concern) period of production which extended from the time the factory was established to 1785.

ROYCROFT POTTERY was made by the Roycrofter community of East Aurora, NY during the late 19th and early 20th centuries. The firm was founded by Elbert Hubbard. Products produced here included pottery, furniture, metalware, jewelry and leather-work.

R. S. PRUSSIA porcelain was produced during the mid-1800s by Erdman Schlegelmilch in Suhl. His brother Reinhold founded a factory in 1869 in Tillowitz in lower Silesia. Both made fine quality porcelain, using both satin and high gloss finishes with comparable decoration. Additionally, both brothers used the same R. S. mark in the same colors, the initials being in memory of their father, Rudolph Schlegelmilch. It has not been determined when production at the two factories ceased.

SAMPSON WARE dates from the early 19th century. The firm was founded in Paris, and reproduced a variety of collectibles wares including Chelsea, Meissen and Oriental Lowestoft, with marks which distinguish their wares as reproductions. The firm is still in production.

SATSUMA is a Japanese pottery having a distinctive creamy crackled glaze decorated with bright enamels and oftentimes Japanese faces. The majority of the ware available today includes the mass produced wares dating from the 1850s. Their quality does not compare to the fine early examples.

SPATTERWARE is a soft paste tableware, laboriously decorated with hand-drawn flowers, birds, buildings, trees, etc., with "spatter" decoration chiefly as a background. It was produced by almost every export potter in Staffordshire, Scotland and Wales, for the American market. A variety of patterns were produced in considerable quantity from the early 1800s to around 1850.

To achieve this type decoration, small bits of sponge was cut into different shapes - leaves, hearts, rosettes, vines, geometrical patterns, etc. - and mounted on the end of a short stick for convenience in dipping into the pigment.

SPONGEWARE, as it is known, is a decorated white earthenware. Color - usually blue, blue/green, brown/tan/blue, or blue/brown - was applied to the white clay base. Because the color was often applied with a color-soaked sponge, the term "spongeware" became common for this ware. A variety of utilitarian items were produced - pitchers, cookie jars, bean pots, water coolers, etc. Marked examples are rare.

STAFFORDSHIRE is a district in England where a variety of pottery and porcelain wares have been produced by many factories in the area.

STICKSPATTER - The term identifies a type of decoration that combines hand painting and transfer-painted decoration. "Spattering" was done with either a sponge or a brush containing a moderate supply of pigment. Stick-spatter was developed from the traditional Staffordshire spatterware, as the earlier ware was time-consuming and expensive to produce. Although the majority of this ware was made in England from the 1850s to the late 1800s, it was also produced in Holland, France and elsewhere. Examples of this later were occasionally marked.

TEA LEAF is a lightweight stone china decorated with copper or gold "tea leaf" sprigs. It was first made by Anthony Shaw of Longport, England during the 1850s. By the late 1800s, other potters in Staffordshire were producing the popular ware for export to the United States. As the result, there is a noticeable version in decoration.

TECO POTTERY, an art pottery line made by the Terra Cotta Tile Works of Terra Cotta, IL. The firm was organized in 1881 by William D. Gates. The Teco line was first made in 1902 and was discontinued during the 1920s.

VAN BRIGGLE POTTERY was established at Colorado Springs, Colorado in 1900 by Artus Van Briggle and his wife Anna. Most of the ware was marked. The first mark included two joined "A's", representing their first two initials. The firm is still in operation.

VILLEROY & BOCH - See Mettlock

WEDGWOOD POTTERY was established by Josiah Wedgwood in 1759 in England. A tremendous variety of fine wares have been produced through the years including basalt, lustre wares, creamware, jasperware, bisque, agate, Queen's Ware and others. The system of marks used by the firm clearly indicates when each piece was made.

Since 1940, the new Wedgwood factory has been located at Barleston.

WELLER POTTERY - Samuel A. Weller established the Weller Pottery in 1872 in Fultonham, Ohio. In 1888, the pottery was moved to Piece Street in Putnam, Ohio - now a part of Zanesville, Ohio. The production of art pottery began in 1893 and, by late 1897, several prestige lines were being produced including Samantha, Touranda and Dickens' Ware. Other later types included Weller's Louwelsa, Eosian, Aurora, Turada and the rare Sicardo which is the most sought after and most expensive today. The firm closed in 1948.

(A-IA '78)   *Gene Harris Antique Center*
HAVILAND, Silver Anniversary Patt., 12 Dinner Plates, 12 Bouillon Cups, 11 Cups, 11 Saucers, 10 Sauce Dishes, 1 Oval Veg. Dish, 2 Platters, Creamer & Sugar, Gravy Boat, Cov. Tureen, Round Veg. Dish, Oblong Relish, 5-8'' Plates, 8-6'' Plates, 2 Butter Pats $910.00

(A-IA '78)   *Gene Harris Antique Center*
HAVILAND, Leonard Vienna Patt., 9-10'' Plates, 12-8½'' Plates, 11-7½'' Plates, 8 Soups, 12 Butter Pats, 12 Bone Dishes, 14 Saucers, 11 Cups, 2 Cov. Tureens, Cov. Gravy W/Plate, Pedestal Compote, Platter, Leaf-Shaped Tray, Sq. Cake Plate, Coffee Pot, & Oval Boat Bowl $425.00

(A-IA '78)   *Gene Harris Antique Center*
HAVILAND, Silver Anniversary Patt. W/ Pink Apple Blossoms, 12-10'' Plates, 13-8½'' Plates, 13-7'' Plates, 12 Soups, 22 Sauce Dishes, 4 Bone Dishes, 10 Butter Pats, 16 Cups, 17 Saucers, 1 Round Bowl, 1-11'' Chop Plate, Relish Dish, Gravy Tureen (Cov.), Platter, Coffee Pot & Cake Plate $1550.00

(A-IA '78)   *Gene Harris Antique Center*
HAVILAND, Purple Violets, No. 148 A., 15-10'' Plates, 13-9'' Plates, 14-8'' Plates, 11-6'' Plates, 16 Soups, 20 Sauce Dishes, 12 Cups, 23 Saucers, 17 Butter Pats, 3 Platters, 3 Oval Veg. Bowls, 2 Cov. Tureens, 3 Pc. Butter, 8-Demi. Cups & Saucers, 4 Extra Saucers $900.00

(A-IA '78)   *Gene Harris Antique Center*
HAVILAND, Forget-Me-Not (Blue Flowers), 13-10'' Dinner Plates, 16-8½'' Plates, 5-7½'' Plates, 13-7½'' Plates, 12 Sauces, 13 Cups, 14 Saucers, 2 Soups, 2 Waste Bowls, 1 Cov. Tureen, 2 Open Bowls, Gravy Boat, Relish Dish, Creamer & Sugar, Water Pitcher & 2 Platters $1100.00

(A-IA '78)   *Gene Harris Antique Center*
HAVILAND, Yellow Princess Patt. W/Gold Trim, 12-10'' Plates, 12-8½'' Plates, 9-7½'' Plates, 11-6'' Plates, 6-5'' Sauces, 6-5½'' Sauces, 7 Butter Pats, 12 Cups (3 Repaired), 19 Saucers, 3 Relish Dishes, Creamer, Sugar, Waste Bowl, Covered Tureen (Lid Cracked) $375.00

(A-IA '78)   *Gene Harris Antique Center*
HAVILAND, 12-10'' Plates, 12-8'' Plates, 11 Cups, 12 Saucers, 12 Soups, 12 Butter Pats, 12 Sauces, 5 Service Pcs. $200.00

(A-IA '78)   *Gene Harris Antique Center*
HAVILAND, 10-10'' Plates, 12 Soups, 10-8'' Plates, 10-7½'' Plates, 11 Sm. Sauces, 7 Reg. Size Sauces, 4 Cups, 9 Saucers, 3 Platters, 2 Cov. Tureens (1 W/Crack), 3 Veg. Bowls, & Soup Tureen $325.00

(A-IA '78)   *Gene Harris Antique Center*
HAVILAND, Yellow Princess Patt., 12-10'' Plates, 9-8'' Plates, 5-6'' Plates, 8 Sauces, 12 Cups, 14 Saucers, 1 Shallow Veg. Bowl $500.00

(A-MA '78)   Richard A. Bourne Co., Inc.

◀ *To the left*

HAND-PAINTED NIPPON CHINA
(ROW I)
LIDDED SUGAR & CREAMER, Non-Matching, Minor Wear To Gold Decoration, Faint Age Crack In Sugar Bowl On Side $30.00
TEA STRAINER, ...$90.00
OVAL RELISH DISH, W/Landscape Scene, 8¼" L. $15.00
(ROW II)
THREE-LEAF-CLOVER SHAPED BOWL, W/Small Handles, Decorated W/Landscape And Birch Tree, 7" Diam. ......
...................................$20.00
PLATE, Decorated W/Windmill, 6⅝" Diam.
...................................$10.00
PLATE, Decorated W/Seascape, Mt. Fujiama In The Background, 7⅛" Diam. .....
...................................$100.00
PLATE, Decorated W/Landscape Surrounded By Fruit & Flowers, 7⅝" Diam. ..
...................................$10.00
(ROW III)
PLATE/PLAQUE, Made In Occupied Japan, Marked "Hadson China" W/Anchor, 8⅛" Diam. $5.00
LARGE PLAQUE, W/Egyptian Desert Scene, 10⅛" Diam. $90.00
PLAQUE, Made In Occupied Japan, Marked "Aiyo China", 8" Diam. $15.00

(A-MA '78)   Richard A. Bourne Co., Inc.
HAND-PAINTED NIPPON CHINA
(ROW I)
ROSE PETAL GINGER JAR OR TEA CADDY, W/Large Yellow Roses .$125.00
MUG, Marbleized Finish W/Band Of Desert Ruins Painted Around Outside, Slight Star-Shaped Crack In Glaze On Bottom, Hold On Handle Is Slightly Worn $40.00
CABINET VASE, Medallion On One Side W/Landscape Scene Surrounded By Flow-
(continued next column)

◀ *To the left*   *(continued)*
ers, 5⅞" H. $40.00
SUGAR SHAKER $90.00
VASE, W/All-Around Snowscape, 6¼" H.
...................................$30.00
(ROW II)
SMALL DIAMOND-SHAPED DISH, W/Flat Ends, Decor. W/Landscape, Lake And Sailboat $10.00
PORCELAIN NAPPY OR ASH TRAY W/HANDLE, Painted W/Nile Scene ..$15.00
DISH, W/Open Handles, Decor. W/River Scene And Boat, 5½" Diam. $20.00
FERNERY, 6" L. $50.00
(ROW III)
RELISH DISH, W/Open Handles, 9" L.
...................................$15.00
OBLONG DISH, W/Tiny Open Handles, Decorated W/Sunset Scene And Sailboats On Calm Water, 8" L. $30.00
CANOE-SHAPED BOAT, Decor. W/Dutch Landscape And Large Windmill, 7" L. .....
...................................$30.00
(ROW IV)
COVERED BISCUIT JAR, 6½" Diam.
...................................$80.00
TWO-PIECE DRESSER SET, Consisting Of Powder Jar & Hair Receiver, Each Supported By French-Style Legs $80.00
BERRY BOWL W/UNDERTRAY, Perforated Bottom In Bowl, Gold And Polychrome Floral Decor. W/Green Border Design, 6" Diam. $110.00

(A-MA '78)   Richard A. Bourne Co., Inc.
HAND-PAINTED NIPPON CHINA

(ROW I)
VASE, W/Egyptian Desert Scene Painted All Around, Green Nippon, 9½" H. ......
...................................$250.00
VASE, W/Scene Of Indian In Canoe Against Background Of Forest Painted Around Entire Body Of Piece, 8¾" H. $250.00
VASE, W/Floral Band Around Bottom And Desert Ruins Around The Main Body Of The Piece, 8¾" H. $200.00

(ROW II)
PAIR OF VASES, (1 Illus.), W/Floral Painting Overall, Large Pink Flowers, 8½" H. ..
...................................$275.00
SEVEN-PIECE NUT SET, (3 Illus.), Including A Large Hand-Painted Bowl And Six Individual Circular Dishes Painted To Match, Bowl Diam. 7¼" $125.00

◀ *To the left*

(A-MA '78)　　　　　*Richard A. Boume Co., Inc.*

DEDHAM POTTERY
(ROW I, L to R)
SMALL PLATE, Duck Patt. (Pre-1929), Minor Edge Roughage Retouched, 6" Diam. $35.00
SMALL PLATE, Rabbit Patt. (Pre-1929), 6" Diam. $40.00
PLATE, Pond Lily Patt. (Pre-1929), 6" Diam. $35.00
(ROW II, L to R)
DISH, Possibly An Early Piece Of Chelsea, Resembles Early Dedham Pieces, Dragon Decor., Two Open Bubbles In Rim, 7⅜" Diam. $90.00
PENTAGONAL DISH, Swan patt. (1929-1943), Maximum Diam. 7⅜" $200.00
HEAVY PLATE OR TEAPOT STAND, Owl Patt., One Rim Chip On Upper Rim, 7½" Diam. $300.00
(ROW III, L to R)
PLATE, Lobster Patt., W/Underglaze Blue Mark Of Numeral & Two Incised Rabbits, 7½"f Diam. $150.00
PLATE, Tapestry Lion Patt. (Pre-1929), 8½" Diam. $275.00
BOWL, Rabbit Patt. (1929-43), Flaring Rim, Dated 1931, 7⅞" Diam. $125.00

(A-MA '78)　　　*Richard A. Boume Co., Inc.*

DEDHAM POTTERY
(ROW I, L to R)
BOWL OR HANDLELESS CUP, Elephant Patt. (1929-1943), 3" Diam. $275.00
BOWL, Elephant Patt., 4½" Diam. $200.00
BOWL, Horse Chestnut Patt. (Pre-1929), Shallow Chip On Rim, Irregular Shape, 5¼" Diam. $50.00
CUP & SAUCER, Small, Rabbit Patt. (1929-1943) $75.00
(ROW II, L to R)
CUP & SAUCER, Grape Patt. (Pre-1929) $60.00
CUP & SAUCER, Large, Rabbit Patt. $80.00
(continued top of next column)

(continued)
PLATE, Concentric Blue Rings On Plain Ground, Underglaze Blue & Incised Rabbit Mark (Pre-1929), 6" Diam. $40.00
(ROW III, L to R)
SUGAR BOWL, Covered, Turtle Patt. (Pre-1929) $175.00
PLATE, Grape Patt. (Pre-1929), 8⅝" Diam. $45.00
TERCENTENARY BOWL, Rabbit Patt., 6⅛" Diam. $75.00

(A-MA '78)　　　*Richard A. Boume Co., Inc.*
PAIR OF OXBLOOD CHELSEA POTTERY VASES Made By Grand-Pa Robinson In Chelsea Before He Moved To Dedham, MA In The Early 1900s. Vases Are Decorated W/Small White Flowers W/ Leaves, Some Splash-On Yellow-Green & Brown Coloring, Mint, 5⅞" H. ...$275.00

(A-MA '78)　　　*Richard A. Boume Co., Inc.*
DEDHAM POTTERY
(ROW I, L to R)
EGG CUP, Rabbit Patt., Initials "DP" Under Foot........................$80.00
CREAMER, Rabbit Patt., Minor Rim Roughage At Spout....................$50.00
OPEN SUGAR BOWL, Rabbit Patt., About Perfect $100.00
PLATE, Rabbit Patt., 6⅛" Diam. ..$40.00
(ROW II, L to R)
PLATE, Rabbit Patt., Discoloration In Rim Between Rabbits, 8½" Diam. $30.00
OBLONG PLATTER, Rabbit Patt., About Perfect, 9¾" L. $150.00
TANKARD-SHAPED CREAMER, Rabbit Patt., 5⅛" H. $150.00
(ROW III, L to R)
BOWL, Rabbit Patt., About Perfect, 8" Diam.........................$110.00
SQUARE BOWL, Unusual Shape, Rabbit Patt., 8½"f Sq. $120.00
BOWL W/Flaring Rim, Rabbit Patt., 7½" Diam. $140.00

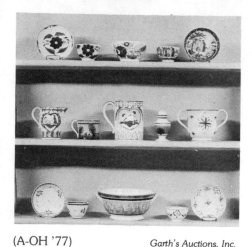

(A-OH '77)   *Garth's Auctions, Inc.*
(ROW I, L to R)
LEEDS CUP & SAUCER, No Handles, Gaudy Single Flower Decor. In Blue, Green, Brown, Yellow & Yellow Ochre, Sm. Flake On Saucer Table Ring..........$100.00
KING'S ROSE BOWL, Professionally Repaired, Base Hairline, 5½'' Diam., 3'' H. .
..............................$50.00
SOFT PASTE CUP & SAUCER, Black Transfer, Yellow Rim, Chip On Saucer Table Ring, Chip & Roughness On Cup ..$15.00
(ROW II, L to R)
PRATT CREAMER, Heart Reserves W/ "Mischievous Sport", & "Sportive—erce", 5 Colors, Minor Chip & Roughness On Spout, 4¾'' H. $195.00
MOCHA MUG, Blue-Green W/Brown Seaweed Decor. & Embossed Rim W/Green & Brown Stripes, Minor Hairline, 3'' H. ......
..............................$145.00
PRATT MUG, Children In Heart Reserves, 5 Colors, 6'' H. $45.00
MOCHA SHAKER, Orange Band W/ Brown Stripes & Brown Seaweed Decor., Minor Roughness, 4½'' H. $220.00
LEEDS LOVING CUP, Blue & Yellow Ochre Decor., Professionally Repaired, 4¾'' H..............................$115.00
(ROW III, L to R)
LEEDS CUP & SAUCER, No Handles, Ribbed W/Sprigs Of Flowers, 4 Colors, Rim Chips On Cup $65.00
MOCHA BOWL, Open Handles, Sand Colored Band W/Earthworm Decor. & White & Drk. Brown Stripes, Green Embossed Rim, Professionally Repaired, 8½'' Diam., 4'' H. $35.00
LEEDS CUP & SAUCER, Floral Design, 4 Colors, Sm. Glaze Flake Near Base Of Cup $70.00

To the right ▶
(L to R)
STAFFORDSHIRE TEAPOT, Blue Transfer Seaweed Design, 9'' H........$40.00
SALT GLAZE TEAPOT, Pewter Lid, Embossed Floral Design, 6'' H. $15.00
SPATTERWARE PLATES, (1 of 6), Underglaze Blue W/Red & Green, 2 W/Edge Chips, 1 Damaged, 9¼'' Diam. $60.00

(A-OH '77)   *Garth's Auctions, Inc.*
(ROW I)
SOFT PASTE PLATE, Polychrome Enameled W/Chinoiserie Decor. W/Purple Luster, 10'' Diam. $90.00
HISTORICAL BLUE STAFFORDSHIRE PLATTER, "R. Hall's Select Views, Gryn, Flintshire Wales, Stone China," Drk. Blue Transfer, Inner Rim Chip, 17'' L. .$180.00
(ROW II, L to R)
HISTORICAL BLUE STAFFORDSHIRE PLATE, "Fair Mount Near Philadelphia," Impressed "Stubbs," Eagle Border, 10¼'' Diam. $95.00
SALT GLAZE SYRUP, Embossed Gothic Arches W/Religous Figures, Lt. Blue Impressed Registry Mark "York Minster Jug, Charles Meigh, Nov. 12, 1846," 7½'' H. .
..............................$135.00
HISTORICAL BLUE STAFFORDSHIRE PLATE, States & "America and Independence," By Clews, 10½'' Diam. ...$160.00
(ROW III, L to R)
SALOPIAN CUP & SAUCER, Blk. Transfer W/Yellow Border, Table Ring Chips ...
..............................$40.00
ENGLISH PORCELAIN CUP & SAUCER, Enameled Chinoiserie Decor., Cup Rim Chip $20.00
CREAMWARE TEAPOT, Inter-twined Rope Handle, Flower Finial, Spout Chip & Rim Hairline, 5½'' H. $80.00
SOFT PASTE CUP & SAUCER, Purple Luster Rim W/Blk. Transfer Of Fulton's Steamer Passing West Point, Cadmus.....
..............................$30.00
STAFFORDSHIRE CUP & SAUCER, Lt. Blue Transfer, "The Valley Of Shenandoah From Jefferson's Rock," Impressed Mark "W.R. & Co." $27.50

(A-OH '77)   *Garth's Auctions, Inc.*

(A-OH '77)   *Garth's Auctions, Inc.*
(ROW I, L to R)
SPONGEWARE CHAMBER POT, Blue & White, 8½'' Diam. $75.00
SPONGEWARE CHAMBER POT, Blue & White, Chipped Base, 8¾'' Diam. ......
..............................$60.00
(ROW II, L to R)
STONEWARE BOWL, Blue Flowers, Impressed "Jugtown Ware," 6'' Diam. $22.50
SPONGEWARE PITCHER, Blue & White, Rim Flakes, 9'' H. $50.00
SPONGEWARE BOWL, Blue & White, Chipped Base, 6½'' Diam. $30.00
(ROW III, L to R)
STONEWARE CROCK, Pale Blue Glaze, 8'' Diam. $12.50
YELLOWWARE BOWL, White Band, Brown Stripes W/Green Seaweed Decor., Interior Glaze Pitting, 12½'' Diam., 6'' H. .
..............................$80.00
SPONGEWARE PLATE,Blue & White, 6¾'' Diam. $40.00

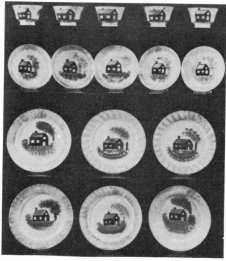

(A-MA '77)   *Richard A. Bourne Co., Inc.*
SPATTERWARE, Partial Set, Schoolhouse Patt., 16 Matching Pcs. W/Pink Spatter Borders, Decor. W/Landscape, Blue House In Center, Yellow Roof, 1 Cup W/Age Crack, Usual Discoloration, Plate Diam. 8⅛'' To 8¼'' $1800.00

(ROW I, L to R)
CANTON PITCHER, Blue & White, Base Chip, 5" H $55.00
CANTON SAUCE PITCHER, Blue & White, 3" H $70.00
ROSE MEDALLION QUATREFOIL DISH, Lemon Peel Glaze, 8¾"x10¾" ...
..................................$175.00
ORIENTAL EXPORT TEAPOT STAND, Lemon Peel Glaze, Polychrome Floral Design, Regilded, 5" Diam..........$55.00
ORIENTAL EXPORT CUP & SAUCER, Border Design In Brown & Orange, Hairlines $35.00
(ROW II)
ROSE MEDALLION TEA SET (13 Pc.), 3 Plates, 7¼" Diam.; Teapot, 9½" H.; Sugar, 3⅝" H.; Waste Bowl (Hairline), 6" Diam.; Creamer, 3½" H.; 6 Cups & Saucers (1 Cup W/Hairline) $170.00
(ROW III, L to R)
ORIENTAL EXPORT PLATE, Blue Underglaze Border & Polychrome Enameled Roses & Other Flowers, 8¾" Diam. $65.00
SAMSON TEA SET (Teapot Pictured), American Eagle Design W/Flowers, Teapot, 5½" H.; Helmet Creamer, 3½" H.; Covered Sugar, 4½" H. $210.00
ORIENTAL EXPORT DISH, Armorial Design, Arms Of Hayes, Lemon Peel Glaze, Gilt & Polychrome Enameling, 8¾" x 10½"
..................................$190.00

(L to R)
KING'S ROSE CREAMER, Shell Pattern W/Broken Pink Border $90.00
KING'S ROSE PLATE, Blue Transfer Border, 7¼" Diam. $160.00
KING'S ROSE CREAMER, Shell Pattern W/Vine Border $75.00

ORIENTAL EXPORT PORCELAIN
19th C., Pink & Gold W/Crest & Rampant Lion & "Semper Fidelis." Marked W/Leaf
(ROW I, L to R)
CUPS AND SAUCERS, (6) $85.00
VEGETABLE DISH & COVER, 9" L., 4¾" H. $45.00
(ROW II, L to R)
LEAF DISHES (3), 7" L. $45.00
TUREEN & TRAY, 11½" L., 8½" H. ...
..................................$130.00
LEAF DISHES, (4), 8½" L. $145.00
(ROW III, L to R)
OPEN SAUCE BOATS & TRAYS (4), 8¼" L. $65.00
VEGETABLE DISH & COVER, 10" L., 5" H. $55.00

COPPER LUSTER
(ROW I, L to R)
CREAMER, Green Ground, Floral Nosegay $50.00
CREAMER, Double Decorated Blue Bands
..................................$50.00
MUG, Blue Band $40.00
(ROW II, L to R)
PITCHERS, (1 of Pr), Animal Head Spouts, Raised Flower Basket Decor., Lt. Blue Ground................$220.00
CREAMER, Varicolored Oval Decor .....
..................................$27.50
CREAMER, Lobed Base, Multicolored Primrose Band $70.00

(ROW I, L to R)
COPPER LUSTER MILK PITCHER, Blue Bands W/Luster Floral Design, 6" H. $37.50
COPPER LUSTER MUG, Cream W/Luster Wavy Lines, 3½" H. $35.00
COPPER LUSTER FLOWER POT, White Band W/Polychrome Floral Decor., 5¾" H. $65.00
COPPER LUSTER MUG, Blue Band W/Luster Floral Design, Minor Base Chips, 3½" H. $22.50
COPPER LUSTER PITCHER, Cream Band W/Luster Floral Design, 5½" H. .....
..................................$25.00
(ROW II, L to R)
MUG, Flo Blue & Copper Luster Stripes On Embossed Surface, 3" H. $45.00
SALT GLAZE TEA SET, 3-Pcs., Inside Of Flange For Lid W/Chips On Sugar & Teapot, 6", 5" & 3¼" H. $75.00
COPPER LUSTER MUG, Cream Band W/Luster Floral Design, 2¾" H ...$30.00
(ROW III, L to R)
IRONSTONE PITCHER, Grey-Green Band, Black & Blue Stripes W/Black Sea Weed, Chip On Spout, 4¾" H ...$40.00
CREAMWARE MUG, Applied Embossed Shepherd On Blue Band, 3¼" H. .$35.00
BLACK JACKFIELD SEATED DOG, Gilt Highlights, 6" H. $25.00
IRONSTONE MUG, Blue Band & Black Transfer Of Horse, Reverse W/Frog, 3" H.
..................................$25.00
IRONSTONE MEASURE, Blue Bands & Black Stripes, Stamped "1 pint", 5" H. ...
..................................$35.00

GAUDY DUTCH
(L to R)
SOUP PLATE, Single Rose Pattern, 10" Diam...........................$270.00
PLATE, Single Rose Pattern, 8¼" Diam.
..................................$180.00
PLATE, Double Rose Pattern, 7¼" Diam.
..................................$150.00
PLATE, Urn Pattern, 5½" Diam. ..$300.00

(A-OH '77)   Garth's Auctions, Inc.

HISTORICAL BLUE STAFFORDSHIRE
(ROW I, L to R)
PLATE, Indian Sport Series, Impressed "Clews," Table Ring Chip, 10" Diam. . . . .
. . . .$27.50
PLATE, Red Transfer, "Shannondall Springs, Virginia," 8" Diam. $40.00
PLATE, "Wardour Castle, Wiltshire," Impressed "Enoch Wood & Sons," Minor Edge Glaze Wear, 10¼" Diam. $15.00
(ROW II, L to R)
PLATE, Red Transfer, "Cattskill Mountain House, U.S.," 10½" Diam. $37.50
CUP & SAUCER, "Hunter With Bow And Arrow And Dogs", Impressed "Adam" . . .
. . . .$27.50
PLATE, Red Transfer, "Palestine," Impressed "Adams," Table Ring Chip, 10½" Diam. $12.00
(ROW III, L to R)
SOUP PLATE, "Writtle Lodge Essex," Wild Rose Border, Impressed "A. Stevenson," Poorly Repaired Rim Flake, 10¼" Diam. $12.50
PLATE, "Oriental Scenery, Mahomedan Mosque & Tomb, I. Hall," 9¾" Diam. . . . .
. . . .$25.00
PLATE, "Faulkhourn Hall," Impressed "A. Stevenson," 10¼" Diam. $15.00

(A-MA '77)   Richard A. Bourne Co., Inc.

(L to R)
PLATE, Med. Blue, "Fair Mount Near Philadelphia", "Stubbs", 10¼" Diam. . . . .
. . . .$130.00
SOUP PLATE, Drk. Blue, "Table Rock, Niagara," Enoch Wood, 10¼" Diam. . . . . .
. . . .$200.00
PLATE, Drk. Blue, America & Independence Series, "Clews," 10½" Diam. $150.00

(A-OH '77)   Garth's Auctions, Inc.

(ROW I, L to R)
GAUDY STAFFORDSHIRE SUGAR BOWL, Red, Blue, Green & Black Floral Decor., 3½" H. $27.50
MINIATURE TEA SET, 3-Pc., Yellow Colored Ware W/Brown & Orange Floral Decor., Minor Wear, Repaired Flake Inside Lid Of Teapot, Sm. Flake On Spout, Teapot-3¼" H., Creamer-2¼" H., Sugar Bowl (not pictured) 2⅝" H. $95.00
GAUDY STICK SPATTER IRONSTONE PLATE, Transfer Scene - Rabbits Playing Tennis, Rim Chip, 9¼" Diam. $45.00
SPATTERWARE CUP & SAUCER, Blue, Peafowl In Red, Green, Yellow Ochre & Black, Minor Rim Roughness On Cup . . . .
. . . .$95.00
(ROW II, L to R)
SPATTERWARE CUP & SAUCER, Brown, Corn Flower In Red & Green, Minor Glaze Wear On Rim Of Cup $195.00
SPATTERWARE CUP & SAUCER, Red, Peafowl In Blue, Yellow, Green & Black . .
. . . .$150.00
SPATTERWARE CUP & SAUCER, Red, Green, & Black, Minor Glaze Wear On Rim Of Cup $90.00
SPATTERWARE CUP & SAUCER, Purple, Cornflower In Red & Green $230.00
(ROW III, L to R)
GAUDY STAFFORDSHIRE SAUCE DISH, Green, Yellow, Red & Black Decor., Edge Hairline, 6¼" Diam. $17.50
SPATTERWARE CUP, Purple, Hairline
. . . .$35.00
GAUDY STAFFORDSHIRE SOUP PLATE, Red, Blue, Green & Black, 9¼" Diam. $27.50
SPATTERWARE CUP, Blue, Peafowl In Blue, Red & Yellow, Rim Chip . .$70.00
GAUDY STAFFORDSHIRE MUG, Red, Blue, Green & Black, Small Rim Hairline, 4" H. $37.50

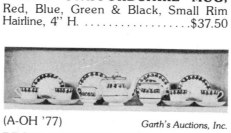

(A-OH '77)   Garth's Auctions, Inc.

BROWN STICK SPATTER, 11 Pc. Child's Tea Set, Teapot-4¾" H., Creamer-2½" H., Sugar-4¼" H., 4 Cups & Saucers, 4 Plates-4¾" Diam., Waste Bowl $65.00

(A-OH '77)   Garth's Auctions, Inc.

HISTORICAL BLUE STAFFORDSHIRE
(ROW I, L to R)
PLATE, Med. Blue Transfer, "Woodlands Near Phila," Impressed "Stubbs," 6¾" Diam. $105.00
PLATTER, Drk. Blue Transfer, "Sancho Panza And The Dutchess", "Clews", 18½" L. $240.00
PLATE, Drk. Blue Transfer, Fruit & Flowers, "Stubbs", 6¾" Diam. $45.00
(ROW II, L to R)
PLATE, Drk. Blue Transfer, "Peace and Plenty," Impressed "Clews," 10" Diam. . .
. . . .$230.00
SUGAR BOWL, "Franklin's Tomb," Impressed "Wood," Repaired, Mismatched Lid, 6" H. $80.00
PLATE, Drk. Blue Transfer, "Harvard College," By R.S.W., 10¼" Diam. $305.00
(ROW III, L to R)
PLATE, Drk. Blue Transfer, "Peace and Plenty," Impressed "Clews," 9" Diam. . . .
. . . .$125.00
MILK PITCHER, Drk. Blue Transfer, Impressed "Clews," 6¼" H. $285.00
PLATE, Drk. Blue Transfer, "America and Independence," Impressed "Clews," 8¾" Diam. $155.00

(A-OH '77)   Garth's Auctions, Inc.

(L to R)
PURPLE LUSTER CUP & SAUCER, Magenta Transfer Of Travelers $7.50
STAFFORDSHIRE BOWL, Lt. Blue Transfer, Ruins Of Gothic Church, 13¼" Diam. $35.00
STICKSPATTER CUP & SAUCER, Blue & White $20.00

(A-OH '77) *Garth's Auctions, Inc.*

HISTORICAL BLUE STAFFORDSHIRE
(ROW I, L to R)
SAUCE BOAT, "Landing Of Lafayette," Drk. Blue, Chipped Base, 5" H. ..$200.00
PLATTER, "Landing Of Gen. Lafayette At Castle Garden, New York, 16 August 1824," Drk. Blue, Impressed "Clews," 17" L. ....
..................................$725.00
BOWL & MATCHING PLATE, "Neptune," Drk. Blue, Plate W/Impressed "Clews," Both W/Edge Flakes, Bowl W/Base Hairline, 6¾" Diam., & 4½" Diam. $80.00
(ROW II, L to R)
PLATE, "Doctor Syntax Taking Possession Of His Living," Impressed "Clews", Med. Blue, Glaze Flaking, 10" Diam. $45.00
TUREEN, Lid Is "Doctor Syntax Pursued By Bull," Base Is "Doctor Syntax Bound To Tree And Drawing From Nature," Impressed "Clews", Drk. Blue, Edge Flakes On Lid, Base Has Chips On Handles, 9" L., 5½" H. ....
..................................$60.00
PLATE, "Doctor Syntax Painting A Portrait," Drk. Blue, Impressed "Clews", 10" Diam. $90.00
(ROW III, L to R)
PLATE, "Landing Of Gen. Lafayette," Impendence," Drk. Blue, Impressed "Clews",
..................................$130.00
PLATTER, States Or "America and Independence," Impressed "Clews", Drk. Blue, 13" L. $500.00
PLATE, States Or "America and Independence," Impressed "Clews", Drk. Blue, 2 Small Glaze Imperfections, 8" Diam. $170.00

(A-OH '77) *Garth's Auctions, Inc.*
HISTORICAL BLUE STAFFORDSHIRE
PLATTER, "Winter View Of Pittsburg, Mass.," "Clews," 16¾" L. $675.00
PITCHER, "America and Independence", Minor Chips, 9¾" H. $150.00

(A-OH '77) *Garth's Auctions, Inc.*
HISTORICAL BLUE STAFFORDSHIRE
(ROW I, L to R)
CREAMER, Drk. Blue Transfer Of Girl Fishing, Hairline, Rim Repair, 5¼" H. $65.00
TUREEN, Drk. Blue Transfer "Oriental Scenery," Palace Of King Of Dehli, I. Hall & Sons, Finial Flake, 13½" L., 11¼" H. ..
..................................$210.00
PLATE, Drk. Blue Transfer, "Woodlands Near Phila.," Eagle Border, 6¾" Diam. $95.00
(ROW II, L to R)
PLATE, Drk. Blue Transfer, "London Views, St. Philips Chapel, Regent Street," Impressed "Wood," 10¼" Diam. $85.00
TODDY, Drk. Blue Transfer, Bridge, Impressed "Peter Morton, Hartford," 4¾" Diam. $75.00
LADLE, Drk. Blue Transfer, Quadraped, Hyenna In Bowl, 7½" L. $75.00
PLATE, Drk. Blue Transfer, "Commodore MacDonnough's Victory," Impressed "E. Wood & Sons," 10" Diam. $235.00
(ROW III, L to R)
SUGAR BOWL, Drk. Blue Transfer, Washington At Tomb, Hairlines & Chips On Lid Flange, 6½" H. $110.00
CUP PLATE, Drk. Blue Transfer, "Castle Garden, Battery, N.Y.," Impressed "Enoch Wood & Sons," 3¾" Diam. $135.00
PLATE, Drk. Blue Transfer, "Park Theatre, New York," 10¼" Diam. $110.00
CUP PLATE, Drk. Blue Transfer, "Castle Garden, Battery N.Y.," Impressed "Wood," 3¾" Diam. $125.00
SAUCE TUREEN, Drk. Blue Transfer, "Landing Of Lafayette" Impressed "Clews," Pinpoint Flakes & Chips On Lid, 5¼" H. .
..................................$335.00

(A-OH '77) *Garth's Auctions, Inc.*

(A-OH '77) *Garth's Auctions, Inc.*
HISTORICAL BLUE STAFFORDSHIRE
(ROW I, L to R)
FOOTED CREAMER, "Wandering Boy," Drk. Blue, Minor Edge Wear, 4¼" H. .....
..................................$65.00
PLATTER, States Or "America And Independence," Drk. Blue, Impressed "Clews", 16¾" L. $850.00
CREAMER, "Girl With Flower Basket," Drk. Blue, Glaze Wear & Rim Edge Repair, 5¼" H. $65.00
(ROW II, L to R)
PLATE, "Washington," Drk. Blue, 2 Small Glaze Imperfections, 7¾" Diam. ...$185.00
PLATE, "Don Quixote and Sancho Panza," Drk. Blue, "Clews," 6¾" Diam. $85.00
FEEDER, Drk. Blue Transfer Of Still Life W/Shell & Vase Of Flowers, Base Mark - "Stone China," Rim Edge Flake, Hairline On Handle, 4½" Diam., 3" H. $120.00
PLATE, "Sancho And The Priest And The Barber," "Clews", Drk. Blue, 7¾" Diam. .
..................................$75.00
(ROW III, L to R)
PLATE, States Or "America And Independence," Impressed "Clews", 2 Chips On Table Ring, 10½" Diam. $115.00
PLATE, "Peace And Plenty", Drk. Blue, 3 Small Glaze Imperfections, Minor Scratch Mark, Impressed "Clews", 9" Diam. $135.00
PLATE, "Buenos Ayres," Drk. Blue, 10" Diam. $75.00

To the left

HISTORICAL STAFFORDSHIRE
(ROW I, L to R)
PLATE, "Sancho Panza's Debate With Teresa," 9" Diam. $95.00
PLATE, "Peace and Plenty," "Clews," 10" Diam. $150.00
PLATE, "Winter View Of Pittsburg, Mass.," "Clews," 8¾" Diam. $130.00
(ROW II, L to R)
PLATE, "Doctor Syntax Reading His Tour," 10½" Diam. $55.00
URN, Wandering Boy, 5¾" H. $90.00
PLATE, "Doctor Syntax Mistakes Gentleman's House For An Inn," "Clews," 10" Diam. $65.00

(A-OH '77) *Garth's Auctions, Inc.*
(ROW I, L to R)
WHITE CLAY GREASE LAMP, Drk. Brown Albany Slip, 4'' H. $180.00
STONEWARE PITCHER, Miniature, Brushed Cobalt Leaf Design $385.00
REDWARE CREAMER, Clear Speckled Glaze, 3¼'' H. $40.00
STONEWARE BANK, Greenish Brown Glaze, 4'' H. $27.50
WHITE CLAY GREASE LAMP, Drk. Brown Albany Slip, Rim Flake, 4¼'' H. $200.00
(ROW II, L to R)
REDWARE JAR, Speckled Shiny Glaze, Base Chips, Rim Wear, 5¾'' H. ...$22.50
REDWARE FISH MOLD, Brown Glaze, Edge Wear, Edge Flakes, 12'' L. ...$45.00
REDWARE JUG, Green & Clear Glaze, Glaze Wear, 7¾'' H. $65.00
(ROW III, L to R)
REDWARE PLATE, Yellow Slip Wavy Line Decor., Clear Glaze, Coggled Edge, 9'' Diam.........................$255.00
REDWARE BOWL, Yellow Slip Decor. Worn, 8½'' Diam., 3½'' H. $95.00
REDWARE BOWL, Glaze W/Yellow Slip Worn, 10½'' Diam., 4¼'' H. $100.00

To the right

(A-OH '77) *Garth's Auctions, Inc.*
HISTORICAL BLUE STAFFORDSHIRE
(ROW I, L to R)
PLATE, "Park Theatre New York", Drk. Blue, 10'' Diam. $150.00
PLATE, "Welcome Lafayette The Nations Guest And Our Country's Glory," Embossed Border, Impressed "Clews", 7¾'' Diam. $320.00
PLATE, Arms Of New York, "Excelsior", Drk. Blue, Broken & Professionally Repaired, 10'' Diam. $160.00
(ROW II, L to R)
PLATE, "The Valentine From Wilkie's Designs," Drk. Blue, Impressed "Clews", Minor Rim Flakes, 9'' Diam. $100.00
TEAPOT, Scene On Side Of 2 Dogs, Drk. Blue, Unmarked, Minor Glaze Wear On Spout & Top Flange, Minor Glaze Flakes Underside Lid, 7¾'' H. $145.00
PLATE, "Christmas Eve From Wilkie's Designs," Impressed "Clews", Drk. Blue, 9'' Diam. $135.00

(A-OH '77) *Garth's Auctions, Inc.*
HISTORICAL BLUE STAFFORDSHIRE
(ROW I, L to R)
TRAY, "The Rabbit on The Way From Wilkie's Designs," Impressed "Clews", Drk. Blue, Rim Flake, 9¾'' L. $100.00
SOUP PLATE, "Playing At Draughts From Wilkie's Designs", Impressed "Clews", Drk. Blue, 8¾'' Diam. $100.00
BOWL, "Hanover Terrace Regents Park", Impressed "Adam Warranted Staffordshire," Drk. Blue, Rim Flake, 8¼'' L. $60.00
(ROW II, L to R)
PLATE, "Doctor Syntax Returned From His Tour," Impressed "Clews", Med. Blue, 2 Small Flakes On Table Ring, 7¼'' Diam. $65.00
PLATE, "The Escape Of The Mouse From Wilkie's Designs," Med. Drk. Blue, Impressed "Clews", Edge Glaze Wear, 10'' Diam. $87.50
CUP & SAUCER, Scene Of 2 Dogs, Impressed "Clews", Drk. Blue, Cup W/Hairline & Chip On Base $60.00
(ROW III, L to R)
PLATE, "Doctor Syntax Drawing After Nature," Med. Blue, 10¼'' Diam. ...$60.00
PLATE, Hunters and Dogs, Impressed "Clews," Minor Wear & Knife Scratches, Rim Chips, 8¾'' Diam. $40.00
PLATE, "Doctor Syntax And The Bees," Impressed "Clews", Med. Blue, Rim Flake, 10'' Diam. $55.00

◄

(A-OH '77) *Garth's Auctions, Inc.*
(ROW I, L to R)
LUSTER PITCHER, Pink & Purple, Embossed Hunting Dogs, 5¾'' H. ...$115.00
HISTORICAL BLUE STAFFORDSHIRE CUP PLATE, Arms of the States Series By F. Mayer, So. Carolina, Med. Drk. Blue, 4¼'' Diam. $225.00
CANARY LUSTER PITCHER, Silver Luster Trim W/Black Transfer "Peace & Plenty," Rim Hairline, 6½'' H. $875.00
HISTORICAL BLUE STAFFORDSHIRE CUP PLATE, Boston Statehouse Mismarked "Scudder's American Museum", Impressed "Stevenson," Drk. Blue, 4¼'' Diam. $535.00
SOFT PASTE TEAPOT, Brown Oriental Scene Transfer, Blue Edge, 4¾'' H. $65.00
(ROW II, L to R)
SOFT PASTE PLATE, Embossed Border W/Polychrome & Purple Luster Floral Decor., 7¾'' Diam. $35.00
STAFFORDSHIRE PLATE, Lt. Blue Transfer Rim W/Black Central Transfer Of "Sulphur Springs, Delaware, Ohio," Edge Chips 9¼'' Diam. $95.00
SOFT PASTE PLATE, Kings Rose W/Polychrome Decor., 8'' Diam. $60.00
(ROW III, L to R)
HISTORICAL BLUE STAFFORDSHIRE PLATE, "Beauties Of America, Library Philadelphia, I & W Ridgway," Drk. Blue, 8¼'' Diam. $115.00
HISTORICAL BLUE STAFFORDSHIRE PLATE, Unmarked Scene Of Early Steamboat, Drk. Blue, 10¼'' Diam. .....$.80.00
HISTORICAL BLUE STAFFORDSHIRE CUP & SAUCER, Impressed "E. Wood & Sons, Burslem", Scene Of Chancellor Livingston ship, Drk. Blue $260.00
HISTORICAL BLUE STAFFORDSHIRE SOUP PLATE, States Or "America and Independence," Drk. Blue, Impressed "Clews", Underside Rim Flake, 8¾'' Diam. .$110.00

(A-OH '77) *Garth's Auctions, Inc.*
(L to R)
PLATE, Don Quixote "Mambrino's Helmet," Med. Drk. Blue, 10'' Diam. $85.00
BOWL, "Washington By The Tomb," Med. Drk. Blue, Base Hairline, Rim Flake, 6¼'' Diam., 3'' H. $130.00
PLATE, Fishing Scene, Impressed "Clews", Med. Blue, Hairline & Flake On Table Ring, 10'' Diam. $35.00

(A-OH '77)   *Garth's Auctions, Inc.*
(ROW I, L to R)
STAFFORDSHIRE WASTE BOWL, Lt. Blue Transfer "Catskill Moss, Valley Of Wyoming," Flake On Rim, Base Chipped, 5½" Diam., 3¼" H. $9.00
STAFFORDSHIRE PLATTER, Lt. Blue Transfer "American Views, Opaque China, T. Godwin Wharf, Baltimore," Rim Chip, 17" L. $20.00
STAFFORDSHIRE BUST, Polychrome Enamel W/Minor Flaking, 7¼" H. $155.00
(ROW II, L to R)
LEEDS SAUCER, Gaudy Blue & Ochre Decor., 5¾" Diam. $27.50
STAFFORDSHIRE PLATTER, Lt. Blue Transfer "Catskill Moss, Near Weehawken," 15" L. $27.50
JACKFIELD COW CREAMER, Black, Worn Gilt Decor., Ear Chipped, 7½" L., 5½" H. $40.00
(ROW III, L to R)
SPATTERWARE PLATE, Blue, White Star Center, 8½" Diam. $120.00
GAUDY "MAASTRICHT" PLATTER, 11¾" L. $22.50
SPATTERWARE TRAY, Blue, W/Red & Green Cornflower, Rim Chip, 9½" L. ....
.........................$135.00

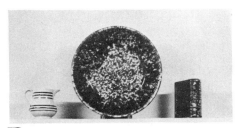

(A-OH '77)   *Garth's Auctions, Inc.*
(L to R)
YELLOWWARE CREAMER, Brown & White Stripes, 4½" H. $25.00
ROCKINGHAM BOWL, Crack, 13" Diam. $20.00
BENNINGTON BOOK BOTTLE, "Separated Spirits G.," Flint Enamel Glaze W/ Green, Sm. Flake Bottom Edge, 5½" H. ..
.........................$210.00

(A-OH '77)   *Garth's Auctions, Inc.*
(ROW I, L to R)
STAFFORDSHIRE TOBY PITCHER, Sponge Decor. On Base W/Drk. Blue Coat, Yellow Knee Breeches & Gilt Stars On Vest, 9½" H. $170.00
ROCKINGHAM TOBY PITCHER, Chips On Base, Toes & Rim, 6¼" H. $55.00
STAFFORDSHIRE TOBY PITCHER, Sponge Decor. On Base & Handle, W/ Yellow Coat, Red Knee Breeches, Blue Buttons, Rim Repair, 10" H. $140.00
(ROW II, L to R)
STAFFORDSHIRE TOBY PITCHER, Polychrome Enameling W/Purple Luster Mug In Hand, Base Mkd. "A. E. Gray & Co., Hanley, England," Rim Flake, 5½" H.
.........................$30.00
ROCKINGHAM TOBY TEAPOT, Sm. Rim Flake, 9½" H. $95.00
STAFFORDSHIRE TOBY PITCHER, Polychrome W/Luster Trim On Coat, Rim Hairline, 5¾" H. $37.50

(A-OH '77)   *Garth's Auctions, Inc.*
(ROW I, L to R)
STAFFORDSHIRE CHIMNEY PIECE, Polychrome W/Gold, Minor Damage To Tree Foliage, Base Flake, 5¾" H. ..$20.00
POTTERY FIGURE, Woman W/Cloak, Early 19th C., Point Of Anchor At Feet W/One Point Missing, 7 Colors, Chipped, Base Hairline, 7" H. $70.00
STAFFORDSHIRE DOG, Rust W/Gold, Yellow & Black, 5¾" H. $35.00
(continued bottom of next column)

(A-OH '77)   *Garth's Auctions, Inc.*
ROCKINGHAM
(ROW I, L to R)
CREAMERS (2), 1 Illus.; 1 W/Fluted & 1 W/Tapered Sides, Spout, Rim & Base Flakes, 4½" H. & 6" H. $17.50
SOAP DISH, 4" x 5¼" x 2¼" H. $45.00
BOWLS (2), 1 Illus.; 1 W/Hairline, 6" Diam., 3¼" H.; 1 W/Beaded Edge, 7¾" Diam., 1¾" H. $35.00
PLATES, (2), 1 Illus.; Minor Chip & Rim Flakes, 9½" & 9¾" Diam. $70.00
CUSTARD CUP & BOWL, Cup 3" Diam., 2¼" H.; Bowl 5¾" Diam., 2¾" H.
.........................$12.50
TOBY CREAMER, Base Chip, 5¾" H. ..
.........................$35.00
(ROW II, L to R)
VASES (2), 1 W/Edge Flake & Chip, 5¾" H. $20.00
COVERED JAR, Chips, 7¼" Diam., 6¾" H. $70.00
(ROW III, L to R)
PITCHER, Peacock Design, 8¼" H. .....
.........................$50.00
BOWL, 9¾" Diam., 4¼" H. $40.00
PLATES (2), 1 Illus.; Flakes, 9½" x 9¾" Diam. $85.00

────────────

◄ *To the left*   *(continued)*

(ROW II, L to R)
MINIATURE STAFFORDSHIRE MUG, Black Transfer Prayer, ¼" Rim Hairline, 2" H. $40.00
POLYCHROME POTTERY BIRDS, (4), 2 W/Base Flakes, 2¾" H. $45.00
STAFFORDSHIRE CHIMNEY PIECE, 2 Dogs & Keg, Polychrome, 4¼" H. .....
.........................$28.00
(ROW III, L to R)
SILVER LUSTER SHAKER, 3½" H. ....
.........................$15.00
STAFFORDSHIRE LAMBS (2), One Pictured, 2" & 2¼" H. $22.50
STAFFORDSHIRE LAMB, Sanded Fleece, 2¼" H. $30.00
MINIATURE PURPLE LUSTER JUG, Magenta Transfer Of House & Stream One Side, Rev: Man Fishing In Rapids, 3" H. ..
.........................$65.00

(A-OH '77)   *Garth's Auctions, Inc.*

COPPER LUSTER
(ROW I, L to R)
PITCHER, Canary Yellow Band W/White Reserves W/Blk. Transfer "Cornwallis", Rev: "Lafayette", Repairs, 6¾" H. $180.00
CREAMER, White Band W/Magenta Transfer Of Animals, Spout Chipped, 5" H. $35.00
CREAMER, Blue W/Embossed Polychrome Flowers In Basket, Figural Spout, 7" H. $100.00
(ROW II, L to R)
CREAMER, Green & Cream Bands W/ Floral Luster Decor., 5¾" H. $70.00
CREAMER, Canary Yellow Band W/White Reserves W/Brick Red Transfer, Minor Flake On Spout, 4¾" H. $75.00
CREAMER, Canary Yellow Band W/White Reserves W/Sepia Transfer, Polychrome Enameling, 4¾" H. $115.00
CREAMER, Pink Luster Band W/Embossed Copper Cows, Top Band Of Green & Purple Luster, 5½" H. $105.00
(ROW III, L to R)
PITCHER, Olive Green Band W/Embossed Polychrome Flowers, Mask Spout, Hairline In Base Of Handle, 8½" H. $65.00
FLOWER POT, 2 Pc., Orange Band W/ Embossed Red Rose W/Copper Leaves, Base Chipped, 6" Diam., 6" H. . . $105.00
PITCHER, White Reserves W/Purple Lustre, "Harrison & Reform", Rev: Eagle W/ Banner "For The Sake Of Thee", Base Hairline, 9½" H. $800.00

(A-PA '77)   *Pennypacker Auction Centre*

SPATTERWARE CUPS & SAUCERS (3), (1 Pictured), Red & Blue Rainbow W/Adams Rose Centers $360.00

(A-OH '77)   *Garth's Auctions, Inc.*

(ROW I, L to R)
SUNDERLAND LUSTER MILK PITCHER, Copper Sanded Band, Spout Chipped, 5½" H. $50.00
SOFT PASTE CUP & SAUCER, Gaudy Red, Yellow & Black Floral, Rim Repair On Cup, Saucer W/Minor Rim Flake . . . $42.50
GAUDY DUTCH CUP & SAUCER, Table Ring Of Cup Chipped $95.00
COPPER LUSTER PITCHER, Wide Orange Band W/Luster Decor $75.00
(ROW II, L to R)
SPATTERWARE PLATE, Red W/Peafowl In Blue, Yellow & Green, Sm. Rim Flakes, 8¼" Diam. $140.00
SILVER LUSTER TEA SET, 3-Pc., Queen Anne Patt., Creamer (Repaired):3¾" H.; Teapot (Sm. Chip On Spout):6" H; Sugar Bowl (Base Chipped):5" H. $130.00
SPATTERWARE PLATE, Blue W/Single Rose Center, Rim Flakes, 8" Diam. $100.00
(ROW III, L to R)
COPPER LUSTER CREAMER, White Band W/Brick Red Transfer, Red & Yellow Under Spout, 4½" H. $75.00
COPPER LUSTER TUMBLERS, (Pr), Enameled Polychrome Flowers, 5" H. $85.00
SILVER RESIST CREAMER, Stripes & Floral Band, Luster Worn, 4¾" H. . $55.00
COPPER LUSTER CREAMER, Blue Band W/Blk. Transfer, "General Jackson, The Hero Of New Orleans", Spout Chipped, 5½" H. $35.00

(A-PA '77)   *Pennypacker Auction Centre*

GAUDY DUTCH
(L to R)
CUP & SAUCER, Single Rose Pattern $180.00
BOWL, Carnation Pattern, 5½" Diam. $150.00
CUP & SAUCER, King's Rose War Bonnet Pattern, Age Mark $55.00
BOWL, Dahlia Pattern, 5½" Diam. $600.00
CUP & SAUCER, Single Rose Pattern $200.00

(A-PA '77)   *Pennypacker Auction Centre*

MINIATURE LEEDS COFFEE POT, Straight Spout, Blue, Orange & Green Decor., 4¾" H. $160.00

(A-OH '77)   *Garth's Auctions, Inc.*

(ROW I, L to R)
REDWARE FOOD MOLD, 2 Embossed Crowns In Base, 6½" L. $15.00
REDWARE FISH BOTTLE, Green Glaze, 6½" L. $380.00
SEWER TILE DOG, Crack & Sm. Hole In Base, 5½" H. $22.50
ROCKINGHAM SOAP DISH, 6" L. $27.50
(ROW II, L to R)
ROCKINGHAM MIXING BOWL, 9¼" Diam. $27.50
SEWER TILE LION, Hand Tooled, Chips On Base, 8¾" L. $22.50
REDWARE TURKS HEAD MOLD, Greenish Cast Glaze, Hairline Crack, 9¼" D. $30.00
(ROW III, L to R)
TREEN FOOTED COVERED JAR, 20th C., 8" H. $15.00
REDWARE FOOTED COVERED JAR, Green & Floral Designs, Possibly Port Neuf Pottery, 6" H. $17.50
HAND LANTERN, Tin W/Brass Top, Red, Blue & Clear Glass Sides W/Hinged Covers, Nickel Plated Brass Font & Burner, German, Sgn., 8¼" H. $25.00

(A-OH '77)   *Garth's Auctions, Inc.*

SPATTERWARE

(ROW I, L to R)

PITCHER, Blue & White, Rim Chips, 10½" H. $115.00

PLATTER, Blue, Sm. Broken Glaze Bubble Near Rim, 17" L. $130.00

(ROW II, L to R)

CUP & SAUCER, Rainbow, Red, Blue & Purple W/Peafowl, Cup Has Rim Flakes, Saucer Has Hairline & Table Ring Chip $125.00

PLATE, Red W/Peafowl Decor. In Green, Yellow & Blue, Edge Wear, Crows Foot On Back, 8¼" Diam. $145.00

CUP & SAUCER, Red & Green Sponge Decor $47.50

(ROW III, L to R)

SOUP PLATE, Blue W/Red Transfer Of Man Capturing Wild Horses, 10½" Diam. $75.00

CUP & SAUCER, Miniature, Blue, Sm. Flake On Rim Of Saucer $40.00

WASTE BOWL, Peafowl Decor., Green, Blue, Red & Black W/Blue Spatter Foot, Rim Wear, 4½" Diam., 3¼" H. . .$155.00

PITCHER, Blue W/Red Transfer Of Cowboys Roping Steer, Handle Hairline, 9½" H. $195.00

(A-PA '77)   *Brown Bros. Gallery*

STAFFORDSHIRE PITCHER, Blue, "Boston State House - City Hall, New York," By Stubbs, 6½" H. $290.00

CHELSEA STYLE PITCHER (1 Of Pr), Lavender Ground, Raised White Floral Swag Accents $80.00

(A-OH '77)   *Garth's Auctions, Inc.*

(ROW I, L to R)

MOCHA PITCHER, Tan Band W/Drk. Brown Seaweed Decor., White, Drk. Brown & Embossed Green Stripes, Sm. Chips On Spout, 6½" H. $105.00

LIVERPOOL PITCHER, Blk. Transfer Of Joined Hands W/Heart, "Happy The Man ..." Rev: Eagle W/Interlocked Circles Of 16 States, Ca.1803, Old Crack, 8" H. $85.00

SILVER RESIST PITCHER, Birds Feeding Young, 6½" H. $190.00

(ROW II, L to R)

LEEDS PLATE, Peafowl In Blue, Blue Feather Edge, 1¼" Hairline, 8¼" Diam. $150.00

YELLOW LUSTER WASTE BOWL, Minor Glaze Wear On Rim, 5" Diam., 3" H. $370.00

SILVER RESIST YELLOW LUSTER PITCHER, Floral Design, Spout Chipped, 5½" Diam. $195.00

GAUDY PLATE, Polychrome Floral Wreath, 8¼" Diam. $105.00

(ROW III, L to R)

PRATT MUG, Children In Heart Shaped Reserves, Rim Chipped & Repaired, 6" H. $145.00

MOCHA BOWL, White W/Blue Band & Fish Worm Decor., 9¾" Diam., 4¾" H. $135.00

MOCHA MUG, Drk. Brown, Tan, White & Blue-Grey Cat Eye Decor., Old Rim Flakes, 5" H. $230.00

To the right ▶

(ROW I, L to R)

PORCELAIN STEIN, Enameled Flowers $45.00

METTLACH STONEWARE STEIN $190.00

METTLACH STEIN, Enameled Decor $350.00

(ROW II, L to R)

METTLACH STEIN $375.00

METTLACH STEIN $350.00

METTLACH STEIN, #2211 . . . .$375.00

ENAMELED GLASS STEIN, Pewter Top $45.00

(ROW III, L to R)

PORCELAIN STEIN $45.00

CRANBERRY PICKLE CASTER, Inverted Thumbprint, Enameled $175.00

STONEWARE STEIN, Pewter Top $50.00

(A-OH '77)   *Garth's Auctions, Inc.*

MINIATURES

(ROW I, L to R)

LEEDS SOFT PASTE CREAMER, Rose Buds In Green, Black, Orange & Brown, Minor Rim Flake, 2⅛" H. $85.00

LEEDS CREAMER, Vining Decor. In Brown, Green & Yellow Ochre, Minor Rim Flake, 2½" H. $115.00

YELLOW LUSTER MUG, Red Transfer Oak Leaf Border, "A Trifle For Margaret", Professionally Repaired Handle, 2¼" H. $145.00

LEEDS CREAMER, Blue & White Chinoiserie Decor., Rim Roughness, 2⅜" H. $60.00

LEEDS CREAMER, Blue & White Chinoiserie Decor., Rim Roughness & Chip, 2" H. $45.00

(ROW II, L to R)

STAFFORDSHIRE DOG, Black, Rust & Yellow Decor., Rust Has Flaking, 3½" H. $30.00

GAUDY WELSH MUG, 2" H. . . .$85.00

GAUDY WELSH MUG, 2⅞" H. .$45.00

GAUDY WELSH MUG, 1¾" H. .$75.00

STAFFORDSHIRE DOG, Rust, Yellow Ochre & Black Decor., 3⅜" H. $55.00

(ROW III, L to R)

LEEDS CUP & SAUCER, Leaf Design In 4 Colors, Saucer-4" Diam. $80.00

SOFT PASTE TUREEN & PLATTER, Blue Transfer Scene Of Farmyard W/Cow, Platter-5¾" L. $85.00

GAUDY STAFFORDSHIRE CUP & SAUCER, Rose, Saucer-4⅝" Diam. $35.00

(A-OH '77)   *Garth's Auctions, Inc.*

(A-OH '77)   *Garth's Auctions, Inc.*
(ROW I, L to R)
BENNINGTON COW CREAMER, Flint Enamel, Green Flecks Sparce In Glaze, Hairline In Base, Missing Lid, 5½" H. $105.00
YELLOW WARE MUG, Bands Of White & Drk. Brown, 3½" H. $37.50
BENNINGTON COW CREAMER, Rockingham Glaze, Base Mkd. W/"N", Base Hairline, Missing Lid, 5½" H. $145.00
(ROW II, L to R)
BENNINGTON TULIP VASE, Flint Enamel, Base & Rim Flake, 9½" H. .$155.00
YELLOW WARE CHAMBER POT, White Band W/Brown Stripes & Blue Seaweed Decor., 9" Diam., 5¼" H. $37.50
ROCKINGHAM CANDLESTICK, Candle Socket Hairline, Minor Base Chips, 9¼" H. $225.00
(ROW III, L to R)
ROCKINGHAM FOOT WARMER, Base Glazing Imperfection, 8¾" H. $85.00
YELLOWWARE PITCHER, W/Brown Stripes, 6½" H. $20.00
PITCHER W/Rockingham Glaze, Embossed Peacock, Sm. Rim Glaze Imperfection, 8" H. $57.50

(A-OH '77)   *Garth's Auctions, Inc.*

(A-OH '77)   *Garth's Auctions, Inc.*
(ROW I, L to R)
REDWARE DOG, Yellow Slip Streaked W/Red & Details In Sgraffito, 5¾" H. $255.00
CHALKWARE DOG, Red, Yellow & Black Decor., 7½" H. $200.00
CHALKWARE FIGURE, Oriental Boy W/ Hobby Horse, Head Cracked, 5" H. $30.00
CHALKWARE CAT, Bullseye Design, 6½" H. $215.00
(ROW II, L to R)
CHALKWARE RAM, Red, Black & Yellow Decor., 7½" H. $380.00
CHALKWARE SQUIRREL, Open Fore Paws, Red, Black & Yellow, 7¼" H. $230.00
CHALKWARE SQUIRREL, Open Fore Paws, Red, Drk. Brown & Yellow, 5" H. $190.00
WHITE CLAY DOG, Drk. Brown Glaze, Base W/"Souvenir 1877, F.M. King Co. 1897", 7¼" H. $50.00

To the left

(ROW I, L to R)
STONEWARE BIRD FEEDER, Brown Mottled Glaze, 8¼" H. $75.00
STONEWARE JARS (1 of 2), 1 W/Brown Glaze & 1 W/Yellowish Glaze W/Brown Speckles (Hairline), 3⅜" H. $15.00
REDWARE COLANDER, Interior Glaze, Rim Flake, 7¾" Diam., 4½" H. . . .$70.00
EARTHENWARE CREAMER, Drk. Brown Pebbly Glaze, 2¾" H. $45.00
NEW GENEVA POTTERY PITCHER, Floral Design, Rim Flakes, 7" H. . . .$85.00
(ROW II, L to R)
REDWARE CANDLE SCONCE, Clear Glaze W/Mottled Yellow, 6½" H. .$230.00
WHITE CLAY LAMB BAKING MOLD, Orange Interior Glaze, Wooden Pegs Hold Halves Together, 10" L. $145.00
REDWARE CANDLE SCONCE, Clear Glaze W/Mottled Yellow & Green, 6½" H. $280.00
(ROW III, L to R)
REDWARE JUG, Clear & Mottled Green Glaze, 5¾" H. $45.00
REDWARE COLANDER, Applied Handle & Feet, Clear Glaze, Hairline, Rim Chips, 9" Diam., 9¾" H. $145.00
REDWARE FOOD MOLD, Ear Of Corn Center, Clear Glaze W/Brown Sponge Work, Applied Feet, 7¾" L. $90.00

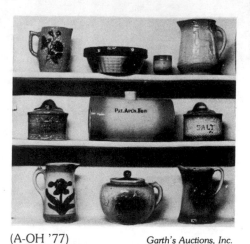

(A-OH '77)   *Garth's Auctions, Inc.*
BLUE & WHITE STONEWARE
(ROW I, L to R)
PITCHER, Embossed Tree Bark W/Roses, Chipped Spout, 6¾" H $25.00
BOWL, Embossed Basket Weave, 9½" Diam. $12.50
CUP, "Nutmeg" In Gilt, 3" H $10.00
PITCHER, Embossed Deer, Spout Roughness, 8½" H $25.00
(ROW II, L to R)
SALT BOX, Embossed Basket Weave & "Salt", Minor Roughness, 5¾" Diam. $35.00
FOOT WARMER, One Side Mkd. "O.K. Footwarmer", Rev: "Logan Pottery Co. Logan, O.", Handle Hairline, 12" L. $20.00
SALT BOX, Embossed Basket Weave, Flowers & "Salt", Hairline, 6" Diam. $56.00
(ROW III, L to R)
PITCHER, Embossed Iris, Base Glaze Wear, 8¼" H $52.50
BEAN POT, Embossed "Boston Baked Beans", Flakes, 7" H $52.50
PITCHER, Embossed Cherries, Spout Roughness, 8½" H $55.00

(A-PA '77)   *Pennypacker Auction Centre*
CHALK FRUIT TREE, 13½" H. $325.00

(D-KC '78) *Fisher's Antiques*
(*ROW I, L to R*)
ROSEVILLE VASE, Donatello, 3" H. ...
.............................$45.00
WELLER PITCHER, Barcelona, 8¾" H.
.............................$95.00
WELLER VASE, Sicardo, Signed, 4½" H.
.............................$150.00
(*ROW II, L to R*)
ROSEVILLE JARDINIERE, Donatello,
4" H. $65.00
**BRUSH McCOY-SYLVAN LINE JARDI-
NIERE,** Dated 1915, 5" H. $65.00
WELLER JARDINIERE, Fairfield, 3½" H.
.............................$65.00

(A-PA '77) *Pennypacker Auction Centre*
SLIPWARE LOAF DISH, Rim Chipped,
14" L. $185.00

(D-AR '78)
SPITTOON W/Blue Sponge Decoration &
Band $65.00

(D-KS '78) *Fisher's Antiques*
(*ROW I, L to R*)
JUGTOWN POTTERY VASE, Salt Glaze,
3½" H. $40.00
ROOKWOOD VASE, Dated 1920, 8½"
H. $45.00
WELLER VASE, Marbellized, 9" H. ....
.............................$45.00
WELLER VASE, Tutone, 7" H. ..$35.00
CLIFTON INDIAN POTTERY VASE,
3½" H. $35.00
(*ROW II, L to R*)
WELLER ROSE HOLDER, Woodcraft,
7" H. $45.00
WELLER VASE, Ardsley, 7½" H. $35.00
REDWING ART POTTERY VASE, 6¾"
H. $25.00
WELLER VASE, Coppertone, 6½" H. ....
.............................$35.00
WELLER FROG, 5" H. $45.00
(*ROW III, L to R*)
TECO VASE, 3¾" H. $40.00
WELLER VASE, Burntwood, 3" H. $30.00
WELLER VASE, Stellar Black, Artist
Signed, 5¾" H. $125.00
MUNCIE POTTERY VASE, 3¾" H. ....
.............................$15.00
WELLER VASE, 3¼" H. $25.00

(A-PA '77) *Pennypacker Auction Centre*
CHALK FIGURE, Girl, 9¾" H. ..$240.00
CHALK FIGURE, English Poodle Dog,
4½" H. $90.00

(D-KS '78) *Fisher's Antiques*
(*ROW I, L to R*)
STONEWARE MONMOUTH VASE, 8"
H. $40.00
WELLER HUDSON VASE, Blue/Gray
Glaze, 8½" H. $75.00
VAN BRIGGLE VASE, Persian Rose
Color, Artist Signed, 6¾" H. $55.00
(*ROW II, L to R*)
WELLER ELEPHANT PLANTER, 4" H.
.............................$30.00
PISGAH FOREST VASE, Crystalline
Glaze, 5" H. $45.00
**PAUL WEBB'S MOUNTAIN BOYS
PLANTER,** By Imperial Porcelain Corp.,
4¼" H. $35.00
(*ROW III, L to R*)
DOG PLANTER, 4½" H. $20.00
WELLER JARDINIERE, Blueware, 7¼"
H. $125.00
DESERT SANDS VASE, 3½" H. $20.00

(D-KS '78) *Fisher's Antiques*
(*L to R*)
WELLER VASE, Dickensware, Second
Line, 12¼" H. $350.00
WELLER VASE, Art Nouveau, 11¼" H.
.............................$150.00

(A-OH '77)   *Garth's Auctions, Inc.*

SPATTERWARE
(ROW I, L to R)
SUGAR BOWL, Blue, Peafowl Decor. In Blue, Red, Green & Black, Green Spatter Base, 5" Diam., 4¼" H. $175.00
CUP AND SAUCER, Purple, Rooster In Red, Yellow, Blue & Black.......$110.00
JAR, Blue, Minor Chips, 6½" H. ..$35.00
CUP AND SAUCER, Green $65.00
CREAMER, Blue & Purple, Red Rose Decor., 4¾" H. $75.00
(ROW II, L to R)
PLATE, Blue, Peafowl Decor. In Red, Blue, Green & Black, Impressed "Adams", 9½" Diam...................$250.00
TEAPOT, Blue, Red Rose Decor., 5" H. $140.00
PLATE, Blue, Peafowl Decor. In Red, Blue, Green & Black, Impressed "Adams", 9½" Diam...................$220.00
(ROW III, L to R)
CUP AND SAUCER, Blue, Rooster In Red, Yellow Ochre, Blue & Black .$320.00
PITCHER, Blue & Purple Rainbow, 7½" H. $150.00
CUP AND SAUCER, Green, Peafowl Decor. In Red, Blue, Green & Black, Minor Rim Chips $185.00

(A-OH '77)   *Garth's Auctions, Inc.*

(ROW I, L to R)
ROCKINGHAM BOWLS, (1 of 2), 1 Cracked & 1 W/Rim Chip, 5½" and 6" Diam. $22.50
ROCKINGHAM BOWL, Exterior W/ Moulded Panels, Overall Glaze Wear, 9¾" Diam. $25.00
YELLOWWARE BOWL, Blue & White Stripes, 6" H. $25.00
(ROW II, L to R)
ROCKINGHAM TURKS HEAD MOLD, 8¾" H. $45.00
ROCKINGHAM BOWL, 9¼" Diam. ....
.................................$40.00
YELLOWWARE MIXING BOWL, Exterior W/Molded Design, Brown & Green Glaze, 8" Diam. $45.00

(A-OH '77)   *Garth's Auctions, Inc.*

(ROW I, L to R)
HISTORICAL BLUE STAFFORDSHIRE CUP PLATE, "Landing Of Lafayette," Impressed "Clews," Hairline, 4⅜" Diam.
.................................$90.00
LEEDS TODDY PLATE, Peafowl In Tree, Green Edge, ½" Hairline, 5½" Diam.
.................................$390.00
WORCESTER DR. WALL CUP & SAUCER, Blue & White, Crescent Mark, Roughness On Cup Table Ring, 4¼" Diam......
.................................$105.00

(ROW II, L to R)
CANARY YELLOW LUSTER MUG, Floral Band, 2¼" H. $210.00
MINIATURE DISHES, (Pr.), Blue & White Willow Patt., Impressed "Wedgwood," 4" L. $75.00
SALOPIAN MUG, Cupid On Lamb, Rim & Base Chips, 2¼" H. $65.00

(ROW III, L to R)
CREAMWARE MUSTARD POT & SAUCER, Brick Red Decor., "Davenport," Flake On Saucer Rim, 3½" H. $30.00
CREAMWARE TEA STRAINER, Brown Greek Key Design, Wedgwood, 3¼" Diam.
.................................$45.00
MOCHA PEPPER POT, Yellow W/Brown Stripes & Seaweed, Repairs, 4½" H. ..
.................................$85.00
CANARY YELLOW MUG, Red Transfer Of "Washington & Lafayette," Hairline In Handle, Base Flake, 2⅜" H. $240.00
LEEDS SOFT PASTE CREAMER, Floral Design, 5 Colors, Old Repairs Rim & Base, 3½" H. $50.00

(ROW IV, L to R)
WOODEN GOING-TO-BED LAMP, Ivory Receptacle For Matches, 2¼" H. ..$35.00
CAST IRON PIG PAPERWEIGHT, "Pig Iron" & "Toledo," 2⅛" H. $27.50
WOODEN BOX, Rose Mulled Decor. W/ Flowers, 4½" L. $180.00
WOODEN SNUFF BOX, 2 Lids, 1 W/ Ivory Inset, 1 W/Concealed Fastener, Oval Ivory Inset In Bottom, 3½" L. $75.00

(A-OH '77)   *Garth's Auctions, Inc.*
(ROW I)
SPONGEWARE BOWLS, Nest Of 4, Tan, Blue & White, Largest W/Crows Foot Damage, 6¼" to 9¼" $82.50
(ROW II, L to R)
SPONGEWARE PITCHER, Brown, Green & White, 7¼" H. $27.50
SPONGEWARE BOWL, Tan, White & Blue, 6½" Diam. $15.00
SPONGEWARE COVERED BOWL, Green & White, Rim & Lid Chips, 6" Diam., 4½" H. $20.00
SPONGEWARE PITCHER, Black & White W/Blue Stripes, Spout Flake, Rim Hairline, 9¾" H. $45.00
(ROW III L toR)
SPONGEWARE BOWL, Tan, Blue & White, Interior Mkd. "It Pays To Trade W/ South Dakota Wheat Growers Ass'n., Rim Flakes, 8½" Diam. $25.00
SPONGEWARE BOWL, Tan, Blue & Cream Colored Ground, Interior Marked As One Above, 7½" Diam. $25.00
SPONGEWARE BOWL, Tan, Blue & White, 9¼" Diam. $25.00

(A-OH '77)   *Garth's Auctions, Inc.*
GAUDY DUTCH TEA SET, OYSTER PATTERN
CUPS & SAUCERS, (6), 2 Cups & 4 Saucers W/Minor Chips $1125.00
TEAPOT, Chip On Spout & Edge Of Lid, 5¾" H. $575.00
CREAMER, 4½" H. $475.00
SUGAR BOWL, Hairline In Base, Chip On Inside Lid, Flange, 5½" H. $400.00
BOWL, 10" Diam., 1½" H. $200.00
WASTE BOWL, Rim Chip, 6¼" Diam., 3¼" H. $150.00

(D-NY '78) *Lee Vines Antiques*
FRENCH ENAMEL VASE, Portrait Of Young Girl, Daisies At Neck & Base, Deep Cranberry Top & Base, 8" H. $750.00

(D-NY '78) *Lee Vines Antiques*
FRENCH FAIENCE PLATE, 1¼" Open Work Border, Hand Painted Scene, Signed "E. Duc", Mkd. "Lille 1767", 9¼" Sq. $95.00

(D-NY '78) *Lee Vines Antiques*
RORSTRAND VASE, Blue W/Irises, Artist Signed, 14" H. $550.00

(D-NY '78) *Lee Vines Antiques*
BOOTH & O'DELL TARRYTOWN POTTERY VASE, Mottled Blue Body W/Limoges Type Large Daisies, Ochre Neck, 18" H. $350.00

(D-NY '78) *Lee Vines Antiques*
CROWN DUCAL WALL PLAQUE, Ca. 1891-1916, By A. Richardson & Co., England, Enameled Lustered Sgrafitto, Signed "C. Rhead", 13⅞" W. $135.00

(D-KS '78) *Fisher's Antiques*
WELLER AURELIAN JARDINIERE, 10½" Diam., 9" H. $350.00

(D-NY '78) *Lee Vines Antiques*
ROOKWOOD SCENIC VELLUM VASE, Signed "Ed Hurley, 1904", 10" H. . . . . . .
. . . .$350.00

(D-NY '78) *Lee Vines Antiques*
ROYAL BAYREUTH VASE, Blue Ground, Portrait Of Girl & Pony Surrounded By Field Flowers, Gold Handles, Blue Mark, 8" H. $295.00

NILOAK POTTERY
(ROW I, L to R)
VASE, Rose, Blue & Ivory $35.00
VASE, Rust, Ivory & Blue $45.00
VASE, Dark Red & Blue $35.00
VASE, Blue, Rose & Ivory $35.00
(ROW II, L to R)
VASE, Rose & Blue $30.00
VASE, Blue, Rose & Ivory $30.00
URN, Dk. Red W/Blue Swirls $50.00
VASE, Blue, Rose & Ivory $30.00
VASE, Rust, Blue & Ivory $35.00
(ROW III, L to R)
VASE, Blue, Ivory & Rose $40.00
VASE, Blue, Ivory & Rose $30.00
FROG, Blue, Ivory & Brown $18.00
PLATE, Blue & Rust $30.00
VASE, Blue, Green & Ivory $35.00
VASE, Blue, Rose & Ivory $40.00

SLEEPY EYE POTTERY PITCHER, Cobalt & White, 8" H..............$225.00

(ROW I, L to R)
HATPIN HOLDER, Pink, 5½" H. .....
.............................$45.00
VASE, Green Jasperware, 4¾" H. $45.00
HANGING HATPIN HOLDER, Grey & Pink, 6¾" H..........$45.00
HATPIN HOLDER, Green & Pink, 5¼" H....................$45.00
(ROW II, L to R)
HATPIN HOLDER, White & Pink, 4¾" H....................$45.00
HATPIN HOLDER, Grey & Pink, 5" H.
.............................$45.00
HATPIN HOLDER, Pink & Green, 5¼" H.
.............................$45.00
HATPIN HOLDER, White & Blue, High Glaze, 5¼" H..................$45.00

(ROW I, L to R)
WELLER VASE, Roma, 6" H. ...$25.00
WELLER VASE, Roma, 8" H. ...$25.00
WELLER ROSE HOLDER, Roma, 8½" H................................$30.00
WELLER VASE, Roma, 5½" H. ..$25.00
(ROW II)
WELLER BREAKFAST SET, Creamer - 4½"; Milk Pitcher - 6½", Sugar 4" $125.00
(ROW III, L to R)
WELLER VASE, Roma, 7" H. ...$25.00
WELLER STANDING VASE, Roma, 6½" H................................$40.00
ROSEVILLE VASE, LaRose, 6½" H. ...
.............................$35.00
NILOAK DOG PLANTER, 5½" L. .....
.............................$20.00
DRYDEN BUFFALO, 4" H. $20.00

(ROW I, L to R)
WELLER VASE, 4" H. $25.00
ROSEVILLE VASE, Blackberry, 4½" H.
.............................$45.00
WELLER VASE, Blue Drapery, 3½" H.
.............................$25.00
WELLER JARDINIERE, Forest Line, 4¾" H................................$45.00
WELLER VASE, 4½" H. $25.00
(ROW II, L to R)
ROYCROFT MAPLE SYRUP JUG, 5" H................................$25.00
WELLER VASE, Warwick, 4¾" H. $45.00
WELLER PITCHER, 6½" H. $45.00
NILOAK FROG PLANTER, High Glaze, 4½" H........................$20.00
GONDER PITCHER, 5½" H. ...$15.00
(ROW III, L to R)
ERPHILLA ART POTTERY VASE, Germany, 5¾" H..................$25.00
WELLER JARDINIER, Patra, 6½" H. ..
.............................$55.00
WELLER VASE, Coppertone, 6¼" H. ....
.............................$45.00

(ROW I, L to R)
OWENS POTTERY VASE, 9" H. $85.00
WELLER NUDE VASE, Brown Orange Peel Background W/Nude In Orange, 9½" H................................$350.00
(ROW II, L to R)
WELLER VASE, Blueware, 10" H. ....
.............................$125.00
OWENS POTTERY VASE, Brown High Glaze, 5" H..................$85.00
THOMAS FORRESTER VASE, Tony Weller Depicted, 9¾" H. $75.00

(A-OH '77)   Garth's Auctions, Inc.
(ROW I, L to R)
HOUND HANDLED PITCHER, Embossed Hunting Scenes, Purple Colored Glaze, Small Pinpoint Flakes, 5½" H. $60.00
REDWARE BOWL, Brown Band W/Swags Of Yellow Slip & Green Dots, Glaze Wear On Center, 12" Diam., 2½" H. . . .$75.00
HOUND HANDLED PITCHER, Embossed Hunting Scenes, Rockingham Glaze, Spout Chips, 7" H. $75.00
(ROW II, L to R)
SEWER TILE SHAVING MUG, Divided, Incised Crosshatching On Exterior, Hand Molded, 4" H. . . . .
STONEWARE CREAMER, Cobalt Blue Brush Marks Around Top, Interior Top Edge Glazed Blue, Rim Chip At Handle, 3¾" H. $85.00
REDWARE FLOWER POT, Attached Saucer, Some Yellow Slip Decor., Cracked, 4¼" H. $22.50
REDWARE FROG, Clear Glaze, Minor Repair To Front Feet & Eye, 5¾" L. $10.00
REDWARE SHAVING MUG, Attached Round Basin, Exterior Has Tooled Bands & Drk. Metallic Glaze, Base Chip, 4" H. . . . .
. . . .$25.00
(ROW III, L to R)
WHITE CLAY HANGING FLOWER POT, Attached Saucer, Exterior Ribbed W/Applied Grecian Maiden Playing Lyre, Coated In Albany Slip, Small Chips, 8½" H. . . . . .
. . . .$55.00
REDWARE BOWL, Cream Slip W/Yellow & Green & Clear Glaze, Minor Glaze Wear, 9" Diam. $30.00
BENNINGTON COVERED JAR, "1849" Mark, Minor Chips Inside Lid Flange . . . . .
. . . .$265.00

(A-PA '77)   Brown Bros. Gallery
REDWARE POURING JUG, Sponged . .
. . . .$300.00
REDWARE PITCHER, 8¼" H. .$160.00
REDWARE CROCK, Manganese Splash, Damaged $130.00

(A-OH '77)   Garth's Auctions, Inc.
(ROW I)
REDWARE BOWL, Applied Open Handles, Clear Shiny Glaze Has Edge Wear, Old Hairlines, 11" Diam., 3¼" H. .$22.50
ROCKINGHAM "MADE DO" COFFEE POT, Iron Handle & Tin Lid W/Wooden Finial Held In Place By Tin Bands, Tin Ring On Spout Needs Resoldering, 11¼" H. . . . .
. . . .$65.00

(ROW II, L to R)
ROCKINGHAM POT, Flaking Glaze, Repaired Mismatched Lid, 7½" Diam., 9½" O.H. $25.00
ROCKINGHAM BOWL, 5¼" Diam., 3½" H. $45.00
ROCKINGHAM TURKS HEAD MOLD, 8¼" Diam. $55.00
(ROW III, L to R)
BENNINGTON FLINT ENAMEL CANDLESTICK, 8" H. $300.00
ROCKINGHAM JAR, No Lid, 8¼" Diam., 6" H. $55.00
ROCKINGHAM PITCHER, 6¼" H. . . . .
. . . .$55.00

(A-PA '77)   Pennypacker Auction Centre
(L to R)
POTTERY SPONGE CAKE DISHES (2), 6½" & 5¾" $90.00
POTTERY ANT TRAP, Incised Rings $10.00
POTTERY SPONGE CAKE DISHES (2), 7" $95.00

(A-OH '77)   Garth's Auctions, Inc.
(ROW I, L to R)
REDWARE BEEHIVE, Unglazed Exterior, Interior W/Pale Green Glaze, Edge Chips, 8" Diam., 9" H. $20.00
WOODEN KEY, For Tightning Rope Beds, 17" L. $55.00
REDWARE JUG, Black Metallic Glaze, 10¼" H. $15.00
(ROW II, L to R)
REDWARE FLOWER POT, Tooled Bands & Stripes Of Yellow Slip, 6" H. $40.00
WOODEN BOWL, Exterior W/Worn Blue Paint, Warped, 12¼" Diam. $70.00
WHITE CLAY FLOWER POT, W/Saucer, Edge Chips, 5¾" Diam., 6" H. $15.00
FLOWER POTS
(ROW III, L to R)
REDWARE, W/Brown Splotches & Clear Glaze, Rim Chip On Saucer, 6" Diam., 5¾" H. $45.00
REDWARE, W/Yellow Slip, 4¼" Diam., 3½" H. $90.00
REDWARE, W/Brown Splotches & Yellowish Glaze, Minor Hairline On Rim & Chips, Base Stamped "LTK," 5½" Diam., 4½" H. $80.00

(A-MA '77)   Richard A. Bourne Co., Inc.
STAFFORDSHIRE
(L to R)
PLATE, Dr. Blue, "Landing Of Gen. Lafayette At Castle Garden, New York, 16th August, 1824", "Clews", 8⅞" Diam. . . . . . .
. . . .$160.00
PLATE, Drk. Blue, "Commodore MacDonough's Victory," Enoch Wood & Sons, 10" Diam. $220.00
PLATE, Lt. Blue, "Landing Of The Fathers," Enoch Wood & Sons, 9⅞" Diam. $125.00

(D-ME '78)   *Hope Farm Antiques*
REDWARE JUG, Sgn. "W. England", Yellow Splotches Design $105.00

(A-OH '77)   *Garth's Auctions, Inc.*
(ROW I, L to R)
REDWARE PITCHER, Greenish-Tan Glaze, Flake On Top Edge, 7¾" H. $15.00
REDWARE LOAF PAN, 4-Line Yellow Slip Decor., Clear Shiny Glaze, Old Chips, 10¾" x 16¼" x 2¾" H. $160.00
EARTHENWARE PITCHER, Mottled Green Glaze, 7¾" H. $35.00
(ROW II, L to R)
REDWARE TURKS HEAD MOLD, Clear Speckled Glaze, 6½" Diam. $35.00
REDWARE PLATE, Yellow Slip Decor., Old Chips, 10" Diam. $170.00
REDWARE FOOD MOLD, Orange, 6½" Diam., 3" H. $17.50
(ROW III, L to R)
REDWARE TURKS HEAD MOLD, Greenish-Clear Glaze, 9" Diam. ...$15.00
WHITE CLAY TURKS HEAD MOLD, Green Exterior, Clear Glaze Interior, Edge Chips, 10½" Diam. $45.00
REDWARE PLATE, Yellow Slip Design W/Green & Clear Shiny Glaze, Old Chips, 8" Diam. $100.00

(A-OH '77)   *Garth's Auctions, Inc.*
REDWARE
(ROW I, L to R)
JAR, Glazed Inside & Out, Base Chip, 4" H. $20.00
JUG, Cream Colored Slip Decor. W/Incised Dashes Near Top, Base Chip & Hairlines, 8" H. $60.00
LAMP, Applied Handle, Worn Amber Glaze, Chips, 4" H. $35.00
(ROW II, L to R)
APPLE BANK, Minor Wear, 2½" H. ....
...................$30.00
MINIATURE EAR OF CORN MOLD, Brown Splotches On Rim, Minor Glaze Wear, 4½" L., 1¾" H. $135.00
POT, Applied Handle, Pouring Spout, Drk. Brown Speckles, Lid Missing, 5¼" H. ....
...................$60.00
MINIATURE TURKS HEAD MOLD, Drk. Brown Glaze Decorates Rim, 4" Diam., 1½" H. $160.00
(ROW III, L to R)
TURKS HEAD MOLD, 6¾" Diam. ......
...................$25.00
MOLD, Fish Shape, Rim W/Drk. Brown Running Glaze, Minor Edge Wear, 11¾" L.
...................$65.00
PUZZLE JUG, Band Of Yellow Slip & Drk. Green Running Glaze, 5½" H. ......
...................$115.00

(A-PA '77)   *Pennypacker Auction Centre*
SLIPWARE LOAF DISH, Crowsfoot Decor., 15¾" L. $525.00

(A-OH '77)   *Garth's Auctions, Inc.*
REDWARE
(ROW I, L to R)
JUG, Black Shiny Glaze, Lip Flake, 5" H.
...................$20.00
JAR, Brown Mottled Glaze, Edge Chips, 5¼" Diam., 5½" H. $7.50
VASE, Tooled Handles, Reddish-Brown Shiny Glaze, Edge Chips, Base Hairline, 6¾" H. $85.00
BOWL, Clear Glaze W/Drk. Brown Speckles, Minor Edge Roughness, 5" Diam. ....
...................$30.00
JUG, Black Shiny Glaze, Minor Glaze Wear, 5½" H. $37.50
(ROW II, L to R)
JUG, Black Shiny Glaze, Handle Chip, Lip Wear, 5½" H. $27.50
LOAF PAN, 3-Line Yellow Slip Decor., Coggled Edge, Edge Chips, 10½" x 16½"
...................$420.00
JAR, Drk. Brown Running Glaze, Inside Edge Rim Chips, 4" Diam., 4½" H. ......
...................$12.50
(ROW III, L to R)
PLATE, Yellow Slip Design, Coggled Edge, 8¼" Diam. $82.50
PITCHER, Yellow Slip W/Brown & Green Running Glaze Covered W/Clear Shiny Glaze, Glaze Flakes & Chips, 8½" H. ....
...................$155.00
PLATE, Brown & Yellow Slip, Clear Shiny Glaze, Coggled Edge, Glaze Flakes, 7½" Diam. $135.00

(A-PA '77)   *Pennypacker Auction Centre*
(L to R)
REDWARE PITCHER, Molded Edge, Drk. Glaze $95.00
REDWARE QUART JAR, Mottled Glaze, Rough Edge $55.00
REDWARE POURING POT, Mottled Glaze & Lid & 3" Glazed Redware Creamer (Not Pictured), 4¾" $100.00

(D-KS '78) *Fisher's Antiques*

STONEWARE
(L to R)
EAGLE POTTERY, 12-Gal., Benton, Ark., 18½" H $75.00
SALT GLAZE BUTTER CHURN, 5-Gal., 17" H $85.00
PICKLE CROCK, 14¾" H $65.00

(D-ME '78) *Hope Farm Antiques*
STONEWARE JUG, 2-Gal., Norton-Worcester, Leaf Design $75.00

(A-OH '77) *Garth's Auctions, Inc.*
STONEWARE
(ROW I, L to R)
BOTTLE, "B" In Cobalt, Impressed "P. PFANNEBECKER, SR.", 10¾" H .$37.50
BOTTLE, Impressed "P. MANSFIELD", Chip At "M", 6¾" H $22.00
JUG, White Stenciled Label On Brownish Green Glaze, "A. ANDRIESSON, Wholesale Liquor Dealer, 172 Federal St., Allegheny, Pa.", Lip Chips, 7½" H $35.00
JUG, 6½" H $15.00
BOTTLE, Impressed "Jones & Co.", Flake On Base & Lip, 11" H $27.50
(ROW II, L to R)
CROCK, Impressed "3", Rim Flake, 6" H $11.00
JAR, Stenciled Cobalt "Jas Hamilton & Co., Greensboro, Pa.", 9½" H $32.50
JUG, 6¾" H $32.50
(ROW III, L to R)
CANNING JAR, Rim Flakes, 9" H $20.00
BOTTLE, Impressed "G. Van Slyke", Glazed Over Chip On Lip & Base, 9" H $16.00
JUG, Cobalt "3" & Flourish, Repaired Rim Chips & Ear For Wire Handle, 8" H $22.50
BOTTLE, Impressed "C. Berry, Hop Beer", 9¾" H $30.00
BOTTLE, Paneled & Blue Stripe On Shoulder, Impressed "Green & Clark", 9¾" H $32.50

(A-PA '77) *Brown Bros. Gallery*
(L to R)
STONEWARE CROCK, Grey, Blue Decor. $65.00
STONEWARE JUG, 2-Gal., Grey, Blue Bouquet Decor. $110.00
STONEWARE CROCK, 2-Gal., Grey, Cover, Blue Cornucopia Decor. ..$120.00

(A-PA '77) *Pennypacker Auction Centre*
STONEWARE
(L to R)
BUTTER CROCK, Double Handle & Blue Leaf Decor. By Satterlett & Mory, Fort Edward, 7½" $55.00
CROCK, 5-Gal., Empressed Cow W/Blue Highlights, By Gardiner Stoneware, Gardiner, Maine $100.00
JUG, 2-Gal., Freehand Bird On Branch, By Adam Caire, Poughkeepsie, N.Y. .....
.................................$80.00

(A-PA '77) *Brown Bros. Gallery*
STONEWARE CROCK, 5-Gal., Grey, Blue Foliated Band, Signed, R. C. Remmey, Philadelphia, Hairline $95.00

(A-PA '77) *Brown Bros. Gallery*
(L to R)
STONEWARE CROCK, Grey $60.00
STONEWARE CROCK, Grey, Blue Tulip Decor. $50.00
STONEWARE CROCK, Grey, Blue Tulip Decor. $50.00

(A-PA '77) *Brown Bros. Gallery*
(L to R)
STONEWARE JUG, Grey, Blue Incised Band $220.00
STONEWARE CROCK, Grey, 4-Gal., Blue Leafage $50.00

(A-OH '77)   *Garth's Auctions, Inc.*

STONEWARE JUG, 5-Gal., Stenciled Sideways, "5", 19" H $45.00
STONEWARE JAR, 3-Gal., Ovoid, Cobalt Blue Brushed Floral Design, Handle Hairline, Chips, 16" H $55.00
STONEWARE JAR, 8-Gal., Stenciled Label: "Williams & Reppert Greensboro, Pa.", Cobalt Brushed Designs, Cracked, 18½" H $50.00
PINE CROCK STAND, Refinished, 42" W., 22" D., 32" H $135.00
STONEWARE JUG, 2-Gal., Stenciled Label: "H.F. Behken, Grocer, 2217 & 2219 Market Street, Wheeling, W.Va.", Spout Chip, 14½" H $40.00
STONEWARE JAR, 2-Gal., Stenciled Label: "H.T. Williams, New Geneva, Pa.", 12½" H $40.00
STONEWARE JAR, Ovoid, Blue Bands, 6½" H $40.00
STONEWARE JAR, Stenciled Label: "T. F. Reppert, Greensboro, Pa.", 9½" H $35.00
STONEWARE JAR, Ovoid, 3 Blue Stripes, 6¾" H $40.00
WROUGHT IRON PEEL, Ram's Handle, 42½" H $55.00
TIN STRAINER, 11" L $25.00
OIL ON CANVAS BOARD, Brown Bull, Ornate Gilt Frame, 12½" x 15" . . .$50.00
WROUGHT IRON PEEL, 41" L .$45.00

(A-OH '77)   *Garth's Auctions, Inc.*

STONEWARE
(ROW I, L to R)
JUG, Blue Transfer Labels; "Casey Bros. Scranton, Pa." & "Pasteur Chamberland Filter Co., Dayton, Ohio", 7½" H .$27.50
BOTTLE, "Vimo, Ginger Beer, Cleveland, Ohio", Base Chip, 6½" H $11.00
BOTTLE, "The Christian Moerlein Brewing Co.", Minor Lip Flake, 10½" H . . .$17.50
BOTTLES (2), 1 Illus., Impressed "Harrington, Southend", & "Josiah Russell", "Bourne Denby", 6½" H. & 7½" H $7.00
JUG, Brown & White, "The Schwartz & Klein Co., Youngstown, Ohio", Lip Chipped, 8¾" H $27.50
(ROW II, L to R)
BOTTLE, Impressed "G.B.", Wooster, Ohio, 10" H $20.00
BOTTLE, "English Brewed Ginger Beer, The M. Shoulder Bottling Works, Akron, Ohio", 7" H $13.00
FLASK, 8" H $37.50
BOTTLE, "English Brewed Ginger Beer, The M. Shoulder Bottling Works, Akron, Ohio", 7" H. $10.00
BOTTLE, Impressed "J.C. Schnell's Sour Mash Kiln Dried Grain Whiskey", 8½" H. $32.50
(ROW III, L to R)
JUG, Brown & White, "High Grade Sherry Wine, Salzman & Siegelman, Brooklyn, N.Y.", 6¾" H. $15.00
BOTTLE, Ceramic Cap, Wire Fastener, "W.K. Wagner, Youngstown, Ohio", 8½" H. $6.00
JUG, Stenciled "S.T. Suit, Suitland, Md. & 1880", Minor Glaze Flakes, 6¾" H.$55.00
BOTTLES, (2), 1 Illus., Tan Glaze W/ "Josiah Russel" 7½" H.; Grey Salt Glaze W/"Dr. Cronk", Hairline, 7¼" H. . .$12.50
JUG, "O'Keefe's Pure Malt Whiskey, Oswego, N.Y.", 7½" H. $17.50

◀ *To the left*

(A-OH '77)   *Garth's Auctions, Inc.*
STONEWARE COOLER, 4-Gal., Impressed "Somerset Potters Works", Incised Birds Highlighted In Cobalt Blue, Chip & Hairline On Base, Wood, Pewter & Iron Spigot Not Pictured, 19" H. $1700.00

(A-OH '77)   *Garth's Auctions, Inc.*
(ROW I, L to R)
STONEWARE JUG, Incised "Hirsch Bros., Louisville, Ky.", Lip Flake, Repaired Handle, 3" H $14.00
STONEWARE JUG, Incised "Kentucky Fruit Vinegar, For Sale By J. Bondarant", Lip Flakes, 2¾" H. $21.00
STONEWARE JUG, Incised "Compliments Of John Cook, 67 McGee St.", 3" H $15.00
STONEWARE INK, 2" H $5.00
STONEWARE JUG, Embossed "Old Kernel Corn", Incised Bottom, "1913", 2¾" H $21.00
STONEWARE JUG, Incised "Compliments Of Hunters Tea Store, 184-11 Washington St.", Base Chip, 2¾" H $25.00
STONEWARE JUG, Impressed "J.W. Russell", Lip Flake, 3" H $17.00
(ROW II, L to R)
CAST IRON BIRDS (2), 1 Illus., Both W/Worn Red Paint, 2½" H $10.00
CAST IRON PIG, Worn White & Black Paint, 2¼" H $40.00
STONEWARE PIG BOTTLE, White Glaze W/Blue Spots, Ear Chipped, 5" L . .$12.50
CABLE PAPERWEIGHT, "Broderick & Bascom, St. Louis, Mo.", Worn Gilt Paint, 3" H $13.00
CAST IRON BIRD, 2¾" H $22.00
(ROW III, L to R)
STONEWARE JUG, Brown & White, "Motto Jug, Detrick Distilling Co., Dayton, O.", 4½" H $22.50
BENTWOOD STORAGE BOX, 6" L $45.00
BENTWOOD STORAGE BOX, 4" L $32.50
STONEWARE JUG, White Glaze, Blue Label, "The Golden Hill, Toledo, Ohio", 4½" H $25.00

(A-PA '77)   *Pennypacker Auction Centre*
POTTERY PIE PLATE, Glazed W/Zig-Zag Slip Decor., 10½" Diam. $290.00
POTTERY PLATE, Glazed Slipware, 7¾" Diam. $150.00

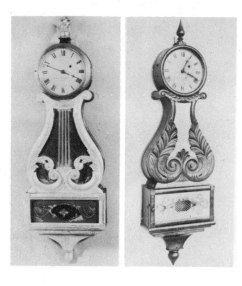

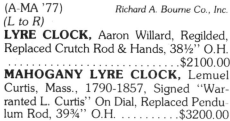

(L to R)
LYRE CLOCK, Aaron Willard, Regilded, Replaced Crutch Rod & Hands, 38½" O.H. $2100.00
MAHOGANY LYRE CLOCK, Lemuel Curtis, Mass., 1790-1857, Signed "Warranted L. Curtis" On Dial, Replaced Pendulum Rod, 39¾" O.H. $3200.00

WAG-ON-WALL CLOCK, Continental, Early 19th C., Orig. Face, Pendulum Swings Man's Eyes, Tongue Goes Back & Forth, Weight Driven Movement W/Strike, Weights Replaced $400.00

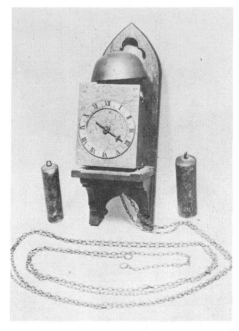

MINIATURE LANTERN CLOCK, Peter Closon, London (1636-1653), 30-Hour Movement Converted To Anchor Escapement, Engraved Brass Dial & Wooden Bracket, Orig. Weights, 7½" H. .$4500.00

(L to R)
BANJO CLOCK, Sawin & Dyer, Boston, Ca. 1820-1825, Mahogany Case, Restored, Dial & Case Door Latches Missing, Professionally Repainted Glass, 42½" O.H. .....
......................................$1500.00
BANJO CLOCK, Unknown American Maker, Door Glass Cracked, Repainted, 33½" O.H. $1000.00

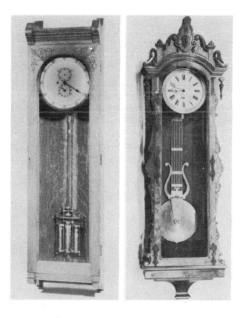

(L to R)
REGULATOR WALL CLOCK, Quarter Oak Case, 60-Beat Regulator Movement, Dead Beat Escapement, Jeweled Pallets, 3-Jar Mercury Pendulum, Second Hand Missing, One Mercury Jar Chipped, 67½" O.H.
......................................$550.00
FRENCH REGULATOR WALL CLOCK, Burled Walnut Faced Case, Porcelain Dial, Pinwheel Escapement, Gridiron Pendulum, 87½" O.H. $3200.00

BRASS LANTERN CLOCK, Thomas Tompion, London, 17th C., 30-Hour Striking & Alarm Movement W/Single Hand, Silvered Chapter & Alarm Rings, Verge Escapement, Back Plate W/"Stirrup And Spurs", Professional Replaced Alarm Mechanism & Pallets, 15" H. $3750.00

(A-MA '77)   *Richard A. Bourne Co., Inc.*
(L to R)
MAHOGANY BRACKET CLOCK,
Thomas Wagstaffe, London, 1756-1793,
8-Day Verge Movement, Brass Dial & Orna-
mentation, 19⅞" O.H. $2100.00
BRASS LANTERN CLOCK, James Grey
(Shaston), English, Late 17th-Early 18th C.,
Verge Movement, Restored Verge Wheels
& Pallets, 14½" O.H. $800.00
ENGLISH BRACKET CLOCK, 18th C.,
Maker Unknown, Hardwood Case W/Brass
Mounts, Brass Circle Over Chapter Ring
Missing, 18" O.H. $750.00

(A-MA '77)   *Richard A. Bourne Co., Inc.*
CLOCK, Claudius Du Chesne, Londini
(1693-1730), Full Quarter Repeater W/
Verge Escapement, Pull-Repeating On Six
Bells, Moon Phase, Tell-Tale Pendulum,
Engraved Back Plate, Ebonized Wood Case,
Professional Restoration, Orig. Brass Key,
18" O.H. $7000.00

(A-MA '77)   *Richard A. Bourne Co., Inc.*
MASSACHUSETTS SHELF CLOCK,
Aaron Willard, Mahogany Case, Orig. Kid-
ney Dial W/Willard Signature, Pediment &
Hinges Replaced, 34½" O.H. ...$4600.00

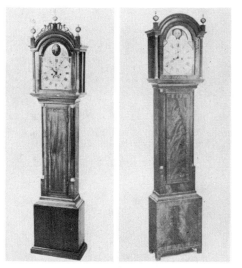

(A-MA '77)   *Richard A. Bourne Co., Inc.*
(L to R)
TALL CLOCK, Simon Willard, Grafton &
Roxbury, Mass., 1753-1848, Mahogany
Case W/String & Band Inlay, Orig. Label
W/Advertisement & Instructions Inside
Door, Orig. Brass Works, Decorated Dial,
Wrought Iron Hands, Lower Front Wood
Panel & Brass Finials Are Replacements,
Approx. 91" O.H. $8000.00
TALL CLOCK, Aaron Willard, Boston,
Mass., Inlaid Mahogany Case W/Broad
Band & String Inlays, Orig. Maker's Paper
Label Inside Door, Brass Works, Decor.
Iron Dial W/Moon Phase, Second Hand &
Pair Wrought Iron Hands, Minor Repairs,
92½" O.H. $7000.00

(A-MA '77)   *Richard A. Bourne Co., Inc.*
PILLAR AND SCROLL SHELF CLOCK,
Eli & Samuel Terry, Plymouth, Conn., 1824-
1827, Orig. Label, Original Wooden Works
& Finials, Upper Glass Cracked In Corner,
Reverse-Painted Lower Glass Is Replace-
ment, 31¼" O.H. $1400.00

(A-MA '77)   *Richard A. Bourne Co., Inc.*
MANTEL OR TABLE CLOCK, Edward
Wicksteed, London (1763-1795), Fusee,
Verge Escapement, Break-Arch Dial, Ebon-
ized Case W/Pineapple Finials, Pull-
Repeating On Two Bells, Orig. Brass Key,
16½" O.H. $2750.00

(A-MA '77)   *Richard A. Bourne Co., Inc.*
(L to R)
CONTINENTAL TALL CLOCK, Refinished Pine Case, Brass Works W/Striking Movement, Brass Covered Dial W/Pewter Motto & Chapter Ring, 82" O.H. $1000.00
TALL CLOCK, David Somerville, British, 18th C., Inlaid Mahogany Case, Orig. Brass Works, Burnished Steel Dial, Wrought Iron Hands, Finials Missing, Minor Restoration To Case, 83½" O.H. $1450.00

(A-OH '77)   *Garth's Auctions, Inc.*
MAHOGANY TALL CASED CLOCK, Wood Inlay In Circle & Oval Designs W/ Cross Banding, Brass Works W/Painted Metal Face, Trim Missing On Bonnet, 90" O.H. $900.00

(A-VA '77)   *Laws Auction & Antiques*
TALL CASED CLOCK, Boston, Mass., Ca. 1750, Japanned, Works Mkd. G. Brown, Boston; Lower Pine Case W/Shaped Single Door W/River & Garden Scene At Lower Base, 6'7" O.H. $3750.00

(A-OH '77)   *Garth's Auctions, Inc.*
TALL CASED CLOCK, Cherry & Walnut Burl, Brass Works, Decor. Metal Face, Calendar Movement & Second Hand, Replaced Finials & Feet, 8'6" O.H. $1150.00

(A-PA '77)   *Brown Bros. Gallery*
WALNUT TALL CASE CLOCK, Brass Dial Inscribed "Jacob Godshalk, Philadelphia", 30 Hr. Brass Movement Calendar Aperture, 7'5" O.H. $3300.00

(A-MA '77)   *Richard A. Bourne Co., Inc.*
(L to R)
TALL CLOCK, Frederick Wingate, Augusta, Maine, 1782-1864, Orig. Adv. Label In Back, Refinished Birch Case, Ebonized Rings, Orig. Brass Works, Wrought Iron Hands, 92" O.H. $3500.00
TALL CLOCK, Works By Thomas Clift, English, 18th C., Orig. Signed Brass Dial W/Cast Iron Fret Decor., Wrought Iron Hands; Case, Solid Cherry Replacement, 76½" O.H. $600.00

(A-MA '77)   *Richard A. Bourne Co., Inc.*
MINIATURE GRANDFATHER CLOCK,
Unknown Maker, Painted Pine Case, 8-Day
Movement Without Strike, Brass Bushed
Iron Plates, Brass Wheels, Banjo-Type
Movement W/Hands, Dial & Weight, Glass
Door Cracked, 28⅞" O.H. $7000.00

(A-MA '77)   *Richard A. Bourne Co., Inc.*
(L to R)
MAHOGANY CASED TALL CLOCK,
Samuel Toulmin, Strand, London, 1747-
1783, Fluted Brass Finials, Orig. Brass Works
W/Engraved Brass Dial, Minute Hand &
Calendar Dial, Strike Or Silent Settings,
Base Is Replacement Of Original, 91" O.H.
..............................$900.00
TALL CLOCK, William Bird (Seagrave),
English, 18th C., Carved Oak Case, Orig.
Brass Works, Second Hand & Calendar Dial,
Applied Brass Chapter Rings, Orig. Wrought
Iron Hands, Minor Repair, 84" O.H. .....
..............................$850.00

(A-OH '77)   *Garth Auctions, Inc.*
CHERRY TALL CASED CLOCK, Inlaid
Bird On Door, Brass Works In Wooden Case
W/Painted Wooden Face Mkd. "H. Dilger
Of Canton", Face Paint Peeling, 90" O.H. .
..............................$900.00

(A-MA '77)   *Richard A. Bourne Co., Inc.*
(L to R)
TALL CLOCK, Benjamin Swan, Augusta,
Maine, Early 19th C., Birch & Wavy Birch
W/Curly Maple Door & Column Supports,
Orig. Brass Works, Signed Dial, Refinished
In Natural, 90½" O.H. $3000.00
TALL CLOCK, James C. Cole, Rochester,
N.H., Early 19th C., Brass Works, Ship
Movement, Wrought Iron Hands, Replaced
Dial, Non-Matching Finials, 83" O.H. .....
..............................$1200.00

To the right ▶

TALL CLOCK By Stephen M. Taber (New
Bedford, MA & Providence, RI, 1777-1862).
Select-grain Mahogany Case W/Unusual
Fan Inlay, Fluted Quarter Columns W/
Brass Stop Fluting, Reticulated Crest; W/
Moon Phase, O.H. 94½" $5,500.00

(A-MA '78)   *Richard A. Bourne Co., Inc.*

(A-PA '77)   *Brown Bros. Gallery*
GRAINED PINE TALL CASE CLOCK,
Brass 8 Day Time & Strike Movement, 7'11"
O.H. $2200.00

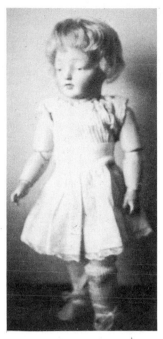

FULPER BABY DOLL, Sleep Blue Eyes, Composition Body, 23" H. $685.00

KESTNER CHARACTER DOLL (Set), 4 Interchangeable Heads, 3 Closed Mouth, Orig. Box, (1 Illus), 11½" H. $2750.00

QUEEN ANNE DOLL, Ca. 1750, Wooden Head, Body & Limbs, Black Glass Eyes, Orig. Clothes, 12" H. $1175.00

JUMEAU DOLL, French "DEP", Ball Jointed Body, Brown Stationary Eyes, 18" H. $295.00

FRENCH SFBJ DOLL, "252" Pouty, Brown Sleep Eyes, Orig. Wig, Composition Baby Body, 8" H. $2175.00

WAX BABY DOLL, Ca. 1600, Poured Wax Head & Arms, Black Glass Eyes, Orig. Box, 9" H. $965.00

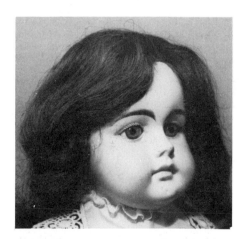

BELTON DOLL, Blue Paperweight Eyes, Orig. Cloth Body, Kid Arms W/Stitched Fingers, Sewn-On Leather Boots, Old Clothes, 24" H. $600.00

POURED WAX DOLL, Cloth Body, Wax Arms & Legs, Inserted Hair, Wire Eyes, 24" H. $675.00

SUPERIOR DOLL, Brown Eyes, Orig. Clothes & Label, 16½" H. $315.00

(A-MA '77)   Richard A. Bourne Co., Inc.

DOLLS

(ROW I, L to R)

COMPOSITION HEAD GIRL, Blonde Mohair Wig, Painted Eyes, Cloth Body, Composition Head, Arms & Legs, Skirt & Knit Sweater, Orig. Undergarments, Signed "MDT", 7" H. $500.00

COMPOSITION DOLL, Blonde Hair, Glass Pupil-Less Eyes, Wooden Hands & Feet, Cloth Body, Blue Polka Dot Dress, Orig., Faded, 11½" H. $25.00

GIRL CARRYING BISQUE DOLL, Blonde Mohair Wig, Blue Eyes, Bisque Hands, Kid Body W/Cloth Legs & Feet, Cotton Dress, Lace Undergarments, Sm. Hole In Forehead, Gown Faded, 12" H. $60.00

NANTUCKET LADY, Composition Head, Painted Brown Eyes, Wire Arms, Wax Hands, Wooden Legs & Feet, Cloth Body, Orig. Silk Gown, Hand Broken, Gown Frail, 9" H. $100.00

(ROW II, L to R)

COMPOSITION BOY, Mohair Wig, Composition Head, Inset Blue Glass Eyes, Bisque Hands, Kid Body & Legs, Wool Suit, Wig Worn, Minor Wear On Nose, Chin & Cheeks, Suit Faded, 15½" H. $50.00

COMPOSITION GIRL, Molded Blonde Hair, Composition Head, Blue Glass Inset Eyes, Kid Body, Arms, Hands, Legs & Feet, Cotton Dress, Orig. Homespun Petticoat, Minor Wear, Costume Faded, Prof. Repair To Crack In Head, 16½" H. $60.00

LADY WITH BASKET, Composition Head, Reddish Mohair Wig, Glass Eyes, Kid Hands, Cloth Body & Legs, Calico Dress, Orig. Petticoat & Pantalets, Face Cracks, Hair Worn, Costume Faded, 16½" H. $30.00

(ROW III, L to R)

GRANDMOTHER DOLL, Composition Head, Gray Lamb's Wool Wig, Painted Eyes, Leather Hands, Cloth Body, Arms &
(continued top of next column)

◀ *To the left*   *(continued)*

Legs, Orig. Gray Dress; Shoes & Hair Worn, 20½" H. $80.00

BRIDE DOLL, Composition Head, Blonde Mohair Wig, Brown Eyes, Kid Body & Jointed Arms, Satin Gown, Forehead Crack, Shoulder Plate Repair, Right Hand Missing, 19½" H. $60.00

SQUASH HEAD DOLL, Composition Head, Blonde Hair, Glass Pupil-Less Eyes, Wooden Hands & Legs, Cloth Body, Orig. Blue Dress & Undergarments, Legs Broken Off, 24½" H. $25.00

(A-MA '77)   Richard A. Bourne Co., Inc.

BISQUE-HEAD DOLLS

(ROW I, L to R)

BISQUE BOY, Blonde Hair, Black Velvet Suit, Kid Body & Legs, Bisque Hands, 13" H. $150.00

GERMAN BISQUE DOLL, American Boy, Set-In Blue Glass Eyes, Closed Mouth, Blonde Hair, Kid Body & Legs W/ Bisque Hands, Groom Costume, 16½" H. $225.00

BISQUE BOY, Molded Blonde Hair, Set-In Drk. Brown Eyes, Closed Mouth, Mkd. "15/0", Cloth Body, No Arms, Red Flannel Suit, 10" H. $75.00

(ROW II, L to R)

BISQUE BOY, Blonde Molded Hair, Painted Blue Eyes, Closed Mouth, Kid Body W/Cloth Legs & Leather Hands, White Shirt & Velvet Pants & Jacket, 18" H. $200.00

BISQUE BOY, German, Molded Hair, Brown Stationary Eyes, Closed Mouth, Cloth Body & Legs W/Bisque Hands, Satin Shirt & Velvet Jacket & Pants, 19" H. $600.00

BISQUE BOY, Blonde, Blue Painted eyes, Cloth Body & Legs W/Bisque Hands, Checkered Pants, White Shirt & Blue Jacket, Leather Boots, Shoulder Plate Repaired, Repair To Nose, 18" H. $100.00

(A-MA '77)   Richard A. Bourne Co., Inc.

DOLLS

(ROW I, L to R)

BISQUE WOMAN, Painted Eyes, Bisque Shoulder Plate, Head, Arms & Legs, Cloth Body, Orig. Taffeta Dress & Underwear, 6¼" H. $225.00

BLONDE WOMAN, Bisque Head, Shoulder Plate, Hands & Legs, Cloth Body, Bridal Gown, Undergarments, 6" H. $275.00

BONNET-TYPE BISQUE HEAD, Painted Eyes, Bisque Arms & Legs, Cloth Body, Velvet Gown, Orig. Cotton Underwear, 7¾" H. $75.00

(ROW II, L to R)

BLONDE BISQUE HEAD, Painted Eyes, Bisque Arms & Legs, Cloth Body, Calico-Type Dress, Underwear, Toes Broken, 6" H. $30.00

BISQUE NIPPON BOY, Painted Eyes, Lace Dress & Petticoat, Paint Worn On Shoes, 7" H. $40.00

BISQUE HAPPY FATS, Painted Eyes & Mouth W/2 Teeth, Pink Gown, 4" H. $175.00

BISQUE ROSE O'NEIL KEWPIE, Painted Hair, Eyes & Mouth, Satin Dress, Signed "O'Neil", 5¼" H. $60.00

BISQUE ROSE O'NEIL KEWPIE, Painted Hair, Eyes & Mouth, No Costume, Signed "O'Neil", 4½" H. $30.00

(ROW III, L to R)

BISQUE HEAD SCOTTISH BOY, Blonde Hair, Painted Eyes, Bisque Shoulder Plate, Arms & Legs, Cloth Body, Scottish Costume, 11" H. $50.00

20TH CENTURY LADY, Bisque Head & Shoulder Plate, Lt. Brown Wig, Painted Eyes & Mouth, Bisque Legs Mkd. "Germany", Cloth Body, Gown Frail & Worn, Right Leg Broken & Missing, 11" H. $75.00

BISQUE BOY, Painted Eyes, Jointed Bisque Arms & Legs, Molded-On Undergarment, Right Leg Broken At Hip, 7½" H. $25.00

(A-MA '77)   *Richard A. Bourne Co., Inc.*
(ROW I, L to R)
CLOTH DOLL, Embroidered Features, Homespun-Type Petticoat, Cotton Dress, 9" H. $30.00
CLOTH DOLLS, Pr., Man & Woman, Hand-Painted Faces, Wooden Legs, Wool Clothing, Knit Sweaters, 7" H. $10.00
CLOTH DOLL, Girl From Norway, Blonde Hair, Painted Features, Felt & Cotton Costume, 7" H. $20.00
CLOTH DOLL, Humpty Dumpty, Face Pencilled On Cardboard, Velvet Costume, Faded, Costume Worn, Sitting Position Ht. 4½" $10.00
CLOTH DOLL, Paper Hands, Brown Glazed Material Costume, Remnants Of Hair, Breaks In Costume, 3½" H. . .$30.00
(ROW II, L to R)
CLOTH DOLL, Inked-In Features, Cotton Dress, Dotted Swiss Undergarments, Hair Worn, Faded Costume, 9" H. $30.00
CLOTH DOLL, From India, Black Thread Hair, Painted Features, Native Costume, Face Stained, 9½" H. $10.00
CLOTH DOLL, Embroidered Eyes, Stuffed Post Body, Flannel Dress, 10" H. . .$10.00
FABRIC DOLL, Crocheted, Blonde Mohair Wig, 10½" H. $90.00

(A-MA '77)   *Richard A. Bourne Co., Inc.*
(ROW I, L to R)
SCHOENHUT GIRL, Wooden W/Painted Features, Brown Wig, Undergarments, Minor Face Crazing, 16½" H. $375.00

(continued bottom of next column)

(A-MA '77)   *Richard A. Bourne Co., Inc.*
(ROW I, L to R)
MILLINER MODEL, Black Pupil-Less Glass Eyes, Cloth Body, Arms & Legs; Kid Hands, Cotton Dress, Paint Flaking, Cracks, 22½" H. $600.00
PAPIER MACHE HEAD DOLL, Painted Brown Eyes, New Cloth Body, Legs, New Kid Arms, Cotton Dress, Undergarments, Shoulder Plate Crack, 19" H. $60.00
PAPIER MACHE HEAD DOLL, Black Pupil-Less Eyes, Painted Mouth, Cloth Body, Legs & Arms, Kid Hands, Wool Dress, Undergarments, Leather Purse, Worn, Dress Motheaten, 21½" H. $550.00
(ROW II, L to R)
PAPIER MACHE HEAD DOLL, Painted Blue Eyes, Cloth Body, Arms & Legs; Arms Stubs W/No Fingers; White Dress, Pantalets, Orig. Greiner Label On Back W/"1858", Shoulder Cracks, Head Loose From Body, 23½" H. $80.00
PAPIER MACHE HEAD DOLL, Painted Blue Eyes, Cloth Body, Legs & Arms, Leather Hands, Cotton Dress, Linen Petticoat, Body Needs Repair, 24" H. . .$50.00
LINEN DOLL, Black Hair, Painted Features W/Black Pupil-Less Eyes, Cotton Body W/Painted Over Linen Hands & Legs, Taffeta Dress, Cotton Petticoat, Nose Rubbed, Paint Worn On Cheek, 22" H. $225.00

◄ *To the left*

IZANNAH WALKER DOLL, Cloth Painted Over, Painted Features & Hair, Cloth Body, Arms & Legs, Undergarments, White Print Dress, Cloth Broken On Head & Hands, Paint Cracked, 17½" H. $700.00
CARVED WOODEN FIGURE, Legs Jointed At Hips & Knees, Cotton Costume, 14½" H. $10.00
(ROW II, L to R)
WOODEN HEAD DOLL, Wooden Hands & Feet, Cloth Body, Undergarments, Quilt-

(A-MA '77)   *Richard A. Bourne Co., Inc.*
CLOTH DOLLS
(ROW I, L to R)
LENCI GIRL, Brown Mohair Wig, Painted Face, Tennis Outfit, Minor Wear On Nose, 14½" H. $210.00
LENCI BOY, Blonde Mohair Wig, Painted Eyes, Costume Flaking, 14½" H. .$225.00
NORWEGIAN DOLL, Brown Mohair Wig, Painted Eyes, Felt Costume, 15" H. $70.00
(ROW II, L to R)
AMERICAN WAR SOLDIER, Printed Cloth Face, Army Uniform, 15" H. .$60.00
HOMEMADE LADY, Painted-On Eyes, Needlework Nose & Mouth, Mesh Netting Hair, Orig. Linen Jacket, Skirt & Blouse, Orig. Undergarments, 14½" H. $50.00
GIRL, Blonde W/Printed-On Face, Boots & Hands, Calico Dress, Homespun Undergarments, Faded, 15" H. $25.00
(ROW III, L to R)
FRENCH DOLLS, Pr., By M. Bernard Ravca, Stockings Stretched Over Silk, Simulated Wooden Shoes, Man - 13"; Lady - 11½" $275.00
ELDERLY COUPLE, Homemade Stockinette Dolls, Mid-19th Century Costumes, Minor Damage, Man - 16" H; Lady - 15" H. $30.00

(continued)

ed Dress, Nose Repaired, Paint Flaked Off Hands & Feet, 20½" H. $300.00
CLOTH HEAD DOLL, Painted Black Hair & Features, Cloth Head, Arms, & Legs Painted Over & Cloth Body, Undergarments, Cotton Dress, Paint Worn, 17½" H.$80.00
CARVED WOODEN DOLL, Wooden Body & Legs & Cloth Arms, Brown Human Hair Wig, Painted Features, Cotton Undergarments, Wool Dress, Minor Paint Wear, 23" H. $75.00

(A-MA '77)   *Richard A. Bourne Co., Inc.*

(L to R)

BLACK-HAIRED CHINA, Set-In Black Pupil-Less Eyes, Cloth Body & Legs W/ Leather Arms, Cotton Undergarments, Print Dress, Break In Left Arm Over Shoulder & Across Front Of Neck, Arm Missing Below Elbow, 17½" H. $175.00

BLACK-HAIRED CHINA, Cloth Body, China Arms & Legs, Cotton Undergarments & Print Dress, Left Hand Missing, Minor Crack In Leg, 14½" H. $50.00

BLACK-HAIRED CHINA, Cloth Body, Legs, & Arms W/Leather Hands, Cotton Petticoat, Wool & Cotton Costume, No Shoulder Plate, Hair Worn, Firing Mark On Cheek, 15¼" H. $10.00

(A-MA '77)   *Richard A. Bourne Co., Inc.*

CHINA-HEAD DOLLS

(L to R)

BLACK-HAIRED CHINA, Boy, Painted Features W/Blue Eyes, Grey Wool Trousers, Tan Tweed Jacket & Cotton Shirt, Neck Broken, 15½" H. $85.00

BROWN-EYED CHINA, Black Hair, Cloth Body, Arms & Legs; Kid Hands, Silk Dress, Undergarments, Shoulder Plate Chipped, Hairline Crack, 14" H. . .$250.00

BLONDE-HAIRED CHINA, "Dolly Madison" Type, Painted Features W/Blue Eyes, Cloth Body, Arms & Legs; Kid Hands, Orig. Costume, Hands In Poor Condition, Nose Rubbed, 15½" H. $75.00

(A-MA '77)   *Richard A. Bourne Co., Inc.*

CHINA-HEAD DOLLS

(ROW I, L to R)

BLACK-HAIR, Blue Painted Eyes, Cloth Body, China Arms & Legs, Black Painted-On Shoes, Right Leg Broken & Reglued, 17½" H. $300.00

BIEDERMEIER DOLL, Human Hair Wig, Blue Painted Eyes, Cloth Body, China Arms & Legs, Painted-On Shoes, 15½" H. $350.00

BLACK-HAIR, Brown Painted Eyes, Cloth Body & Legs, Kid Arms, Leather Slippers, Finger Missing, 18" H. $125.00

BLACK-HAIR, Brush Marks Across Front, Blue Painted Eyes, Cloth Body, China Arms & Legs, Minute Chip On Back Of Head, 16½" H. $200.00

(ROW II, L to R)

BLACK-HAIR, Brown Painted Eyes, Cloth Body & Legs, Kid Arms, 16½" H. $400.00

BLACK-HAIR, Blue Painted Eyes, China Arms, Cloth Upper Body Fitted Onto Box Which Is Sewing Cabinet, 16" H. .$125.00

BLACK-HAIR, Brush Marks At Side Of Face, Blue Painted Eyes, Cloth Body, China Arms & Legs, Left Leg & Boot Repaired & Repainted, 16½" H. $75.00

BLACK-HAIR, Blue Painted Eyes, Cloth Body & Legs, China Arms, 18" H.$100.00

To the right

(ROW II, L to R)

BLACK-HAIRED CHINA, Painted Blue Eyes, Cloth Body, Arms & Legs, Petticoat, Checked Dress, Few Face Pits, 23½" H. $150.00

BLACK-HAIRED CHINA, Painted Blue Eyes, Cloth Body & Legs, Leather Arms, Undergarments, Silk Dress, 24" H.$150.00

BLACK-HAIRED CHINA, Painted Blue Eyes, Cloth Body, Legs & Arms, Wooden Hands, Undergarments, Print Dress, 27" H. $150.00

(A-MA '77)   *Richard A. Bourne Co., Inc.*

CHINA HEAD DOLLS

(ROW I, L to R)

BLACK-HAIRED CHINA, Decorated Features W/Blue Eyes, Cloth Body; China Arms & Legs, Taffeta Costume, Undergarments, Paint Worn, Shoulder Plate Hairline, 15" H. $125.00

BLACK-HAIRED CHINA, Painted Features W/Blue Eyes, Cloth Body; China Arms & Legs, Taffeta Gown Faded, 15½" H. $800.00

BLACK-HAIRED CHINA, Painted Features W/Blue Eyes, Cloth Body, Arms & Legs; Kid Arms, Wool Dress, Petticoat, Sm. Firing Mark, Shoulder Plate Blemish, 16½" H. $100.00

(ROW II, L to R)

BLACK-HAIRED CHINA, Painted Features W/Blue Eyes, Cloth Body, China Arms & Legs, Bee Wakeman Costume, Undergarments, Dress Worn, Arm Firing Marks, Leg Crack, 20½" H. $125.00

BLACK-HAIRED CHINA, Painted Features W/Blue Eyes, Cloth Body, China Arms & Legs, Lace Costume, Undergarments, Minor Knee Flaw, Crack In Shoulder Plate, 18" H. $175.00

BLACK-HAIRED CHINA, Painted Features W/Blue Eyes, Cloth Body & Legs, Leather Hands & Arms To Elbows, Navy Blue Dress, Undergarments, Shoulder Plate Crack, Hair Worn, 16½" H. $75.00

(A-MA '77)   *Richard A. Bourne Co., Inc.*

(D-VA '78)   *Melton's Antiques*
STEINER BISQUE DOLL, French, Negro, Orig. Wig, Jointed Body, 12" H. . .$2275.00

(D-VA '78)   *Melton's Antiques*
MILLINER MODEL DOLL, Hair Braided & Made Into Bun In Back (Molded); Real Hair In Front, 18" H. $795.00

(D-VA '78)   *Melton's Antiques*
K STAR R DOLL, Negro, "101" (Marie), Orig. Wig, Old Clothes, 21" H. . .$3950.00

(D-VA '78)   *Melton's Antiques*
K STAR R DOLL, "114" Pouty, 11" H. . .
. . . .$1250.00

(D-VA '78)   *Melton's Antiques*
K STAR R DOLL, "114", Glass Eyes, Pouty, Human Hair Wig, Ball Jointed Body, 25" H. $3750.00

(D-VA '78)   *Melton's Antiques*
JUMEAU DOLL, Tete, Brown Paperweight Eyes, Head & Body Signed, Old Clothes, 22" H. $1495.00

(D-VA '78)   *Melton's Antiques*
KESTNER GIBSON GIRL DOLL, Sleep Blue Eyes, Orig. Wig, Kid Body, Bisque Arms, 17" H. $1175.00

(D-VA '78)   *Melton's Antiques*
PARIAN DOLL, Cloth Body, Bisque Limbs, 17" H. $385.00

(D-VA '78)   *Melton's Antiques*
JUMEAU DOLL, Mechanical, Head Mkd. "Tete Jumeau", Paperweight Eyes, Bisque Forearms, Plays Music, Orig. Label, 10" O.H. $3950.00

(A-MA '77)   Richard A. Bourne Co., Inc.

DOLLS
(ROW I, L to R)
WAX OVER COMPOSITION, Brown Wig, Blue Glass Eyes, Cloth Body, Mkd. "J. Lagmann's Patent, Mar. 25th, 1874", Minor Damage To Fingers, 28" H......$120.00
WAX OVER COMPOSITION, Cloth Body, Kid Arms, China Legs (Do Not Match), 28" H........................$100.00
WAX OVER COMPOSITION, Cloth Body, Composition Arms & Legs, Toe Broken, 23" H.................$60.00
(ROW II, L to R)
WAX OVER COMPOSITION, Cloth Body To Waist, Bisque Arms & Legs, 18th C. Costume, Minor Damage, 15" H. .....
.................................$160.00
POURED WAX DOLL, Blonde Human Hair Wig, Cloth Body, Wax Over Composition Arms, 13½" H............$100.00
WAX OVER COMPOSITION, Brown Wig, Open & Shut Eyes, Cloth Body, 10½" H........................$75.00
WAX OVER COMPOSITION, 2 Women Dolls, Cloth Bodies, Blonde Wigs, Stationary Eyes, Colonial Costume, Both 11½" H. ..
.................................$95.00

(A-MA '77)   Richard A. Bourne Co., Inc.

(A-MA '77)   Richard A. Bourne Co., Inc.

(ROW I, L to R)
WAX OVER COMPOSITION BABY, Set-In Blue Glass Eyes, Wooden Legs & Lower Arms W/Composition Hands, Voice Box, Head & Face Cracks, Minor Paint Flaking, 11" H......................$50.00
RELIGIOUS FIGURE, "Infant of Prague", Wax Head W/Blonde Wig, Painted Features & Blue Eyes, Wax Hands & Feet, Cloth Body, Undergarments, Velvet Dress, 15" H.
.................................$75.00
WAX OVER COMPOSITION TWO-FACED DOLL, Brown Human Hair Wig, Blue Glass Threaded Eyes, Cloth Body W/Composition Arms & Legs, Undergarments, Dotted Swiss Dress, Minor Crack At Eye On Face W/Closed Mouth; Chin Broken On Other Face; Cloth Broken At Knees, 15" H.
.................................$90.00
(ROW II, L to R)
WAX LADY, Blonde Wig, Set-In Blue Glass Eyes, Wax Hands & Arms, Cloth Body & Legs, Cotton Undergarments, Silk Dress, Dress Faded, Needs Cleaning, 20" H. .....
.................................$250.00
WAX OVER COMPOSITION DOLL, Blonde Wig, Set-In Blue Glass Eyes, Cloth Body, Cotton Undergarments, Silk Dress, Head Rewaxed, Wig & Dress Worn, 20½" H
.................................$25.00
WAX OVER COMPOSITION DOLL, Kid Body, Petticoat, Figured Dress, Wax Worn, 21" H...................$75.00

◄*To the left*
WAX OVER COMPOSITION DOLL, Brown Mohair Wig, Stationery Glass Eyes, Kid Arms, Cloth Body & Legs, Orig. Taffeta Costume, Undergarments, Minor Crazing, Crack In Jaw & Shoulder, 23½" H. $75.00
WAX OVER COMPOSITION DOLL, Orig. Drk. Brown Wig, Pupil-less Black Glass Eyes, Cotton Body & Legs, Kid Arms, Green Dress, Undergarments, Crackling On Face & Shoulder Plate, Gown Worn, 23" H.
.................................$50.00

(A-MA '77)   Richard A. Bourne Co., Inc.

(L to R)
WAX OVER COMPOSITION DOLL, Brown Human Hair Wig, Set-In Brown Glass Eyes, Painted Features, Swivel Neck On Bisque Shoulder Plate, Kid Body, Arms & Legs, White Undergarments, Wool Dress, Neck Cracked, 35" H..........$175.00
WAX OVER COMPOSITION DOLL, Brown Human Hair Wig, Blue Glass Eyes, Painted Mouth, Cloth Body & Legs, Undergarments, Cotton Print Dress, Nose & Right Shoulder Cracked, 26" H........$75.00
WAX OVER COMPOSITION DOLL, Blonde Mohair Wig, Cloth Body, Set-In Blue Threaded Glass Eyes, Painted Features, Cotton Undergarments, Silk Costume, Wax Cracked On Forehead & Legs, Wig Worn & Soiled, 27½" H.....$75.00

(A-MA '77)   Richard A. Bourne Co., Inc.

(L to R)
METAL HEAD DOLL, Ash Blonde Mohair Wig, Glass Eyes, Bisque Hands, Kid Body W/Cloth Legs & Feet, Silk Dress, Lace Undergarments, Signed "Minerva", Finger Chipped, Paint Rubbed On Nose .$130.00
METAL HEAD DOLL, Molded Blonde Hair, Inset Glass Eyes, Painted Mouth, Molded Celluloid Hands, Cloth Body, Legs, Feet & Arms, Organdy Dress, Lace Undergarments, 14½" H.................$175.00
METAL HEAD BOY DOLL, Blonde Hair, Painted Eyes, Brows & Mouth, Cloth Arms, Hands, Body, Legs & Feet, Checked Suit, Minor Paint Loss, Suit Soiled & Faded, 11" H........................$70.00

(A-MA '77)   *Richard A. Bourne Co., Inc.*

WAX OVER COMPOSITION DOLL, Orig. Drk. Brown Wig, Set In Blue Glass Eyes, Kid Arms, Cloth Body & Legs, Orig. Taffeta Dress, Undergarments, Face Cracked, Worm Damage In Arms, Dress Faded, 26" H. $75.00
POURED WAX DOLL, Blonde Mohair Wig, Open & Shut Brown Eyes, Cloth Body & Legs, Kid Arms, Orig. Costume, 24" H. $125.00

(A-MA '77)   *Richard A. Bourne Co., Inc.*

MILLINER MODEL, Lady, Blue-Green Eyes, Taffeta & Lace Costume, Undergarments, Face Repainted, Minor Shoulder Plate Crazing, 27¾" H. $350.00
MILLINER MODEL, Lady, Painted Features W/Blue Eyes, Orig. Taffeta & Linen Costume Worn, Minor Chip, Crack & Break In Kid On Legs, 21" H. $600.00

(A-MA '77)   *Richard A. Bourne Co., Inc.*
(ROW I, L to R)

POURED WAX DOLL, Orig. Blonde Mohair Wig, Open & Shut Blue Glass Eyes, Cloth Body, Poured Wax Arms, Dotted-Swiss Dress, Undergarments, Crack In Shoulder Plate, 17½" H. $175.00
WAX OVER COMPOSITION DOLL, Blonde Mohair Wig, Open & Shut Blue Threaded Eyes, Cloth Body, Voice Box (not working), Composition Arms & Legs, Orig. Cotton Dress, Wax Off Back Of Ear, Face & Shoulder Plate Soiled, 16½" H. $50.00
WAX OVER COMPOSITION DOLL, Reddish-Blonde Wig, Cloth Body, Arms & Legs, Set-In Pupil-less Black Glass Eyes, Red Dress, Cotton Pantalets, Nose Rubbed, Chips, Worm Holes, 13½" H. $70.00
(ROW II, L to R)
POURED WAX DOLL, Orig. Blonde Wig, Set In Blue Glass Eyes, Poured Wax Arms, Hands & Legs; Cloth Body, Orig. Costume, Flannel Undergarment, Costume Slightly Soiled, 17½" H. $500.00
POURED WAX DOLL, Orig. Blonde Mohair Wig, Set In Blue Glass Eyes; Poured Wax Arms; Kid Body, Legs &Feet; Orig. Brocade Costume, French Undergarments, Fingers Broken On Right Hand, Costume Needs Repair, 17" H. $450.00
WAX OVER COMPOSITION DOLL, Lt. Brown Mohair Wig, Set In Blue Threaded Eyes, Wax Over Composition Arms & Legs; Cloth Body; Green Linen-Like Dress, Undergarments, Face & Shoulder Plate Rewaxed, 15" H. $75.00

◀ *To the left*
(A-MA '77)   *Richard A. Bourne Co., Inc.*
RAG DOLL, Inked-On Features, Cotton Dress Worn, 14" H. $25.00
CLOTH DOLL, Black Mammy, Painted Features, Wooden Feet, 11½" H. . .$50.00
CLOTH DOLL, Man, Knitted Eyes, Stockinette Body, Knit Costume, 17½" H. $10.00

(A-MA '77)   *Richard A. Bourne Co., Inc.*

DOLLS

(ROW I, L to R)
MILLINER MODEL, Silk Gown W/Orig. Silk Pantalets, Cracks, Repairs, 8" H. $50.00
MILLINER MODEL, Brunette Girl, Silk Dress W/Orig. Undergarment, Minor Flaking, Slight Age Cracks, 9¼" H. $60.00
MILLINER MODEL, Brunette Girl, Orig. Cotton Dress & Lace Undergarments, Crack, Flaking, 10" L. $70.00
MILLINER MODEL, Brunette Girl, Faded Undergarments, Flaking, Cracks, 8¾" H. $50.00

(ROW II, L to R)
MILLINER MODEL, Boy or Man, Orig. Velvet Coat, Satin Vest & Pants, Cotton Shirt, Brush Marks Around Face & Arm Loose, 10½" H. $200.00
MILLINER MODEL, Girl In Old Costume, Gown Faded, Flaking, 10½" H. . . .$70.00
MILLINER MODEL, Girl, Net Overskirt & Linen Blouse, Cracks, Paint Flaking, Arm Loose, 9¼" H. $40.00
MILLINER MODEL, Woman In Orig. Brocade Gown W/Cotton Undergarments, Gown Worn, Nose Worn, Cracks, 12¼" H. $450.00

(ROW III, L to R)
MILLINER MODEL, Lady In Taffeta Dress, Paint Flaking, Leg Broken, 13½" H. $275.00
MILLINER MODEL, Lady In Calico 2-Pc. Dress, Cracks, Foot Missing, 12" H. $70.00
MILLINER MODEL, Lady In Cotton Gown, Cracks, Paint Worn, Paper Petticoat, 13" H. $150.00

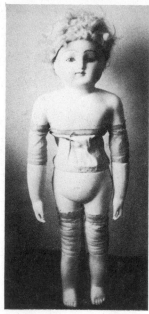

(D-VA '78)   *Melton's Antiques*
ARMAND MARSEILLE DOLL, Brown
Sleep Eyes, Ball Jointed Body, 24" H. . . . .
. . . .$155.00

(D-VA '78)   *Melton's Antiques*
K STAR R DOLL, "117" Pouty, Sleep
Eyes, Human Hair Wig, Ball Jointed Body,
25" H. $2550.00

(D-VA '78)   *Melton's Antiques*
STEINER DOLL, Paperweight Eyes, Cloth
Sections Inserted Between Bisque Sections,
Motchmann Type Body, 18" H. .$1750.00

(D-VA '78)   *Melton's Antiques*
COMIC CHARACTER DOLL, "Mortiz",
Bisque, Swivel Neck, Jointed Shoulders &
Hips, 6½" H. $1100.00

(D-VA '78)   *Melton's Antiques*
A.M. CHARACTER BABY DOLL, "990",
Sleep Eyes, 21" H. $295.00

(D-VA '78)   *Melton's Antiques*
BRU DOLL, "Circle Dot", Marked, Human
Hair Wig, Kid Body, Bisque Arms, Old
Clothes, 17" H. $4850.00

(D-VA '78)   *Melton's Antiques*
GERMAN BISQUE DOLL, Blue Sleep
Eyes, Human Hair Wig, Jointed Kid Body,
Orig. Clothes, 23" H. $225.00

(D-VA '78)   *Melton's Antiques*
MILLINER MODEL DOLL, Orig. Clothes,
20" H. $575.00

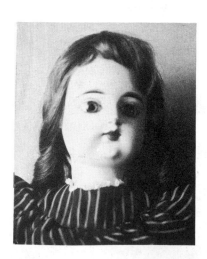

(D-VA '78)   *Melton's Antiques*
FRENCH F.G. DOLL, Paperweight Eyes,
Human Hair Wig, Composition Body, 25"
H. $1075.00

(A-MA '77)   Richard A. Bourne Co., Inc.

PARIAN-HEADED DOLLS
(ROW I, L to R)

BLONDE PARIAN, Blue Painted Eyes, New Cloth Body, Bisque Arms & Legs, 19" H. $300.00
BLONDE PARIAN, Blue Painted Eyes, Cloth Body & Legs, Kid Arms, Leather Slippers, 21½" H. $225.00
BLONDE PARIAN, Blue Painted Eyes, Cloth Body & Legs, New Bisque Arms, 18" H. $225.00
BLONDE PARIAN, Blue Painted Eyes, Cloth Body, Bisque Arms & Legs, Repair To Ear & Shoulder Plate, 16" H. $300.00
(ROW II, L to R)

BROWN-HAIRED PARIAN, Blue Painted Eyes, New Cloth Body, Bisque Arms & Legs, 15½" H. $250.00
BROWN-HAIRED PARIAN, Blue Painted Eyes, Cloth Body & Legs, Bisque Arms, 18" H. $250.00
BLONDE, Blue Painted Eyes, Cloth Body, Bisque Arms & Legs, 16" H. $225.00
BLONDE, Blue Painted Eyes, Cloth Body, Bisque Arms & Legs, Repaired Fingers, 14" H. $200.00

(A-MA '77)   Richard A. Bourne Co., Inc.
(ROW I, L to R)

PARIAN HEAD DOLL, Blonde, Painted Blue Eyes, Cloth Body, Carved Wooden Arms, Hands & Feet, Crack In Shoulder Plate, 17" H. $35.00
BISQUE HEAD DOLL, Mkd. "DEP" W/ Horseshoe Mark & Numerals "1900-3-0", Blonde Wig, Fixed Blue Glass Eyes, Composition Body, 15½" H. $100.00
CHINA HEAD DOLL, Black Hair, Painted Blue Eyes, Cloth Body & Legs, Leather Hands, 18" H. $125.00
(ROW II, L to R)

BISQUE HEAD DOLL, Numeral "8" On Head, Fixed Brown Glass Eyes, Painted Mouth, Blonde Mohair Wig, Kid Body, 20" H. $400.00
CHINA HEAD DOLL, Painted Blue Eyes, Cotton Body, China Hands & Feet, Left Hand Thumb Missing, Right Hand Fingers Worn, 21½" H. $37.00
BISQUE HEAD NURSE DOLL, By Armand Marseille, Mkd. W/"AM" Mark & "4-0½DEP" & "370", Brown Sleep Eyes, Jointed Kid Body W/Cotton Legs & Bisque Hands, 21" H. $70.00

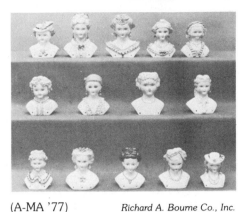

(A-MA '77)   Richard A. Bourne Co., Inc.

PARIAN DOLL HEADS
(ROW I, L to R)

BROWN HAIR, Molded-On Yellow Hat, Right Shoulder Repair, 4½" H. . . .$500.00
BLONDE HAIR, "5AF" On Shoulder Plate, Repairs, 5½" H. $275.00
BLONDE HAIR, Hair Repair & To Ruffle Around Shoulder Plate, Worn Spot On Cheek, 5¼" H. $250.00
BLONDE HAIR, Blue Painted Eyes, Earrings, Ruffles Repaired, 4½" H. . .$125.00
BLONDE HAIR, Molded Ribbon Of Copper Lustre Framing Face, Flat Swivel Neck, Repairs To Neck & Necklace, Head Retouched, 4¼" H. $375.00
(ROW II, L to R)

BLONDE HAIR, Chest Plate & Decor. Repairs, 4½" H. $125.00
BLUE GLASS EYES, Painted Shoulder Decor., Shoulder Plate Repair, 4½" H. $275.00
BLONDE CURLS, Beads Repainted, 4¾" H. $200.00
BLONDE HAIR, Molded Collar & Tie, 4¼" H. $300.00
(ROW III, L to R)

BLONDE HAIR, Ruffles Around Neck & Over Shoulders, 3¾" H. $250.00
BLONDE HAIR, Touched Up, Shoulder Plate Repaired, 4" H. $100.00
BLACK HAIR, Blue Painted Eyes, Left Ear Repair, 4½" H. $100.00
BLONDE HAIR, Blue Painted Eyes, 4" H. $250.00
BLONDE CURLS, Blue Painted Eyes, Minor Repair To Curls, 3¼" H. . .$325.00

(A-MA '77)   Richard A. Bourne Co., Inc.
(L to R)

BISQUE HEAD, Lt. Brown Wig, Swivel Neck, 5½" H. $350.00
BISQUE HEAD, Lt. Brown Wig, Swivel Neck, "10" On Back Of Head, Replaced Eyes, 5¼" H. $340.00
BISQUE HEAD, Lt. Brown Wig, Swivel Neck, Pierced Ears, 4" H. $425.00
BISQUE HEAD, Blonde Wig, Swivel Neck, Shoulder Plate Repair Neck & Forehead, 3" H. $60.00

To the right ▶

(L to R)

BLACK-HAIRED CHINA, Painted Blue Eyes, Cloth Body & Legs, Leather Arms & Hands, Undergarments, Sheer Dress, Hands Damaged, Dress Worn, 13" H. $50.00
BLACK-HAIRED CHINA, Painted Blue Eyes, Cloth Body & Legs, China Arms, Undergarments, Silk Dress, Shoulder Place & Face Pitted, Eyebrows Worn, Nose Rubbed, 15½" H. $90.00
PINK-TONED CHINA, Black Hair, Painted Blue Eyes, Cloth Body & Legs, Kid Arms, Cotton Undergarments, Silk Taffeta Dress, 13½" H. $100.00

(A-MA '77)   Richard A. Bourne Co., Inc.

(A-MA '77)   *Richard A. Bourne Co., Inc.*

BISQUE HEAD DOLLS
(ROW I, L to R)
KAISER BABY, Bisque Head W/Painted Brown Hair, Open & Shut Mouth, Painted Blue Eyes, Composition Body, Arms & Legs, White Petticoat, Head Mkd. "36/K*R/100", Arm & Leg Cracks, 14" H. $325.00
CHARACTER DOLL, Bisque Head, Painted Blue Eyes, Open & Shut Mouth, Composition Body, Arms & Legs; Blue Flannel Sailor Suit, Mkd. "36/D*R/100", Thumbs Missing, Body Cracks, Paint Missing, 15" H. ...
....$125.00
GERMAN STRUNG DOLL, Bisque Head W/Blonde Mohair Wig, Open & Shut Brown Eyes, Open Mouth W/2 Teeth, Composition Body & Legs, White Flannel Petticoat, Mkd. "Made In Germany 11/143", Arm Reglued, 17½" H. $275.00
(ROW II, L to R)
BISQUE HEAD, Blonde Mohair Wig, Blue Eyes, Open & Shut Mouth, Composition Body, Arms & Legs, White Petticoat, Signed "211" & "J.D.K.", Minor Wear, 10½" H. $300.00
BYE-LO BABY, Bisque Head, Cloth Body & Composition Hands, Diaper & Petticoat, Signed "1923 By Grace Storey Putnam", Hands In Poor Condition, 10¼" H. ......
....$200.00
GOGGLY-EYED DOLL, Bisque Head W/Blue-Grey Eyes, Watermelon Mouth, Lt. Brown Hair, Composition Body, Arms & Legs, Blue & White Romper Costume, Undergarment, Cracks In Composition, Mkd. "241/0" $1100.00

(A-MA '77)   *Richard A. Bourne Co., Inc.*

BISQUE HEAD DOLLS
(ROW I, L to R)
GERMAN STRUNG DOLL, Brown Mohair Wig, Brown Glass Eyes, Composition Body & Arms, Wooden Legs & Feet, Undergarments, Cotton & Lace Dress, Body Signed "Trademark" and "Schultz Mark", 20" H.
....$400.00
GERMAN STRUNG DOLL, Blonde Mohair Wig, Open & Shut Blue Eyes, Composition Body, Arms, & Legs, Signed "S & H/DEP/7/Germany", Undergarments, Silk & Net Dress, 20" H. $425.00
GERMAN STRUNG DOLL, Blonde Wig, Blue-Gray Stationary Eyes, Composition Body, Arms & Legs, Undergarments, Bride's Dress, Signed "Armand Marseille/Germany 390/A3M", Minor Breaks In Dress, 20" H.
....$125.00
(ROW II, L to R)
GERMAN STRUNG DOLL, Brown Wig W/Hairnet, Blue Open & Shut Eyes, Composition Body, Arms & Legs, Undergarments, Silk Dress, 25" H. $150.00
GERMAN BISQUE DOLL, Solid Dome Head, Blonde Wig, Stationary Blue Glass Eyes, Cloth Body, Legs, Feet & Arms, Undergarments, Silk & Linen Dress, Moth Holes, 27½" H. $325.00

◄ *To the left*

L to R)

GERMAN BISQUE HEAD VIOLINIST, Set In Blue Glass Eyes; 4 Teeth, Mohair Wig, Carved Wood Hands & Legs, Orig. Frayed Costume, Working Condition, 14" H. $600.00
BISQUE HEAD MAROTTE, Set In Blue Glass Eyes; Closed Mouth; Blonde Mohair Wig, French Liberty Cap; Satin & Brocade Costume Soiled; Working Condition, 15" O.H. $200.00

(A-MA '77)   *Richard A. Bourne Co., Inc.*

CHARACTER DOLLS
(ROW I, L to R)
OLD LADY, Kid Head, Thread Glasses Sewn Over Eyes, Grey Human Hair Wig, Taffeta Costume, No Arms, 10" H. $30.00
"JEFF" Made In Switzerland, Ceramic Head, Hands & Feet W/Metal Jointed Body, Cotton Costume, 8" H. $50.00
"MUTT", Mate To Preceding Doll, 6½" H.
....$45.00
"NUTHEAD", (2), Hickory Nut Heads, Painted Faces, Orig. Costumes, 1 W/Wooden Arms, 1 W/Wired Taped Arms, Both Without Legs, Period Costumes, Costumes Soiled, 1 W/Arm Missing, 7" H. ...$10.00
"NUTHEAD", Hickory Nut Head, White Wool Wig, Painted-On Features W/Closed Eyes, Hands Made Of Seeds, Cotton Batting Body, Wire Legs Covered W/Fiber, Wooden Feet, Ribbon Costume, 4" H. ....
....$20.00
(ROW II, L to R)
MOTHER GOOSE & HOT MUFFIN LADY, Composition Heads, Hands & Legs, Cloth Bodies, Gray Mohair Wigs, Muffin Lady's Head In Poor Condition, Minor Moth Damage to Costume, 13½" & 11½" O.H.
....$25.00
ADMIRAL DEWEY, Bisque Head, Composition Body, Arms & Legs; Admiral's Costume, Left Foot Damaged, Moth Damage To Costume, 14½" H. $375.00
(ROW III, L to R)
IRISH FOLK DOLL, Papier Mache Head W/Painted Features, Lt. Brown Wooly Wig, Soft Fiber Body Over Wire Frame, Native Costume, Red Flannel Petticoat, Standing Ht. 18"; Seated - 11½" H. $30.00
EMMETT KELLY'S "WILLIE THE CLOWN", Molded Rubber Head & Hands, Cloth Body, Arms, Legs & Feet; Brown Wig, Painted Features, Baby Berry Toy, New York City, Clothes Soiled, 21" H. ..$40.00

(A-MA '77)   Richard A. Bourne Co., Inc.
PAPIER MACHE HEAD DOLLS
(ROW I, L to R)
FISHERWOMAN, Painted Eyes, Mouth & Hair; Carved Wooden Hands, Composition Legs & Feet, "La Paire" Mkd. In Pencil, Orig. Costume Faded & Soiled, Nose Worn, Age Cracks, 7" H. $50.00
CHARACTER LADY, Wooden Arms, Legs & Body, Stub Hands & Feet, Print Dress, Petticoat & Pantalets, Head Broken, Cracks, 11" H. $20.00
GIRL, Painted Features, Cloth Body & Legs; Kid Hands; Cotton Dress & Undergarments, Chest Plate Cracks, Clothes Worn, 16" H. $140.00
GIRL, Cloth Body & Legs; Kid Arms; Cotton Dress, Undergarments, Head Broken & Repainted, Shoulder Plate Cracks, Fingers Broken, 17" H. $35.00
(ROW II, L to R)
BLONDE GREINER DOLL, Painted Features, Orig. Cloth Body, Arms & Legs & Label "8", Cotton Dress & Undergarments, Head Damaged, Forehead Piece Missing, Nose Broken Off, Hair Worn, 24" H. $60.00
SUPERIOR-TYPE DOLL, Blonde W/ Painted Features, Cloth Body & Legs, Print Dress, Undergarments, Ear Cracked, Hands In Poor Condition, 16" H. $50.00
SUPERIOR-TYPE DOLL, Painted-On Black Hair, Cloth Body, Leather Arms & Hands, Silk Dress, Undergarments, Signed "M&S" W/"2015", Paint Worn, 23" H. $60.00

(D-VA '78)   Melton's Antiques
POURED WAX DOLL, Inserted Hair, Orig. Clothes, 11" H. $575.00

(A-MA '77)   Richard A. Bourne Co., Inc.
(ROW I, L to R)
PAPIER MACHE HEAD, Milliner Model W/Kid Body, Arms & Legs, Painted Features, Silk Dress, Undergarments, Neck Cracks, Paint Flaking, Dress Worn, 10½" H. $100.00
PAPIER MACHE HEAD, Net Overskirt & Velvet Bodice Gown, Hair Worn, Paint Flaking, Gown Soiled, 11½" H. . . .$50.00
PAPIER MACHE HEAD, Silk Dress, Kid Legs, Shoulder Crack, Paint Flaking, 11½" H. $90.00
PAPIER MACHE HEAD, Net Overskirt, Undergarments, Shoulder Plate Crack, Gown Soiled, 13½" H. $50.00
(ROW II, L to R)
PAPIER MACHE HEAD, Milliner Model, Cotton Dress, Long Pantalets, Shoulder Plate Crack, Soiled Dress, 15" H. . .$70.00
PAPIER MACHE HEAD, Net Dress, Undergarments, Paint Flaking, Shoulder Plate Checks, Dress Soiled, 14¼" H. $50.00
PAPIER MACHE HEAD, Silk Dress, Undergarment, Face Checks, Shoulder Plate Crack, Dress Worn, 15½" H. $175.00
PAPIER MACHE HEAD, White Dress, Undergarments, Head Mended, Shoulder Plate & Back Checks, 16½" H. $75.00
(ROW III, L to R)
PAPIER MACHE HEAD, Cotton Print Dress, Petticoat, Face Checks, Shoulder Plate Crack, Dress Worn, Paint Flaking, 15½" H. $40.00
PAPIER MACHE HEAD, Net Overdress, Pink Underskirt, Chest Plate Crack, Paint Flaking, Dress Soiled, 17½" H. . . .$250.00
PAPIER MACHE HEAD, Silk Dress, Face & Shoulder Plate Checked, Legs Broken, Paint Flaking, Dress Worn, 18½" H. $100.00

(A-MA '77)   Richard A. Bourne Co., Inc.
(ROW I, L to R)
PAPIER MACHE, Milliner Body, Kid, Wooden Arms & Legs, Orig. Cotton Dress, Petticoat, Neck Cracks, Soiled Dress, 6½" H. $75.00
PAPIER MACHE, Milliner Body, Blue Dress & Petticoat, Paint Flaked On Arms & Legs, Paint Worn From Face & Hair, 7½" H. $30.00
PAPIER MACHE, Milliner Body, Cotton Dress, Petticoat, Cracked Shoulder Plate, Arms Broken & Taped, Dress Soiled, 7½" H. $35.00
PAPIER MACHE, Milliner Body W/Painted Features, Cotton Dress, Pantalets, Face & Shoulder Plate Checks, Hands Do Not Match, 9¼" H. $70.00
(ROW II, L to R)
PAPIER MACHE, Milliner Body, Net Dress, Linen Petticoat, Neck Checks, Dress Soiled, 10" H. $275.00
PAPIER MACHE, Milliner Body, Cotton Dress, Petticoat, Shoulder Plate Cracks, Paint Flaked, 10½" H. $45.00
PAPIER MACHE, Boy-Type Head, Milliner Body, Velvet Jacket & Pants, Nose Rubbed, Cracks, Costume Soiled, 12½" H. $60.00
(ROW III, L to R)
PAPIER MACHE, Milliner Body, Pink & White Dress, Undergarments, Shoulder Plate Crazed, Dress Soiled, 12¾" H. $375.00
PAPIER MACHE, Milliner Body, Cotton Dress & Petticoat, Head Chipped, Shoulder Plate Cracks, Neck Checks, Dress & Undergarments Soiled, 11½" H. $25.00
PAPIER MACHE, Milliner Body, Lace & Velvet Dress, Cotton Petticoat, Face & Hair Crazed, Cracks, Dress Soiled, 12" H. $40.00

(A-MA '77)   *Richard A. Bourne Co., Inc.*
AUTOMATONS
MECHANICAL CYCLE W/RIDER,
Gesso Over Cloth Head, Painted Hair &
Features; Wood Body, Metal Hands & Feet;
Working Condition, Costume Soiled, 9" H.,
10½" O.L. $700.00
MECHANICAL CYCLE W/RIDER,
Identical To Preceding, Head Of Girl, Work-
ing Condition, 9" H., 10½" O.L. .$550.00

(A-MA '77)   *Richard A. Bourne Co., Inc.*
FRENCH PORCELAIN DOLL, "Roh-
mer" Type, Blonde Mohair Wig, Blue Glass
Inset Eyes, Kid Body, Wooden Legs & Upper
Arms Covered W/Kid, Porcelain Lower
Arms, Taffeta Dress, 14½" H. . . .$2500.00

(A-MA '77)   *Richard A. Bourne Co., Inc.*
(L to R)
FRENCH FASHION DOLL, Blonde Wig,
Blue Threaded Glass Eyes, Swivel Neck,
Kid Body, Arms & Legs, Undergarments,
Taffeta Dress, 21" H. $800.00
BISQUE DOLL, Human Hiar Wig, Set-In
Blue Eyes, Cloth Body & Legs, W/Leather
Hands, Undergarments, Cotton Dress,
22' H. $225.00
FRENCH FASHION DOLL, Brown Hu-
man Hair Wig, Stationary Blue Glass Eyes,
Swivel Neck, Cloth Body & Legs W/Bisque
Hands, Signed "E Depose J", Petticoat,
Taffeta Dress, Dress Worn, 19½" H. . . . . .
. . . .$1000.00

(A-MA '77)   *Richard A. Bourne Co., Inc.*
(L to R)
FRENCH FASHION DOLL, Blonde
Human Hair Wig, Stationary Blue Glass
Eyes, Swivel Neck, Kid Body, Arms & Legs,
Undergarments, Silk Dress, 18" H. . . . . . .
. . . .$900.00
FRENCH FASHION DOLL, Blonde Mo-
hair Wig, Stationary Blue Glass Eyes, Swivel
Neck, Kid Body, Arms & Legs, Cotton Un-
dergarments, Taffeta Dress, 17" H. . . . . . .
. . . .$1100.00
FRENCH FASHION DOLL, Blonde Hu-
man Hair Wig, Stationary Blue Glass Eyes,
Wooden Body, Arms & Legs, Cotton Under-
garments, Wool Dress, Minor Flaking On
Body, 18" H. $700.00

(A-MA '77)   *Richard A. Bourne Co., Inc.*
FRENCH FASHION DOLLS
(ROW I, L to R)
BLONDE WIG, Blue Brown Glass Eyes,
Swivel Neck, Kid Body, Arms & Legs, 15"
H. $800.00
BLONDE MOHAIR WIG, Blue-Gray
Blown Glass Eyes, Swivel Neck, Kid Body,
Arms & Legs, Silk Dress, Ankle Broken, 16"
H. $650.00
(ROW II, L to R)
BROWN HUMAN HAIR WIG, Blue Blown
Glass Eyes, Swivel Neck, Kid Body, Arms &
Legs, 14½" H. $800.00
BROWN WIG, Brown Blown Glass Eyes,
Kid Body & Feet, Bisque Hands, Impressed
"I", Minor Flaw In Left Chin, 10" H. . . . . .
. . . .$700.00
LT. BROWN WIG, Gray Blown Glass Eyes,
Swivel Neck, Kid Body, Arms & Legs, Red
& Tan, 14" H. $700.00

(A-MA '77)   *Richard A. Bourne Co., Inc.*
(L to R)
FRENCH FASHION DOLL, Blonde Mo-
hair Wig, Stationary Lt. Blue Eyes, Jointed
Body, Kid Covered W/Elastic Holding Legs
To Body, Brass Upper Arms Fit Into Wooden
Socket, Dressed As Catherine de Medici,
Cotton Undergarments, Brocade Gown,
Left Arm Loose At Elbow, 18" H. $800.00
FRENCH FASHION DOLL, Brown Hu-
man Hair Wig, Stationary Gray Glass Eyes,
Kig Body & Legs, Bisque Arms To Elbows,
Cotton Undergarments, Knit Wool Petticoat,
Linen Dress, Neck Chip, Left Arm Loose,
Dress Soiled, 17" H. $400.00
FRENCH FASHION DOLL, Brown Hu-
man Hair Wig, Stationary Blue Glass Eyes,
Swivel Neck, Wooden Jointed Body & Arms,
Taffeta Petticoat, Gold & Velvet Gown Of
Elizabethan Period, Cheek Crack, 17½" H.
. . . .$550.00

(A-MA '77)   *Richard A. Bourne Co., Inc.*
(ROW I, L to R)
PARIAN HEAD, Painted Eyes, 4¾" H. . .
. . . .$125.00
PARIAN HEAD, Blue Glass Eyes, Swivel
Neck, 4¼" H. $425.00
PARIAN HEAD, Blonde Hair, Blue Paint-
ed Eyes, 4¼" H. $150.00
PARIAN HEAD, Brown Hair, "VI" Inside
Shoulder Plate, Minor Chips, 4¼" H. . . . . .
. . . .$100.00
(ROW II, L to R)
PARIAN HEAD, Blonde Curls, Blue Glass
Eyes, 4 Painted Teeth, 4¼" H. . . .$350.00
PARIAN HEAD, Blonde Curls, Blue Paint-
ed Eyes, 4" H. $80.00
PARIAN HEAD, Brown Curls, Blue Paint-
ed Eyes, "Lazy Question Mark" Inside
Shoulder Plate, 3¾" H. $450.00
PARIAN HEAD, Blue Glass Eyes, Blonde
Hair, Swivel Neck, 3¾" H. $350.00
PARIAN HEAD, Blonde Hair, Blue Paint-
ed Eyes, Nose Repair, 4½' H. $75.00

(A-MA '77)   Richard A. Bourne Co., Inc.

(ROW I, L to R)
PINE CHURCH, American, 19th C., Hinged Front Roof Inlaid W/Abalone-Shell Hearts, Orig. Finish W/Minor Wear, 17" L., 13" D., 16" H. $320.00
WOODEN CHURCH, Hinged Back Door, Inside Fitted W/Minister, Organist, Organ, Pews & Pulpit, Minor Restoration Necessary, Repainted, 11½" L., 9" W., 20¼" H. $175.00
(ROW II, L to R)
WOOD & LITHOGRAPH DOLL-HOUSE, Furnished W/Oriental Ivory & Victorian Furnishings, Paper Worn & Faded, Needs Restoration, Finial Missing On Roof, 17" L., 10½" D., 17½" H. $650.00
ONE-ROOM DOLLHOUSE, Furnished, Wallpapered, Fireplace, Carpet; White W/Green Roof, 2 Red Chimneys, Repainted, 20" O.L., 13½" D., 15¼" H. $175.00

(A-MA '77)   Richard A. Bourne Co., Inc.
DOLLHOUSE, Dining Room, Living Room, Nursery & Twin Bedroom, Upper & Lower Hall, Conventional 20th Century Furnishings, Carpeted, Draped, Paintings, Repainted, 38" L., 19" D., 50" H. $300.00

(A-MA '77)   Richard A. Bourne Co., Inc.
DOLLHOUSE, Roof & Glass-Paneled Doors Open To Four Lge. Rooms Including Completely Equipped Kitchen, Front Of Roof Hinged To Reveal Two Attic Rooms, Dining Room Complete W/Fireplaces, China, Paintings, Etc., Living Room W/Victorian Furnishings & Decor. For Christmas, Includes Dollhouse Doll, Pets, Tiny Bonnet Baby, Presents Under Tree, Draperies; Electrically Lighted; Painted Yellow W/Green Roof, Two Wooden Chimneys, Doors W/Locks, Painted Shutters On Windows; Minor Wear, Paint Slightly Flaking, 39" L., 25" W., 56" H. $2000.00

To the right ▶

(ROW I, L to R)
WOOD & LITHOGRAPH DOLLHOUSE FURNITURE, 6" L. Sofa, 5 Side Chairs 4¾" H., Piano 4" H., Bench Table, Floor Lamp, Sm. Pedestal, Minor Wear ....
...............................$80.00
WOOD & LITHOGRAPH BIRDHOUSE, By R. Bliss Company, Plastic Burd, Base 3½" L., 2¾" H. $80.00
(ROW II, L to R)
WOOD & LITHOGRAPH DOLL-HOUSE, Worn & Faded, 11½" H. ......
...............................$150.00
WOOD & LITHOGRAPH DOLL-HOUSE, 2 Wooden Figures, 13" H. ......
...............................$310.00
(ROW III, L to R)
WOOD & PAPER-FACED DOLL-HOUSE, Applied & Painted Sides & Front, Incised Brick-Style Chimney, Worn, Paint Retouched, 17½" H. $100.00
LITHOGRAPH HIGHCHAIR, "The Alphabet Chair", Letters Lithographed & Applied To Wooden Back, Paper Faded, Ball From Top Of Spindle Missing, 12" H.
...............................$60.00

(A-MA '77)   Richard A. Bourne Co., Inc.

(A-MA '77)   Richard A. Bourne Co., Inc.
DOLLHOUSE, 19th Century Style W/Clapboard Siding & Shingled Roof, Four Rooms W/Hallways & Stairway, Victorian & Conventional Furnishings, Papered Walls, Carpeted, Draped, Fireplaces, Exterior Weathered, Window Shutters Missing, 52½" L., 26" W., 43" H. $3600.00

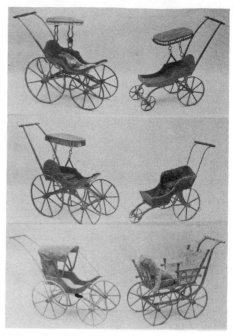

(A-MA '77)   *Richard A. Bourne Co., Inc.*
DOLLHOUSE, Victorian Mansion W/
Four Rooms, Victorian & Empire Style Furnishings, Crank Telephone & Treadle Sewing Machine, Partially Repainted, Needs Painting, Pieces of Gingerbread Broken Off & Missing, 41¾" L., 27½" W., 57" H.; Cut-Down Table W/Stand Adds Another 23¾" In Ht. $3300.00

(A-MA '77)   *Richard A. Bourne Co., Inc.*
DOLLHOUSE, Swiss Chalet Style W/
Yellow Exterior & Stencil Designs, Victorian Oak Base On Casters, 4 Lg. Rooms, Contains 14 Dolls (maid, four ladies, seven children & two infants), Victorian Furnishings, Attic Room In Top W/Christmas Tree, Trunk & Santa Claus, 51" L., 24" D., 76½" H. $2800.00

(A-MA '77)   *Richard A. Bourne Co., Inc.*
(ROW I, L to R)
DOLL'S SURREY, 19th C., Red Decorated Body W/Stencil Decor., Fringed Top, Cushion, Red Upholstery, Flaking, Minor Paint Wear $160.00
DOLL'S SURREY, Fringed Top, Orig. Paint W/Striping, Cotton Balls Around Edge, Replaced Front Axle $60.00
(ROW II, L to R)
DOLL'S SURREY, Orig. Blue Paint W/
Striping, Adjustable Fringed Top, Paint Flaking $160.00
DOLL'S CARRIAGE, Orig. Wood & Paint, Replaced Upholstery $100.00
(ROW III, L to R)
DOLL'S STROLLER, Collapsible Leather top W/Several Sm. Holes, Orig. Black Paint W/Stencil Decor. $90.00
DOLL'S CARRIAGE, Wicker Weaving Around Body, Worn Stuffed Dog In Carriage, Carriage Reupholstered In Modern Chintz $75.00

◀ *To the left*
(ROW I, L to R)
DOLL TRUNK W/Two China Dolls (8" & 3" H.), Red Imitation Leather W/Black Trim & Nail Heads, Trunk Contains Hat Boxes, Trinkets, Doll Wardrobe, 10" L., 6¾" D., 5½" H. $800.00
DOLL TRUNK, Red Imitation Leather, Black Leather Flap, Straps & Nail Heads, Stamped On Lid "Sam'l. J. Denton", Handles Missing, 12" L., 8" D., 7¼" H.
. . . .$60.00
(ROW II, L to R)
DOLL TRUNK, Black Imitation Leather W/Leather Flaps W/Red Band & Nail Heads, 8" L., 5½" D., 4¼" H. $30.00
WOODEN TRUNK, Skin Covered, Leather Bands & Nail Heads, 8¼" L., 5" D., 4" H. $90.00

(A-MA '77)   *Richard A. Bourne Co., Inc.*

(A-MA '77)   *Richard A. Bourne Co., Inc.*
MINIATURE DOLLHOUSE FURNITURE
(L to R)
SHAVING MIRROR, Mahogany Frame & Stand W/Beveled Glass Mirror, 4" H. . . . . . .
. . . .$30.00
ROSEWOOD DRUM TABLE, Revolving Top, Velvet-Lined Edge, Tilting Top, Minor Chip On Table Edge, 3" Diam., 3½" H. When Top Tilted $40.00
BRASS TEAKETTLE W/DOWN-HEARTH TRIVET, Sm. Dent In Teakettle, Trivet: 3½" L., 2¾" W., 3½" H.; Teakettle: 3½" H. $50.00

(A-VA '77) *Laws Auction & Antiques*
COMB-BACK WINDSOR ARM CHAIR,
Pennsylvania, Saddle Seat, Old Finish . . . . .
. . . .$1050.00

◄ *To the left*
(A-PA '77) *Brown Bros. Gallery*
COMB-BACK WINDSOR ARM CHAIR
. . . .$850.00

(A-OH '77) *Garth's Auctions, Inc.*
COMB-BACK WINDSOR ARM CHAIR,
Worn Green Paint $2350.00

(A-VA '77) *Laws Auction & Antiques*
COMB-BACK WINDSOR ARM CHAIR,
Cupid's Bow Scroll Crest, Single Board Seat,
Ca. 1780-1800 . . . .$600.00

(A-PA '77) *Pennypacker Auction Centre*
WINDSOR WRITING CHAIR, Signed
On Base, "A. Motzer", Stenciled . . . .
. . . .$2000.00

(A-VA '77) *Laws Auction & Antiques*
COMB-BACK WINDSOR ROCKER,
New England, Ca. 1800, Molded Seat . . . .
. . . .$475.00
CANDLESTAND, Amer., 18th C., 18"
Diam., 26½" H. $300.00

(A-VA '77) *Laws Auction & Antiques*
RODBACK WINDSOR SIDE CHAIRS,
Set Of 4, New England $325.00

◄ *To the left*
(A-PA '77) *Brown Bros. Gallery*
WINDSOR BIRD-CAGE SIDE CHAIR
(1 of 3), Set $570.00
WINDSOR ARMCHAIR $400.00

(A-PA '77)   *Pennypacker Auction Centre*
(L to R)
COMB-BACK WINDSOR ARM CHAIR
W/Carved Ears, Bottle Turnings & "H"
Stretcher, 25" W., 44" H. $2600.00
HIGH BACK WINDSOR ARM CHAIR
W/Knuckle Arms, "H" Stretcher, Blunt
Arrow Feet, 43" H. $2000.00

(A-VA '77)   *Laws Auction & Antiques*
NEW ENGLAND WINDSOR ROCKER,
Curly Maple, Plank Seat, Ca. 1800 . . . .
. . . .$475.00
**PENNSYLVANIA SERPENTINE TOP
TEA TABLE,** Ca. 1760-70, Top 31" x 32",
28" H. $500.00

(A-MA '77)   *Richard A. Bourne Co., Inc.*
CHILD'S WINDSOR ARM CHAIR, American, Late 18th-Early 19th C., Orig.
Black Paint W/Stenciled Striping . .$450.00
**MINIATURE CHILD'S BLANKET
CHEST,** American, Late 18th-Early 19th
C., 6-Board Const., Orig. Blue Paint, 20½"
O.L. $275.00
CHILD'S HITCHCOCK SIDE CHAIR,
Orig. Rush Seat, Minor Repair $70.00

(A-MA '77)   *Richard A. Bourne Co. Inc.*
WINDSOR ARM CHAIR, American, 18th
or Early 19th C., Pine Plank Seat, Oak Arms
& Crest, Refinished $900.00
QUEEN ANNE CANDLESTAND, American, 18th C., Orig. Black Paint . . .$500.00
BANISTER-BACK SIDE CHAIR, American, 18th C., Grained Finish, Rush Seat
Worn $300.00

(A-MA '77)   *Richard A. Bourne Co. Inc.*
BANISTER-BACK ARM CHAIR, American, 18th C., Old Black Paint & Rush Seat
. . . .$1000.00
HEPPLEWHITE MAHOGANY CANDLESTAND, American, 18th C. .$700.00
STEP-DOWN WINDSOR SIDE CHAIR,
American, 19th C., Orig. Black Paint, Chalk
Figures In Bottom Of Pine Plank Seat . . . .
. . . .$100.00

(A-PA '77)   *Brown Bros. Gallery*
CHILD'S WINDSOR PLANK CHAIR,
Buttermilk Paint $70.00

(A-PA '77)   *Pennypacker Auction Centre*
BIRD-CAGE WINDSOR SIDE CHAIR
W/Bent Back $70.00

(A-PA '77)   *Brown Bros. Gallery*
**CHILD'S SHERATON WINDSOR ARM
CHAIR,** Orig. Decor. $220.00

(A-VA '77)   *Laws Auction & Antiques*
BANISTER-BACK SIDE CHAIR, 18th
C., New England, Maple, Woven Seat,
Ca. 1720-50 . . . .$225.00

BOW-BACK WINDSOR ARM CHAIR,
Amer., 18th C., Vase Turnings, Molded
Seat, Probably RI or CT Origin, 21" W.,
18" D., 35" H. $375.00
CHILD'S WINDSOR CHAIR, Amer.,
Ca. 1780-90, 24" H. $300.00
WINDSOR ARM CHAIR, Amer., Ca.
1780-1800, Probably RI Origin, 37" H. . . .
. . . .$425.00

BOW-BACK WINDSOR ARM CHAIR,
Mass., Ca. 1780-1800, Saddle Seat . . . . . .
. . . .$650.00

WINDSOR BOW-BACK ARM CHAIR
. . . .$950.00

WINDSOR BRACE BACK CHAIR . . . .
. . . .$400.00

WINDSOR FANBACK SIDE CHAIR . .
. . . .$300.00

WINDSOR ARM CHAIR $575.00

ROD-BACK WINDSOR SIDE CHAIRS,
Set of 6, Plant Seats $275.00

To the right ▶
HOOP-BACK WINDSOR SIDE CHAIR
. . . .$300.00

(D-CT '78)
BANISTER-BACK SIDE CHAIR, Maple, Ca. 1740 Massachusetts, 42" H. Chair Back Features A Wavy Cresting W/Both The Tail Of A Fish & The Head Of A Wolf, Orig. Finish, New Seat $650.00

(D-VA '78)   *William C. & Hazel G. Adams*
BANISTER-BACK CHAIR, Legs Extended $175.00

(D-VA '78)   *William C. & Hazel G. Adams*
LADDERBACK CHAIRS, (Set of 4), Maple W/Some Curly Maple $400.00

(A-MA '77)   *Richard A. Bourne Co. Inc.*
BANISTER-BACK ARM CHAIR, American, 18th C., Splint Seat, Refinished .....
.... $600.00
CHILD'S LADDER BACK ARM CHAIR, Scandinavian, 18th or Early 19th C., Rush Seat, Orig. Cond. $150.00
PINE AND MAPLE TAVERN TABLE, American, 18th C., Natural Finish, 39¼" L., 23" W., 26" H., (Drop Leaf - 8½") ......
.... $800.00

(A-MA '77)   *Richard A. Bourne Co., Inc.*
BANISTER-BACK SIDE CHAIR, American, 18th C., Replaced Rush Seat, Refinished W/Mahogany Stain $800.00
QUEEN ANNE OVAL TAVERN TABLE, American, 18th C., Fruitwood Base, Walnut Top, Refinished, 29¾" L., 23¼" W., 28" H.
.... $700.00
QUEEN ANNE ROUNDABOUT CHAIR, American, 18th C., Slip Commode Seat Under Cushion, Mahogany $700.00

(A-PA '77)   *Brown Bros. Gallery*
PENNSYLVANIA LADDER BACK ARM-CHAIR, 5 Arched Slats, Orig. Grained Decor. $775.00

(A-PA '77)   *Brown Bros. Gallery*
SHERATON LADDER BACK CHAIRS, (1 of 3), Rush Seats, Orig. Decor $195.00

(A-PA '77)   *Brown Bros. Gallery*
LADDER BACK ROCKER, Slat Back ..
.... $50.00

(A-VA '78)   *Laws*
CHIPPENDALE SIDE CHAIRS, (Set of 4), Late 19th C., Slip Seats $475.00

(A-PA '77) *Pennypacker Auction Centre*
QUEEN ANNE CORNER CHAIR, Cherry, Mass., 1740-1760, 27½" W., 30½" H.
. . . .$2150.00

(A-PA '77) *Brown Bros. Gallery*
SPINDLE BACK PLANK ROCKER, Grained, Orig. Decor $170.00

(A-PA '77) *Pennypacker Auction Centre*
BOSTON ROCKER, Orig. Strip & Floral Decor On Yellow Ground $115.00

(A-VA '77) *Laws Auction & Antiques*
CORNER ARM CHAIR, Mass., 18th C., Woven Rush Seat $300.00

(A-PA '77) *Brown Bros. Gallery*
CHILD'S HIGH CHAIR W/Orig. Decor.
. . . .$250.00

(A-PA '77) *Brown Bros. Gallery*
ARROWBACK PLANK YOUTH CHAIR, Orig. Graining & Decor $80.00

◀ *To the left*
(A-VA '77) *Laws Auction & Antiques*
CORNER CHAIR, New England, Ca. 1730, Cherry & Maple, Country Rush Seat, Refinished, 22" W., 22" D., 30" H. . . . . . .
. . . .$350.00

(A-VA '77) *Laws Auction & Antiques*
CARVER CHAIRS, Set Of 4, 1 Arm & 3 Side, Work Shop Of Wallace Nutting . . . . .
. . . .$550.00

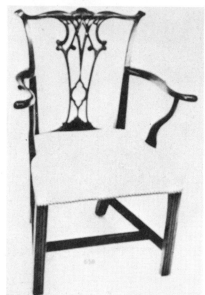

(A-VA '77)   *Laws Auction & Antiques*
CHIPPENDALE ARM CHAIR, 18th C., Ca. 1770-80, Walnut, Upholstered, 22" W., 18" D., 36" H. $525.00

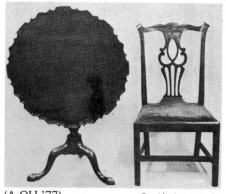

(A-OH '77)   *Garth's Auctions, Inc.*
TILT TOP TEA TABLE, Mahogany, 1-Pc. Pie Crust Top, Refinished, Mid 19th C., 31" Diam., 27½" H. $300.00
CHIPPENDALE SIDE CHAIR, Mahogany, Slip Seat W/Red Plush Upholstering, Old Finish $350.00

(A-VA '77)   *Laws Auction & Antiques*
CHIPPENDALE ROCKING CHAIR, "Amer., Ca. 1760-70, Cherrywood, Converted From Side Chair $180.00
CHIPPENDALE SIDE CHAIR, Amer., Ca. 1760-70, Cherrywood, 38" H. (Matches Rocking Chair $190.00

(A-VA '78)   *Laws Auction & Antiques*
CHIPPENDALE SIDE CHAIRS (Set Of 3), Seats Upholstered In Cream & White Silk $250.00

(A-VA '77)   *Laws Auction & Antiques*
CHIPPENDALE DINING ROOM CHAIRS, Set Of 6, Slip Seats, 1 Arm & 5 Side Chairs $2000.00

(A-MA '77)   *Richard A. Bourne Co. Inc.*
COUNTRY CHIPPENDALE SIDE CHAIR, American, 18th C., Orig. Black Finish, Rush Seat Replaced W/Upholstery $325.00
QUEEN ANNE FRUITWOOD CANDLESTAND, American, 18th C., Orig. Finish, Top W/Age Splits & Old Nail Repairs, Replaced & Reglued Leg $150.00
COUNTRY CHIPPENDALE SIDE CHAIR, American, 18th C., Old Black Finish, Rush Seat Replaced W/Upholstery, Metal Braces On Back Legs $75.00

(A-VA '78)   *Laws Auction & Antiques*
QUEEN ANNE SAVERY TYPE SIDE CHAIR, 18th C., Pennsylvania, Walnut, Ca. 1760 . . . .$800.00

(A-VA '77)   *Laws Auction & Antiques*
HITCHCOCK SIDE CHAIRS, Orig. Stencil Decor., Cane Seats, Ca. 1830 . . . .$350.00

(A-PA '77)   *Pennypacker Auction Centre*
WALNUT CHIPPENDALE FOOT STOOL, Needlepoint Top $875.00

◄ *To the left*
(A-MA '77)   *Robert C. Eldred Co., Inc.*
ENGLISH CHIPPENDALE DINING CHAIRS, Set Of 6 (2 Illus.), 6 Side Chairs & 1 Armchair, Gros Point Needlework Upholstered Slip Seats $2800.00
PIE CRUST TILT TOP TABLE, Mahogany, 30½" Diam., XVIII Century . .$400.00

(D-MO '78)
VICTORIAN ROCKER, New Upholstery
. . . .$295.00

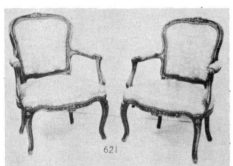

(A-VA '78)   *Laws Auction & Antiques*
LOUIS XV ARM CHAIRS, Pr., Overall
Floral Carving, Floral Cartouche Design
Silk Material $1200.00

(A-VA '78)   *Laws Auction & Antiques*
**SPANISH FOOT HIGH BACK QUEEN
ANNE CHAIR,** 18th C., Walnut, Tooled
Leather Back & Seat Upholstery, Ca. 1730
. . . .$400.00

(A-PA '77)   *Pennypacker Auction Centre*
MORAVIAN TYPE CHAIR $30.00

(A-PA '77)   *Pennypacker Auction Centre*
FRUITWOOD MORAVIAN CHAIR,
Small $300.00

(A-VA '78)   *Laws Auction & Antiques*
QUEEN ANNE COUNTRY SIDE CHAIR,
New England Orig., Ca. 1730, 41" H. . . . .
. . . .$225.00
**HEPPLEWHITE TRIFID SPIDER LEG
CANDLESTAND,** Ca. 1780-90, CT Orig-
ing, Refinished, 28" H., 18" Diam. . . . . . .
. . . .$280.00

(A-VA '78)   *Laws Auction & Antiques*
TIGER MAPLE DESK, Storage Interior,
Ca. 1790-1800, 38" H., 33" W. . .$700.00
**TIGER MAPLE SHERATON SIDE
CHAIR** W/Woven Hickory Seat, Ca. 1800
. . . .$50.00

(A-VA '78)   *Laws Auction & Antiques*
CIRCULAR CANDLESTAND W/Bulb-
ous Turned Shaft, Snake Feet, Ca. 1790,
27½" H., 20½" Diam. $275.00
**CHIPPENDALE MAHOGANY SIDE
CHAIR,** Upholstered Slip Seat W/Beaded
Legs Connected By Beaded Box Stretchers,
Old Patina, Ca. 1770, Phil. Origin . . . .
. . . .$225.00

(A-PA '77)   *Brown Bros. Gallery*
WINDSOR STICK BACK SETTEE,
Duck Bill Arms, 6'5" L. $2600.00

A-PA '77)   *Brown Bros. Gallery*
SHERATON WINDSOR STICK BACK
SETTEE, Orig. Grained & Stenciled Decor.
..............................$1600.00

(D-VA '78)   *William C. & Hazel G. Adams*
EMPIRE SOFA, Ca. 1820-1830, N.Y.
Mahogany, Orig. Horsehair Upholstery,
68½" L., 22½" D., 34½" H. ...$1200.00

(D-VA '78)   *William C. & Hazel G. Adams*
EMPIRE SOFA, Ca., 1820-1830, Amer.,
Mahogany, Deep Red Damask Upholstery,
84" L., 23" D., 34" H. $1950.00

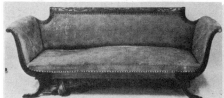

(A-OH '78)   *Garth's Auctions, Inc.*
FEDERAL STYLE SOFA, Reeded &
Carved Mahogany Frame, Worn Green Up-
holstery, Brass Paw Castor Missing, Repairs
Necessary, 84" L. $100.00

(A-OH '77)   *Garth's Auctions, Inc.*
SHERATON SOFA, Carved Mahogany,
Ornamented By Acanthus Leaves & Star
Floral Design, Carved Crest, Swagged Drap-
ery, Stylized Sheaves W/Bow Ties, Orig.
Finish W/Green Velvet Upholstery, 73" L.,
37" H. $3000.00

(A-VA '77)   *Laws Auction & Antiques*
CHIPPENDALE STYLE HUMP BACK
SOFA, Mahogany Wood Carved Ends,
Gadrooned Molded Skirt, Gold & Blue Floral
Striped Brocade Upholstery, 84" L. ......
.............................$675.00

(A-OH '77)   *Garth's Auctions, Inc.*
REEDED LYRE MAHOGANY SOFA,
Moss Green Velvet Upholstery, Repaired
Foot, 76" L. $325.00
HAND COLORED LITHOGRAPH,
"American Winter Scene", By Joseph Hoo-
ver, Phila., Pine Frame, 30" x 36" $150.00

(A-PA '77)   *Brown Bros. Gallery*
(L to R)
WINDSOR ARMCHAIR, Bamboo Turn-
ings $450.00
SIMILAR ARMCHAIR $550.00

(A-VA '77)   *Laws Auction & Antiques*
PHILADELPHIA WINDSOR ARM
CHAIR, 18th C., Signed Chapman, Ma-
hogany, Orig. Indian Red Paint ...$850.00
BETTY LAMP, American, 18th-19th Cen-
tury, Copper, Orig. Staple To Hang & Wick
Pick $85.00
CHERRY CANDLESTAND, New Eng-
land, Ca. 1770-80, Sq. Ovolu Cornered Top,
Top: 17" x 18", 27½" H. $250.00

(A-VA '77)   *Laws Auction & Antiques*
BOW BACK WINDSOR ARM CHAIRS,
Set Of 8, Saddle Seats $1900.00

(D-VA '78)   *William C. & Hazel G. Adams*
WINDSOR CHAIR, Labeled Wallace
Nutting, Reproduction $175.00

(A-OH '77)   *Garth's Auctions, Inc.*
BRASS BED, Mother of Pearl Bands . . . .
. . . .$900.00

(A-OH '77)   *Garth's Auctions, Inc.*
JENNY LIND YOUTH BED, Walnut, Made Into Bench W/Red, White & Blue Print Cushion, 22" x 50" x 30" H. $150.00
DROP LEAF TABLE, Walnut, Doll Size, 14" W. $30.00

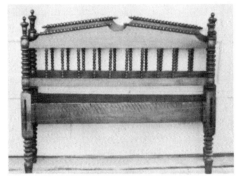

(D-WA '78)
MAPLE SPOOL BED W/Orig. Finish, Three-Quarter Size, Ca. 1860, Ohio Origin
. . . .$290.00

(A-MA '77)   *Richard A. Bourne Co. Inc.*
PINE SETTLE, American, 18th C., Made Of Broad Plank, 2 Removable Lids, Refinished, 75" L., 17½" D., 49" Back Height .
. . . .$550.00

(A-MA '77)   *Robert C. Eldred Co., Inc.*
BRASS STORE WEIGHTS, Set Of Nine, 2 oz. To 28 lbs. $150.00
EARLY SETTLE, Original Finish, 57" L. .
. . . .$350.00

(A-OH '77)   *Garth's Auctions, Inc.*
COUNTRY EMPIRE SETTEE, Black Paint, Arms Repaired, 82" L., 22" D., 34" H. $210.00

(A-ME '77)   *Julia's Auction Service*
WINDSOR SETTEE, All Orig., Refinished, 77½" L. $1250.00

(A-OH '77)   *Garth's Auctions, Inc.*
SETTEE, Modern Black Paint W/Gold Striping, 85" L. $235.00
CURRIER & IVES PRINT, "American Homestead, Autumn", Margins Slightly Trimmed, Old Pine Frame, 12½" x 16½"
. . . .$215.00
CURRIER & IVES PRINT, "American Homestead, Spring", Margins Slightly Trimmed, Curly Maple Frame, 12½" x 16½" . .
. . . .$235.00
CURRIER & IVES PRINT, "American Homestead, Winter", Margins Slightly Trimmed, Old Cherry Frame, 12½" x 16½" . .
. . . .$410.00
CURRIER & IVES PRINT, "American Homestead, Summer", Margins Slightly Trimmed, Curly Maple Frame, 12½" x 16½"
. . . .$260.00

(A-OH '77)   *Garth's Auctions, Inc.*
SETTEE W/White Paint W/Green, Black, Brown & Yellow Striping W/Floral & Foliage Work, Minor Wear, One Arm Old Replacement, & One Spindle Missing, 78" L., 28½" D. $600.00

(A-OH '77)   *Garth's Auctions, Inc.*
SETTEE W/Orig. Brown Paint W/Yellow & Black Striping & Hand Painted Floral Work On Crest, 71½" L. $750.00

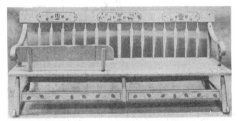

(A-OH '78)   *Garth's Auctions, Inc.*
ARROWBACK MAMMY BENCH, Modern Cream Colored Paint W/Pennsylvania Dutch Designs In Red & Green, Minor Repairs, 70" L. $210.00

(A-OH '78)   *Garth's Auctions, Inc.*
WINDSOR SETTEE, Refinished, 75½" W., 18½" D., 16" H. Seat $950.00

(A-VA '77)   *Laws Auction & Antiques*
WINDSOR SETTEE W/Scrolled Ear Fanback W/Blunt Arrow Turned Legs & Bobbin Stretchers, Sgn. Wallace Nutting (Label Affixed To Underside Of Seat, 87" L. . . . .
. . . .$1000.00

(A-OH '77)　　　　　　*Garth's Auctions, Inc.*
CUPBOARD, Orig. Red Paint W/Graining In Curly Maple On Door, Interior Has Shelves, Door Reversed, 30¾" W., 20" D., (35¾" x 22½" At Cornice), 67½" H. $410.00

(A-MA '77)　　　　　*Richard A. Bourne Co., Inc.*
CUPBOARD, American, 19th C., Shelves In Both Sections, Refinished In Lt. Gray Antique Finish, 49½" L., 22" D., 83" H. $400.00

(A-OH '77)　　　　　　*Garth's Auctions, Inc.*
STONEWARE JUG, 2-Gal., Impressed "H. Purdy, Ohio", Cobalt Blue Flower, 14" H. $135.00
STONEWARE JAR, 4-Gal., Stenciled Cobalt "Williams & Reppert, Greensboro, Pa.", Base Hairlines, 14" H. $27.50
STONEWARE JUG, 3-Gal., Impressed "Sipe & Sons, W---port, Pa.", Cobalt Blue Flower, 14" H. $50.00
PINE CUPBOARD, Refinished, Replaced Cornice, 48" W., 11½" D., 87" H. $285.00

(A-OH '77)　　　　　　*Garth's Auctions, Inc.*
POPLAR CUPBOARD, Refinished W/ Wooden Knobs Added, 40" W., 19½" D., 77" H. $475.00

(A-OH '77)　　　　　　*Garth's Auctions, Inc.*
ARCHITECTURAL CORNER CUPBOARD, Pine, 2-Pc., Orig. White, Red & Green Paint; Minor Repair, 55¾" W., 30" D., 82" H. $700.00

To the right ▶

(A-OH '77)　　　　　　*Garth's Auctions, Inc.*
CORNER CUPBOARD, Paint Removed To Show Orig. Yellow, Bottom Door Cut For Double Door, 42½" W., 22½" D., 88½" H. $1350.00

(A-PA '77)   *Pennypacker Auction Centre*
PINE PIE SAFE, 12 Perforated Tin Panels In Pinwheel Decor. $275.00

(A-OH '77)   *Garth's Auctions, Inc.*
WALNUT CUPBOARD, Refinished, 46½" W., 21½" D., 79" H. $400.00
STONEWARE JAR, Cobalt Brushed Tulip Design, Minor Chips, 11¾" H. $50.00
STONEWARE JAR, 2-Gal., Cobalt Slip Foliage Design, Impressed "New York Stoneware Co., Fort Edward, N.Y.", 14" H. $45.00
STONEWARE JAR, 2-Gal., Stenciled Label: "T.F. Reppert, Greensboro, Pa.", Cobalt Brushed Design, 11¾" H. ..$45.00

(A-OH '78)   *Garth's Auctions, Inc.*
WALNUT CORNER CUPBOARD, Upper Shelves W/Notches Cut For Spoons, White Porcelain Knobs, 54½" W., 84¾" H. ....
...............................$800.00

(A-OH '77)   *Garth Auctions, Inc.*
CHERRY CORNER CUPBOARD, Old Varnish Finish, Ends Of Cornice Missing, 46" W., 21" D., 80" H. $525.00

To the right ▶

(A-OH '77)   *Garth's Auctions, Inc.*
CHERRY & CURLY MAPLE CUPBOARD, Ivory Escutcheons, Mortised & Pinned Joints, Paneled Back, Refinished, Knobs Replaced, 44½" W., 18½" D., 82½" H. $650.00

(A-OH '77)   *Garth Auctions, Inc.*
SHAKER PINE CUPBOARD, Orig., Reddish-Brown Paint, Maine or Groveland, 41½" W., 16" D., 79" H. $1500.00

(D-VA '78)   *William C. & Hazel G. Adams*
**BROKEN ARCH CORNER CUP-
BOARD,** Ca. 1790, Virginia, Walnut, Heart
Pine Secondary Wood, Requires 40" Cor-
ner, 8'2" O.H. $3900.00

(A-PA '77)   *Brown Bros. Gallery*
TWO-PIECE CORNER CUPBOARD,
Tiger Maple, 6'1" H. $3200.00

(D-MA '78)   *Crazy Horse Antiques*
SHAKER KITCHEN CUPBOARD, Ca.
1840-50, Hancock, Ma., Poplar .$2700.00

(A-VA '77)   *Laws Auction & Antiques*
WALNUT PIE SAFE, Amer., Ca. 1850-60,
3 Punched Tin Panels, 42" W., 18" D.,
55" H. $400.00

(A-OH '77)   *Garth Auctions, Inc.*
APPLEWOOD CLOTHES PRESS,
Dovetailed Drawers, 2-Part, Orig. Oval
Brasses, Restored, 43" W., Under Cornice,
46½" W. At Cornice, 18" D., 77¾" H. . . .
. . . .$500.00

(A-MA '77)   *Richard A. Bourne Co., Inc.*
DRY SINK, Pennsylvania 19th C., Poplar
W/Cherry Finish, 48" L., 20" D., 57¼"
O.H. $750.00

◄ *To the left*

(A-OH '77)   *Garth's Auctions, Inc.*
ENGLISH OAK CUPBOARD, 2-Pc.,
Mortised & Pinned Constr., Replaced Cor-
nice & Hinges, Old Finish 1 Door W/Repair
At Hinge, 42" W., 19" D., 76" H. . . . .
. . . .$475.00
DELFT CHARGER (1 of Pr.), Blue &
White W/Vase Of Flowers, Old Rim Chips,
12¼" Diam., 2¼" H. $500.00
DELFT CHARGER, Polychrome Floral
Decor., 14" Diam., 2½" H. $240.00

(A-MA '77) *Richard A. Bourne Co., Inc.*
MAHOGANY CORNER CABINET, American, 18th C., 51" W., 28" D., 82" H.
..................................$1100.00

(A-OH '77) *Garth Auctions, Inc.*
PINE IRISH COUNTRY CORNER CUPBOARD, Center Door Opens To Center Compartment, Refinished W/Minor Feet Repair, Blue Interior, 44" W., 76¼" H. ....
...............................$450.00
INDIAN BASKET, Geometric Diamond Pattern, Worn Rim, 17" Diam., 7½" H. ..
.................................$80.00

(A-OH '77) *Garth's Auctions, Inc.*
MAPLE CUPBOARD, Dovetailed Drawers, Refinished, Base & Base Frame Replaced, Repairs, 44" W., 22" D., 87½" H.
...............................$475.00
CLEAR BLOWN JAR, 2 Applied Rings & Lid W/Applied Handle, 12½" H. ..$50.00
CLEAR BLOWN JAR, Applied Rings & Lid W/Applied Handle, 12¼" H. ..$50.00
CLEAR BLOWN JAR, Applied Rings & Lid W/Applied Handle, 12½" H. ..$50.00

◄ *To the left*
(A-OH '77) *Garth's Auctions, Inc.*
PINE ARCHITECTURAL CORNER CUPBOARD, Continuous Molding, Cornice Missing, Worn Blue-Grey Paint, Interior W/Worn Red Paint, 46" W., 18½" D., 85" H. $1525.00
(ROW I, L to R)
REDWARE JUG, Grey Glaze W/Black & White Speckles, 5½" H. $20.00
CARVED WOODEN HEAD, White Face W/Red Mouth, Black Eyes, Brown Paint On Hair, 11¾" H. $165.00
REDWARE BOTTLE, Greenish Shiny Glaze, 6½" H. $60.00
(ROW II, L to R)
WOODEN NOGGIN, Hinged Lid, Carved, 20th C., 7½" H. $25.00
WOODEN SHORE BIRD, Carved, Speckled White, Grey & Black Paint, Head Repaired, Replaced Beak, 9" W., 7¼" H.
....................................$95.00
TREEN CANISTER, Turned Rings W/ Brown Stain, Inset Bottom & Matching Turned Lid, 9½" H. $37.50
(ROW III, L to R)
REDWARE JUG, Drk. Green Glaze W/ Orange Spots, Tooled Rings At Shoulder, Minor Glaze Flakes, 7¾" H. $85.00
WOODEN CANDLESTICK, 3 Inset Cut-Out Feet, Tin Drip Pan, Green Paint, 6½" H. $187.00
REDWARE JUG, Greenish Clear Shiny Glaze W/Orange Spots, Tooled Rings At Shoulder, Minor Glaze Flakes Around Lip, 7¾" H. $125.00
(ROW IV, L to R)
WOODEN SHORE BIRD, Carved, Worn Brown & White Combed Paint, Branded "T. Rogers", Modern Metal Base, 8" W., 7½" H. $155.00
WOODEN SHORE BIRD, Carved, Old Grey & Black Paint, Modern Metal Base, 9" W., 11½" H. $45.00
WOODEN SHORE BIRD, Carved From ½" Thick Wood, Weathered Paint, Modern Metal Base, 6½" W., 7½" H. $50.00

(A-MA '77) *Richard A. Bourne Co., Inc.*
PENNSYLVANIA CUPBOARD, Late 18th-Early 19th C., Walnut & Poplar, Cast Pewter Handles, 43¼" L., 17" D., 72¾" O.H. $800.00

(A-OH '77)   *Garth's Auctions, Inc.*
PINE CUPBOARD, Orig. Grained Decor.,
Brown Over Yellow Ground, Cornice Old
Replacement, 34" W., 18½" D., 71½" H.
.............................$600.00
STONEWARE BOTTLE, 9" H. ..$16.00
STONEWARE FLASK, 8" H. $75.00
STONEWARE JUG, Impressed "Good-
win Webster", Blue Splashes, Crows Feet,
12" H........................$27.50
STONEWARE INK BOTTLE, Impressed
"Giessen Blue", 6¼" H............$7.00
STONEWARE BOTTLE, 10" H. ..$9.00

(A-MA '77)   *Richard A. Bourne Co., Inc.*
COUNTRY PINE CUPBOARD, Lower
Section American, 18th C., Upper Section
Custom-Made Addition Of Old Wood, Re-
stored & Refinished, 46½" W., 21½" D.,
73¾" H......................$550.00

(A-MA '77)   *Robert C. Eldred Co., Inc.*
ENGLISH OAK COURT CUPBOARD,
Dated 1706, Paneled Doors & Sides, Carv-
ing On Upper Section, 61½" L., 63½" H.
.............................$1000.00

◄ *To the left*

(A-VA '77)   *Laws Auction & Antiques*
QUEEN ANNE CORNER CUPBOARD,
18th C., 2-Pc., Pine, Doors Open To Expose
Demi-Lune Interior W/Shaped Shelves,
Takes 34" Corner, 85" H. $1600.00

(A-VA '78)   *Laws*
CHIPPENDALE CORNER CABINET,
18th C., Mahogany, Takes 32" Corner,
85" H........................$900.00

(A-OH '77)   *Garth's Auctions, Inc.*
**PENNSYLVANIA ARCHITECTURAL
CORNER CUPBOARD,** Poplar W/Orig.
Red & Black Graining, Interior W/Modern
Blue Paint, Latches Missing, Back Dated
"1802", 57" W., 32" D., 9' 8½" H. .....
.............................$2350.00

(A-OH '77)   *Garth's Auctions, Inc.*
MAHOGANY CHIPPENDALE OXBOW DESK, Dovetailed Drawers W/Fitted Interior, Replaced Brasses & Bottom Drawers, 42" W., 23" D., 43" H., 32¼" Writing Ht. $725.00

(A-VA '77)   *Laws Auction & Antiques*
18th CENTURY MAHOGANY DESK, W/Serpentine Front, Secret Storage, Ca. 1760-80, North Shore Or Boston Origin, 44" H. $1550.00

(A-OH '77)   *Garth's Auctions, Inc.*
COUNTRY SHERATON CHEST OF DRAWERS, Cherry, Cockbeaded Dovetailed Drawers, Paneled Ends, 41" W., 19½" D., 45" H. $290.00
VICTORIAN BRASS CANDLESTICKS, Pr., Push-Ups, 7¾" H. $77.50
BRASS STUDENT LAMP, Drk. Green Cased W/White, Bottom Edge Of Shade Chipped, Electrified, Needs Rewiring, 21" H. $180.00
BRASS CANDLESTICK, 18th C., Side Push-Up, Minor Soldered Repair, 8¼" H. $55.00
BRASS CANDLESTICK, 18th C., Side Push-Up W/Heavy Knob, 6" H. . . .$90.00

(A-ME '77)   *Julia's Auction Service*
CHILD'S WILLIAM & MARY SLANT FRONT DESK, Amer., Cherry W/Pine Secondary Wood, Replaced Brass Hdwe., Replaced Foot, 24½" W., 12½" D., 33" H. $800.00

(A-OH)   *Garth's Auctions, Inc.*
MAHOGANY DESK, Dovetailed, Cockbeaded Drawers Have Figured Mahogany Veneer On Pine, Fitted Interior W/Pigeon Holes & 5 Dovetailed Drawers, Back Board Replaced W/Plywood, 36" W., 19½" D., 40" H. $325.00

(A-MA '77)   *Robert C. Eldred Co., Inc.*
EMPIRE CREDENZA, French, Ca. 1840, Ebony and Ormolu W/Semi-Precious Stone & Ivory Encrustations On Central Panel, 49¾" W., 49¾" H. $600.00

(A-VA '78)   *Laws*
PLANTATION DESK, 18th C., American Tiger Maple, Storage Interior, 33" W., 21" D., 38" H. $700.00
SHERATON SIDE CHAIR, Tiger Maple, Woven Hickory Seat, Ca. 1800 . . .$700.00

(A-VA '78)   *Laws*
CHIPPENDALE DROP FRONT DESK, 18th C., Ca. 1760-70, Mahogany, Inlaid Molded Edge Drop, Satinwood Inlay Fitted Interior, Cockbeaded Edging, Pierced Chippendale Brass Bail Pulls, 44" W., 21" D., 42" H. $1350.00

(A-OH '77)   *Garth's Auctions, Inc.*
WALNUT SECRETARY, Dovetailed
Drawer & Well W/Slant Top Lift Lid, 2
Interior Shelves, Refinished, Lock Hasp
Missing, 39" W., 24½" D., 93" H.$650.00
WOVEN SPLIT WOOD BASKET, 18"
x 12½" x 12" H.................$42.50

(D-MA '78)   *Crazy Horse Antiques*
SHAKER TRUSTEE'S DESK, Ca. 1830-
40, Hancock, Ma., Pine $6400.00

(A-VA '77)   *Laws Auction & Antiques*
HEPPLEWHITE TAMBOUR DESK, Ma-
hogany, Inlaid, Felt Lined Flip Down Writing
Surface, 33½" W., 19" D., 46" H. $800.00

(A-MA '77)   *Richard A. Bourne Co., Inc.*
CHIPPENDALE MAHOGANY DESK,
Mass., 18th C., 9 Drawers & 8 Pigeonholes,
41½" L. $4250.00

(D-MA '78)   *Crazy Horse Antiques*
SHAKER WORK DESK, Ca. 1810-20,
Canterbury, N.H., Pine $2800.00

(A-OH '77)   *Garth's Auctions, Inc.*
EMPIRE BUTLER'S DESK, Curly Maple,
Dovetailed, Cockbeaded Drawers, Top
Drawer Opens For Desk, Interior W/7
Drawers, Pigeon Holes, Inlaid Walnut Shield
Escutcheons, Hardware Replaced W/Clear
Lacy Knobs, (1 Missing), Old Finish, 45" W.,
22¾" D., 49½" H. $575.00

(A-PA '77)   *Brown Bros. Gallery*
**HEPPLEWHITE MAHOGANY BU-
REAU,** Reeded Stiles, French Bracket Feet
.............................$900.00
DRESSER MIRROR, Two-Tier ..$250.00

(A-OH '77) *Garth's Auctions, Inc.*
PINE DOME TOP DECORATED TRUNK, Cream Ground W/Blue-Green Bands & Swags, Red Border Stripes, "S.R." On Top, Interior W/Newspaper Dated "1819", Springfield, Mass., Minor Wear, 29" W., 14" D., 13" H. $145.00

(A-OH '77) *Garth's Auctions, Inc.*
PINE PENNSYLVANIA BLANKET CHEST, Dovetailed Case & 2 Overlapping Drawers, Iron Strap Hinges, Orig. Paint, Sgn. "Peter Miller 1804"; Some Molding Replacement On Ends, Restored Drawer Front, Replaced Bear Trap Lock, 49½" x 23" x 23½" H. $1800.00

(A-VA '78) *Laws*
PARTNER'S DESK, Mahogany, Green Leather Inset Writing Surface Framed W/Gilt Greek Key Design; One Side Fitted W/9-Drawer Compartments, The Other Having A Cabinet Door & Three Simulated Drawer Fronts Concealing A Cabinet Door, Ca. 1850, 36" W., 54" L., 30" H. . .$1100.00
TIFFANY STUDIOS DESK SET, 10-Pc., Zodiac Pattern, Green Bronze Patina; Triple Tier Paper Or Letter Holder, Memo Pad Holder, Receipt Holder, Pen Tray, Inkwell W/Insert, Calendar Stand, Stamp Box, Thermometer, Desk Pad Ends, Each Signed Tiffany Studios, N.Y. & Numbered . . . .
. . . .$1000.00

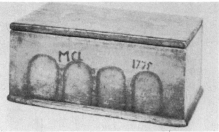

(A-PA '77) *Brown Bros. Gallery*
PENNSYLVANIA DUTCH MINIATURE CHEST, Decor. & Dated 1775, Strap Hinges $600.00

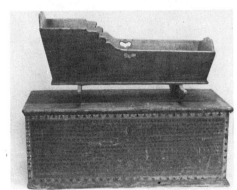

(A OH '77) *Garth's Auctions, Inc.*
PINE BLANKET CHEST, Dovetailed Const., Brown "Vinegar Painting" On Lt. Ground, Border Of Red & Black Diamonds On White Ground, Bear Trap Lock, Strap Hinges, Till Missing, 51½" W., 22½" D., 20" H. $130.00
MAPLE CRADLE, Dovetailed Const., Orig. Worn Brown Finish, Old Repair To Headboard End, 44½" W., 18" D., 21' H.
. . . .$135.00

(A-MA '77) *Richard A. Bourne Co., Inc.*
MAHOGANY TAMBOUR SECRETARY, American, 18th C., Fold Out Lid, Sm. Cupboard Between Tambour Doors, Minor Restorations, 40" W., 19" D., 82½" O.H.
. . . .$1300.00

(A-MA '77) *Richard A. Bourne Co., Inc.*
TIGER MAPLE SLANT-FRONT SECRETARY, American, 19th C., Removable Top, Lid Folds Out W/Working Interior W/4 Pigeonholes and 2 Drawers, Refinished In Natural Wood, Replaced Lid Hinges, 35¾" W., 32" D., 79¾" H. $600.00

(A-VA '77) *Laws Auction & Antiques*
GEORGIAN SECRETARY, Burled Fruitwood, Brass Plates, Bales & Escutcheons, Dropped Writing Surface W/Engraved Gold-Brown Inset Leather Writing Surface, 41½" W., 20¼" D., 88" H. $3750.00

(A-VA '77) *Laws Auction & Antiques*
WALNUT SLANT FRONT DESK, Pennsylvania, Ca. 1770, Blind Dovetailed Top Thumbnail Molded Drop, 39" W., 20" D., 43½" H. $1500.00

(A-PA '77) *Brown Bros. Gallery*
TIGER MAPLE SLANT TOP DESK, Fitted Interior, Replaced Ogee Feet $2700.00

(A-VA '78) *Laws*
WILLIAM AND MARY DESK, 18th C., Massachusetts, Burl Walnut Veneer, 31" W., 18" D., 40" H. $2000.00

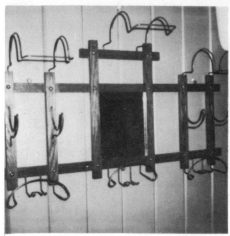

(D-KS '78) *Fisher's Antiques*
COAT, GLOVE & HAT RACK, Oak, 22" x 32" L. $85.00

(A-MA '77) *Richard A. Bourne Co., Inc.*
ADAM-STYLE ARCHITECTURAL LOOKING GLASS, English Or Continental, 19th C., Carved & Gilded, Piece Molding Missing & 1 Rosette, 37¼" H. $50.00

(A-OH '77) *Garth's Auctions, Inc.*
CONVEX MIRROR, Gilded Carved Wood & Gesso Frame, Minor Flaking Of Gilt, 35" W., 60" H. $1450.00

(A-ME '77) *Julia's Auction Service*
FEDERAL CONVEX MIRROR, Phoenix Crest, Regilted, 26" Diam. $425.00

◀ *To the left*

(A-MA '77) *Richard A. Bourne Co., Inc.*
LOUIS XV STYLE LOOKING GLASS, Foliate Scrolled Gilt Frame & Beveled Glass, 50½" H. $175.00
LOUIS XV STYLE MIRROR BRACKET SHELVES, Pr., Rococo Style W/Phoenix Bird Pediments, Gilded $200.00

(A-PA '77) *Brown Bros. Gallery*
SHERATON ARCHITECTURAL MIR-ROR, 29" H. $140.00

(A-VA '78) *Laws*
SHERATON WASHSTAND, Mahogany, Dovetailed Gallery Back, Ca. 1800, 26" W., 18" D., 36" H. $300.00

(A-VA '77) *Laws Auction & Antiques*
FEDERAL BASIN STAND, Mass., Ca. 1800, Mahogany, Dovetailed Scrolled Backsplash, 18" W., 18" D., 38" H. . .$300.00

(A-PA '77) *Brown Bros. Gallery*
SHERATON ARCHITECTURAL MIR-ROR, 21½" H. $90.00

(A-VA '77) *Laws Auction & Antiques*
FEDERAL BASIN STAND, New England, Ca. 1810, Mahogany, 24" W., 16" D., 40" H. $275.00

(A-VA '77) *Laws Auction & Antiques*
SHERATON CANTERBURY, Mahogany, 1 Draw In Base W/Thumbnail Edge & Bear-ins Brass Pulls, Brass Block-Castered Feet, 14" W., 20" L., 20" H. $325.00

◀ *To the left*

(A-PA '77) *Brown Bros. Gallery*
SHERATON ARCHITECTURAL MIR-ROR, Mahogany 25" H. $100.00
SHERATON CHILD'S ROCKER, Rush Seat $100.00

(A-MA '77) *Richard A. Bourne Co., Inc.*
WATER BENCH, Pennsylvania, 19th C., Poplar W/Cherry Finish, 22" W., 13¼" D., 47¼" H. $350.00
HANGING CANDLE BOX, Pine, Red Finish, 10" W., 5½" D., 16½" H. .$50.00
CHOPPING BOWL, Maple, Orig., 20¼" L. $80.00
TAVERN TABLE, American, 18th C., Pine, 23¼" Plank Top, 35¾" L., 23¼" W., 29" H. $325.00

(A-OH '77)   *Garth's Auctions, Inc.*
QUEEN ANNE HIGHBOY, Maple W/
Pine Sides, Dovetailed Drawers, Refinished,
Hardware & Apron Drops Replaced, 34½"
W., 38" W. At Cornice, 18½" D., 70½" H.
..............................$3400.00
WOODEN CARVED BOWL, Weathered
White, 22¾" L., 7¼" H. $70.00

(A-OH '78)   *Garth's Auctions, Inc.*
MAPLE QUEEN ANNE HIGHBOY,
Dovetailed Drawers, Replaced Brasses, Re-
finished, 39½" W., 20" D., 69" H. ......
.............................$6400.00

(A-VA '77)   *Laws Auction & Antiques*
**QUEEN ANNE BONNET TOP HIGH-
BOY,** Boston, Mass., 18th C., Walnut,
Brass Bale Plates & Escutcheons, 37" W.,
20" D., 78" H. $6400.00

(A-VA '77)   *Laws Auction & Antiques*
**PHILADELPHIA QUEEN ANNE HIGH-
BOY,** 18th C., Walnut, Tulip & Poplar ...
.............................$4250.00

(A-OH '77)   *Garth's Auctions, Inc.*
MAPLE QUEEN ANNE HIGHBOY,
Dovetailed Const., Refinished W/Replaced
Brasses, Top Drawer Of Base Signed In
Pencil "Albert Hale Claremont, N.H.", 36"
W., (29¼" W. At Cornice), 19" D., 78½" H.
.............................$3100.00

(A-VA '77)   *Laws Auction & Antiques*
DUNLAP SCHOOL HIGHBOY, New
Hampshire, Ca. 1740, Maple, Drawers W/
Thumbnail Molding & Brass Batwing Pulls,
39" W., 19½" D., 81½" H. $3750.00

(A-OH '77) *Garth Auctions, Inc.*
POPLAR CHIPPENDALE CHEST,
Dovetailed Const., 2 False Drawers, Hinged
Lid, Orig. Red Paint, Brass Bails & Escut-
cheons, 41" W., 19¾" D., 41¾" H. . . . . .
. . . .$1550.00
WOODEN DUCK DECOY, Merganser
W/Orig. Painted Decor., Branded "P",
13" L. $185.00
WOODEN STORAGE BOX, "Finger"
Joints, 13½" L. $175.00
WOODEN STORAGE BOX, Lid W/Glued
Repair, 9¾" L. . . . .
WOODEN DUCK DECOY, Orig. Paint,
Branded "P", 14½" L. $47.50

(A-OH '77) *Garth's Auctions, Inc.*
PINE MULE CHEST, Dovetailed Draw-
ers, Orig. Reddish-Brown Graining Over
Yellow Ground, 43½" W., 18½" D., 42" H.
. . . .$350.00
WOODEN CHURCH BIRD HOUSE,
Grey, White & Red Paint, Metal Roof, Minor
Damage, 25" L., 13" W., 30" H. .$107.50

(A-MA '77) *Richard A. Bourne Co. Inc.*
**HEPPLEWHITE SWELL-FRONT BU-
REAU,** American, 18th C., Mahogany W/
Rosewood Band Inlay, Minor Loss Of Ve-
neer & Inlay, 36" L. $700.00

(A-MA '77) *Richard A. Bourne Co. Inc.*
**GEORGIAN MAHOGANY SWELL-
FRONT BUREAU,** English, Late 18th-
Early 19th C., Orig. Pulls, Length At Waist:
40½" $475.00

(D-MO '78) *Old House Antiques*
QUEEN ANNE HIGHBOY, Walnut Flame
Veneer Drawer Fronts, Ca. 1740, 6'8" H. .
. . . .$16,500.00

(A-OH '77) *Garth's Auctions, Inc.*
CHERRY CHEST OF DRAWERS, Dove-
tailed Cockbeaded Drawers W/Clear
Pressed & Sanded Glass Knobs, Replaced
Feet & Top, 42" W., 22" D., 51" H. . . . . .
. . . .$410.00
BRASS VICTORIAN CANDLESTICKS,
Pr., Push-Ups, 8¾" H. $65.00
WALNUT BOX, Dovetailed W/Herring-
bone & Star Inlay, 5½" x 5¾" x 14" . . . .
. . . .$80.00

(A-VA '77) *Laws Auction & Antiques*
CHIPPENDALE CHEST, Maple, Signed
"Wallace Nutting", Brass Plates & Bales,
Inset Paneled Sides, 36" W., 19" D., 37" H.
. . . .$500.00

(A-VA '78)   *Laws*
CHIPPENDALE CHEST, Figured Mahogany, Line Inlay, Batwing Brasses, 41" W., 20½" D., 37" H. $625.00

(D-VA '78)   *William C. & Hazel G. Adams*
GALLERY TOP CHEST, Mahogany Veneered On White Pine, Orig. Milk Glass Knobs, Chest: 38¾" W., 43" H.; Top: 32" W., 12" O.H. $600.00

(A-VA '77)   *Laws Auction & Antiques*
CHIPPENDALE TALL CHEST, Amer., Ca. 1780-90, Curly Maple, Drawers W/ Thumbnail Molding, Brass Pulls, 39" W., 20" D., 59½" H. $1800.00

(A-PA '77)   *Brown Bros. Gallery*
CHIPPENDALE CHERRY BUREAU $900.00

(A-VA '78)   *Laws Auction & Antiques*
HEPPLEWHITE BOW FRONT BUREAU W/Satinwood Band Inlay, Cockbead Molding On Drawers, Oval Brass Plates W/Lion Head Centers, Ca. 1800, 35" H., 36" W., 20" D. $800.00

(A-VA '78)   *Laws*
GEORGIAN STYLE QUEEN ANNE LOOKING GLASS, Ca. 1850-60, 16" W., 30" H. $425.00
BACHELOR'S CHEST, 18th C., Mahogany W/Ebony & Satinwood Inlay, Engraved Brass Pulls, 31½" W., 18" D., 31" H. . . . .
. . . .$950.00

(A-PA '77)   *Brown Bros. Gallery*
HEPPLEWHITE MAHOGANY BUREAU, Satinwood Line Inlay $500.00

(A-VA '77)   *Laws Auction & Antiques*
HEPPLEWHITE BOWFRONT CHEST, Amer., Top W/Banded Inlay Lip, Drawers W/Cockbeaded Molding, Satinwood Panels W/Brass Pulls, 33¾" W., 20" D., 36" H. $425.00

(A-VA '77) *Laws Auction & Antiques*
HEPPLEWHITE CHEST ON CHEST, English, Ca. 1790-1800, Top Case W/ Molded Crown, Banded Inlay, Lower Case W/Echoing Box & Urn Inlay, 42" W., 21" D., 70" H. $1500.00

(A-VA '78) *Laws*
BONNET TOP CHEST-ON-CHEST, 18th C., Massachusetts, Cherry, Beaded Drawers, Brass Bail Pulls, 41" W., 21" D., 83" H. $4000.00

(D-VA '78) *William C. & Hazel G. Adams*
ARMOIR, Ca. 1830, N.Y., Mahogany W/Poplar & Pine Secondary Woods, 48½" W., 91¾" H. $3900.00

(A-MA '77) *Richard A. Bourne Co., Inc.*
QUEEN ANNE CURLY MAPLE CHEST-ON-FRAME, Southern New Hampshire, 18th C., Replaced Base, Foot Reglued, Refinished In Natural Wood, Replaced Hardware, 36" L. At Waist, 60⅜" H. $2000.00

(A-VA '78) *Laws*
CHIPPENDALE CHEST-ON-CHEST, English, 18th C., Ca. 1780-90, Mahogany, Cockbeaded Molding, Brass Escutcheons & Bail Plates, 45" W., 21" D., 67" H. $1200.00

(A-PA '77) *Brown Bros. Gallery*
QUEEN ANNE CHEST ON FRAME, Tiger Maple, Cabriole Legs W/ Grooved Dutch Feet, Scalloped Skirt $6600.00

(A-VA '77)   *Laws Auction & Antiques*
QUEEN ANNE BONNET TOP HIGH-BOY, Curly Maple & Pine, 18th C., Up-swich, Ma., Ca. 1750, 38" W., 19" D., 82" H. $13,500.00

(D-NH '78)   *Old Town Farm Antiques*
MAPLE QUEEN ANNE CHEST ON CHEST, C. 1780, 18½" D., 39" W., 6'7" H. $6500.00

(A-VA '78)   *Laws*
QUEEN ANNE BONNET TOP HIGH-BOY, 18th C., Connecticut, 37" W., 19" D., 80" H. $8500.00

(A-OH '77)   *Garth's Auctions, Inc.*
WILLIAM & MARY HIGHBOY, Walnut W/Walnut Burl & Herringbone Crossbanded Drawer Fronts, Brass Drop Pulls & Escutch-eons, Refinished, Restoration, 39⅜" W., 22⅛" D., 60⅝" H. $8500.00

(D-NH '78)   *Old Town Farm Antiques*
QUEEN ANNE HIGHBOY, Figured Ma-ple, Ca. 1780, 19" D., 37" W., 6'6" H. $10,500.00

(A-VA '78)   *Laws*
RHODE ISLAND QUEEN ANNE HIGH-BOY, Maple, Lower Case 37½" W., 5'7" H. $2000.00

(A-PA '77)   *Brown Bros. Gallery*
PHILADELPHIA WALNUT HIGHBOY,
Swan Neck Cresting Flame Finials, Shell
Carved Top & bottom Center Drawers,
Fluted Quarter Columns, Shell Carved
Skirt, Leaf Carved Knees, Ball & Claw Feet,
8'1" H., 43" W., 21" D., Ca. 1765-80 . . .
. . . .$15,000.00

(A-VA '78)   *Laws*
KOREAN HIGH CHEST, Elm & Pear
Wood, Brass Fittings, Ca. 1800 . . .$400.00

(D-NH '78)   *Old Town Farm Antiques*
QUEEN ANNE TIGER MAPLE CHEST,
C. 1760, 50" H., 36" W., 17½" D. . . . . . .
. . . .$6600.00

(A-VA '78)   *Laws*
PENNSYLVANIA CHEST ON FRAME,
18th C., Walnut, Thumbnail Molding, Brass
Bail Plates, 40" W., 23" D., 64" H. . . . . .
. . . .$4000.00

(D-OH '78)
SHAKER PINE WARDROBE, 38" W.,
13¼" D., 8' H. $3000.00

(A-PA '77)   *Brown Bros. Gallery*
EMPIRE TIGER MAPLE BUREAU . . . . .
. . . .$325.00

(D-CO '78)
EASTLAKE OAK DRESSER W/Orig.
Pulls $550.00

(D-AZ '78)
WALNUT CHEST, 8 Dovetailed Drawers, 28" W., 32" H. $175.00

(A-VA '77)   *Laws Auction & Antiques*
CHIPPENDALE CHEST, Phila., Ca. 1770, Molded Edge Top, Cockbeaded Drawers, Brass Pulls $2300.00

(D-ME '78)   *Hope Farm Antiques*
CHIPPENDALE BLANKET CHEST, Pine $525.00

(D-VA '78)   *William C. & Hazel G. Adams*
MINIATURE EMPIRE CHEST OF DRAWERS, Amer., Mahogany W/Poplar & Pine Secondary Woods, Ebony Front Columns & Legs, 19" W., 11½" D., 20½" H. $950.00

(A-MA '77)   *Richard A. Bourne Co., Inc.*
MAPLE CHEST OF DRAWERS, American, 18th C., Refinished, Hardware A Modern Replacement, 34" W., 17" D., 41" H. $1400.00

(A-VA '77)   *Laws Auction & Antiques*
BLANKET CHEST, Amer., Ca. 1830, Molded Edge Top Lifts For Storage Over Dovetailed Case W/Cabinet Doors Beneath, 46" W., 23" D., 40" H. $225.00

(A-PA '77)   *Brown Bros. Gallery*
PENNSYLVANIA DUTCH DOWER CHEST, W/Orig. Tulip Decor., Strap Hinges, Bracket Feet $4200.00

(A-MA '77)   *Richard A. Bourne Co., Inc.*
CHIPPENDALE PINE BLANKET CHEST, American, 18th C., Hinged Top, Refinished, 35½" H. $350.00

(A-MA '77)   *Richard A. Bourne Co., Inc.*
CHIPPENDALE CHERRY BUREAU, American, 18th C., Replaced Hardware, Minor Repairs, 39" H. $2200.00

(A-PA '77)   *Pennypacker Auction Centre*
MINIATURE WEBBER BOX, Flower Decor. Top Of Lid, Front Decor. W/1848 & Sarah M. Shaffer, Trees & House, Sides W/ Tulips, 10½" L., 6" D., 6" H. ..$1900.00

(A-MA '77)   *Richard A. Bourne Co. Inc.*
SHERATON SHAVING STAND, American, 19th C., Mahogany W/String Inlay, 19" L., 20" O.H. $150.00
SHERATON SWELL-FRONT BUREAU, American, C. 1800-1810, Cherry, Orig. Drawer Pulls & Escutcheons, 40¼" L. . . . .
. . . .$425.00

(A-OH '77)   *Garth's Auctions, Inc.*
CHEST OF DRAWERS, American Pine Cottage Furniture, Dovetailed Drawers, Grained & Painted W/Brown Lattice Work & Leaves, Mirror Frame Has Repair, 38½" W., 17½" D., 70" O.H. $70.00
CHALK BULLDOG, Repainted Black & White W/Red Mouth & Button Eyes, 16" H.
. . . .$15.00

To the right ▶

(D-MO '78)
PINE CHEST, Dovetailed, Refinished, 18" D., 26" W., 24" H. $190.00

(A-OH '78)   *Garth's Auctions, Inc.*
QUEEN ANNE CURLY MAPLE CHEST, Dovetailed Drawers, Replaced Brasses, Refinished, 36¼" W., 18" D., (19" x 38" at Cornice), 47" H. $4250.00
SHELF CLOCK, Birch W/Bracket Feet, Painted Wooden Dial, Brass Bail Handle, Replaced Works, Hands Original, 18" H. . . .
. . . .$510.00

(A-VA '77)   *Laws Auction & Antiques*
FRENCH MARBLE TOP COMMODE, Inlaid Panel, Ormolu Trim, 42" W., 16" D., 39" H. $950.00
FRENCH ROSEWOOD CHEST, 1 Drawer Over Drop Front Writing Surface W/ Fitted Compartments, Inlaid Floral Panels & Applied Ormolu Trim, 26" W., 13½" D., 48" H. $700.00

(A-MA '77)   *Richard A. Bourne Co. Inc.*
PINE BLANKET CHEST, American, 18th C., Hinged Lid, Natural Finish, 35¾" L., 18" D., 42" O.H. $325.00

(A-OH '77)   *Garth Auctions, Inc.*
GRAINED BLANKET CHEST, Pine, Dovetailed Case, Till & Wrought Iron Strap Hinges, Drk. Reddish Brown Over Lt. Salmon, Orig. Cond., 42" W., 22" D., 28½" H.
. . . .$750.00
CARDBOARD STORAGE BOX, Wallpaper Covered, Yellow & Red Painted Paper, Minor Edge Wear, 11" x 13½" x 12" H. .
. . . .$320.00

(A-MA '77)   *Richard A. Bourne Co. Inc.*
SIX-BOARD BLANKET CHEST, New England, C. 1800, Hinged Top, Signed On Back W/"SP" & Date 1800, Refinished In Natural Wood, 42" L. $275.00

(A-OH '77)   *Garth's Auctions, Inc.*
PINE & POPLAR KAS, Orig. Flame Graining, 2 Int. Dovetailed Drawers, Minor Molding Replacement Under Cornice, 74¼" W. (at cornice), 20¾" D., 83¼" H. ......
................................$625.00

(A-OH '77)   *Garth's Auctions, Inc.*
COUNTRY KAS, Curly Maple Front & Cornice, Poplar Sides, 2 Dovetailed Walnut & Poplar Drawers, 6 Walnut Clothes Hooks, Orig. Hardware, 57½" W. At Cornice, 21" D., 78½" H. $825.00

(A-OH '77)   *Garth's Auctions, Inc.*
ROSE MULLED PINE KAS, Decor. W/ Red, Green, White & Black, On Blue Ground, Dated "1802", Wrought Iron Lock & Hinges, One Interior Shelf, Base Molding & Section Of Cornice Replaced, 42½" W., 17" D., 72½" H. $875.00

(A-OH '77)   *Garth's Auctions, Inc.*
ENGLISH CLOTHES PRESS, Pine, Dovetailed Cockbeaded Drawers, Base Molding Incomplete, Replaced Foot, No Shelves, Orig. Reddish Brown Graining Worn, 47" W., 22" D., 76" H. ...$350.00

 To the left

(A-PA '77)   *Pennypacker Auction Centre*
KAS, Walnut, Lancaster Co., All Orig., Sgn. & Dated 1776, H. 7'7" ..$24,000.00

(A-VA '78)   *Laws*
HEPPLEWHITE LINEN PRESS, 18th C., Massachusetts, Cherry, 44½" W., 19" D., 7' H. $800.00

(A-OH '77)   *Garth's Auctions, Inc.*
WALNUT OHIO KAS, Dovetailed Drawers, 1 Interior Shelf, Refinished, 22½" D., 60" W., (26" x 66½" At Cornice), 85" H.
................................$410.00

(A-PA '77)   *Pennypacker Auction Centre*
DOUGH BOX, Dovetailed Const., Pegged
Lift Top, 29½" W., 43" L. $750.00

(A-VA '77)   *Laws Auction & Antiques*
SAWBUCK TABLE, Amer., Ca. 1760-80,
Orig. Scrub Finish, 45" W., 32" D., 27" H.
.............................$1000.00

(A-MA '77)   *Richard A. Bourne Co., Inc.*
SAWBUCK TABLE, American, 18th C.,
2-Plank Top W/Oak Base, Refinished, 83"
L., 33¼" W., 28" H. $550.00

(A-VA '78)   *Laws Auction & Antiques*
**GEORGE II DOUBLE TOP TEA OR
GAME TABLE,** Mahogany, Felt Covered,
Recessed Pockets For Chips, 30" W., 28½"
H...........................$1650.00

(A-VA '77)   *Laws Auction & Antiques*
DROP LEAF REFRACTORY TABLE,
18th C., Double Swing Sq. Gate Legs, Pinned, Mortise & Tenion Construction, 7'8"
W., 23" (Closed), 61" L. (Open), 28½" H.
.............................$1650.00

(A-VA '77)   *Laws Auctions & Antiques*
CHIPPENDALE DROP LEAF TABLE,
Mass., Ca. 1760-80, Single Board Top,
17¼" L. (Closed), 46" (Open), 52½" W.,
28" H........................$625.00

◀ *To the left*

(D-ME '78)   *Hope Farm Antiques*
DROP LEAF HARVEST TABLE, Ca.
1840, 6' L. $825.00

(A-VA '78)   *Laws Auction & Antiques*
QUEEN ANNE DROP LEAF TABLE,
Ca. 1760, Figured Mahogany, Single Board
Top, Swing Gate Legs, L. 17" (Closed),
58" (Open), 49" W., 27½" H. ..$1000.00

(A-MA '77)   *Richard A. Bourne Co., Inc.*
**WALNUT QUEEN ANNE DROP-LEAF
TABLE,** American, 18th C., Refinished,
44" L., 44" Diam. Open, 26½" H. ......
.............................$1100.00

(A-VA '78)   *Laws Auction & Antiques*
**CHIPPENDALE DOUBLE TOP CARD
TABLE,** Mahogany, Serpentine Shaped
Top Opens To Tray Top Gaming Table,
Fitted Storage Interior, Side Candle Or Chip
Drawer, L: 14" (Closed), 28" (Open), 29½"
W., 29" H. $1500.00

(A-VA '77)   *Laws Auction & Antiques*
QUEEN ANNE DROP LEAF TABLE,
Ca. 1740, Walnut, Gateleg Const., 16" L.
(Closed, 49" L. (Open), 48" W. . .$800.00

(A-VA '77)   *Laws Auction & Antiques*
QUEEN ANNE DROP LEAF TABLE,
Boston, Mass., Ca. 1720, Maple, 37" L.,
12" W. (Closed), 28" H. $1000.00

(A-VA '77)   *Laws Auction & Antiques*
CHERRYWOOD DROP LEAF TABLE,
American, Ca. 1750, Molded Top, Cantered
Drawer, Leaves Supported By Swing Butter-
fly Supports, 15" L., 40" W. (Closed), 40"
(Open), 26" H. $500.00

(A-VA '77)   *Laws Auction & Antiques*
DROP LEAF TABLE, Molded Single
Board Top & Drops, Cabriole Legs Termi-
nate In Hairy Claw & Ball Feet. Attributed
To Workshop Of Benjamin Randolph, Phil-
adelphia, Ca. 1760-80, 29" H., 55" L.
(Open), 46" W. $900.00

(A-OH '77)   *Garth's Auctions, Inc.*
AMERICAN EMPIRE SIDEBOARD, Ma-
hogany and Flame Grained Mahogany Ve-
neer On Pine, Dovetailed Construction,
77" W., 28" D., 53½" H. $125.00
GOUT STOOL, Mahogany, Orig. Worn
Leather, End & Center Adjustable, 24" W.,
12" D., 14" H. $150.00
GIRANDOLES, Set Of 3, Gilt Brass W/
Marble Base & Cut Prisms, Center Piece
Has Minor Breaks In Brass, 14" H. & 18"
H. $50.00

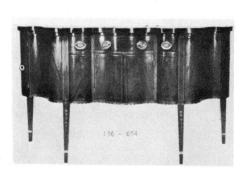

(A-VA '77)   *Laws Auction & Antiques*
**HEPPLEWHITE MAHOGANY SIDE-
BOARD,** Amer., W/Inlay, Ca. 1790-1800
. . . .$1700.00

(A-MA '77)   *Richard A. Bourne Co., Inc.*
FEDERAL MAHOGANY SIDEBOARD,
Mass., 18th C., Minor Scratches, 72" L.,
29" D., 39¾" H. $700.00

(A-VA '77)   *Laws Auction & Antiques*
FEDERAL SIDEBOARD, Amer., Mass.,
1790-1810, Mahogany, Molded Top W/
4 Porringer Cups Over Reeded Balusters,
Compartmented Drawers W/Cockbead
Moldings & Period Brasses, 5'8" W., 20" D.,
40" H. $650.00

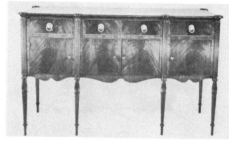

(A-MA '77)   *Richard A. Bourne Co., Inc.*
**SHERATON MAHOGANY SIDE-
BOARD,** American, 19th C., Crotch-Grain
Facings, 64" L., 21½" D., 39¾" H. . . . . . .
. . . .$500.00

(A-VA '77)   *Laws Auction & Antiques*
MAHOGANY BANQUET TABLE, Ca.
1800, 3-Part, Molded Sides & Tilt Top, Brass
Casters, 47½" W., L: 105" To 143" Extended (Two Leaves), 29" H. $1700.00

(A-PA '77)   Pennypacker Auction Centre
CHIPPENDALE TRIPOD DISH TOP TEA TABLE, Mahogany, Crotch & Swirl Grained Wood, 1-Pc., Shell & Acanthus Leaf Carved Legs, Phila., 1760-1780, 34" Diam., 28" H. $6000.00

(A-PA '77)   Pennypacker Auction Centre
WALNUT TEA TABLE, Tilt Top, Snake Feet & Hesitant Shells Carved On Knees $375.00

(A-VA '77)   Laws Auction & Antiques
ELLIPSE TILT-TOP CANDLESTAND, Amer., New England, Ca. 1780-1800, Curly Maple, Top: 25" x 18", 28½" H. .$775.00

(A-MA '77)   Richard A. Bourne Co., Inc.
CHIPPENDALE MAHOGANY PIE-CRUST TABLE, American, 18th C., Minor Restoration $525.00

(A-PA '77)   Pennypacker Auction Centre
MAPLE TILT TOP TABLE $310.00

(A-VA '77)   Laws Auction & Antiques
HEPPLEWHITE TILT-TOP TABLE, Cherry, Ellipse-Shaped Top, Top: 29" x 16¾", 26½" H. $225.00

(A-MA '77)   Richard A. Bourne Co., Inc.
PINE TAVERN TABLE, American, 18th C., Maple Legs, Refinished, 67" L., 37" W., 29¼" H. $300.00

To the right ▶

PINE AND MAPLE STAND, American, 18th C., Natural Finish, Top Has Age Split, 23¾" L., 17½" W., 27" H. $1300.00
JACOBEAN TAVERN TABLE, American or English 17th C., Refinished, 35" L., 22⅝" W., 29" H. $950.00
THUMB-BACK SIDE CHAIR, American, 19th C., Rush Seat, Natural Finish, Traces Red Stain $90.00

(A-MA '77)   Richard A. Bourne Co., Inc.

(A-VA '77)   *Laws Auction & Antiques*
MAHOGANY TEA TABLE, Boston, Mass.,
Ca. 1760-80, Curly Maple Block, 33¾"
Diam., 28" H. $425.00

(A-VA '77)   *Laws Auction & Antiques*
CANDLESTAND, Black W/Gold Decor.,
N.E. Origin, Late 18th or Early 19th Century,
32½" H. $425.00

(A-VA '77)   *Laws Auction & Antiques*
**PENNSYLVANIA   CHERRYWOOD
CHAIR TABLE,** Lift Top Storage Seat,
Ca. 1790-1800, Top: 48" x 32", 30" H.
. . . .$500.00

(A-VA '77)   *Laws Auction & Antiques*
**NEW ENGLAND CHERRYWOOD TA-
BLE,** Tilt-Top, Recessed Rounded Corners
Framed By Light Line Inlay, Top: 30" x
31", 27½" H. $250.00

(A-VA '77)   *Laws Auction & Antiques*
**MAHOGANY DISH TOP CANDLE
STAND** W/Padded Snake Feet, Ca. 1770,
Top 18½" x 19" , 29" H. $800.00

(A-MA '77)   *Richard A. Bourne Co. Inc.*
**QUEEN ANNE DROP-LEAF CHERRY
TABLE,** American, 18th C., Refinished In
Natural Wood, Butterfly Repairs To Age
Split, 38" L., 42" W. (Open), 28" H. . . . .
. . . .$1000.00
**QUEEN ANNE CURLY MAPLE TAV-
ERN TABLE,** American, 18th C., Refin-
ished In Natural Wood, Top Needs Refin-
ishing, 34" L., .24½" W., 26" H. $2750.00

◄ *To the left*

(A-MA '77)   *Richard A. Bourne Co., Inc.*
TAVERN TABLE, American, 18th C.,
Pine & Hardwoods, Natural Finish, 53½"
L., 29¼" D., 26¾" H. $400.00

(D-VA '78)   *William C. & Hazel G. Adams*
EMPIRE TABLE, N.Y. State, Grained
Mahogany W/White Pine & Chestnut Secondary Woods, Orig. Ebony Decor., 40" x
51" Extended; 29¼" H. $750.00

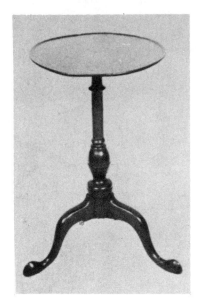

(A-VA '77)   *Laws Auction & Antiques*
HEPPLEWHITE CELLARETTE, Amer., Ca. 1790, Mahogany, Lift Top, Inlay, Sides W/Brass Lifts, 14" W., 14" D., 22½" H. $450.00

(A-PA '77)   *Brown Bros. Gallery*
QUEEN ANNE MAHOGANY DISH TOP TABLE, Top 18½" Diam. . .$725.00

(A-PA '77)   *Brown Bros. Gallery*
SHERATON TIGER MAPLE TILT TOP TABLE, Unique Conch Shell Inlay $1100.00

(A-VA '77)   *Laws Auction & Antiques*
SHERATON PEMBROKE TABLE, Mahogany, 1-Board Top & Ovolu Cornered Drops, Brass Casters, Ca. 1800, 36" W., 21½" L., 29" H. (Closed), 42" (Open) $250.00

(A-PA '77)   *Brown Bros. Gallery*
SHERATON CHERRY TILT TOP STAND, Cut Corner Top $220.00

(A-MA '77)   *Richard A. Bourne Co. Inc.*
CENTENNIAL QUEEN ANNE CANDLE-STAND, Maple $170.00
QUEEN ANNE TAVERN TABLE, Maple, American, 18th C., Refinished, 31¼" L., 23" W., 24½" H. $1800.00
QUEEN ANNE CANDLESTAND, American, 18th C., Hardwood, Minor Repair $850.00

(A-PA '77)   *Brown Bros. Gallery*
QUEEN ANNE MAPLE TEA TABLE $2600.00

(A-VA '78)   *Laws*
CHIPPENDALE PIE CRUST BIRD CAGE TILT TOP TEA TABLE, 18th C., Mahogany, 28" Diam., 27" H. . . .$450.00

(D-VA '78)   *William C. & Hazel G. Adams*
SEWING TABLE, Amer., (Southern), Mahogany W/Poplar & Pine Secondary Wood, 20" W., 19" D., 28¾" H. $350.00

(A-PA '77)   *Brown Bros. Gallery*
EMPIRE WORKTABLE, Tiger Maple . . .
. . . . $375.00

(A-VA '77)   *Laws Auction & Antiques*
SHERATON DROP LEAF WORK TABLE, Phila., Ca. 1800, Mahogany, Orig. Brasses & Finish, Cockbeaded Drawers, 35" W. W/Leaves Extended, 18" W., 28" H. $475.00

(D-VA '78)   *William C. & Hazel G. Adams*
GAMING TABLE, Amer., Mahogany W/Oak & Cherry Secondary Woods, 34¾" W., 16¾" D., 29" H. $4500.00

(A-MA '77)   *Richard A. Bourne Co. Inc.*
FEDERAL FLY-LEAF CARD TABLE, American, 18th C., Mahogany W/Fine String Inlay, Minor Age Split In Top $450.00

(A-VA '77)   *Laws Auction & Antiques*
SHERATON LIFT TOP SEWING TABLE, New York, Ca. 1790, Reeded Lift Top Opens To Well W/2 Compartments, Flame Grained & Tiger Striped Mahogany & Poplar Secondary Woods, All Orig., 24¾" W., 13" D., 28" H. $1400.00

To the right ▶

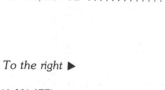

(A-VA '77)   *Laws Auction & Antiques*
SHERATON SEWING TABLE, New England, Ca. 1800-10. Mahogany, Ovolu Corner Top, Banded Inlay, 20" W., 14½" D., 27½" H. $700.00

(A-PA '77)   *Pennypacker Auction Centre*
MAHOGANY CHILD'S DROP LEAF TABLE $55.00

(A-VA '77) *Laws Auction & Antiques*
PENNSYLVANIA QUEEN ANNE LOW-BOY, Walnut & Pine, Ca. 1750 . $3750.00

(A-MA '77) *Richard A. Bourne Co., Inc.*
QUEEN ANNE DRESSING TABLE, English, 18th C., Burled Walnut Facings, Q.A. Style Replacement Hardware, 31¾" L.
.............................$1500.00

(A-VA '78) *Laws Auction & Antiques*
AMERICAN QUEEN ANNE LOWBOY, Walnut, Ca. 1820-30, 29" W., 20" D., 30" H. $650.00
IRON ANDIRONS, Pr., 18th C., Ca. 1760, 14" H. $190.00

(A-VA '78) *Laws Auction & Antiques*
QUEEN ANNE DESK ON FRAME, 18th C., Massachusetts, Maple, Interior W/Pigeon Holes Above Sm. Drawers, 37" W., 40" H.
..............................$1450.00

(A-ME '77) *Julia's Auction Service*
BASKET, Fine Weave, 7" L. $65.00
SHERATON STAND, Hardwood, 1-Drawer, Orig. Red Paint $250.00

(A-VA '78) *Laws Auction & Antiques*
PEMBROKE TABLE, American, Mahogany, Molded Edge Top, Ovolu Drop Leaves, Ca. 1800; L: 37½" (Open), 20" (Closed), 31" W., 28" H. $700.00

(A-VA '78) *Laws Auction & Antiques*
QUEEN ANNE LOWBOY, 18th C., Philadelphia, Walnut, 36" W., 23" D., 29½" H.
..............................$2650.00

(A-VA '78) *Laws Auction & Antiques*
CHIPPENDALE BEDSIDE TABLE, Mahogany, Tray Top, Ca. 1780-90, 24½" W., 20" D., 31" H. $550.00

(A-PA '77) *Brown Bros. Gallery*
WALNUT TABLE, Single Drawer, Turned Legs & Stretcher Base, Dated 1747, Pa. Origin $1000.00

AGATA GLASS was patented by Joseph Locke of the New England Glass Company of Cambridge, Massachusetts in 1877. The application of a metallic stain left a mottled design characteristic of agata, hence the name.

AMBER GLASS is the name of any glassware having a yellowish-brown color. It became popular during the last quarter of the nineteenth century.

AMBERINA GLASS was patented by The New England Glass Company in 1883. It is generally recognized as a clear yellow glass shading to a deep red or fuschia at the top. When the colors are opposite, it is known as reversed amberina. It was machine-pressed into molds, free blown, cut and pattern molded. Almost every glass factory here and in Europe produced this ware, however, few pieces were ever marked.

AMETHYST GLASS - The term identifies any glassware made in the proper dark purple shade. It became popular after the Civil War.

ART GLASS is a general term given to various types of ornamental glass made to be decorative rather than functional. It dates primarily from the late Victorian period to the present day and, during the span of time glassmakers have achieved fantastic effects of shape, color, pattern, texture and decoration.

AVENTURINE GLASS - The Venetians are credited with the discovery of Aventurine during the 1860s. It was produced by various mixes of copper in yellow glass. When the finished pieces were broken, ground or crushed, they were used as a decorative material by glassblowers. Therefore, a piece of Aventurine glass consists of many tiny glittering particles on the body of the object, suggestive of sprinkled gold crumbs or dust. Other colors in Aventurine are known to exist.

BACCARAT GLASS was first made in France in 1765 by La Compagnie des Cristalleries de Baccarat - until the firm went bankrupt. Production began for the second time during the 1820s and the firm is still in operation, producing fine glasswares and paperweights. Baccarat is famous for its earlier paperweights made during the last half of the 19th century.

BOHEMIAN GLASS is named for its country of origin. It is an ornate, overlay, or flashed glassware, popular during the Victorian era.

BRISTOL GLASS is a lightweight opaque glass, oftentimes having a light bluish tint, and decorated with enamels. The ware is a product of Briston, England - a glass center since the 1700s.

BURMESE - Frederick Shirley developed this shaded art glass at the now famous old Mt. Washington Glass Company in New Bedford, Massachusetts, and patented his discovery under the trade name of "Burmese" on December 15, 1885. The ware was also made in England by Thomas Webb & Sons.

Burmese is a hand-blown glass with the exception of a few pieces that were pattern molded. The latter are either ribbed, hobnail or diamond quilted in design. This ware is found in two textures or finishes: the original glazed or shiny finish, and the dull, velvety, satin finish. It is a homogeneous glass (single-layered) that was never lined, cased or plated. Although its color varies slightly, it always shades from a delicate yellow at the base to a lovely salmon-pink at the top. The blending of colors is so gradual that it is difficult to determine where one color ends and the other begins.

CAMBRIDGE glasswares were produced by the Cambridge Glass Company in Ohio from 1901 until the firm closed in 1954.

CAMEO GLASS can be defined as any glass in which the surface has been cut away to leave a design in relief. Cutting is accomplished by the use of hand cutting tools, wheel cutting and hydrofluoric acid. This ware can be clear or colored glass of a single layer, or glass with multiple layers of clear or colored glass.

Although Cameo glass has been produced for centuries, the majority available today dates from the late 1800s. It has been produced in England, France and other parts of Europe, as well as the United States. The most famous of the French masters of Cameo wares was Emile Galle'.

CANDY CONTAINERS were used for holding tiny candy pellets. These were produced in a variety of shapes — locomotives, cars, boats, guns, etc. for children.

CARNIVAL GLASS was an inexpensive, pressed, iridescent glassware made from about 1900 through the 1920s. It was made in quantities by Northwood Glass Company; Fenton Art Glass Company and others, to compete with the expensive art glass of the period. Originally called "Taffeta" glass, the ware became known as "Carnival" glass during the 1920s when carnivals gave examples as premiums or prizes.

CORALENE - The term Coralene denotes a type of decoration rather than a kind of glass - consisting of many tiny beads, either of colored or transparent glass - decorating the surface. The most popular design used resembled coral or seaweed - hence the name.

CRACKLE GLASS - This type of art glass was an invention of the Venetians that spread rapidly to other countries. It is made by plunging red-hot glass into cold water, then reheating and reblowing it, thus producing an unusual outer surface which appears to be covered with a multitude of tiny fractures, but is perfectly smooth to the touch.

CRANBERRY GLASS - The term "Cranberry Glass" refers to color only, not to a particular type of glass. It is undoubtedly the most familiar colored glass known to collectors. This ware was blown or molded, and oftentimes decorated with enamels.

CROWN MILANO glass was made by Frederick Shirley at the Mt. Washington Glass Company, New Bedford, MA., from 1886-1888. It is ivory in color with satin finish, and was embellished with floral sprays, scrolls and gold enamel.

CROWN TUSCAN glass has a pink-opaque body. It was originally produced in 1936 by A. J. Bennett, President of the Cambridge Glass Company of Cambridge, Ohio. The line was discontinued in 1954. Occasionally referred to as Royal Crown Tuscan, this ware was named for a scenic area in Italy, and it has been said that its color was taken from the flesh-colored sky at sunrise. When trans-illuminated, examples do have all of the blaze of a sunrise — a characteristic that is even applied to new examples of the ware reproduced by Mrs. Elizabeth Degenhart of Crystal Art Glass, and Harold D. Bennett, Guernsey Glass Company of Carbridge, Ohio.

CUSTARD GLASS was manufactured in the United States for a period of about thirty years (1885-1915). Although Harry Northwood was the first and largest manufacturer of custard glass, it was also produced by the Heisey Glass Company, Diamond Glass Company, Fenton Art Glass Company and a number of others.

The name Custard Glass is derived from its "custard yellow" color which may shade light yellow to ivory to light green glass that is opaque to opalescent. Most pieces have a fiery opalescence when held to light. Both the color and glow of this ware comes from the use of uranium salts in the glass. It is generally a heavy type pressed glass made in a variety of different patterns.

CUT OVERLAY - The term identifies pieces of glassware usually having a milk-white exterior that has been cased with cranberry, blue or amber glass. Other type examples are deep blue, amber or cranberry on crystal glass, and the majority of pieces have been decorated with dainty flowers. Although Bohemian glass manufacturers produced some very choice pieces during the nineteenth century, fine examples were also made in America, as well as in France and England.

DAUM NANCY is the mark found on pieces of French cameo glass made by Arguste & Antonin Daum, after 1875.

DURAND ART GLASS was made by Victor Durand from 1879 to 1935 at the Durand Art Glass Works in Vineland, New Jersey. The glass resembles Tiffany in quality. Drawn white feather designs and thinly drawn glass threading (quite brittle) applied around the main body of the ware, are striking examples of Durand creations on an iridescent surface.

FLASHED WARES were popular during the late 19th century. They were made by partially coating the inner surface of an object with a thin plating of glass or another, more dominant color - usually red. These pieces can readily be identified by holding the object to the light and examining the rim, as it will show more than one layer of glass. Many pieces of "Rubina Crystal" (cranberry to clear), "Blue Amberina" (blue to amber), and "Rubina Verde" (cranberry to green), were manufactured in this way.

FINDLAY or ONYX art glass was manufactured about 1890 for only a short time by the

Dalzell Gilmore Leighton Company of Findlay, Ohio.

FRANCISWARE is a hobnail glassware with frosted or clear glass hobs and stained amber rims and tops. It was produced during the late 1880s by Hobbs, Brockunier & Company.

FRY GLASS was made by the H.C. Fry Company, Rochester, PA from 1901, when the firm was organized, until 1934 when operations ceased. The firm specialized in the manufacture of cut glassware. The production of their famous "Foval" glass did not begin until the 1920s. The firm also produced a variety of glass specialties, oven wares and etched glass.

GALLE' glass was made in Nancy, France by Emile Galle' at the Galle Factory founded in 1874. The firm produced both enameled and cameo glass, pottery, furniture and other Art Nouveau items. After Galle's death in 1904, the factory continued operating until 1935.

GREENTOWN glass was made in Greentown, IN by the Indiana Tumbler & Goblet Company from 1894 until 1903. The firm produced a variety of pressed glass wares in addition to milk and chocolate glass.

GUNDERSEN peachblow is a more recent type art glass produced in 1952 by the Gundersen-Pairpoint Glass Works of New Bedford, MA, successors to the Mt. Washington Glass Co. Gundersen pieces have a soft satin finish shading from white at the base to a deep rose at the top.

HOBNAIL - The term hobnail identifies any glassware having "bumps" - flattened, rounded or pointed - over the outer surface of the glass. A variety of patterns exists. Many of the fine early examples were produced by Hobbs, Brockunier & Co., Wheeling, W.Va., and The New England Glass Company.

HOLLY AMBER, originally known as "Golden Agate," is a pressed glass pattern which features holly berries and leaves over its glossy surface. Its color shades from golden brown tones to opalescent streaks. This ware was produced by the Indiana Tumbler and Goblet Company for only six months, from January 1, to June 13, 1903. Examples are rare and expensive.

IMPERIAL GLASS - The Imperial Glass Company of Bellaire, Ohio, was organized in 1901 by a group of prominent citizens of Wheeling, West Virginia. A variety of fine art glass, in addition to Carnival glass, was produced by the firm. The two trademarks which identified the ware were issued in June, 1914. One consisted of the firm's name, "Imperial," and the other included a cross formed by double-pointed arrows. The latter trademark was changed in September of the same year from the arrow cross to what was known as a "German" cross. The overlapping "IG" cipher was adopted by Imperial in 1949, and appears on practically all of their present production - including reproduced Carnival glass.

LATTICINO is the name given to articles of glass in which a network of tiny milk-white lines appear, crisscrossing between two walls of glass. It is a type of Filigree glassware developed during the 16th century by the Venetians.

LEGRAS GLASS - cameo, acid cut and enameled glass wares - were made by August J.F. Legras at Saint-Denis, France from 1864-1914.

LOETZ GLASS was made in Austria just before the turn of the century. As Loetz worked in the Tiffany factory before returning to Austria, much of his glass is similar in appearance to Tiffany wares. Loetz glass is oftentimes marked "Loetz" or "Loetz-Austria."

LUTZ GLASS was made by Nicholas Lutz, a Frenchman, who worked at the Boston and Sandwich Glass Company from 1870 to 1888 when it closed. He also produced fine glass at the Mt. Washington Glass Company and later at the Union Glass Company. Lutz is noted for two different types of glass - striped and threaded wares. Other glass houses also produced similar glass and these wares were known as Lutz-type.

MARY GREGORY was an artist for the Boston & Sandwich Glass Company during the last quarter of the 19th century. She decorated glass ware with white enamel figures of young children engaged in playing, collecting butterflies, etc. in white on transparent glass, both clear and colored. Today, the term "Mary Gregory" glass applies to any glassware that remotely resembles her work.

MERCURY GLASS is a double-walled glass that dates from the 1850s to about 1910. It was made in England as well as the United States during this period. Its interior, usually in the form of vases, is lined with flashing mercury, giving the items an allover silvery appearance. The entrance hole in the base of each piece was sealed over. Many pieces were decorated.

MILK GLASS is an opaque pressed glassware, usually of milk-white color, although green, amethyst, black, and shades of blue were made. Milk glass was produced in quantity in the United States during the 1880s, in a variety of patterns.

MILLEFIORI - This decorative glassware is considered to be a special of the Venetians. It is sometimes called "glass of a thousand flowers," and has been made for centuries. Very thin colored glass rods are arranged in bundles, then fused together with heat. When the piece of glass is sliced across, it has a design like that of many small flowers. These tiny wafer thin slices are then embedded in larger masses of glass, enlarged and shaped.

MOSER GLASS was made by Kolomon Moser at Carlsbad. The ware is considered to be another type of Art Nouveau glass as it was produced during its heyday - during the early 1900s. Principal colors included amethyst, cranberry, green and blue, with fancy enameled decoration.

MOTHER-OF-PEARL, often abbreviated in descriptions as M.O.P., is glass composed of two or more layers, with a pattern showing through to the outer surface. The pattern, caused by internal air traps, is created by expanding the inside layer of molten glass into molds with varying designs. And when another layer of glass is applied, this brings out the design. Then the final layer of glass is then acid dipped, and the result is Mother of Pearl Satin Ware. Patterns are numerous. The most frequently found are the Diamond Quilted, Raindrop and Herringbone. This ware can be one solid color, a single color shading light to dark, two colors blended or a variety of colors which includes the rainbow effect. In addition, many pieces are decorated with colorful enamels, coralene beading, and other applied glass decorations.

NAILSEA glass was first produced in England from 1788 to 1873. The characteristics that identify this ware are the "pulled" loopings and swirls of colored glass over the body of the object.

NEW ENGLAND PEACHBLOW - Patented in 1886 by the New England Glass Company. It is a single-layered glass shading single-layered glass shading from opaque white at the base to deep rose-red or from opaque white at the base to deep rose-red or raspberry at the top. Some pieces have a glossy surface, but most were given an acid bath to produce a soft, matte finish.

NEW MARTINSVILLE PEACHBLOW GLASS was produced from 1901-1907 at New Martinsville, PA.

OPALESCENT GLASS - The term refers to glasswares which have a milky white effect in the glass, usually on a colored ground. There are three basic types of this ware. Presently, the most popular includes pressed glass patterns found in table settings. Here, the opalescence appears at the top rim, the base, or a combination of both. On blown or mold-blown glass, the pattern itself consists of this milky effect — such as Spanish Lace. Another example is the opalescent points on some pieces of hobnail glass. These wares are lighter weight. And the third group includes opalescent novelties, primarily of the pressed variety.

PAMONA glass was invented in 1884 by Joseph Locke at the New England Glass Company.

PEKING GLASS is a type of Chinese cameo glass produced from the 1700s, well into the nineteenth century.

PHOENIX GLASS - The firm was established in Beaver County, Pennsylvania during the late 1800s, and produced a variety of commercial glasswares. During the 1930s the factory made a desirable sculptured gift-type glassware which has become very collectible in recent years. Vases, lamps, bowls, ginger jars, candlesticks, etc. were made until the 1950s in various colors with a satin finish.

PIGEON BLOOD is a bright reddish-orange glass ware dating from the early 1900s.

PRESSED GLASS was the inexpensive glassware produced in quantity to fill the increasing demand for tablewares when Americans moved away from the simple table utensils of pioneer times. During the 1820s, ingenious Yankees invented and perfected machinery for successfully pressing glass. And about 1865, manufacturers began to color their products. Literally hundreds of different patterns were produced.

ROSALINE GLASS is a product of the Steuben Glass Works of Corning, NY. The firm was founded by Frederick Carter & T.C. Hawkes, Sr. Rosaline is a rose-colored jade glass or colored alabaster. The firm is now owned by the Corning Glass Company, which is presently producing fine glass of exceptional quality.

ROYAL FLEMISH ART GLASS was made by the Mt. Washington Glass Works during the 1880s. It has an acid finish which may consist of one or more colors, decorated with raised gold enameled lines separating into sections. Fanciful painted enamel designs also decorate this ware. Royal Flemish glass is marked "RF," with the letter "R" reversed and backed to the letter "F", within a four-sided orange-red diamond mark.

SANDWICH GLASS - One of the most interesting and enduring pages from America's past is Sandwich Glass produced by the famous Boston and Sandwich Glass Company at Sandwich, Massachusetts. The firm began operations in 1825, and the glass flourished until 1888 when the factory closed. Despite the popularity of Sandwich Glass, little is known about its founder, Deming Jarvis.

The Sandwich Glass house turned out hundreds of designs in both plain and figured patterns, in colors and crystal, so that no one type could be considered entirely typical - but the best known is the "lacy" glass produced here. The variety and multitude of designs and patterns produced by the company over the years is a tribute to its greatness.

SILVER DEPOSIT GLASS was made during the late 19th and early 20th centuries. Silver was deposited on the glass surface by a chemical process so that a pattern appeared against a clear or colored ground. This ware is sometimes referred to as "silver overlay."

SLAG GLASS was originally known as "Mosaic" and "Marble Glass" because of its streaked appearance. Production in the United States began about 1880. The largest producer of this ware was Challinor, Taylor & Company. The various slag mixtures are: purple, butterscotch, blue, orange, green and chocolate. A small quantity of Pink Slag was also produced in the Inverted Fan & Feather pattern. Examples are rare and expensive.

SPANISH LACE is a Victorian glass pattern that is easily identified by its distinct opalescent flower and leaf pattern. It belongs to the shaded opalescent glass family.

STEUBEN - The Steuben Glass Works was founded in 1904 by Frederick Carter, an Englishman, and T.G. Hawkes, Sr., at Corning,

New York. In 1918, the firm was purchased by the Corning Glass Company. However, Steuben remained with the firm, designing a bounty of fine art glass of exceptional quality.

STIEGEL-TYPE GLASS - Henry William Stiegel founded America's first flint glass factory during the 1760s at Manheim, PA. Stiegel glass is flint or crystal glass, it is thin and clear, and has a bell-like ring when tapped. The ware is quite brittle and fragile. Designs were painted free-hand on the glass - birds, animals and architectural motifs, surrounded by leaves and flowers. The engraved glass resulted from craftsmen etching the glass surface with a copper wheel, then cutting the desired patterns.

It is extremely difficult to identify with certainty, a piece of original Stiegel glass. Part of the problem resulted from the lack of an identifying mark on the products. Additionally, many of the craftsmen moved to other areas after the Stiegel plant closed - producing a similar glass product. Therefore, when one is uncertain about the origin of this type ware, it is referred to as "Stiegel-type" glass.

TIFFANY GLASS was made by Louis Comfort Tiffany, one of America's outstanding glass designers of the Art Nouveau period, from about 1870 to the 1930s. Tiffany's designs included a variety of lamps, bronze work, silver, pottery and stained glass windows. Practically all items made were marked "L.C. Tiffany" or "L.C.T." in addition to the word "Favrille" - the French word for color.

TORTOISE SHELL GLASS - As the name indicates, this type glassware resembles the color of tortoise shell and has deep rich brown tones combined with amber and cream-colored shades. Tortoise Shell Glass was originally produced in 1880 by Francis Pohl, a German chemist. It was also made in the United States by the Sandwich Glass Works and other glass houses during the late 1800s.

VAL ST. LAMBERT Cristalleries, located in Belgium, was founded in 1825 and the firm is still in operation.

VASA MURRHINA glassware was produced in quantity at the Vasa Murrhina Art Glass Company of Sandwich, MA during the late 1900s. John C. DeVoy, Assignor to the firm, registered a patent on July 1, 1884, for the process of decorating glassware with particles of mica flakes (coated with copper, gold, nickel or silver) sandwiched between an inner layer of glass which is opaque, and an outer layer of clear or transparent colored glass. The ware was also produced by other American glass firms and in England.

VASELINE GLASS - The term "Vaseline" refers to color only, as it resembles the greenish-yellow color typical of the oily petroleum jelly known as Vaseline. This ware has been produced in a variety of patterns both here and in Europe — from the late 1800s. It has been made in both clear and opaque yellow, Vaseline combined with clear glass, and occasionally the two colors are combined in one piece.

WAVECREST GLASS is an opaque white glassware made from the late 1890s by French factories and the Pairpoint Manufacturing Company at New Bedford, Mass. Items were decorated by the C.F. Monroe Company of Meriden, Ct., with painted pastel enamels. The name Wavecrest was used after 1898 with the initials of the Company "C.F.M. Co." Operations ceased during World War I.

WEBB GLASS was made by Thomas Webb & Sons of Stourbridge, England during the late Victorian period. The firm produced a variety of different types of art and cameo glass.

WHEELING PEACHBLOW - With its simple lines and delicate shadings, Wheeling Peachblow was produced soon after 1883 by J.H. Hobbs, Brockunier & Company at Wheeling, West Virginia. It is a two-layered glass lined or cased inside with an opaque, milk-white type of plated glassware. The outer layer shades from a bright yellow at the base to a mahogany red at the top. The majority of pieces produced are in the glossy finish.

(A-MA '78)   Richard A. Bourne Co., Inc.

◄ *To the left*

(ROW I)
SET OF THREE AMBERINA CANDLE ORNAMENTS, (1 Illus.), "Diamond Quilted" Pattern With Threading, Each With Opalescent Glass "Jewel" In Center And Holder To Slide Over The Candle, One Has Minute Damage To Threading $375.00
SET OF FOUR AMBERINA SQUARE ICE CREAM DISHES, (1 Illus.), "Daisy And Button" Pattern, Deep Color, One W/ Minute Rim Nick $225.00
PLATED SILVER FIGURAL MATCH HOLDER By James W. Tufts, Boston, In The Form Of A Flemish Boy Holding A Paneled Amberina Lily Vase $400.00
(ROW II)
WHEELING PEACHBLOW STICK VASE, With Deep Amber Rigaree Around Base Of Neck, Deepest Possible Color, 8" H. $725.00
OUTSTANDING AMBERINA BERRY BOWL, Boat-Shaped, "Daisy And Button" Pattern, 10¼" L. $300.00
BARBER'S BOTTLE, Opalescent Cranberry Glass With Opalescent Stars And Stripes $100.00
(ROW III)
CRUET, Mottled Coloring Of Brown, Cranberry Over Pale Yellow With Clear Faintly-Reeded Applied Handle $70.00
APRICOT-COLORED AVENTURINE PITCHER, Squared Top, Clear Amber Reeded Applied Handle, Gold-Colored Flecks, Diamond Quilted Pattern, 5¼" H. $225.00
BLUE-COLORED AVENTURINE PITCHER, Squared Top, Clear Reeded Applied Handle, With Silver Flecking, Diamond Quilted Pattern, 5¼" H. . . .$200.00

(A-MA '78)   Richard A. Bourne Co., Inc.
ENGLISH PAPERWEIGHT, By Whitefriars, Concentric Rings Of Pink, White, Blue, Green, and Other Colors, 2⅝" Diam. $150.00
LARGE POINSETTIA PAPERWEIGHT, The Clear Glass Has A Bluish Tint. Center Is A Large And Very Well Set Red Poinsettia W/White And Red Single Cane In Center, W/Six Green Leaves, 2¾" Diam. $325.00
RECTANGULAR PAPERWEIGHT, By The Gayner Glass Works, Salem, New Jersey, Aqua-Colored And Shows A Bottle With The Name Of The Works On It, 4¼" L., 2⅝" W., 1¼" H. $90.00
OLD CHINESE PAPERWEIGHT, Containing A Well-Set Vivid Red Poinsettia W/ Yellow Cane In Center, Green Stem W/ Two Leaves, Leaf On Left Side Is Imperfectly Formed, 3" Diam. $30.00

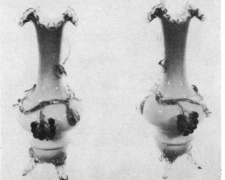

(A-MA '78)   Richard A. Bourne Co., Inc.

◄ *To the left*

(ROW I)
CASED VICTORIAN ART GLASS VASES With Elaborate Applied Art Work, Each With A Cherry Bough Of Amber Branches And Leaves, Two Ripe Red Cherries And A Single Blossom. The Shaped And Ruffled Top Is Clear Amber Glass. The Body Color Is White At Bottom Shading To A Soft Blue At Top, Annealing Marks Around Base Of Neck Of One, 8¾" H. $700.00

(ROW II)
CASED PEACHBLOW-COLORED ART GLASS VASES, Shade From Pale Pink To Deepest Pink At The Top, The Ruffled Rims Are Clear Amber, And Each Vase Is Supported By Three Clear Amber Feet, Minor Damage To Vines & One W/2 Chipped Feet $350.00

(A-MA '77)

Richard A. Bourne Co., Inc.

MISCELLANEOUS COLORED GLASS
(ROW I, L to R)
BOTTLE, Powder Horn Shape, Drk. Olive-Amber W/Opaque Pale Blue Loopings, 14" L. $325.00
TUMBLER, Beaker Form, Amethyst, Flaring Rim, 2⅞" Diam., 3¼" H. $10.00
TUMBLER, Barrel Shape, Amethyst, 1¼" Diam., 3½" H. $25.00
(ROW II, L to R)
VINEGAR BOTTLE, Amethyst, Midwestern, 16-Rib Pattern, Swirled, Minus Stopper, 5⅝" H. $140.00
VINEGAR BOTTLE, Cobalt Blue, 20-Rib Pattern, Swirled, Tooled Pouring Lip, Minus Stopper, 6" H. $50.00
VINEGAR BOTTLE, Cobalt Blue, 18-Rib Pattern, Swirled, Period Stopper, 7" O.H. $40.00
STIEGEL-TYPE BOWLS, Amethyst, Expanded Diamond Pattern, 23-Diamond Mold, Pair, 4½" Diam., 3⅝" H. ..$225.00

(A-MA '78)   *Richard A. Bourne Co., Inc.*

LUTZ-TYPE THREADED GLASS MINIATURE FINGER BOWL & UNDERTRAY, Pale Blue W/Bright Green Threading $50.00
LUTZ-TYPE THREADED FINGER BOWL, Amberina Threading Over Cran-Cranberry W/Amber Applied Threading, Finger Bowl Has Opalescent Bottom, Minute Nicks In Threading Only $25.00
LUTZ-TYPE THREADED FINGER BOWL, Amberina Threading Over Cranberry "Diamond Quilted" Patt., Minor Damage To Threading................$70.00

(A-MA '78)   *Richard A. Bourne Co., Inc.*

ETCHED & CUT GLASS
(ROW I, L to R)
CANDY DISH W/Applied Handle, Minimal Roughage, 5" Diam.........$25.00
CANDY DISH W/Applied Handle, Slight Rim Roughage Only, 6" Diam. $25.00
OBLONG RELISH DISH, Minimal Roughage, 11¾" L. $40.00
(ROW II, L to R)
LAMP GLOBES, Pr., Maximum Diam. Of Opening 2¾"; Diameter Of Globes Approx. 6" $75.00
BOWL, "Strawberry Diamond" Patt., 8" Diam........................$110.00
SALAD DRESSING MIX BOTTLE By Hawkes, Signed, Etched W/Decorative Flowers, Direction Lines For "Oil" & "Vinegar". Stopper Is Silver W/Blue Enamel Top $55.00

(ROW III, L to R)
DECANTER W/Exceptional Engraved Scene Of Fox Who Has Just Missed Catching A Duck Seen In Flight To His Left. Orig. Stopper Engraved To Match, 10⅝" H. ...
..................................$130.00
COMPOTE On High Standard, 8½" H. ...
..................................$50.00
TRUMPET VASE, 11¾" H. $40.00
COMPOTE On High Standard, Thumbprint-Cut Stem, 8½" H. $55.00

◄ *To the left*

BULBOUS PITCHER By Pairpoint, Black Applied Handle, 5¼" H. $140.00
COCKTAIL GLASSES (1 of Pr.) By Pairpoint $225.00
AVENTURINE VASE, Pigeon-Blood Red W/Gold Particles, 9¼" H. $90.00
FRENCH CAMEO GLASS VASE Sgn. "Daum Nancy France." Black Foot W/Mottled Pink, Red, Amber & White Body; Cameo Cutting Of Flowers Silhouetted Against Red-Orange Ground, 10" H. .....
..................................$425.00

(A-MA '78)   *Richard A. Bourne Co., Inc.*

(A-MA '78)   *Richard A. Bourne Co., Inc.*

◀ *To the left*

(ROW I)
PINK AND WHITE SWIRLED SATIN GLASS VASE, Squarish Shape W/Square, Slightly-Flaring Top, Five Frosted Colorless Applied Feet, Slight Roughage To One Foot, 4½" H. $70.00
THREE MATCHING PIECES OF SATIN GLASS, Low Bowl W/Ruffled And Scalloped Rim, Small Vase W/Ruffled Top, And Small Tumbler Or Jar, Unusual Satin-Glass-Like Herringbone Patt., No Opaque Liner, Glass Is Translucent Frosty Cranberry Color W/Delicate Black And Gold Decor. Of Cat-O-Nine-Tails And Other Rushes, Bowl, 5½" Diam., Vase, 5½" H., Tumbler, 3¼" H. $225.00

(ROW II)
CASED PEACHBLOW WEBB-TYPE VASE, W/Black And Gold Decor. Of Insects And Flowers, Rich Full Color, 5¼" H. $100.00
WEBB DECORATED CASED PEACHBLOW VASE, W/Clear Amber Applied Handles And Enamel Decor. Of Colorful Flowers On Both Sides Done In Fine Detail $200.00
CASED ART WORK PEACHBLOW VASE, Peachblow Coloring W/Clear Amber Ruffled Lip and Applied Art Work Flower W/Two Leaves & Vine Form Handle, One Leaf Chipped, 5¾" H. $85.00
PEACHBLOW SATIN FINISH VASE, Signed "Rococo" Art Glass, Decorated W/Bird & Flower, 7" H. $125.00

(ROW III)
FINE LARGE SATIN FINISH VASE, Peachblow Color, Decor. W/Fruit & Flowers, Rich Coloring, 9¼" H. $175.00
WEBB CASED PEACHBLOW VASE, W/Clear Applied Handles And Overall Decor. Of Blue And White Flowers With Gold Stems And Berries, Slight Roughage To Art Work In One Area Of Handle, 6¾" H. . .$275.00
CASED WEBB PEACHBLOW VASE, W/Gold Decor. Of Flowers And Branches, 7½" H. $250.00

(ROW IV)
OUTSTANDING SATIN GLASS EWER, W/Plated Silver Mountings And Lid, Globular Pinched Body W/Overall Gold Leaf And Flower Decoration W/Tied Cord Around Neck, 8" H. $400.00
SATIN GLASS BOWL, White Shading To Blue Exterior W/Soft Rich Pink Interior Shading To Blue At Edges, Bowl Is Melon Ribbed And Has Ribbon Candy Ruffled And Scalloped Edge. 10" Sq., 4¾" H. $750.00

To the right ▶

(ROW I, L. to R)
GUNDERSON GLASS PEACHBLOW VASE, Small W/Pouring Lip, Light Color, Satin Finish, 4" H. $40.00
BURMESE MUSTARD POT, W/Plated Silver Cover $70.00
PEACHBLOW FOOTED CREAMER, Satin Finish, Deep Color, White Reeded Applied Handle $85.00
PEACHBLOW CUPS & SAUCERS, Pr., Deep Color, White Reeded Applied Handles $175.00

(ROW II, L to R)
EARLY PEACHBLOW VASE, Similar In Coloring To Mt. Washington Peachblow, W/Turned-Down Three-Scallop Rim, 5" H. $55.00
PEACHBLOW SATIN-FINISH TALL STEMMED SHERBETS, Pr. $160.00
HEAVY PEACHBLOW SATIN-FINISH TUMBLER $60.00
PEACHBLOW SATIN-FINISH SUGAR, ...$80.00

(ROW III, L to R)
PEACHBLOW COMPOTE, W/Deeply Scalloped Rim, Dull Finish, 6¾" Diam., 5" H. $120.00
PEACHBLOW TRUMPET VASES, Pr., Delicate Color, Well Formed, 9¼" H. $90.00
PEACHBLOW CRUET, Excellent Deep Color, White Reeded Applied Handle, Original Peachblow Stopper $160.00

(A-MA '78)   *Richard A. Bourne Co., Inc.*

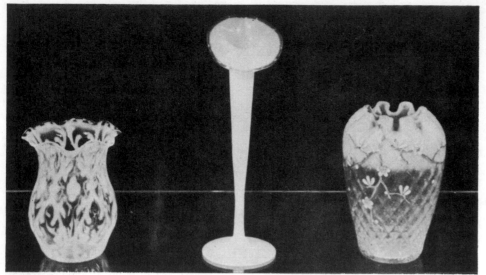

(A-MA '78)   Richard A. Bourne Co., Inc.

To the left ◄

SPANISH LACE VASE, Pale Yellow W/
Opalescent Pattern, 5½" H. $55.00
**FRY FOVAL GLASS TRUMPET-FORM
BUD VASE,** Ruffled Top Has Faint Green
Edge, 10¼" H. $100.00
DIAMOND QUILTED GLASS VASE,
Clear To Pale Pink Opalescence At Top,
Enamel Floral Decoration, 6½" H. .$60.00

(A-MA '78)   Richard A. Bourne Co., Inc.

(ROW I, L to R)
**LUSTRE GLASS FINGER BOWL &
UNDERTRAY** W/Green Rim. Made By
Emil J. Larson While Working For Durand,
Vineland, NJ, 1925-1932, Accompanied By
Certificate Sgn. By Larson $125.00
**STEUBEN GOLD AURENE UNDER-
TRAY** For Sherbet, 5" Diam. $50.00
**STEUBEN YELLOW JADE CUP &
SAUCER** W/White Alabaster Applied Han-
dle, Unsigned $40.00
(ROW II, L to R)
**TEN-PANELED GOLD RUBY GLASS
PLATE** By Carder While Working For
Durand, 1925-32, Accompanied By Certi-
ficate Of Authentication $70.00
TEN-PANELED GREEN GLASS PLATE
By Carder, While Working For Durand,
Accompanied By Certificate, 8¾" Diam. . .
. . . .$60.00
TEN-PANELED LUSTRE GLASS PLATE
W/Gold Ruby Rim & Opalescence In Body.
Made By Carder At Vineland, Certificate
Of Authentication, 8¼" Diam. $75.00
(ROW III, L to R)
TEN-PANELED LUSTRE GLASS VASE
W/Regular Air Traps, Made By Carder While
At Vineland, Certificate Of Authentication,
6¾" H. $200.00
LUSTRE GLASS VASE, Circular Foot,
Trumpet Shape W/Cut & Etched Design,
Made By Carder At Vineland, 10" H. . . . . .
. . . .$125.00
**STEUBEN VERRE DE SOIE ETCHED
GLASS VASE** W/Fleur-de-lis, Swag &
Wreath Etching, Unsigned, 6" H. .$120.00
PALE AMBER TAZZA By Carder, While
Working At Sinclaire, Bath, NY, Ca. 1922,
Certificate Of Authentication By Mr. Carder,
7-3/16" H. $80.00

To the right ▶

(ROW I, L to R)
NINE-PC. Decor. Amberina Beverage Set
W/Handled Mugs, Each Piece W/Overall
Decor. In Heavy Enamel Of Colorful Flow-
ers & Matching Applied Amber Handle . . .
. . . .$900.00

(ROW II, L to R)
AMBERINA SUGAR SHAKER W/Pew-
ter Top, Patt. Of Two Vertical Panels Of
Diamond Quilting Separated By Vertical
Ribbed Panels $190.00
AMBERINA DECANTER OR CARAFE,
"Inverted Thumbprint" Patt., 1 Qt. Capa-
city $95.00
AMBERINA VASE, Elongated "Inverted
Thumbprint" Patt., 6¼" H. $120.00
AMBERINA PICKLE JAR, "Hobnail"
Patt., Made To Be Used In Holder $120.00
AMBERIAN PICKLE JAR, "Daisy & But-
ton" Patt., Deep Fuchsia Color At Top. . . .
. . . .$90.00
AMBERINA CREAMER, "Inverted
Thumbprint" Patt., Ruffled Top & Clear
Amber Applied Handle, 5½" H. . .$130.00

(ROW III, L to R)
AMBERINA BULBOUS PITCHER, "In-
verted Thumbprint" Patt. W/Enamel Decor.
Of Fruit Blossoms, Clear Applied Amber
Handle. $210.00
AMBERINA WATER PITCHER W/Square
Top, "Hobnail" Patt., Clear Amber Applied
Handle, Deep Mt. Washington Type Color.
. . . .$275.00
AMBERINA QT. DECANTER, Reverse
Coloring, "Inverted Thumbprint" Patt.,
Amberina Stopper Not Orig., Minute Spots
Of Sickness In Decanter $125.00
AMBERINA PICKLE CASTOR, Melon-
ribbed Shape, "Inverted Thumbprint" Patt.,
W/Plated Silver Holder & Lid (Replacement)
. . . .$275.00

(A-MA '78)   Richard A. Bourne Co., Inc.

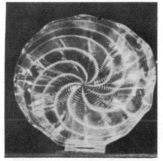

(A-MA '78)   Richard A. Bourne Co., Inc.

**LUTZ-TYPE THREADED GLASS UN-
DERTRAY,** Amber Base Color W/Blue &
Opaque Pinwheel Pattern, Ruffled Rim,
Minor Damage On Bottom, 5¾" Diam. . . .
. . . .$40.00

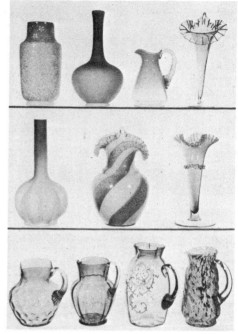

(A-MI '78)   C. B. Charles Galleries, Inc.

(ROW I, L to R)

STEVENS & WILLIAMS OVERLAY OPALENE VASE, Crimped Top, Rose Motif, 5¾"
H. $45.00
WEBB SATIN GLASS PERFUME BOTTLE, Silver Mount & Hinged Lid, Signed, 3¼" H.
....$170.00
STEUBEN AURENE LIGHT SHADES (2), Peacock Feather Patt., 5" H. $150.00
MOUNT WASHINGTON MUSTARD POT, Silver Hinged Top, Handle & Spoon, 4½"
O.H. $85.00
TIFFANY CENTERPIECE, Gold Iridescent Intaglio, Signed "8425K L.C. Tiffany Favril",
Lotus Pad Patt., 13½" Diam., 2¾" H. $600.00
(ROW II, L to R)
LE GRAS FRENCH CAMEO VASE, Enamel Decor., Signed, 7½" H. $325.00
IMPERIAL VASE, Blue Iridescent, Striped Flower Form, Unsigned, 10¼" H. ...$100.00
WEBB SATIN GLASS JAM JAR, Coralene On Pink Mother-Of-Pearl, 6" H. ...$250.00
GALLE FRENCH CAMEO VASE, Berry & Leaf Patt. In Green On Pink Ground, Signed,
8½" H. $450.00
TIFFANY IRIDESCENT CYPRIOTE VASE, Signed "L.C.T. K1371", 13" H. $4600.00
(ROW III, L to R)
MOUNT WASHINGTON SALT & PEPPER SHAKERS, Pr., Floral Decor., 2" H. .....
....$90.00
CLEAR OVERSHOT PITCHER, Clear Applied Handle, 7¼" H. $30.00
GOLD & BLUE IRIDESCENT VASE, Drapery Patt., 7" H. $150.00
AURENE BUD VASE, Gold & Blue, Signed "Aurene 234", 8" H. $200.00
LE GRAS FRENCH CAMEO VASE, Enamel Decor., Signed, 6" H. $275.00
(ROW IV, L to R)
TIFFANY TUMBLER, Gold Iridescent, Signed "7303H L.C. Tiffany Favrile", Victoria patt.,
5¾" H. $310.00
STEUBEN BLUE AURENE ON CALCITE COMPOTE, Unsigned, 4¼" H. $275.00
MOSER CRANBERRY GLASS COMPOTE, Gold Enamel Decor., Signed, Faceted Sur-
face, 12⅝" H. $275.00
BRISTOL VASES, Pr., Burnt Orange Ground, Dogwood Patt., 10" H. $80.00

(A-MA '78)   Richard A. Bourne Co., Inc.

(ROW I, L to R)
**ENGLISH PEACHBLOW SATIN GLASS
VASE** W/Overall Decor. Of Yellow Flowers,
Gold Stems & Foliage, 9¼" H. $110.00
PEACHBLOW SATIN GLASS VASE,
English, 10½" H. $190.00
TALL CREAMER, Opalescent Salmon
Pink W/Amber Applied Reeded Handle,
Ground Pontil $65.00
**CRANBERRY JACK-IN-THE-PULPIT
VASE,** Clear Foot, Cranberry Stem & Finely
Ruffled Rim, 10⅝" H. $50.00

(ROW II, L to R)
PEACHBLOW VASE, Satin Finish, Stick
Type W/Large Melon Ribs Around Bottom,
Small Inner Rim Nick, 12" H. $150.00
CASED GLASS VASE, Cranberry On
Pink Shot W/Silver Flecks & White Spiral
Bands, Ruffled Edge, One-Inch Check In
Outer Casing In Shoulder, 11¼" H. ......
............................$60.00
TRUMPET VASE, Opalescent Cranberry
W/Clear Foot & Clear Applied Rigaree,
Ruffled Rim, Trefoil Shape At Top, 10½" H.
............................$65.00

(ROW III, L to R)
CRANBERRY GLASS PITCHER "In-
verted Thumbprint" Patt. W/Clear Applied
Handle & Squared Top, Shallow Flakes
Around Pontil Which Occurred During The
Making $110.00
DEEP CRANBERRY GLASS PITCHER
W/Vertical Panels & Clear Reeded & Ap-
plied Handle $110.00
ENGLISH VASE, Shading From Faint
Salmon Pink To Vivid Medium Fuchsia Col-
or, W/Salmon Pink Applied Handle &
Enamel Decor $70.00
SPANGLE GLASS PITCHER, Yellow,
White & Amethyst In Clear Casing W/Clear
Applied Handle, Molded-In Swirled Design
............................$40.00

◄ *To the left*

(A-MI '78)

C. B. Charles Galleries, Inc.

◄ *To the left*

(ROW I, L to R)
STEUBEN BLUE AURENE VASE, Signed "Aurene 6307", 13¾" H. $650.00
GALLE CAMEO VASE, 3-Color, Tree Motif, Signed, 16¼" H. $700.00
TIFFANY BON BON PLATE, Gold Iridescent, Signed, "L.C.T.", 6" Diam. .$175.00
TIFFANY PINCHED CORDIAL CUP, Gold Iridescent, Signed "L.C.T.", 1¾" H. $160.00
TIFFANY SALT CELLAR, Gold Iridescent, Signed, Fluted Rim, 2⅞" Diam., 1¼" H. $160.00

(ROW II, L to R)
TIFFANY PINCHED CORDIAL CUP, Brown Iridescent, Signed "L.C.T. T4414", 1¾" H. $120.00
TIFFANY LATTICE DECORATED VASE, Blue Iridescent, Signed "L.C. Tiffany-Favrile 7130C", 6¼" H. . . .$2600.00
STEUBEN GOLD AURENE CALCITE SHERBET, W/Underplate, Unsigned, Plate, 6" Diam., 4½" H. $110.00
STEUBEN GOLD AURENE CALCITE SHERBET, W/Underplate, Unsigned, Plate, 6" Diam., 4½" H. $110.00
FROSTED GLASS & BRASS OIL LAMP, Handpainted Floral Design On Shade & Base, Brass Fittings In Griffin Design, Lamp, 15" H., Panel 21½" H. $300.00

(ROW III, L to R)
STEUBEN GOLD AURENE CALCITE SHERBET, W/Underplate, Unsigned, Plate, 6" Diam., 4½" H. $110.00
MOSER VASE, Polychrome Enamel, Leaf patt., Signed, 7⅜" H. $135.00
MOUNT WASHINGTON SALT SHAKER, Melon Shape, Handpainted Floral Decor., 1¾" H. $30.00
SALT CELLAR, Pastel Iridescent, Ovoid Shape, Fluted Rim, 2" L., 1⅜" H. .$20.00
SALT CELLAR, Pastel Iridescent, Round, Fluted Rim, 1⅞" Diam., 1" H. $15.00
NEW MARTINSVILLE SALT CELLAR, Iridescent, Round, Fluted Rim, Unsigned, 1⅞" Diam., 1¼" H. $15.00
SALT CELLAR, Pastel Iridescent, Ovoid Shape, Fluted Rim, 2¼" L., 1¼" H. $15.00

(ROW IV, L to R)
TIFFANY TRI-HANDLED INTAGLIO CUT LOVING CUP, Signed "L.C. Tffany Favrile 389G", 7½" H. $2500.00
MOSER CHAMPAGNE GLASSES, (Set of 6), Enamel Decor., Polychrome Floral Motif On French Blue Ground, Signed, 7¼" H. $375.00
MOSER FINGER BOWLS (Set of 6), Enamel Decor., Polychrome Floral Motif On French Blue Ground, 4¾" Diam., 2¼" H. $350.00
MOSER WINE GLASSES (Set of 4), Enamel Decor., Polychrome Floral Motif On French Blue Ground, 8⅞" H. $250.00
THREADED GLASS CREAMER & SUGAR, White Stripe On Peach Ground, Applied Handle & Feet, Creamer - 4½" H. $70.00

(A-MA '78)   *Richard A. Bourne Co., Inc.*

(ROW I)
BACCARAT THREE-COLOR CAMEO VASE, With Morning Glories And Other Pink Flowers Over A Profusion Of Green Leaves On White Satin Finished Ground, *(continued next column)*

◄ *To the left*   *(continued)*
10½" H. $650.00
VAL ST. LAMBERT CAMEO GLASS VASE, Amethyst Vines And Flowers On Colorless Frosted Ground With Clear Amethyst Lip, Signed, 9¾" H. $325.00
OVERLAY CAMEO-STYLE VASE, Probably English, With Vivid Cranberry-Colored Body And Abstract Wave-Like Overlay Of Opaque Glass Having A Rough Finish And Touched W/Gold. The Clear Cranberry Part Of The Glass Is Decorated With Flowers In Gold, 11¾" H. . .$150.00
(ROW II)
HONESDALE ACID CUT VASE, Green Cut To Colorless Frosted Glass With Gold Striping And Highlights. Signed, Signature Is Worn But Visible In Pontil, 6¾" H. $175.00
PEKING CAMEO GLASS VASE, Red Flowers Cut To Opaque White Ground, With Red Lip And Foot, On Teakwood Base, 9¾" H., Minute Foot Damage $175.00
BACCARAT CAMEO VASE, With Green Daisy-Like Flowers Against A Colorless Background Of Engraved Leaves; Green Wave Border Around Top. Vase Is Square, Unsigned, 10" H. $200.00

(D-NY '78)   *Lee Vines Antiques*
TIFFANY BON BON DISH, Flower Form, Stretched Edge, Gold W/Lavender & Blue Iridescence, Signed, 5" H. $450.00

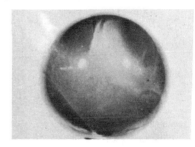

(A-MA '78)   *Richard A. Bourne Co., Inc.*
WITCH BALL, Brilliant Rainbow Coloring In Blue, Cranberry & White In Abstract Arrangement $90.00

(D-NY '78)   *Lee Vines Antiques*
WAVECREST GLOVE BOX, Blue Satin W/Cream Panels Outlined In Foliate Scrolls, Enameled Armeria Blooms & Leaves, Beaded Dots, Ormolu Rims, Signed, 8½" L., 4⅛" W., 3½" H. $675.00

(A-MI '78)   *C. B. Charles Galleries, Inc.*
(ROW I, L to R)
BRISTOL BUD VASES, Pr., Butterfly, Bird & Rose Patt., 1 Clockwise, One Counterclockwise, 6¼" H., ...$30.00
DOROTHY C. THORPE PERFUME BOTTLE, Rose Motif, Paper Label, 6⅞" H. . . . . . .
. . . .$50.00
WAVECREST PIN DISH, Brass Mount, Signed, 2¾" Diam., 1⅝" H. $40.00
PRESSED GLASS PEDESTAL JELLY DISH, Bull's Eye & Diamond Patt., Etched Lip, 4⅛" Diam., 5" H. $15.00
PRESSED GLASS PEDESTAL FRUIT BOWL, Bull's Eye & Diamond Patt., 6½" Diam., 7⅞" H. $25.00
(ROW II, L to R)
NORTHWOOD CARNIVAL GLASS BASKET, Green Pastel, Woven Wicker Patt., 3¼" H. $70.00
OVERSHOT GLASS PITCHER, Clear Body, Azure Neck, Applied Clear Handle, 7¾" H. $50.00
LOETZ IRIDESCENT VASE, Shades Peach At Base To Green At Neck, Signed, 8⅝" H. $150.00
BACCARAT CELERY DISH, Amberina, Fluted Edge, Signed, 9½" L., 3¼" W., 1½" H. $35.00
BACCARAT ROOSTERS, Pr., Signed, 2¾" H. $35.00
(ROW III, L to R)
GALLE MINIATURE CAMEO VASE, Mauve Floral Patt., Cream Ground, Signed, 4¼" H. $150.00
LOETZ MINIATURE CRATERED VASE, Green Iridescent, Unsigned, 3" H. $40.00
TIFFANY LIQUEUR GLASS, Gold Iridescent, Signed "L.C.T. Favrile", 4⅜" H. $110.00
GREEN SATIN GLASS ROSE BOWL, Gold W/Blue Floral Decor, 10¼" Diam., 4" H. $100.00
VASA MURRHINA VASE, Pink, Crimped Top, 5 Clear Applied Feet, 6½" H. . . .$50.00
IMPERIAL FLARE VASE, Pastel Iridescent, Tulip Form, 8¼" H. $30.00
(ROW IV, L to R)
TIFFANY BOWL, Gold Iridescent, Signed "L.C.T. Favrile", 6" Diam., 2½" H. . .$275.00
GREENTOWN HONEY DISH, Dewey Patt., Minor Rim Chip, 4¾" H. $25.00
PERFUME BOTTLE, Gold Enamel, Floral Patt., 7¼" H. $50.00
STEUBEN BOWL, Gold Calcite, Unsigned, 10¼" Diam., 3⅛" H. $150.00

(D-NY '78)   *Lee Vines Antiques*
BRIDE'S BASKET, Melon Ribbed, Bowl Shading From Rose To Pink, Mkd., Southington Co., Bowl: 11" W.; 11¼" O.H. . . .
. . . .$350.00

To the right ▶

(A-MI '78)   *C. B. Charles Galleries, Inc.*

(ROW I, L to R)
TIFFANY PANELED GOLD DORE TABLE LAMP, Yellow, Signed "Tiffany Studios N.Y. 1924", 3-Light, Shade, 14" Diam., 7½" H., 21½" H. $2800.00
RUBINA VERDE VASE, Gold & White Enamel Floral Patt., Crimped Top, 8" H. $90.00
SATIN GLASS VASE, Pink Mother-Of-Pearl, Herringbone Patt., Fluted Top, 7⅜" H. $175.00
MOSER PLATFORM & FOOTED VASE, Gold & Polychrome Enameled Decor., Double Fan Patt., 16½" H. $325.00
THREADED GLASS FINGER BOWL, Underplate, Pink, Bowl, 5½" Diam., 3" H. $50.00

(ROW II, L to R)
AMBER INVERTED CORALENE THUMBPRINT TUMBLER, Floral Design, 3¾" H. $60.00
YELLOW AIR TRAP SATIN GLASS VASE, Raindrop Patt., Crimped Top, 5¼" H. $120.00
STEVENS & WILLIAMS VASE, Signed "S&W Stourbridge Art Glass", Overlay Acanthus Leaf Design, 5" H. $150.00
TIFFANY BOWL, Gold Iridescent, Signed "427N L.C. Tiffany Favrile", 10" Diam., 2⅜" H. $450.00
GALLE FRENCH CAMEO VASE, Mauve & Blue Alpine Scene, Signed, 9¾" H. $700.00

(ROW III, L to R)
TRANSLUCENT RED TIFFANY VASE, Signed "L.C. Tiffany Favrile 6658K", 6½" H. $4000.00
THREE CUP SWEETMEAT EPERGNE, Threaded & Overlay Glass, Circular Beveled Mirror Base, 10⅜" H. $185.00
TIFFANY NUT BOWL W/6 Nut Cups, Gold Iridescent, Signed "L.C. Tiffany Favrile E1630", Paper Label, Swirl Patt., 8¾" H. $900.00

(ROW IV, L to R)
TIFFANY GOLD IRIDESCENT VASE, Signed "L.C. Tiffany Favrile," Paper Label, Swirl Patt., 8¾" H. $1200.00
SATIN GLASS JEWEL BOX, Mauve Floral & Figural Decor., Gold Ormolu Fittings & Base, 5½" L., 4¼" W., 4½" H. . .$225.00
DAUM NANCY CAMEO VASE, Burnt Orange & Black Lily Design On Gold Field, Signed, 13¼" H. $550.00
BRIDE'S BASKET, Cased Glass, Crimped Flare Rim, Cranberry & White, 11" Diam., 3⅜" H. $50.00

(D-NY '78)   *Lee Vines Antiques*
BRIDE'S BASKET, Deep Rose, Clear Rim, White Exterior, "Wilcox" Silver Holder, 10" W., Holder: 10½" H. $225.00

(D-NY '78)   *Lee Vines Antiques*
BRIDE'S BASKET, Pink W/Large Enamelled Daisies, Gold Leaves, 10½" W.; Holder By James W. Tufts, 11¼" H. $300.00

◄ *To the left*

(A-MI '78)   *C. B. Charles Galleries, Inc.*

(ROW I, L to R)
TIFFANY VASE, Black Iridescent, Signed "L.C. Tiffany Inc. Favrile W5129", Paper Label, Pull-Up Patt., 8" H. $3500.00
GALLE CAMEO VIOLET VASE, Mauve Floral Design, Signed, 3¼" H. ...$225.00
TIFFANY SALT CELLAR, Gold Iridescent, Signed, "L.C.T. Favrile", 1¼" H. ....
....$130.00
TIFFANY TRUMPET VASE, Gold Iridescent, Signed "9679N 1548 L.C. Tiffany Favrile", 8⅝" H. $400.00
TIFFANY GLADIOLA VASE, Paper Weight Glass, Signed "3280P Louis C. Tiffany Favrile", 20" H. $6250.00
HAWKES TEAR DROP CANDLESTICKS, Emerald Green, Signed, 14" H.
....$250.00

(ROW II, L to R)
STEVENS & WILLIAMS VASE, Opalescent, Crimped Top, 10⅛" H. $100.00
WEBB VASE, Gold Enamel & Polychrome Crane & Floral Patt., Unsigned, 10⅛" H. .
....$200.00
THREADED CUSTARD GLASS VASE, Pink, Applied Transparent Green Wave-Form Base, 3¼" H. $55.00
LOETZ VASE, Green Iridescent, Spider Web Decor., Unsigned, 10⅝" H. .$100.00
CARDER ROSALENE SHERBET, Unsigned, 5" Diam., 2½" H. $140.00
BURMESE NUT DISH, 4⅝" Diam., 1⅜" H. $150.00

(ROW III, L to R)
CARDER SHERBET & UNDERPLATE, Green Jade, Unsigned, 5⅞" Diam., 4¼" O. H. $100.00
WEBB PEACH BLOW VASES, Pr., Gold Enamel Butterfly & Plum Blossom Design, Unsigned, 6½" H. $600.00
TIFFANY VASE, Iridescent, Flower-Form, Paper Label, Pulled Decor., 4¾" Diam., 10⅛" H. $900.00
DURAND CANDLESTICKS, Pr., Mushroom Shape, Amber Base W/Raspberry Top, White Pulled-Up Floral Patt., 3½" H. .....
....$325.00

(ROW IV, L to R)
VENETIAN CANED GLASS PLATE, Gold & White Filigree, 7⅛" Diam. .$35.00
BURMESE LILY VASE, Lip Design, 12" H. $475.00
DAUM NANCY ENAMELED COLUMBINE CAMEO VASE, 4-Color, Floral Patt., Yellow Field, Signed, 9" H. ....
....$450.00
MOUNT WASHINGTON PEACH BLOW VASE, 10¾" H. $550.00
TIFFANY FRUIT BOWL, Gold Iridescent, Signed "3510N L.C. Tiffany Favrile", 7⅝" Diam., 2⅝" H. $425.00
LOETZ PINCHED BOTTLE-VASE, Four-Armed, Green Iridescent, Signed, 6⅜" H. $350.00

(D-NY '78)   *Lee Vines Antiques*
BRIDE'S BASKET, Cased Opalescent Bowl W/Gold Iridescence & Lge. Gold Flowers & Leaves, Wilcox Silver Holder W/2 Cherubs Each Side, Bowl: 12¼" W.; 19¾" H. $335.00

(D-NY '78)   *Lee Vines Antiques*
MINI-BASKET, Body Ribbed W/Opal Lines, Turned Down Rose-Pink Collar, Green Looped Ladle, Applied Pink & Opal Flower W/Green Leaves, 7½" H., 4" W.
....$135.00

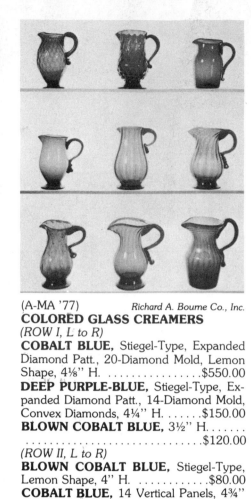

(A-MA '77)   *Richard A. Bourne Co., Inc.*

COLORED GLASS CREAMERS
(ROW I, L to R)
COBALT BLUE, Stiegel-Type, Expanded Diamond Patt., 20-Diamond Mold, Lemon Shape, 4⅛" H. $550.00
DEEP PURPLE-BLUE, Stiegel-Type, Expanded Diamond Patt., 14-Diamond Mold, Convex Diamonds, 4¼" H. $150.00
BLOWN COBALT BLUE, 3½" H. $120.00
(ROW II, L to R)
BLOWN COBALT BLUE, Stiegel-Type, Lemon Shape, 4" H. $80.00
COBALT BLUE, 14 Vertical Panels, 4¾" H. $130.00
COBALT BLUE, 16-Rib Pattern, Swirled, 4¾" H. $180.00
(ROW III, L to R)
COBALT BLUE, Stiegel-Type, Expanded Diamond Patt., 11-Diamond Mold, Folded-In Lip, 4¾" H. $150.00
COBALT BLUE, Stiegel-Type, 20 Vertical Ribs, Folded-In Lip, 5" H. $175.00
AMETHYST, Stiegel-Type, 24 Vertical Ribs, Horizontal Ribbed Band, No Foot, 5¼" H. $250.00

(A-MI '78)   *C. B. Charles Galleries, Inc.*

(ROW I, L to R)
STEUBEN ROSALINE CENTERPIECE, Cast Silver Base, Unsigned, 10½" Diam., 8" H. $150.00
BRISTOL VASE, Ivory, Castle Scene, 10⅝" H. $40.00
FROSTED RUBINA CRYSTAL VASE, Hobnail Patt., 8½" H. $90.00
BRISTOL LUSTRES, Pr., Pale Aqua, Gold Enamel & Polychrome Decor., 14⅜" H. $200.00
(ROW II, L to R)
SATIN BRISTOL VASES, Pr., Floral Design, Blue, Green & Brown, 7⅝" H. $35.00
IMPERIAL STRETCH GLASS COMPOTE, Amberina, 5¾" Diam., 4½" H. $60.00
BRISTOL VASES, Pr., Pink, Daisy Patt., 9½" H. $90.00
PATTERN GLASS COMPOTE, Three Face Design, 6½" H. $85.00
BRISTOL VASE, White, Peony Design, 12½" H. $35.00
(ROW III, L to R)
VENETIAN SHERBET, White Filigree, Caned & Gold, Swirled, Clear Glass Decor., 4⅛" H. $15.00
BRISTOL VASES, Pr., Floral Design, 11¼" H. $80.00
RUBINA CRYSTAL DISH, Clear Applied Feet, 8¾" Across; 3¾" H. $60.00
BRISTOL VASE, White, Country Scene, 9⅛" H. $25.00
(ROW IV, L to R)
CRANBERRY GLASS PITCHER, Hobnail Patt., Applied Clear Turned Handle, 5⅞" H. $100.00
CRANBERRY GLASS VASE, Raindrop Patt., 3⅝" H. $45.00
HAWKES PERFUME BOTTLE, Reverse Etching On Base, Floral & Geometric Design, Monogramed Silver Top, Signed, 7" H. $130.00
STEUBEN CALCITE LAMP SHADE, Gold Aurene Lining, Unsigned, 5½" H. ...$90.00
BRISTOL VASE, Olive, Floral Design, 12¼" H. $45.00
PURPLE SLAG COMPOTE, Bust Of Jenny Lind Stem, 8½" Diam., 7¾" H. $65.00

(D-MO '78)

SEVEN BOTTLE CASTOR SET, Silver Plated Frame $250.00

◄ *To the left*

(A-MI '78)   *C. B. Charles Galleries, Inc.*

(ROW I, L to R)
GALLE MINIATURE CAMEO VASE, Brown Thistle Patt., Gold Ground, Signed, 4½" H. $225.00
TIFFANY GOLD DECORATED OVER-LAY VASE, Heavy Bas Relief Work Of Leaves & Vines, Signed "L.C. Tiffany Favrile BZZ6C, 14" H. $3700.00
LOETZ VASE, Tulip Form, Unsigned, 9" H. $180.00
BOHEMIAN RED IRIDESCENT SQUAT VASE, Spider Webbing Decor., 4¾" H. $70.00
OPALESCENT VASE, Milky White, Tropical Fish Motif, 2 Seahorse Handles, 6⅞" H. $80.00
PEACH BLOW CRUET, Applied Handle & Overlay Floral Decor., 7¼" H. .$100.00

(Row II, L to R)
DURAND GOLD IRIDESCENT VASE, Unsigned, 6¾" H. $225.00
BRISTOL PITCHER, Smoke, Sparrow & Dogwood Patt., 13⅞" H. $60.00
WEBB BASE, Coralene On Satin Glass, Signed, 7½" H. $350.00
AURENE COCKTAIL GLASS, Gold, Signed "Aurene", 5" H. $110.00
RAINBOW GLASS PINCH VASE, Gold Enamel & White Decor. At Collar, 5½" H. $150.00
TIFFANY VASE, Flower Form, Signed "L.C.T. T3373", Opalescent Exterior, Color Pulled Up Through Stem, Gold Iridescent Lining Of Cup, 4½" Diam., 11½" H. $2300.00

(ROW III, L to R)
WHEELING PEACHBLOW GLOSSY TUMBLER, 3½" H. $150.00
TIFFANY BOWL, Yellow Pastel, Signed "1925 L.C.T. Favrile", Laurel Leaf Design, 6" Diam., 1¾" H. $275.00
SANDWICH GLASS WHALE OIL LAMP BASE, Thumbprint Design, 18" H. $100.00
AMBERINA VASE, Polychrome & Gold Enamel Decor., Crimped Top, Floral Design, 9½" H. $175.00
(ROW IV, L to R)
AURENE COLOGNE ATOMIZER, Gold, Unsigned, 7⅜" H. $120.00
OVERSHOT VASE, Inverted Pale Green, Scalloped Top, Applied Glass Decor., 7½" H. $50.00
TIFFANY FINGER BOWL, Gold Iridescent, Signed "L.C.T.", 4¼" Diam., 2⅜" H. $205.00
MARY GREGORY GOBLET, Teal Blue, Young Girl W/Flower Patt., 6⅛" H. $80.00
FRENCH MARBLE GLASS VASE, Polychrome & Gold Enamel Decor. At Collar, Foot & Neck, 10⅝" H. $80.00
GALLE BLOW OUT PLUM VASE, Beige Ground W/Green Leaves & Fruit, Signed, 15¼" H. $3500.00

(D-NY '78)   *Lee Vines Antiques*
STEUBEN AURENE FAN VASE, Blue Decor., Signed, 5" W., 8" H. $850.00

(D-NY '78)   *Lee Vines Antiques*
DAUM NANCY CAMEO VASE, Iridescent Yellow Chipped Background W/Cut & Enameled Teasel & Leaves, Enameled Neck, 4" H. $250.00

(A-MA '78)   Richard A. Bourne Co., Inc.

STEUBEN GLASS
(ROW I, L to R)
JACK-IN-THE-PULPIT VASE, Amber Threading-Style Art Work Applied Around Rim. Entire Body Filled W/Regularly Placed Air Traps, Unsigned, 4¾" H. $40.00
LOT OF 3 PIECES OF STEUBEN, Finger Bowl Signed "F Carder" & Marked, Matching Undertray & Tall Stemmed Pale Green Wine Glass W/Applied Threading .$200.00
(ROW II, L to R)
CANDLESTICKS, Pr., Citron Or Topaz Glass W/Wide Rims & Black Threading, Signed, 6" H. $150.00
VASE (Center), "Inverted Thumbprint" Patt. W/Dark Amber Applied Threading, Unsigned, Minor Damage To Threading Around Lower Area, 6" H. $40.00
(ROW III, L to R)
VASE, "Diamond Quilted" Patt. W/Black Threading Around Upper Rim & Neck, Signed, 6½" H. $70.00
VASE W/Regular Air Traps &Cranberry Threading Around Ruffled Rim, Unsigned, Minor Damage To Threading, 8¾" H. . . . .
. . . .$40.00
VASE, Pale Blue W/Regular Air Traps & Clear Threading Around Neck, Signed "Steuben, F. Carder" For Dr. Kopins By Mr. Carder, 7¾" H. $90.00

(A-MA '78)   Richard A. Bourne Co., Inc.

LUTZ-TYPE THREADED FINGER BOWL & UNDERTRAY, Amber Color . .
. . . .$35.00
LUTZ-TYPE THREADED GLASS FINGER BOWL & UNDERTRAY, Apricot & Cranberry Color, Minute Damage To Threading $40.00
STEVENS & WILLIAMS TYPE THREADED GLASS FINGER BOWL, Blue Threading On Clear Glass, Trefoil-Shaped Finger Bowl W/Vertical Ribbing . . .
. . . .$70.00

(A-MA '78)   Richard A. Bourne Co., Inc.

(See photo above) ▲

(ROW I)
SIX-PIECE BEVERAGE SET, Tall Pitcher W/Applied Blue Handle & Five Matching Tumblers, "Inverted Thumbprint" Patt. W/Mary Gregory Type Decor. Minute Rim Roughage On Some Pieces $200.00

(ROW II)
LARGE DECORATED VASE, Shading Clear To Deep Amethyst W/Enameled Flowers, 10¼" H. $125.00
COBALT BLUE VASA MURRHINA BEEHIVE PITCHER By Hobbs, Brock-unier & Co., Wheeling; Silver Flicks, Clear Applied Handle $50.00
SAPPHIRE BLUE BLOWN GLASS WA-TER PITCHER W/Gold & Enamel Decor. Of Flowers, Clear Blue Applied Reeded Handle $70.00

(ROW III)
IRIDESCENT PURPLE-BLUE VASES, Pr. Austrian, Sgn., Decor W/Yellow Poppies, Leaves, Stems & Blue Around Base Represents Water Or Soil, 10½" H. .$100.00
BLACK BLOWN GLASS VASE, English, Decor. W/Soft Blue Flowers & Insects, 11½" H. $60.00
AMETHYST VASE, Austrian W/Rainbow Iridescence & Clear Applied Serpent Wound Around Stem, Minute Nicks In Rim, 10" H.
. . . .$40.00

(D-FL '78)
STEUBEN WINE DECANTER, W/2 Of 6 Matching Wines, Vertical Ribbed, Amethyst $450.00

(D-NY '78) *Lee Vines Antiques*
CASED PITCHER & FIVE TUMBLERS, Lt. Cranberry Interior, Custard Exterior, Deep Cranberry Applied Handle, Enameled Leaves & Orange Throated Swallow, Pitcher: 9¼" H. $395.00

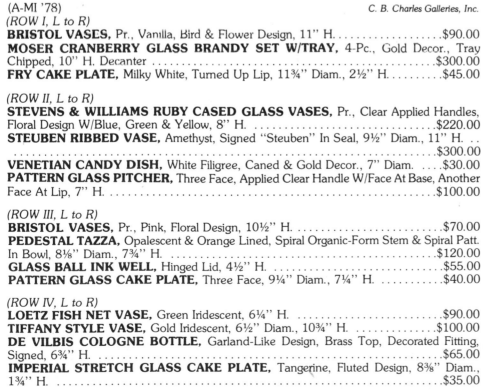

(A-MI '78) *C. B. Charles Galleries, Inc.*
(ROW I, L to R)
BRISTOL VASES, Pr., Vanilla, Bird & Flower Design, 11" H. $90.00
MOSER CRANBERRY GLASS BRANDY SET W/TRAY, 4-Pc., Gold Decor., Tray Chipped, 10" H. Decanter $300.00
FRY CAKE PLATE, Milky White, Turned Up Lip, 11¾" Diam., 2½" H. $45.00

(ROW II, L to R)
STEVENS & WILLIAMS RUBY CASED GLASS VASES, Pr., Clear Applied Handles, Floral Design W/Blue, Green & Yellow, 8" H. $220.00
STEUBEN RIBBED VASE, Amethyst, Signed "Steuben" In Seal, 9½" Diam., 11" H. . .
. . . .$300.00
VENETIAN CANDY DISH, White Filigree, Caned & Gold Decor., 7" Diam. $30.00
PATTERN GLASS PITCHER, Three Face, Applied Clear Handle W/Face At Base, Another Face At Lip, 7" H. $100.00

(ROW III, L to R)
BRISTOL VASES, Pr., Pink, Floral Design, 10½" H. $70.00
PEDESTAL TAZZA, Opalescent & Orange Lined, Spiral Organic-Form Stem & Spiral Patt. In Bowl, 8⅛" Diam., 7¾" H. $120.00
GLASS BALL INK WELL, Hinged Lid, 4½" H. $55.00
PATTERN GLASS CAKE PLATE, Three Face, 9¼" Diam., 7¼" H. $40.00

(ROW IV, L to R)
LOETZ FISH NET VASE, Green Iridescent, 6¼" H. $90.00
TIFFANY STYLE VASE, Gold Iridescent, 6½" Diam., 10¾" H. $100.00
DE VILBIS COLOGNE BOTTLE, Garland-Like Design, Brass Top, Decorated Fitting, Signed, 6¾" H. $65.00
IMPERIAL STRETCH GLASS CAKE PLATE, Tangerine, Fluted Design, 8⅜" Diam., 1¾" H. $35.00

(D-NY '78) *Lee Vines Antiques*
DAUM NANCY TUMBLER, Cameo Cut Mistletoe W/White Jewelled Berries On Cranberry Chipped Ground, Signed 3½" H. $200.00

◀ *To the left*

(A-MI '78)   *C. B. Charles Galleries, Inc.*
(ROW I, L to R)
WEBB ROSE BOWL, Topaz Overlay, Tri-Footed, Unsigned, 3⅝" Diam., 5⅛" H. $100.00
BRISTOL PORTRAIT VASES, Pr., Green Field, Clover & Dogwood Floral Patt., 14¾" H. $90.00
MOSER VASE, Polychrome & Gold Enamel, Applied Parrot Decor., Bronze Mount, Signed, 22½" H. $1800.00
(ROW II, L to R)
WAVECREST BISCUIT JAR, Lily Patt., Silver Mount, Handle & Lid, Unsigned, 8½" H. $100.00
MARY GREGORY TANKARD PITCHER, Amber, Cavalier W/Trumpet Enameled Patt., Unsigned, 12⅜" H. ...$110.00
WEBB PEACH BLOW VASE, Unsigned, 7⅛" H. $250.00
BURMESE BOWL, Crimped Top, 4" Diam., 2½" H. $150.00
TIFFANY TRUMPET VASE, Pink Pastel, Signed "L.C.T. Favrile, 1886", Intaglio Base, 9⅜" H. $400.00
BOHEMIAN RUBY OVERLAY LIQUERS, (4), 5½" H. $50.00
(ROW III, L to R)
DAUM NANCY CAMEO GLASS POWDER BOWL, Signed In Pattern On Top, Etched On Bottom, Bowl, 4¼" Diam. ....
............................$300.00
CASED RAINBOW GLASS CRUET, Crimped Top, Applied Clear Handle, 7" H.
............................$60.00
PINCH VASE, Shaded Gold & Iridescent, Flare Top, Applied Clear Glass Decor. At Neck, 4¼" H. $25.00
(ROW IV, L to R)
SATIN GLASS PINCH VASE, Butterscotch Mother-Of-Pearl, Raindrop Patt., 8¾" H. $175.00
MOUNT WASHINGTON MUSTARD POT, Violet Patt., Silver Mount & Spoon, 3¼" H. $70.00
TIFFANY GOLD DORE TABLE LAMP, Metal Sculptured Shade Signed "Tiffany Studios N.Y. 1412", Base Signed "Tiffany Studios, N.Y. 539", Shade, 12" Diam., 7" H. 18½" H. $2000.00
LOETZ CRATERED VASE, Iridescent, Applied Shell-Form Decor., Unsigned, 5¼" H. $45.00
RUBY EGERMANN DINNER BELL, Grape & Vine Patt., 5⅞" H. $30.00
FRY FOVAL GLASS CREAMER & SUGAR, Milky White, Opalescent W/Green Opaline Applied Handles, Creamer, 3½" H.
............................$125.00

(D-NY '78)   *Lee Vines Antiques*
BRIDE'S BASKET, Shaded Rose W/Clear Rim, Meriden Base W/Cherubs, Silver Base, 4¾" D., Bowl 11" W., 14¼" H. .$600.00

◀ *To the left*

(D-NY '78)   *Lee Vines Antiques*
VICTORIAN BUD VASE, Sapphire Blue Insert W/Mary Gregory Type Enameled Flowers In Numbered Silver Holder, 7½" H.
............................$95.00

To the right ▶

(A-MA '78)   Richard A. Bourne Co., Inc.

TUMBLERS

(ROW I, L to R)
OPALESCENT, Signed, "Holly" Patt. By Northwood $55.00
OPALESCENT, Signed, Drapery Design By Northwood $20.00
OPALESCENT GREEN, "Inverted Thumbprint" Patt., About Perfect ...$5.00
OPAQUE OPALESCENT, "Hobnail" Patt. $10.00
CUSTARD GLASS, "Intaglio" Patt. By Northwood, About Perfect $60.00

(ROW II, L to R)
CUSTARD GLASS, "Chrysanthemum Sprig" Patt., Attrib. To Northwood .$80.00
CUSTARD GLASS, Signed, Hand Painted Roses, By Heisey $40.00
CUSTARD GLASS, "Krystol" Patt., Souvenir Of "Coshocton, O." $22.00
CUSTARD GLASS, Pr., Iris Design By Northwood $130.00

(ROW III, L to R)
FROSTED & DECORATED, "Wild Rose W/Bowknot" Patt. $20.00
FROSTED W/SILVER STAIN (AMBER) BARS, "Klondike" Or Amberette" Patt., Shallow Chip On Bottom Has Been Slightly Ground $40.00
"BLUEBIRD & STRAWBERRY" Patt., Chip On Bottom Ring Of Tumbler .$10.00
CLEAR, "Palm Beach" Patt. $30.00
CLEAR, "Daisy & Button W/Narcissus" Patt. $15.00

(ROW IV, L to R)
CLEAR, Variant Of "Daisy" Patt. W/Fired-On Reddish-Purple Flowers & Gold Decor. $12.00
CLEAR, Six Petaled Flowers Around Side, Flowers Have Reddish-Amethyst Fired-On Coloring W/Gold Centers $5.00
CLEAR, "Three Fruit" Patt., Chip In Foot Ring $5.00
PRES-CUT CLEAR, W/Ruby Flash Panels & Heavy Gold Decor., Two Panels Have Faint Nicks $20.00
"LEAF & FLOWER" Patt. W/Amber Flash Decor., Two Minute Flakes On Bottom Of Foot Ring $10.00

(ROW V, L to R)
CLEAR, "Cherry Lattice" Patt. By Northwood W/Amethyst Flash & Gold Decor. $10.00
CLEAR & APRICOT OPALESCENT, "Inverted Diamond Point" Patt., Minute Rim Roughage $5.00
CLEAR, "Wyoming" Patt. W/Gold Decor $35.00
VASELINE GLASS, "Daisy & Button" Patt. W/Patt. In Base $35.00
ETCHED AMBER FLASH TO CLEAR GLASS, "Esther" Patt. $15.00

(A-MA '78)   Richard A. Bourne Co., Inc.

IRIDESCENT BLUE TEN-PANELED VASE, Signed "L C Tiffany Favrile", Cylindrical Shape, Slightly Scalloped Rim And Squat Bell-Shaped Foot Extensions. 15⅛" H. $650.00
VASIFORM NIGHT LAMP, Signed Louis C. Tiffany", Exterior Coloring Is Greenish W/Abstract Feather Pattern, When Lighted It Shades Yellow At Bottom To Red In Center And Retains Its Green Coloring At Top, A Lace-Like Bronze Fitting Fits In The Top And Supports The Lamp, Cord Is Mounted At Lower Part Of Base Through A Hole With Bronze Fitting Around It Which Is Original To The Piece, 19¾" H. $1200.00
IRIDESCENT GOLD TIFFANY CANDLE HOLDER, Signed "L C T" And Bearing Orig. Paper Label On Pontil. The Candle Holder Is In A White And Green Feather Patt., Has Ten Panels At The Base Which Swirl Towards The Top, And Is Fitted W/A Spring-Loaded Candle Holder And Shade Holder, 14⅝" H. $550.00

(A-MA '78)   Richard A. Bourne Co., Inc.

(ROW I)
TIFFANY INDIVIDUAL SALT, Iridescent Gold, Eight-Panel Design W/Pinched-In Scalloped Top $85.00
MINIATURE VASE, Signed "L C T", Iridescent Gold, Base Has Four Foot Extensions And Ruffled Top, 2⅞" H. ...$225.00
SMALL VASE OR WHISKEY GLASS, Signed "L C T", Iridescent Gold W/Pinched Sides, 2⅞" H. $160.00
MINIATURE VASE, Signed "L C Tiffany Favrile", Iridescent Gold, Eight-Panel Design, 3" H. $175.00
TIFFANY VASE, Signed "L C Tiffany Favrile", Retains Original Green And Gold Tiffany Label, Iridescent Gold, Eight-Panel Design W/Pinched Sides, Applied Ring Around Neck, Slightly Scalloped Top, 4" H. $275.00
TIFFANY FINGER BOWL, Iridescent Bluish-Gold, Ten-Paneled W/Scalloped Rim $150.00

(ROW II)
TIFFANY TAZZA OR SMALL COMPOTE, Signed In Bottom "L C Tiffany Favrile" And "1702", Retains Original Green And Gold Tiffany Label. Bluish Iridescent Gold, 6⅜" Diam., 6¼" H. ..$250.00
PAIR OF EXTREMELY RARE TRUMPET FORM VASES, By Quezal, One Is Signed W/Silver Signature In Pontil. Deep Iridescent Blue, 6⅛" & 5¾" H. $700.00
IRIDESCENT GOLD TIFFANY VASE, Signed "L C T" 6½" H. $220.00
(ROW III)
IRIDESCENT GOLD TIFFANY BOWL, W/Ruffled Edge, Unsigned, Bears Remains Of White Tiffany Label, 7¾" Diam. $150.00
IRIDESCENT GOLD CANDLE HOLDER, With Spring-Loaded Glass Holder, Silver Plated Mounting And Matching Iridescent Gold Shade, Shade Signed "LCT", Base Signed & Numbered, 13¼" H. $450.00
LARGE IRIDESCENT GOLD TIFFANY BOWL, Signed "L C Tiffany Favrile", Bowl Is Ten-Paneled And Has Slightly Scalloped Rim, 9¾" Diam. $350.00

◄ *To the left*

(A-MA '78) *Richard A. Bourne Co., Inc.*
(ROW I, L to R)
PEACHBLOW OPEN SUGAR, By Mt. Washington, W/Wishbone Feet & Applied Strawberry In Pontil, Appears To Have Minute Damage & Regluing, 4¼" Diam.
.................................$1000.00
NEW ENGLAND PEACHBLOW (WILD ROSE) TUMBLER, Deep Color .$250.00
MINIATURE BURMESE BOWL, W/Elaborate Ruffled & Scalloped Rim, 3⅝" Diam.
.................................$200.00
(ROW II, L to R)
BURMESE MINIATURE VASE, Decor. Satin Finish, Painted W/Two Barn Owls Perched On Pine Bough, 3⅜" H. .$625.00
BURMESE VASE, By Mt. Washington, Bulbous Body W/Square Top Decorated W/Oak Leaves & Acorns, Satin Finish, 2⅞" H. $425.00
BURMESE CABINET VASE, By Webb, Decor. W/Elaborately Ruffled Rim, Decor. W/Leaves & Berries, Satin Finish, 3⅝" H.
.................................$300.00
(ROW III, L to R)
BURMESE DECORATED TUMBLER, By Mt. Washington, W/Satin Finish & Frame Of Roses & Wreaths Encircling Verse, "The Cowslip Is A Country Lass, / The Violet Is A Nun;— / But I Will Woo The Dainty Rose, / The Queen Of Every One. / Thomas Hood"........................$1100.00
BURMESE CREAMER, By Mt. Washington, Satin Finish, Rich Color, Typical Mt. Washington Form W/Applied Handle & Ribbon Candy Ruffled Rim, ¼" Check In Rim, 5¼" H. $140.00
BURMESE VASE, Simple Conical Shape W/Flaring Ribbon Candy Ruffled Rim, 4¼" H............................$225.00

◄ *To the left*

TUMBLERS
(ROW I, L to R)
POMONA, Second Grind W/Blue Cornflower $40.00
CLEAR GLASS, "Triple Daisy" Patt. W/Ruby Flash Key Design In Rim $10.00
CLEAR, W/Mary Gregory-Type Decor. Of Boy Holding Flower, Slight Rim Roughage
.................................$12.00
SWIRLED, W/Reverse-Swirl Patt. In Pastel Shaded Multi-Coloring $20.00
(ROW II, L to R)
AMBER FLASHED BOHEMIAN, W/Two Pictorial Panels & One Plain, Slight Nick In Rim $10.00
BOHEMIAN-TYPE HEAVY PANELED, Clear W/Amber Panels Etched W/Vintage Design $30.00
OVERSHOT RUBENA LEMONADE GLASS, Cranberry To Clear $60.00
AMBER PRESSED GLASS, By Bryce Bros., Pittsburgh, "Wheat & Barley" Patt., Originally Issued As "Duquesne" Patt. ....
.................................$17.00

(ROW III, L to R)
"ESTHER" PATTERN, Clear W/Silver Stain (Amber) Band, One Chip In Foot ...
.................................$5.00
GERMAN, Amber W/Applied Strawberries & Well-Painted Armorial Decor., Tiny Annealing Check In Bottom $15.00
FRENCH OVERLAY, Ruby To Clear W/Gold Rim.......................$25.00
OPAQUE WHITE SATIN-FINISH, Possibly Mt. Washington, About Perfect $25.00
(ROW IV, L to R)
OVERLAY, Attributed To Carlsbad, Green Cut To Clear W/Elaborate Designs Of Deers & Trees, Both Cameo & Intaglio Cutting.........................$60.00
ETCHED, Gold Decor., Signed On Bottom "G Cet Co/5th Ave/New York Verreries de Nancy/France $30.00
MOSER-TYPE, Amethyst To Clear, Panel Cut $25.00
PINK SATIN-FINISH, Cased & W/Diamond Quilting...................$45.00

(A-MA '78) *Richard A. Bourne Co., Inc.*

To the right ▶

(L to R)
CIRCULAR LATTICINIO TRAY, Blue & White In A Sunburst From The Center. 11⅛" Diam. $75.00
BLOWN GLASS WHIMSY, Nailsea. In The Form Of A Pipe, Cranberry, Opaque White & Clear Loopings. Approx. 14½" L. $120.00

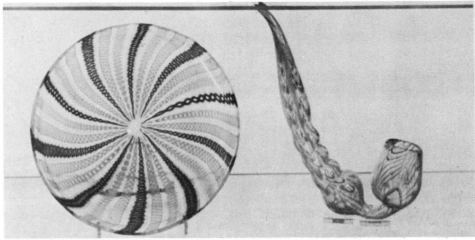

(A-MA '78)   *Richard A. Bourne Co., Inc.*

(A-MA '78)   *Richard A. Bourne Co., Inc.*
(ROW I, L to R)
AUSTRIAN LOETZ-TYPE ART GLASS VASE, Iridescent Deep Red W/Blue Leaf-Like Swirled Sides. Sides Pinched In Three Areas. Flat Top Pinched In Three Areas To Correspond To Pinching Of The Body 10¾" H. $70.00
FRENCH CAMEO GLASS VASE, Has Rough-Cut Colorless Glass Ground, Large White & Purple Iris W/Dragonfly Above The White Iris. Leaves Are Cameo Glass; Flower Blossoms, Buds, Dragonflys Are Painted In Heavy Enamel, 10⅜" H. $200.00
AUSTRIAN ART GLASS VASE, Interesting Coloring W/Pink & Opaque Feather-Like Designs On Clear Green Ground, 16" H. $60.00
(ROW II, L to R)
FRENCH ART GLASS VASE, Signed "Schneider" On Top Of Foot & "France" In Pontil. Cluthra-Like Glass In Rich Reds W/Black Circular Foot & Black Applied Handles, 11¾" H. $150.00
BELGIAN ART GLASS VASE, Mkd. "Made In Belgium". Satin Finish W/Pink, Yellow & Opaque Mottling, Black Foot. Decor. W/Flowers On Both Sides, 14⅝" H. $130.00
CONTINENTAL ART GLASS VASE, W/ Signature Which Appears To Be "Mado" On Upper Side Of Vase. Piece Made Of Heavy Glass, Satin Finish, Shading To Orange & Opaque Mottling At Top & Dark Brown At Bottom. Decor. W/Blue & Pink Berries & Foliage, 11⅞" H. $80.00

(A-MA '78)   *Richard A. Bourne Co., Inc.*
TUMBLERS
(ROW I, L to R)
VASA MURRHINA, Cape Cod Glass Co., Mid-Nineteenth C. $40.00
HEAVY ART GLASS, Probably Sandwich Or Cape Cod Glass Co., "Acanthus Leaf" Patt. W/Mottled Cranberry & White On Amber Ground, About Perfect $45.00
PRESSED RAINBOW GLASS, Predominantly Amber, Green & Cranberry In A Foliage Patt., About Perfect, Ground Rim Was Probably Accomplished At The Factory $10.00
RAINBOW-COLORED, Probably Boston & Sandwich Glass Co., "Frosted Ivy" Patt., Minor Chip On Inner Rim & Slight Roughage $15.00
(ROW II, L to R)
SWIRLED AMBERINA, Sandwich Or Mt. Washington, One Minute Rim Flake $50.00
VASA MURRHINA, Probably Cape Cod Glass Works, Sandwich, Mass., Tortoise

(continued next column)

◀ *To the left*   *(continued)*
Shell Mottled Coloring, Two Small Nicks In Rim $5.00
WESTERN POMONA, Decor. W/Flowers & Fern Leaves, Faintly Frosted Surface W/Faint Amber Band At Top, Very Minute Rim Roughage $25.00
POMONA, Rare, First Grind, Blue Cornflower, About Perfect $80.00
(ROW III, L to R)
BLUE & OPALESCENT, W/Random Opalescent Maze-Like Design, About Perfect $35.00
PELOTON, Heavy Clear & Aqua Enamel Decor. Of Flowers, About Perfect . .$70.00
CRANBERRY GLASS LEMONADE, Decor. W/Gold, White & Blue Decor., About Perfect $35.00
SATIN GLASS, Blue To White Diamond Quilted Mother-Of-Pearl Design, About Perfect, Few Minute Bubbles $90.00
(ROW IV, L to R)
CASED GLASS, Ivory White Exterior Decor. W/Flowers, Soft Pink Interior, Minute Inner Rim Chips $25.00
SWIRLED PINK, Similar To Pink Slag But With Heat-Developed Color, Roughage Around Entire Rim $25.00
PINK CASED OPAL GLASS, Nine Swirls, Color Similar To Pink Slag, Heat-Developed Color, Sm. Rim Chip & Light Roughage $20.00
RUBENA, Cranberry, Vertical Ribbing, Decor. Of House & Lge. Gold Flowers, About Perfect $40.00
(ROW V, L to R)
FRENCH DOUBLE CUT OVERLAY, White Cut To Clear W/Applied Paperweight Ring Around Rim, About Perfect . . $130.00
TRIPLE OVERLAY, Probably French, Lt. Blue To White To Clear, Double Panel & Star Cutting, Inner Rim W/Ground Area To Remove Roughage $70.00
DOUBLE CUT OVERLAY, Probably French, Cobalt Blue Cut To Clear, About Perfect $35.00
CUT OVERLAY, DURAND, Made By Emil Larson Between 1925 & 1932, W/Witnessed Document Of Facts, About Perfect $110.00

(A-MA '78)   Richard A. Bourne Co., Inc.
RUBY FLASH GLASS LAMP FILLER,
Unusual Form, Made Of Clear Glass W/
Areas Of Ruby Flash Applique & Gold,
Green & Blue Decor. W/Red Applied

(A-MA '78)   Richard A. Bourne Co., Inc.
COBALT BLUE LEAD CRYSTAL VASE,
Hexagonal Shape W/Vertical Panels, 8" H.
...............................$70.00

(A-MA '78)   Richard A. Bourne Co., Inc.
**LAVENDER CUT LITHYALIN GLASS
VASE** (Bohemian), Tip Of One Sawtooth
On Base Chipped, 6½" H. $200.00

(A-MA '78)   Richard A. Bourne Co., Inc.
AVENTURINE FLOWER BOWL, Pos-
sibly English, Rich Red Ground Color W/
Green Aventurine In Abstract Arrangement,
Decor. W/Large Sunflower, 3⅞" H. $60.00

(A-MA '78)   Richard A. Bourne Co., Inc.
COBALT BLUE FOOTED TUMBLER,
Inverted Bead-Like Drapery Patt., Hex-
agonal Foot, Minor Foot Roughage From
Mold..........................$50.00

(A-MA '78)   Richard A. Bourne Co., Inc.

(ROW I)
MILLEFIORI TOOTHPICK, With Slight-
ly Flaring And Scalloped Rim, 2" H. $80.00
SQUAT CRACKLE GLASS VASE,
Opaque Crackling Over Deep Cobalt Blue,
Similar To Durand, 2" H. $50.00
MILLEFIORI MINIATURE VASE, Ame-
thyst With White Canes, 3" H. $60.00
(ROW II)
SPANGLE GLASS VASE, Shot With
Gold Flecks, Melon Ribbed And Swirled
And Mottled Colors Of Deep And Pale Reds,
Greys And Greens, Slight Roughage Around
Top, 3½" H. $40.00
DECORATED OPAL GLASS VASE,
Attributed To Dudley, Stourbridge, England,
Overall Decoration In Elaborate Lace-Like
Designs Using Many Colors, 4¾" H. .....
...............................$40.00
ART GLASS MUG, W/Reeded Satin-Fin-
ish Colorless Applied Handle, Vivid Colors,
Strong Pattern, 3¼" H. $90.00

(ROW III)
IRIDESCENT GOLD OPEN SUGAR,
Maker Unknown, With Iridescent Colorless
Applied Handle And Circular Foot, 5" H.
...............................$90.00
**MILLEFIORI COVERED PITCHER OR
CHOCOLATE POT,** Brilliant And Colorful
Canes Well Set With Striped Handle To
Match, 7½" H. $125.00

(A-MA '78)   Richard A. Bourne Co., Inc.
(ROW I)
PINK SLAG GLASS SAUCE DISH, "In-
verted Fan And Feather" Pattern, With Four
Ball Feet $225.00
PINK SLAG GLASS SUGAR BOWL,
"Inverted Fan & Feather" Pattern, Minus
Cover........................$100.00
**MT. WASHINGTON SIGNED CROWN
MILANO VASE,** Stick Type, With Three
Applied Leaves At Base Of Neck, Overall
Decoration Of Flowers In Many Colors, One
Applied Leaf Repaired ....7⅞" H. $400.00
**JAR WITH PLATED SILVER MOUNT-
INGS,** By Smith Brothers, Signed, Soft
Satin Finish Tan Color Decorated With
Daisies $250.00
(ROW II)
**SATIN FINISH DECORATED MT.
WASHINGTON TYPE VASE,** Yellow-tan
Color At Top, Pink Around Bottom, Squat
Shaped, Decorated With Flowers In Brown,
White And Yellow, Ruffled Top, 5½" H.,
6" Diam. $90.00
**HOLLY AMBER SPOON HOLDER OR
MARMALADE JAR,** Tiny Nick On Foot
Ring $200.00
SIGNED "LUSTRE ART" VASE, Irides-
cent Leaves And Vines On Vivid Iridescent
White Ground, Iridescent Gold-Orange In-
terior, 7" H. $175.00
MERCURY GLASS CUP AND SAUCER,
Boston & Sandwich Glass Co., With Etched
Vines And Birds, Clear Applied Handle,
And Gold Mercury Interior $80.00

(ROW III)
MT. WASHINGTON TYPE JAR, With
Decoration Of Autumn Leaves And Berries,
Two Minute Nicks In Rim, 5½" H. ..$90.00
MT. WASHINGTON ROSE BOWL,
Large White Satin Finish With Decoration
Of Large Clovers, 6" Diam. $180.00
**VASA MURRHINA TYPE COVERED
BUTTER DISH,** White Cased Glass With
Abstract Meanderings Of Greyish-Brown
Shot With Silver Flecks Throughout, Two
Minor Nicks On Under Rim Of Base ......
...............................$75.00

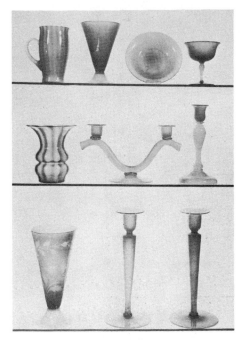

(A-MA '78)   Richard A. Bourne Co., Inc.

TUMBLERS

(ROW I, L to R)
OPALESCENT BLUE GLASS, "Inverted Fan & Feather" Patt. W/Gold Decor. $45.00
EMERALD GREEN GLASS, "Inverted Fan & Feather" Patt. W/Gold Decor. $45.00
BLUE BARREL-SHAPE, W/Gold Decor. Floral Panels $10.00
AMETHYST GLASS, "S-Repeat" Patt. W/Gold Decor. $25.00

(ROW II, L to R)
EMERALD GREEN GLASS, "Delaware" Patt. W/Gold Decor. $40.00
EMERALD GREEN GLASS, Signed, By Northwood, Gold Decor. $35.00
IRIDESCENT PALE AMETHYST GLASS, Swirled & W/Four Oval Rosetted Medallions, Upper Rim Roughage . . .$7.00
EMERALD GREEN GLASS, "Esther" Patt. W/Gold Decor. $25.00

(ROW III, L to R)
EMERALD GREEN GLASS, "Colorado" Patt. W/Gold Decor., Mkd. "Souvenir of York, Pa." $7.00
RUBY FLASH GLASS, Gold Decor. "Carnation" Patt. By New Martinsville Glass Co. $30.00
AMBERINA, "Hobnail" Patt. $120.00
AMBERINA, Signed, By Baccarat, Swirled Design, Worn On Inside & Has Small Chips On Foot Ring $50.00

(ROW IV, L to R)
TALL COBALT BLUE GLASS, Unidentified Patt. In Bull's Eye & Flute Design $20.00
COBALT BLUE GLASS, Signed, "Mirror" "Inverted Thumbprint" Patt., By Heisey $35.00
DEEP AMETHYST GLASS, "Croesus" Patt. W/Gold Decor. $60.00
MILK GLASS, Deeply-Molded Patt. Of Open Rose, Stems & Bud W/Drk. Brown Fired-On Finish, Typical Of That Found On Miniature Lamps $7.00

(A-MA '78)   Richard A. Bourne Co., Inc.
RUBENA VERDE GLASS
(ROW I, L to R)
SALT & PEPPER SHAKERS, Pr., "Inverted Thumbprint" Patt., Orig. Tops . . . . .
. . . .$100.00
TUMBLERS (3), "Hobnail" Patt., One W/Small Rim Nick, (1 Illus.) $125.00
SYRUP PITCHER, Opalescent Hobnails, Orig. Pewter Top & Applied Handle, Chip & Minute Roughage To Hobs On Lower Extremities Of The Piece $175.00
FINGER BOWL, "Hobnail" Patt., Ruffled Rim $70.00
(ROW II, L to R)
BLOWN MOLDED VASE, Strawberry In Pontil, Foot Has Small Nick On Tip, 6" H.
. . . .$85.00
BERRY BOWL, "Hobnail" Patt., Opalescent Hobnails & Square Ruffled Rim, 8" Sq. $80.00
CELERY VASE, "Inverted Thumbprint" Patt., Small Nick, 6¼" H. $50.00
(ROW III, L to R)
PITCHER, "Hobnail" Patt., Applied Handle, One Hob Mostly Chipped Off $120.00
PITCHER, "Thumbprint" Patt., Squared Top & Applied Handle $140.00

(A-MA '78)   Richard A. Bourne Co., Inc.

IRIDESCENT PINK AND GOLD FLUTED BOWL, New Martinsville Peachblow, 5" Diam. $40.00
OPALESCENT PANELED ROSE BOWL, English, Faint Iridescence Or Gold-Washed Interior, 4¼" Diam. $40.00
OPALESCENT VASELINE PANELED BLOWN GLASS BOWL, Probably Webb, With Eight Panels, Top Is Octagon Shape, 5" Diam. $60.00

(A-MA '78)   Richard A. Bourne Co., Inc.

(ROW I)
STEUBEN RIBBED LEMONADE, Jade-Green With Alabaster Handle, Unsigned . .
. . . .$40.00
JADE-GREEN STEUBEN CONICAL-SHAPED GOBLET WITH ALABASTER FOOT, Signed $80.00
STEUBEN JADE-GREEN SHERBET, With Alabaster Stem, Signed, Together With **JADE-GREEN UNDERTRAY.** . . . .
. . . .$90.00
(ROW II)
TRANSLUCENT JADE-GREEN PANELED VASE, Waisted Body, Unsigned, 6" H. $90.00
DOUBLE CANDLEHOLDER, Translucent Jade-Green Arm With Alabaster Foot And Sockets, Unsigned, 6¼" H., 11" I. $120.00
JADE-GREEN AND ALABASTER CANDLESTICK, Pale Jade-Green Socket And Foot With Alabaster Stem, Unsigned, 8½" H. $70.00
(ROW III)
SIGNED STEUBEN VASE, Trumpet Or Conical Form With Jade Body And Alabaster Foot, Cut And Etched Flowers Around Entire Vase, 10" H. $250.00
PAIR OF TALL JADE-GREEN CANDLESTICKS, Unsigned, 12" H. .$175.00

(D-CA '78)
NEW ENGLAND PEACHBLOW SOCK DARNER $200.00

(A-MA '77)   *Richard A. Bourne Co., Inc.*

ART GLASS & OTHER COLORED GLASS
(ROW I, L to R)
BARBER'S BOTTLE, Amethyst, White Enameled Forget-Me-Nots, 7¼" H. ......
.................................$40.00
BARBER'S BOTTLES (Pr), 1 Illus., Amber, White Enameled Forget-Me-Nots, Minor Chemical Deposit, 8" H. $35.00
COLOGNE BOTTLE, Cobalt Blue, White Enamel Mary Gregory Type Decor., 8⅞" H.
.................................$35.00
COLOGNE BOTTLE, Cranberry W/Opalescent Swirling & Lip, 8½" H. $90.00
(ROW II, L to R)
BLOWN GLASS HYACINTH VASES, (Pr), 1 Illus., Amethyst, 8" & 7¾" H. ....
.................................$25.00
BLOWN GLASS COLOGNE BOTTLES (Pr), 1 Illus., Deep Cobalt Blue, 10¾" & 11" H. $50.00
FLASH GLASS CELERY VASE, Ruby, Paneled, Boston & Sandwich Glass Co., Normal Wear To Flashing, 8⅝" H.$150.00
FLUID LAMP, Cobalt Blue, Princess Feather Pattern, 8" H. $125.00
(ROW III, L to R)
ART GLASS VASE, French 19th C., Blue & White Spiral Pattern W/Applied Handles, Foot W/Chip, 8½"H. $60.00
DOUBLE CUT OVERLAY DECANTER, French 19th C., White Cut To Clear W/Gold Decor., Applied Strap Handle, 13" O.H. $140.00
LATTICINIO VASE, Venetian Blue & White, 9½" H. $55.00

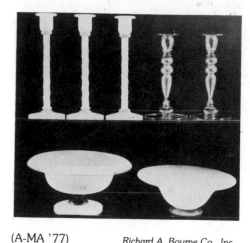

(A-MA '77)   *Richard A. Bourne Co., Inc.*
ART GLASS
(ROW I, L to R)
CANDLESTICKS, Pr., H.C. Fry Glass Co., Rochester, Pa., Ca. 1920, Opalescent W/Green Wafers & Green Spiral Threading, 12" H. $250.00
CANDLESTICK, H.C. Fry Glass Co., Ca. 1920, Opalescent W/Blue Wafers & Clear Spiral Threading, 12" H. $75.00
STEUBEN TOPAZ CANDLESTICKS, Pr., Applied Blue Rims, Unsigned, 9¾" H.
.................................$125.00
(ROW II, L to R)
FOVAL GLASS CENTERPIECE BOWL, H.C. Fry Glass Co., Ca. 1920, Opalescent Body, Turned-Down Rim Edged In Blue W/Purple-Blue Opaque Stem, 12½" Diam., 6½" H. $100.00
FOVAL GLASS CENTERPIECE BOWL, H.C. Fry Glass Co., Cal 1920, Opalescent Bowl W/Opaque Green Circular Foot, 11½" Diam., 4⅛" H. $85.00

(A-MA '77)   *Richard A. Bourne Co., Inc.*
ART GLASS
(ROW I, L to R)
TAZZAS, Pr., Cobalt Blue, Cut & Etched Grapes, Leaves & Vines, 8½" Diam., 7⅜" H. $100.00
PAIRPOINT COMPOTE, Amber, Paperweight Knop Stem W/Air Traps, 12¼" Diam., 7⅜" H. $75.00
URN, Pairpoint Glass Works, Amber, Clear Paperweight Knop Stem W/Air Traps, 6⅛" Diam., 12" H. $90.00
(ROW II)
CENTERPIECE SET, Cobalt Blue, 3-Pc., Cut & Etched Grapes, Leaves & Vines, Candlestick Repaired & Foot Chipped, Bowl: 12" Diam., 5¼" H.; Candlesticks: 8⅛" H. $150.00

(A-MA '77)   *Richard A. Bourne Co., Inc.*
ART GLASS
(ROW I, L to R)
CHRISTMAS SALT, Cobalt Blue, Orig. Dated Pewter Shaker, Minus Breaker .....
.................................$40.00
MINIATURE AMBERINA MUG, Inverted Thumbprint, Cranberry Shading To Amber
.................................$70.00
AMBERINA WHISKEY GLASS, "Baby Diamond-Quilted", Deep Fuchsia At Top, 2½" H. $150.00
AMBERINA CABINET VASE, Deep Fuchsia At Top, Amber Rigaree Around Neck, 3⅜" H. $150.00
(ROW II, L to R)
CRANBERRY GLASS CREAMER, Gold & Enameled Decor., 3½" H. $100.00
PAIRPOINT BURMESE SUGAR & CREAMER, Ca. 1950, Yellow Applied Handles, 1 W/Orig. Label.......$170.00
(ROW III, L to R)
SANDWICH AMBERINA TUMBLER, Inverted Thumbprint $50.00
LIBBY AMBERINA JACK-IN-THE-PULPIT VASE, Decor. W/Forget-Me-Nots & Gold "World's Fair/1893", 7⅝" H. .....
.................................$475.00
AMBERINA TRUMPET VASE, Deep Coloring, Vertical Paneling, 7" H. $300.00

(A-VA '78)   *Laws*
GEORGE III STERLING CASTOR SET, By Peter & Ann Bateman, 8 Silver Topped Glass Bottles & Engraved Footed Tray ....
.................................$500.00

◀ *To the left*

(A-MA '77   *Richard A. Bourne Co., Inc.*
INKWELLS
(ROW I, L to R)
PITKIN-TYPE, Olive-Green, 36-Rib, Swirled, Rim Chip, 1-5/16" H., 2⅜" Sq. . . .
. . . .$425.00
BLOWN THREE MOLD, Olive-Green, Minor Bruise & Wear, 2-3/16" Diam., 1½" H. $40.00
BLOWN THREE MOLD, Olive-Green, Edge Chips, 2⅜" Diam., 1⅝" H. . .$45.00
BLOWN THREE MOLD, Olive-Green, 2¼" Diam., 1½" H. $65.00
(ROW II, L to R)
BLOWN THREE MOLD, Olive-Green, 2⅜" Diam., 1⅞" H. $90.00
BLOWN THREE MOLD, Olive-Amber, 2⅝" Diam., 1¾" H. $90.00
BLOWN THREE MOLD, Olive-Green, 2⅜" Diam., 1-9/16" H. $80.00
(ROW III, L to R)
BLOWN THREE MOLD, Olive-Green, Minor Base Wear, 2¼" Diam., 1-13/16" H.
. . . .$85.00
BLOWN THREE MOLD, Olive-Green, Collar Chip, Minor Base Wear, 2⅜" Diam., 1⅝" H. $50.00
BLOWN THREE MOLD, Olive-Green, Base Bruise, 2¼" Diam., 1-9/16" H. . . . . .
. . . .$20.00
(ROW IV, L to R)
BLOWN THREE MOLD, Olive-Green, Collar Nick, 2¾" Diam., 1¾" H. . .$70.00
BLOWN THREE MOLD, Olive-Green, 2-11/16" Diam., 1¾" H. $95.00
BLOWN THREE MOLD, Olive-Green, 2-11/16" Diam., 2" H. $80.00

◀ *To the left*

(D-NY '78)   *Lee Vines Antiques*
WEBB CAMEO CUT FIGURAL SCENT BOTTLE, Blue To White W/Silver Tail, 6" L. $1850.00

(D-AL '78)
CUT GLASS CARAFE, Water, Pinwheels W/Notched Prisms On Neck, 8" H. . . . . . .
. . . .$190.00

(D-NY '78)   *Lee Vines Antiques*
WEBB CAMEO CUT SNUFF BOTTLE, Cut To Simulate Peking Glass, By Kionel Price For Daughter, "Dear May" Cut Into Bottle $4000.00

(D-NY '78)   *Lee Vines Antiques*
MOTHER OF PEARL SNUFF BOTTLE, W/Adventurine Stopper, Flat On One Side, Convex On Reverse, Drk. Spot On Flat Side is Paint, 2½" H. $200.00

(A-MA '77)   *Richard A. Bourne Co., Inc.*

(ROW I, L to R)
CANDLESTICKS, Pr., Opalescent Blue
Petticoat Dolphin, Bakewell, Pears & Co.,
Pittsburgh, Ca. 1870's, 1 W/Minor Base
Roughage, 6½" H. $300.00
CANDLESTICK, Opalescent Vaseline
Petticoat Dolphin, Bakewell, Pears & Co.,
Pittsburgh, Ca. 1870's, 6½" H. $75.00
CANDLESTICK, Opalescent & Clear
Petticoat Dolphin, Bakewell, Pears & Co.,
Pittsburgh, Ca. 1870's, 6⅝" H. $75.00
ROW II, L to R)
CANDLESTICKS, Pr. Black Amethyst
Glass Socket & Foot Decor. W/Sterling
Silver Overlay, Paperweight-Type Knop
Stem, 4" H. $90.00
CANDLESTICK, Amethyst, Pairpoint
Glass Co., New Bedford, Ca. 1920's, High-
Drip Catch, Foot W/Copper-Wheel Engrav-
ing Of Grapes, Vines & Other Designs,
Paperweight Knop Stem, 11¾" H. .$60.00
CANDLESTICK, H.P. Sinclaire & Co.,
Corning, N.Y., Ca. 1910-1920, Amber,
Engraved Design Of Compotes Filled W/
Fruit, 12" H. $50.00
(ROW III)
BLOWN CANDLESTICKS, Pr., Central
Glass Co., Wheeling, W. Va., Amethyst
Paneled Bases W/Opaque White Lips,
15" H. $375.00

To the right ▶
**FRY FOVAL HANDLED LEMONADE &
UNDERTRAY,** Opalescent W/Soft Powder
Blue Applied Handle $80.00

(A-MA '78)   *Richard A. Bourne Co., Inc.*

(See photo above) ▲
(ROW I)
MT. WASHINGTON-TYPE BOWL W/8
Swirled Panels, Peachblow Shading W/
Painted Yellow Flowers & Green Leaves,
Ruffled Top, 2½" H. $55.00
NEW ENGLAND PEACHBLOW VASE,
Supported By 5 Feet (Minute Roughage),
4¼" H. $100.00
BURMESE VASE, Glossy Surface, White
Beaded Decor. Around Top, Three Swal-
lows In Flight Painted On Side, 4⅝" H.
...............................$60.00
FINDLAY ONYX GLASS MUFFINEER
W/Orig. Brass Screw Top, 5½" H. $160.00
(ROW II)
AGATA TOOTHPICK HOLDER, Un-
usual Deep Color, In-Turned Ruffled Top,
2⅜" H. $90.00
AGATA TUMBLER W/Good Mottling ...
...............................$80.00
CONDIMENT SET, Plated Silver Holder
By James W. Tufts, Boston. Pink Cased
Glass Decor. Shakers. Frame Includes Nap-
kin Ring & Shelf Below $200.00

(A-MA '78)   *Richard A. Bourne Co., Inc.*

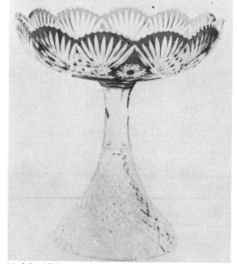

(A-MA '78)   *Richard A. Bourne Co., Inc.*
DOUBLE CUT OVERLAY COMPOTE,
Minute Roughage On Side, 10" H. $400.00

(A-MA '78)   *Richard A. Bourne Co., Inc.*
JACK-IN-THE-PULPIT VASE "Diamond
Quilted" Patt. W/Rainbow-Colored Mot-
tling & Opalescence Around Rim, 5⅝" H.
...............................$50.00

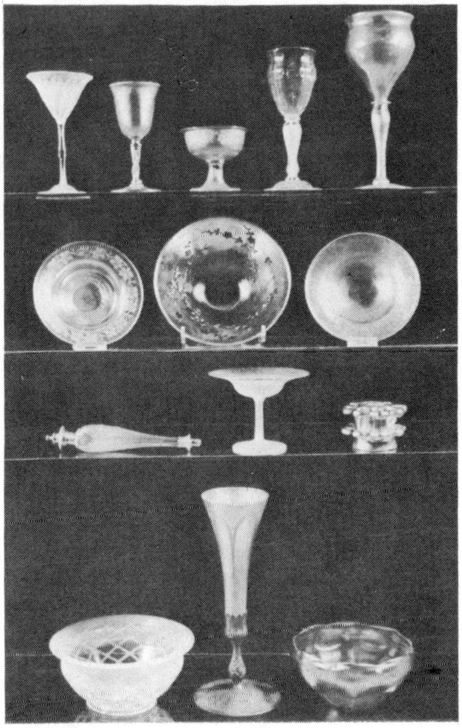

(A-MA '77) *Richard A. Bourne Co., Inc.*

TIFFANY GLASS

(ROW I, L to R)

WINE GLASS, Opalescent Amethyst W/ Clear Stem & Opalescent Foot, Signed "L.C. Tiffany Favrile", 6⅜" H. . . .$300.00

WINE GOBLET, Iridescent Bronze Bowl, Iridescent Blue Twist Stem & Iridescent Bluish-Gold Foot, Signed "L.C.T. Favrile 1241", 5⅞" H. $200.00

SHERBET, Iridescent Gold W/Engraved Band Of Grapes & Vines, Signed "L.C.T. Favrile", 3¾" Diam., 3⅜" H. $200.00

WINE GOBLET, Yellow-Green W/Paneled Foot & Bowl W/Frosted Air Trap In Stem, Unsigned, Orig. White Label, 7⅝" H. $100.00

CHALICE, Iridescent Gold, Signed "L.C.T. Favrile 1267", 9¼" H. $225.00

(ROW II, L to R)

CANDY DISH, Footed, Iridescent Gold W/Engraved Band Of Grape Vines & Leaves, Signed "L.C. Tiffany Favrile M", 6" Diam., 2" H. $300.00

BOWL, Iridescent Blue W/Incised Dogwood Blossoms & Branches, Signed "L.C.T. Favrile 1990", 7⅝" Diam., 3⅞" H. $550.00

CANDY DISH, Footed, Iridescent Gold, Signed "L.C.T. Tiffany, Inc. Favrile M", 6¼" Diam., 2" H. $175.00

(ROW III, L to R)

SCENT BOTTLE, Silver Mounted W/Frosted & Iridescent Glass Body W/Amber & Black Inset Glass Decor., Signed "Tiffany & Co., Sterling 1752", 8¾" O.L. .$350.00

TAZZA, Pastel Glass W/Iridescent Blue Rim, Opalescent Bowl, Stem & Foot W/ Feather-Like Patt., Signed "L.C.T. Favrile 1701", 5⅝" Diam., 4½" H. $350.00

FLOWER HOLDER, Iridescent Gold Stand W/Double Flower Holders, Signed "L.C.T. Favrile 6", Minor Nicks, 3⅝" Diam.,

(continued top of next column)

◀ *To the left* *(continued)*

2⅜" H. $100.00

(ROW IV, L to R)

PASTEL BOWL, Greenish Aqua Rim W/ Opalescent Diamond Quilting On Clear Glass, Signed "L.C. Tiffany-Favrile 1896", 8¼" Diam., 3¾" H. $375.00

VASE, Iridescent Gold, Feather Design Outlined In Iridescent Green, Signed "L.C.T." & "Tiffany Studios New York 1048", 11¾" H. $400.00

BOWL, Iridescent Gold W/8-Panel Sides, Signed "L.C.T. Favrile", Minor Wear, 7" Diam., 3¼" H. $175.00

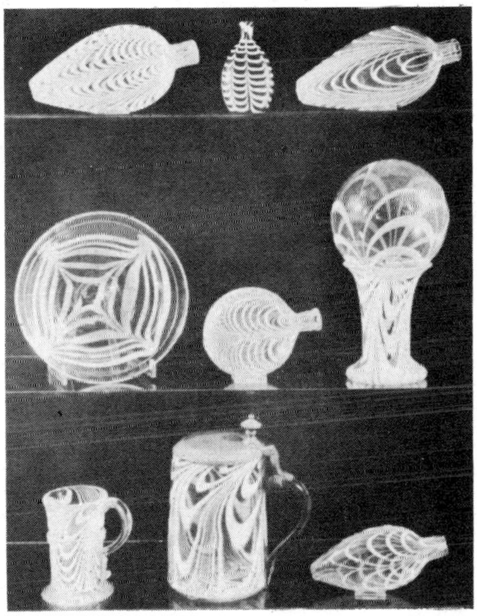

(A-MA '77) *Richard A. Bourne Co., Inc.*

LOOP DECORATED GLASS

(ROW I, L to R)

FLASK, South Jersey, Clear W/Opaque White Loopings, Bottom Chip, 8½" L. $30.00

POCKET FLASK, Golden-Amber, White Loopings, 4⅜" H. $120.00

FLASK, South Jersey, Clear W/Opaque White Loopings, Minor Chemical Deposit, 8¼" L. $40.00

(ROW II, L to R)

BOWL, South Jersey, Clear W/4 Swags Opalescent White Loopings, Folded Rim, Pontil Mark, 8¾" Diam., 3¾" H. . .$50.00

BLOWN FLASK, South Jersey, Clear W/ 5 Swags White White Loopings, Few Open Pits, 6½" L. $50.00

WITCH BALL & STAND, South Jersey, Clear W/Opaque White Loopings, Ball Diam.: 6"; Vase: 6" H., 11" O.H. $110.00

(ROW III, L to R)

BLOWN GLASS PRESENTATION MUG, Clear Leaded Glass W/Opaque White Loopings, Body & Handle Check, 3¼" Diam., 5½" H. $40.00

BLOWN GLASS STEIN, Clear Glass Body W/Opaque White Swirled Loopings, Pewter Hinged Lid, Mug Ht: 7¾"; Base Diam.: 5½"; 9½" O.H. $80.00

FLASK, South Jersey, Clear W/4 Swags White Loopings, Minor Roughage, 7¼" L. $50.00

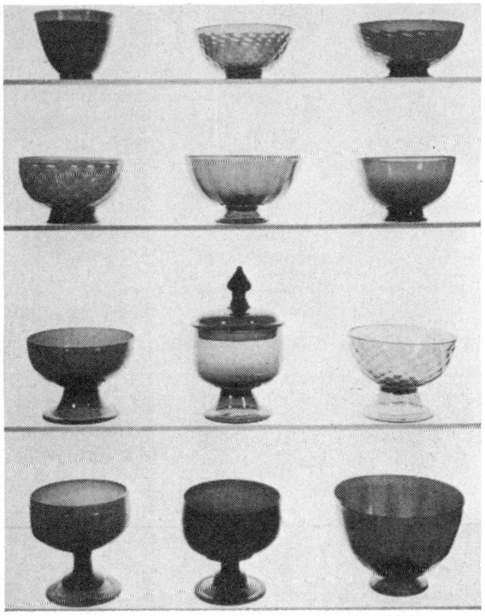

(A-MA '77) *Richard A. Bourne Co., Inc.*

EARLY COLORED GLASS BOWLS

(ROW I, L to R)

BAPTISMAL, Blown, Red-Amber, Applied Milk-White Threading Around Rim, 3½" Diam., 2¾" H. $125.00

BAPTISMAL, Cobalt-Blue, 20-Diamond Design, 4¼" Diam., 2¼" H. $200.00

BAPTISMAL, Cobalt-Blue, Pattern Molded W/22-Diamond Design, 4¾" Diam., 2½" H. $350.00

(ROW II, L to R)

BAPTISMAL BOWL, Cobalt Blue, Pattern Molded In 17-Diamond Design, 4½" Diam., 2¾" H. $100.00

BAPTISMAL BOWL, Cobalt Blue, Pattern Molded W/16 Vertical Ribs, 5" Diam., 2⅞" H. $200.00

BAPTISMAL BOWL, Cobalt Blue, 4¼" Diam., 2¾" H. $125.00

(ROW III, L to R)

BAPTISMAL BOWL, Blown Glass, Cobalt Blue, 4¾" Diam., 3½" H. $200.00

SUGAR BOWL, Blown Glass, Cobalt Blue, 3⅞" Diam., 6⅝" O.H. $450.00

BAPTISMAL BOWL, Blown Glass, Sapphire Blue, Pattern Molded In 16-Diamond Design, 4⅝" Diam., 3½" H. $500.00

(ROW IV, L to R)

BAPTISMAL BOWL, Blown Glass, Cobalt Blue, 4¼" Diam., 4½" H. $125.00

BAPTISMAL BOWL, Blown Glass, Amethyst, 4½" Diam., 4½" H. $125.00

FOOTED BOWL, Blown Glass, Cobalt Blue, Pattern Molded in 12-Panel Design, 5¾" Diam., 4¼" H. $200.00

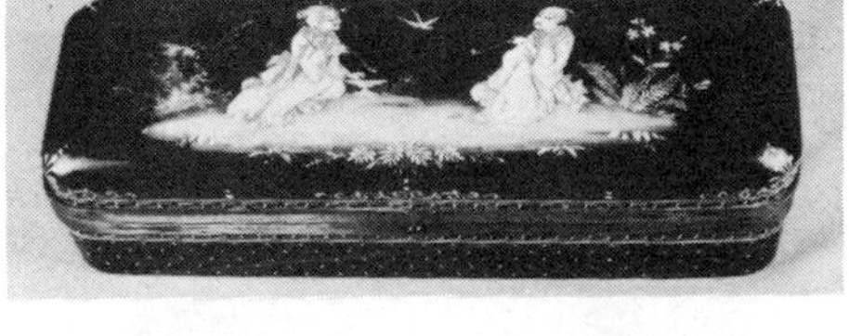

(D-NY '78) *Lee Vines Antiques*

COBALT BLUE GLOVE BOX, Hinged, Enameled & Detailed Oriental Couple Sitting In Garden, Silver Rims, Base Dot Decorated, 11¾" L., 3⅞" W., 3⅜" H. $325.00

(A-OH '77)   *Garth's Auctions, Inc.*
(ROW I, L to R)
CLEAR FLINT SALT, "Loop", 2½" H. .
. . . .$5.00
CLEAR LACY DISH, "Butterfly Variant",
Edge Chips, 8" L. $20.00
CLEAR LACY HONEY DISH, "Roman
Rosette", 4" Diam. $10.00
CLEAR FLINT SALT, "Loop", 2¾" H. .
. . . .$6.00
(ROW II, L to R)
CLEAR LACY BOWLS, Pr., "Peacock
Eye", Rayed Center, 6" Diam. $20.00
CLEAR BLOWN WINES, (1 of 6), Applied
Foot, 4¼" H. $78.00
CLEAR PRESSED LAMP, Applied Han-
dle & Brass Ring, 2¼" H. $20.00
CLEAR BLOWN TUMBLER, "Steigle
Type Copper Wheel Engraving Of Tulip &
Other Flowers, 3" H. $37.50
(ROW III, L to R)
CLEAR LACY PLATE, "Roman Rosette",
7½" Diam. $22.50
CLEAR LACY BOWL, "Oak Leaf", 8¼"
Diam. $32.50
CLEAR LACY BOWLS (1 of Pr), "Star
Medallion", Edge Chips, 6¼" Diam.
. . . .$30.00

(A-MA '77)   *Richard A. Bourne Co., Inc.*
TIFFANY GLASS
(ROW I, L to R)
CANDLESTICKS, Pr., Lt. Green, Paneled
Foot, 1 Signed "L.C.T. Favrile 8"; 1 Signed
"L.C.T.", 7¾" H. $550.00
DECANTER, Iridescent Pale Gold, Pinched
Sides, 1 Pt. Size, Signed "L.C.T. R7946",
9⅛" H. $450.00
COMPOTE, Iridescent Gold, Signed
"L.C.T. Favrile", White & Green & Gold
Labels, 6" Diam., 6" H. $225.00
(ROW II, L to R)
VASE, Iridescent Bronze, Gold & Blue,
W/Zig-Zag Green & Bronze Shoulder Decor.,
Signed "L.C. Tiffany Favrile 2711M", 8⅜"
H. $2100.00
JACK-IN-THE-PULPIT VASE, Iride-
scent Gold, Signed "L.C.T. Y9178", 13¾"
H. $1000.00
VASE, Iridescent Gold, Bluish Iridescent
Foot, Signed "L.C. Tiffany - Favrile 1730",
9⅞" H. $200.00
TRUMPET VASE, Blue & Opalescent
Pastel, Signed "L.C. Tiffany-Favrille 1885",
Orig. Green & Gold Label, 10½" H. . . . . .
. . . .$900.00

(A-MA '77)   *Richard A. Bourne Co., Inc.*
TIFFANY GLASS
(ROW I, L to R)
SALT, Iridescent Gold, Cauldron Form,
Signed "L.C.T.", 2⅛" Diam., 1¼" H. . . . .
. . . .$120.00
PANELED BOWL, Iridescent Gold, Signed
"L.C.T. Favrile", 3" Diam., 1½" H. . . . . . .
. . . .$120.00
MASTER SALT, Iridescent Gold, Ribbon
Edge, Signed "L.C.T.", 2⅝" Diam., 1" H.
. . . .$110.00
SALT, Iridescent Gold, Ribbon Edge,
Signed "L.C.T.", 2½" Diam., 1" H. . . . . .
. . . .$100.00
(ROW II, L to R)
CABINET VASE, Iridescent Gold Amber,
Paneled Neck, Signed "L.C.T. K731",
Orig. Label, 2¾" H. $350.00
CABINET VASE, Iridescent Bluish Gold
Amber, Applied Flowers & Stems In Deep
Relief, Signed "L.C.T.-8568", Orig. Label,
2⅝" H. $600.00
CABINET VASE, Opalescent Amber,
Marble-Like Swirling, Signed "X1792", Orig.
Label, 2⅞" H. $350.00
CABINET VASE, Iridescent Gold W/Iri-
descent Lavender Scroll Work, Signed
"L.C.T. B1115", Orig. Label, 3" H. . . . . . .
. . . .$400.00
(ROW III, L to R)
FINGER BOWL, Iridescent Gold, 12 Pan-
els W/Band Of 24 Double Honeycomb Cuts,
Signed "L.C.T. Favrile", 4-3/16" Diam.,
2⅜" H. $175.00
ART GLASS BOWL, Iridescent Gold, 4
Kettle-Like Feet, 8 Panels, Signed "L.C.T.",
Orig. Label, Minor Nick, 4⅜" Diam., 2¾" H.
. . . .$200.00
ART GLASS VASE, Iridescent Gold, Ab-
stract Pinched Style, Signed "L.C.T. H343",
4⅛" H. $275.00
(ROW IV, L to R)
ART GLASS SAUCE DISH, Iridescent
Blue, 10 Paneled Side, Signed "17.54 L.C.T.
Favrile", Orig. Green & Gold Label, 4⅞"
Diam., 1¼" H. $275.00
ART GLASS CANDY DISH, Iridescent
Gold, Flower Form, Signed "L.C.T. Y4933",
5½" Diam., 4⅛" H. $275.00
ART GLASS CANDY DISH, Iridescent
Gold, Flower Form, Signed "L.C.T. Y4932",
5⅝" Diam., 4" H. $325.00

(A-MA '77)   *Richard A. Bourne Co., Inc.*

◀ *To the left*

FRENCH LACY GLASS
(ROW I, L to R)
SALT, Clear, Wire Twist Handle .$130.00
CANDLESTICK, Clear, By Baccarat,
Minor Roughage, 6½" H. $15.00
PLATE, Clear, By Baccarat, Minor Chip,
7⅝" Diam. $25.00
BOWL, Clear, Frosted Stippled Band W/
Raised Garland Of Flowers & Tassels, Cover
W/Acanthus Leaf Design $140.00
(ROW II, L to R)
CUP & SAUCER, Amber, By Baccarat,
Chipped $80.00
RELISH DISH, Clear, Rim Roughage &
1" Check In Foot, 9⅛" L., 3¼" H. $45.00
(ROW III, L to R)
PLATE, Amber, Band Of Roses W/Sun-
burst, Minor Nick, 7¾" Diam. $40.00
PLATE, Cobalt Blue, Minor Roughage,
8¾" Diam. $90.00

PRESSED GLASS

(ROW I, L to R)

SUGAR BOWL, Hobnail W/Thumbprint Base, Lt. Blue $45.00

SUGAR BOWL, Forget-Me-Not, Pink Satin Finish W/Frosted Knob, Cased, Quilted $90.00

SUGAR BOWL, Pale Vaseline, Swirled, Opalescent Knob, 2" Heat Check . .$60.00

SUGAR BOWL, "Delaware," Gold Decor., Emerald Green, Lid Chipped & Reglued $30.00

(ROW II, L to R)

SUGAR BOWL, "Colorado or Lacy Medallion," Gold Decor., Emerald Green . .$50.00

SUGAR BOWL, "Tulip," Gold Decor., Light Green $40.00

SUGAR BOWL, Heart & Foliage Designs W/Gold Decor., Paneled, Cobalt Blue $70.00

CASED GLASS PICKLE JAR, Spangle Glass, Artwork Handle, Minor Roughage $20.00

(ROW III, L to R)

SUGAR BOWL, Pointed Panel Daisy & Button, Ca. 1894, Lt. Blue $50.00

SUGAR BOWL, "Inverted Thumbprint," Vaseline $25.00

SUGAR BOWL, "Inverted Thumbprint," Amber $40.00

SUGAR BOWL, "Daisy & Button V-Ornament, Vaseline, Sm. Chips & Lt. Roughage $60.00

(ROW IV, L to R)

PICKLE JAR, Inverted Thumbprint, Cranberry W/Clear Applied Artwork Knob, Minor Roughage $55.00

SUGAR BOWL, "Wildflower," Amber $40.00

PICKLE JAR, Inverted Thumbprint, Yellow-Green, Clear Applied Knob, Rim Chips. $40.00

RUBY FLASH GLASS SUGAR BOWL, "Henrietta," Rim Nick $50.00

CLEAR PRESSED GLASS

(ROW I, L to R)

WINE GLASSES (1 of 8), "Primrose" $90.00

WINE GLASSES (1 of 5), "Ashburton", Flint $120.00

BAR TUMBLERS (1 of Pr.), "Diagonal Band", Flint $60.00

WHISKEY TUMBLER, "Brilliant", Flint $30.00

(ROW II, L to R)

CRUET, Similar To "Palmette", Orig. Stopper $20.00

SPILLS, 2, "Harp", Flint, Both W/Minor Roughage $25.00

GOBLETS (1 of 2), "Diamond Point", Flint $80.00

(ROW III, L to R)

WATERFORD-TYPE PITCHER, Possibly Pittsburgh $40.00

COMPOTE, "Loop", Boston & Sandwich Glass Co., Foot Chipped, Flint, 7½" Diam., 6" H. $60.00

(ROW IV, L to R)

SWEETMEAT, "Loop", Boston & Sandwich Glass Co., Minor Roughage .$110.00

CELERY VASE, "Loop", Boston & Sandwich Glass Co., Flint, Minor Roughage $45.00

PRESSED GLASS

(L to R)

SUGAR BOWL, "Thousand Eye," Opalescent $60.00

SUGAR BOWL, "Thousand Eye," Amber $45.00

SUGAR BOWL, Diamond Quilted, Vaseline $35.00

BOHEMIAN SUGAR BOWL, Cut Designs & Ruby Flash Decor. $140.00

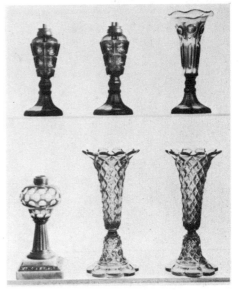

(ROW I, L to R)

AMETHYST WHALE OIL LAMPS, "Three-Printie" Patt., Boston & Sandwich Glass Co., Orig. Pewter Collars & Double Drop Whale Oil Burners, Minor Foot Chip, 8¼" H. $1300.00

AMETHYST VASE, "Ellipse & Bullseye" Patt., Boston & Sandwich Glass Co., 9½" H. $400.00

(ROW II, L to R)

FLUID LAMP, Boston & Sandwich Glass Co., Double-Cut Overlay Font In Amethyst Cut To Clear, Marble Base, Brass Molding, Orig. Brass Collar, 9¼" H. $550.00

RED-AMBER VASES, Pr., "Diamond Patt.", Minor Chip & Nick On One, 12" H. $325.00

(ROW I, L to R)

CUT GLASS BOWL $85.00

CUT GLASS JAR, Amber Cut To Clear $200.00

CUT GLASS BOWL $85.00

(ROW II, L to R)

CUT GLASS DISH $175.00

CUT GLASS CELERY VASE $65.00

CUT GLASS BOWL, Signed "Libbey" $120.00

"CABLE" PATTERN, FLINT GLASS
(ROW I, L to R)
EGG CUP, Clear, Roughage On Cover ..
...............................$140.00
EGG CUPS, (14), Clear, One W/Chipped
Foot $325.00
HANDLED WHISKEY, Clear, Cracks
Under Handle $17.00
FOOTED SALT, Clear $35.00
CHAMPAGNES, (Set-6), Clear .$1250.00
LADIES' GOBLETS, (Set-4), Clear .....
..............................$210.00

(ROW II, L to R)
INDIVIDUAL SALTS, (Set-9), Four W/
Rim Roughage $30.00
HONEY DISHES, (Set-13), Clear ....
..............................$80.00
SAUCE DISHES, (14), 9 "Cable", 5 "Ca-
ble & Fan", Few W/Chips $40.00
PLATES, (Set-8), Clear, 6¼" Diam. ..
..............................$250.00
OPALESCENT BLOWN BOBECHE, Ap-
plied Molded "Cable" Rim $50.00

(ROW III, L to R)
BUTTER DISH, Clear, Sm. Bruise On
Finial, Chipped Base $30.00
TUMBLERS, (2), Clear $210.00
SYRUP PITCHER, Hinged Pewter Top,
Clear, 1½" Crack On Handle $55.00
SPOONHOLDER, Clear, "Cable & Fan"
..............................$30.00

(ROW IV, L to R)
PINT DECANTER, Clear, Orig. Stopper
..............................$210.00
QUART DECANTER, Clear, Pewter Bar
Stopper W/Vasa Murrhina Marble, Dent In
Stopper, Minor Flaking $140.00
QUART DECANTER, Clear, Bar Lip &
Pewter Bar Stopper W/Blue & Opalescent
Swirled Sandwich Marble $100.00
QUART DECANTER, Clear, "Cable"
Stopper $120.00

(ROW I, L to R)
CLEAR FLINT COLOGNES, Pr., Star &
Punty W/Matching Stoppers, 1 W/Bruise,
4¾" H. $125.00
CLEAR FLINT WINE, Ashburton Variant,
3½" H. $7.50
CLEAR FLINT WINE, Excelsior Variant,
3¾" H. $17.50
CLEAR FLINT WINE, Tulip & Sawtooth,
3¾" H. $20.00
CLEAR FLINT WINE, Ribbed Bellflower,
Base Flake, 4" H. $11.00
(ROW II, L to R)
CLEAR PETTICOAT LAMP, Sandwich
Moon & Star, Brass Collar, Handle Flakes,
3½" H. $50.00
CLEAR FLINT WINE, Honeycomb, 3½"
H. $10.00
CLEAR FLINT FOOTED BOWL, Sand-
wich Moon & Star, 4½" Diam., 3½" H. ..
..............................$55.00
CLEAR FLINT WINE, Horn Of Plenty,
3⅞" H. $30.00
CLEAR PETTICOAT LAMP, Coin Spot
W/Applied Handle & Brass Collar, 4" H. ...
..............................$55.00

(ROW III, L to R)
CLEAR FLINT COLOGNES, Pr., Sand-
wich Moon & Star, Stoppers Vary, 9½" H.
..............................$90.00
CLEAR FLINT SPILL HOLDER, Sand-
wich Moon & Star, Minor Interior Base Wear,
4⅜" H. $37.50
CLEAR FLINT COMPOTE, Almond
Thumbprint, 8" H. $45.00
CLEAR FLINT CREAMER, Sandwich
Moon & Star, Applied Handle $65.00

(L to R)
PRESSED GLASS GOBLETS, (2), Mag-
net & Grape Patt., Flint $80.00
PRESSED GLASS COMPOTE, Plume
Patt., Clear, 7½" Diam., 4½" H. .$100.00
PRESSED GLASS WHALE OIL LAMP,
Star & Punty Patt., Clear, 10½" H. .....
..............................$100.00

CLEAR BLOWN GLASS
(ROW I, L to R)
WHISKEY GLASS, Stiegel-Type, Etched
Band Of Leaves, 2⅞" H. $35.00
WHISKEY GLASS, Stiegel-Type, Etched
Drapery & Leaf Band, 3" H. $25.00
FLIP GLASS, Stiegel-Type, Engraved,
3⅜" H. $35.00
TUMBLER, Paneled, Octagonal, Engraved
Band, 4" H. $35.00
(ROW II, L to R)
PINT MUG, Stiegel-Type, Strap Handle,
Engraved Basket Of Flowers, 4⅞" H. .....
..............................$100.00
PINT MUG, Stiegel-Type, Strap Handle,
Engraved Sunflower, 4⅜" H. $80.00
PINT MUG, Stiegel-Type, Bulbous, En-
graved Tulip, Minor Chemical Deposit,
5¾" H. $35.00
(ROW III, L to R)
PINT MUG, Stiegel-Type, Strap Handle,
Engraved Sunburst W/Singing Bird, 5½" H.
..............................$150.00
QUART MUG, Stiegel-Type, Strap Handle,
Engraved Tulip Plant, Firing Check, 6½" H.
..............................$50.00
PINT TANKARD, Stiegel-Type, Clear,
Hinged Pewter Top, Engraved Masonic Em-
blems & Date 1796, 7¾" H. $250.00
(ROW IV, L to R)
TEA CADDY, Stiegel-Type, Screw Top,
Engraved Basket Of Flowers, Screw Top
Chips, 7¼" H. $75.00
QUART DECANTERS, (Pr), 1 Illus.,
Amelung-Type, Drapery Etching & Cutting,
Period Stoppers, One W/Chip In Neck &
Reglued, Other W/Minor Chemical Deposit.
..............................$25.00
QUART DECANTER, Blown & Pattern
Molded, Engraved Great Seal Of The United
States & "Liberty"; Panel W/"American
Independence", Ribbed Design, Sunburst
Period Stopper, 10⅜" H. $800.00

(A-OH '77)   Richard A. Bourne Co., Inc.
(ROW I, L to R)
LIBBEY CANDLESTICKS, Pr., Black,
Signed $460.00
ART NOUVEAU VASE, Gilded Metal
Mountings $120.00
PATE DE VERRE NIGHT LIGHT, Signed
"Argy Rousseau" $375.00
CORALENE VASE $160.00
(ROW II, L to R)
WEDGWOOD TOBACCO JAR . . . . . .
. . . . $125.00
LIBBEY AMBERINA VASE, 2 Handled
. . . . $290.00
DURAND VASE, Gold, Signed "Durand"
In Vase $500.00
**MINIATURE AMBERINA TRI-CORNER
TOOTHPICK** $200.00
LIBBEY AMBERINA VASES, Pr.,
Signed, (1 Illus.) $750.00

(A-MA '77)   Richard A. Bourne Co., Inc.
STIEGEL-TYPE GLASSWARE
(ROW I, L to R)
FLIP GLASS, Clear, Etched W/Tulip,
4⅝" Diam., 10" H. $325.00
FLIP GLASS, Clear, 12 Sunken Panels,
Etched, 5½" Diam., 7" H. $135.00
FLIP GLASS, Clear Blown, Engraved
Band, 4⅞" Diam., 6" H. $60.00
(ROW II, L to R)
FLIP GLASS, Plain Blown, Engraved,
5⅛" Diam., 6½" H. $70.00
FLIP GLASS, Plain, Engraved Flowers,
6" Diam., 6½" H. $50.00

(A-MA '77)   Richard A. Bourne Co., Inc.
ART GLASS
(ROW I, L to R)
PEACHBLOW SUGAR BOWL, Mt.
Washington Glass Co., 3⅝" Diam., 1-15/16"
H. $1300.00
BURMESE SUGAR BOWL, Mt. Wash-
ington Glass Co., 3½" Diam., 1-15/16" H.
. . . . $250.00
STRIPED GLASS SUGAR BOWL, Opal-
escent Body W/Pink Striping & Pink & White
Striped Handles, 4" Diam., 2" H. . . $75.00
(ROW II, L to R)
BURMESE SUGAR BOWL, Mt. Wash-
ington Glass Co., Ribbon Candy Ruffled
Rim, 4" Diam., 3" H. $300.00
CROWN MILANO SUGAR BOWL, Mt.
Washington Glass Co., Floral Spray Decor.,
Signed "CM", 4½" Diam., 4¼" O.H. . . . .
. . . . $850.00
TIFFANY PANELED FINGER BOWL,
Iridescent Gold, Signed "L.C.T. R3647",
4¼" Diam., 2¼" H. $150.00
(ROW III, L to R)
**WHEELING PEACHBLOW SUGAR
BOWL,** 3¾" H. $450.00
AMBERINA SUGAR BOWL, Mt. Wash-
ington Glass Co., Fuchsia, Amber Wish-
bone Feet W/Applied Strawberry In Pontil,
4¼" Diam., 3" H. $450.00

(A-MA '77)   Richard A. Bourne Co., Inc.
(L to R)
MILK GLASS FLUID LAMP, Columbian
Coin Patt., Opaque White, 8" H. . $200.00
MILK GLASS FLUID LAMP, Unidenti-
fied Grape Patt., Opaque White, 3" Check
On Socket, 7¾" H. $35.00
PRESSED GLASS PICKLE JAR, Vase-
line Patt., Plated Silver Holder & Tongs . . .
. . . . $90.00
PRESSED GLASS COMPOTE, Dia-
mond Thumbprint Patt., Clear, 10½" Diam.,
8" H. $60.00

(A-MA '77)   Richard A. Bourne Co., Inc.
"CABLE" PATTERN, FLINT GLASS
(ROW I, L to R)
BAR TUMBLER, Clear, Nick On Foot . . . .
. . . . $130.00
TUMBLER, Clear, Oversized $240.00
WHALE OIL LAMP, Clear, Applied Han-
dle, Brass Collar $80.00
CREAMER, Clear, "Cable & Fan", Ap-
plied Handle, Chipped Foot $80.00
COVERED SUGAR, Clear, "Cable &
Fan" $75.00

(ROW II, L to R)
CRUETS, (2), Clear, Applied Handles,
Non-Matching Replacement Stoppers . . . . .
. . . . $50.00
FLUID LAMPS, (2), Original Fixtures &
Chimneys, 12¼" H. $130.00
WHALE OIL LAMPS, (2), Clear, "Cable
& Fan", 8¼" H. $150.00
LAMP, Clear, Pewter Collar, Collar Nicks,
7" H. $80.00
CELERY VASE, Clear, "Cable & Fan" . .
. . . . $30.00

(ROW III, L to R)
PITCHER, Clear, Applied Handle, Crack
Under Handle, 8½" H. $25.00
FLUID LAMP, Clear, "Cable & Fan",
Brass Stem & Collar, Marble Base, 10¾" H.
. . . . $70.00
GOBLETS, (Set-14), Clear $550.00
CASTOR SET, Unsigned Amer. Pewter
Base W/5 Clear Bottles Including Mustard,
2 Shakers & 2 Cruets $275.00
(ROW IV, L to R)
COMPOTE, Clear, Chipped Foot Ring,
7¼" Diam., 4" H. $15.00
COMPOTE, Clear, "Cable & Fan", Cover
W/Rim Nicks, 8⅛" Diam., 10½" H. . . . . . .
. . . . $270.00
COMPOTE, Clear, 8¼" Diam., 4½" H. . . .
. . . . $25.00

PRESSED GLASS
(ROW I, L to R)

EGG CUPS, (Set of 18), Cable, Flint, 7 W/ Grayish Hue, 11 Clear, (1 Illus) . . . $475.00

GOBLETS, (Set of 17), Flint, Cable, 1 W/Rim Nick, (1 Illus) $625.00

BAR LIP DECANTER, Qt., Cable, Flint, Clear $100.00

WINES (Set of 6), Paneled Thistle, 1 W/Rim Bruise, (1 Illus) $100.00

(ROW II, L to R)

CRUET, Paneled Thistle, Clear, Stopper Not Orig. $15.00

BUTTER DISH, Paneled Thistle, Clear . .
. . . . $65.00

CAKE STAND, Paneled Thistle, Clear . . .
. . . . $15.00

SALT SHAKER, Paneled Thistle, Clear, Silver Plated Top $17.00

(ROW III, L to R)

COMPOTES, Pr., Paneled Thistle, 5'' Diam., 5'' H. (1 Illus) $30.00

PITCHER, Paneled Thistle, Greenish Tint
. . . . $25.00

COMPOTES, Pr., Paneled Thistle, 1 W/ Minor Stem Nick, 6'' Diam., 8'' H., (1 Illus)
. . . . $30.00

(ROW IV, L to R)

CAKE PLATE, Clear, Paneled Thistle, 10'' Diam., 5'' H. $20.00

CELERY VASES, Pr., Clear, Paneled Thistle, Not Quite Matched, 9¼'' H., (1 Illus) $30.00

SANDWICH PLATES, (Set of 5), Clear, Paneled Thistle, 1 W/Crack, 7¼'' Sq., (1 Illus) $70.00

PRESSED GLASS — FROSTED LION PATTERN
(ROW I, L to R)

FOOTED SAUCE DISHES (1 of 8), Minor Edge Roughness, 3⅞'' Diam. $30.00

EGG CUPS (1 of 2), 1 W/Base Check, 1 W/ Foot Ring Nick $15.00

GOBLETS, (1 of 3) $100.00

SPOONHOLDER $15.00

MARMALADE JAR, Edge Chips, Cover Missing $10.00

(ROW II, L to R)

CREAMER, Minor Roughness $25.00

SUGAR BOWL, Lion Knob, Frosted Foot
. . . . $40.00

SUGAR BOWL, Lion Head Knob, Few Nicks $45.00

DISH, Crouched Lion Knob, Frosted Foot, 7'' L., 7¼'' H. $50.00

(ROW III, L to R)

CELERY VASE $25.00

COVERED DISH, Frosted Foot Ring, Crouched Lion Knob, Minor Roughage, Minor Crack On Lion, 8¾'' L., 8'' H. . . . . .
. . . . $30.00

WATER PITCHER, Shallow Crack, 9'' O.H. $25.00

(ROW IV)

COMPOTES, Pr., Lion's Head Finial, Each W/Sm. Chip, 8'' Diam., 11½'' H. . . .
. . . . $140.00

PRESSED CLEAR GLASS
(ROW I, L to R)

SUGAR BOWL, Open Rose $35.00

SUGAR BOWL, Frosted Ribbon . . $40.00

SUGAR BOWL, Dewdrop With Star, Bowl Rim Roughage $35.00

SUGAR BOWL, Classic, Minor Chip . . . .
. . . . $70.00

(ROW II, L to R)

SUGAR BOWL, Quilted Forget-Me-Not, Rim Nicks On Bowl $30.00

SUGAR BOWL, Thumbprint $50.00

SUGAR BOWL, Hobnail, 5 Ball Feet, Minor Roughness $30.00

SUGAR BOWL, Beaded Grape Medallion $30.00

(ROW III, L to R)

SUGAR BOWL, Thumbprint, Roughage On Edge Of Cover $35.00

SUGAR BOWL, Frosted Lion, Frosted Reclining Lions Around Foot Ring . $75.00

MARMALADE JAR, Hand $40.00

SUGAR BOWL, Blown & Engraved, Bands Of Lge. Flowers, Star Cut Knob . . $190.00

(ROW IV, L to R)

SUGAR BOWL, Gothic Arches, 8 Scallops, Rim Chip $10.00

SUGAR BOWL, Thumbprint $30.00

SUGAR BOWL, Moon & Star $25.00

CREAMER, Excelsior Flint, Molded-On Handle $35.00

◀ *To the left*

(L to R)

FLINT GLASS SUGAR BOWL, Ca. 1840-1850, Cobalt Blue, Minor Flakes & Nick, 9⅛'' O.H. $350.00

SUGAR BOWL, Sawtooth Patt., Cobalt Blue, Chipped, Roughage $300.00

SUGAR BOWL, Oval Ellipses In Band Around Top, Olive-Green, 3½'' Across Flats; Bowl - 3¾'' H., 6-3/16'' O.H. . . . . . .
. . . . $500.00

PRESSED GLASS
(ROW I, L to R)
TUMBLER, One Of 3 W/Applied Handle, Paneled, 3¾" H. $12.50
CELERY BOAT, Amber, Daisy & Button Patt., 13¾" L. $17.50
TUMBLER, Clear, Paneled Finecut, 3¾" H. $3.00
(ROW II, L to R)
GOBLET, Amber, Cane Patt., 6" H. ......
............$6.00
BOWL, Blue, Paneled Daisy Patt., 8¾" x 10½" x 5¼" H. $35.00
GOBLET, Pr., Amber, Basket Weave Patt.
............$16.00
(ROW II, L to R)
PITCHER, Blue, Cane Patt., 8½" H. ....
............$45.00
BOWL, Amber, Daisy & Button Patt. W/ Cross Bar $45.00
PITCHER, Paneled Finecut, Clear, 9" H. ..
............$27.50

(ROW I, L to R)
HONEY DISH, Clear, Lacy, Roman Rosette Pattern, 3¾" Diam. $10.00
PLATE, Clear, Lacy, Peacock Eye Border & Thistle Center, Minor Edge Flakes, 8" Diam.
............$52.50
HONEY DISH, Clear, Flint, Rayed Peacock Eye Pattern, 4¼" Diam. $7.00
(ROW II, L to R)
PLATE, Clear, Lacy, Lyre Alternates W/ Lattice Work In Rim, 6" Diam. $20.00
OCTAGONAL BOWL, Clear, Lacy, Beehive & Thistle Pattern, Edge Flakes, 9¼" Diam. $37.50
BOWL, Clear, Lacy, Rayed Peacock Eye Pattern, Edge Chips, 5¾" Diam. $10.00

PRESSED GLASS
(ROW I, L to R)
CANDLESTICKS, Pr., Clear, Similar But Not Exact Pair, Minor Pinpoint Flakes, 7½" & 7¾" H. $35.00
OPEN SUGAR, Clear, Flint, Vernon Honeycomb Pattern, 5¼" H. $11.00
COVERED DISH, Clear, Flint, Horn Of Plenty Pattern, Sm. Rim Chips, 6" L. .....
............$45.00
GOBLET, Clear, Flint, Elongated Thumbprint Pattern, Foot Not Completely Filled Out, 5¾" H. $8.00
(ROW II, L to R)
DECANTER, Clear, Arches & Bullseye Pattern, Flake On Lip, 8½" H. $10.00
TUMBLER, Clear, Flint, Block Pattern W/ 2 Horizontal Elongated Thumbprints Each Block, 4¾" H. $10.00
COMPOTE, Clear, Flint, Waffle Pattern, Rim Flake, Minor Roughness, 6" Diam., 8" H. $17.50
TUMBLER, Clear, Flint, Elongated Thumbprint Pattern, 2 Base Flakes, 5" H. ....
............$21.00
VASE, Clear, Washington Pattern, 7½" H.
............$12.00
(ROW III, L to R)
PANELED TULIP VASE, Clear, Flint, Foot & Bowl W/Pinpoint Flakes, 9¾" H. ...
............$42.50
COMPOTE, Clear, Flint, Star Pattern, Base Flake, 5¾" Diam., 5½" H. $9.00
OPEN SUGAR, Clear, Flint, Cable W/Ring, 4¾" Diam., 4½" H. $12.00
VASE, Clear, Blown, Knop Stem, Applied Bowl & Foot, Polished Pontil, 8¾" H. .....
............$20.00

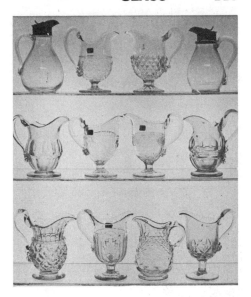

PRESSED GLASS
(ROW I, L to R)
SYRUPER, Clear, Applied Handle, Tin Lid, 6¾" H. $15.00
CREAMER, Clear, Oak Wreath Pattern, Applied Handle, 6¼" H. $22.50
CREAMER, Clear, Sawtooth Pattern, Applied Handle, 6" H. $25.00
SYRUPER, Clear, Applied Handle, Tin Lid, 6" H. $15.00
(ROW II, L to R)
CREAMER, Clear, Applied Handle, Ashburton Pattern, Polished Pontil, 5¾" H....
............$72.50
CREAMER, Clear, Applied Handle, Paneled Acorn Band Pattern, 5¾" H...$17.50
CREAMER, Clear, Applied Handle, Forget-Me-Not & Scroll Pattern $25.00
CREAMER, Clear, Applied Handle, Argus Pattern, Polished Pontil, 2 Heat Checks Near Handle, 6¼" H. $50.00
(ROW III, L to R)
CREAMER, Clear, Applied Handle, 4 Petal Pattern, Heat Check At Base Of Handle, 6¾" H. $27.50
CREAMER, Clear, Applied Handle, Magnet & Grape Pattern, 6½" H.........$32.50
CREAMER, Clear, Honeycomb Pattern, Wheel Engraved Under Handle, "Pat 1865", Polished Pontil, 5¾" H. $100.00
CREAMER, Clear, Applied Handle, Squared Star Pattern, 6½" H. $17.50

To the left
(L to R)
SAUCE, Clear, Blown, 3-Mold, Concaved At Center, Sm. Broken Bubble In Center, 5¾" Diam. $30.00
TUMBLER, Clear, Flint, Bellflower Pattern, 3½" H. $35.00
GOBLET, Clear, Flint, Bellflower Pattern, 6" H. $20.00
CONDIMENT BOTTLES (Pr.), Clear, Flint, Bellflower Pattern, Both W/Lip Chips, 5¾" H. $12.50
PLATE, Clear, Flint, Bellflower Pattern W/Scalloped Edge, Edge Chips, 6¼" Diam.
............$20.00

(A-MA '77)   *Richard A. Bourne Co., Inc.*
PRESSED GLASS, "BEADED GRAPE MEDALLION" PATTERN
(ROW I, L to R)
SALTS (1 of 3), Clear, 2 W/Sm. Rim Nicks
....$20.00
HONEY DISHES, (1 of 6), 1 W/½" Rim
Check $20.00
CORDIALS (1 of 4)..................$80.00
EGG CUPS (1 of 8) $110.00
SAUCE DISHES (1 of 8), Minor Edge
Roughage $45.00
(ROW II, L to R)
RELISH DISH, Sm. Chip Under Rim, 8"
L. $5.00
BUTTER DISHES (2) $55.00
SUGAR BOWL, Rim Chips $30.00
(ROW III, L to R)
GOBLETS (1 of 10) $160.00
SPOONHOLDERS (1 of 3), Flint .$25.00
COMPOTE, 8½" Diam., 5⅛" H. .$25.00
(ROW IV, L to R)
COVERED DISH, Marked "Mould Patd.
May 11, 1869", Minor Rim Chips, 9¼" L.
....$35.00
COVERED DISH, Marked "Mould Patd.
May 11, 1869", Minor Nicks On Rim, 10¼"
L. $45.00
(ROW V, L to R)
CELERY VASE $20.00
CASTER SET, Pewter Caster Holder, 5-
Bottle $65.00
WATER PITCHER, 2½" Crack In Upper
Section Of Handle $10.00

(A-MA '78)
*Richard A. Bourne
Co., Inc.*
OPAQUE GREEN FOUR-PIECE CONDIMENT SET, Clover Shaped Tray, Shakers & Cruet....................$250.00

(A-MA '77)   *Richard A. Bourne Co., Inc.*
CLEAR PRESSED GLASS
(ROW I, L to R)
FLINT GLASS MASTER SALT, "Bullseye & Fleur-de-Lis" $35.00
FLINT GLASS BUTTER DISHES (1 of Pr), "Bullseye & Fleur-de-Lis", Minor Rim Roughage $130.00
FLINT GLASS EGG CUPS (1 of 6), "Paneled Diamond Point" $60.00
FLINT GLASS SPOONHOLDER, "Morning Glory" $110.00
FLINT GLASS GOBLETS (1 of 6), "Bullseye And Fleur-de-Lis" $250.00
(ROW II, L to R)
FLINT GLASS GOBLETS (1 of 10), "Waffle and Thumbprint", 1 W/Chip in Foot, 3 W/Minor Roughage To Feet......$225.00
FLINT GLASS COMPOTE, "Bullseye & Fleur-de-Lis", Minor Ring Nicks, 8" Diam., 4" H. $50.00
FLINT GLASS CANDLESTICKS, (1 of Pr.), "Loop And Petal", 1 W/¾" Heat Check In Socket & Ground Petals, 6¾" H. ....
....$85.00
(ROW III, L to R)
WHALE OIL LAMPS, Pr., "Heart", Brass Collars, Minor Roughage, 10¾" H. ....
....$225.00
FLINT GLASS CELERY VASE, "Diamond Thumbprint", 9⅜" H. $55.00
FLINT GLASS BAR-LIP QUART DECANTERS (1 of Pr), "Bullseye and Fleur-de-Lis", Chips In Foot Rings $90.00

To the right
(A-MA '77)   *Richard A. Bourne Co., Inc.*
(L to R)
PAPERWEIGHT VASE, Iridescent Gold W/Decor. Of Vines & Incised Cut Green Leaves, Signed "Louis C. Tiffany-Favrile 1666", 12⅛" H. $950.00
TRUMPET VASE, Iridescent Gold, Paneled, Signed "L.C. Tiffany-Inc. Favrile 1544 816N", 16¼" H. $400.00
FLOWER-FORM VASE, Opalescent Iridescent Gold & Green, Signed "Tiffany W2488", 12¼" H. $1500.00

(A-MA '77)   *Richard A. Bourne Co., Inc.*
CLEAR PRESSED GLASS
(ROW I, L to R)
FLINT GLASS SUGAR, "Loop", Minor Chips On Base $60.00
FLINT GLASS MID-SIZE DECANTER, "Star", Non-Matching Stopper, 11" O.H.
....$20.00
FLINT GLASS DECANTERS, (1 of Pr.), "Ashburton", Orig. Stoppers, One Stopper Chipped, 11½" & 11¼" H. $130.00
LAMP, "Bullseye & Fleur-de-Lis", Orig. Double Divergent Camphene Burner, 10" H. $130.00
QUART DECANTER, "Bellflower", Professionally Repaired Stopper, 13" H. ......
....$80.00
(ROW II, L to R)
CASTER SET, Pewter Holder W/5 Matching "New England Pineapple" Bottles ....
....$130.00
FLINT GLASS BOWL, "Bellflower", 7¾" Diam. $50.00
CASTOR SET, Pewter Holder W/5 "Roman Key" Flint Glass Bottles $100.00
(ROW II, L to R)
FLINT GLASS COMPOTE, "Bellflower", Minor Chips On Foot Ring, 9" Diam., 8¾" H. ....
FLINT GLASS FLUID LAMPS, (1 of Pr.), "Ellipse", Double Divergent Camphene Burners, Minor Chips, 11" H. $175.00
FLINT GLASS COMPOTE, "Bellflower", 9" Diam., 9" H. $90.00

(A-MA '77)   *Richard A. Bourne Co., Inc.*
(ROW I, L to R)

MILK GLASS SUGAR BOWL, "Strawberry Patt.", Opaque White, Minor Roughage $30.00
MILK GLASS SUGAR BOWL, "Princess Feather Patt.", Opaque White, Maude B. Feld Label $75.00
OPALESCENT SUGAR BOWL, Boston & Sandwich, "Loop Patt.", Minor Roughage & Nick $90.00
(ROW II, L to R)
MILK GLASS SUGAR BOWL, "Sawtooth Patt.", Opaque White, Boston & Sandwich Glass Co. $60.00
MILK GLASS SUGAR BOWL, "Blackberry Patt.," Opaque White $35.00
OPALESCENT & CLEAR SUGAR BOWL, "Beatty Honeycomb Patt.", Minor Roughage $50.00
(ROW III, L to R)
CHOCOLATE GLASS SUGAR BOWL, "Cactus Patt.", Greentown Glass Co., Indiana $75.00
PURPLE SLAG SUGAR BOWL, Paneled Design $120.00

(A-MA '77)   *Richard A. Bourne Co., Inc.*
MILK GLASS COVERED ANIMAL DISHES
(ROW I, L to R)
RECLINING DOG, Blue & White, 5½" L., 4" H. $40.00
RECLINING CAT, Blue & White, Sm. Chips, 5½" L., 4⅛" H. $40.00
NESTING HEN, 5½" L., 4½" H. $40.00
(ROW II, L to R)
RECLINING RABBIT, 5⅜" L., 4¼" H. $45.00
RECLINING DOG, Boston & Sandwich Glass Co., Minor Roughage, 4¾" L., 3⅞" H. $325.00
NESTING HEN, Blue & White, 5½" L., 4½" H. $40.00
(ROW III, L to R)
NESTING DUCK, Sm. Tail Chip, 1 Glass Eye Missing, 8" L., 5" H. $70.00
NESTING HEN, Blue & White, Glass Eyes Missing, 7" L., 6" H. $30.00
(ROW IV, L to R)
BATTLESHIP "MAINE", Flakes & Roughage, 7¾" L., 3⅝" H. $25.00
NESTING HEN, Tail Chipped, 5½" L., 4½" H. $10.00
NESTING HEN, Blue, Tail Chips, Glass Eyes Missing, Base Warped, 7" L., 6¼" H. $35.00

(A-MA '77)   *Richard A. Bourne Co., Inc.*
PRESSED GLASS — PANELED THISTLE PATTERN
(ROW I, L to R)
FOOTED SALTS (1 of 5) $35.00
MINIATURE HONEY DISHES, Pr., 1 Misshapen (1 Illus) $15.00
FOOTED MASTER SALTS (1 of 4) .....
.... $50.00
COMPOTES (1 of 2), Not Matched Pr., 5¼" & 5½" Diam., 5" H. $15.00
(ROW II, L to R)
ROSE BOWL, 6" Diam. $20.00
SUGAR BOWL $15.00
CELERY VASES, (1 of Pr.) $35.00
COMPOTE, 8" Diam., 7" H. $15.00
(ROW III, L to R)
BERRY BOWL, 10" Diam. $20.00
BOWL, 8" Diam. $15.00
(ROW IV, L to R)
BERRY BOWL, 10" Diam. $20.00
PLATES, (1 of 7), 10¼" Diam. ... $70.00

(A-MA '77)   *Richard A. Bourne Co., Inc.*
(L to R)
STIEGEL-TYPE SUGAR BOWL, "Diamond Diaper" Patt., 11-Diamond Design, Cobalt Blue, Bowl: 4¼" Diam., 4½" H.; Cover: 4¾" Diam., 6" O.H. $1500.00
LACY PURPLE-BLUE BOWL, Boston & Sandwich Glass Co., Non-Lacy Cover, Minor Flakes & Chips $1250.00
LACY SAPPHIRE BLUE SUGAR BOWL, Minor Flakes, Nick & Roughage .$1100.00

(A-MA '77)   *Richard A. Bourne Co., Inc.*
(L to R)
DOUBLE CUT OVERLAY SUGAR BOWL, Blue Cut To Clear, Mirror Patt., Sunburst Cut Base $350.00
LACY TRANSLUCENT POWDER BLUE SUGAR BOWL, Boston & Sandwich Glass Co., Gothic Arch Patt., Minor Roughage & Chip $1200.00
LACY PEACOCK BLUE SUGAR BOWL, Boston & Sandwich Glass Co., Gothic Arch Patt., Minor Roughage & Flake, & Chip ...
.... $900.00

(D-NY '78)   *Lee Vines Antiques*
PRESSED GLASS CELERY VASE, Actress Patt., H.M.S. Pinafore Scenes, 9" H.
.... $150.00

(A-MA '77)   *Richard A. Bourne Co., Inc.*

STIEGEL-TYPE ENAMELED GLASS
(ROW I, L to R)
BRIDE'S BOTTLE, Milky Opaque Blue, Floral Decor. W/Blue, Red & Yellow, Lip Chip, 4½" H. $60.00
BRIDE'S BOTTLE, Clear W/Dove & Flower Decor. In 5 Colors, Orig. Pewter Collar, Paint Chipped, 5⅛" H. $50.00
BRIDE'S BOTTLE, Clear W/3-Color Floral Design, Orig. Pewter Collar & Screw Top, 5¼" H. $60.00
BRIDE'S BOTTLE, Clear W/5-Color Fruit Decor., Pewter Collar, Tool Marks, 5⅝" H. $55.00
(ROW II, L to R)
HALF-PINT MUG, Clear W/6-Color Decor. Of Building & Flowering Plants, Strap Handle, 2⅝" Diam., 3¾" H. $45.00
REMEMBRANCE MUG, Clear W/Rib-Molded Bottom, Floral Vignette W/"Remember Me" On Blue Ground, 3⅝" Diam., 4⅜" H. $15.00
MUG, Clear W/6-Color Rooster & Flower Decor., Strap Handle, Paint Flakes, 3" Diam., 5" H. $100.00
BRIDE'S BOTTLE, Clear W/Figure Of Woman One Side; Rev: German Verse, Floral Panels, 6-Colors, Orig. Pewter Collar, Paint Flaking, 6¾" H. $60.00
(ROW III, L to R)
BRIDE'S BOTTLE, Clear W/6-Color Floral Decor., Orig. Pewter Collar, Glass Foggy, 7¾" H. $40.00
MUG, Continental 18th C., Opaque Opalescent Blue, Strap Handle, 6-Color Scenic Decor., 3¾" Diam., 6½" H. $70.00
BRIDE'S BOTTLE, Clear W/Floral Design In 4 Colors, Lip Chip, Missing Pewter Collar, 6¼" H. $50.00

To the right ▶

(A-MA '77)   *Richard A. Bourne Co., Inc.*

PRESSED GLASS COMPOTES, (2), Sandwich "Star" Patt., Clear, 12" Diam., 9½" H. $275.00
CARYATID FIGURAL STAND, Boston & Sandwich Glass Co., Etched Bowl Inset, 21¼" H. $150.00

(A-OH '77)   *Garth's Auctions, Inc.*
(ROW I, L to R)
LAMP, Clear, Pressed Base & Blown Spherical Font, Single Spout Whale Oil Burner, Base Flake, 4⅜" H. $17.00
CREAMER, Clear, Blown, Applied Handle, 4" H. $13.00
WINE, Clear, Blown, Ribbed Bowl, Sm. Rim Flake, 3½" H. $25.00
CREAMER, Clear, Blown In Tumbler Mold, 9 Panels, Applied Handle, 4¼" H. ..$30.00
FOOTED CUP, Aqua, Blown, Ribbed, Applied Amber Olive Handle, 3¼" H. $12.50
(ROW II, L to R)
CRUET, Smokey Grey, Blown, Applied Foot & Hollow Handle, 7½" H. $5.00
LAMP, Clear, Blown, Applied Foot & Font, Brass Collar, 6" H. $27.50
FLIP, Pale Green, Blown, Folded Over Lip, 5" H. $52.00
DECANTER, Clear, Applied Lip, Bullseye Variant, 6½" H. $32.50
SYRUPER, Clear, Blown, 3-Mold, Applied Handle & Pewter Lid $77.50
(ROW III, L to R)
VASE, Clear, Flint, Pillar Mold, Baluster Stem, Ground Pontil, 9" H. $30.00
VASE, Canary, Blown, Applied Foot, Ground Pontil, 8½" H. $75.00
VASE, Clear, Blown, Pillar Mold, Knop Stem, Applied Foot & Bowl, 8½" H. ......
..............................$22.50

(A-MA '77)   *Richard A. Bourne Co., Inc.*

PRESSED GLASS
(ROW I, L to R)
SUGAR BOWL, Smocking, Rim Roughage
..............................$40.00
SUGAR BOWL, Excelsior $60.00
SUGAR BOWL, Broad Band Around Top, Gothic-Like Arches In Band Around Bottom Half, Roughage $30.00
SUGAR BOWL $170.00
(ROW II, L to R)
SUGAR BOWL, Thumbprint, Edge Roughage, Sm. Chips $50.00
SUGAR BOWL, Ashburton, Minor Rim Nicks On Cover $40.00
SUGAR BOWL, Cable With Ring, Cover Rim Roughage $45.00
SUGAR BOWL, Waffle and Thumbprint .
..............................$90.00
(ROW III, L to R)
SUGAR BOWL, Sawtooth, Minor Roughage $35.00
SUGAR BOWL, Paneled Diamond Point, Minor Knob Nick $30.00
SUGAR BOWL, New England Pineapple, Rim Roughage, Minor Knob Nick ..$50.00
SUGAR BOWL, Moon And Star, Edge Nick, Rim Roughage $45.00
(ROW IV, L to R)
SUGAR BOWL, Colonial, Minor Chip ...
..............................$65.00
SUGAR BOWL, Bellflower $55.00
SUGAR BOWL, Ribbed Ivy, Minor Flakes
..............................$60.00
SUGAR BOWL, Hamilton, Knob Chip ...
..............................$25.00
(ROW V, L to R)
SUGAR BOWL, Westward Ho ..$100.00
SUGAR BOWL, Frosted Eagle, Minor Nick $70.00
SUGAR BOWL, United States Coin — Half Dollar, Minor Nicks & Roughage ..$150.00
COMPOTE, Three-Face $65.00

(A-MA '77)   Richard A. Bourne Co., Inc.

COLORED PATTERN-MOLDED FOOTED MASTER SALTS
(ROW I, L to R)
PALE AMETHYST, Vertical & Swirled Ribbing, 22-Rib, Minor Rim Nick, 3" Diam., 2⅝" H. $150.00
EMERALD GREEN, Stiegel-Type, 26 Vertical Ribs, 2⅝" Diam., 3⅛" H. ...$600.00
DEEP COBALT BLUE, Stiegel-Type, Diamond-Daisy Design, 2½" Diam., 2¾" H. .
.................................$400.00
COBALT BLUE, Stiegel-Type, Checkered-Diamond Design, 2¼" Diam., 2⅞" H. ....
.................................$600.00
(ROW II, L to R)
DEEP COBALT BLUE, Stiegel-Type, Expanded Diamond Patt., 14-Diamond Mold, Inner Rim Chip, 2½" Diam., 3" H. ......
.................................$150.00
DEEP COBALT BLUE, Stiegel-Type, Expanded Diamond Patt., 18-Diamond Mold, 2⅜" Diam., 2-15/16" H. $200.00
DEEP COBALT BLUE, Stiegel-Type, Expanded Diamond Patt., 11-Diamond Mold, Flower Form Foot, Inner Rim Chip, 2⅝" Diam., 3⅛" H. $150.00
COBALT BLUE, Stiegel-Type, Expanded Diamond Patt., 11-Diamond Mold, 2¾" Diam., 2⅞" H. $175.00
(ROW III, L to R)
COBALT BLUE, Stiegel-Type, Expanded Diamond Patt., 11-Diamond Mold, 2⅝" Diam., 2⅞" H. $175.00
COBALT BLUE, Stiegel-Type, Expanded Diamond Patt., 11-Diamond Mold, 2¾" Diam., 3" H. $150.00
DEEP COBALT BLUE, Stiegel-Type, 15 Vertical Ribs, 2⅝" Diam., 3⅛" H. $175.00
COBALT BLUE, Stiegel-Type, Expanded Diamond Patt., 11-Diamond Mold, 2¾" Diam., 2⅞" H. $120.00
(ROW IV, L to R)
COBALT BLUE, Stiegel-Type, Expanded Diamond Patt., 11 or 12-Diamond Mold, Minor Inner Rim Nick, 2¾" Diam., 3" H. .
.................................$50.00
MEDIUM COBALT BLUE, Stiegel-Type, 24 Vertical Ribs, Swirled, 2¼" Diam., 3" H.
.................................$50.00
COBALT BLUE, Stiegel-Type, 26 Vertical Ribs, Swirled, 2⅜" Diam., 3" H. ..$75.00
COBALT BLUE, Stiegel-Type, Expanded Diamond Patt., 11-Diamond Mold, 2⅝" Diam., 2⅞" H. $110.00
COBALT BLUE, Stiegel-Type, 12 Vertical Ribs, 2½" Diam., 3" H. $100.00

(A-OH '77)   Garth's Auctions, Inc.

(ROW I, L to R)
FRUIT JAR, Aqua, "Mason's Patent Nov. 30th, 1858", Zinc Lid, 5¾" H. $10.00
FRUIT JAR, Aqua, "Trade Mark, Lightning" Matching Glass Lid, Wire Fastener, 5½" H. $100.00
FRUIT JAR, Clear, "Flaccus Bros.", Threaded Glass Lid Mkd. "Simplex", Minor Sickness, 6" H. $25.00
FRUIT JAR, Aqua, "Millville" & Partial Patent Infor. On Rev., Matching Glass Lid W/Iron Screw Fastener, Chipped Lid, 5" H.
.................................$45.00
FRUIT JAR, Aqua, "Mason's Patent, Nov. 30, 57", Old English Print, Glass Lid & Zinc Cap, 5½" H. $40.00
FRUIT JAR, Clear, "Crystal Jar", Matching Threaded Glass Lid, 6" H. $37.50

(ROW II, L to R)
FRUIT JAR, Aqua, "Woodbury Improved", Matching Glass Lid W/Zinc Cap, 7½" H. ...
.................................$27.50
FRUIT JAR, Clear, "Perfection", Matching Glass Lid W/Zinc Cap, 7½" H. $50.00
FRUIT JAR, Aqua, "Mason's Patent Nov. 30th, 1858", Zinc Lid, 5¾" H. $7.50
FRUIT JAR, Drk. Amber, "Trademark, Lightening", Matching Glass Lid & Wire Fastener, Sm. Lip Chip, Minor Sickness, 6½" H. $32.50
FRUIT JAR, Aqua, "Cohansey", Matching Glass Lid & Wire Fastener, 7" H. ..$24.00

(ROW III, L to R)
FRUIT JAR, Aqua, "Mason's Patent Nov. 30th, 1858", Whittled Mold, Rim Chips, Zinc Lid, 9¼" H. $5.00
FRUIT JAR, Pale Yellow-Green, "Mason's Patent Nov. 30th, 1858", No Lid, 9" H. ..
.................................$17.00
FRUIT JAR, Aqua, Applied Lip & Iron Pontil, Blown 2-Part Mold, 9" H. ..$35.00
FRUIT JAR, Aqua, Mkd., "Cohansey Glass Mfg. Co.", 9" H. $92.50
FRUIT JAR, Aqua, "Mason Fruit Jar", Zinc Lid, 8¾" H. $5.00

(A-OH '77)   Garth's Auctions, Inc.

(ROW I, L to R)
FRUIT JAR, Aqua, "Magic Fruit Jar, Wm. McCully & Co., Pittsburg, Pa., Pat. By R. M. Dalby, June 6, 1866", Matching Glass Lid W/Iron Fastener & Tightening Screw, Lip Flake, 8½" H. $305.00
INSULATOR, Pale Green, "Hemingray-60", 5" H. $2.50
FRUIT JAR, Green, "Flaccus Bros. etc.", Matching Glass Cap, 6" H. $550.00
INSULATORS (2), 1 Illus., Green One Mkd. "K.C.G.W.", Chipped, 4" H.; Lt. Blue One Mkd. "W. Brookfield, 4 S. Cliff St., N.J.", Base Chip, 4¼" H. $3.00
FRUIT JAR, Aqua, "Victory, Pat. Feb. 9th, 1864, Re.isd June 22, 1867", Glass Lid, Zinc Cap, 7¼" H. $27.50
(ROW II, L to R)
FRUIT JAR, Aqua, "Whitemore's Patent, Rochester, N.Y.", Matching Glass Lid, Wire Fastener, 9" H. $225.00
INSULATOR, Aqua, "O.V.C. Co.", 4" H.
.................................$3.00
FRUIT JAR, Amber, 2-Part Whittled Mold, "Trade Mark, Lightening", Glass Lid, Wire Fastener, Chipped Lip, 8" H. $25.00
INSULATORS, (2), 1 Illus., Aqua One Mkd. "Lynchburg", Chipped, 4" H.; Clear One W/Patent Dated "Dec. 19, 1871", Chipped, 3¾" H. $5.00
FRUIT JAR, Aqua, "The Van Vliet Jar Of 1881", Glass Lid, Wire & Iron Fastener, Threaded Screw, 8¼" H. $305.00
(ROW III, L to R)
FRUIT JAR, Aqua, Glass Lid, Metal Fastener, Lip Chipped, 9¾" H. $80.00
INSULATOR, Drk. Aqua, "Gayner", 4½" H. $3.00
FRUIT JAR, Aqua, Blown 2-Part Mold, Iron Pontil, 8¾" H. $45.00
INSULATOR, Drk. Aqua, "F.M. Locke & Co., Victor, N.Y. Pat. May 22, 1894", Base Chips, 3½" H. $3.00
FRUIT JAR, Aqua, "Clarke Fruit Jar Co., Cleveland, O.", Glass Lid, Metal Fastener, 9" H. $50.00

(A-MA '77)   *Richard A. Bourne Co., Inc.*

FREE-BLOWN & PATTERN-MOLDED FLASKS & BOTTLES
(ROW I, L to R)
HALF-PINT HIP FLASK, Golden-Amber, Zanesville, 24-Rib, Swirled, Minor Damage, 4¾" H. $125.00
HALF-PINT HIP FLASK, Red-Amber, Zanesville, 24-Vertical Rib, Chemical Deposits, 4¾" H. $100.00
HALF-PINT HIP FLASK, Red-Amber, Zanesville, 24-Vertical Rib, Minor Rim Nick, 5¼" H. $175.00
(ROW II, L to R)
HALF-PINT HIP FLASK, Red-Amber, Zanesville, 14-Vertical Rib, Chemical Deposit On Side, 5" H. $150.00
HALF-PINT HIP FLASK, Amethyst, Mantua, 16-Rib, Swirled, 6" H. ...$300.00
PINT FLASK, Amethyst, Stiegel, 26-Diamond, 6" H. $1000.00
(ROW III, L to R)
PINT FLASK, Olive-Green, Pontil & Sheared Lip, 7' H. $50.00
PINT FLASK, Golden-Amber, Kent, Ohio, 20-Vertical Rib, 6¾" H. $400.00
PINT FLASK, Golden-Amber, Ohio, 18-Rib, Swirled, 6¼" H. $350.00

(A-MA '77)   *Richard A. Bourne Co., Inc.*

(L to R)
SHEAF OF WHEAT CALABASH BOTTLE, Qt., Amber, Lip Nicks, Cloudy Interior, 9" H. $25.00
ANCHOR FLASK, Qt., Golden-Amber, 9⅜" H. $10.00
FLASK, Qt., Emerald Green, Five-Pointed Star One Side; Rev: Plain, Chemical Deposit, 9⅛" H. $75.00

(A-MA '77)   *Richard A. Bourne Co., Inc.*

(ROW I, L to R)
BALTIMORE MONUMENT, ½ Pt., Emerald Green, 6" H. $950.00
BALTIMORE MONUMENT, ½ Pt., Golden Amber, 6⅛" H. $1050.00
BALTIMORE MONUMENT — EAR OF CORN, Qt., Golden-Amber, 8⅜" H. .....
..............................$400.00
(ROW II, L to R)
CABIN BOTTLE, Reddish-Amber or Tobacco Brown, 7¾" H. $500.00
SUNBURST, Pt., Olive-Green, 7½" H. ..
..............................$500.00
SUNBURST, Pt., Golden-Olive, 7⅝" H. ..
..............................$1100.00
(ROW III, L to R)
SUNBURST, Pt., Olive-Amber, 7¾" H. ...
..............................$250.00
SUNBURST, ½ Pt., Greenish-Olive-Amber, 5¾" H. $200.00
SUNBURST, ½ Pt., Clear Olive-Green, 6¾" H. $150.00
SUNBURST, ¾ Pt., Blue-Green, 7" H. ..
..............................$190.00

(A-MA '77)   *Richard A. Bourne Co., Inc.*

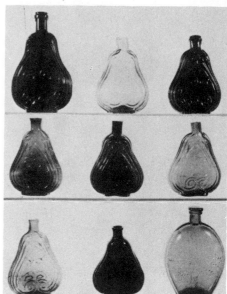

(A-MA '77)   *Richard A. Bourne Co., Inc.*

(ROW I, L to R)
SCROLL, Qt., Golden-Amber, 9" H. ....
..............................$600.00
SCROLL, Pt., Yellow-Green, 6⅞" H. ....
..............................$425.00
SCROLL, Pt., Olive-Green, 6⅞" H. .....
..............................$500.00
(ROW II, L to R)
SCROLL, Pt., Golden-Amber, Rim Chip, 7" H. $400.00
SCROLL, Pt., Olive-Green, Rim Roughage, 7" H. $500.00
SCROLL, Pt., Golden-Amber, Rough Sheared Lip, 6⅞" H. $550.00
(ROW III, L to R)
SCROLL, Pt., Med. Blue-Green, 7" H. ....
..............................$350.00
SCROLL, Pt., Reddish-Amber or Tobacco Brown, 6½" H. $650.00
TREE, Qt., Golden-Amber, 8¼" H. ......
..............................$500.00

To the left

PICTORIAL & HISTORICAL FLASKS
(ROW I, L to R)
AMERICAN FLAG One Side; Rev: "New Granite Glass Works, Stoddard, N.H.", Pt., Golden-Amber, 7⅛" H. $1900.00
AMERICAN EAGLE, Pt., Olive-Yellow, Monongahela & Early Pittsburgh District, 6½" H. $6400.00
WASHINGTON-EAGLE, Pt., Lt. Green, Frederick Lorenz, Pittsburgh, 6⅞" H. ......
..............................$1100.00
(ROW II, L to R)
EAGLE-FLOWER, Pt., Aquamarine, Midwestern, Double Ringed Neck, 7" H. ......
..............................$450.00
PORTRAIT, Pt., Blue-Green, Wheat Price & Co., Wheeling, W. Va., Cracked, 6¾" H.
..............................$600.00
EAGLE & ROSETTED FLOWER, Pt., Aquamarine, 7" H. $750.00
BALTIMORE MONUMENT, Pt., Aquamarine, Cloudy, 6½" H. $350.00

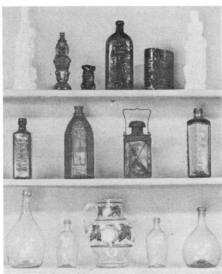

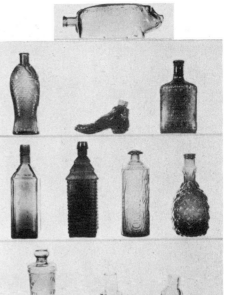

(A-OH '77)   *Garth's Auctions, Inc.*
(ROW I, L to R)
BITTERS BOTTLE, Amber, "National Bitters", Patent 1867", ...$152.50
BOTTLE, Deep Aqua, Applied Double Headed Eagle Seal Mkd. "Zare", 13¾" H. $25.00
BLOWN BOTTLE, Green, 3-Part Mold, 12½" H. $40.00
BITTERS BOTTLE, Yellow-Amber, Indian Maiden, "Brown's Celebrated Indian Herb Bitters", "Patented Feb. 11, 1868", Lip Flake, 12¼" H. $65.00
BLOWN WINE BOTTLE, Cobalt Blue, Pontil Mark, 13¼" H. $95.00
(ROW II, L to R)
LOG CABIN BITTERS BOTTLE, Drk. Amber, "Drake's 1860 Plantation Bitters", "Patented 1862", Interior Residue, 19" H. $40.00
FLASK, Half-Pint, Amber, Urn & Cornucopia, 5½" H. $85.00
FLASK, Pint, Olive-Green, Taylor & Washington, Dyottsville Glass Works, Broken Blister, 7½" H. $435.00
FLASK, Half-Pint, Olive-Amber, Double Eagle, 6" H. $67.50
LOG CABIN BITTERS BOTTLE, Amber, "Drake's 1860 Plantation Bitters", "Patented 1862", Minor Interior Residue, 10¼" H. $40.00
(ROW III, L to R)
WINE BOTTLE, Olive-Amber, Blown In 3-Part Mold, High Kick-Up, 10" H. $10.00
GIN BOTTLE, Olive, Remains Of Lead Foil Seal, 9½" H. $9.00
FLASK, Qt., Amber, Eagle & "Liberty", Rev: "Willington Glass Co. West Willington, Conn.", Dirty Interior, 8½" H. $97.50
BOTTLES, (2), Whiskey W/Kick-Up, 10½" H., and Olive Green Gin Bottle, 9¼" H. $35.00

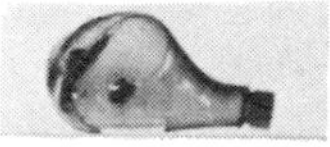

(A-MA '77)   *Richard A. Bourne Co., Inc.*
CANDY BOTTLE, Amber, Ham Form, Screw Top, Fairton Glass Works, Fairton, N.J., 6" L. $25.00

(A-OH '77)   *Garth's Auctions, Inc.*
(ROW I, L to R)
FIGURAL BOTTLE, Milk Glass, Bear Wrapped Around Post, Satin Finish, "Depose", 11¼" H. $37.50
FIGURAL BOTTLE, Cobalt Blue, Poodle, 8" H. $5.00
FIGURAL JAR, Black Amethyst, Bear, Minor Flakes, 3¾" H. $65.00
BOTTLE, Amber, "Warner's Safe Kidney & Liver Cure, Rochester, N.Y.", Sm. Base Blister, 9½" H. $7.50
CERAMIC BOOK BOTTLE, "History of Holland", Blue Glaze, Corner Chip, 5½" H. $15.00
FIGURAL BOTTLE, Milk Glass, Bear, Base Hairline, 11" H. $17.50
(ROW II, L to R)
BOTTLE, Olive Green, Aromatic Schnapps, 8" H. $20.00
INK BOTTLE, Cobalt Blue, "Carters", 9¾" H. $37.50
LANTERN BOTTLE, Olive Green, Incased In Tin, 7¾" H. Plus Handle $55.00
BOTTLE, "Dr. Townsends Sarsaparilla", Green, Pontiled, 9¼" H. $52.50
(ROW III, L to R)
BLOWN CLUB BOTTLE, Aqua, 10" H. $35.00
HALF PINT FLASK, Aqua, Double Eagle, 6¼" H. $37.50
CLEAR BLOWN PITCHER, Enameled Decor., 9" H. $65.00
HALF PINT FLASK, Aqua, Union & Clasped Hands, Rev: Eagle & Banner, 6½" H. $32.50
BLOWN GLOBULAR BOTTLE, Aqua, Sick, 8" H. $20.00

(A-OH '77   *Garth's Auctions, Inc.*
CALABASH BOTTLE, Aqua, "Jenny Lind", Rev: Glass Factory, Iron Pontil, 9¾" H. $87.50

(A-MA '77)   *Richard A. Bourne Co., Inc.*
FIGURAL, WINE & SPIRIT, MEDICINE, BITTERS, BLACKING, CANDY & OTHER BOTTLES
(ROW I)
BITTERS BOTTLE, Amber, Pig Form, "Suffolk Bitters" W/"Philbrook & Tucker, Boston", 10" L. $140.00
(ROW II)
BITTERS BOTTLE, Amber, For Dr. Fisch's Bitters, Unlettered, By Whitney Bros. Glassworks, Glassboro, N.J., 8¼" H. $7.00
CANDY BOTTLE, Foot W/Worn-Out Shoe, Black Amethyst Glass W/Screw Top, Screw Top Split, 6" L. $55.00
BITTERS BOTTLE, Amber, "Royal Pepsin Stomach Bitters, L. & A. Scharff Sole Agents, St. Louis, U.S. & Canada", 7½" H. $22.00
(ROW III, L to R)
BITTERS BOTTLE, Amber, "Doyle's Hop Bitters", 1872, 9½" H. $20.00
BITTERS BOTTLE, Amber, "S.T. Drakes /1860/Plantation/X/Bitters" 9¾" H. $40.00
TIPPECANOE BITTERS BOTTLE, "H.H. Warner & Co.,", & "Bottle Pat. Nov. 20, '83", Rochester, N.Y.", Amber, 9" H. $55.00
PINEAPPLE BITTERS BOTTLE, Amber, "W. & Co. N.Y.", Pontil Mark In Base, 8½" H. $175.00
(ROW IV, L to R)
CANNON BITTERS BOTTLE, Golden Amber, "A.M. Bininger & Co. 19 Broad St. N.Y.", Roughage & Sm. Rim Chips, 12½" H. $125.00
FIGURAL COLOGNE BOTTLE, Pink Glass In Owl Form W/Painted Eyes, 3 Sm. Lip Nicks, 10" H. $40.00
FIGURAL COLOGNE BOTTLE, Amber, Seated Dog W/Painted Eyes, Tears, Muzzle, Mount & Neck Ribbon, Base Cracks, Lip Chips, 9⅝" H. $2.00

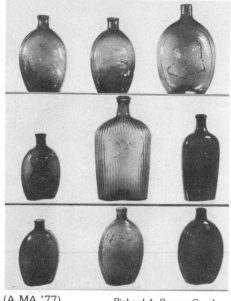

(A-MA '77)   *Richard A. Bourne Co., Inc.*

PICTORIAL & HISTORICAL FLASKS
(ROW I, L to R)
WASHINGTON-TAYLOR, Pt., Golden-Amber, 6¾" H. $100.00
WASHINGTON-TAYLOR, Pt., Golden-Amber, Chemical Deposit, 6¾" H. . . . . . .
. . . .$150.00
WASHINGTON-TAYLOR, Qt., Yellow-Amber, 8¼" H. $300.00
(ROW II, L to R)
PORTRAIT, Pt., Olive-Amber, 6" H. . . . .
. . . .$125.00
EAGLE, Qt., Emerald Green, Minor Wear, 9½" H. $850.00
EAGLE, Pt., Amber, Minor Wear, 7¾" H. .
. . . .$70.00
(ROW III, L to R)
EAGLE, ½ Pt., Golden-Amber, Coventry, Conn., Open Bubble On Side, Minor Rim Flake, 5¾" H. $50.00
EAGLE-CORNUCOPIA, Pt., Golden-Amber, Chemical Deposit, 6¾" H. .$40.00
EAGLE-CORNUCOPIA, Pt., Olive-Green, Lip Chips, 6⅝" H. $40.00

(A-MA '77)   *Richard A. Bourne Co., Inc.*
PICTORIAL & HISTORICAL FLASKS
(ROW I, L to R)
FLASK, Pt., Olive-Amber, 6-Pointed Star One Side; Rev: 6-Pointed Star W/Raised Arm & Clenched Fist, High Point Wear, Open Bubble In Rib, 7⅝" H. $50.00
FLASK, Pt., Olive-Amber, 6-Pointed Star One Side; Rev: 6-Pointed Star W/Raised Arm & Clenched Fist, Lip Bruise, 7¾" H. . .
. . . .$80.00
FLORA TEMPLE FLASK, Pt., Drk. Amber or Tobacco Brown, Lip Chip, 8⅜" H. . . . . .
. . . .$175.00
FLORA TEMPLE FLASK, Pt., Emerald Green, 8⅝" H. $400.00

(A-MA '77   *Richard A. Bourne Co., Inc.*
(ROW I, L to R)
JENNY LIND CALABASH BOTTLE, Qt., Aquamarine, 10¼" H. $150.00
JENNY LIND CALABASH BOTTLE, Qt., Aquamarine, 10" H. $125.00
JENNY LIND CALABASH BOTTLE, Qt., Aquamarine, 9" H. $30.00
(ROW II, L to R)
JENNY LIND FLASK, Pt., Aquamarine, 6⅞" H. $900.00
EAGLE-CORNUCOPIA FLASK, ½ Pt., Aquamarine, Monangahela & Early Pittsburgh District, 5⅜" H. $450.00
EAGLE FLASK, Pt., Aquamarine, Louisville, Ky. Glass Works, Cloudy, 7½" H. . . .
. . . .$50.00
(ROW III, L to R)
EAGLE-TREE FLASK, Pt., Aquamarine, Kensington Glass Works, Phila., 6½" H. . .
. . . .$150.00
EAGLE-FLAG FLASK, Qt., Aquamarine, Coffin & Hay, Hammonton, N.J., Lip Flake, 8" H. $130.00
EAGLE-GRAPES FLASK, Qt., Aquamarine, Cloudy, 7¾" H. $100.00

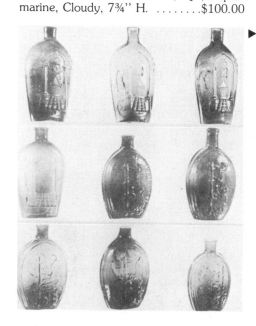

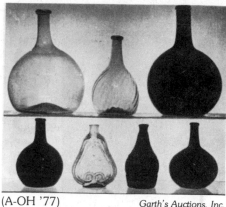

(A-OH '77)   *Garth's Auctions, Inc.*
(ROW I, L to R)
ZANESVILLE BLOWN GLOBULAR BOTTLE, Aqua, Star Bruise, 11¼" H. . . .
. . . .$65.00
ZANESVILLE BLOWN CLUB BOTTLE, Aqua, 24 Swirled Ribs, 8½" H. . .$105.00
ZANESVILLE BLOWN GLOBULAR BOTTLE, Amber, 24 Swirled Ribs, 12" H.
. . . .$450.00
(ROW II, L to R)
ZANESVILLE BLOWN GLOBULAR BOTTLE, Amber, 24 Swirled Ribs, 7½" H.
. . . .$250.00
SCROLL FLASK, Aqua, Louisville Glass Works, Shallow Broken Blister On Interior Near Lip, 7" H. $105.00
BLOWN 3-MOLD BOTTLE, Olive-Amber, Keene, N.H., 7" H. $425.00
GLOBULAR BOTTLE, Amber, Blown, 24 Swirled Ribs, Sm. Broken Blisters, 7¼" H.
. . . .$275.00

(A-OH '77)   *Garth's Auctions, Inc.*
BLOWN CHESTNUT BOTTLE, Violet, 18 Vertical Ribs, Reproduction, 20th C., 5¾" H. $55.00

To the left

(A-MA '77)   *Richard A. Bourne Co., Inc.*
PICTORIAL & HISTORICAL FLASKS
(ROW I, L to R)
MASONIC-EAGLE, Pt., Olive-Amber, Minor Chemical Deposit, 7½" H. . . .$110.00
MASONIC-EAGLE, Pt., Olive-Amber, 7¾" H. $175.00
MASONIC-EAGLE, Pt., Olive-Amber, 7¾" H. $200.00
(ROW II, L to R)
MASONIC-EAGLE, Pt., Olive-Green, 7½" H. $200.00
RAILROAD, Pt., Olive-Green, 6¾" H. . . .
. . . .$125.00
RAILROAD, Pt., Olive-Green, Chipped, 7⅝" H. $200.00
(ROW III, L to R)
RAILROAD-EAGLE, Pt., Olive-Amber, 6⅞" H. $125.00
RAILROAD-EAGLE, Pt., Amber, Rim Chip, 6¾" H. $70.00
RAILROAD-EAGLE, Pt., Olive-Amber, 5⅞" H. $175.00

(A-MA '77)   *Richard A. Bourne Co., Inc.*

FIGURAL, WINE & SPIRIT, MEDICINE, BITTERS, BLACKING, CANDY AND OTHER BOTTLES
(ROW I, L to R)
PRESSED GLASS CANDY CONTAINERS (2), Clear, Duck & Rabbit, Chip on Duck Base, Nick On Base Of Rabbit: 4⅜" H., Duck: 2⅞" H. $30.00
PRESSED GLASS CANDY JAR, Clear, Buddha Form, Amber Stopper, Signed "Vanline's", 6½" H. $12.00
PRESSED GLASS BOTTLE, Clear, Horse's Hoof Form, Metal Screw Cap W/ "Gordon's Hoof Ointment", 5½" H. . . . . . .
. . . .$35.00
(ROW II, L to R)
PRESSED GLASS CANDY BOTTLES, Pr. (1 Illus.), Clear, Powder Horn Form, Screw Tops, 8½" L. $25.00
PRESSED GLASS CANDY BOTTLE, Clear, Revolver Form, Screw Top Missing, 1½" Check On Barrel, Roughage, Chemical Deposit Inside, 8" L. $2.00
COLOGNE BOTTLE, Bunch of Grapes, Chemical Deposits, 6" L. $10.00
(ROW III, L to R)
CLEAR FIGURAL BOTTLE, Punch Form, Chemical Deposit In Bottom, Screw Top Missing, 8½" H. $5.00
CLEAR FIGURAL COLOGNE BOTTLE, Seated Cat W/Painted On Eyes, Nose, Mouth & Ribbon, 11⅛" H. $15.00
PRESSED GLASS COLOGNE BOTTLE, Clear, Santa Claus Form, Minor Chemical Deposit Inside, 12⅛" H. . .$25.00

(A-OH '77)   *Garth's Auctions, Inc.*
(L to R)
PITKIN FLASK, Olive-Green, ½ Post, 24 Swirled & Vertical Ribs, Sick, 6½" H. .
. . . .$200.00
CHESTNUT FLASK, Pale Emerald Green, 25 Slightly Swirled Ribs, Broken Blister, 6½" H. $135.00

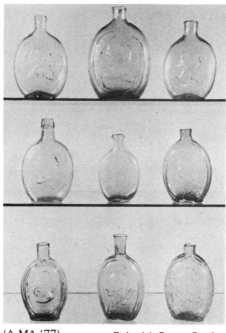

(A-MA '77)   *Richard A. Bourne Co., Inc.*
PICTORIAL & HISTORICAL FLASKS
(ROW I, L to R)
WASHINGTON-TAYLOR, Pt., Aquamarine, Phila., Chemical Deposit, Minor Rim Nick, 7" H. $40.00
WASHINGTON-TAYLOR, Qt., Aquamarine, Phila., Chemical Deposit, 8" H. . . .
. . . .$30.00
WASHINGTON-TAYLOR, Pt., Aquamarine, Phila., 6⅝" H. $80.00
(ROW II, L to R)
WASHINGTON-TAYLOR, Pt., Aquamarine, Cracked, 7¼" H. $5.00
WASHINGTON-SHEAF, ½ Pt., Aquamarine, Bottom Cloudy, 6" H. $20.00
JACKSON-EAGLE, Pt., Lt. Green, James Taylor & Co., Lip Nicked, 6¼" H. . . . .
. . . .$600.00
(ROW III, L to R)
TAYLOR-RINGGOLD, Pt., Aquamarine, 6⅝" H. $75.00
TAYLOR-BALTIMORE MONUMENT, Pt., Aquamarine, Cloudy, 7½" H. . . . .
. . . .$100.00
LAFAYETTE-EAGLE, Pt., Aquamarine, Kensington Glass Works, Phila., Neck Chipped, 6⅝" H. $125.00

(A-MA '77)   *Richard A. Bourne Co., Inc.*
PICTORIAL & HISTORICAL FLASKS
(ROW I, L to R)
DOUBLE EAGLE, ½ Pt., Olive-Amber, 6¼" H. $40.00
DOUBLE EAGLE, ½ Pt., Drk. Amber, 6½" H. $35.00
DOUBLE-EAGLE, Pt., Drk. Amber, High Point & Base Wear, 7½" H. $25.00
(ROW II, L to R)
UNION-CLASPED HANDS, ½ Pt., Golden-Amber, 6⅜" H. $35.00
UNION-CLASPED HANDS, ½ Pt., Drk. Amber, 6½" H. $35.00
SHEAF OF WHEAT, ½ Pt., Olive-Amber, Minor Damage, 6⅛" H. $4.00
SHEAF OF WHEAT, ½ Pt., Olive-Green, Minor Damage, Chemical Deposit, 6⅛" H. .
. . . .$10.00
(ROW III, L to R)
SHEAF OF WHEAT, Pt., Olive-Amber, 7⅝" H. $40.00
SHEAF OF WHEAT, Qt., Drk. Amber or Tobacco Brown, Rim Nick & Chip, 9" H. . .
. . . .$35.00
FLASK, Pt., Olive Green, Ballet Dancer One Side; Rev: Soldier Carrying Gun, Lip Bruise, 8⅛" H. $300.00

◀ *To the left*

(A-OH '77)   *Garth's Auctions, Inc.*
(ROW I, L to R)
GLOBULAR BOTTLE, Yellow-Amber, 24 Swirled Ribs, Zanesville, 7¾" H. . . . . . .
. . . .$425.00
FLASK, Aqua Chestnut, 24 Swirled Ribs, Zanesville, 6¾" H. $85.00
GLOBULAR BOTTLE, Aqua, 24 Swirled Ribs, Zanesville, 7¼" H. $85.00
(ROW II, L to R)
PITKIN, Yellow-Olive, ½ Post W/35 Vertical & Swirled Ribs, 7" H. $160.00
BOTTLE, Aqua, 24 Swirled Ribs, Zanesville, 8½" H. $55.00
DOUBLE EAGLE FLASK, Yellow-Amber, Iron Pontil, Heat Check In Neck, 7½" H.
. . . .$105.00

(A-OH '77)   *Garth's Auctions, Inc.*

TIN COOKIE CUTTERS
(ROW I)
HORSE, 4" H. $16.00
BOUQUET OF FLOWERS, 4¼" H. .....
..........................$6.00
CROWING ROOSTER, 4¼" H. ..$16.00
(ROW II)
SMALL ROOSTER, 3" H. $5.00
DEER W/ANTLERS, 4¾" H. $41.00
POUTER PIGEON, 3" H. $8.00
(ROW III)
EAGLE, 3½" H. $17.00
COD FISH, 2½" H. $7.00
DOG, 2½" H. $7.00
(ROW IV)
RUNNING DOG, 3" H. $9.00
CRIMPED EDGE HEART, 3½" H. .....
..........................$13.00
BIRD LANDING, 2½" H. $10.00

(A-OH '77)   *Garth's Auctions, Inc.*

TIN COOKIE CUTTERS
CROW $17.00
DUTCH LADY $13.00
MAN $12.00
LARGE ROOSTER $31.00
DOVE IN FLIGHT $26.00
SEATED CAT $18.00
DUTCH HEART $36.00
TULIP $41.00
DOG $13.00
GUINEA PIG $21.00
REINDEER $12.00
SANTA CLAUS W/PACK $2.00
LION $5.00
FISH $9.00
HORSE $15.00
LARGE EAGLE $34.00
FAT MOUSE $17.00
BOOT $19.00
WHALE $20.00
BIRD, LANDING $10.00

(A-OH '77)   *Garth's Auctions, Inc.*

TIN COOKIE CUTTERS
EAGLE, 3¼" H. $15.00
BIRD, 2½" H. $6.00
ROOSTER, 3¼" H. $16.00
PRIMITIVE WOMAN, 2¾" H. ...$9.00
CHICKEN, 2¼" H. $8.00
SWAN, 3" H. $4.00
BIRD, Resoldered Handle, 2¼" L. $15.00
MAN, 5¼" H. $9.00
BOOT, 3¾" H. $22.00
WOMAN, 5" H. $11.00

(A-OH '77)   *Garth's Auctions, Inc.*

TIN COOKIE CUTTER, Rabbit ...$5.00
TIN CHOCOLATE MOLD, Chick ......
..........................$7.00
TIN CHOCOLATE MOLD, Fish ...$6.00
TIN CHOCOLATE MOLD, Dog ...$6.00
IRON CHOPPING KNIFE, Brass Mounted Wooden Handle, 6" L. $12.50
TIN COOKIE CUTTER, Bird $5.00
TIN COOKIE CUTTER, Bird $5.00
TIN COOKIE CUTTER, Bear $5.00
TIN COOKIE CUTTER, Running Animal
..........................$5.00

(A-OH '77)   *Garth's Auctions, Inc.*

TIN COOKIE CUTTERS
(ROW I, L to R)
BIRD $12.00
BIRD $3.00
HORSE, Crimped Mane & Tail, 4½" L.
..........................$40.00
(ROW II, L to R)
STAR $1.00
BIRD IN FLIGHT $11.00
SWIRLED DESIGN, Cylindrical Handle.
..........................$7.00
(ROW III, L to R)
BIRD $16.00
BIRD, Resoldered $27.00
ROOSTER $21.00
(ROW IV, L to R)
FISH, Crimped Fin $15.00
FISH $20.00

(A-OH '77)   *Garth's Auctions, Inc.*

TIN COOKIE CUTTERS
BIRD, 2½" L. $10.00
FISH, 4¼" L. $40.00
RUNNING DOG, 3¼" L. $15.00
TWO WOMEN, 2⅜" & 3" H. $14.00
WOMAN W/CRIMPED SKIRT, 3" H.
..........................$8.00
FISH, 3" L. $8.00
WOMAN WITH HAT, 3" H. $22.50
PIG, 3¼" L. $26.00
DOG, 2¾" L. $22.00
BIRD IN FLIGHT, 3½" L. $40.00
HAND & HEART, 3¾" H. $132.50
ROOSTER, 3" H. $12.00
MAN IN MOON, 4½" H. $23.00
SEATED DOG, 3¼" H. $16.00
CAST IRON COOKIE BOARD, "Gingerbread Man", 5¾" x 11¼" H. $105.00

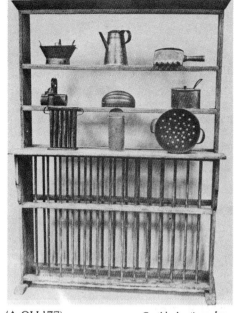

(A-OH '77)   *Garth's Auctions, Inc.*
(ROW I, L to R)
IRONSTONE PITCHER, Embossed Surface W/Blue & Black Glaze, 8½" H. $42.50
YELLOW WARE BOWL, Back W/Impressed Signature In Shield, Words Indistinct, 10" x 13" $32.50
MORTAR & PESTLE, Iron, Mortar - 6" H. $27.50
STONEWARE FOOT WARMER, Impressed "Dorchester Pottery Works, Boston, Mass.", 10¾" H. $20.00
(ROW II, L to R)
CANNON, Cast Bronze In Cast Iron Frame, Workable, Barrel - 7½" L. $65.00
ROUND TABLE, Doll Size, 6¾" Diam., 5¾" H. $15.00
CUSTARD CUP, Blue & White Kitchen Spatter, 4' Diam. $13.00
BURL MALLET, Stamped "S. Lee", 15" L. $17.50
(ROW III, L to R)
MORTAR & PESTLE, Walnut, 6½" H. $27.50
STONEWARE JAR, Impressed "Messenger Bros. 55 Bromfield St.", Base Chipped, 9" H. $17.50
MORTAR & PESTLE, Lignum Vitae, 6¼" H. $40.00

(A-OH '77)   *Garth's Auctions, Inc.*
(ROW I, L to R)
TURNED WOODEN BOWL, Red Exterior, Worn White Painted Interior, 7" Diam. $22.50
SHAKER SEWING BOX, Interior Lined W/Gold Paper W/Black Dots, 7¾" Diam., 3⅜" H. $30.00
TURNED WOODEN BOWL, Green Exterior, Rim Chip & Age Crack, 5" Diam. $13.00
TURNED WOODEN BOWL, Worn Blue Paint, 7½" Diam. $27.50
(ROW II, L to R)
TIN LAMP FILLER, Zinc Lid & Copper Cap On Spout, 9½" H. $15.00
WALNUT BOX, Diamond Shaped Black Inlaid Escutcheon, Signed "Sister A. Brookes. T. Fisher, '99", Key, 3" x 5" x 9" $45.00
WOODEN SCRUB BRUSHES (2) $12.50
SHAKER COFFEE POT, Tin, 6½" H. $25.00
(ROW III, L to R)
TURNED WOODEN BOWL, Worn Grey Painted Exterior, Warped, 8½" x 7¾" $30.00
TURNED WOODEN BOWL, Traces Red Paint On Exterior, 6" Diam. $30.00
SHAKER STORAGE BOX, Wooden, Lid W/Repaired Split, 9" L. $60.00
SHAKER STORAGE BOX, Wooden, Stitched Joints, Old Drk. Green Paint, 6" L., 2¼" H. $47.50
TURNED WOODEN BOWL, Worn Brown Painted Exterior, 5¼" Diam. $35.00
TURNED WOODEN BOWL, Grey Painted Exterior W/Red Beneath, 7" Diam. $22.50
TURNED WOODEN BOWL, Brown Painted Exterior, 6" Diam. $22.00

(A-OH '77)   *Garth's Auctions, Inc.*
PINE PEWTER CUPBOARD, Worn Orange-Brown Paint, Back Boards Missing On Top Section, Mortised construction, 54" W., 16" D., 76½" H. $660.00
TIN UTENSILS
(ROW I, L to R)
ANGEL FOOD CAKE PAN, W/Cooling Rack, 10" Diam. $7.00
SIDE SPOUT COFFEE POT, 9½" H. $27.00
MULTI-SPOUT POURER, 8" W. $107.50
(ROW II, L to R)
LAMP, Horizontal Font, Brass Burner, Worn Green Paint, No Chimney, 6¾" W. $27.50
MELON RIBBED FOOD MOLD, Minor Repair, 9" L. $21.00
CONTAINER, Cast Iron Handle, 8½" W. $25.00
(ROW III, L to R)
CANDLE MOLD, 12 Tube, 11" H. $26.00
GRATER, Triangular Shaped Punching, 11½" H. $10.00
SIEVE, 11¼" Diam. $18.00

(D-ME '78)
TIN GOOSENECK TEAKETTLE, Shaker $165.00

(D-MA '78)
CHERRY SPRINGERLE ROLLING PIN, 18" L. $165.00

(D-OH '78)
IRON APPLE PEELER, Pa. Patent, Complete & Working $45.00

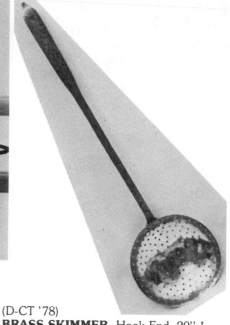

(A-OH '77) *Garth's Auctions, Inc.*
WOODEN BUTTER PRINT, Floral Star, 3¼" Diam. $22.50
WOODEN BUTTER PRINT, Pineapple, 3½" Diam. $5.00
WOODEN BUTTER PRINT, Pomegranate, 3¼" Diam. $20.00
WOODEN BUTTER PRINT, Stars & Leaves, 3⅛" Diam. $20.00
WOODEN BUTTER PRINT, Flower W/ Foliage, 3⅝" Diam. $20.00
BURL SCOOP, Side Damaged, Age Crack, 13" L. $385.00
WOODEN BUTTER PRINT, Pomegranate, 3¾" Diam. $22.50
WOODEN BUTTER PRINT, Leaf Design, 3¾" Diam. $22.50
WOODEN BUTTER PRINT, Geometric, 4⅛" Diam. $85.00
HORN SPOON, Engraving Of Teepee On Bowl, 15" L. $30.00
WOODEN BUTTER PRINT, Star Shaped Flower, No Handle, 4" Diam. $22.50

(A-OH '77) *Garth's Auctions, Inc.*
(ROW I, L to R)
NUTMEG GRATER, Tin, 6½" H. . .$2.00
WICK TRIMMER, Iron, 6" L. $10.50
VEGETABLE WASHER, 5½" H. $15.00
NUTMEG GRATER, Tin, 5½" H. . .$5.00
(ROW II, L to R)
CHOCOLATE MOLD, Tin, 4½" W. $9.00
BUTTER PRINT, Thistle, Miniature, 1¼" Diam., 2" L. $31.00
TOMMY CANDLE HOLDER, Wrought Iron, 9" L. $42.50
(ROW III, L to R)
BUTTER PRINT, Wooden, Sheaves Of Wheat, 2½" x 4¼" $17.50
FLOWER POT, Stoneware, Albany Slip, 3" H. $75.00
BUTTER PRINT, Wooden, Cow, Age Cracks, 3⅝" Diam. $125.00

(D-CT '78)
BRASS SKIMMER, Hook End, 20" L. $80.00

(D-CO '78)
BRASS COFFEE GRINDER . . .$100.00

(A-PA '77) *Pennypacker Auction Centre*
LADLE, Brass Bowl, Wrought Iron Handle, Arro. 1821, A.A.V.D. Tulip & Dots Decor., 19½" L. $500.00

(A-PA '77 *Pennypacker Auction Centre*
BUTTER PRINT, Two Sides Unequal In Size, 4½" & 3¾" Diam., Daisy Sprigs Prints $170.00
BUTTER PRINT, Harp Center Surrounded By Four Fish, Berry Border $55.00
BUTTER PRINT, Cow, Long Handle $75.00

(D-PA '78)
BUTTER BOX, Walnut, Dovetailed, Wrought Iron Handle, 6½" D., 16" W., 21" H. $245.00

(D-NJ '78)
BRASS SKIMMER, W/Iron Handle $50.00

(D-KS '78)   *Fisher's Antiques*
(TOP)
WOODEN LEMON SQUEEZER, 10½"
L. $40.00
(L to R)
WOODEN SPOON, Advertising, 13" L. .
. . . .$5.00
WOODEN COOKIE ROLLING PIN, 15"
L. $45.00
WOODEN OLIVE DIPPER, German, 5
Holes In Center Of Bowl, 12" L. . .$25.00
WOODEN POTATO MASHER, 10½" L.
. . . .$20.00
CAST IRON EGG BEATER, 10" L. . . . .
. . . .$15.00
CHOPPING KNIFE, 5¼" $10.00
CORK SCREW, 4" L. $6.00

(A-OH '77)   *Garth's Auctions, Inc.*
CAST IRON
(ROW I, L to R)
PAPERWEIGHT, Pig, 3" L. $20.00
EAGLE, Worn Gilt, 8¼" Wingspan . . . . . .
. . . .$14.00
PAPERWEIGHT, Pig, 3" L. $20.00
(ROW II, L to R)
BIRD, Black, Worn, 4" L. $12.00
DUCK, White, 5¾" L. $12.00
BIRD, White, 4" L. $12.00
(ROW III, L to R)
BIRDS, Pr., 4" L. $22.50
EAGLE & ARROW, Old Gilt, 7¼" Wing-
span $17.50
(ROW IV, L to R)
BIRD, 5¾" L. $5.00
FISH, 7" L. $50.00
BANK, Dog, 5½" L. $27.50

(A-OH '77)   *Garth's Auctions, Inc.*
(ROW I, L to R)
DOG BOOK ENDS, Cast Iron, Both
Halves, 6" L. $10.00
TASSEL WEIGHTS, (4), Cast Iron, 4½"
H. $14.00
QUAIL, Bronze, Wooden Base, 4½" H. . .
. . . .$155.00
(ROW II, L to R)
TASSEL WEIGHTS, Pr., Cast Iron, 10¼"
H. $9.00
FIGURE OF MAN, Cast Iron, 8" H. . . . . .
. . . .$10.00
STAG BANK, Cast Iron, Traces Black
Paint, 10" H. $67.50
CANDLESTICK, Cast Iron, Sq. Base,
6" H. $8.00
(ROW III, L to R)
MERCURY THERMOMETER, Engraved
Brass Back Set Into Cast Iron Ivy Frame, 8"
H. $10.00
SHOOTING GALLERY FIGURES, Pr.,
Deer, 7½" H. $25.00
MECHANICAL BANK, Cast Iron, "Ma-
gician Bank", 8" H. $45.00
SEATED DOG, Cast Iron, Worn Paint,
5½" H. $13.00

(A-OH '77)   *Garth's Auctions, Inc.*
BRASS SHIP'S BELL, Clapper & Hanging Bracket, 9¾" H. $75.00

(A-PA '77)   *Pennypacker Auction Centre*
(L to R)
PEWTER PLATE, American, B. Barns,
7¾" Diam., ...$175.00
PEWTER BOWL, American, B. Barns,
Phila., Pa., 6½" Diam. $400.00

(A-OH '77)   *Garth's Auctions, Inc.*
WROUGHT IRON FORK, Tooled Han-
dle, 23" L. $45.00
WROUGHT IRON FORK, 16" L. . . . . . .
. . . .$20.00
**WROUGHT IRON RAM'S HORN
HINGE,** Single, 6¼" L. $12.00
MINIATURE CANNON, Iron Barrel,
Wooden Carriage W/Old Blue Paint, 9½" L.
. . . .$85.00
FRAME From 1-Pc. Wood W/Applied
Composition Decor., 4½" x 5¼" . .$26.00
WROUGHT IRON TOMAHAWK, 17¼"
L. $20.00
WROUGHT IRON SPATULA, 4¾" L.
. . . .$42.50
TIN CANDLE ARM, From Sconce Or
Chandelier, Crimped Pan, Traces Gold
Japanning, Pan - 3½" Diam., 7½" O.L.
. . . .$50.00
WROUGHT IRON FORK, Tooled Han-
dle, 16" L. $32.50

(A-OH '77)   *Garth's Auctions, Inc.*
(L to R)
PEWTER COFFEE POT, Incised Floral
Design, Cast Finial, 10" H. $45.00
PEWTER HOT WATER BOTTLE, Screw
On Cap W/Handle, Inner Pewter Seal,
Dent, 12½" L. $45.00

(A-PA '77)   *Pennypacker Auction Centre*
(L to R)
PEWTER WATER PITCHER, American,
Hinged Lid, Signed "Boardman", 9½" H.
. . . .$240.00
PEWTER COFFEE POT, American,
Signed "G. Richardson", 11" H. .$270.00
TIN COFFEE POT, Eagle Spout . .$80.00

(A-OH '77)   *Garth's Auctions, Inc.*
(L to R)
FORK, Iron W/Cast Handle, 15" L. . . . . .
. . . .$10.00
STRAINER, Wrought Iron & Brass,
Stamped, "F.B.S., Canton, Ohio, Pat. Jan.
26, '86", 16" L. $70.00
TASTER, Wrought Iron, Handle Stamped
"J. Schmidt, 1843", 10" L. $150.00
CHOPPING KNIFE, Wrought Iron,
Stamped "Camfield", Wooden Handle,
7" W.
SPATULA, Wrought Iron, 11½" L. . . . . . .
. . . .$22.50
STRAINER, Wrought Iron & Brass, 9" L.
. . . .$80.00
FORK, Wrought Iron, 14" L. $15.00
TASTER, Wrought Iron & Brass, 10½" L.
. . . .$35.00
SPATULA, Wrought Iron & Brass, 15½" L.
. . . .$45.00
SPATULA, Wrought Iron, Handle Stamped
W/"W. Ankerman", 15½" L. $75.00

(D-MO '78)
COPPER WASH BOILER $65.00

(A-PA '77)   *Pennypakcer Auction Centre*
(L to R)
COPPER MEASURES (5), 2¼" to 5½"
. . . .$110.00
COPPER MEASURES (2), 8" & 10" . . .
. . . .$70.00

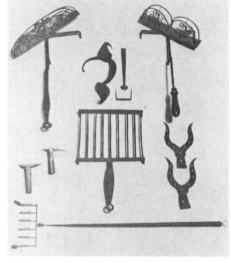

(A-OH '77)   *Garth's Auctions, Inc.*
WROUGHT IRON
TOASTER, Repaired Foot, 20½" L. . . . . .
. . . .$135.00
THUMB LATCH, W/Rod & Staple, 13½"
L. $375.00
TOASTER, Turned Wooden Handle, 21½"
L. $145.00
BROILER, 17½" L. $135.00
DOUGH SCRAPER, Worm Eaten Wood-
en Handle, 4" L. $70.00
DOUGH SCRAPER, Iron Handle, 4" L.
. . . .$75.00
HINGES, Pr., Pitchfork Shape, 8½" L. . .
. . . .$150.00
TOASTER, Pencil Post Handle, 31½" L.
. . . .$95.00

To the right ▶

(A-OH '77)   *Garth's Auctions, Inc.*
(ROW I, L to R)
CHOPPING KNIFE, Turned Wooden
Handle, Blade Stamped "W. Greaves &
Sons", 5½" W. $5.00
CHOPPING KNIFE, Wooden Handle,
9¼" W. $25.00
CHOPPING KNIFE, Wooden Handle,
5¾" W. $10.00
(ROW II, L to R)
CHOPPING KNIFE, Wooden Handle,
Blade Has Rust Damage, 5¼" W. $5.00
IRON ELBOW BOX LOCK, No Keeper
Or Second Handle, 4¼" x 6" $7.50
CHOPPING KNIFE, Curved Supports,
Wooden Handle, 7" W. $22.50
WROUGHT IRON "S" HOOK, 5" L. . .
. . . .$5.00
LEATHER CUTTING TOOL, Wooden
Handle, Signed "A.F. Deharty", 6" L. . . .
. . . .$2.00
(ROW III, L to R)
CHOPPING KNIVES
Wooden Handle, Blade Split, 5½" W. . . . .
. . . .$5.00
Turned Wooden Handle, 7¼" W. . .$25.00
Wooden Handle, 6¼" W. $10.00

(A-OH '77)   *Garth's Auctions, Inc.*
CHOPPING KNIVES
(ROW I, L to R)
Wooden Handle, 6¼" W. $20.00
Wooden Handle, 5" W. $32.50
Wooden Handle & Metal Rod Supports,
6" W. $15.00
(ROW II, L to R)
Shaped Blade, Wooden Handle, 6½" W. . .
. . . .$20.00
MEDALLION, Cast Pewter, "John A.
Logan", 4" x 5½" $45.00
Goose Neck Handle, 13" L. $45.00
Wooden Handle, Blade Corner Damaged,
5½" W. $15.00
(ROW III, L to R)
Wooden Handle, 5¾" W. $17.50
Wooden Handle W/Turned Knobs, 8" W.
. . . .$52.50
Wooden Handle, 6" W. $15.00

(A-OH '77)   *Garth's Auctions, Inc.*
**CAST WHITE METAL CHOCOLATE
MOLD,** Rabbits, 4½" x 10¼" $17.50

(A-MA '77)   *Richard A. Bourne Co., Inc.*
(ROW I)
PINE KNIFE BOX, Orig. Reddish Finish .
. . . .$50.00
PINE KNIFE BOX, Dovetailed, Red . . . . .
. . . .$70.00
(ROW II)
SUGAR FIRKIN, Restored & Redecorated
. . . .$20.00
PINE FOOTSTOOL, Old Red Finish . . . .
. . . .$55.00
(ROW III)
CRANBERRY SCOOP, Patent Date
June 2, 1899, Curly Maple Sides . .$90.00
PINE HANGING SALT BOX, Hand
Forged Nails, Red Paint $150.00

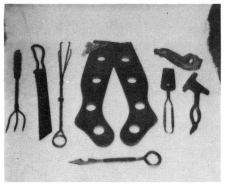

(D-KS '78)   *Fisher's Antiques*
(L to R)
MEAT FORK, 12" L. $5.00
BREAD KNIFE, 14" L. $7.00
WIRE CHIMNEY CLEANER, 14" L. . . .
. . . .$10.00
WOODEN STOCKING STRETCHERS,
15", Pr. $25.00
ADVERTISING SPATULA, 9½" L. . . . .
. . . .$7.00
CAST IRON MEAT TENDERIZER, 7" L.
. . . .$15.00
(TOP RIGHT)
TIN CHOCOLATE MOLD, Pipe Design,
5" L. $35.00
(BOTTOM CENTER)
**ADVERTISING ICE PICK & BOTTLE
OPENER,** 8" L. $15.00

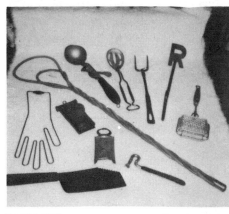

(D-KS '78)   *Fisher's Antiques*
(TOP RIGHT)
ICE CREAM SCOOP, Patent 1895, 11" L.
. . . .$15.00
**ADVERTISING BOTTLE OPENER/
BEATER,** Dated 1914, 11" L. $15.00
CAST IRON MEAT FORK, 12¾" L. . . .
. . . .$12.00
BRANDING IRON, Brass Stamp, Franklin
Blackleg Serum Co., 11¼" L. $15.00
WIRE SOAP SAVER, 9" L. $15.00
(DIAGONAL)
"RIZ" FEATHER PILLOW BEATER,
27¼" L. $25.00
(BOTTOM LEFT)
WIRE GLOVE STRETCHER, 10¾" L. . .
. . . .$15.00
NUTMEG GRATER, Tin & Wood, 4½" L.
. . . .$35.00
MINIATURE NUTMEG GRATER, Tin,
4½" L. $5.00
**ADVERTISING CIGAR BOX OPENER
& HAMMER,** Dated 1897, 5½" L. . . . . . .
. . . .$20.00
MEAT CLEAVER & TENDERIZER,
10" L. $15.00

(D-KS '78)   *Fisher's Antiques*
(LEFT — TOP TO BOTTOM)
**WOODEN HANDMADE MEAT TEN-
DERIZER,** 10" L. $12.50
WOODEN GLOVE POWDERER, 5¾"
L. $25.00
WOODEN BUTTER PADDLE, Hand
Decorated, 9½" $25.00
(CENTER)
STONEWARE ROLLING PIN, Wild-
flower Design, 14" L. $65.00
(RIGHT — TOP TO BOTTOM)
STONEWARE MEAT TENDERIZER,
Wildflower Design, 9" L. $65.00
WOODEN SUGAR SCOOP, 7½" L. . . .
. . . .$35.00
WIRE PAN SCRATCHER, 10" L. . . . . .
. . . .$17.00

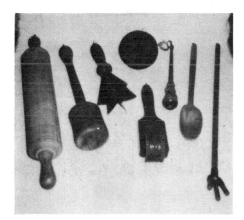

(D-KS '78)   *Fisher's Antiques*
(L to R)
WOODEN NOODLE ROLLING PIN,
18" L. $40.00
WOODEN MASHER, 13½" L. . .$12.00
VEGETABLE CHOPPER, 9½" L. . . . . .
. . . .$15.00
CHERRY SWIZZEL STICK, 10¼" L. . .
. . . .$35.00
WOODEN SPOON, 14½" L. $6.00
**WOODEN MAYTAG "DIPSY DOOZY"
CLOTHES FORK,** 20½" L. $25.00
(CENTER TOP)
WOODEN BUTTER PRINT, Heart Patt.,
4" Diam. $45.00
(CENTER BOTTOM)
WOODEN COOKIE ROLLER, German,
Fruit & Nut Design, 9½" L. $40.00

(A-PA '77)   *Pennypacker Auction Centre*
WROUGHT IRON BREAD TOASTER,
Six-Heart Design, Long Handle . . .$225.00

(A-PA '77)   *Pennypacker Auction Centre*
SWIVEL BASE TOASTER, Eight Rattail
Designs, Long Handle $300.00

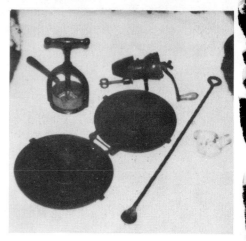

(A-OH '77)   *Garth's Auctions, Inc.*
(ROW I, L to R)
BRASS HANGING TOBACCO BOX,
Polished, 6½" W., 3" D., 5¾" H. .$40.00
YELLOWWARE FOOD MOLD, Ear Of
Corn Center, 7¼" x 9" x 4" H. . . .$45.00
HANGING COMB CASE, Woven Stripes
Of Tin W/Tin "Curls", 8½" W., 3¾" D.,
7½" H. $22.50
(ROW II, L to R)
WALLPAPER COVERED BOX, Blue &
White Printed On Faded Purple Ground,
6¼" Diam., 4¾" H. $92.50
SPRUCE GUM BOX, Carved From 1-Pc.
Wood W/Sliding Lid, Friezian Type Carving
All Sides, 3½" x 6½" x 1¾" $145.00
TREEN PONCE SANDER $35.00
TREEN WARE BOX, Red Sponging On
Yellow Ground, Glued Cracks In Lid &
Base, 6¼" Diam., 6" H. $10.00
(ROW III, L to R)
YELLOWWARE FOOD MOLD, Swirled
Center, 6¼" Diam., 3¼" H. $16.00
TREEN WARE COMPOTE, Orig. Drk.
Green Paint W/Red & Yellow Striping, 8½"
Diam., 5" H. $100.00
YELLOWWARE FOOD MOLD, Swirled
Center, Rim Hairline, 6¼" Diam., 3¾" H.
. . . .$15.00

(A-OH '77)   *Stratford Auction Center*
**MINIATURE SALESMAN'S SAMPLE
TINS**
(ROW I, L to R)
BUSTER BROWN MUSTARD . . .$22.50
LOG CABIN SYRUP $52.50
ROCKFORD WATCHES TRAY .$37.50
INDIAN BOTTLE OPENER, Metal . . . .
. . . .$12.00
RUNKEL COCOA $20.00
ROYAL BAKING POWDER $5.00
(ROW II, L to R)
MONARCH COCOA $17.50
TEAS $15.00
KLEIN'S COCOA $20.00
BOSCUL COFFEE BANK $27.50
NESTLES FOOD $15.00
DILL'S ADHESIVE PLASTER . .$15.00
DR. LeGEARE HEALING POWDER . . .
. . . .$10.00
MONARCH COCOA $17.50
(ROW III, L to R)
MENTHOLATUM $15.00
COTTOLENE $15.00
CRACKER JACK TIN BANK . . .$52.50
DOP TIP TRAY $37.50
POSTUM CEREAL $700
COLGATE BABY TALC $30.00
JOHNSON'S POWDERED WAX . . . . .
. . . .$15.00
TEAS $15.00
KLEIN'S COCOA $20.00

(D-KS '78)   *Fisher's Antiques*
(TOP)
CAST IRON MEAT PRESS $20.00
CAST IRON NUTMEG GRATER . . . . . .
. . . .$35.00
(BOTTOM)
CAST IRON WAFFLE IRON, Assorted
Design, 8" Diam. $20.00
CAST IRON TASTING SPOON, 22¼" L.
. . . .$20.00
SPONGEWARE SALT & PEPPER, 1-
Piece, 3" $35.00

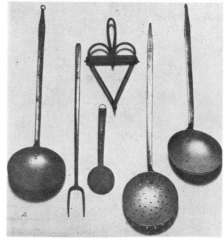

(A-OH '77)   *Garth's Auctions, Inc.*
UTENSILS
(L to R)
WROUGHT IRON & BRASS DIPPER,
Handle Stamped "J. Schmidt, 1884", 10"
L. $140.00
WROUGHT IRON FORK, Handle Signed
"J. Schmidt," 1842", 17½" L. . . .$135.00
WROUGHT IRON TRIVET, 9½" L. . . . .
. . . .$45.00
TIN SPOON, 8½" L. $10.00
**WROUGHT IRON & BRASS STRAIN-
ER,** Handle Stamped "J. Schmidt, 1848",
20" L. $180.00
WROUGHT IRON & BRASS DIPPER,
Handle Stamped "J. Schmidt, 1848, 18" L.
. . . .$160.00

(D-PA '78)
WOODEN PEEL, Pine, 20" L. . . .$85.00

(D-PA '78)
PINE CUTTING BOARD, 25" L. . . . . . .
. . . .$65.00

(A-OH '77)   *Garth's Auctions, Inc.*
TREEN WARE
(ROW I, L to R)
WINES, (2), 1 Drk. & 1 Light, 2¾" & 2⅞"
....$15.00
WINE (1¾" H.) & **NEEDLE CASE,** W/
Threaded Top W/Age Checks, 3" H. .....
....$19.00
SNUFF BOX, 3¼" Diam. $12.50
(ROW II, L to R)
JAR, Wire Handle, Chipped Finial, 3½" H.
....$70.00
JAR, Wire Handle, 2¾" H. $67.50
JAR, Wire Handle, 3" H. $80.00
JAR, Wire Handle, 3½" H. $65.00
(ROW III, L to R)
PEARS (Pr.), Salt & Pepper Shakers, 3" H.
....$35.00
SALT, 2¾" Diam., 2" H. $15.00
PEAR BOX, 3½" H. $35.00
TRAVELING NUTMEG GRATER,
Threaded Lid, Ivory & Punched Metal
Grater, Chipped, 2½" H. $77.50

To the right
(ROW I, L to R)
BLOCK TIN SCOOP, 10½" L. ...$6.00
TIN SPICE CHEST, Wooden Knobs,
9¾" W., 13¾" H. $80.00
TIN FOOD MOLD, Marked "France",
10½" L. $20.00
(ROW II, L to R)
TIN ABC PLATE, "Mary Had A Little
Lamb", 8" Diam. $45.00
TIN ADVERTISING LARD BUCKET,
"1776-1876 Naphey's Lard, Philadelphia",
Base Resoldered, 2½" H. $10.50
TIN FOOD MOLD, Melon Ribbed, 6¾" L.
....$15.00
TIN ABC PLATE, "Who Killed Cock Rob-
in", 7¾" Diam. $37.50
(ROW III, L to R)
COPPER POT, Iron Handle, Dovetailed
Const., 6½" Diam., 5" H. $47.50
TIN TURKS HEAD MOLD, Swirled, 11"
Diam. $11.00
COPPER SAUCE PAN, Turned Wooden
Handle, Dovetailed Const., Marked Base,
5" H. $47.50

(A-OH '77)   *Garth's Auctions, Inc.*
(ROW I, L to R)
TREEN JAR, Lignum Vitae, Base Age
Checks, 6" H. $90.00
TREEN COMPOTE, Walnut, 20th C., 6½"
Diam., 8½" H. $35.00
TREEN JAR, Wire Handle, 5¼" H. .....
....$95.00
(ROW II, L to R)
TIN "A.B.C." PLATE, 6" Diam. ..$20.00
TREEN SANDER, 3" H. $20.00
TIN MELON RIBBED FOOD MOLD,
10" L. $15.00
TREEN JAR, Covered, Turned Rings, Red
Stain, 4¾" H. $12.50
TREEN DIPPER, Made 1-Pc. Wood, 4"
Diam., 7¾" L. $67.50
(ROW III, L to R)
TREEN MORTAR & PESTLE, Age
Crack, 6¼" H. $35.00
TIN MELON RIBBED FOOD MOLD,
"Kreamer", 8½" L. $15.00
TIN FOOD MOLD, Embossed Rose, 5¼"
L. $37.50
TIN FOOD MOLD, Red Center, "Ger-
many", 6¼" H. $12.50

(A-OH '77)   *Garth's Auctions, Inc.*

(A-OH '77)   *Garth's Auctions, Inc.*
TREEN FOOTED JAR, Wire Handle, 7"
Diam., 7" H. $140.00
TREEN FOOTED JAR, Wire Handle,
Cracked Base, 6½" Diam., 6" H. ..$80.00
TREEN FOOTED JAR, Wire Handle, 6¼"
Diam., 5" H. $105.00
(ROW II, L to R)
TREEN JAR, Traces Orig. Decor., Var-
nished, 4¾" H. $135.00
TREEN JAR, Refinished, Chipped Lid,
7¼" H. $65.00
TREEN JAR, Part Of Lid Flange Missing,
5¼" Diam. $7.50
(ROW III, L to R)
TREEN BOX, 1 Pc. Wood, 7⅝" H. .....
....$25.00
FISH CUTTING BOARD, 13½" L. .....
....$40.00
TURNED CUP, Attached Turned Handle,
9¼" L. $5.00

(D-MA '78)
MAPLE CHOPPING BOWL, Unusual
Shape, 5" H., 11¼" W., 19" L. ..$145.00

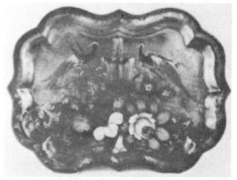

(A-PA '77   *Pennypacker Auction Centre*
TIN CHIPPENDALE TRAY, Decor. W/
Peacock, Fountain & Flowers, 30" $60.00

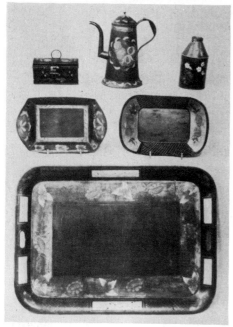

(A-MA '77)   *Richard A. Bourne Co., Inc.*

TOLEWARE

(ROW I)

DOME-TOP BOX, Hasp, Tulips & Berries, 6½" L. $40.00

COFFEEPOT, Orig. Decor., 10½" H. $800.00

CANNISTER, 8" H. $25.00

(ROW II)

MUFFIN TRAY, 12½" L. $175.00

MUFFIN TRAY, 12½" L. $35.00

(ROW III)

OBLONG TRAY, 28" L. $60.00

(A-OH '77)   *Garth's Auctions, Inc.*

CAST IRON WAFFLE IRON, Wrought Iron Handles, 28" L. $30.00

CAST IRON PARLOR STOVE, "Stanley's Patent No. 2", Decor. W/Pr. Of Maidens & Basket Of Fruit, 26" W., 16½" D. 35" H. $405.00

WROUGHT IRON STRAP HINGES, (1 of 2), 44" L. $20.00

WROUGHT IRON PEEL, 46" L. $125.00

WROUGHT IRON ADJUSTABLE SAW-TOOTH TRAMMEL, 30" L. Closed $45.00

TIN PITCHER, Iron Handle, Worn Alligatored Paint, 12¼" H. $27.50

WROUGHT IRON ADJUSTABLE TRAMMEL, 37" L. Closed $25.00

WROUGHT IRON PEAL, Ram's Horn Handle, 50" L. $65.00

WROUGHT IRON STRAP HINGE, 45½" L. $10.00

(A-OH '77)   *Garth's Auctions, Inc.*

PINE SHELVES, Drk. Graining, 27" W., 8" D., 33½" H. $230.00

(ROW I, L to R)

TIN CANDLE LANTERN, Clear Blown Globe, Black Paint, 11" H. $145.00

TOLE TEA CADDY, Red Ground W/ Blue, Green, Yellow, White & Black, 5¼" H. $815.00

TIN WHALE OIL LAMP, Gimbal Type Font, 4¾" Diam., 8" H. $125.00

(ROW II, L to R)

TOLE PITCHER, Brown Japanning W/ Yellow Stripe, Worn, 5½" H. $20.00

TOLE COFFEE POT, Worn Black Ground W/Yellow, Red, Green, Blue, Ochre & White, 8" H. $280.00

TOLE TEA CADDY, Black Ground W/ Yellow, Red, Green & White, Minor Wear, 5¾" H. $200.00

(ROW III, L to R)

TOLE CREAMER, Black Ground W/Red, Yellow, Green & White, Minor Wear, 4¼" H. $230.00

TOLE TRAY, Drk. Brown Japanning W/ Crystalized Center & Floral Band in Yellow, Red, Green, Orange & White, Minor Wear, 8¾" x 12¼" $265.00

TOLE SUGAR BOWL, Drk. Japanned Ground Worn, Yellow & Red, 4" Diam., 3½" H. $145.00

(A-PA '77)   *Pennypacker Auction Centre*

TOLEWARE

(ROW I, L to R)

COFFEE POT, Goose Neck Spout, Onion Flower Decor., 11" H. $320.00

COFFEE POT, Spout On Side, 8½" H. $190.00

CREAMER, W/Lid, Red Decor . . .$77.50

COFFEE POT, Straight Front, Pour Spout, Fruit & Feather Decor., 8¾" H. . .$700.00

COFFEE POT, Goose Neck Spout, Tomato Flower Dec. $550.00

(ROW II, L to R)

BREAD TRAY, Tulip Flower Center, 13¾" L. $200.00

TEA CADDY, 5¼" H. $155.00

BOX, Hinged Lid, 7½" L. $55.00

BREAD TRAY, Adams Rose Floral Bouquet Center, 10½" L. $250.00

(A-PA '77)   *Pennypacker Auction Centre*

TOLEWARE

COFFEE POT, Onion Flower Decor., Goose Neck Spout, 11" H. $320.00

COFFEE POT, Poppy Decor., Pour Spout, 8" H. $145.00

DEED BOX, Strawberry Decor. . .$125.00

COFFEE POT, Fruit & Feather Decor., Straight Front, Pour Spout, 8¾" H. $700.00

(A-PA '77)   *Pennypacker Auction Centre*

WROUGHT IRON POPCORN POPPER $40.00

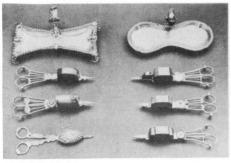

(A-MA '77)   Richard A. Bourne Co., Inc.

SILVER
(ROW I)
GEORGIAN SNUFFER TRAY, Henry Hallsworth, London, 1773, 8 Oz. Troy . . . .
. . . .$325.00
GEORGIAN SNUFFER TRAY, John Parker & Edward Wakelin, London, 1764, Foliate-Form Handle, 6 Oz. Troy .$275.00
(ROW II)
GEORGIAN CANDLE SNUFFER, Polished Steel Snuffer W/Silver Handles & Applied Crest, Unascribed Hallmarks . . . . .
. . . .$75.00
GEORGIAN CANDLE SNUFFER, William Bayley, London, 1805, Polished Steel W/Silver Handles, Scissors-Type . . . .
. . . .$200.00
(ROW III)
SHEFFIELD PLATED CANDLE SNUFFERS, Pr., Scissors-Type $50.00
IRISH CANDLE SNUFFER, James Scott, Dublin, 1798,Engraved, Scissors-Type . . . .
. . . .$300.00
(ROW IV)
CONTINENTAL CANDLE SNUFFERS, Pr., Unascribed Hallmarks $150.00
GEORGIAN CANDLE SNUFFER, Scissors-Type, Polished Steel W/Silver Handles, Unascribed Hallmarks $125.00

(A-OH '77)   Garth's Auctions, Inc.
TIN COOKIE CUTTERS
WOMAN, 5" H. $14.00
PIG, 6" L. $23.00
WOMAN, W/Outstretched Arms, 4¾" H.
. . . .$12.00
GOOSE, 4" W. $7.00
RUNNING HORSE, 6" W. $65.00
BIRD, Oversize Beak, Handle Missing, 4¼" W. $12.00
BIRD, Small, 2¾" W. $6.00
FISH, 5¾" W. $55.00
CRIMPED EDGE, Two Tulips In Center, 2¾" Sq. $3.00

(A-MA '77)   Richard A. Bourne Co., Inc.
SILVER
(ROW I, L to R)
JAMES II CANDLESTICK, Pierre Harach, London, 1685, Engraved Crest On Base, 5¼ Oz. Troy, 3⅝" H. $1300.00
WILLIAM & MARY CANDLESTICK, Anthony Nelme, London, 1691, Engraved Crest On Base, 5 Oz. Troy, 3⅝" H. . . . . . .
. . . . $1300.00
GEORGE III CIRCULAR SALT, 18th C., Hallmarks Obscured, 1⅞ Oz. Troy . . . .
. . . .$60.00
GEORGIAN SAUCE-BOAT, London, 1765, Illegible Maker's Mark, 3½ Oz. Troy.
. . . .$150.00
(ROW II, L to R)
GEORGE II CREAMER, London, 1775, 2 Front Feet Repaired, Minor Dent, 2¼ Oz. Troy $100.00
GEORGIAN TEAPOT W/Matching Stand, Charles Hougham, London, 1791, Teapot W/Wooden Handle & Finial, Sm. Chip On Finial, 19 Oz. Troy $1300.00
(ROW III)
WILLIAM IV LADLE, "King's" Pattern, London, 1832, Handle Engraved "Cook", 8 Oz. Troy $150.00

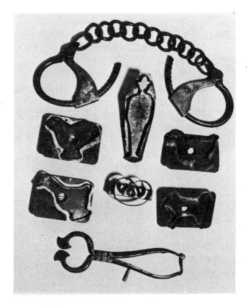

(A-OH '77)   Garth's Auctions, Inc.
SILVER
(ROW I, L to R)
TEAPOT, London Hallmarks, "W.S." & Date Letter For 1758-59, Victorian Embossed Floral Designs, Wooden Handle, 11" H. $530.00
MASTER SALTS (Pr.), London, 1767-78, Embossed Floral Design, 2½" Diam. . . . . .
. . . .$105.00
MUFFINEER, London Hallmarks, William Grundy, 1749-50, Monogramed "G", 9" H.
. . . .$600.00
TEAPOT, London Hallmarks, Thomas Whipham, 1743-44, Victorian Embossed Floral Designs W/Birds, Etc., 10" H. . . . . . .
. . . .$435.00
(ROW II, L to R)
LOVING CUP, London Hallmarks, George Smith II and Thomas Hayter, 1795-96, Hollow Handles Dented, One W/Initials "W.W.", 6" H. $250.00
MASTER SALTS, (Pr.), London Hallmarks, Simeon Coley, 1763-64, Embossed Floral Designs, 2½" Diam. $130.00
CREAM PITCHER, London Hallmarks, John Edward Terrey, 1817-18, 7½" H. . . .
. . . .$90.00
SALVER, London Hallmarks, John Crouch I, & Thomas Hannam, Sm. Hole In Center, Cast Ball & Claw Feet, Engraved Crest In Center, 8" Diam. $300.00

◄ *To the left*

(A-OH '77)   Garth's Auctions, Inc.
IRON HANDCUFFS, Pr. $30.00
TIN COOKIE CUTTER, Chicken, 4" W.
. . . .$5.00
TIN COOKIE CUTTER, Man W/Hat, 6" H. $22.50
TIN COOKIE CUTTER, Duck, 4" W. . . .
. . . .$6.00
TIN COOKIE CUTTER, Duck, 4" W. . . .
. . . .$5.00
TIN COOKIE CUTTER, Pretzel, 2¾" W.
. . . .$7.00
TIN COOKIE CUTTER, Dog, 4" W. . . . .
. . . .$5.00
IRON SUGAR NIPPERS, 9¼" L. . . . . . .
. . . .$65.00

(A-MA '77)   *Richard A. Bourne Co., Inc.*

PEWTER
(ROW I, L to R)
BEAKER, American, Unmarked, 3⅛" H.
..................................$70.00
BEAKER, American, Unmarked, 2⅞" H.
3" Diam........................$40.00
SOAP DISH, Ashbil Griswold, Meriden,
Conn., 1802-1842, "A.G." Touch, Hinged
Lid, 4⅜" Diam., 1¾" H.........$400.00
SUNDIAL, Unmarked, 4½" Diam. ......
..................................$100.00
CUSPIDOR, William Savage Touch, Mid-
dletown, Conn., Ca. 1830, 6¼" Diam.,
3¼" H........................$325.00

(ROW II, L to R)
PORRINGER, Crown Handle, New Eng-
land, 18th C., IC Mark, 4¼" Diam. ......
..................................$200.00
PORRINGER, Crown Handle, New Eng-
land, 18th C., IC Mark, 4¾" Diam. ......
..................................$275.00
TEAPOT, Freeman Porter, Westbrook,
Maine, 1835-1860's, 7" H. $225.00
BASIN, American, Eagle Touch, 6⅝"
Diam.........................$150.00

(ROW III, L to R)
BASIN, Thomas D. & Sherman Board-
man, Hartford, Conn., 1819-1830, Straight-
Line Touch, 7⅞" Diam.........$375.00
BASIN, American, Edward Danforth
Touch, Small Dents, 7⅞" Diam. ..$225.00
BASIN, American, Thomas Danforth
Boardman Touch, 8" Diam. $150.00

(ROW IV, L to R)
COMMUNION FLAGON, William Calder,
Providence, R.I., 1817-1856, Straight-Line
Touch, 11" H. $600.00
PITCHER, 2-Qt., Rufus Dunham, West-
brook, Main, 1837-1861, Straight-Line
Touch $275.00
CASTOR SET, Rufus Dunham, Westbrook,
Maine, 1837-1861, Straight-Line Touch,
5 Matching Bottles $200.00

(A-MA '77)   *Richard A. Bourne Co., Inc.*

PEWTER
(ROW I, L to R)
WHALE OIL LAMP, Morey & Ober, Bos-
ton, 1852-1855, Double Divergent Cam-
phene Burner, 4½" H..........$110.00
SPARKING LAMP, American, Unmarked,
Base Slightly Bent, 5¼" H. $130.00
WHALE OIL LAMP, American, Unmarked,
5¾" H.......................$125.00
WHALE OIL LAMP, American, Unmarked,
6½" H.......................$125.00
WHALE OIL LAMP, Signed, Reed & Bar-
ton, "4" Mark, 7" H. $170.00
(ROW II, L to R)
PORRINGER, Crown Handle, 4¼" Diam.
..................................$300.00
PORRINGER, American, Unmarked,
Lee-Type Handle Resoldered, 5" Diam.
..................................$75.00
PORRINGER, New England, 18th C.,
Unmarked, Minor Dents, 5¼" Diam. .....
..................................$150.00
INK WELL, Unmarked, Glass Jar, Few
Dents $50.00
(ROW III)
BASINS, Pr., American, Unmarked, Bot-
toms Dented, 9⅛" Diam........$100.00
(ROW IV, L to R)
TEAPOT, Engraved Band Of Vines &
Leaves Around Center, Dented, Bottom Re-
placed W/Tin $100.00
TEAPOT, American, Signed, Samuel Simp-
son, Yalesville, Conn., 1835-1852, Straight-
Line Touch $275.00
TEAPOT, American, Signed, James H.
Putnam, Malden, Mass., 1830-1835 ......
..................................$170.00

(A-OH '77)   *Garth's Auctions, Inc.*
PEWTER FLAGON, Unmarked, 10" H. .
..................................$255.00

(A-MA '77)   *Richard A. Bourne Co., Inc.*
PEWTER
(ROW I, L to R)
HAND LAMP, Signed, Morey & Ober,
Boston, 1852-1855, Double Divergent Cam-
phene Burner W/Pewter Caps, Number
"1", 5¼" H. $200.00
WHALE OIL LAMPS, Pr., American,
Unsigned, 6½" H. $300.00
LAMP, Roswell Gleason, Dorchester, Mass.,
1822-1871, Straight Line Touch, Double
Divergent Brass Camphene Burner, 9"
H...........................$280.00
LAMP, Samuel Rust, New York City, 1837-
1845, Double Divergent Brass Camphene
Burner, 7" H. $180.00
(ROW II, L to R)
PORRINGER, American, Unmarked,
Heart & Crescent Handle, 3⅜" Diam. ....
..................................$110.00
PORRINGER, Signed, William Calder,
Providence, R.I., Eagle Touch, 4¼" Diam.
..................................$575.00
PORRINGER, American, Unmarked,
Old English Style Handle, 4¼" Diam.
..................................$140.00
PORRINGER, American, Unmarked,
Crown Handle, 4⅝" Diam. $200.00
PORRINGER, American, Unmarked, Flow-
er Handle $250.00
(ROW III, L to R)
SUGAR BOWL, George Richardson, Sr.,
Boston, 1818-1828 & Cranston, R.I., 1828-
1845 ....$1600.00
SUGAR BOWL, Ashbil Griswold, Meriden,
Conn., 1802-1842, Eagle Touch ..$400.00
TEAPOT, George Richardson, Boston,
1818-1828 & Cranston, R.I., 1828-1845,
Marked "G. Richardson/No. 3/Warranted",
Minor Dents Around Base $250.00
(ROW IV, L to R)
CHALICES, American, Unmarked,
Matched Pair $450.00
BEAKER, Continental, 6⅝" H. ...$90.00
PINT MEASURE, English, Victorian, Mon-
ogrammed, Engraving On Bottom ..$60.00
SYRUP JUG, American, Unmarked .....
..................................$130.00

AMERICAN PEWTER
(A-OH '77)   *Garth's Auctions, Inc.*
AMERICAN PEWTER
(ROW I, L to R)
COFFEE POT, Eagle Touch Mark, "Boardman & Co., New York", 12" H. $305.00
CHARGER, 2 Eagle Touch Marks, "Boardman Warranted", 12½" Diam. . . .$350.00
CANDLESTICK, Battered, 9¾" H. $55.00
PITCHER, Strainer Spout, "Homan & Co. Cincinnati", Repair In Base, 12" H. $175.00
(ROW II, L to R)
CREAMER, "Sellow & Co. Cincinnati", Minor Dent, 5½" H. $190.00
TEAPOT, Touch Mark "Putnam", Battered Base, 8½" H. $170.00
SUGAR BOWL, "Sellow & Co. Cincinnati", 7½" H. $190.00
(ROW III, L to R)
CANDLESTICKS, Pr., 9¾" H. .$160.00
COFFEE POT, "Sellow & Co. Cincinnati", Solder Repair In Base, 10½" H. .$195.00
PLATE, 10¼" Diam. $55.00

(A-OH '77)   *Garth's Auctions, Inc.*
(ROW I, L to R)
PEWTER GREASE LAMP, Double Wick, 8¼" H. $95.00
PEWTER CHARGER, London Maker's Touch Marks, Repaired Rim Hole, 18" Diam. $140.00
PEWTER CLOCK LAMP, Clear Blown Font W/Roman Numerals On Frame, Touch Mark "...10 N 10 ..., Camona" W/Star In Center, Repaired Base, 16" H. $245.00
(ROW II, L to R)
BRASS FLEMISH SPOUT LAMP, Hanging Pan, Polished, 8½" H. $105.00
PEWTER WHALE OIL LAMPS, Pr., Double Spout Burners, 8" H. $210.00
MINIATURE BRASS CANDLESTICKS, Pr., Sheet Brass, One Repaired, 4½" H. $50.00
BRASS QUEEN ANNE CANDLESTICK, 7" H. $160.00
(ROW III, L to R)
PEWTER WHALE OIL LAMP, Brass & Tin Double Spout Burner Damaged, 8¾" H. $90.00
PEWTER BURNING FLUID LAMP, Newell Patent, W/Snuffer, 3¾" H. $180.00
PEWTER & TIN FUNNEL, Slightly Battered, 4½" L. $20.00
PEWTER LAMP, Wooden Handle, Battered Base, 2¼" Diam., 6" L. $80.00
PEWTER LAMP, Lard Burner, 8" H. $235.00

(A-MA '77)   *Richard A. Bourne Co., Inc.*
SILVER
(ROW I)
GEORGE III COFFEEPOT, Robert Swanson, London, 1765, Wooden Handle, 29 Oz. Troy $1100.00
GEORGIAN CIRCULAR WAITER, Ebenezer Coker, London, 1771, Engraved Crest, 32 Oz. Troy.............$1400.00
(ROW II)
GEORGIAN PLATTER, London, 1789, Unrecorded Maker "WL", Minor Wear, 16¼" L., 39 Oz. Troy..........$750.00
GEORGE III PLATTER, Daniel Smith & Robert Sharp, London, 1785, Engraved Crest, 12" L., 14 Oz. Troy.......$275.00

(A-OH '77)   *Garth's Auctions, Inc.*
(L to R)
PEWTER WHALE OIL LAMP, Brass Collar Soldered Over Orig. Threaded Opening In Font, Brass Double Spout Burner, Signed "Smith & Co.", 7½" H.........$105.00
PEWTER PORRINGER, "The Mer..-Wilson Co.", 4" Diam. $25.00
PEWTER TANKARD, "James Yates ½ Pint", 3⅝" H. $80.00
PEWTER CREAMER, Incised Floral Design, Mkd. "XI", 5¾" H. $36.00

(A-MA '77)   *Richard A. Bourne Co., Inc.*
SILVER
RUSSIAN HOT WATER KETTLE ON STAND, Various Hallmarks W/"84" Mark W/Date 1880, Ivory Inset Underside Handle, Gold-Washed Interior, Engraved Crest, 32 Oz. Troy $400.00
RUSSIAN TEAPOT, CREAMER & SUGAR, Identical Marks To Preceding Piece & Identical Crest, 27½ Oz. Troy Total. $350.00

(A-VA '78)   *Laws*
FRENCH SILVER WEDDING BOWLS, Pr., 19th C., Caryatid Figures For Handles, Feet W/Chain Link Motif, 1838 Mark & Maker's Hallmark, 7" Diam., 5¾" H. $500.00

(A-VA '77)   *Laws*
GEORGE JENSEN TEA OR COFFEE SERVICE, Cosmos Pattern, Serving Tray (27" x 17½"); Tea Urn; Coffeepot; Teapot; Covered Sugar Bowl; Creamer & Waste Bowl; Orb Design W/Stylized Bowl Base $4500.00

To the right ▶
(ROW I, L to R)

TIN COVERED PAIL, Type Used To Carry Home Beer From Saloon, 4¼" H. $7.00

TWO CYLINDRICAL GRATERS, "Nutmeg", 7½" H., Pat. Aug. 6, 01 . . . . .$9.00

TIN FUNNEL W/Long Tubular Handle, Used For Making PA Dutch Funnel Cakes (Drechter Kuchel). Recipe Attached, 18" L. $31.00

(ROW II, L to R)

TIN MOLD In Shape Of Fish, 9½" L. $10.00

OVAL TIN MOLD, Eagle In High Relief, Copper Washed In Tin, 5" x 7" x 4½" H. $90.00

OVAL TIN MOLD, Pineapple In High Relief, Copper Washed In Tin, 5¼" H. $57.50

OVAL TIN MOLD, Ear Of Corn In High Relief, Copper Washed In Tin, 4¾" H. $45.00

TIN MOLD In Shape Of Fish, 11" L. $12.50

(ROW III, L to R)

TIN TEAPOT W/Wooden Finial, Top Of Handle Resoldered To Pot, 7¾" H. $12.50

TWO PIECES OF TIN, Grater W/Fold Down Hinge & Small Tin Container W/ Cover $15.00

NESTING TIN CAKE PANS, 7, Size Ranges From 3" Diam. To 10½" Diam. . . .$22.50

TWO PIECES OF TIN, Cookie Cutter W/ Cylindrical Handle Mkd. "Rumford." Civil War Era Drinking Cup, 2½" H. $2.00

EARLY TIN MILK PAIL W/Cover, 7¾" H. $11.00

(A-OH '78)   *Garth's Auctions, Inc.*

(A-MA '78)   *Richard A. Bourne Co., Inc.*

(ROW I, L to R)

COIN SILVER TEA SERVICE By James Hamill, New York, Ca. 1816. Dolphin Finials & A Band Of Grapes & Vine Around Shoulder, Minor Denting On Creamer, Foot Of Sugar Bowl Slightly Bent. 49 oz. Troy. $600.00

(continued bottom of next column)

(A-MA '78)   *Richard A. Bourne Co., Inc.*

◀ *To the left*   (continued)

(ROW II, L to R)

COIN SILVER TEA SERVICE By Peter Chitry, New York, Ca. 1814. Fluted Body W/Leaf Molding & Grape Vine Band Around Shoulder & Bases, Few Minor Dents. 62 oz. Troy $875.00

(ROW III, L to R)

CASED FIVE-PIECE COIN SILVER TEA SERVICE By Bigelow Broners, Kennard, Boston, MA 1845. Globular Shapes W/Elaborate Chased Design, Paw Feet & Floral Finials. 92 oz. Troy $575.00

◀ *To the left*

PEWTER

(ROW I, L to R)

SMALL CAMPHENE LAMP By Capen & Molineus, (N.Y.C., 1848-1854, Dorchester MA, 1844-1847). "No. 4". Cap For Burner Missing, Pewter Is Slightly Dark In Some Areas, Minor Dents $200.00

WHALE OIL LAMP By Smith & Co. W/ Orig. Double-Drop Whale Oil Burner, Minor Dents $350.00

WHALE OIL LAMP W/Double-Divergent Camphene Burners, Lamp & Caps Slightly Bent, Burner Complete W/Orig. Wicks, Well Preserved $175.00

SUGAR BOWL, Wooden Finial Is Partially Broken Away, Pewter Somewhat Bent, One Handle Needs Resoldering At Top $120.00

(ROW II, L to R)

MATCHING SUGAR & CREAMER By James Dixon & Son, London, Finial On Cover Slightly Bent $150.00

UNMARKED TEAPOT, American, Wooden Finial Missing $60.00

PIGEON-BREASTED TEAPOT By Roswell Gleason (Dorchester, MA 1822-1871), Has Few Small Dents $225.00

(ROW III, L to R)

UNMARKED TALL COFFEE OR TEAPOT, Foot Ring Needs Resolder To Base, Finial Slightly Dented Inward $125.00

TEAPOT By Lorenzo L. Williams (Philadelphia, 1838-1842), Cover & Handle Slightly Bent & Needs Straightened $125.00

(A-OH '77)   *Garth's Auctions, Inc.*
TIN LANTERN, Frame W/Worn Black & Blue Paint, 3 Reverse Painted Glass Panels, 4th Side Has Door, Font & Oil Burner Replaced, 12½" Sq., 29" H. $140.00

(A-PA '77)   *Pennypacker Auction Centre*
(L to R)
TIN MILK WARMER, Door & Whale Oil Lamp Burner, 2 Milk Holders On Top, 10½" H. $60.00
TIN SWINGING WHALE OIL KETTLE LAMP, Handle, Saucer Base $400.00
TIN WHALE OIL LAMP, Oil Font, Signed "C.F. Rees, Pat. June 12, 1866, Millersville, Lancaster, Pa." 10" H. $80.00
TIN WALL SCONCE, Crimped Overhang For Smoke Bell, 10½" H. $200.00
TIN WHALE OIL LAMP, Green Decor., Signed "C.F. Rees, Pat. June 12, 1866, Millersville, Lancaster, Pa.", 10" H. . . . . . .
. . . . $80.00

(A-PA '77)   *Pennypacker Auction Centre*

(A-OH '77)   *Garth's Auctions, Inc.*
(ROW I, L to R)
TIN CANDLE LANTERN, Black Paint, 10½" H. Plus Wire Ring Handle . . . $22.50
PEWTER SAUCER BASE CHAMBER STICK, 7¾" Diam., 4¾" H. $92.50
TIN TWELVE TUBE CANDLE MOLD, 10½" H. $50.00
(ROW II, L to R)
TIN LIGHTING DEVICE, Hanging Basket W/Double Cone Font & Single Tubular Spout, 8½" H. $55.00
TIN FOUR TUBE CANDLE MOLD, 10" H. $25.00
OIL LAMP, Stoneware Base & Font, Brass Burner, Hairline In Font, 9¾" H. . . $25.00
TIN SINGLE TUBE CANDLE MOLD, 10¼" H. $57.50
TIN DOUBLE CRUSIE LAMP, Cover & Pick, 9½" H. $25.00
(ROW III, L to R)
TIN LANTERN, Candle Socket W/Font & Whale Oil Burner, 10" H. Plus Hanger .
. . . . $27.50
IRON FOUR SPOUT GREASE LAMP, 3½" H. Plus Wire Chain & Hook . . $22.50
PEWTER COOKIE BOARD, Mounted On Wood, 4¼" x 7¼" $75.00
IRON DOUBLE CRUSIE LAMP, 6½" H. Plus Hanger $32.50
SHEET METAL FOLDING CANDLE LAMP, Galvanized, Isinglass Panels, "The Stonebridge Folding Lantern, Pat'd. 1908, N.Y.C.", 10" H. Plus Handle $15.00

◀ *To the left*

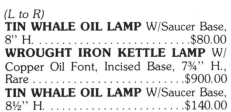

(L to R)
TIN WHALE OIL LAMP W/Saucer Base, 8" H. $80.00
WROUGHT IRON KETTLE LAMP W/ Copper Oil Font, Incised Base, 7¾" H., Rare $900.00
TIN WHALE OIL LAMP W/Saucer Base, 8½" H. $140.00

(A-PA '77)   *Pennypacker Auction Centre*
TIN MILK WARMER, Door, Whale Oil Lamp Insert, Stencil Decor., 8" H. . $55.00
TIN WHALE OIL LAMP, Handle, 7" Saucer Pan $60.00
TIN TINDER LIGHTER, Candle Holder Lid, Round $70.00
TIN FAT LAMP HOLDER, Matching Tin Fat Lamp, 11" H. $200.00
TIN WHALE OIL LAMP, Saucer Base, Stenciled, Archer's Patent June, 1842-Philadelphia, Pa., 7½" H. $270.00

(A-MA '77)   *Richard A. Bourne Co., Inc.*
(ROW I, L to R)
PEWTER WHALE OIL LAMP, American, Roswell Gleason, Orig. Double Drop Whale Oil Burner, 6½" H. $275.00
PEWTER WHALE OIL LAMP, American, Unmarked, Minus Burner, 4½" H. . $90.00
PEWTER WHALE OIL LAMPS, Pr., American, Roswell Gleason, Brass Burner Holders (Burner Missing From One), 9¼" H.
. . . . $550.00

(ROW II, L to R)
WALNUT LANTERN, Top Board Split, 10" H. $160.00
TIN CANDLE MOLD, 12-Part, for 10" Candles $70.00

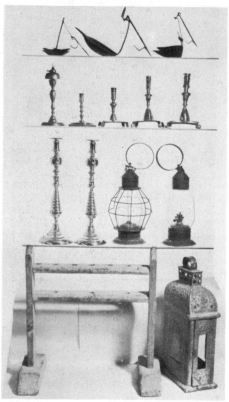

(A-PA '77)   *Pennypacker Auction Centre*
BRASS PETER DERR BETTY LAMP,
Wrought Iron Holder Mkd. "P.D. 1842"
..................................$725.00

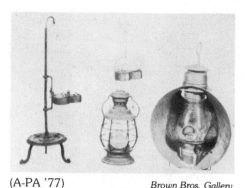

(A-PA '77)   *Brown Bros. Gallery*
IRON BETTY LAMP W/Adjustable Stand
.........................$375.00
BETTY LAMP, Iron, Hanging.....$90.00
RAILROAD LANTERN, Copper, Grill
W/Bull's-eye Lens, Removable Simplex
Burner $325.00
TIN DRIVING LANTERN No. 20, Mkd.
"C.T.Ham Mfg. Co.", Bull's-eye Chimney.
..................................$90.00

(A-MA '77)   *Richard A. Bourne Co., Inc.*
LIGHTING DEVICES
(ROW I, L to R)
IRON HANGING SPOUT LAMP, 4
Spouts & Pick...................$80.00
HANGING SINGLE CRUSIE, W/ Hanger
..................................$70.00
HANGING DOUBLE CRUSIE, W/
Hanger...........................$40.00
(ROW II, L to R)
BRASS WHALE OIL LAMP, Cap Lid &
Single Drop Oil Burner, 9¾" H. ...$35.00
BRASS CANDLESTICK, Bell Metal Base,
5¼" H...........................$75.00
BRASS CANDLESTICK, Continental,
6¼" H...........................$50.00
BRASS CANDLESTICK, 8¼" H. ......
..................................$55.00
BRASS CANDLESTICK, 8¾" H. .....
..................................$50.00
(ROW III, L to R)
BRASS CANDLESTICKS, Pr., English,
One W/Threaded Base $110.00
TIN POLICE LANTERN, Wire Globe
Guard, Globe Engraved "Police", Double-
Drop Whale Oil Lamp...........$200.00
TIN LAMP, Blown Glass Globe, Orig.
Attached Tin Reservoir $80.00
(ROW IV, L to R)
WOODEN CANDLE HOLDER, Natural
Weathered Finish $125.00
**PIERCED TIN DOUBLE CANDLE LAN-
TERN,** 4 Windows, 2 W/Replacement
Glass, 2 W/No Glass, 19" O.H. ..$250.00

To the right ▶

(A-PA '77)   *Pennypacker Auction Centre*
BRASS PETER DERR KETTLE LAMP,
Wrought Iron Stand, Mkd. "P.D. 1853"
..................................$1850.00

(A-PA '77)   *Pennypacker Auction Centre*
COPPER PETER DERR BETTY LAMP,
Wrought Iron Holder Mkd. "P. Derr, 1838",
Med. Size $950.00

(A-MA '77)   *Richard A. Bourne Co., Inc.*
BRASS
(ROW I, L to R)
CANDLESTICKS (1 of Pr.), Pushups,
Thumbprint To Pushup Missing On Each,
5¼" H. $55.00
CANDLESTICKS (1 of Pr.), 6¾" Diam.,
4½" H. $90.00
CANDLESTICKS (1 of Pr.), Knop Stems,
Pushups, One Pushup Missing, 5¼" H. ...
..................................$55.00
CANDLESTICKS (1 of Pr), "Jack-Of-
Diamonds" Pattern, Both Pushups Missing,
9" H. $80.00
(ROW II, L to R)
CANDLESTICKS, Pr., Pushups, 10" H. .
..................................$150.00
WHALE OIL LANTERN, Sandwich Pres-
entation Type Shade Etched W/"GWR",
17⅜" O.H. $450.00

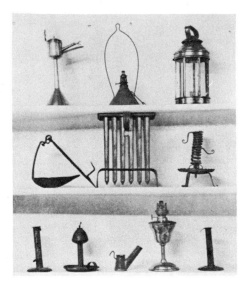

(A-OH '77)   Garth's Auctions, Inc.
(ROW I, L to R)
BRASS LIGHTING DEVICE, Conical Base, Font W/Removable Lid, Polished, 11½" H. $65.00
TIN HANGING LAMP, Conical Font, Brass Burner, 15" H. $10.00
TIN CANDLE LANTERN, 7 Glass Panels, Hinged Vent, 11½" H. $110.00
(ROW II, L to R)
WROUGHT IRON GREASE LAMP, 6½" H. Plus Hanger $115.00
TIN CANDLE MOLD, 12-Tube, 10½" H. $45.00
WROUGHT IRON CANDLE HOLDER, Adjustable W/Crimped Pan, 3 Legs, Rusted, 8½" H. $35.00
(ROW III, L to R)
IRON HOG SCRAPER CANDLESTICK, Pushup & Lip Hanger, 6" H. $37.50
TIN WHALE OIL LAMP, Traces Dk. Brown Japanning, 5" Diam., 6¼" H. .....
....$50.00
TIN SINGLE SPOUT MINER'S LAMP, 3½" H. $7.00
BRASS OIL LAMP, Weighted Base, Solder Repair At Base Of Font & Burner, 10" H.
....$22.50
IRON HOG SCRAPER CANDLESTICK, Pushup & Lip Hanger, 6" H. $40.00

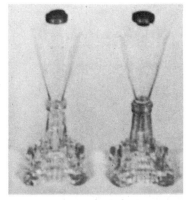

(A-PA '77)   Brown Bros. Gallery
FLINT GLASS WHALE OIL LAMPS, Pr., Blown & Molded, Stepped Bases .....
....$140.00

(A-MA '77)   Richard A. Bourne Co., Inc.
PEWTER
(ROW I, L to R)
HAND LAMP, American, Unmarked, Double Divergent Camphene Burner, 4¼" H. $100.00
WHALE OIL LAMP, American, Unmarked, Single Drop Burner, Foot Ring Needs Resoldered, Dented, 4½" H. $30.00
TABLE LAMP, American, Unmarked, Double Divergent Camphene Burner, 9" O.H.
....$175.00
FLAGON, Continental, Lid Resoldered, Dented, 7½" H. $70.00
(ROW II, L to R)
WHALE OIL LAMPS, Pair, William Calder, Providence, R.I., 1817-1856, Signed W/Straight-Line Touch, Minus Burners, 9" H.
....$475.00
DOUBLE SPOUT LAMP, Continental, Mangled Spouts, 13½" H. $60.00
TIME LAMP, German, Glass Reservoir, Pewter Bent, Reservoir Broken $40.00

(A-MA '77)   Richard A. Bourne Co., Inc.
(ROW I, L to R)
LITHOPHANE SHADE, 6-Paneled, Scenes, Bottom Diam., 10½"; Top Diam., 6½"; 6" H. $200.00
LITHOPHANE SHADE, 6-Paneled, Scenes, Bottom Diam., 10¼"; Top Diam., 6¼"; 6½" H. $200.00
LITHOPHANE SHADE, 6-Paneled, Scenes, Bottom Diam., 10¼"; Top Diam., 6½"; 6½" H. $275.00
(ROW II, L to R)
LITHOPHANE SHADE, 5-Paneled, Scenes, Bottom Diam., 9"; Top Diam., 5¾"; 6¼" H. $150.00
LAMP SHADE, 5-Paneled, Painted Silhouettes In Black On Opaque White Glass,
(continued bottom of next column)

(A-OH '77)   Garth's Auctions, Inc.
(ROW I, L to R)
TIN CANDLE LANTERN, Star Decor., Triangle Vents, 15" H. $40.00
MINIATURE BRASS FLAT IRON, Wooden Handle & Insert, 4" L., 5½" H. $50.00
TIN LANTERN, Ring To Hold Oil Font, Font & Burner Missing, Needs Repair, 15" H. $30.00
MINIATURE WROUGHT IRON FLAT IRON, 4¼" L., 2¼" H. $22.50
TIN RAILROAD LANTERN, Clear Hand Blown Globe, Top W/"C. R.R.", Glass Font W/Brass Collar, Worn Brown Japanning, 15" H. $75.00
(ROW II, L to R)
SHEET IRON CONICAL LAMP, Cast Iron Handle & Screw Cap W/Star Design, Chain & Hanger, 5½" H. $30.00
TIN AND BRASS MINER'S LAMP, "Patent Dd D. William, Jan. 10, 1882", Dented, 5¼" H. $20.00
COPPER LAMP, Resoldered, 3½" H. ...
....$12.50
MINIATURE TIN LAMP, Reflector, Brass "Acorn" Burner & Chimney, Worn Red Japanning, 6" H. $35.00
TIN WHALE OIL LANTERN, 3 Sliding Tin Panels, Folding Handle, Worn Brown Paint, Removable Tin Font, 5½" H. ......
....$30.00
(ROW III, L to R)
TIN LANTERN, 2 Hinged Doors, Worn Brown Japanning, Traces Of Decor., 11" H.
....$40.00
TIN LANTERN, Brass Cap, Clear Glass Globe, Glass Font W/Brass Oil Burner, Globe Chipped, 9¾" H. $55.00
TIN LANTERN, 3 Isinglass Panels, Sliding Tin Door, Tin Font, Whale Oil Burner, Worn Brown Japanning, 9½" H. $40.00

(continued)
Bottom Diam., 9¼"; Top Diam., 5¾"; 6½" H. $100.00
HALL LANTERN, Boston & Sandwich Glass Co., Ca. 1850-1860, Metal Frame, 6 Cut & Frosted Panels W/Orig. Blown Glass Smoke Bell, Electrified, 10" H., 8½" Diam. $125.00

(A-MI '78)   *C. B. Charles Galleries, Inc.*
TIFFANY LILY LAMP $6500.00

(A-MA '78)   *Richard A. Bourne Co., Inc.*

(A-MA '78)   *Richard A. Bourne Co., Inc.*
TABLE LAMP, Iridescent Gold, Has Twelve-Paneled Circular Foot and Matching Twelve-Paneled Iridescent Gold Shade, Unsigned, 15" H. $650.00

(A-MA. '78)   *Richard A. Bourne Co., Inc.*
ART NOUVEAU TABLE LAMP, Tall Bronze-Finished Metal Base & Octagonal Bent Glass Art Nouveau Shade W/Elaborate Reticulated Design Over Panels In Bronzed Metal Finish, One Panel Cracked, Otherwise About Perfect, 28" O.H. $425.00

(A-MA '78)   *Richard A. Bourne Co., Inc.*

◀ *To the left*

TIFFANY NEWEL POST LAMP, Simple Bronze Mounting W/Iridescent Green & Gold Feather Patt. Globe, Signed "LCT", One Small Chip On Under-Rim Of Globe, Globe 8" H. $350.00

◀ *To the left*

LAMP SHADES

(ROW I, L to R)
SIGNED "QUEZAL" THREADED LAMP SHADE, Abstract Threading In Iridescent Gold W/Matching Heart-Shaped Leaves On Iridescent Ivory Ground $70.00
SIGNED "QUEZAL" ART NOUVEAU LAMP SHADE, Green Threading Over White Ground W/Iridescent Gold Leaf Design $60.00
SIGNED STEUBEN ART NOUVEAU LAMP SHADE, Blue, Gold & White Aurene In Blue Feather Design $110.00
SIGNED STEUBEN ART NOUVEAU LAMP SHADE, Gold & White Aurene In Feather Design $80.00

(ROW II, L to R)
SIGNED "QUEZAL" ART NOUVEAU LAMP SHADE, Gold & Ivory Feather Design $85.00
SIGNED STEUBEN ART NOUVEAU LAMP SHADE, Iridescent Gold W/Green & White Meander Design On Border .....
.... $170.00
BELL-SHAPED OPALESCENT VASE-LINE LAMP SHADE, Opalescent Bowknot & Swag Design $50.00
SIGNED "QUEZAL" ART NOUVEAU LAMP SHADE, Iridescent Gold & Green On White $95.00

(ROW III, L to R)
ART NOUVEAU LAMP SHADES, (Set Of 4), Matched, Iridescent Green, Gold & White Feather Design, 3 Have Minute Rim Nicks & Slight Rim Roughage, (1 Illus.) ...
.... $375.00
SIGNED AURENE ART NOUVEAU LAMP SHADES, (Set Of 3), Matched, By Steuben, Green, Gold & White Aurene In Feather Design, 2 Have Minute Rim Nicks (1 Illus.) $250.00
ART NOUVEAU LAMP SHADE, Gold & Ivory In Feather Design $60.00
SIGNED "QUEZAL" ART NOUVEAU LAMP SHADE, Gold & Ivory Feather Design, Slightly Larger Than Average .....
.... $90.00

(ROW IV, L to R)
ART GLASS LAMP SHADE, Possibly Stevens & Williams, Ruffled Rim, Opaque White Loopings In Clear Shading To Cranberry, Minor Rim Chips $50.00
ART NOUVEAU LAMP SHADES, Pr., Iridescent Yellow, Green, & Brown In Feather Design, Both Retain Orig. Labels Of Iris Glass Co., Fostoria, Ohio, (1 Illus.) ....
.... $270.00
SIGNED STEUBEN GOLD AURENE TEN-PANELED LAMP SHADE, Two Small Nicks In Small Rim $60.00
CONICAL-SHAPED TEN-PANELED LAMP SHADE, Iridescent Gold, Signed "LCT", Signature Not Guaranteed . $60.00

(A-PA '77)   *Brown Bros. Gallery*
STAINED GLASS TABLE LAMP, Brass Base, Shade 20" Diam. $600.00

(A-MA '77)   *Richard A. Bourne Co., Inc.*
MINIATURE LAMP BASES
(ROW I, L to R)
PEDESTAL LAMP BASE, Amber, Brass Collar, 5⅞" H. $60.00
LAMP BASE, Opaque White Nutmeg, Orig. Brass Collar, 2½' H. $25.00
SPIRIT LAMP BASE, Lt. Green, 3½" H. $10.00
(ROW II, L to R)
LAMP BASE, Amethyst, Lip Roughage, 4½" H. $20.00
LAMP BASE, Emerald Green, Basketweave Patt., 3¼" H. $25.00
LAMP BASE, Clear Pressed Glass, Orig. Brass Collar, 4½" H. $20.00
(ROW III, L to R)
LAMP BASE, Opaque White or Milk Glass, Incurved Paneling, Orig. Brass Collar, 2⅞" H. $17.00
LAMP BASE, Opaque Blue, Globular, Orig. Brass Collar, & Oil Fixture, 4" H. $30.00
LAMP BASE, Opaque Blue, Orig. Brass Collar & Burner, 4½" H. $25.00

(D-NY '77)   *Lee Vines Antiques*
MINIATURE LAMP, Cranberry, Swirled, 8½" H. $250.00

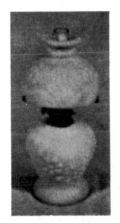

(A-PA '77)   *Brown Bros. Gallery*
MINIATURE SATIN GLASS OIL LAMP, Embossed Floral Design Over Surface $160.00

(A-MA '77)   *Robert C. Eldred Co., Inc.*
TRIPLE OVERLAY FLUID LAMPS, Pr., Both Pedestals & Fonts Cut From Deep Blue To White To Clear, Double Marble Bases W/Ormolu Molds, 25" H. $600.00

(D-NY '77)   *Lee Vines Antiques*
MINIATURE LAMP, "Nellie Bly", Smith #219, Pink Daisies On Milk Glass Base, Frosted Shade, 8" H. $250.00

(D-NY '77)   *Lee Vines Antiques*
MINIATURE LAMP, (Smith #370), Iridescent Cranberry W/Embossed & Beaded Swirled Body & Shade W/Greyish Overshot Between Ribs, 8¾" H. $325.00

(A-MA '78)   *Richard A. Bourne Co., Inc.*
PAIRPOINT TABLE LAMP, Sgn., Copper Base W/Embossed Hand-Painted Glass Shade. Diam. Of Shade Approx. 16", O.H. 25" $3,100.00

(A-MA '77)   *Richard A. Bourne Co., Inc.*

(ROW I, L to R)
FLUID LAMP, Boston & Sandwich Glass Co., Ca. 1860's, Double Cut Overlay Font Cranberry Cut To Clear, Brass Stem, Marble Base, Open Air Bubble In Font, 8½" H. $100.00
FLUID LAMP, Boston & Sandwich Glass Co., Ca. 1860's, Threaded Font, Aqua W/White Spiral Swirls, Brass Stem, Marble Base, 8½" H..................$125.00
FLUID LAMP, Boston & Sandwich Glass Co., Ca. 1860's, Glass Font, Opaque White W/Cranberry Loopings, Brass Stem, Marble Foot, 8½" H. $250.00
(ROW II, L to R)
FLUID LAMP, Chocolate Glass, Greentown, Indiana Glass Works, "Wild Rose W/ Bowknot" Patt., 8½" H. $400.00
FLUID LAMP, Greentown, Indiana Glass Works, "Wild Rose W/Bowknot" Patt., Clear Font W/Chocolate Glass Base, 9¼" H. $400.00
FLUID LAMP, Boston & Sandwich Glass Co., Ca. 1860's, Double-Cut Overlay Glass Font, Cranberry Cut To Clear, Engraved Vine & Floral Band, Opaque White Glass Base, Decor. Worn, 10½" H. $300.00

(A-IA '78)   *Gene Harris Antique Center*
PAIRPOINT PUFFY TABLE LAMP (2" Crack) $440.00
PAIRPOINT PUFFY BOUDIOR W/Butterfly $900.00

(A-MA '77)   *Robert C. Eldred Co., Inc.*
CRYSTAL FESTOONED CANDELABRA, Pr., English, Adam Period Of XVIII Century, Cylindrical Gilt Bronze Standards, Cut Glass Finials, Acanthus Leaf Scrolled Branches, Beaded Bobeches, Cut Crystal Pendants, 27" H. $550.00

◄ *To the left*

(D-NY '77)   *Lee Vines Antiques*
MARTELE CANDLESTICKS, Pr., Sterling Silver, 9" H. $1500.00

(A-MA '77)   *Richard A. Bourne Co., Inc.*
(ROW I)
GIRANDOLES, Pr., Boston & Sandwich Glass Co., Ca. 1850-1860, Gold-Washed, Marble Bases, Translucent White "Star & Punty" Patt., Peg Lamps W/Camphene Burners, Sandwich Cut Crystal Prisms, Minor Nicks, 14" H. $900.00
(ROW II)
GIRANDOLE, Boston & Sandwich Glass Co., Ca. 1850-1860, Gold-Washed, Marble Base, Translucent White Sandwich "Acanthus Leaf" Patt. Peg Lamps Fitted W/Double-Drop Camphene Burner & Brass Collar, Sandwich Cut Crystal Prisms, 1 Peg Lamp Chipped, 19½" H. $1000.00

(A-MA '77)   *Richard A. Bourne Co., Inc.*
LAMPS
(ROW I, L to R)
SPARKING LAMP, Clear, Ribbed, Orig. Brass Collar & Fluid Lamp Burner, 5½" H. $35.00
SPARKING LAMP, Clear, Minus Collar, Base Chip, 5½" H. $30.00
WHALE OIL LAMP, Clear, Boston & Sandwich Glass Co., Etched W/Berries & Acorns, Orig. Pewter Collar, 6¼" H. .....
.................................$100.00

(A-MA '78)   *Richard A. Bourne Co., Inc.*

LAMPS
(ROW I, L to R)

FAIRY LAMP, Satin Glass Peachblow Color, Complete W/Clear Glass Liner & Orig. Red Cross Night Light Candle, 4½" H. $400.00

BURMESE FAIRY LAMP, W/Burmese Chimney & Base, Heavy Patented Base Mkd. Inside "S. Clarke Patent Trade Mark Fairy", 4½" H. $375.00

FAIRY LAMP, W/Jeweled Gilded Brass Base & Swirled Pink Satin Glass Globe, Retains Period Candle, 4¾" H. $150.00
(ROW II, L to R)

MINIATURE FLUID LAMP, Clear & Mottled Cranberry & Opaque White Glass, Base W/Pinwheel Design & Supported By Four Clear, Reeded & Scrolled Feet, Matching Globe W/Scalloped Rim, 7" H. $100.00

ART NOUVEAU FLUID LAMP, Iridescent Blue Abstract Design On Iridescent Green Ground, Squat Cylindrical Shape W/Partially Frosted Chimney & Orig. Oil Fixture, Diameter Of Base 4½"; 11¼" H. .$100.00

FLUID OR MINIATURE LAMP, Opaque Glass W/Satin Finish, Decor. W/Blossoms & Leaves, 3¾" Diam.; Height To Collar 2½" $60.00

MINIATURE LAMP, Blue Cut Velvet Satin Glass, Frosted Or Satin-Finished Applied Foot, Orig. Oil Fixture & Chimney, Height To Collar 4" $80.00
(ROW III, L to R)

CRANBERRY PEG LAMPS, Pr., Centers Of Candlesticks Painted Black W/Embossed Princess Feather-Like Design, Peg Lamps Are Cranberry Glass W/Yellow & Gold Enamel Decor. & Retain Orig. Fixtures, Height To Collars 13" $260.00

(continued top of next column)

◀ *To the left*   *(continued)*

SATIN GLASS PEG LAMP, Salmon Pink W/Opaque White Swirls, Made In Three Parts, Base Of Matching Glass In Typical Fairy Lamp Base As Is The Swirled Chimney Which Has Been Ground On Two Sides To Allow Air To Enter, Chip On Tip Of One Foot, 12½" H. $375.00

(A-OH '78)   *Garth's Auctions, Inc.*
(ROW I, L to R)

QUILTED CHRISTMAS LIGHT, Golden Amber, Rim Roughness, 3½" H. . .$40.00

QUILTED CHRISTMAS LIGHT, Green, Rim Chips, 3½" H. $40.00

QUILTED CHRISTMAS LIGHT, Amethyst, Rim Chips, 3½" H. $50.00

TIN SKATER'S LAMP, Amethyst Globe, 7" H $165.00

QUILTED CHRISTMAS LIGHT, Deep Amber, Rim Chips, 3½" H. $42.50

QUILTED CHRISTMAS LIGHT, Cobalt Blue, 3½" H. $37.50

QUILTED CHRISTMAS LIGHT, Emerald Green, 3½" H. $35.00
(ROW II, L to R)

WROUGHT IRON RUSH LIGHT HOLDER, Scrolled Counter Weight, Cast Iron Base, 9½" H. $95.00

TIN FLASK, No Lid, 4½" H. $12.50

WROUGHT IRON DOUGH SCRAPER, 3½" W. $10.00

TIN OIL LAMP, Brass Burner, Glass Cracked, 6¾" O.H. $37.50

TIN LAMP, Saucer Base, Central Wick Supports, Needs Solder Repair, 6½" H. $12.50
(ROW III, L to R)

TIN CYLINDERICAL CANDLE BOX, 13" L., 4¼" Diam. $335.00

TIN HAND LAMP, Conical Font & Brass Burner, Tubular Wick, Hinged Shade W/ Isinglass Window, 3¾" H. $50.00

TIN LAMP FILLER, Resoldered Handle, 6½" H. $50.00

(A-MI '78)   *C. B. Charles Galleries, Inc.*
TURTLE BACK HANGING LAMP . . . . .
. . . .$9000.00
▶

(A-MA '77)   *Richard A. Bourne Co., Inc.*
COLORED CHRISTMAS LIGHTS
(ROW I, L to R)

LIGHT GREEN LIGHT, Stiegel, Pattern Molded In 12-Diamond Design W/Folded Lip, 2⅛" Diam., 2½" H. $60.00

SMOKY PLUM LIGHT, Gold-Amber Folded Lip, 12-Diamond Design, 2¼" Diam., 4¾" H. $75.00

AMETHYST LIGHT, Stiegel, Pattern Molded In 12-Diamond Design, 2½" Diam., 2⅞" H. $100.00

COBALT BLUE LIGHT, Blown & Pattern Molded in 18-Diamond Design, 3" Diam., 3" H. $35.00
(ROW II, L to R)

LIGHT YELLOW-GREEN LIGHT, Stiegel, Opalescent Folded Lip, Opalescence In Pontil, 14-Diamond Design, 2⅞" Diam., 4" H. $100.00

LIGHT ELECTRIC-BLUE LIGHT, Stiegel, Pattern Molded In 14-Diamond Design, 3" Diam., 3⅝" H. $120.00

EMERALD GREEN LIGHT, Pattern Molded In 18-Diamond Design, 2⅞" Diam., 3¼" H. $50.00
(ROW III, L to R)

DEEP COBALT BLUE LIGHT, Stiegel, 20-Diamond Design, 2¾" Diam., 4¼" H. $150.00

AMETHYST LIGHT, Stiegel-Type, Pattern Molded In 14-Diamond Design, 2⅝" Diam., 3⅞" H. $80.00

AMETHYST LIGHT, Stiegel-Type, Pattern Molded In 14-Diamond Design, Cracked, 3" Diam., 3¾" H. $50.00

(A-MA '77)   *Richard A. Bourne Co., Inc.*

LAMPS
(ROW I, L to R)
SPARKING LAMP, Clear Blown Three Mold, Orig. Tin Single-Drop Whale Oil Burner, 2" H. $250.00
SPARKING LAMP, Clear Blown, Burner Missing, 2¾" Diam., 1¾" H. $45.00
SPARKING LAMP, Clear Blown, Orig. Tin Double-Drop Burner, 2½" Diam., 2" H. $80.00
SPARKING LAMP, Clear Blown, Minus Burner, 3½" H. $70.00
(ROW II, L to R)
SPARKING LAMP, Clear Blown, Orig. Single-Drop Whale Oil Burner, 2⅞" H. ....
SPARKING LAMP, Clear Blown, Orig. Single-Drop Whale Oil Burner, 3" H. .....
..................................$60.00
LAMP, Clear Blown, Minus Burner, 3" H. $30.00
(ROW III, L to R)
LAMP, Clear Blown, Folded Lip, Globular Font, Minus Collar, 4" H. $80.00
MOLDED PEG LAMP, Clear, 12-Panel, Orig. Brass Collar, Double-Drop Brass Whale Oil Burner, 3" Diam., 4½" H. .....
..................................$70.00
SPARKING LAMP, Clear Blown, Globular Font, Amethyst Tint, Rough Finish At Top, 4¼" H. $40.00

(A-MA '77)   *Richard A. Bourne Co., Inc.*
WHALE OIL LAMP, Frosted, Pressed Glass Base, Minus Collar, Foot Chipped, 8½" H. $40.00
WHALE OIL LAMP, Pressed Glass Base, Minus Collar, Minor Roughage, 9½" H. ....
..................................$35.00
WHALE OIL LAMP, Quatrefoil Pressed Glass Base, Minus Collar, Foot Chip, Minor Roughage, 7¾" H. $30.00

(A-MA '77)   *Richard A. Bourne Co., Inc.*
(ROW I, L to R)
FLUID LAMP, "Bellflower" Pattern Font, Brass Stem & Collar, Marble Base, 8½" H.
..................................$70.00
FLUID LAMP, "Honeycomb" Pattern Flint Glass Font, Brass Stem Collar, Marble Base, 9½" H. $50.00
CANDLESTICK, Clear, Boston & Sandwich Glass Co., 9" H. $40.00
CANDLESTICKS (1 of 3), Clear, Boston & Sandwich Glass Co., 7½" H. ...$90.00
(ROW II, L to R)
CANDLESTICKS, (1 of Pr.), Clear, Boston & Sandwich Glass Co., Minor Roughage On Foot, 9⅞" H. $90.00
WHALE OIL LAMPS, Pr., Clear, "Star and Punty" Pattern, Boston & Sandwich Glass Co., Orig. Pewter Collars, Minor Roughage & Heat Check Under Collar, 10¾" H. .
..................................$175.00
(ROW III, L to R)
FLUID LAMP, Pressed Glass W/Opalescent Striped & Swirled Cranberry Glass Font, 9¼" H. $190.00
FLUID LAMP, Pressed Glass W/Opalescent Striped & Swirled Blue Glass Font, 9¼" H. $110.00
FLUID LAMP, Pressed Flint Glass Font, Brass Collar & Stem, Opaque White Pressed Glass Base, 11¼" H. $50.00

(A-MA '77)   *Richard A. Bourne Co., Inc.*
WHALE OIL LAMP, Clear, 12-Panel, Free Blown, Minus Collar, 6½" H. $100.00
WHALE OIL LAMP, Clear Blown, Minus Collar, 9¼" H. $125.00

(A-MA '77)   *Garth's Auctions, Inc.*
(ROW I, L to R)
CLEAR PRESSED LAMP, Applied Handle, "Pat. App. For 1877", Brass Collar & Burner, Globe Missing, 3" H. $30.00
CLEAR BLOWN LAMP, Applied Handle & Base, No Burner, Base Incomplete, 3" H.
..................................$50.00
CLEAR PRESSED LAMP, Applied Handle, Brass Collar Mkd. "Pat'd Apr. 13, 1875, Mar. 2, 1878", Kerosene Burner, 4¾" H. .
..................................$20.00
CLEAR BURNING FLUID LAMP, Made In 2-Part Mold, Applied Handle, Pewter Collar, Single Spout Burner, 4" H. .$50.00
CLEAR PRESSED LAMP, Brass Collar & Burner, Globe Missing, 1⅞" H. $8.00
CLEAR PRESSED BURNING FLUID LAMP, 8-Panel, Pewter Collar, Single Spout Burner & Cap, 4¼" H. $77.50
(ROW II, L to R)
CLEAR LAMP, Made In 2-Part Mold, Applied Handle, Cut Floral Design, Brass Collar, Double Whale Oil Burner, 4⅛" H. .....
..................................$50.00
MINIATURE LAMP, Clear Pressed Font, Opaque Powder Blue Paneled Base, Brass Collar & Burner, Milk Glass Globe, 6¼" H.
..................................$45.00
CLEAR BLOWN LAMP, Polished Pontil, Brass Collar, Pewter Whale Oil Burner, 5¼" H. $85.00
CLEAR PRESSED LAMP, Flowers & Leaves On Font, Brass "Pearl" Burner & Chimney, 6¾" H. $25.00
CLEAR LAMP, Made In 2-Part Mold, Applied Handle, Pewter Collar, Whale Oil burner, 4½" H. $50.00
(ROW III, L to R)
CLEAR CANDLESTICK, Pressed Base, Blown Hollow Bulbous Stem, Blown Candle Socket, 10" H. $125.00
CLEAR CANDLESTICK, Pressed Lacy Base, Blown Stem & Candle Socket, Minor Roughness On Base, 7¾" H. $205.00
CLEAR PRESSED MINIATURE LAMP, Floral Patt. On Font & Chimney, Brass Collar & Burner, 9½" H. $45.00
CLEAR CANDLESTICK, Pressed Stepped Base, Blown Bulbous Stem & Blown Candle Socket, Base Chipped, 10¾" H.$95.00

(A-MA '77) *Richard A. Bourne Co., Inc.*

(ROW I, L to R)
CANDLESTICKS, Pr., Boston & Sandwich Glass Co., Blue Socket W/Translucent White Stems & Bases, 7⅜" H. ......
................................$400.00
CANDLESTICK, Pittsburg, Ca. 1840-1850, Blue Socket W/Translucent White Base, 6¾" H. $325.00
DOLPHIN CANDLESTICK, Pittsburg, Ca. 1840's, Translucent Blue, Minor Chips, 6⅞" H. $200.00
CANDLESTICK, Boston & Sandwich Glass Co., Ca. 1840, Translucent Blue Upper Half, White Lower Section, 8½" H
................................$450.00
(ROW II, L to R)
ACANTHUS LEAF CANDLESTICKS, Boston & Sandwich Glass Co., Ca. 1840's, Blue Font W/Translucent White Clambroth Stems & Bases, Chips & Roughage, 9½" H.
................................$700.00
DOLPHIN CANDLESTICK, Boston & Sandwich Glass Co., Translucent Blue Top W/Raised Dolphins & Shells & Translucent White Clambroth Base, 10¼" H. ..$850.00
PETAL-TOP COLUMNAR CANDLESTICKS, Pr., Boston & Sandwich Glass Co., Ca. 1840's, Translucent Yellow-Green, Minor Flaking & Chip, 9⅛" H. ...$900.00
(ROW III, L to R)
PETAL-TOP COLUMNAR CANDLESTICKS, Pr., Boston & Sandwich Glass Co., Ca. 1840's, Translucent Blue & White, Minor Chip & Roughage, 9⅛" H. $950.00
DOLPHIN CANDLESTICK, Boston & Sandwich Glass Co., Ca. 1840's, Blue Petal Socket W/Translucent White Dolphin & Base, 1½" Check In Dolphin Tail, 10¼" H.
................................$325.00
PETAL-TOP COLUMNAR CANDLESTICKS, Pr., Boston & Sandwich Glass Co., Ca. 1840's, Translucent Purple-Blue Sockets W/Translucent White Clambroth Bases, Minor Rim Edge Nicks, 9¼" H. ....
................................$575.00

(A-MA '77) *Richard A. Bourne Co., Inc.*
(ROW I, L to R)
CANDLESTICK, Boston & Sandwich Glass Co., Canary Yellow, 6¾" H. .$70.00
CANDLESTICKS, Pr., Canary Yellow, 7½" H. $210.00
FLINT GLASS CANDLESTICKS, Pr., Boston & Sandwich Glass Co., Loop & Petal Patt., Canary Yellow, Roughage, 6¾" H. .
................................$150.00
FLINT GLASS DOLPHIN CANDLESTICK, Boston & Sandwich Glass Co., Canary Yellow, Minor Nicks, 9½" H.$160.00
(ROW II, L to R)
FLINT GLASS CANDLESTICKS, Pr., Boston & Sandwich Glass Co., Amethyst, 8¼" H. $700.00
FLINT GLASS CANDLESTICK, Med. Cobalt Blue, New England Glass Co., 9" H.
................................$350.00
FLINT GLASS CANDLESTICK, Amethyst, New England Glass Co., Minor Roughage, 7⅝" H. $375.00
CANDLESTICKS, Pr., Honey Amber, ¼" Heat Check In One, 9" H. $400.00
(ROW III, L to R)
CANDLESTICKS, Pr., Deep Cobalt Blue, Both W/Heavy Annealing Lines, 6¼" H. ...
................................$300.00
FLINT GLASS CANDLESTICKS, Pr., New England Glass Co., Canary Yellow, 1 W/Minor Chip & 1 W/Nick, 9" H. $300.00
FLINT GLASS CANDLESTICKS, Pr., Cobalt Blue, 1 W/1½" Check In Socket, 9" H. $475.00
(ROW IV, L to R)
FLINT GLASS DOLPHIN CANDLESTICKS, Pr., Boston & Sandwich Glass Co., Canary Yellow, 1 W/Chip; 1 W/Roughage, 9¾" H. $450.00
FLINT GLASS CANDLESTICK, Boston & Sandwich Glass Co., Yellow-Green, Shallow Flake, 9" H. $250.00
FLINT GLASS DOLPHIN CANDLESTICKS, Pr., Boston & Sandwich Glass Co., Canary Yellow, Minor Chips & Nicks, 10¼" H. $400.00

(A-MA '77) *Richard A. Bourne Co., Inc.*
LAMPS
(ROW I, L to R)
FLUID LAMP, Boston & Sandwich Glass Co., Ca. 1860, Triple-Cut Overlay Font, Rose To White To Clear, Fluted Milk Glass Base, 14" H. $800.00
FLUID LAMP, Boston & Sandwich Glass Co., Ca. 1860, Triple-Cut Overlay Font, Rose To White To Clear, Sandwich Cutting, Milk Glass Base, 13" H. $750.00
FLUID LAMP, Boston & Sandwich Glass Co., Ca. 1860, Blown Glass Font Of Opaque Blue & Clear Spirals, Milk Glass Base, Heat Check In Wafer Of Font, 11" H. ...$200.00
(ROW II, L to R)
BANQUET LAMP, Boston & Sandwich Glass Co., Ca. 1860, Double-Cut Overlay Font, White Cut To Cranberry, Double-Stepped Marble & Bronze Base, Blown Cut & Frosted Globe, Electrified, 28" H. ....
................................$1000.00
FLUID LAMP, Gold-Bronze, Cut & Frosted Sandwich Glass Globe, Patented Lamp W/ Fuel Reservoir, Electrified, 33" H. ..$300.00

(A-PA '77) *Brown Bros. Gallery*
(L to R)
PEWTER CANDLESTICKS, Pr., 8" H. .
................................$150.00
BRASS CANDLESTICKS, Pr., 10" H. ..
................................$140.00
BRASS CANDLESTICKS, Pr., 7" H. ....
................................$100.00

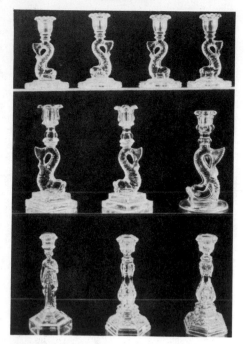

(A-MA '77)　　　*Richard A. Bourne Co., Inc.*
(ROW I, L to R)
FLINT GLASS DOLPHIN CANDLE-STICKS, Pr., Clear, 12-Panel Socket, Midwestern Bullseye Scalloping, 6½" H.
..............................$200.00
FLINT GLASS DOLPHIN CANDLE-STICKS, Pr., Clear, 12-Panel Socket, Midwestern Bullseye Scalloping, Minor Flake, 6½" H. $125.00
(ROW II, L to R)
DOLPHIN CANDLESTICKS, Pr., Boston & Sandwich Glass Co., Clear, Minor Chips & Roughage, 10" H. $250.00
DOLPHIN CANDLESTICK, Clear, Ca. 1850's, 9¼" H. $260.00
(ROW III, L to R)
CARYATID CANDLESTICK, Boston & Sandwich Glass Co., Clear, Ca. 1840-1850, 9⅝" H. $300.00
ACANTHUS LEAF CANDLESTICKS, Pr., Boston & Sandwich Glass Co., Clear, Minor Chips & Roughage, 9⅜" H. ......
..............................$250.00

(A-MA '77)　　　*Richard A. Bourne Co., Inc.*
(ROW I, L to R)
FLINT GLASS CANDLESTICK, Boston & Sandwich Glass Co., Purple-Blue, Minor Nicks & Roughage, 6⅝" H. $175.00
CANDLESTICK, Pittsburgh, Ca., 1840's, Grayish Translucent Blue, Minor Chips, 9½" H. $700.00
FLINT GLASS CANDLESTICK, New England Glass Co., Cobalt Blue, Minor Chips & Roughage, 9⅜" H. $250.00
FLINT GLASS CANDLESTICK, Pittsburgh, Ca. 1840's, Deep Purple-Blue, Socket W/Heat Check, 9¾" H. $200.00
(ROW II, L to R)
FLINT GLASS CANDLESTICKS, Pr., Pittsburgh, Ca. 1840's, Deep Purple-Blue, Chips & Crack, 9¾" H. $250.00
CRUCIFIX CANDLESTICK, New England Glass Co., Ca. 1860's, Emerald Green, 11⅜" H. $300.00
CRUCIFIX CANDLESTICK, New England Glass Co., Translucent Med. Blue, Minor Chips, 11⅜" H. $425.00
(ROW III, L to R)
CRUCIFIX CANDLESTICK, Translucent Jade Green, Tiny Check, Roughage, 11⅜" H. $400.00
CRUCIFIX CANDLESTICK, Clear, Citron Color, Minor Roughage, 9¾" H. ......
..............................$600.00
CRUCIFIX CANDLESTICK, Translucent Power Blue, Heavy Annealing Lines, 9¾" H. $500.00

◀ *To the left*

(A-PA '77)　　　*Pennypacker Auction Centre*
SANDWICH GLASS ALABASTER CANDLESTICK, Blue & White, Dolphin Pattern $160.00
SANDWICH GLASS ALABASTER LAMP, Blue, Double Font, By Ripley & Co., 1870, 13½" H. $525.00

(A-MA '77)　　　*Richard A. Bourne Co., Inc.*
(ROW I, L to R)
FLINT GLASS FLUID LAMPS, Pr., Boston & Sandwich Glass Co., Ca. 1840-1850, "Three Printie" Patt., Med. Cobalt Blue, Pewter Whale Oil Burners, Minor Chips & Flake, 9¾" H. $650.00
FLINT GLASS FLUID LAMP, Boston & Sandwich Glass Co., Ca. 1840-1850, Loop Patt., Sapphire Blue, Double-Drop Pewter & Tin Camphere Burner, Pewter Collar, Minor Flake, 8¼" H. $375.00
(ROW II, L to R)
FLINT GLASS FLUID LAMP, Boston & Sandwich Glass Co., Ca. 1840-1850, Loop Patt., Emerald Green, Double-Drop Whale Oil Burner, Pewter Collar, Minor Flake & Chip, 9¾" H. $700.00
FLINT GLASS FLUID LAMPS, Pr., Boston & Sandwich Co., Ca. 1840-1850, Loop Patt., Cobalt Blue, Pewter & Tin Double-Drop Whale Oil Burner, Orig. Pewter Collars, Minor Flakes & Roughage, 9¾" H. ..
..............................$650.00

(ROW III, L to R)
SPILL HOLDER, Boston & Sandwich Glass Co., Ca. 1840-1850, Star & Punty Patt., Translucent Jade Green, Minor Roughage & Flakes, 4⅞" H. $1600.00
FLUID LAMP, Boston & Sandwich Glass Co., Ca. 1840-1850, Star & Punty Patt., Translucent Jade-Green, Double-Drop Camphene Burner, Orig. Brass Collar, Gold "Presentation" Decor., Minor Flake, Gold Decor. Worn, 10⅝" H. $1250.00
FLUID LAMP, Boston & Sandwich Glass Co., Ca. 1840-1850, Star & Punty Patt., Translucent Lapis Blue, Double-Drop Camphene Burner, Orig. Brass Collar, 10⅝" H.
..............................$1500.00
FLINT GLASS WHALE OIL LAMP, Boston & Sandwich Glass Co., Ca. 1840-1850, "Four Printie" Patt., Purple-Blue, Orig. Brass Collar, Foot Chipped, 11¼" H. ....
..............................$450.00

(A-MA '77)   Richard A. Bourne Co., Inc.

FLUID LAMPS, Pr., Boston & Sandwich Glass Co., Ca. 1830-1840, Trefoil Bases W/Raised Figures Of American Eagle W/ Spread Wings, Blown Knop Stems, Brass Holders, Frosted Globes & Peg Lamps W/ Pewter Collars & Whale Oil Burners, Chips, Flakes & Roughage, 16¾" O.H. .$1200.00

(A-MA '77)   Richard A. Bourne Co., Inc.

(Row I)
"APPLE SAUCE" LAMP, 3-Part Clear Glass Lamp W/Four-Barrel Base & Edison 2-Pc. Chimney, Pressed Glass Match Holder In Base, Opaque White Shade, 21" H. ...
.............................$200.00

(ROW II)
BACCARAT LUSTRES, Pr., Bowl-Shaped Lustres W/Inner Candleholders & Foliate Bobeche, Fluted Feet, Acid Frosted Overall, Cut Crystal Prisms, Minor Nick, 10" Diam., 14" H. $400.00

(A-MA '77)   Richard A. Bourne Co., Inc.
(ROW I, L to R)
WHALE OIL LAMPS, Pr., New England Glass Co., Ca. 1835-1845, Emerald Green, Pewter Collars & Double-Drop Whale Oil Burners, 6½" H. $900.00
FLUID LAMP, New England Glass Co., Orig. Pewter Collar, Cobalt Blue, 8" H. ....
..................................$700.00
WHALE OIL LAMP, Boston & Sandwich Glass Co., "Three-Printie" Patt., Peacock Green, Pewter Collar W/Double-Drop Whale Oil Burner, 8" H. $700.00
WHALE OIL LAMP, New England Glass Co., Ca. 1835-1845, Loop Patt., Emerald Green, Orig. Pewter Collar, Double-Drop Whale Oil Burner, Minor Chip, 7½" H. ...
..................................$400.00
(ROW II, L to R)
WHALE OIL LAMPS, Pr., Free-Blown, Cobalt Blue, Five-Stepped Pressed Glass Bases, Orig. Tin & Cork Double-Drop Whale Oil Burners, Minor Chips & Roughage, 8¼" H. $900.00
BLOWN GLASS LAMP FILLER, Cobalt Blue, Minor Roughage, 8⅝" H. ..$400.00
FLUID LAMP, New England Area, Ca. 1835-1845, Ellipse & Circle Patt., Amethyst, Pewter Collar, Double-Drop Brass Camphene Burner, 8" H. $700.00
(ROW III, L to R)
FLUID LAMPS, Pr., New England Glass Co., Ca. 1835-1845, Emerald Green, 1 W/Brass Collar & 1 W/Pewter Collar, Minor Chips & Roughage, 9¾" H. $850.00
FLUID LAMP, New England Glass Co., Ca. 1835-1845, Purple-Blue, Orig. Pewter Collar, Nicks, 8¾" H. $300.00
FLUID LAMP, New England Glass Co., Ca. 1835-1845, Plum-Hued Amethyst, Orig. Pewter Collar & Brass & Pewter Double Divergent Camphene Burner W/Caps, Minor Chips, 8⅞" H. $350.00
FLUID LAMP, New England Area, 1835-1845, Ellipse & Circle Patt., Amethyst, Orig. Brass Collar, Double Divergent Brass Camphene Burner W/Cap, Minor Chip & Roughage, 10" H. $350.00

(A-MA '77)   Richard A. Bourne Co., Inc.
(ROW I, L to R)
FLINT GLASS WHALE OIL LAMP, Boston & Sandwich Glass Co., Ca. 1840-1850, Loop Patt., Canary Yellow, Orig. Brass Collar, 8⅞" H. $250.00
FLINT GLASS FLUID LAMP, Boston & Sandwich Glass Co., Ca. 1840-1850, Bullseye & Ellipse Patt., Canary Yellow, Foot Chipped, 8¼" H. $300.00
FLINT GLASS WHALE OIL LAMP, Boston & Sandwich Glass Co., Ca. 1840-1850, Ellipse Patt., Canary Yellow, 11⅛" H. ..
..................................$400.00
FLUID LAMPS, Pr., Boston & Sandwich Glass Co., Ca. 1840-1850, Loop Fonts On Monumental Or Plinth Bases, Orig. Brass Collars, 1 W/Minor Chips, 11" H. .$800.00
(ROW II, L to R)
FLUID LAMP, Boston & Sandwich Glass Co., Ca. 1840-1850, Acanthus Patt., Translucent Blue & White, Orig. Brass Collar, Minor Chip, 11½" H. $450.00
FLUID LAMPS, Pr., Boston & Sandwich Glass Co., Ca. 1840-1850, Tulip Patt., Translucent Purple-Blue & White, Orig. Pewter Collars, Minor Flake & Roughage, 12½" H. $700.00
FLUID LAMPS, Boston & Sandwich Glass Co., Ca. 1840-1850, Star & Punty Patt., Translucent Jade Green, Brass Collars, Stencil-Gilded Brass Stems, Marble Bases, Gilt Worn, 10¾" H. $700.00
(ROW III, L to R)
FLINT GLASS FLUID LAMP, Boston & Sandwich Glass Co., Ca. 1840-1850, Onion Patt., Translucent Powder Blue, 13½" H. ..
..................................$1300.00
MATCH HOLDERS, Pr., Boston & Sandwich Glass Co., Ca. 1840-1850, Onion Patt., Translucent Powder Blue, 5" L., 3⅜" W., 1½" H. $300.00
DOUBLE FONT, Ripley & Co., Translucent Blue Double Font W/Match Holder On Opaque White Milk Glass Base, Minor Roughage, 12⅛" H. $550.00

(A-OH '77)   *Garth's Auctions, Inc.*
OIL ON CANVAS, Backed On Masonite & Cleaned, Gilt Frame, 47½" x 55" $1050.00

(A-PA '77)   *Pennypacker Auction Centre*
FRAKTUR VORSCHRIFT, Colorful Flowers & Figures, 8" x 13" $95.00

(A-OH '77)   *Garth's Auctions, Inc.*
FRAKTUR CERTIFICATE, "1842", 2 Garlands Of Roses, Angel & Pr. of Birds, Paper Stained, Framed, 15½" x 16¼" $365.00
FRAKTUR BIRTH CERTIFICATE, German Recording Of Birth In 1792, Milford, Northampton County, Dated 1810, Hearts & Flowers In Red, Yellow, Blue, Green & Black, Paper Edge Uneven, Framed, 6¼" x 9¼" $210.00
WATERCOLOR, Bird, Red & Drk. Brownish Green, Walnut Frame, 7" x 8¼" $85.00

(A-OH '77)   *Garth's Auctions, Inc.*
OIL PAINTING On Canvas, Orig. Cond. W/One Minute Repair, Attributed To Horace Bundy, Vermont, Unframed, 24¼" x 28¼" $950.00

(A-PA '77)   *Pennypacker Auction Centre*
SAMPLER, By Sarah N. Phillips, July 19, 1831, Oak Frame, 16" x 16" $210.00

(D-NY '78)   *Lee Vines Antiques*
ROOKWOOD PLAQUE, Scenic View, "Garden Of The Gods", Signed E. Dier, 1898, Plaque: 3½" x 6½"; W/Frame: 9½" x 12½" $750.00

(A-PA '77)   *Pennypacker Auction Centre*
FRAKTUR VORSCHRIFT, Colorful Capital Letters, 8" x 12" $105.00

(A-PA '77)   *Brown Bros. Gallery*
SAMPLER, By Mary A. Boone, 1835, Tiger Maple Frame $170.00

(A-PA '77)   *Brown Bros. Gallery*
CURRIER & IVES FOLIO PRINT, "Gen. Butler & Dexter", Large $375.00

(A-OH '77)   *Garth's Auctions, Inc.*

(ROW I, L to R)

SILHOUETTE, Hollow Cut, Paper Has Stain, 3" Diam. $25.00

SILHOUETTES, Pr., Hollow Cut, Young Girls, Highlighted W/Pencil, Black Painted Wooden Frames — One W/Repair, 5¼" Diam. $240.00

SILHOUETTE, Hollow Cut, Boy, Embossed Brass Frame, Paper Has Tears, 2¾" x 3¾" $35.00

(ROW II, L to R)

SILHOUETTE, Ink, Gentleman, Gold Highlights, "R. Bloye, 1813", Burl Veneer Frame, 5¾" x 6¾" $145.00

SILHOUETTE, Hollow Cut, Mkd. "Peale Museum", Old Frame, 7" x 8¼" .$150.00

SILHOUETTE, Ink, Gentleman, Gold Matt & Rosewood On Pine Frame, 5½" x 6½" $155.00

(ROW III, L to R)

SILHOUETTE, Hollow Cut, Gentleman, Moulded Frame, Black Paint, 5¼" x 6¼" $35.00

SILHOUETTE, Pen & Ink, Lady In Fancy Hat, Frame Inlaid W/Dolphins, 4" Sq. $75.00

SILHOUETTE, Hollow Cut, Boy, Mkd. "D. Green", Paper In Poor Condition, Pine Frame, 5¼" x 6¼" $55.00

SILHOUETTE, Hollow Cut, Boy, Turned Frame W/Black Paint, 5" Diam. . . .$25.00

(A-OH '77)   *Garth's Auctions, Inc.*

(ROW I, L to R)

MINIATURE ON IVORY, Lady W/Red Beads, Purple Dress, Gilt Brass Case W/ Window In Back, 2¾" H. $145.00

MINIATURE ON IVORY, Gentleman, Gold Case, 2½" H. $225.00

MINIATURE ON IVORY, Gentleman, Brass Case, Window In Back W/Coat Swatch & Lock Of Hair, Minor Repair To Base, 2½" H. $115.00

(ROW II, L to R)

MINIATURE ON IVORY, Child, Minor Water Damage, Brass Case Needs Repair, 1¾" H. $105.00

MINIATURE ON IVORY, Gentleman, Brown Coat, Embossed Brass On Wood Frame, 2¾" x 3½" $155.00

MINIATURE ON IVORY, Gentleman, Gold Case, 1½" H. $135.00

(ROW III, L to R)

MINIATURE ON IVORY, Gentleman, Window In Back W/Orig. Swatch Of Cloth From Subject's Coat, 2⅞" H. $375.00

MINIATURE ON IVORY, Lady, Gold Case W/Lens In Back, 2½" x 3⅛" $145.00

MINIATURE ON IVORY, Gentleman, Gold Case W/Lens In Back W/Swatch Of Subject's Coat, 3" H. $135.00

(A-MA '77)   *Richard A. Bourne Co., Inc.*

CURRIER AND IVES

FOLIO LITHOGRAPH, "American Brook Trout", Period Frame, Small $90.00

FOLIO LITHOGRAPH, "A Frontier Settlement", Slight Fading, Worn Edge Of Print, Period Frame, Medium $175.00

(A-MA '77)   *Robert C. Eldred, Co., Inc.*

RUSSIAN ICON, XIX Century, Three Saints, Silver Gilt & Enamel Riza, Touch of Ivan Petrovich Klebnikov, Within Gilt Bronze Case W/Glass Cover, 18½" x 16½" $5000.00

◀ *To the left*

(A-MA '77)   *Robert C. Eldred Co., Inc.*

RUSSIAN ICON, XIX Century, Our Lady Of Kazanskaya, Repousse Silver Gilt Riza, Moskow 1881, Enameled Spandrels & Halos, Touched W/St. George And The Dragon, and Mark Of Anton Kuzmichev, 14" x 12¼" $2300.00

(A-MA '77)   *Robert C. Eldred Co., Inc.*

RUSSIAN ICON, XIX Century, Dormition Of The Virgin, Repousse & Enamel Riza, 10½" x 12¼" $2200.00

FACHROALO KAZAK PRAYER RUG,
Green Mihrab On Brick Red Ground W/
Small Geometric Motifs; Ivory Major Border
W/Leaf & Wine Glass Design, 5'3" x 32'8"
.................................$650.00

HOOKED RUG, Wool, Gold Zig-Zag
Border, Grey Ground, Made In 1912 To
Commemorate 1812 Alliance Of U.S. &
Britain, 3'10" x 5'5½" $135.00

SHIRVAN RUG, Red & White Diamond
Medallions On Deep Blue Field; Ivory Major
Border W/Crab Design Flanked By Treeton
Minor Borders, 4' x 6'9" $2600.00
MALAYER SAROUK RUG, Rust, Light
Blue, Ivory, Green, Gold & Salmon W/
Dark Blue Field, Geometric Floral Design
Surrounds Large Medallion, 4'7" x 7' ....
.................................$825.00
LENKORAN TALISH RUG, W/Classic De-
sign Of Three Turtle Shaped Medallions In
Ivory, Rust, Green, Blue & Tan On Brown
Field. 4'3" x 8'1" $2000.00

KAZAK RUG, White Center Medallion W/
Blue Latchhooks On Red Field W/Smaller
Diamond Medallions, Leaf & Wine Glass
Design On White Border, 5'2" x 7'6" ....
.................................$900.00

SAROUK RUG, Deep Blue Field Centered
By Brick Red Medallion & All Over Floral
Design; Blue Border W/Geometric Flower-
ing Vine, 4'1" x 7' $1350.00

BLUE & WHITE QUILT, Acorn Leaf
Patt., 80" x 84" $190.00

DOUBLE WEDDING RING QUILT
80" x 84" $175.00

KAZAK RUG, 3 Blue & White Medallions
On Brick Red Field; Green Major Border
Flanked By Red & White Treeton Minor
Borders, 4'11" x 7'1" $900.00

(A-OH '77)   *Garth's Auctions, Inc.*
JACQUARD COVERLET, Single Weave, 2-Pc., Blue & White, Vintage Border, Corners Signed "Louise Yager 1853", 90" x 70" $115.00

(A-OH '77)   *Garth's Auctions, Inc.*
QUILT, Red, Blue-Grey & White W/Pieced Star & Applique Vining Border W/Smaller Stars, 78" Sq. $255.00

(A-OH '77)   *Garth's Auctions, Inc.*
APPLIQUE QUILT, Pinwheels Of Blue, Green & Pink W/Scalloped Stylized Floral Border On Yellow Ground, 78" Sq. $255.00

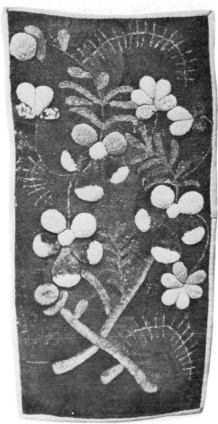

(A-OH '77)   *Garth's Auctions, Inc.*
HOOKED RUG, Sculptured, Waldoboro Type, W/Drk. Brown Ground, Sheared Flowers In White, Red & Brown, 18¾" x 39" $300.00

(A-VA '78)   *Laws*
TURKISH SILK PRAYER RUG, Rust Field W/Flowering Tree In Ivory, Blue & Gold; Deep Blue Border W/Floral Design & Gold Minor Borders W/Vine Motif, 4'3" x 5'11".......................$1800.00

(A-OH '77)   *Garth's Auctions, Inc.*
INDIAN RUG, Yei, Stock Of Corn W/ Yellow, Red, Black, Grey and White, Weather Run W/"Sugar", Minor Wear, 51½" x 77" $250.00

(A-OH '77)   *Garth's Auctions, Inc.*
INDIAN RUG, Early Tes-nos-pao, Red, White, Grey & Blue-Black, 50" x 97" $355.00

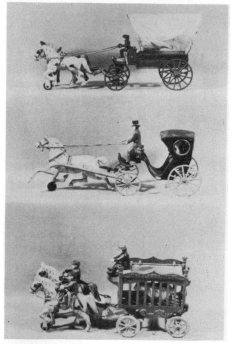

CAST IRON TOYS
COVERED WAGON $225.00
LADY'S CARRIAGE, Female Passenger
Inside, Driver In Red Livery, White Horse .
. . . .$225.00
CIRCUS WAGON, White Horses, No
Harness $400.00

(A-OH '77)   Garth's Auctions, Inc.
TIN TOYS
(ROW I, L to R)
PICKUP TRUCK, Friction, Red, Yellow
& Blue, 19" L. $32.50
TOURING CAR, Windup, 1 Rider Missing
Arm, Paint Worn, 8" L. $360.00
(ROW II, L to R)
SEDAN, Friction, Black W/Gold Stripe,
17¾" L. $75.00
CAR WITH DRIVER, Windup, Germany,
6¼" L. $125.00
CAR WITH DRIVER, Windup, Coupe,
Germany, 6¼" L. $130.00
(ROW III, L to R)
COUPE, Friction, Blue W/Gold Stripe,
17½" L. $35.00
PICKUP WITH DRIVER, Windup, Ger-
many, 7¾" L. $65.00

(A-MA '77)   Garth's Auctions Inc.
(ROW I)
TIN FRICTION TOY, Ladder Truck, Worn
Orig. Paint, 22" L. $50.00
WOODEN JUMPING JACK, Composi-
tion Face, Red, White & Blue Costume,
17" O.A.L. $17.50
(ROW II, L to R)
TIN WIND-UP TOY, Black Lady Sweep-
ing, Spring Will Not Hold, "Lindstrom Corp.
U.S.A.", 8" H. $7.00
TIN WIND-UP TOY, Balloon Man W/
Monkeys, Eyes Move, Working Condi-
tion, 6½" H. $27.50
FRENCH TOY HORSE RACING GAME,
"Jeude Course, M.J. & Co.", Japanned
Horses & Jockeys, Green Flocked Track,
In Wooden Box W/Lid, 7½" Sq., 4" H. . .
. . . .$65.00
PULL TOY, Tin "Ice" Wagon W/Cast
Iron Horse & Driver, Orig. Worn Paint, 10"
L. $22.50
(ROW III, L to R)
TIN PULL TOY, Camel W/Worn Green &
Yellow Paint, 8" L. $130.00
TIN WIND-UP TOY, "Bunny", Working
Condition, "Lindstrom Tool & Toy Co.
U.S.A.", 5½" H. $15.00
TIN WIND-UP TOY, Pecking Hen, Work-
ing Condition, Yellow & Red Worn Paint,
5½" H. $50.00
TIN FRICTION TOY, Goose On Wheels,
Rusted Paint, 8" L. $40.00

To the right ▶

TOYS
(ROW I, L to R)
FIREMAN ON LADDER, Windup, "Louis
Marx & Co.", 22" H. $40.00
CAROUSEL, Windup, Germany, Worn
Polychrome, 6¾" Diam., 12" H. . .$80.00
FERRIS WHEEL, Windup, "Hy-Lo, Buf-
falo Toys", 14½" H. $39.00
(ROW II, L to R)
SHOOTING GALLERY CHICKENS,
Cast Iron, Red & White, 10¼" L., 4½" H.
. . . .$11.00
FIRE PATROL, Cast Iron, 1 Fireman Mis-
sing, 18¾" L. $205.00

(A-OH '77)   Garth's Auctions, Inc.
(ROW I, L to R)
TIN WIND-UP TOY, "George The Drum-
mer Boy", by Marx, Working Condition, 9"
H. $25.00
TIN WIND-UP TOY, "Ferris Wheel" by J.
Chein, 16¼" H. $22.50
TIN WIND-UP TOY, "No. 27 Drum Ma-
jor", By Wolverine, Working Condition,
Drum Sticks Missing, Minor Wear, 13½" H.
. . . .$27.50
(ROW II, L to R)
TIN WIND-UP TOY, Monkey W/Hoola
Hoop, "Made In Japan", Working Condi-
tion, 9" H. $12.50
TIN WIND-UP TOY, Passenger Ship,
"Made In U.S. Zone, Germany", Key Mis-
sing, Paint Worn, 19¾" L. $45.00
TIN WIND-UP DOG, Dog Tossing Candy
In Mouth, Working Condition, "Made In
Japan", 5½" H. $5.00
(ROW III, L to R)
TIN CHICKEN, Clucks When Crank
Turned, "Made In U.S.A.", 7¾" H. . . . . .
. . . .$5.00
CAST IRON TOY, "Overland Circus", 6
Musicians & Driver, "Made In U.S.A.", Re-
painted, 15½" L. $50.00
TIN CHURCH BANK, "J. Chein", 4" H.
. . . .$10.00

(A-OH '77)   Garth's Auctions, Inc.

(ROW I, L to R)

CIRCULAR BLOCKS, Set of 10, Mid-19th C., Mounted On Board W/Screws, Each W/Lithographed Paper Surface W/Letters, Verse & Pictures, Minor Wear $35.00
JACK-IN-THE-BOX BLOCK, Clown Inside, Working $22.00
WOODEN BLOCKS, Set Of 9, Orig. Box Entitled "The Embossing Company's Toy Blocks No. 77", Box Worn........$7.00
RAGGEDY ANN SAFETY BLOCKS, Boxed Set $7.00
PICTURE BLOCKS, Partial Set of 8, Mid-19th C., Worn $5.00

(ROW II, L to R)

WOODEN BLOCKS, Nest of 3, 19th C., Lithographed Animals, Letters, Etc. .$12.00
WOODEN BLOCKS, Set of 26, Letters & Pictures Faded $15.00
BLOCKS, Nest of 4, Heavy Pasteboard W/Pictures & Letters, Minor Wear, Faded $5.00
WOODEN BLOCKS, Nest of 4, Lithographed Pictures Of Animals, Scenes Of Children, Letters, Minor Wear, 1 or 2 Blocks May Be Missing $15.00

(ROW III, L to R)

BLOCKS, Boxed Set, "World's Tower Picture Building Blocks", Mfg. By W. S. Reed Toy Company, Leominster, Mass., Minor Wear $55.00
ARCHITECTURAL ANCHOR BOX, American/German, 19th C., Cased In Wooden Box W/Stones In 3 Colors, Includes Instruction Book, Minor Wear $5.00
FLAT BLOCKS, Lot of 36, Wood W/Applied Lithographs Of Pictures, Letters & Writing, Minor Wear $30.00

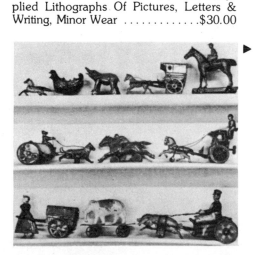

(ROW I, L to R)

TIN BATTERY POWERED TANK, "Made In Japan", 8½" L. $5.00
TIN WIND-UP TOY, Alligator by J. Chein, Working Condition, Minor Wear, 15" L. $12.50
TIN PULL TOY, Passenger Ship "S.S. America", "Wyandotte Toys", Scratched Paint, 12" L. $2.00

(ROW II, L to R)

TIN WIND-UP TOY, Caterpillar By Marx, Metal Bent Around Rear Wheel, Key Missing, 9" L.........................$6.00
TIN WIND-UP TOY, Caterpillar Tractor By Marx, Not Working, 8" L.......$4.00
CAST WHITE METAL TOY BULLDOZER, "Hubley", Worn Paint, 10¼" L. $11.00

(ROW III)

SHEET METAL TRACTOR & TRAILER, Driver's Seat & Hitch Missing, Worn Red & Blue Paint, Unmarked, 16" L. Tractor, 11½" L. Trailer $9.00

To the left

TIN TOYS

(ROW I, L to R)

HORSE & CART, Pull, Orig. Paint Worn, Iron Wheels, 5¼" L. $42.50
ELEPHANT, Pull, "Made In Germany", Transfer Decor., 3" L.............$28.50
HORSE & DELIVERY WAGON, Pull, 5¼" L. $37.50
POLO PLAYER, Pull, 4¼" L. $52.50

(ROW II, L to R)

MONKEY & DOG CART, Windup, "Joko", Germany, 6" L. $45.00
JOCKEY ON HORSE, Wind-Up, Bavaria, ⅛ Wheel Missing, 5" L. $5.00
HANSOM CAB, Wind-Up, 5¾" L. $65.00

(ROW III, L to R)

LADY PULLING CART, Friction, "Depose, R.F.", Wheels Resoldered, 5" L... ....$67.50
ELEPHANT, Pull, White W/Red Blanket, Green Base W/Iron Wheels, 4½" L...... ....$37.50
BUTCHER BOY & PIG CART, Wind-Up, Germany, "Marke Stocke, D.R.G.M.", 8" L. $110.00

(ROW I, L to R)

PARROT PIP-SQUEAK, Composition, Red, Yellow & Blue Cloth Trim, Cloth Covering Base Damaged, 6¼" H. $50.00
LEATHER FIRE BUCKET, Miniature, 3¾" H. $40.00
TOY VIEWER, Scroll Of Handcolored Lithograph Scenes Travel In Opening In Cardboard Box, 8" x 5" x 2¼" ..$125.00
TOY BALANCING MAN, Wooden, Iron Counter Weight, Man - 7" H., 17" O.H. $120.00
JACK-IN-THE-BOX, Cardboard Barrel, Man's Head Painted Composition W/Cloth Covered Spring Loaded Top Hat, Some Wear, Barrell - 4¼" H.........$140.00

(ROW II, L to R)

FINGER ACTIVATED TOY, Wooden, Covered W/Printed Paper, "The Chicken Dispute", 8½" x 4" $65.00
ANIMATED TOY, Paper Dancing Girl & Musicians, Handcolored Figures & Background, Glass Front, Sides Covered W/Marbleized Paper, Non-Workable, 2¼" x 7¼" x 9¼" $100.00
NOAH'S ARK, Wooden, 10 Animals, 2 People, Cream Colored W/Black & Yellow, Red Roof, 8¾" L. $80.00

(ROW III, L to R)

CARVED WOODEN FIGURAL BOXES, Pr., Tops Are Ladies Wearing Folk Costumes, One On Left W/Some Wear, 7½" H. $65.00
BURL CANDLE HOLDER, Cap Shape, 2½" H. $52.50
JACK IN THE BOX, Wooden, 2 White Haired Men W/Painted Composition Heads, Box Covered W/Red & White Printed Paper, 4" x 2" x 4" H. (open) $95.00
RABBIT PIP-SQUEAK, Composition Head, Glass Eyes, White Rabbit Fur, Works, 6½" L., 5½" H. $105.00
TOY PAIL, Stave Construction, Orig. White Paint W/Red Stenciling, Stars, Flags, Horses & "Good Boy", 4¾" Diam., 4¼" H...... ....$47.50

HORSE & WATER WAGON, Pull, Green & Brown, Iron Wheels, Minor Damage, 7¼" W. $57.50
HORSE & WATER WAGON, Pull, White & Blue, Iron Wheels, 6¾" L. $162.50

(A-OH '77)   Garth's Auctions, Inc.
(ROW I, L to R)
TIN WIND-UP TOY, Carousel W/Swans & Airplanes, "Wyandotte Toys, U.S.A.", 5" H. $16.00
TIN FRICTION TOY, Horse & Buckboard, Worn Paint, 7½" L. $6.00
TIN TOY CANNON, Worn Paint, Barrel Dented, 7½" L. $17.00
TIN CAR, Lever Activated, "Japan", 5¼" L. $20.00
(ROW II, L to R)
TIN AIRPLANE, Wheels Turn Propeller, Incomplete Tail, 7½" L. $1.00
TIN WIND-UP TOY, Pool Player, Balls, Workable Condition, 5" W., 14" L. ......
TIN FRICTION TOY, Fire Truck, "Japan", 6¼" L. $5.00
(ROW III, L to R)
TIN CLOWN BANK, "J. Chein", 5" H. $12.00
TIN WIND-UP TOY, Cobbler W/Cloth Coat, Working Condition, "Japan", 6" H. $10.00
TIN WIND-UP TOY, "Dog Patch 4", "Unique Art", Mammy Yokum Missing Arm, Working Condition, 7½" H. ..$40.00
TIN WIND-UP TOY, Dancing Bear, "J. Chein", Working Condition, 4½" H. ......
....$13.00
TIN LAYING HEN, "Wyandotte Toys, U.S.A.", Orig. Cardboard Box, "Susie The Happy Hen", Box Repaired, Has Eggs, 7" H. $8.00

(A-OH '77)   Garth's Auctions, Inc.
TOYS
(ROW I, L to R)
CAROUSEL, 4 Men In Canoes, Tin, Wind-up, Propellers W/Paper Vanes, Orig., Polychrome Paint, Finial Missing, 11" H. ......
....$425.00
CAROUSEL, 4 Bi-Planes & Pilots, Tin, Wind-Up, Paper Vanes Incomplete, Flag Finial, 17" H. $1200.00
ROTATING BLIMPS, 2 Cars W/Passengers, Tin Wind-Up, Orig. Paint, 11¼" H. ...
....$490.00
(ROW II, L to R)
LITTLE ORPHAN ANNIE, Tin, Wind-Up, Harold Gray, Orig. Box, 5" H. ...$225.00
AMOS & ANDY FRESH AIR TAXI CAB, Tin, Wind-Up, Louis Marx, Orig. Cardboard box, 8" L. $275.00
TOONERVILLE TROLLEY, Tin, Wind-Up, Fontaine Fox, 7½" H. $425.00
(ROW III, L to R)
ICE WAGON & HORSE TEAM, Cast Iron, Driver Missing, 12" L. $50.00
DANCING MAN & WOMAN, Tin, Wind-Up, 8" H. $215.00
LIMOUSINE, Cast Iron, "Made By Arcade Mfg. Co.", 12½" L. $92.50

(A-OH '77)   Garth's Auctions, Inc.
(ROW I, L to R)
WIND-UP TOY HORSE, Cloth Covered Wooden & Metal Body, Rabbit Fur Mane & Tail, Key Missing, 6¼" L. $11.00
CAST IRON PULL TOY, Horse W/Sheet Metal Wagon, Worn Red, Yellow & Black Paint, 6½" L. $30.00
TIN WIND-UP TOY, "Tidy Tim" by Marx, Minor Paint Scratches, Working Condition, 8½" L., 7½" H. $27.50
(ROW II, L to R)
SHEET METAL WIND-UP TOY, Caterpillar Tractor by "Structo, Pat. Sept. ;28, 1920", Worn Red & Green Paint, Working Condition, 8¼" L. $37.50
TIN ANIMATED TOY, Climbing Monkey, Worn Red, Yellow & Brown Paint, Flocked Green Coat, Working Condition, 8" H. ....
....$22.50
TIN FRICTION TOY, Child Riding Duck, Worn Green, Yellow, & White Paint W/ Rust Damage, Works Complete, Needs Adjustment, 7½" H. $42.50
(ROW III, L to R)
TIN WIND-UP TOY, "G.I. Joe & The K-9 Pups", "Unique Art", Working Condition, 9" H. $13.00
TIN WIND-UP TOY, W/Squeak Box, Bird On Perch, "Made In Germany", 4" H. $11.00
TIN WIND-UP TOY, "Zilotone", Made By "Wolverine", 3 Metal Records Play 3 Tunes, Working Condition, 7½" W., 7" H. ......
....$155.00
TIN WIND-UP TOY, "Kiddy Cyclist", by "Unique Art", Does Not Run, 9" H. ....
....$13.00

(A-OH '77)   Garth's Auctions, Inc.
CAST WHITE METAL RABBITS, Pr., Brown & White, "Germany", 1½" H. ....
....$5.00
WOODEN NOAH'S ARK, Red & Black, 10¾" L. $52.50
CAST WHITE METAL BUFFALO, "Germany", 3½" L. $6.00

(A-OH '77)   Garth's Auctions, Inc.
(ROW I, L to R)
CAST WHITE METAL ANIMALS (2), Cat & Elephant, "Germany", Worn Paint, Cat - 2" H. $7.00
CAST WHITE METAL HORSE, Black W/Tan Harness, 3½" L. $1.00
CAST WHITE METAL DEER, "Ger-
(continued bottom of next column)

◄ To the left   (continued)
many", Antlers Bent, Worn Paint, 2½" H. $3.50
CAST WHITE METAL COWS (3), Brown & White, Black & White, & Brown, "Made In England", 3" L. (One Pictured In Row III) $7.00
(ROW II, L to R)
COMPOSITION ANIMALS, (2), Horse & Dog, Painted, 2¾" H. $2.00
COMPOSITION ANIMALS, (2), Sheep, 2" L. $4.00

(A-OH '78) *Garth's Auctions, Inc.*
(ROW I, L to R)
CAST IRON BANK, Aunt Jemima, Worn Orig. Silver & Blue Paint, 5¾" H. .$70.00
REDWARE BANK, Jug, Painted Finish, Base Chips, 4" H. $37.00
REDWARE BANK, Multicolored Painted Enamel Decor., 8" H. $51.00
REDWARE BANK, Apple, Worn Red Paint, 2½" H. $46.00
CAST IRON BANK, Clown, Traces Orig. Gold Paint, 6¼" H. $30.00
(ROW II, L to R)
CAST IRON MECHANICAL BANK, "Tammany", Worn Orig. Polychrome Paint, "Pat'd. Aug. 20, 1872", Minor Rust, 4¼" H. $65.00
CAST IRON BANK, Pig, Worn Orig. Gold Paint, 7½" L. $40.00
CAST IRON MECHANICAL BANK, Frog, Base Mkd. "Bank", Worn Orig. Polychrome Paint, "Pat'd. Aug. 20, 1872", Minor Rust, 4¼" H. $105.00
CAST IRON BANK, Lion, Worn Orig. Gold Paint, 5¼" H. $32.50
STONEWARE BANK, Albany Slip, "Greta" Painted On Side, 7" H. $45.00
(ROW III, L to R)
CAST IRON BANK, Jumbo, Worn Gold & Red Paint, 4¾" H. $42.50
ROCKINGHAM BANK, Queen Victoria, Broken Base, 5½" H. $47.50
WOODEN BANK, London Bobby, Spring Head, Polychrome Enamel, 11" H. .$3.00
STONEWARE BANK, Albany Slip, Decoupage Flowers, 4½" H. $21.00
CAST IRON BANK, St. Bernard, Traces Gold Paint, 5½" H. $32.50

(A-OH '77) *Garth's Auctions, Inc.*

(A-OH '78) *Garth's Auctions, Inc.*
CAST IRON BANKS
(ROW I, L to R)
JUMBO, Orig. Gold & Red Paint, 3" H. .
................................$17.50
DOG, Worn Blue Paint, 4½" H. ..$21.00
PIG, No Paint, 7¼" L. $32.50
CAT WITH BALL, No Paint, 5½" L. ....
................................$75.00
PIG, Worn Orig. Gold Paint, 2⅞" H. ....
................................$35.00
(ROW II, L to R)
AUNT JEMIMA, Orig. Polychrome Paint, Minor Wear, 5¼" H. $77.50
JOLLY NIGGER, Pat. Mar. 14, '82, Orig. Red, Yellow & Black Paint, Minor Wear, Mechanical, 6½" H. $85.00
FEMALE DEER, Alligatored Paint, 5" H. .
................................$25.00
REARING HORSE, Worn Orig. Gold Paint, 6¾" H. $40.00
(ROW III, L to R)
IXL SAFE, Pat. July 1881, Worn Orig. Black & Green Paint, 3½" H. $22.00
TURKEY, Worn Orig. Gold Paint, 3½" H.
................................$52.50
COIN DEPOSIT BANK, Combination Safe W/Vintage Embossed Sides & Pull Up Handle, 4" H. $20.00
MAIN STREET TROLLEY, Orig. Worn Gold Paint, Replaced Connecting Screw, 6½" L. $137.50
TIN BANK, Monkey Tips Hat When Coin Deposited, "J. Chein", 5" H. $27.50
TIN BANK, Mascot Safe, Green W/Dog On Door In Red, White & Black, Printed Combination On Bottom, 4" H. $17.50

To the left
TIN TOYS
(ROW I, L to R)
PORTER WITH TRUNK, "Germany", Windup, 6" L., 5½" H. $30.00
JUMPING MONKEY, Wind-Up, "Germany", 5" L., 4½" H. $5.00
TOURING CAR, Wind-Up, Marked "S.G. A.W.", 5¾" L. $107.50
WALKING DOG, Wind-Up, "Made In Germany", 6½" L. $290.00
(ROW II, L to R)
POPEYE, Windup, 7¾" H. $55.00
PEACOCK, Windup, "Ebo, Pao-Pao, Germany, D.R.G.M.", Bellows For Squeak, 9¾" L. $65.00
JUMPING DOG, Wind-Up, "Made In Germany, S.G." 6" H. $17.50
WANNA BUY A DUCK?, Wind-Up, Marx, 8" H. $120.00

(A-OH '78) *Garth's Auctions, Inc.*
CAST IRON BANKS
(ROW I, L to R)
CLOWN, Worn Orig. Gold & Red Paint, 6¼" H. $30.00
POLAR BEAR, Worn White Paint, 5¼" H.
................................$37.50
STATUE OF LIBERTY, Worn Orig. Gold & Red Paint, 6" H. $60.00
SMILING MAN, W/Derby, Worn Orig. Red, White, Grey, Cream Paint, 5½" H. ..
................................$85.00
SOLDIER, Oriental Features, Worn Orig. Gold & Red Paint, 6" H. $60.00
(ROW II, L to R)
"BILLIKEN", Worn Orig. Gold & Red Paint, 4" H. $35.00
JUMBO, Worn Orig. Gold Paint, 2⅜" H. ..
................................$65.00
LION, Worn Orig. Gold Paint, 3¾" H. ..
................................$67.50
"BILLIKEN, Worn Orig. Gold & Red Paint, 4" H. $25.00
(ROW III, L to R)
JUMBO, Worn Orig. Silver, Red & Bold Paint, 5½" H. $57.50
DOG, Traces Black Paint, 3¾" H. .$27.50
HORSE, HORSESHOE, GIRL & DOG, "Good Luck", Worn Orig. Gold & Black Paint, 4⅛" H. $95.50
REARING HORSE, Worn Orig. Gold Paint, Minor Casting Imperfection, 5" H. .$47.50
(ROW IV, L to R)
BOXER DOG, Worn Brown & White Paint, 5¼" H. $30.00
PIG, Gold & Red Paint, 2⅞" H. ..$25.00
JUMBO, Worn Orig. Gold Paint, 3" H. ..
................................$30.00
DONKEY, Worn Orig. Gold Paint, 4½" H.
................................$27.50

(A-OH '77) *Garth's Auctions, Inc.*
CLOWN IN HOOP, Windup, Red & Gold Paint Worn, 6½" Diam. $90.00

(A-OH '78)   *Garth's Auctions, Inc.*

CAST IRON BANKS

(ROW I, L to R)
BLACK MAN, Worn Orig. Gold Paint,
5¼" H. $110.00
JUMBO, Worn Orig. Gold & Red Paint,
4¾" H. $35.00
TEDDY ROOSEVELT, Worn Orig. Gold
& Red Paint, 5⅛" H. $90.00
STAG, Orig. Gold & Red Paint, 6¼" H. ..
...................................$35.00
AUNT JEMIMA, Worn Orig. Gold Paint,
Minor Rust, 5¾" H. $50.00

(ROW II, L to R)
LION, Worn Orig. Gold & Red Paint, 4" H.
...................................$22.50
HOUSE, Worn Orig. Silver & Red Paint,
4¼" H. $32.50
HOUSE, Unpainted, 3⅛" H. $20.00
SAFE, "The J. & E. Stevens Co., Etc.",
Pat. Datesd 1897, Key Missing, Worn Nickel
Plating, 4⅛" H. $22.00
LION, Orig. Gold Paint Worn, 3¾" H. ....
...................................$22.50

(ROW III, L to R)
SAFE, "Sport" Bank W/Scenes Of Animals,
Worn Orig. Gold Paint, Pat. Date 1882, Kay,
3" H. $32.50
DOUBLE FACED BLACK BOY, Worn
Orig. Gold & Black Paint, 3⅛" H. .$65.00
PIG, "A Christmas Roast", Traces Gold
Paint, 7¼" L., 3¼" H. $70.00
TURKEY, Worn Orig. Gold Paint, 3½" H.
...................................$52.50
SAFE, Combination Lock, Worn Orig.
Black Paint, 4" H. $23.00

(ROW IV, L to R)
PRESTO BANK, Pat. APD, Worn Orig.
Gold & Red Paint, 4½" H. $135.00
PRANCING HORSE, Worn Orig. Gold
Paint, 4" H. $27.50
BEEHIVE, Worn Orig. Gold Paint, 2½" H.
...................................$42.50
BABY, Asleep In Cradle W/Bird Perched
On Headboard, No Paint, Minor Rust, 3¾"
L., 3¼" H. $28.00
REARING HORSE, Worn Orig. Gold
Paint, 5⅛" H. $52.50

(A-OH '78)   *Garth's Auctions, Inc.*

CAST IRON MECHANICAL BANKS
(ROW I, L to R)
BANK, "Always Did Spise A Mule", Tail
Broken & Spring Replaced, Worn Orig. Poly-
chrome Paint, "Pat'd. Apr. 27, 1897" ....
..................................$175.00
BANK, Owl, Head Swings, Glass Eyes &
Worn Orig. Paint, 7½" H. $215.00
BANK, Bank Building, Worn Orig. White
& Red Paint, 4¼" H. $25.00
BANK, "Always Did Spise A Mule", Worn
Orig. Polychrome Paint, "Pat'd. Apr. 22,
1872", Coin Hole Cover Damaged, 8¼" H.
..................................$265.00

(ROW II, L to R)
BANK, Punch & Judy, Worn Orig. Poly-
chrome Paint, "Buffalo, N.Y. U.S.A.", List
Of Patents, 7½" H. $300.00
BANK, Clown, Worn Orig. Gold & Red
Paint W/Minor Rust, 6¼" H. $32.00
BANK, Lion & Monkey, Minor Damage,
Worn Orig. Polychrome Paint, 8½" H. ...
...................................$45.00
BANK, Soldier W/Oriental Features, Worn
Red Paint, 6" H. $7.00
BANK, Wurlitzer, Green Paint Worn, Interi-
or Mechanism Not Working, 7½" H. .....
...................................$40.00

(ROW III, L to R)
BANK, House W/Dog On Dish, Traces
Green Paint, 4¾" H. $205.00
BANK, Lion, Worn Orig. Gold Paint, 4" H.
...................................$25.00
BANK, Work Horse, Worn Orig. White,
Green, Black & Tan Paint, Edge Break On
Base, 8½" H. $90.00
BANK, Football Player, Repair To Head,
Orig. Paint Worn, 5¾" H. $60.00
BANK, Domed Building W/Statue Finial,
Traces Orig. Bronze Gilding, 8¾" H. .....
..................................$270.00

(A-OH '77)   *Garth's Auctions, Inc.*

(A-OH '78)   *Garth's Auctions, Inc.*
CAST IRON BANKS
"JOLLY NIGGER", Mechanical, "Pat.
Mar. 14, '82", Worn Orig. Paint, Copper
Bottom W/Cover Plate Mkd. "Pat. Feb. 2,
1875", 6½" H. $105.00
HOUSE, Worn Orig. Gold Paint, 3" H. ...
...................................$17.50
MECHANICAL, Dog Jumps Out & Mule
Kicks, Orig. Pale Blue, Red, & Drk. Blue,
Minor Repair & Wear, Mkd. "Pat. Aug. 3,
1860", 5¼" H. $275.00
BANK BUILDING, Worn Orig. White &
Blue Paint, 3⅜" H. $25.00
HUMPTY DUMPTY, Mkd. "Buffalo, N.Y.,
U.S.A.", Orig. Red, Yellow, Blue & White
Paint, Minor Wear, 7¾" H. $225.00
(ROW II, L to R)
CAMEL, Worn Orig. Gold & Red Paint,
Minor Rust, 4¾" H. $50.00
BANK BUILDING, Traces Gold Paint,
3¼" H. $42.50
JONAH AND THE WHALE, Mechanical,
"Pat. July 15, 1890", Orig. Polychrome
Paint Worn, Coin Hole Cover Replaced,
10¼" L., 5" H. $435.00
U.S. MAIL, Orig. Silver & Red Paint, 3½"
H. $20.00
HORSE, Worn Orig. Gold Paint, 4¼" H. .
...................................$25.00

(ROW III, L to R)
EAGLE AND EAGLETS, Mechanical,
Orig. Polychrome Paint, "Pat. Jan. 23,
1883", 5¾" H. $225.00
WILLIAM TELL, Mechanical, Worn Orig.
Polychrome Paint, "Patented June 23,
1896", Minor Repair, 6½" H. $175.00
BANK BUILDING, Orig. Silver Paint W/
Traces Of Gold, 3⅝" H. $17.50
REARING HORSE, Orig. Gold Paint,
Worn, 7½" H. $45.00

To the left
TIN TOYS
(L to R)
HORSE, Pull, Orig. Yellow Paint W/Red
& Black, Green Base W/Iron Wheels, 9" L.,
6⅜" H. $112.50
▶ **HORSE & WHEELS,** Pull, Wooden Plat-
form, Animated Figure W/Composition
Head, Tin Arms, Yellow Cloth Costume
W/Brown & Yellow hat, 13½" L., 10½"
H. $155.00
ROCKING HORSE, White W/Black, Red,
Blue & Brown, 6" L., 5¼" H. ...$215.00

(A-OH '77)   *Garth's Auctions, Inc.*
TIN TOYS
(ROW I, L to R)
AIRPLANES ON SPIRAL, "Made In Germany", 7" H. $95.00
CLOWN MUSICIANS, Wind-Up, Worn Polychrome, 12" L., 8" H. $295.00
DACHSHUND, Wind-Up, Brown, Tail Missing, 7" L. $17.50
(ROW II, L to R)
CAR, "Wind Up, "Made In Germany, D.R.G.M.", 5½" L. $155.00
JOCKEY ON HORSE, Wind-Up, "Germany, D.R.G.M.", Key Missing, 5" L., 4½" H. $10.00
BIRD IN CAGE, Wind-Up, 8¾" H. $95.00
PLANE, "Aero, Aero, Germany", 4" L. ...
...................................$15.00
BOY & SAINT BERNARD, Windup, 6¾" L. $165.00
(ROW III, L to R)
TOONERVILLE TROLLEY, Windup, "Fontaine Fox", 5¼" L., 7¼" H. ....
...................................$265.00
LIL ABNER & DOGPATCH BAND, Wind-Up, Unique Mfg. Co., 8¼" H. $85.00
BLACK BOY, Wind-Up, 6½" H. ...
...................................$87.50
CAMEL, Wind-Up, Yellow, 5¼" H. ....
...................................$42.50

(A-MA '77)   *Richard A. Bourne Co., Inc.*
TIN MAGIC LANTERN PROJECTOR, One Glass Slide & Miniature Kerosene Lamp, Paint Flaking, 10½" O.H. ..$17.00
TIN MAGIC LANTERN, or Glass Slide Projector W/Metal Kerosene Burner, Minus Slides, Blue Finish, 11" H. $22.00
BRASS SLIDE PROJECTOR, or Magic Lantern W/Brass Kerosene Burner & Glass Slide Holder, 4 Glass Slides (1 Damaged), Mounted On Wooden Base, 11¼" H. ....
...................................$40.00

(A-OH '77)   *Garth's Auctions, Inc.*
TOYS
(ROW I, L to R)
WHEEL BARROW, Cast Iron, Gold & Red, 6½" L. $13.00
BABY BUGGY, Cast Iron, Tan & Silver, 4¼" H. $22.00
SCALES, Cast Iron, Tin Tray & 4 Brass Weights, Silver, 5¾" L. $40.00
IRON, Tin, Blue, 3½" H. $13.00
STOVE, Cast White Metal, "Daisy", Gold, 4¼" H. $11.00
IRON, Tin, Blue W/Red Handle, 5" H. ....
...................................$7.00

(ROW II, L to R)
PLAY STORE REGISTER, Tin & Brass, "Durable Toy & Novelty Co., New York & Cleveland", Black, 4" H. $9.00
RAILROAD ENGINE, COAL CAR & PASSENGER CARS, Tin, Pull, Polychrome, Engine Stenciled "Apollo", No Connecting Hooks, 23½" L. $300.00
(ROW III, L to R)
TRANSFER WAGON, Cast Iron, 3 Horses & Driver, Wagon Bolted To Team, 19" L.
...................................$175.00
YELLOW CAB, Cast Iron, "Arcade", Orange, White & Black, 7¾" L. ..$255.00

(A-MA '77)   *Richard A. Bourne Co., Inc.*
(ROW I, L to R)
TIN MAGIC LANTERN, Or Slide Projector W/Glass Slide & Kerosene Burner, Paint Flaking, 10½" H. $15.00
TIN MAGIC LANTERN SLIDE PROJECTOR, Kerosene Burner & chimney, Red & Black Paint, 11½" H. $22.00
MOTION PICTURE PROJECTOR, Hand-Cranked, Blued Sheet Metal W/Stack & Old Film, 12" O.H. $20.00
(ROW II, L to R)
MICKEY MOUSE TALKIE PROJECTOR, Orig. Box, Records & Films, Speaker Horn $225.00

(A-OH '77)   *Garth's Auctions, Inc.*
TIN TOYS
(ROW I, L to R)
DUCK PULLING BASKET, Wind-Up, "Quack-Quack, D.R.G.M. Lehmann, Germany", 1 Foot Of Duck Broken, 7¾" L. ..
...................................$60.00
ELECTRIC CAR, W/Man & Boy, Wind-Up, "Lehmann, Made In Germany", 5" L. ....
...................................$205.00
HOPPING RABBIT, Wind-Up, Grey & White Paint, Red Trim, 4½" L. $10.00
STAGECOACH, Wind-Up, 8¾" L. ......
...................................$77.50

(ROW II, L to R)
BI-PLANE, Wind-Up, Paper Propeller Blades Missing, 6" L. $445.00
BEE, Green & Red Japanning, 1 Paper Blade Intact, "Brevete S.G.D.G.", 8" L. ..
...................................$28.00
CAR, Driver & Passenger, Wind-Up, "Lehmann", 5½" L., 5½" H. $305.00
PARROT, Wind-Up, 11½" H. $82.50
BUCKING BRONCO, Wild West, Wind-Up, "Lehmann", 6½" L. $70.00
MAN PUSHING WOMAN IN CART, Friction, "Schutz Marke E.P.L.", 6½" W., 5" H. $200.00
(ROW III, L to R)
BOY ON MOTORCYCLE, Wind-Up, Marked "Ki Co.", 8⅜" L., 6½" H. ......
...................................$160.00
HAPPY HOOLIGAN, Wind-Up, "J. Chein & Co., Made In USA", 6" H. $130.00
MAN IN ELECTRIC CAR, Wind-Up, "D.R.G.M. Germany", 5½" L., 5½" H. ..
...................................$120.00
CAT PUSHING CAGE W/2 Mice, Windup, 8¼" L., 6¼" H. $180.00

(A-MA '77)   *Richard A. Bourne Co., Inc.*
ELECTRIC SLIDE PROJECTOR W/ Cord, Orig. Bluing, 15¼" H. $20.00
MICKEY MOUSE PROJECTOR, Hand-Cranked W/Electric Light & Remains Of Old Film, Red & Green Paint, 12" H. ....
...................................$50.00

(A-MA '77)   *Richard A. Bourne Co., Inc.*
(ROW I, L to R)
CAST IRON BELL PULL TOY, Blue
Horse, Wagon-Like Piece W/Nickel Plated
Bells & Wheels, 14½" L. $25.00
PULL TOY, Pressed & Weighted Tin Boy
On Horse, 3½" L., 4" H. $45.00
TIN PULL TOY, Lion On Platform W/4
Wheels, Minor Paint Wear, 4½" L., 3¼"
H. $35.00
(ROW II, L to R)
BELL PULL TOY, Cast Iron Rider, Tin
Horse & Cart W/Nickel Plated Wheels &
Bell, 8½" L., 4¼" H. $50.00
TIN PULL TOY, Running Horse, Figure
Wearing Gun Belt, 2 Tin Bells, 9" L. .....
...............................$70.00
PULL TOY, Cast Metal Figures Riding
Seesaw, Bell In Center Rings, 6¼" L. ....
...............................$140.00
(ROW II, L to R)
**DOUBLE RIDING WESTERN FIG-
URES,** Mounted On Metal Frame W/
Wheels, Each W/Sleigh Bells, Traces Of
Paint, 9½" L., 4" H. $50.00
TRICYCLE PULL TOY, Wooden Rider
W/Metal Arms & Legs, Metal Wheels, Rust-
ed, Faded Paint, Arm Missing, 8¼" L. ....
...............................$40.00
PULL TOY, Nickel-Plated Wheels, By
Gong Bell Mfg. Co., Ca. 1924, 2 Wooden
Clown-Like Figures Rock When Toy Pulled,
7" Diam. Wheels, 10" L. $25.00

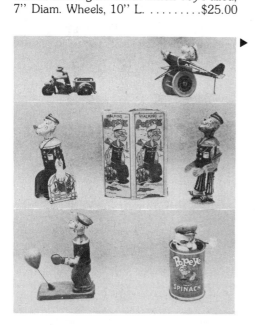

(A-MA '77)   *Richard A. Bourne Co., Inc.*
(ROW I, L to R)
CAST IRON TOY STOVE, "The Royal",
Cast White Metal W/Pipe, 2 Fry Pans,
Spatula & Sauce Pan, 10" L., 8½" O.H. .
...............................$50.00
CAST IRON KITCHEN RANGE, "48"
On Door, Painted Green, Both Lids Missing,
5½" H., 4½" O.L. $20.00
CAST IRON GAS RANGE, Use In Doll-
house, Red Paint, 3" L., 4¼" O.H. $15.00
CHILD'S SEWING MACHINE, Hand
Operated, Stencil Decor., Slightly Rusted ..
...............................$10.00
CHILD'S CASIGE SEWING MACHINE,
Hand Operated, Working Cond....$15.00
CHILD'S SEWING MACHINE, Hand
Operated, Wheel Rusted, Working Cond. .
...............................$10.00
(ROW II, L to R)
CHILD'S CAST IRON & TIN STOVE,
Mkd. "Qualified Range Co., Ft Recovery",
Six Burners, Temp. Gauge In Door, Working
Model, 12½" L., O.D. 9" At Base, 20¾"
H...............................$250.00
CHILD'S TOY WASHING MACHINE,
Hand Operated, "Modern Miss", By C. G.
Wood Company, Girard, Pa., Nickle Plate
Worn Slightly & Pitted, 11" H. $30.00
CHILD'S CAST IRON STOVE, "Baby"
Model, 15" L., 8½" D., 9¼" O.H. .$90.00

To the left
(A-MA '77)   *Richard A. Bourne Co., Inc.*
(ROW I)
**CAST IRON POPEYE ON MOTOR-
CYCLE,** "Spinach" On Side, 3 Rubber
Tires, 5½" L. $190.00
TIN WIND-UP POPEYE THE PILOT,
By Marx, Ca. 1940, Working Condition,
Plane 7" L., 8" Wingspan, 5" H. .$250.00
(ROW II, L to R)
TIN WIND-UP POPEYE FIGURE, By
Marx, Ca. 1930, W/Orig. Box, Box Deterio-
rated, Minor Rusting & Faded Finish On
Popeye Figure, Working Condition, 8" H. .
...............................$90.00
MECHANICAL WALKING POPEYE,
Parrot Cages Missing, Replaced Arms, Finish
Rusted & Worn, Workable, 8" H. ..$20.00
(ROW III, L to R)
TIN WIND-UP POPEYE FIGURE, Pitted
& Rusted, Mechanism Does Not Work, 7½"
H. $90.00
POPEYE IN SPINACH CAN, By Mattel,
Plastic Popeye Pops Out Of Can When Lid
Removed, Cover Missing, 4¼" H. ....
...............................$30.00

(A-MA '77)   *Richard A. Bourne Co., Inc.*
(ROW I, L to R)
**WOOD & LITHOGRAPH HOOK &
LADDER,** Some Lithograph Lost & Re-
placed & Colored In On riders, 31½" L.
...............................$560.00
HORSE & WAGON, Wooden Horse W/
Metal Legs Activated By Rods Connected
To Cast Iron Wheels, Red Paint, Horse
Lithographed Both Sides, 13" L. ..$20.00
(ROW II, L to R)
WOOD & LITHOGRAPH BLOCK SET,
Noah's Ark On Wheels, Removable Roof,
9 Blocks W/Animals & Letters, Minor Wear,
11½" L. $80.00
TIGER IN CAGE ON WHEELS, Wooden
Tiger W/Lithographed Sides, Red & Black
Cage, Minor Wear, 11½" L. $120.00
**LITHOGRAPHED EQUESTRIAN MIL-
ITARY FIGURES,** Set Of 4, 2 Represent
Gen. Pershing, 1 A Soldier Of Minor Rank &
1 Of Field Marshall Haig, Faded, 13" H. ..
...............................$40.00

(A-MA '77)   *Richard A. Bourne Co., Inc.*
(ROW I, L to R)
TOY MILK WAGON W/2 Brown Stuffed
Horses W/Horsehair Tails & Manes, Teddy
Bear, 11 Milk Cans, Minor Wear ..$200.00
WAGON W/2 Stuffed Cloth Horses W/
Horsehair Tails and Manes, Santa Claus
Figure, Sign W/"S Claus Dealer In Good
Things" $325.00
(ROW II, L to R)
STUFFED HORSE, Mohair Covered W/
Horsehair Tail & Mane, Burlap Saddle Blan-
ket, Minor Wear $45.00
CHILD'S PEDAL WAGON, Carved
Wooden Horse W/Horsehair Tail & Mane,
Pump Action Attached To Stirrups, Handle-
bars, Restored, Tail & Mane Are Replace-
ments, Working Condition $130.00

(A-MA '77) *Richard A. Bourne Co., Inc.*
(ROW I, L to R)
FARM OR HAY WAGON W/DRIVER, Ca. 1885, Yellow Wagon & Box W/Red Wheels, Driver Unfinished, 5" L. ..$35.00
IRON SURREY W/LADY PASSENGER, Blue Surrey, Black Horse, 6¾" L. ..$45.00
CAST IRON SULKY W/DRIVER, Ca. 1920, Silver Driver & Horse, Red Wheels, Minor Paint Wear, 4¾" L. $30.00
(ROW II, L to R)
CIRCUS WAGONS, Pr. Double Team of Horses, 1 Black & 1 White, 1 Cage W/Polar Bear & 1 W/Lion, Horses Retouched, 8½" L. $120.00
CAST IRON SURREY, Black Horse, Break In Bottom Repaired, 5¾" L. .$20.00
(ROW III, L to R)
HORSE-DRAWN WAGON, Blue Paint W/Cast Iron Driver, 5⅛" L. ...$30.00
CIRCUS WAGON, Light Cast Metal, Cage W/Polar Bear, 8½" L. $20.00
CAST IRON ELEPHANT-DRAWN CART, Girl Driver W/Blond Hair, Red Hat & Orange Costume, Silver Wagon, Finish Worn, 7½" L. $70.00

(A-OH '77) *Garth's Auctions, Inc.*
TIN TOYS
(ROW I, L to R)
FIRE TRUCK LADDER WAGON, 5 Firemen, Windup, "Made In Germany", 4¼" L. $40.00
FIRE TRUCK LADDER WAGON, 5 Firemen, Windup, "Made In Germany", 4¼" L. $40.00
BOY ON SLED, Windup, "Germany, J.D.", 4½" L. $95.00
TOONERVILLE TROLLEY, Copyright 1922 By Fontaine Fox, 1⅞" H. ..$245.00
(ROW II, L to R)
SWINGING CLOWN, "C.D.Kenny Co.", 4¼" H. $80.00
ROOSTER, PUll, 3¼" L. $32.50
EXPRESS BOY, Windup, "Gesche, D.R.G.M. Germany", 2¾" L. $22.50
GIRL ON HORSE, Rocking, 3¾" L., 3¾" H. $50.00
(ROW III, L to R)
SEWING MACHINE, "Made In Germany", 3¼" L., 3¾" H. $40.00
BABY CARRIAGE, W/Baby, "Made In Germany", 3¾" L., 2½" H. $60.00
BABY CARRIAGE, W/Baby, "Made In Germany", 3½" L., 2½" H. $80.00
HORSE & CARRIAGE, 5½" L., 3¼" H. $95.00

(A-OH '77) *Garth's Auctions, Inc.*
(ROW I)
WOODEN ANIMALS (30), From A Noah's Ark, Cut Out W/Jig-Saw & Hand Painted, Minor Damage To Tails & Ears, Tallest - 11½"; Smallest - 1" H. $125.00
(ROW II, L to R)
TIN WIND-UP TOY, Cowboy On Horseback, "Alps, Made In Japan", Working Condition, 5¾" L. $9.00
TIN WIND-UP TOY, Cat & Ball, "Made In Japan", Working Condition, 6" L. $3.00
TIN WIND-UP TOY, Turtle, "Made In U.S.A.", Working Condition, 5" L. $4.00
TIN WIND-UP TOY, Cat W/Plastic Head & Tail, "Japan", 5" L. ...$3.00
TIN WIND-UP TOY, Rabbit W/Basket, "J. Chein", 6½" L. $2.00
(ROW III, L to R)
TIN WIND-UP TOY, "Coo-Coo Car" By Marx, Working Condition, Paint Worn, 8" L. $35.00
TIN BATTERY OPERATED FORD, "Made In Japan", 10¼" L. $12.50
TIN FRICTION CAR, "Test Drive" By "Daiya, Japan", Paint Alligatored, 6½" L. $5.00

(A-MA '77) *Richard A. Bourne Co., Inc.*
(ROW I)
LIONEL MICKEY MOUSE HAND CAR, Composition Mickey & Minnie Mouse, Key Wind $400.00
TIN MECHANICAL BANK, Donald Duck "Teller" Sticks Out Tongue & Pulls In Coin. $50.00
(ROW II, L to R)
MICKEY MOUSE WASHING MACHINE, Tin W/Lithographed Figures Of Mickey & Minnie, Wringer & Plunger Action Crank, Minor Dent In Wringer $120.00
COMPOSITION MICKEY MOUSE FIGURE, Paint Flaking, 5" H. $80.00
MICKEY MOUSE DRUMMER PULL TOY, By Fisher Price, Movable Arms, Slightly Soiled & Faded, Working Condition ....
...............................$30.00

(A-PA '77) *Pennypacker Auction Centre*
CARVED WOODEN DANCING DOLL, China Head Mounted On Wooden Platform & Bordered By Metal Frame W/2 Old Bells.
...............................$260.00

(A-PA '77) *Pennypacker Auction Centre*
WOODEN MINSTREL TOY, Black Face & White Face Men $220.00

(A-MA '77)   *Richard A. Bourne Co., Inc.*
(ROW I, L to R)

CAST IRON HORSE-DRAWN CAR-RIAGE, Tin Fenders, Replaced Driver, 17" O.L. $375.00

CAST IRON ANDY GUMP IN CAR NO. 348, Arcade Mfg. Co., Freeport, Ill., Paint Worn & Retouched, Radiator Cap Missing, 7¼" L. $240.00

CAST IRON HUBER STEAM ROLLER, Ca. 1929, By Hubley Toy Co., Hubley Label, 8" O.L. $150.00

WAGON, Pulled By Mule, Driven By Black Man In Hat, Varnished, 9½" O.L. .$50.00
(ROW II, L to R)

CAST IRON CARRIAGE, Lady Passenger, Minor Paint Wear, 15½" O.L. $150.00

PULL TOY, Woman Riding Donkey, 6" O.L., 6¾" H. $40.00

CAST IRON CARRIAGE, Man In Blue Suit, 7½" L. $70.00

CAST IRON ICE WAGON, 10" O.L. ....
.....................$25.00
(ROW III, L to R)

FRINGE-TOP CAST IRON SURREY, Driver & Passenger, 13" L. $25.00

CAST IRON STAGECOACH, Driver, 4 Horses (2 White - 2 Grey), Mail Bag, 17" L. $25.00

CAST IRON FARM WAGON, Driver, 2 Horses, 10½" L. $15.00
(ROW IV, L to R)

CAST IRON SANTA CLAUS IN SLEIGH, 2 Reindeer, Mkd. "Mechanical Replicas, Boonesville, New York", 16" L.
.....................$40.00

CAST IRON SURREY, 2 Brown Horses, Western-Style Driver & Lady Passenger, 11½" L. $25.00

CAST IRON COVERED WAGON, 2 Black Horses, Canvas Cover Soiled W/Dust, 11½" O.L. $20.00

(A-MA '77)   *Richard A. Bourne Co., Inc.*
ROCKING HORSE, Carved Wooden Dapple Gray Hobby Horse W/Leather Saddle, Horsehair Tail & Mane, Repainted $150.00
CHILD'S WAGON, Red Body, Iron Wheels, Repainted $40.00

(A-MA '77)   *Richard A. Bourne Co., Inc.*
(ROW I, L to R)

CAST IRON FIRE EQUIPMENT PIECES, (3), 12" Hook & Ladder, 10½" Chief's Wagon & 10" Pumper, Drivers & Horses $75.00

PUMPER TRUCK, Iron Wheels, Radiator Break, Rear Wheel Replacement, Paint Worn & Rusted, 6" L. $20.00
(ROW II, L to R)

HORSE-DRAWN HOOK & LADDER, Front & Rear Drivers, 3 Ladders, Repainted, 30" O.L. $170.00

CAST IRON STEAM PUMPER, 3 Horses, Driver & Rear Attendant, Rubber Hoses, 22" O.L. $50.00
(ROW III, L to R)

HORSE-DRAWN PUMPER, Driver, 3 Horses W/Bell, Paint Worn, 18" L. ....
.....................$150.00

CAST IRON HOOK & LADDER, 2 Drivers, 2 Horses W/Bell, Replacement Ladders, Minor Paint Wear $85.00
(ROW V, L to R)

CAST IRON HOOK AND LADDER, 2 Horses W/Wheel Activated Bell, 2 Drivers, Wooden Ladders, 1 Driver A Replacement, 27" L. $190.00

CAST IRON FIRE HOSE CART, 1 Horse, Driver, Hose Reel W/Rope Simulating Hose, Bell, Wooden Heel Under Horse's Forehoof Broken, 15" L. $300.00

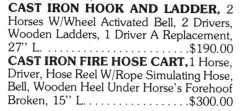

(A-MA '77)   *Richard A. Bourne Co., Inc.*
(TOP)

TOY WAGON W/Walking Teddy Bear Pulling & Steiff Teddy Bear In Wagon, Wagon W/Wooden Body W/"Express" ....
.....................$150.00

(BOTTOM)

WAGON W/2 Stuffed Mohair-Covered Black Horses, Leather Harnesses, Minor Wear, Squeaker On One Bear Not Working.
.....................$175.00

(A-MA '77)   *Richard A. Bourne Co., Inc.*
(ROW I, L to R)

CAST IRON FARM WAGIN, Black Horse, Red Wagon W/White Wheels, 14½" L. ...
.....................$110.00

CAST IRON SAND & GRAVEL WAGON, Minor Paint Loss, 15" L. $80.00

CAST IRON FARM WAGON, 2 Oxen, Minus Rider, 14½" L. $50.00
(ROW II, L to R)

FARM WAGON, Black Horse, Wooden Bottom, 13" L. $375.00

FARM WAGON, 1 Black & 1 White Horse, Driver, 14" L. $70.00

OVERLAND CIRCUS WAGON, 2 Horses W/Lion In Cage, Driver, 14" L. ...
.....................$140.00
(ROW III, L to R)

OVERLAND CIRCUS WAGON, 2 White Horses, 1 W/Rider, Man Playing Calliope, 14" L. $325.00
(ROW III, L to R)

OVERLAND CIRCUS WAGON, 2 White Horses, 1 W/Rider, Cage W/Polar Bear, 14" L. $200.00

OVERLAND CIRCUS WAGON, 2 White Horses, 1 W/Rider, Man Playing Calliope, 14" L. $325.00

CAST IRON OVERLAND CIRCUS WAGON, 2 White Horses, 1 W/Rider, Driver & 6-Pc. Band, 15½" L. $400.00
(ROW IV)

CAST IRON BUDWEISER BEER WAGON, 8 Clydesdale Horses, 2 Figures, Kegs Of Beer, Mounted On Board, 33" L. .....
.....................$120.00

(A-MA '77)   *Richard A. Bourne Co., Inc.*
CHILD'S SLEIGH, Blue Velvet Upholstered Seat, Red Body W/Black Stripes, Wooden Undercarriage, Metal Runners, Minor Wear..................$170.00
IRISH MAIL VELOCIPEDE, Ca. 1910, Reupholstered Seat, Rubber Worn Off Front Tire, Working Condition $125.00

(ROW I, L to R)
MECHANICAL TIN TOY CAR, "Uncle Wiggily's Crazy Car", Germany, Ca. 1920, Howard R. Garis Copyright, No Bumpers, Mechanism Not Working, Orig. Paint, 9¼" L. $550.00
AMOS & ANDY AIR TAXI CAB COMPANY, Tin, 2 Figures & Dog, By Marx, Ca. 1930, Paint Retouched, 8" L. $100.00
MECHANICAL AUTO, "The Tut-Tut" By Lehmann, Ca. 1910, Working Condition, 7" L. $275.00
(ROW II, L to R)
TIN AUTOMOBILE, Blackened, Motor Not Working, 7" L. $30.00
TIN OPEN ROADSTER, Made In Germany By Orobr., Working Condition, 6" L. $95.00
TIN DELIVERY WAGON, 3-Wheeled, By Lehmann, Ca. 1910, Gears Do Not Mesh, Repairable $310.00
TIN AUTOMOBILE, Working Mechanism, 5½" L. $90.00
(ROW III, L to R)
TOONERVILLE TROLLEY, By H. Fisher & Co., Copyright 1922 By Fontaine Fox, Mechanism Does Not Work, Repairable, Age-Darkened Paint, 5" L. $170.00
SNOOPY GUS HOOK & LADDER, Truck Only By Marx & Co., N.Y., Hook & Ladder Missing, 7¾" L. $40.00
TIN MECHANICAL "INTERSTATE" BUS, Driver, Minor Paint Wear, Minor Dents, Mechanism Does Not Work, 10" L. $120.00
(ROW IV, L to R)
TIN YELLOW TAXI, By Mohawk Toys, Minor Paint Wear & Denting Of Sides, Mechanism Does Not Work, 7" L. $40.00
TIN RAPID DELIVERY TRUCK NO. 10, Slightly Bent, Mechanism Missing, 7¾" L. $40.00
TIN MOTORCYCLE POLICEMAN, By Marx, Ca. 1930, Minor Paint Wear, Working Condition, 8½" L. $50.00

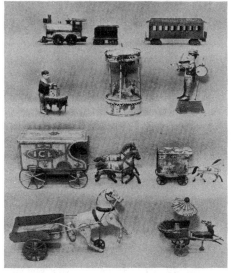

(ROW I)
TIN TOY STEAM LOCOMOTIVE, Brass Burner, Mkd. "Dart" - Trademark of M.C.F. Co., 1887, Paint Crazed On Passenger Car, 8" Locomotive, 4" Tender, 9½" Car. $400.00
(ROW II, L to R)
TIN MECHANICAL MAGICIAN TOY, German, Ca. 1900, Magician Lifts Cover From Box & Head Appears & Arm Waves Wand, Paint Flaking, 5½" H. $425.00
TIN MECHANICAL MERRY-GO-ROUND, German, 3 Carousel Figures Revolve Around Pole, Music Box Plays Several Notes, Papier Mache Horses & Riders, Pole Bent, 10" H. $175.00
TIN ONE-MAN BAND, German, Wind-Up Mechanism, Paint Flaking, Spring Broken, 10" H. $175.00
(ROW III)
TIN ICE WAGON, 2 Lithographed Tin Horses, Lithographed Wagon W/Cast Iron Wheels, Paint Flaking, Rear Wheel Broken, 17" L. $200.00
TIN WAGON, Driver, Wagon Painted Blue, Iron Wheel, Minor Paint Flaking, 9¾" L. $90.00
(ROW IV)
TIN HORSE & CART, Blue Cart W/Cast Iron Wheels, Silver Horse W/Hinged Legs, Paint Worn On Wheels, 17" L. $45.00
CART, Drawn By Reindeer, Straw Umbrella & Carriage, Mounted On Tin Frame W/Tin Wheels, Worn, 9" L. $45.00

(L to R)
TIN AUTOMOBILE, Friction Drive, Red Paint W/Gold Striping, Radiator Painted Green W/Minor Dents, 11" L. $90.00
WOOD & STEEL AUTOMOBILE, Friction Drive, 3 Cast Iron Figures, 10½" L. $175.00

(ROW I, L to R)
HORSE & WAGON, Stuffed Horse W/ Mohair Hide & Mane, Human Hair Tail, Mounted On Wheeled Platform, "U.S. Mail" Wagon W/Lithographed Paper On Side, Minor Wear, 22" O.L., Horse - 9" H. $50.00
PAPIER MACHE ELEPHANT, On Wheels, Glass Paperweight Eyes & Ivory-Like Tusks, 10" L., 7" H. $25.00
PAPIER MACHE ELEPHANT, Mounted On Platform, Back Split, Saddle Worn, 9" L., 7" H. $20.00
(ROW II, L to R)
MILK DELIVERY WAGON, Horse On Wheeled Platform W/White Wagon W/ Borden's Advertising, Horse's Hide Worn, 17" L., 8" H. $40.00
PAPIER MACHE SHEEP FIGURES, (2), Wool-Like Cotton Coats, 1 Mounted On Wheeled Platform, 1 Fitted W/Wheels On Feet, Both W/Green Glass Eyes, 9" L., 8" & 9" H. $40.00
(ROW III)
SHEEP, Flock Of 4, All Mounted On Wheeled Platforms, Simulated Wool Coats Of Various Materials, Coats Soiled, Smallest: 6" L., 6" H., Largest: 10" L., 8" H. $75.00

(Top to Bottom)
TIN LOCOMOTIVE & TENDER, Red W/White Outlining Stripes, Friction Motor Missing, Paint Worn, Wheels Rusted & Bent, 17" L. $25.00
WOOD & TIN LOCOMOTIVE & TENDER, "Clark's Hill Climber", Friction Engine Missing, Red Paint W/Stenciled Decor., Paint Flaking, 6 Sm. Wheels Missing, 17½" L. $90.00

(A-MA '77)   *Richard A. Bourne Co., Inc.*
(ROW I, L to R)
TOY AIRSHIPS, (5), Tin Twin Engine Fighter, Made In Japan; Cast Iron Dirigible W/"Zep", Traces Silver Finish; Seaplane W/"SeaGull", Pusher Type Engine, Propeller Missing; Metal Clipper W/4 Engines, 1 Propeller Missing; Aluminum Seaplane W/ Spring Drive, Twin Engine, "Silver Eagle". $60.00
(ROW II, L to R)
THE FLYING JENNY, Sheet Metal, Remains of "U.S. Mail" One Side, U.S.A.F. Star On Wings, Paint Worn, 15½" L......
....$40.00
WOODEN AIRPLANES (2), Bi-Plane, World War I Type, Red Paint Flaking; Twin-Engine Seaplane, Silver Paint W/U.S. Stars On Wings; Bi-Plane 11¾" L.; Seaplane 9" L. $30.00
(ROW III, L to R)
METAL MONOPLANE, Friction Engine, Yellow Fuselage & Red Wings, British A.F. Symbol On Wings, Paint Flaking, Upper Tail Assembly Missing, 13" L. $10.00
STEELCRAFT STEEL AIRPLANE, Modeled After "Spirit Of St. Louis", U.S.A.F. Star On Wings, Paint Worn, Replaced Propeller, 24" L. $20.00
(ROW IV)
STEEL ZEPPELIN, Model Of Akron, Push Or Riding Toy W/3 Wheels & 3 Engines W/Propellers, 1 Wheel Geared & Arm Missing, Silver Paint Worn & Spotted, 30" L. .
....$55.00

To the right ▶
(A-OH '77)   *Garth's Auctions, Inc.*
STEAM LOCOMOTIVE, Working Model, "Osceola", Matching Coal Car, Brass & Iron W/Wooden Cab, Needs Restoration, Wooden Top Of Cab Split & Repaired, Engine - 40" L., Coal Car - 16" L.......
....$395.00
STEAM THRESHING ENGINE, Wooden Model, Moving Parts, Red, Black & Yellow Paint, Minor Restoration, Custom-Built Plexiglass Case, 41" L. $325.00

(A-MA '77)   *Richard A. Bourne Co., Inc.*
(ROW I, L to R)
STEAM OPERATED PADDLE WHEEL BOAT, Tin, "Water Witch", Walking Beam Excursion Type, 12¼" L. $725.00
TIN WARSHIP, 2 Guns & Turret, Captain At Helm & Man W/Gun Aft, Spring Broken, Paint Flaking, Wind-Up Mechanism Broken, 10½" L., 5½" H. $60.00
(ROW II, L to R)
TIN OCEAN LINER, Red & Blue Hulled W/2 Stacks, Single Mast W/Flag, Crank, Wind-Up Mechanism Not Working, 9" O.L. $60.00
TIN FRICTION SHIP W/4 Wooden Lifeboats, Paint Worn, 12½" L. $65.00
(ROW III, L to R)
FRICTION WARSHIP, Minor Paint Scratches, 10" L. $50.00
TIN WIND-UP LAUNCH, Propeller Missing, Paint Flaking, Rails Damaged, Rudder Bent, 10" O.L. $25.00
(ROW IV, L to R)
STEAM LAUNCH, Figures Under Canopy, Crewman On Bow, Canopy Worn, Wind-Up Mechanism Does Not Work, 8" L. .$55.00
TIN DIVING SUBMARINE, By Wolverine Supply Mfg. Co. Of Pittsburgh, W/Orig. Box, 12½" L. $30.00

(A-MA '77)   *Richard A. Bourne Co., Inc.*
(ROW I, L to R)
CAST IRON LOCOMOTIVE, Attached Tender Mkd. "1085", Black Paint, 8⅞" O.L. $35.00
CAST IRON LOCOMOTIVE, Tender & 5 Passenger Cars, 27" L. $80.00
(ROW II)
CAST IRON LOCOMOTIVE, Tender W/ "23", Passenger Car Mkd. "New York Central & Hudson River R.R." & "892", Gondola Mkd. "H.T.R.R.", 10" Locomotive, 37" O.L. $280.00
(ROW III)
CAST IRON LOCOMOTIVE, Tender & 3 Passenger Cars, 1 Red, 1 White, 1 Blue, Mkd. "Pennsylvania Lines" & "Rouin", Paint Aged, 7¾" Locomotive, 41" O.L. ..
....$100.00
(ROW IV, L to R)
CAST IRON TROLLEY, Repainted Yellow & Red, 8" L. $45.00
CAST IRON TRAIN, Locomotive, Tender & 2 Cargo Cars, Mkd. "M.C.R.R.", 7½" Locomotive, 22" O.L. $55.00
(ROW V, L to R)
CAST IRON LOCOMOTIVE & TENDER, Benton Toy Co., Kenton, Ohio, Tender Mkd. "NYC RR CO", Black Paint, Minor Repairs, 9" Engine, 14" O.L. $50.00
CAST IRON LOCOMOTIVE W/Tender & Passenger Car, Traces Silver Paint, Wheels Repainted, 6" Engine, 16" O.L. ...$45.00

(A-MA '77)   *Richard A. Bourne Co., Inc.*
(Top to Bottom)
LIONEL LOCOMOTIVE NO. 10, Ca. 1925-29, Freight Set W/No. 515 Tank Car; No. 512 Flat Car Loaded W/6 Wooden Barrels; No. 513 Cattle Car; No. 516 Dump Car; No. 517 Caboose; Rail Missing On Tank Car, Operable, 11½" Locomotive $190.00
LIONEL LOCOMOTIVE, Ca. 1926-30, Repainted, Cab Loose, Operable, 10¼" L. Locomotive $50.00

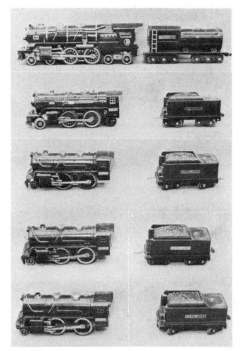

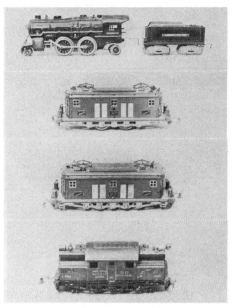

(A-MA '77)   *Richard A. Bourne Co., Inc.*
(Top to Bottom)
LIONEL LOCOMOTIVE NO. 8, Ca.
1925-32 W/Baggage Car No. 332, Pullman
Car No. 339, Observation Car No. 341,
Locomotive Top Repainted, Operable,
10¾" Locomotive $110.00
LIONEL LOCOMOTIVE NO. 8, Ca.
1925-32, Passenger Set W/Mail Car No.
332, Pullman Car No. 337, Observation Car
No. 338, Minor Paint Scratches, Operable,
10¾" Locomotive $215.00
LIONEL LOCOMOTIVE NO. 8, Recon-
structed Power Unit W/Pullman No. 337,
Observation Car No. 338, Paint On Passenger Cars Crazed & Dulled, Operable, 10¾"
Locomotive $110.00

(A-MA '77)   *Richard A. Bourne Co., Inc.*
(ROW I, L to R)
**TIN ELECTRIC LOCOMOTIVE W/
TENDER** & Winnertown Transformer
1012, By Winner Toy Corporation, Tender
Mkd. "Winner Lines No. 1016", Ca. 1931-
32, Operable, Light Missing, 7" L. .$50.00
**TIN ELECTRIC "LIONEL JUNIOR"
LOCOMOTIVE & TENDER,** Ca. 1934-
35, Minor Paint Wear, 8" Locomotive . . . .
. . . .$35.00
(ROW II, L to R)
**LIONEL PETER RABBIT TIN WIND-UP
HAND CAR,** Basket W/Cardboard Egg,
Ca. 1936, Operable, 8½" L. $250.00
**MICKEY MOUSE TIN WIND-UP LO-
COMOTIVE & FREIGHT CAR,** By Marx,
Not Operable, Worn Paint, 10½" Loco-
motive $100.00
(ROW III)
MICKEY MOUSE CIRCUS TRAIN,
Lionel, Ca. 1935, Locomotive & 3 Tin Cars,
Operable, Worn Paint, Minor Rusting, 7¼"
Locomotive $300.00

(A-MA '77)   *Richard A. Bourne Co., Inc.*
(Top to Bottom)
**LIONEL STEAM LOCOMOTIVE NO.
400,** Ca. 1931-39, W/Tender No. 400T,
Operable, 18½" Locomotive $800.00
**LIONEL BUILD-A-LOCO NO. 390E
STEAM LOCOMOTIVE** W/Tender No.
384T, Wheels Deteriorated, Minor Restora-
tion Necessary, Operable, 13¾" Locomo-
tive $235.00
**LIONEL BUILD-A-LOCO STEAM
LOCOMOTIVE** W/Tender No. 384T,
Mail Car No. 332, Pullman No. 337, & Ob-
servation Car No. 336, Macy Special Issue
Cars, Operable, 12" Locomotive . . . .
. . . .$350.00
**LIONEL BUILD-A-LOCO NO. 384E
STEAM LOCOMOTIVE,** Ca. 1930-32,
Unnumbered Lionel Tender; Four Flat Cars
No. 511; Two Loaded W/Lumber, One
W/Boxes; Searchlight Car No. 520; Gondola
No. 512; and Caboose No. 517; Minor Wear,
Operable, 12½" Locomotive $175.00
**LIONEL BUILD-A-LOCO STEAM LO-
COMOTIVE,** Ca. 1932-32, Tender No.
384T; Freight Train W/Gondola No. 512;
Cattle Car No. 513; Refrigerator Car No.
514R; Caboose No. 517; Minor Paint
Scratches, Cow Catcher Broken On Loco-
motive, Operable, 12" Locomotive . . . .
. . . .$140.00

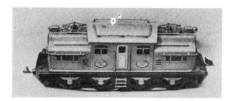

(A-MA '77)   *Richard A. Bourne Co., Inc.*
LIONEL LOCOMOTIVE NO. 480E,
Ca. 1927-36, Passenger Train W/No. 418
Power Car; Parlor & Baggage Car No. 419;
Observation Car No. 490, Wheels Deterio-
rated, 16½" Locomotive $650.00

(A-MA '77)   *Richard A. Bourne Co., Inc.*
(Top to Bottom)
**AMERICAN FLYER STEAM LOCO-
MOTIVE NO. 4670** W/Tender No. 4671,
Freight Train W/Tank Car No. 4010; Flat Car
No. 4023; Flat Car No. 4022; Two Gondolas
No. 4017; Caboose No. 4021, Locomotive
Wheel Chipped & Repaired, 14½" L. . . . .
. . . .$300.00
**AMERICAN FLYER LOCOMOTIVE
NO. 4678** W/Two Pullman Cars No. 4341,
Observation Car No. 4342, Operable, 14½"
Locomotive $225.00
**AMERICAN FLYER LOCOMOTIVE
NO. 4678** W/Two Club Cars No. 4340,
Pullman Car No. 4331, Pullman Car No.
4332, Paint Scratches On Engine, Minus
Headlamp, 14½" Locomotive $170.00
IVES NO. 3242 LOCOMOTIVE, W/
Passenger, Buffet & Observation Cars,
Cars Need Restoration, Paint Scratched On
Engine, 12" Locomotive $90.00

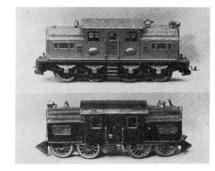

(A-MA '77)   *Richard A. Bourne Co., Inc.*
(Top to Bottom)
LIONEL NO. 402E LOCOMOTIVE, Ca.
1926-28; W/Freight Set Of Flat Car No.
211 W/Load Of Logs; Gondola No. 212;
Cattle Car No. 213; Automobile & Furniture
Car No. 214; Oil Car No. 215; Side Dump
Car No. 218; Caboose No. 217; Minor Wear,
Operable, 16½" Locomotive $400.00
LIONEL NO. 42 ELECTRIC ENGINE,
Ca. 1915, W/Parlor Car No. 18; Observation
Car No. 190; Complete W/Box, Operable,
16½" Locomotive $250.00

(A-MA '77)   *Richard A. Bourne Co., Inc.*
(ROW I)
TIN "MARKIN" LOCOMOTIVE, W/
9½" Locomotive, 5¼" Tender, 6½" Pas-
senger Car, Operable, Spring-Driven Works,
Paint Flaking $70.00
(ROW II, L to R)
**CAST IRON "IVES NO. 17" WIND-UP
LOCOMOTIVE,** Tin Tender, Operable,
Works Not Guaranteed, 7" Locomotive . . .
. . . .$55.00
CAST IRON WIND-UP LOCOMOTIVE,
Tin Tender Mkd. "American Flyer Line",
Ca. 1910-1915, Operable, Works Not Guar-
anteed, 7" Locomotive $65.00
(ROW III, L to R)
**CAST IRON "IVES" WIND-UP LOCO-
MOTIVE,** Tin Tender Mkd. "B.&O.R.R.",
Operable, Locomotive Chipped, Tender
Scratched & Rail Broken, Works Not Guar-
anteed, 7" L. $20.00
CAST IRON WIND-UP LOCOMOTIVE,
"American Flyer", Tin Tender W/"160",
Minor Wear, 6¼" L. $15.00
(ROW IV, L to R)
**CAST IRON "IVES NO. 17" WIND-UP
LOCOMOTIVE,** Electric Works, Operable,
Works Not Guaranteed, 6¾" Locomotive .
. . . .$25.00
CAST IRON WIND-UP LOCOMOTIVE,
"American Flyer", Operable, Minus Brake,
Repaired, Traces Iron-Colored Paint, Works
Not Guaranteed. 6½" Locomotive .$10.00
(ROW V, L to R)
**CAST IRON WIND-UP LOCOMOTIVE
& TENDER,** Operable, Black Paint Flaking,
Works Not Guaranteed, 6½" Locomotive .
. . . .$20.00
**CAST IRON WIND-UP LOCOMOTIVE
& TENDER,** Mechanism Does Not Work,
Bolt Replaces Car Hitch, Tender Repainted,
6" Locomotive $20.00
(ROW IV, L to R)
**CAST IRON "IVES NO. 6" LOCOMO-
TIVE & TIN TENDER,** Ca. 1910-15,
Tender Repainted, Works Not Guaran-
teed, 6" Locomotive $25.00
**CAST IRON WIND-UP LOCOMOTIVE
& TIN TENDER,** Mechanism Does Not
Work, Tender Repainted, 2 Halves Of Loco-
motive Loose, 6¼" L. $15.00

(A-MA '77)   *Richard A. Bourne Co., Inc.*
(ROW I, L to R)
**BING TYPE TIN WIND-UP LOCOMO-
tive,** Gondola, 2 Passenger Cars, Baggage
Car & Misc. Car, Locomotive Mkd. "J.D.P.
France 464", Four Mkd. "Bing", Operable,
Minor Rusting, 7" Locomotive $40.00
**CAST IRON WIND-UP LOCOMOTIVE
NO. 444,** Operable, 8½" L. $70.00
(ROW II, L to R)
ENGLISH-STYLE LOCOMOTIVE, For-
ward & Reverse Mechanism Workable,
Cement Car, Livestock Car & Wine Vat
Car, Minor Wear, 6½" L. $60.00
**CAST IRON "IVES" IRON WIND-UP
LOCOMOTIVE,** Ca. 1912, Tin Tender,
Minor Paint Scratches, Operable, 5¾"
Locomotive $175.00
(ROW III, L to R)
**CAST IRON IVES NO. 6 WIND-UP
LOCOMOTIVE,** Ca. 1910-15, Tin Tender
Mkd. "F E No. 1", Operable, 6¾' Locomo-
tive $50.00
CAST IRON WIND-UP LOCOMOTIVE,
Minus Tender, Operable, 6½" L. . .$20.00
(ROW IV, L to R)
CAST IRON WIND-UP LOCOMOTIVE
W/Overland Flyer & Tin Tender, Operable,
Tender Bent, 7¾" Locomotive $45.00
CAST IRON WIND-UP LOCOMOTIVE,
Operable, 6" L. $15.00
(ROW V, L to R)
**TIN WIND-UP LOCOMOTIVE & TEN-
DER,** Red & Black, Operable, Tender Re-
painted, 7" Locomotive $10.00
TIN WIND-UP LOCOMOTIVE W/Electric
Light, Red Paint, Operable, Paint Worn,
Cow Catcher Bent, 8" L. $10.00

(A-MA '77)   *Richard A. Bourne Co., Inc.*
(ROW I, L to R)
ELECTRIC LOCOMOTIVE NO. 3238,
Caboose No. 67, New York New Haven &
Hartford Railroad Freight Car, Flat Car
Loaded W/Lumber, Canadian & Pacific Flat
Car No. 64387 & Gondola No. 63, Stenciled
Numbers, Surface Slightly Pitted & Rough-
ened, Operable, 9¾" Locomotive $150.00
**LIONEL ELECTRIC LOCOMOTIVE
NO. 152,** Ca. 1917-27, Minor Repair To
Electric Light, Operable, 7" O.L. . . .$20.00
**LIONEL ELECTRIC LOCOMOTIVE
NO. 152,** Ca. 1917-27, Operable, 7" L.
. . . .$30.00
(ROW II)
**LIONEL ELECTRIC LOCOMOTIVE
NO. 154,** Ca. 1917-23, Two No. 602 &
One No. 601 Passenger Car, Paint Marred
& Scratched, Engine Inoperable, 7" L.
Locomotive $50.00
(ROW III)
**LIONEL ELECTRIC LOCOMOTIVE
NO. 252,** Ca. 1926-32, Two No. 629 &
One No. 630 Passenger Cars, Railroad
Cars Repainted & Engine Inoperable, 8"
L. Locomotive $40.00
(ROW IV)
**LIONEL ELECTRIC LOCOMOTIVE
NO. 252,** Ca. 1926-32, Two No. 629 Cars
& One No. 630 Passenger Cars, Cars Re-
painted, Runs Poorly, 8" L. Locomotive . .
. . . .$50.00
(ROW V)
**LIONEL ELECTRIC LOCOMOTIVE
NO. 252,** Ca. 1926-32, Two No. 607 &
One No. 608 Passenger Cars, Headlamp
Repainted, Operable, 8" L. Locomotive . . .
. . . .$125.00
(ROW VI)
**LIONEL ELECTRIC LOCOMOTIVE
NO. 253,** Ca. 1925-32, Two No. 529 &
One No. 530 Passenger Cars, Paint
Scratched & Worn, Operable, 9" L. Loco-
motive $125.00

◄ *To the left*

(A-MA '77)   *Richard A. Bourne Co., Inc.*
LIONEL TROLLEY, Ca. 1906-10, Restored, Operable, 10¾" L. Locomotive . . .
. . . .$160.00

(A-OH '77) *Garth's Auctions, Inc.*
(ROW I, L to R)

PISTOL, Conv. Perc W/Perc. Cap Shield, Part Round Bbl., Engraved Brass Hdwe., Mask Type Butt Cap, Grained Stock . . . . . .
. . . .$155.00
SHARPS PISTOL, 4 Bbl., 30 Cal., "Sold By Tipping & Lawden, England" Mkd. On Frame, Nickel Plated Frame, Gutta Percha Grips, SN3470 . . . .$135.00
GAULOIS SQUEEZE PISTOL, 8mm., Floral Etched Receiver & Bbl., Mottled Rubber Grip, SN3151 . . . .$210.00
(ROW II)
PISTOLS, Pr., F.L. Center Hammer, O/U Bbl., Mkd. "Lambert, Libert", Swivel Priming Pans, Checkered Grips, 41 Cal., C1800 . . .
. . . .$360.00
(ROW III, L to R)
REMINGTON ARMY REVOLVER, New Model Perc., Reblued, Nickel Plated Trigger Guard, SN124201 . . . .$145.00
COLT RIFLE-REVOLVER, Bisley Mod. 41, Nickel Plated, 5½" Bbl., SN256039 . . . . . .
. . . .$220.00
(ROW IV, L to R)
ENGLISH HOLSTER PISTOL, F.L. Mil., Lock Dtd. 1808, Brass Trimmed Fittings, Eng. Proof Mkd. Bbl., 67 Cal. $370.00
PISTOL, Perc. Under Hammer, Part Round Bbl., Walnut Stock, 10" L. $70.00

(A-OH '77) *Garth's Auctions, Inc.*
(ROW I)

PISTOLS, Pr., Conv. F.L., Brass Trim W/ Carved Stock, Arabic Mkd. Bbls., Chased Bbls. W/Silver Inlay, 18" L $235.00
(ROW II)
PISTOL, Engr. Conv. F.L., Lock & Bbl. Signed "Penzneter In Wein", Raised Carved Stock, 65 Cal., 22" L. $360.00
ENGLISH PEPPER BOX, 5 SHOT REVOLVER, Iron Trim, Engraved, Side Mtd. Hammer W/Slide Safety, 36 Cal., Mkd., "G. Clough & Son Bath", Flash Deflector . . . . .
. . . .$225.00
SPRINGFIELD PISTOL CARBINE, U.S. Mod. 1855, Maynard Primer, Ramrod Missing, Rear Sight, 17½" L. $260.00
(ROW III, L to R)
PISTOL, U.S. North Mod. 1819 F.L., Lock Dtd. 1821, 15¾" L. $270.00
REVOLVER, Ivory Grips, Cooper Engr., 31 Cal., SN3369 . . . .$375.00
PISTOL, Perc. Center Hammer Tip Down, 17 Cal., Mkd. "Rieger In Munchen", Panel Stock, SN2716 . . . .$45.00
FRENCH NAVAL PERC. PISTOL, Belt Hook, Mod. 1837, Swivel Ramrod, 58 Cal., 12" L. $190.00
(ROW IV)
TARGET PISTOL, Eng. F. L., Mkd. "Joseph Haig No. 1 Piccadilly, London", Engraved Iron Fittings, Round Checkered Grips, 66 Cal., 13½" L. $355.00
STARR REVOLVER, Single Action Perc., Pat. 1856, 8" Bbl., SN52117 . . . .$180.00

◀ *To the left*

(Top to Bottom)
U.S. NORTH CONTRACT FLINT LOCK PISTOL, Model 1816, Lock Plates Stamped "S North U (Eagle) S Midl tn Conn', Barrel Stamped "P US RJ", Walnut Stock W/ "LS" Inspector Marks, Walnut Stock, Correck Replacement Ramrod Of Hickory W/ Slotted Steel Tip, Minor Pitting . . .$750.00
U.S. CONTRACT FLINT LOCK PISTOL, By "R Johnson Middn Conn. 1842", 98% Plus Orig. Case Hardened Colors On Lock Plate, Blued Trigger, Walnut Stock W/"HH" & "WAT" Inspector Marks $1200.00
U.S. PERCUSSION PISTOL, Model 1842, Lock Plate Mkd. "US H. Aston Mdl tn Conn 1848", Barrel Tang Dated 1848 & Barrel Stamped "US SM P", Walnut Stock W/"NWP" & "WAT" Inspector Marks . . . .
. . . .$600.00
REMINGTON NAVY REVOLVER, New Model, 75% to 80% Orig. Blue On Barrel & Loading Lever, Brass Trigger Guard, Walnut Grips $600.00

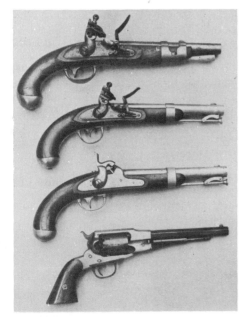

(A-MA '78) *Richard A. Bourne Co., Inc.*

(A-MA '78) *Richard A. Bourne Co., Inc.*
WEAPONS
(Top to Bottom)
U.S. MAGAZINE RIFLE, Chaffee-Reese, Model 1882, Walnut Full Stock W/"SWP 1884" Inspection Marks, Minor Wear . . . . .
. . . .$650.00
U.S. SPRINGFIELD WARD BURTON BOLT-ACTION RIFLE, Model 1871, Walnut Full Stock W/"ELA" & "JWR" Inspection Marks $625.00
REMINGTON LEE NAVY RIFLE, Model 1879, Barrel Stamped "P WM F" W/Anchor; Action Stamped "The Lee Arms Co., Bridgeport, Conn. USA Patented Nov. 4, 1879", 60% to 70% Orig. Blue Finish $450.00
U.S. ARMY CONTRACT REMINGTON LEE MAGAZINE RIFLE, Model 1882, Barrel Stamped "VP" & "US"; Action Stamped "The Lee Arms Co., Bridgeport, Conn. USA Patented Nov. 4, 1879", Parts Retain 75% Plus Orig. Finish, Minor Crack On Left Side Of Action $500.00
U.S. REMINGTON LEE NAVAL RIFLE, Model 1885, Action Stamped "Remington Arms Co., Ilion, N.Y. USA, Sole Manufacturers & Agents, Patented Nov. 4, 1879"; "USA (Anchor) No. 3282 HHE", 30% Orig. Finish, Comb Of Butt Stamped W/Rack Number "144" $375.00
U.S. SPRINGFIELD RIFLED MUSKET, Dated 1865 Lock & Barrel, Blued Rear Sight, 90% Orig. Case Hardening, Walnut Stock W/"STT" & "ELA" Inspection Marks, Minor Chip $900.00

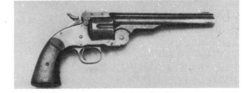

(A-MA '77) *Richard A. Bourne Co., Inc.*
SMITH & WESSON SCHOFIELD REVOLVER, First Model, Serial Number 112, 70% to 75% Orig. Blue On Barrel, Butt Stamped "US", Walnut Grips W/Inspector's Mark On Left Side $1200.00

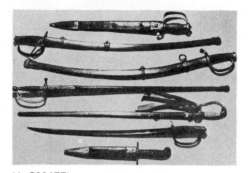

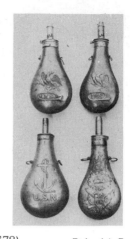

(A-OH '77)   *Garth's Auctions, Inc.*
(TOP TO BOTTOM)
FOOT ARTILLERY SWORD, Brass Hilt, Black Leather Scabbard Trimmed In Brass, Fish Scale Grip W/Eagle & Shield, Blade Mkd. "1843. R.P.", Rev: "N.F. Ames, Springfield", Hilt Mkd. "J.C.B.", 27" L. $300.00
CAVALRY SABER, Brass Engraved Hilt & Iron Scabbard, Blade Mkd. "Horstmann Bros. & Co. New York", 39" L. . .$150.00
LIGHT ARTILLERY SWORD, Brass Hilt & Iron Scabbard, Blade Mkd. "U.S., M.M., 1864", Rev: "Ames" Mark, 39" L. $140.00
NON-COMMISSIONED OFFICER'S SWORD, Brass Hilt, Black Leather Scabbard Trimmed In Brass, Blade Mkd. "U.S., J.C.W., 1865", Rev: "Made By Ames Mfg. Co.", Hilt Mkd. "A.D.K.", 39¾" L. $95.00
INFANTRY OFFICER'S SWORD, Brass Hilt & Engraved Scabbard, Cast Eagle On Hilt & Whale Bone Grip, Blade Engraved & Design Made By Bluing; Red, White & Blue Ribbon On Scabbard, 37¾" L. . . .$115.00
NAVY CUTLASS, Brass Hilt, Blade Mkd. "U.S.N., D.R., 1864, P.G.G.", & Anchor, Rev: "Ames Mfg. Co., Chicapee, Mass.", Hilt Marked "22", 32" L. $125.00
LONG BLADED KNIFE, Brass & Walnut Hilt & Black Leather Scabbard Tipped In Brass, Blade Mkd. "U.S., W.D.", Rev: "Ames Mfg. Co. Cabotville, 1848", Brass Hilt Mkd. "W.D., J.W.R.", 19" L. $560.00

(A-MA '78)   *Richard A. Bourne Co., Inc.*
U.S. MILITARY IRON PINCER MOLD, Stamped "Hall's Rifle" $160.00
"COLT'S PATENT" MARKED DRAGOON MOLD, Brass, Inspected "WAT" W/Iron Sprue Cutter $275.00
"COLT'S PATENT" BRASS .31 POCKET MODEL MOLD $70.00
BRASS MOLD, Casting Two .54 Caliber Conical Bullets W/3 Grooves, Fitted W/Iron Sprue Cutter, 7½" Overall $100.00
COMBINATION BULLET MOLD, PRIMER, DE-PRIMER LOADING TOOL, Marlin Firearms Co., New Haven, Ct. Patent October 4, 1881, In Caliber .32-.40, 80% Plus Orig. Blue Finish, Orig. Pigskin Leather Carrying Case $110.00
CIVIL WAR .44 CALIBER MILITARY GANG MOLD, Iron Body Casting 6 Bullets, Heavy Iron Sprue Cutter, Walnut Handles, Brass Ferrules, Minor Pitting $160.00
"US" MARKED IRON MOLD, Casting .54 Caliber Round Ball, 7¼" Overall $130.00
BULLET MOLD, All Iron, Casting Conical Bullet W/3 Grooves Of About .52 Caliber, Automatic Fitting To Form Concave Depression At Back Of Bullet $80.00
BULLET MOLD, All Iron, Sprue Mechanism Mkd. "TKL", Casts Bullet W/Hole Directly Down The Middle $80.00

(A-MA '78)   *Richard A. Bourne Co., Inc.*
POWDER FLASKS
(Row I, L to R)
U.S. MILITARY STYLE, Embossed Both Sides W/American Eagle & "US", Dated 1833, Triangular Carrying Rings . .$475.00
U.S. MILITARY STYLE, Embossed Both Sides W/American Eagle & "US", Dated 1832, Mkd. "R Dingee New York", Minor Dents $200.00
(ROW II, L to R)
USN FOWLED ANCHOR, Embossed Both Sides, Mkd. "Stimson 1845", Minor Seam Split $400.00
BATTY PEACE, Embossed Both Sides, Top Mkd. "Batty 1854 ADK" $250.00

(A-MA '78)   *Richard A. Bourne Co., Inc.*
POWDER FLASKS
(Row I, L to R)
U.S. MILITARY STYLE, Embossed Both Sides W/American Eagle & "US", Dated 1833, Mkd. "R Dingee New York", Spout Top Missing, Minor Dents, Needs Repair $250.00
"PUBLIC PROPERTY", One Side Embossed W/Bugle & "Public Property", One Side Embossed W/Bugle Only, Minor Dents & Blemishes, Restored Spout $175.00
(Row II, L to R)
BATTY-STYLE PEACE, Top Mkd. "N.P. Ames 1838" & "MS" Twice, Minor Dent At Bottom $225.00
BATTY-STYLE PEACE, Top Mkd. "N.P. Ames 1838", Restored Spout, Minor Seam Split $125.00

(A-MA '78)   *Richard A. Bourne Co., Inc.*
(Top to Bottom)
LEE VERTICAL-ACTION MILITARY RIFLE, Model 1875, 50% Thinning Blue On Barrel, Walnut Stock W/Some Handling/Rack Marks, "E.L.A." Inspector's Mark $650.00
SHARPS NAVAL CONTRACT RIFLE, Model 1855, 28" Round Barrel Fitted For Bayonet, Stamped W/Naval Anchor, Walnut Stock, Minor Pitting Overall $900.00

(A-MA '78)   *Richard E. Bourne, Inc.*
LABELED WOODEN POWDER CASK W/Orig. Paper Label On End $225.00

(A-OH '77) *Garth's Auctions, Inc.*
(TOP TO BOTTOM)
CUTLASS, C. 1800, Iron Figure "8" Hilt, Curved Steel Blade, Hilt Stamped "U.S.", 31¼" L. $285.00
CUTLASS, C. 1917, Blade W/Orig. Blueing, Never Sharpened, Marked "U.S.N.", Steel Hilt W/Wooden Grips, Leather Scabbard, 30¼" L. $105.00
MUSICIAN'S SWORD, Brass Hilt, Leather Brass Trimmed Scabbard, Blade Marked "U.S., C.S.L., 1864", Rev: "Ames Mfg. Co., Chicapee", 35¼" L. $90.00
MILITARY NON-COMMISSIONED OFFICER'S SWORD, Brass Hilt W/Shield Of Stars & Stripes & Knight's Head, Ivory Grip, Leather Brass Trimmed Scabbard, Blade Marked "Germany", 35" L. ..$25.00
SWORD BAYONET, Brass Hilt, Black Leather Brass Tipped Scabbard, Unmarked, 28¼" L. $220.00
FOOT ARTILLERY SWORD, Brass Hilt, Black Leather Brass Trimmed Scabbard, Fish Scale Grip W/Eagle & Shield, Blade Marked "N.P. Ames, Springfield", Rev: "United States, 1835", Hilt W/"W.S.' and "8 Sect., E., 3., Pgt", White Buff Belt 26" L. $310.00
BAYONET, Model 1917, Blade Marked "U.S." Stamped Over British Property Mark, Rev: "1918 Remington", Leather Scabbard, 22¾" L. $20.00
NAVY CUTLASS, Model 1917, Steel Hilt, Unmarked Blade W/Orig. Blueing & Never Sharpened, Russet Leather Scabbard, 30¾" L. $25.00

(A-MA '78) *Richard A. Bourne Co., Inc.*
COLT MARTIALLY-MARKED DRAGOON REVOLVER, Second Model, Matching Serial Numbers 10279 Throughout, Stamped "New Hampshire" On Left Side Of Barrel, 10% Orig. Blue Finish, Cylinder W/Engraved Scene & Ormsby Signature (Model US M.R. COLT'S Patent), Brass Backstrap & Trigger Guard, Walnut Grips W/"JCB" & "WAT" Inspector Marks .....
.................$6500.00

(A-OH '77) *Garth's Auctions, Inc.*
(ROW I)
PISTOL, Wheel Lock, 59 Cal., Stock W/ Maker's Crest, Butt Stock Inlaid W/Ivory, Part Oct. Bbl. 24" L. $675.00
PISTOL, U.S. Mod. 1841 Perc., Mkd. "H. Aston", Inspection Marks $225.00
(ROW II, L to R)
PISTOL, U.S. Mod. 1816 F.L., Mkd. "S. North", 15½" L. $210.00
PISTOL, U.S. Boclock Navy Martial, Lock & Bbl. Mkd. "Ames Springfield 1845" ......
.................$300.00
PISTOL, French Mod., 1877 St. Etienee F.L., SN80, Frizzen Spring Replaced, Brass Trim W/Brass Ramrod $290.00
(ROW III)
PISTOL, U.S. Mod., 1816 F.L., Lock Mkd. "S. North Middleton, Conn", Ramrod Missing, Inspector's Marks $240.00
PISTOL, European Tip Up, 17 Cal., Engraved Hdwe. W/Silver Mask Butt Cap, Set Trigger, Side Hammer, Ammo. Compartment .....
.................$180.00
(ROW IV)
PISTOL, French Cavalry, Ring Hammer, 72 Cal., Brass Trim, Ramrod Missing, SN405
.................$180.00
PISTOL, Spanish Mod., 1824 F.L., Swivel Ramrod, 70 Cal., Brass Barrel Band, Trigger Guard & Butt Cap, Lock Mkd. "Estado De Guano Joiatdo", 14" L. $160.00

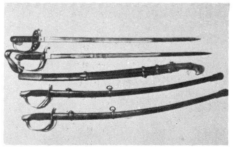

(A-OH '77) *Garth's Auctions, Inc.*
(TOP TO BOTTOM)
WILKENSON SWORD, Scabbard, Etched Blade, Pierced Basket Guard, SN28904 ...
.................$85.00
ENGLISH ARTILLERY SWORD, Leather Covered Scabbard, "Robert Mole & Sons, Maker's", Ribbed Hand Guard, M8723 ...
.................$80.00
RUSSIAN COSSACK SWORD, Moisin Nangate Needle, Bayonet, Scabbard, DTD1940 ....$135.00
U.S. CAVALRY SWORD, "Ames 1864", Scabbard $115.00
U.S. CAVALRY SWORD, "Emerson Silver, Trenton, 1864", Scabbard $105.00

(A-OH '77) *Garth's Auctions, Inc.*
(ROW I, L to R)
PISTOL W/Holster, Czech. "CZ" Mod. 38, 9mm., SN241002 ....$95.00
WALTHER PISTOL, W/Nazi Marks, Mod. PP, 22 Cal., Orig. Holster, SN214794P ...
.................$275.00
MAUSER MIL. PISTOL, 10 Shot W/Cone Hammer, SN450 ....$645.00
(ROW II, L to R)
JAPANESE NAMBU PISTOL, Holster, Nambu Mod. 1914, 8mm., Clip W/Matching SN, SN34434 ....$145.00
WALTHER PISTOL, P 38, Nazi Marked, Holster Nazi Marked W/Extra Magazine, SN 25643 ....$340.00
GERMAN LUGER, 1940 Dtd. Breech W/43 On Toggle, Auto. Pistol, Matched 1936 Type Holster & 2 Matched Clips, All W/SN 1262H
.................$375.00
(ROW III, L to R)
GERMAN NAVY FLARE PISTOL, W.W.I., Single Shot, 27mm., Bell Shaped Muzzle, Brass Parts, SN2097 ....$45.00
LUGER SNAIL DRUM MAGAZINE, 32 Shot, Original, SN595032 ....$190.00
JAPANESE NAMBU PISTOL, Mod. 1914, 8mm., SN47252 ....$155.00

(A-MA '78) *Richard A. Bourne Co., Inc.*
(Top to Bottom)
WARNER CIVIL WAR SADDLE RING CARBINE, Brass Frame, Stamped "Greene Rifle Works, Worcester, Mass., Pat'd 1864", Initials "MM" On Barrel, Butt Plate & Stock, Case Hardened Hammer & Trigger, Walnut Stock $1600.00
DOUBLE PERCUSSION SHOTGUN, .12 Gauge, 32" Barrell Mkd. "London Fine Twist", Lock Plates Engraved "E Lovell SAV GEO", Walnut Checkered Stock W/ Cap Box $200.00
CIVIL WAR CONTRACT .58 MUSKET, Savage R.F.A. Co., Middletown, Conn., 1864, Steel Parts, Walnut Stock ....
.................$500.00

(A-OH '77)   *Garth's Auctions, Inc.*
CARVED COCONUT SHELL, Furry Face One End W/Open Circular Mouth, Hooded Eyes; Also, Carved Eagle, Cannon, Hammer, Cornucopia & Crown, Medallions W/2 Profiles, Lions, Hearts, Arrow and 2 Loop Like Ears, 4¾" L. $170.00
COPPER PISTOL SHOT FLASK, Brass Fitting, Decor. W/Embossed Turkeys Both Sides, 4⅜" L. $130.00
CURLY MAPLE KENTUCKY RIFLE, Half-Stock, Stock Has Checkering & Low Relief Covering, Inlaid Silver Crescent W/ "A", Brass Engraved Patch Box & Inlaid Engraved Brass Oval W/American Eagle, Percussion Lock Signed "Benedict Roray, Warranted", Engraved Barrer W/"H.B.", Removable Back Sight, Barrel - 41½" L., 57½" O.A. $660.00
ENGRAVED POWDER HORN, Animals, Man, Tulips, Fish & Hex Signs, "Tommes M.N.", 8¾" L. $210.00
ENGRAVED POWDER HORN, Birds, Flowers & Date "1813", 10¾" L. $300.00

(A-OH '77)   *Garth's Auctions, Inc.*
(TOP TO BOTTOM)
COACH GUN, F. L. Blunderbuss, Lock Mkd. "Brander & Potts London", Checkered Wrist, Brass Hdwe., 14" Bbl. . . . . . .
. . . .$350.00
SEMI-AUTO. RIFLE, German Mod. G-43, Sniper Scope, Sling, SN2066 . . . .$400.00
MUSKETOON, French Mod. 1829, Long Range Rear Sight, Matching Ramrod, SN373
. . . .$250.00
SHOTGUN-RIFLE, German Drillings, 16 Ga. - 7.8 x 57, Receiver Decor. W/Deer Scenes, Engraved Breeches, Mkd. "Aug. June, Suhl", SN196 . . . .$290.00
MAUSER TRAINING RIFLE, 4mm Single Shot, Bolt Action, Mkd. "JGA Buscher Sport Model, Nurnberg", SN2194 . . . . . .$100.00

(A-OH '77)   *Garth's Auctions, Inc.*
COLT POLICE PISTOL, New Model, #1862, Matching Serial #'s 19965, 5 Shot, 36 Cal., 9½" L. $280.00
COLT POCKET PISTOL, Matching Serial #'s 11776, Engraved Cylinder, 5 Shot, 36 Cal., 11½" L. $260.00
CIVIL WAR DRUM, Hand Painted Oval Medallion, Sling & Drum Sticks, 16½" Diam., 16¾" H. $900.00
U.S. RIFLE, Model 1855, 61 Cal. Percussion, Serial #3167, Lock W/"E. Whitney U.S., New Haven 1855", Brass Patch Box, 33" Barrel, 49" L. $450.00
NAVY CUTLASS, Brass Hilt, Blade Marked "U.S.N., 1862, D.R.P." & Anchor, Rev: "Ames, etc.", Leather Scabbard (Not Shown), 32¼" L. $160.00
AMMUNITION POUCH, Leather, 2 Tin Compartments, "J.B. Thakter, Portland, Me. 1862", Brass "U.S." Medallion, 9¼" L.
. . . .$65.00
OFFICER'S GAUNTLETS, Pr., Yellow Suede, Size 8½, Civil War $85.00
LEATHER BELT, "U.S." Brown Buckle .
. . . .$55.00
COLT NAVY PISTOL, Model 1851, Matching Serial #'s 77580, 6 Shot, 36 Cal., 13¼" L. $420.00
SPRINGFIELD MUSKET, Removable Stock, "U.S. Springfield 1856", Eagle On Percussion Lock, 12" Barrel, 18" Overall, 29" W/Stock $1800.00
COLT RIFLE, Model 1863, Percussion Lock W/Eagle, Walnut Stock & Matching Bayonet W/Black Leather Brass Tipped Scabbard (Bayonet Not Shown), 40" Barrel, 56" Overall $900.00

(A-MA '78)   *Richard A. Bourne Co., Inc.*
ADAMS PATENT .36 DOUBLE ACTION PERCUSSION REVOLVER, Mass. Arms Co., Chicopee Falls, 30% to 40% Orig. Blue Finish, Checkered Walnut Grips, Trigger Return Spring Defective $350.00

(A-OH '77)   *Garth's Auctions, Inc.*
(TOP TO BOTTOM)
KENTUCKY RIFLE, Full Stick, Conv., C.M. Stock, Brass Patch Box, "J.M. In Silver
. . . .$260.00
RIFLE-SHOTGUN, Perc., Swivel Breech, Paneled Sides, Wooden Patch Box, Lock Mkd. "Ant. Baumann In Munchen", Set Trigger, 30" Bbl $350.00
FLINTLOCK MUSKET, British, Brown Bess, Brass Fittings, 37¼" Bbl., SN206 . . .
. . . .$410.00
RIFLE-SHOTGUN, Perc., Mkd. "Adam Kuchen Reuter In Regensburg", Ornate Back Action Locks, Wooden Patch Box, Carved Wooden Trigger, Set Trigger . . . . .
. . . .$410.00
GERMAN SHOTGUN-RIFLE, 16 ga., 7.8 x 57, Mkd. "Jmann Meffert-Suhl", Telescope Mounts, Engraved Pheasant & Duck Scenes, SN60917 . . . .$170.00
SCHUTZEN TARGET RIFLE, Drop Block Action, 7.6mm., Mkd. "E. Schmidt & Habermann", Receiver Decor. W/Hunting Scenes, Breech Block Mkd. "System Reform", SN22501 . . . .$325.00

(A-MA '78)   *Richard A. Bourne Co., Inc.*
CARTRIDGE BOX, Leather, Interior W/ Wooden Block Drilled W/Two Rows Of Twenty Holes For Paper Cartridges, 7½" L.
. . . .$45.00

(A-MA '78)   *Richard A. Bourne Co., Inc.*
(Top to Bottom)
SMITH & WESSON AMERICAN REVOLVER, First Model, Serial Number 989, 40% to 50% Orig. Blue On Barrel, Oil-Finished Walnut Grips, Minor Wear .$1200.00
COLT SINGLE-ACTION .45 CALIBER REVOLVER, Model 1873, 7½" Barrel, Serial Number 114266, 50% Orig. Blue On Barrel, Walnut Grips $2100.00

(A-OH '78)   *Garth's Auctions, Inc.*

◀ *To the left*

POPLAR DRESSING TABLE, Dovetailed Drawers, Replaced Hardware, Worn Refinishing, 37" W., 24" D., 40¼" H. $230.00

WOVEN SPLIT WOOD WOOL BASKET, Bentwood Handles, Reed Feet, Rim Weaving Incomplete, 21½" x 28" x 12½" $47.50

BIRDSEYE MAPLE SIDE CHAIRS, (Set of 4), New Cane Seats, Refinished $300.00

NILOAK POTTERY CANDLESTICKS, Pr., 9½" H. $55.00

NILOAK POTTERY VASE, Base W/ Orig. Paper Label, 4¼" H. $17.00

OIL ON CANVAS, Winter Scene - Shepherd & Flock, Gilt Frame, 24" x 31" $85.00

OIL ON CANVAS, Country Church W/ Sleigh & Horse, Gilt Frame, 14" x 21" $62.50

(A-OH '78)   *Garth's Auctions, Inc.*

BANISTER BACK ARMCHAIR, New Rush Seat, Restoration, Worn Black Paint $175.00

CURLY MAPLE QUEEN ANNE TABLE, Dovetailed Drawer, Replaced Drawer & Top, Worn Brown Finish, 21" Sq., 27½" H. $880.00

WOVEN REED BASKET, Wooden Handle, Natural, Brown & Tan, Minor Wear, 9½" x 16" x 8½" O.H. $22.00

INDIAN BASKET, Drk. Brown Woven Design, Minor Rim Break, 6¼" x 9" x 2¼" H. $27.50

BURL BOWL, Age Crack In Side, 6" Diam., 2½" H. $130.00

WATERCOLOR ON PAPER MINIATURES (3), Man, Woman & Child, Old Gilt Frames, 8½" x 9" and 7½" x 8" $235.00

(A-OH '78)   *Garth's Auctions, Inc*

COUNTRY CAPTAIN'S CHAIRS, Pr., Refinished $75.00

WOVEN SPLIT WOOD MARKET BASKET, Faded Red & Blue & Natural Woven Design, 13½" x 16½" x 16½" $37.50

POPLAR BLANKET CHEST, Dovetailed, Till, Old Red Paint Varnished, 44" W., 18½" D., 26" H. $95.00

STONEWARE JUG, Brownish Green Glaze, Raised Lettering Label "Weber . . . Akron, O.", 9¼" H. $15.00

STONEWARE JAR, 2-Gal., Stenciled Label, "T.F. Reppert, Greensboro, Pa.", 12¼" H. $32.50

POTTERY JUG, Applied Handle, Shiny Drk. Green To Matt Finish Red Glaze, 11¼" H. $12.00

CURRIER & IVES PRINT, Small Folio, "The Two Pets", Margins Trimmed, Paper Tear, Beveled Frame, 12¾" x 16¾" $17.50

CURRIER & IVES PRINT, Small Folio, "The Home Of Scott", Margins Trimmed, Minor Stains, 13¼" x 17¼" $60.00

CURRIER & IVES PRINT, Small Folio, "My Little White Kittens", Gilt Frame, 13" x 16¼" $42.50

CURRIER & IVES PRINT, Small Folio, "Little Barefoot", Margins Trimmed, Walnut Frame, 14" x 18" $42.50

(A-OH '78)   *Garth's Auctions, Inc.*

POPLAR BLANKET CHEST, Dovetailed, Till, Brown Varnish Graining Over Light Ground, Replaced Hinges, 48½" W., 21¾" D., 27¼" H. $130.00

RYE STRAW BASKET, Hole In Center, Rim Break, 12½" Diam., 3" H. . . .$10.00

WOODEN DECOY, Preening Mallard, C. 1973, 10½" L. $20.00

POPLAR BOX, Dovetailed, Orig. Brown Paint W/Black Striping & Red Rectangles W/Inverted Corners, Alligatored, Edge Wear, Replaced Lock & Hasp, 26" W., 12¾" D., 9¼" H. $40.00

RYE STRAW BASKET, 11" Diam., 4¾" H. $30.00

WOODEN DECOY, Bufflehead Drake, Working Repaint, 13" L. $25.00

PUNCHED TIN PAUL REVERE LANTERN, Black Paint Flaking, 13½" O.H. $45.00

WOODEN DECOY, Bufflehead Hen, Working Repaint, 12½" L. $22.50

(A-PA '77)   *Brown Bros. Gallery*

PENNA. BRASS BED WARMER, Long Handle $210.00

(A-OH '78)   *Garth's Auctions, Inc.*

PINE & POPLAR DRY SINK, Orig. Tan & White Steel Comb Graining, Zinc Lined Well, 48" W., 19½" D., 47½" H. .$360.00

CARVED WOODEN FISH, Brown & Gold W/White Dots And Yellow, Minor Tail & Fin Damage, 20th C. Folk Art, 36½" L. $135.00

WOODEN BOARD, Hollowed Section One End, Red Paint W/Black Letters, 3½" x 42" $5.00

(A-OH '77)   *Garth's Auctions, Inc.*
LADDER BACK CHAIR, Worn Leather
Seat, "Old Minorcan Chair" On Middle
Slat, Top Slat Incomplete $25.00
POPLAR DOUGH BOX, Dovetailed
Const., Reddish-Brown Graining, Free Hand
Yellow Brush Work, Missing Lid, 34½" W.,
23½" D., 26½" H. $155.00
PINE UTENSIL RACK, 15 Wrought Iron
Hooks, 58½" L. $105.00
**BRASS AND WROUGHT IRON DIP-
PER,** Sm. Handle Break, 21½" L. . . . . . .
. . . . $45.00
WROUGHT IRON FORK, 16¾" L. . . . .
. . . . $20.00
WROUGHT IRON FORK, 24½" L. . . . .
. . . . $17.50
WROUGHT IRON DIPPER, Hole For
Hanging, 17" L. $20.00
WROUGHT IRON TASTER, 14¼" L. . . .
. . . . $27.50
**WROUGHT IRON & BRASS STRAIN-
ER,** 18" L. $50.00

(A-OH '78)   *Garth's Auctions, Inc.*
PINE FOOTSTOOL, Drk. Red Paint, 7½"
x 14" x 7¼" H. $70.00
SIDE CHAIRS, Pr., Orig. Brown Graining
Over Mustard Ground W/Black Striping,
Minor Wear $30.00
TILT TOP CANDLESTAND, Pine Top,
Hardwood Base, Varnish Finish, 16¾" x
19¾" x 27" H. $140.00
OPALESCENT CANDLESTICK, Petal
Socket, Base Flakes, 7¼" H. $30.00
CURRIER & IVES PRINT, Small Folio,
"Ferns", Trimmed Margins, Gilt Frame,
12" x 16" $25.00
MIRROR, Two-Part, Acorn Drop Cornice
(Several Acorns Missing), Orig. Reverse
Painting Of House, 14" x 26½" . . . $35.00

(A-OH '78)   *Garth's Auctions, Inc.*
WOODEN DECOY, Battery Goose, Outer-
bank, Back Bay, Va., Working Repaint &
Repair To Bill, 24½" L. $55.00
PINE MULE CHEST, 1-Board Ends, Cut-
Out Feet, Dovetailed Drawer, Lift Lid, Orig.
Staple Hinges, Replaced Engraved Brasses,
Minor Restoration, Heavy Varnish, 38" W.,
17½" D., 32½" H. $310.00
ARROWBACK SIDE CHAIRS, (Set of
5), Refinished $125.00
WOODEN DECOY, Coot, By Al Wragg,
Michigan, Stamped "W.B.", C. 1974, 12"
L. $20.00
TIN LANTERNS, Pr., Orig. Oil Burners,
Brass Name Plate, "Raymount Proust,
Constricteur, Paris", 11½" O.H. . . . $25.00
BURL BOWL, Side Repair, 14" Diam., 6"
H. $305.00
OIL ON CANVAS PAINTING, Maid Of
The Mist & Niagara Falls, Gilt Frame, 15½"
x 20½" $25.00
SAMPLER ON HOMESPUN, Bible Verse,
Vining Border, "A.A. Evans 1855, Aged 7
Years", Red, Blue, Green, Pink, Violet,
Yellow & Tan, Framed, 18" x 19" $255.00

(A-VA '78)   *Laws*
ENGLISH REGENCY SIDEBOARD,
Grained Mahogany Molded Top, Wine
Slide Drawer, Overall Light & Drk. Line
Inlay, Ca. 1820, 77" W., 28" D., 37" H. . .
. . . . $625.00
**MAHOGANY URN FORM KNIFE
BOXES** In The Sheraton Style On Square
Plinths W/Ogee Bracket Feet, 25" H. . . . .
. . . . $475.00
PORTRAIT ON CANVAS, 19th C. Oil . .
. . . . $175.00

To the right ▶

STONEWARE JAR, 2-Gal., Impressed
Label "Whites Utica", Bird In Cobalt Blue
Slip, Glazing Imperfection, 14" H. . . . . . .
. . . . $95.00
**COUNTRY SHERATON BLANKET
CHEST,** Walnut, Mortised Const., Dove-
tailed Drawers, Orig. Brasses, Till & Secret
Door, 50" W., 22" D., 30" H. . . . $420.00
MINIATURE JELLY CUPBOARD, Pine,
Dovetailed Drawers & Gallery, Yellow Grain-
ing W/Red Striping & Reserves W/Land-
scape Scenes On Top & Doors, Minor Wear,
17¾" W., 8¾" D., 23" H. $245.00
WOVEN SPLIT WOOD BASKET, Wood-
en Handles, 21½" D., 12" H. $45.00
CARVED WOODEN BIRD, Black-Bellied
Plover, New England, New Base, 8½" H. . .
. . . . $80.00
CURRIER & IVES LITHOGRAPH,
Small Folio, "Up The Hudson", Trimmed
Margins, Beveled Cherry Frame, 14" x 17"
. . . . $80.00

(A-OH '77)   *Garth's Auctions, Inc.*

(A-OH '78)　　　　　*Garth's Auctions, Inc.*

LADDERBACK ROCKING CHAIR, New Paper Rush Seat, Refinished . . $45.00
WROUGHT IRON STATIONARY BROILER, 14" W $70.00
COUNTRY HEPPLEWHITE DROP LEAF TABLE, Walnut, Worn Varnish Finish, 1-Board Wide Top, 20" x 36" W/10½" Leaves, 29" H. $290.00
WROUGHT IRON TRIVET, Triangular, 15" W. $70.00
STONEWARE JAR, 2-Gal., Impressed Label "H.H. Cowden, Harrisburg", Pebbly Finish W/Blue Floral Medallion Center, 9¾" H. $70.00
WOODEN & COMPOSITION FIGURE OF JOHNNY WALKER, Alligatored Finish, Repaired Arm, 13" H. $30.00
ROCKINGHAM PITCHER, Hunting Scenes, Hairline & Rim Repairs, 9¼" H. $15.00
YARN SWIFT, Clamps To Table, 22" H. $37.50
LITHOGRAPH, Handcolored, By "Sarony and Major", "Capitulation Of Monterey", Margins Trimmed, Framed, 11¾" x 15¾" $20.00
SPENCERIAN CALLIGRAPHY DRAWING, "Home Sweet Home", C. Kadle, Penman", Birds & Poem, Worn Gilt Frame, 22" x 28" $12.50

(A-OH '78)　　　　　*Garth's Auctions, Inc.*

PINE CORNER CUPBOARD, Old Refinishing Mellowed To Warm Brown, Marred, 30" W., 18" D., 68" H. $610.00
MAPLE JOINT STOOL, Replaced Pine Top, Mortised Stretcher, Minor Repairs, Refinished, 14" x 19" x 20" H. . . $360.00
SHOW TOWEL, Pink Cross Stitch On Homespun, Flowers, Peacocks, Pennsylvania Ladies, Deer & Alphabet, "Cafin 1795", Drawn Work Band At Bottom, 10½" x 54" $800.00
PEWTER PORRINGER, Touch Mark On Handle & Inside Bottom, Both Illegible, 5" Diam. $160.00
PEWTER CREAMER, Cast Hollow Handle W/Break At Base, Unmarked, 4¾" H. $35.00
PEWTER HANGING WALL POCKET, Wedding Initials, 5" H. $130.00
PEWTER PLATE, Rim Has Wedding Initials, Touch Marks Not Clear, 9¼" Diam. $60.00

(A-OH '78)　　　　　*Garth's Auctions, Inc.*

WALLACE NUTTING WINDSOR SIDE CHAIR, Worn Orig. Finish, Branded Signature "Wallace Nutting", Repair To Seat & One Spindle $410.00
QUEEN ANNE SWING LEG DROP LEAF TABLE, Walnut, Braced Split In Leaf, Arm Of Swing Leg Replaced, Minor Restoration, 12¼" x 36" W/14" Leaves, 28¼" H. $600.00
STERLING SILVER BOWL, Repousse Rim W/Roses, Grapes, Strawberries, Mkd. "The Loring Andrews Co., Cincinnati, U.S.A.", Minor Dents, 9" Diam., 3¼" H. $65.00
TELESCOPING CANDLESTICK, Silver On Copper, Adjustable, 8½" to 10½" H. $25.00
PAPER CUT-OUT, Abraham & Isaac & The Sacrifice, Foreign Inscription & Date "1840", Blue Paper Background, Mahogany Frame, 10¾" x 12¼" $100.00
BAROMETER, Rosewood On Pine, Silvered Metal Dials W/Convex Mirror In Center, Working Condition, 37" H. . . . $150.00

(D-MA '78)
CANADIAN GOOSE DECOY, Hand Carved, Glass Eyes, Repainted, 10" H., 18" L. $165.00

To the right ▶

TAVERN TABLE, Maple Base & Pine 1-Board Top, Refinished, Replaced Top, 22" x 32" x 24½" H. $390.00
POPLAR FOOT WARMER, Wrought Iron Handle, Sliding Cover, Removable Coal Basket, Red Paint, 9" x 9¼" x 8" H. $77.50
WINDSOR SIDE CHAIR, Refinished $385.00
BURL BOWL, 15½" Diam., 5" H. $380.00
OIL ON CANVAS PAINTING, Old Man Walking Along Stream, Stenciled Label "J. Rodenmayer, Balt. Md", 15½" x 19½" $85.00

(A-OH '78)　　　　　*Garth's Auctions, Inc.*

(A-OH '77)   *Garth's Auctions, Inc.*
HEPPLEWHITE CABIN DESK, Rosewood & Mahogany, Dovetailed Drawers W/ Applied Beading, Slant Top, Fold Our Writing Surface, Orig., Hdwe., Old Finish, Minor Repairs, 35¾" W., 22" D., 37" H. (Closed)
....$800.00
CAST IRON DUCKS, Pr., 1 W/Head Up, 1 W/Head Down, Mkd. "Copyright R.M.B.", 11½" H. $75.00

(A-OH '77)   *Garth's Auctions, Inc.*
ENGLISH CHIPPENDALE DESK, Mahogany on Pine, Dovetailed Drawers, Interior W/Pigeon Holes & 6 Drawers, Replaced Ogee Feet & Brass Bails, Veneer Repair, 48" W., 19½" D., 42" H., 31½" Writing Ht. $500.00
CLEAR FLINT LAMPS, Pr., Sq. Base, Bigler Fonts Separated By Wafers, Both W/Base Chips, Brass Collars, 11½" H. ...
....$85.00
GUADY STAFFORDSHIRE TEA SET, Green & Purple Floral Decor. W/Brick Red, Creamer - 4¼" H. (Spout Chipped); Teapot - 7" H. (Hairline In Base & Top Of Handle), & 5 Handless Cups & Saucers (3 Cups W/ Hairlines) $160.00
CONVEX MIRROR, Wooden Frame W/Carved Wooden & Gesso Eagle, Regilded W/Gold Leaf, 22" Diam., 29" H. ..
....$250.00

(A-OH '77)   *Garth's Auctions, Inc.*
ENGLISH CHIPPENDALE SIDE CHAIR, Mahogany, Foliage Carved In Low Relief On Crest Rail $250.00
ENGLISH CHEST OF DRAWERS, Mahogany, 3 Dovetailed Drawers, Pull Out Shelf Under Top, Restored Feet, Replaced Hdwe. & Molding Around Top Added, Refinished, 34" W., (Top 35½" W.), 19¼" D., 30¾" H. $500.00
BRASS MID-DRIP CANDLESTICK, Paw Feet, 12¼" H. $55.00
INLAID SERPENTINE FRONT KNIFE BOX, Interior W/Inlay W/Compass Star On Inside Of Lid, Repair Necessary, Back Of Base Broken Out At Hinge, 14¾" H. ......
....$75.00
SAMPLER, Dated "1795", Alphabets & Strawberry Trees W/Peacock & Goose, Fabric Deteriorated, Birdseye Veneer Frame - 8¾" x 12¼" $30.00
SAMPLER ON HOMESPUN, Alphabets W/Crowns & Floral Border In Red & Green, "Isabella Crawford, Aged 8 Years, 30 March 18", Frame - 17" x 21½" .....
....$45.00

(A-OH '77)   *Garth's Auctions, Inc.*
PINE SHAKER TIN CUPBOARD, Canterbury, Rebuilt Drawers, 17½" W., 12½" D., 69" H. $270.00
PAPIER MACHE LAMB, Butcher Shop Trade Sign, Replaced Ear, 33" L., 18" H.
....$200.00
WOODEN BOOT MAKER'S SIGN, Black Paint, Wrought Iron Brackets, Replaced Heel, 28" H. $150.00
WOODEN HORSE, Alligatored Black & Red Paint, Side From Merry-Go-Round Car, 31" L. $105.00

◄ *To the left*

(A-OH '77)   *Garth's Auctions, Inc.*
WOODEN DECOY, Canvas Back Hen, Michigan, Old Working Repaint, 15¼" L.
....$35.00
PINE BLANKET CHEST, Dovetailed Const., Till, Orig. Brown Graining On Coral Ground, Reset Hinges, 37¾" L., 21" D., 24" H. $190.00
WOODEN DECOY, Canvas Back Drake, Michigan, Old Paint, 17" L. $45.00
WOODEN DECOY, Redhead Drake, Keel, Overpainting 13½" L. $55.00
BIRCH TALL POST BED, Orig. Rope Rails, Exterior Measurements: 57" x 79" x 66" H. $925.00
PAINTING ON VELVET, Castle In Ruins, Gilt Frame, 23½" x 30¼" $80.00

(A-OH '77)   Garth's Auctions, Inc.
WINDSOR SIDE CHAIR, Cleaned Down
To Old Red $330.00
COUNTRY TAVERN TABLE, Birch
Base, Poplar Breadboard Top, Refinished,
24¾" x 35½" x 28¾" H. $120.00
DOLL SIZE CRIB, Black Paint, Repaired
Legs, 14" x 21½" x 16½" H. $60.00
PAPIER MACHE OWL, Glass Eyes, "De-
catur, Illinois, Pat. Pend", Minor Wear,
14½" H. $20.00
TOLE DOCUMENT BOX, Drk. Brown
Japanning, Minor Wear & Touch Up, 6" x
6½" x 9½" $65.00
WOODEN SHOREBIRD, Life Size Cur-
lew, 20th C., 14" H. $75.00
TOLE DEED BOX, Drk. Ground W/Orig.
Yellow & Red Decor., Minor Flaking, Brass
Bail Handle, 4½" x 5½" x 8¾" . . .$75.00
HANDCOLORED LITHOGRAPH, Lge.
Folio, "View Of The River And Shipping At
Limehouse", Framed, 26" x 36" . .$65.00

(A-OH '77)   Garth's Auctions, Inc.
COUNTRY QUEEN ANNE TEA TABLE,
Replaced Top, Restored Feet, Refinished,
25" x 35" x 28" H. $450.00
CANDLE MOLD, 24 Pewter Tubes, Wood-
en Frame, 5½" x 19" x 16" H. . .$410.00
BALLOON BACK SIDE CHAIRS (Set Of
6), Orig. Brown Paint W/Yellow Striping &
Stenciled Fruit, Minor Wear $375.00
WOODEN DUCK DECOY, Comb Paint-
ed Feathers, 16" L. $80.00
PINE BOX, Dovetailed, Grey Paint W/
Brown Borders, "T.H. Sargent", Leather
Strap Handle, 8" x 12" x 4" $40.00
HANGING WALL SCONCES, Pr., Oval
Mirror Inserts, 14" W., 12½" H. . .$185.00
OIL ON CANVAS PORTRAIT, Young
Woman, Orig. Stretcher Canvas, 25" x
30¼" $170.00

(A-OH '77)   Garth's Auctions, Inc.
WOODEN HOBBY HORSE, Worn Paint,
46½" L. $110.00
PINE STAND, Dovetailed Drawer, Red &
Black Graining W/Striping, Minor Wear,
18" x 24" x 29¾" H. $75.00
WINDSOR SIDE CHAIR, Refinished . . .
. . . .$135.00
TRAMP ART BOX, 3 Lidded Compart-
ments, 12" x 17" x 6½" H. $65.00
SPENCERIAN PEN & INK DRAWING,
Eagle, Silver Gilt Frame, 17½" x 21½" . . .
. . . .$135.00
CARVED PINE FRAME, Leprechaun
Form, Refinished & Fitted W/Mirror, 23" H.
. . . .$335.00

(A-OH '77)   Garth's Auctions, Inc.
CANE SEAT SIDE CHAIRS, (Set of 4),
Curly Maple, Sabre Leg, Refinished . . . . . .
. . . .$180.00
PINE DRESSING TABLE, Dovetailed
Drawers, 1-Board Top, Refinished, 37" x
17¾" x 32" H. $120.00
PINE DOME TOP BOX, Brown Graining
W/Red & Cream Striping & Initials "P.G.",
Iron Handles, 30" x 14" x 11¾" .$140.00
ROCKINGHAM SEATED DOG, Incised
"James Hill", Base Chips, 10" H. $125.00
ROCKINGHAM SPITTOON, 14¼"
Diam., 6¼" H. $65.00
ROCKINGHAM SEATED DOG, Rust
Coat W/Yellow & Black, Black Flaked, Base
Chip, 9¼" H. $40.00
OIL ON CANVAS PAINTING, Boat &
Mountain Lake, Gilt Frame, Minor Patch On
Canvas, 18½" x 29½" $105.00

(A-OH '77)   Garth's Auctions, Inc.

◀ *To the left*

**MAHOGANY QUEEN ANNE SIDE
CHAIR,** Restoration $475.00
HEPPLEWHITE INLAID CARD TABLE,
Mahogany, Inlay Repaired, 36" W., 18¼"
D., 29¼" H. $1150.00
ROSE MEDALLION MOON URN, Birds
Of Paradise & Butterflies, Orange Peel Glaze,
Flake On Lid Underside, 22½" H. . . . . . .
. . . .$1225.00
ORIENTAL PORCELAIN VASES, Pr.,
Blue & White, 10" H. $155.00
**HISTORICAL BLUE STAFFORDSHIRE
TUREEN,** Open Work Handles, "Dixcove
On The Gold Coast, Africa", Enoch Wood,
Cracked & Glaze Flakes On Handle, 15¼"
L., 11¼" H. $350.00
BANJO CLOCK, Orig. Reverse Painting,
Glass In Midsection Old Repaint & Flaking,
Bottom Board Incomplete, 32" H. . . . . . .
. . . .$1000.00
OIL ON CANVAS PAINTINGS, Pr.,
European Castles, Ornate Gilt Frames,
16½" x 20½" $750.00

(A-OH '77)   *Garth's Auctions, Inc.*

BANISTER BACK SIDE CHAIR, Old Black Paint W/Gold Striping, Worn Woven Seat $110.00
WALNUT CUPBOARD, 1-Pc., Late 19th C., Board & Batten Doors, Refinished, 27" W., 16½" D., 77" H. $400.00
STONEWARE JUG, 5-Gal., Impressed "Weading & Belding, Brantford, Ohio", Cobalt Blue Brushed Floral Design, Glaze Wear, 18½" H. $65.00
CHARCOAL ON PAPER DRAWING, Bearded Gentleman, Pine Frame Partially Stripped Of Black Paint, 10¼" x 11½" . . .
. . . .$25.00
CHARCOAL ON PAPER DRAWING, Bearded Gentleman, Wooden Frame, Built Up Gesso Decor., & Worn Gilding, 12½" x 18" $25.00

(A-OH '77)   *Garth's Auctions, Inc.*

CARVED FOLK ART EAGLE, Late 19th C., Tip Of Bill Repaired, 25" H. . .$410.00
COUNTRY SHERATON JELLY CUPBOARD, Dovetailed Drawers, Orig. Red Graining Over Yellow Ground, Poplar & Other Woods, Front Foot & Knobs Replaced, 44¼" W., 20½" D., 49" H. $425.00
CARVED WOODEN LION'S HEAD, Worn Pale Yellow & Red Paint, Base Chip, Modern Wooden Stand, 13½" H. . .$70.00
WOODEN CHURCH MODEL, Orig. Red, Gold & Black Paint, Cut-Out Tracery In Windows, Removable Steeple, Replaced Roof, Minor Damage To Steeple, 14" W., 21" D., 27" H. $90.00
SHAVING MIRROR, Painted Red W/ Gold Decor., Turned Wooden Base, Old Mirror Glass, 16½" H. $20.00

(A-OH '77)   *Garth's Auctions, Inc.*

WINDSOR STEP DOWN CHAIRS, Pr., Refinished $160.00
CHEST OF DRAWERS, American Pine Decorated Cottage Furniture, Dovetailed Drawers & Gallery Back, 40½" W., 19½" D., 36" H. $115.00
CAST IRON SHEEP BOOK ENDS, Pr., 7¼" H. $40.00
WOODEN LEATHER COVERED TRUNK, Brass Studs, Iron Hasp & Lock, Brass Bail Handle, Interior Lines W/Newspaper - "Bell's Weekly Messenger", 8" x 9" x 13" $40.00
OIL ON CANVAS PAINTING, Subject Is "John William Schuckers, Sr. b. 1804, d. 1839, Massillion, Ohio", Unframed, Orig. Stretcher, 17" x 21" $295.00
INDIAN RUG, Yei, 29" x 30" . . .$90.00
INDIAN CEREMONIAL CANE, One Piece Root W/Carved Snakes Heads & Fish, Drk. Brown Painted Stripes, 34½" L. . . . . .
. . . .$75.00

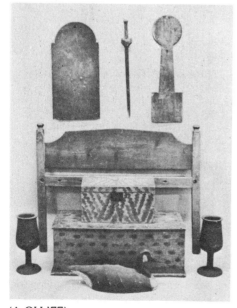

(A-OH '77)   *Garth's Auctions, Inc.*

◀ *To the left*

GOOSE DECOY, Canvas Over Frame Forms Body, Wooden Head, Black & White Paint, 22½" L. $65.00
CAST IRON VASES, Pr., 1 W/Cast Name "Clyde", 14" H. $125.00
PINE TRUNK, Staple Hinges, Grey-Green Paint W/Drk. Green Dots, Lid Initialed "E. L., M30, 1809", 32¼" W., 14" D., 12½" H.
. . . .$375.00
PINE DOME TOP BOX, Iron Hasp & Lock, Orig. Black On Yellow Ground Decor., 18" W., 10¾" D., 10½" H. $255.00
ROPE BED, Maple Posts, Pine Headboard, Orig. Side Rails, Refinished, 44¼" x 81" . .
. . . .$135.00
PINE COOKIE BOARD, 13" x 26" . . . .
. . . .$32.50
WOODEN SWORD, Traces Blue Paint, 26" L. $10.00
BACK BOARD FOR BANJO CLOCK, 8¾" x 28½" $17.00

(A-OH '77)   *Garth's Auctions, Inc.*

PINE DOME TOP BOX, Dovetailed, Orig. Blue Paint W/Stenciled Red Tulips & Flowers W/Blue Leaves, Iron Lock, Hasp Missing, Edge Wear, 30" W., 14" D., 11" H.
. . . .$150.00
BENCH, Old Red Paint, 12" x 78" x 6½" H. $230.00
SEWER TILE LIONS, Pr. Hand Molded, 28½" L., 15" H. $700.00
WOODEN SIGN, Iron Bound, White, 29¾" x 48" $215.00

(A-MA '77) *Richard A. Bourne Co., Inc.*
CHINESE CHIPPENDALE HANGING SHELF, English, 18th C., Minor Damage, Unrestored, 35" L., 5" D., 51¼" O H $700.00

(ROW I)
ENGLISH PORCELAIN CUP & SAUCER, Chinoiserie Decor., Saucer W/Slight Age Crack $30.00

(ROW II)
STAFFORDSHIRE MILK PITCHER, Raised Figures Of Hunting Dogs, Pink, Green & Yellow Lustre Decor., Minor Spout Chip, 4⅞" H. $70.00
LEEDS CREAM PITCHER, Cobalt Blue Decor., 3¼" H. $40.00

(ROW III)
BROMLEY WARE CUPS & SAUCERS, Pr., Minor Discoloration On Saucer .$65.00

(A-OH '77) *Garth's Auctions, Inc.*
CAST IRON HORSE WINDMILL WEIGHT, Flaking Black Paint Shows White Beneath, 17½" W., 18¾" H. $70.00
POPLAR BLANKET CHEST, Dovetailed Const., Till W/Lid Missing, Strap Hinges, Bear Trap Lock Missing, Worn Decor., Brown Vinegar Painting W/Panels In Blue Outlined In White, Blue Feet, Red Molding, One Back Foot Incomplete, 51½" W., 22" D., 22¾" H. $725.00
STONEWARE JUG, 3-Gal., Ovoid, Brush Blue Cobalt Design, Impressed "L. Seymour, Troy Factory", 15½" H. $35.00
TRAMP ART MIRROR, Drawer In Base, 13" W., 33½" H. $200.00
STONEWARE JUG, 2-Gal., Cobalt Blue Slip Design, Crack In Base, 13½" H. $45.00

(A-OH '77) *Garth's Auctions, Inc.*
HEPPLEWHITE CHEST OF DRAWERS, Cherry W/Inlaid Mahogany Facade, Dovetailed Cockbeaded Drawers, Orig. Brasses W/Worn Gilt Finish, Minor Damage, Chipped Feet, 46" W., 20¼" D., 36" H. . .$800.00
VICTORIAN BRASS CANDLESTICKS, Pr., Pushups, Polished, 11¾" H. . .$85.00
BENTWOOD BRIDE'S BOX, Pine W/ Orig. Green, Yellow, White, Black & Salmon Decor. On Red Ground, 15" x 9" x 6" H. 320.00
N. CURRIER LITHOGRAPH, "The Cares Of A Family", Large Folio, Trimmed Margins, Pine Frame, 26¾" x 33½" $260.00

To the right ▶

(A-OH '77) *Garth's Auctions, Inc.*
APOTHECARY CHEST, 35 Drawers, Cherry W/Poplar Drawer Fronts, Refinished W/New Top & Bracket Feet, 45" W., 12" D., 31" H. $325.00
STONEWARE PITCHER, Impressed Numbers, "Maurine A. Knight, Germ Proof Chemical Stoneware, Akron, Ohio, U.S.A.", 12¾" H. $37.50
STONEWARE VASE, Brown Sponged Glaze, Base Mkd. "E Houghton & Co. Dalton, Ohio", 11" H. $35.00
STONEWARE PITCHER, White Glaze W/Blue Brushed Man, 10" H. $85.00
STONEWARE PITCHER, Mkd. "Akron, Ohio" Shield, 12½" H. $40.00
TIN CANDLE SCONCES, Tin, Glass Enclosed Candle Enclosure W/Hinged Door, Pr. $95.00
OIL ON CANVAS PORTRAIT, Colonial Gentleman, 20th C., Unframed, 15" x 18" $45.00

(A-OH '77) *Garth's Auctions, Inc.*
CAST IRON HITCHING POST, Old Paint, Arm Missing, 46½" H. $190.00
CAST IRON COFFEE GRINDER, "Enterprise Mfg. Co. Philadelphia, Pa.", "American Pat. Oct. 31, '79", Tin & Brass Hopper, Worn Paint, Wheels 25" Diam., 42" H. $260.00

(A-OH '78)   Garth's Auctions, Inc.

WINDSOR WRITING ARM CHAIR, Dovetailed Drawer, Refinished $325.00

MAHOGANY ON PINE BOX, 5 Dovetailed Drawers, 13" W., 12½" D., 8¼" H. $55.00

PINE BENCH, Orig. Red Stain, 10" D., 35¼" W., 23¾" H. $180.00

OVOID STONEWARE JUG, Impressed "Charlestown", Base Hairline, Rim Flake, 14" H. $50.00

STONEWARE JAR, 2-Gal., Impressed "Ottman Bros., Fort Edwards N.Y.", Cobalt Blue Floral Design, 14" H. $70.00

WOODEN BOX, Covered W/Blue, White & Gold Wallpaper, Leather Hinge, 16" x 8½" x 5" $15.00

COPPER EAGLE WEATHERVANE, Traces Gold Leaf, No Standard, Repaired, 34½" Wingspan, 35" H. $375.00

WROUGHT IRON FIREPLACE FORK, 45½" L. $62.50

WATERCOLOR MEMORIAL, "Sacred To Memory Of Ruthe Ingersoll", Paper Creased & Torn, Framed, 12¾" x 16¾" $150.00

◄ *To the left*
(A-OH '77)   *Garth's Auctions, Inc.*

STONEWARE JAR, Brushed Cobalt Leaf Design, Impressed "P. Her .", Rim Flakes, 12" H. $22.50

STONEWARE JUG, Cobalt Blue Floral Design, Impressed "Haxstry & Co. Fort Edwards, N.Y.", 11" H. $45.00

STONEWARE JAR, Brushed Cobalt Leaf Design, 10" H. $25.00

BUCKET BENCH, Oak W/Worn Modern Green Paint, 28½" W., 15½" D., 25" H. $95.00

STONEWARE JAR, 3 Cobalt Stripes, 8" H. $25.00

STONEWARE JAR, Impressed "1", 9" H. $12.50

STONEWARE CANNING JAR, Stenciled "A.P. Donaghho, Parkersburg, W. Va." Rim Chips, 8" H. $20.00

STONEWARE BOTTLE, Paneled W/Cobalt Blue Around Neck, Impressed "D.S.", Lip Roughness, 10" H. $26.00

STONEWARE BOTTLE, 9" H. $7.00

STONEWARE BOTTLE, Greenish Glaze, Impressed "Newton & Co. California Beer", Lip Chip, 10¼" H. $19.00

STONEWARE BOTTLE, Greenish Glaze, Impressed "J. Weir", 9¼" H. $22.00

WINDSOR SIDE CHAIR, Refinished $110.00

INDIAN RUG, Yei W/Grey Ground & Red, Brown, White, Blue & Black, 34" Sq. $160.00

WROUGHT IRON REVOLVING BROILER, Needs Minor Repair, 11½" Diam., 27" L. $90.00

(A-OH '77)   *Garth's Auctions, Inc.*

DESK, Pine, Lift Up Lid, 62" W., 18" D., 32½" H. $130.00

CARRIAGE LAMPS, Pr., Sheet Metal W/ Cast Ornamentation & Embossed Cut Out Swags On Finial, Beveled Glass Lenses W/ Mirror Finish Interior, One W/Kerosene Burner, "White Mfg. Co.", 40" H. $425.00

FOOD CHOPPING MACHINE, Cast Iron Mechanism, Tin Drum, Wooden Base, Signed & Patent Dated, 16" L., 12½" H. $45.00

PINE TRUNK, Iron Sides, Strap Hinges, Old Red Paint, Wallpaper Lining, 30" x 18" x 16" $30.00

MECHANICAL BELLOWS, Brass Pulleys, Wood & Sheet Iron Housing, Wooden Base, Pulley Belts Missing, 30¾" L.O.A., 11½" H. $60.00

SHIP MODEL, Wooden, From Sag Harbor, N.Y., Orig. Worn Paint, Minor Repair Necessary, 19th C., 42" L. $170.00

◄ *To the left*
(A-OH '77)   *Garth's Auctions, Inc.*

WILLIAM & MARY CHEST OF DRAWERS, Walnut & Oak, Dovetailed Drawers, Replaced Brass Hdwe. & Turned Feet, Refinished, 38¼" W., 21¾" D., 38⅞" H. $800.00

PEWTER PLATE, "Townsend & Compton, London" Touch, 7¾" Diam. . . $57.50

PEWTER TEAPOT, American, Resoldered At Spout & Handle, Wooden Disc Missing From Finial, 7½" H. $175.00

CUTLERY BOX, Walnut Veneer On Pine, Cast Brass Hasp & Lock, Lid Handle Missing, Minor Veneer Damage, 9" W., 7" D., 12¾" H. $45.00

PEWTER FLATWARE, 36 Pc. Set, Spoons & Forks Mkd. "Neu Platina", Knives have Steel Blades $50.00

PEWTER CHARGER, "London" Touch Marks, Pitted Surface, 20¼" H. . . $115.00

PEWTER PLATE, "London" Touch Marks, 7¾" Diam. $50.00

To the right ▶

(A-OH '78)   *Garth's Auctions, Inc.*

PINE & POPLAR BLANKET CHEST, Dovetailed Bracket Feet W/2 Overlapping Drawers Flanked By Fluted Dividers, Original Hardware Including Bear Trap Lock & Key, (Escutcheon Gone), Brass Bail Handles & Iron Strap Hinges, Original Worn Brown & Yellow Stamp Graining Over A White Ground W/Dark Blue Feet & Faded Red Moulding, 49½" W., 22¾" Deep, 28¾" H. $900.00
REDWARE MILK PAN, Clear Interior Glaze, Hairline, 13¼" D. $50.00
FLARED WOVEN SPLIT WOOD BAS- KETS, Pr., W/Wooden Bases, Upholstery Tacks Around Base & Rim, Black & Pale Blue Paint, 10½" D., 6" H., Plus Handles $130.00
REDWARE OVOID JAR, Interior Glaze, Rim Hairline, 12" H. $65.00
FRAKTUR CERTIFICATE, W/Printed Rectangular Text Block, Printed Top Border & Hand Drawn Boldly Stylized Floral Border W/Mermaids In The Bottom Corners, Good Colors, Red, Blue, Yellow, Shades Of Green & Brown, Records Birth Of "Daniel Achenbach in 1781, Northampton County, Pennsylvania", By Arnold Hoevelmann, 16½" x 19¾" $1200.00
FRAKTUR CERTIFICATE, Printed From Same Block As Above, Hand Drawn Stylized Floral Borders W/Deer In One Corner & A Pelican In The Other, Good Colors, Red, Blue, Green, Yellow & Black, Records Birth Of Jacob Luzz in 1778, Cumberland County, Pennsylvania, Old Paper Repair On Left Margin, By Arnold Hoevelmann, 16½" x 19¾" $1300.00

(A-MA '78)   *Richard A. Bourne Co., Inc.*

CIVIL WAR CARTRIDGE BOX, Complete W/Orig. Shoulder Belt, Mfg. By Watertown Arsenal, 1864, Complete W/"US" Oval Plate On Pouch Cover & Brass Round Eagle Cross Belt Plate $180.00

(A-OH '78) . . . .*Garth's Auctions, Inc.*

FOLK ART CARVING, Wooden Horse W/Wood And Composition Cowboy, Polychrome Paint, 16" L., 11½" H. ...$30.00
PAINTED HIGHCHAIR, Orig. Green Paint W/Dark Green And Black Striping And Stenciled Fruit In A Basket Crest. Wear On Foot Rest And Arms, Rest Of Paint Is In Very Fine Condition, 37¼" H. ...$200.00
CHERRY COUNTRY CHIPPENDALE DROP LEAF SWING LEG TABLE, Square Legs With Beaded Corners And Inside Chamfer. 3 Board Top, 14" x 42' x 28½" H. $950.00

(continued next column)

SIX YARN "TURKEY WORK" FLOW- ER SQUARES Sewn Together Into A Mat, 17" x 25½" $17.50
OCTAGONAL TOLE TRAY, Gold Crystalized Ground With A White Band And Black And Yellow Striping, Some Wear, 5¾" x 8½" $80.00
TOLE DEED BOX, Black Ground W/ White Band Decor. In Red And Green, Some Wear, 8" x 4" x 4½" $45.00
TOLE MATCH BOX, Black Ground W/ Red, Yellow And Green Floral Painting, Has Wear, 4¾" W. $62.50
OCTAGONAL TOLE TRAY, Crystalized Ground And White Band With Red And Green Floral Decoration, Some Wear, 6" x 9" $35.00
SAMPLER ON HOMESPUN, Vining Border W/Urns And Baskets Of Flowers, Gate W/Little Man On Top, And Verse, "Mary Nelson Finished This Work Jan. 29, 1831", Green, Brown, Tan, Yellow And Black, Letters Have Wear And Some Are Restored, Framed, 18" Sq. $190.00
OIL ON CANVAS, Still Life Of Pineapple, Roses, Grapes, Strawberries, And Other Fruit, Cleaned And Rebacked, Very Good Color, Old Gilt Frame, 25¾" x 28¾" $425.00
SAMPLER ON HOMESPUN, Floral Border W/Architectural Frame For Verse, Trees, Flowers, Adam & Eve, Serpent, Ducks And "Caroline Dawson 1838", Good Color, Green, Red, Brown, Gold And White, Minor Damage And 2 Small Holes, Framed, 13¾" x 18½" $250.00

◀ *To the left*

(A-OH '77)   *Garth's Auctions, Inc.*
MAHOGANY HANGING CORNER CUPBOARD, Reverse Gilt Decor. Pane In Center, Line Inlay In Drk., 29" W., 18½" D., 40½" H. $220.00
CHERRY QUEEN ANNE SIDE CHAIR, Slip Seat, Replaced Center Splat, 1 Foot Chipped, Refinished $425.00
TOLE COFFEE POT, Red Ground W/ Floral Painting In Green, Blue, Yellow & White, Decor. By JoAnn Shank, 11" H. ...
.................................$370.00
WATERCOLOR, Floral W/Gilt Frame, 17¼" x 20¾" $115.00
LEATHER MASONIC APRON, Painted Gold, Blue & Other Colors, Framed, 16¾" x 20" $105.00

(A-OH '77)   *Garth's Auctions, Inc.*
SHAKER ARM CHAIR ROCKER, Child Size, Green Woven Tape Seat, Orig. Finish, Size "0" $380.00
DOLL CRADLE, Woven Split Wood, 20" L. $30.00
PINE LABEL CABINET, Interior Originally Divided Into 144 Pigeon Holes, From West Family, Mt. Lebanon, 29" W., 6½" D., 62½" H. $225.00
SHAKER ASH CARRIER, Sheet Iron W/ Wrought Iron Handle, Hancock, 22" L. ....
.................................$35.00
WOODEN SHADOW DECOY, White Winged Scoter, Old Black & White Paint, 44" L. $22.50

(A-MA '77)   *Robert C. Eldred Co., Inc.*

◀ *To the left*

RED TOLE CHESTNUT URNS, Pr., Ca. 1790, Decor. W/Marine Paintings Depicting French Warships, Ram's Head Loose Ring Handles, 11" H. $450.00

(A-OH '77)   *Garth's Auctions, Inc.*
PINE BLANKET CHEST, Dovetailed Const., Till, Orig. Red Paint, Reset Hinges, 50¼" W., 21½" D., 23" H. $300.00
STONEWARE CROCK, 1½ Gal., Stenciled "W.T. Chaffey & Co., Agents, 264 Liberty St., Pitts.", Base Hairline, 9" H. ....
.................................$35.00
BURL BOWL, 23" Diam., 8" H. ....
.................................$775.00
STONEWARE CROCK, Brushed Cobalt Design W/"1½", 10" H. $60.00
OIL ON ACADEMY BOARD PAINTING, Front Yard Scene W/Children, Dog, Parents W/Baby & House, Paper Label "F.W. Devoe & Co. New York" On Back, Shadow Box Frame, 21¼" x 25¼" $175.00

(A-OH '78)   *Garth's Auctions, Inc.*
POPLAR BLANKET CHEST, Worn Orig. Blue Paint, Dovetailed Const., Till, 47½" W., 21½" D., 24" H. $300.00
PINE APOTHECARY CHEST, Dovetailed Drawers, Paint Removed To Show Orig. Blue W/Worn Black Drawer Numbers, 1 Drawer Replaced, 36¼" W., 9½" D., 27¾" H. $360.00
TIN HAND LAMP, Double Spout Burner, 3¾" H. $45.00
TIN LARD LAMP, Saucer Base, 6¾" H. .
.................................$110.00
TIN HAND LAMP, Heat Shield By Handle, Double Spout Whale Oil Burner, 3" H. ...
.................................$45.00

(A-OH '77)   *Garth's Auctions, Inc.*
PINE CUPBOARD, Dovetailed Case, 3 Adjustable Shelves, Old Drk. Paint, 27" W., 11" D., 36" H. $130.00
SABRE LEG SIDE CHAIRS (1 of 3), Curly Maple & Birdseye Maple, 1 Cane Seat Needs Repair, Refinished $135.00
WOODEN ADJUSTABLE LIGHTING DEVICE, Double Taper Holder On Threaded Standard, 12" H. $380.00
WOODEN JAR, Age Crack In Base Held By Staples & Wire Band, 11" Diam., 8" H.
.................................$35.00
TOLE LIGHTING DEVICE, Green W/ Yellow Striping, Removable Shade, Clear Lamp, Brass Single Spout Burning Fluid Burner, 11" O.H. $285.00
HANGING WOODEN TOWEL RACK, 24" W., 10" D., 26½" H. $80.00
GILDED FEDERAL MIRROR, Reverse Painting, Scene Of House & Trees, Minor Flaking, 13" x 25" $185.00

(A-PA '77)   *Pennypacker Auction Centre*
FISH STORE SYMBOL, Wooden, Weathered, 45½" L.................$120.00

(A-PA '77)   *Brown Bros. Gallery*
(L to R)
REDWARE PITCHER $160.00
HEPPLEWHITE DRESSING MIRROR
.................................$250.00
SPLINT OAK NUTTING BASKET, Small
.................................$65.00

(A-OH '77)   *Garth's Auctions, Inc.*
ARROW BACK ARM CHAIR, Refinished.
.................................$65.00
COUNTRY CANDLESTAND, Cherry & Curly Maple, Refinished, 13¾" x 16½" x 27¼" H....................$270.00
TURTLE BACK BELLOWS, Yellow, Green, Black, Gold & Red, 17¼" L. .....
.................................$85.00
LEEDS CHARGER, Blue Feather Edge, Bird Sitting On Tree In Center, 4 Colors, 12¼" Diam..................$600.00
THEOREM ON PAPER, Yellow Finch In Cherry Tree, Gilt Frame, 12" x 15½" ....
.................................$75.00
PAPER CUT-OUT, "Remembrance Token", Poem & "April 6, 1882", Cherry On Pine Frame, 10" x 12" $85.00

(A-OH '77)   *Garth's Auctions, Inc.*
WINDSOR ROCKER, White Paint Cleaned Off To Show Orig. Coral W/Traces Of Red Striping & Gilt Stenciling ..$120.00
CURLY MAPLE STAND, 14½" x 20" x 28¾" H....................$85.00
WOVEN SPLIT WOOD BASKET, Wooden Handle, Minor Repair Needed, 11" Diam., 10" H. $33.50
BENTWOOD STORAGE BOX, Worn Drk. Paint, 4 Fingers In Base, 1 In Top, 9¼" L..............................$105.00
BENTWOOD STORAGE BOX, Worn Varnish Finish, 2 Fingers In Base, 1 In Top, 6¼" L. $65.00
REDWARE MILK BOWL, Interior W/ Yellow Slip, Wavy & Straight Lines, Clear Glaze, Old Rim Chips, 13¾" Diam., 5½" H.
.................................$70.00
N. CURRIER PRINT, "The High Bridge At Harlem, N.Y.", Bottom Edge Torn & Margins Trimmed, Framed, 13¼" x 17"
.................................$145.00
ALPHABET SAMPLER, Birdseye Veneer Frame, 20" x 22" $50.00

(A-PA '77)   *Pennypacker Auction Centre*

(A-PA '77)   *Pennypacker Auction Centre*
LEHN BUCKET, Colorful, 10½" Diam., 8¼" H. $800.00

(A-OH '77)   *Garth's Auctions, Inc.*
COUNTRY CAPTAIN'S CHAIR, Old Red Paint........................$70.00
PINE HEPPLEWHITE TABLE, 1-Board Top, Refinished, 21½" x 32" x 29" H. ....
.................................$160.00
STONEWARE COOLER, 3-Gal., Impressed "New York Stoneware Co. Fort Edwards, N.Y.", Cobalt Blue Highlights, Rim Chip, 12¾" H..............$25.00
WOODEN BOWL, Worn Blue Paint On Ext., 22" Diam. $105.00
OIL ON BOARD, Still Life, Pine Frame, 12¾" x 16½" $25.00
OIL ON WOODEN PANEL, Cow In Wooden Stream, 14¼" x 20" $65.00
WROUGHT IRON & BRASS UTENSILS, Pr., Dipper & Strainer, 17½" x 16" $55.00
WROUGHT IRON TRIVET, 8¼" L. .....
.................................$140.00
WROUGHT IRON UTENSILS, Pr., Dipper & Strainer, 18½" x 19".......$50.00
PINE MEAT BOARD, Wrought Iron Hooks, No Finish, 27" L. $60.00

To the left

(L to R)
▶ **LEHN CUP & SAUCER,** Miniature, Decorated $270.00
LEHN CUP & SAUCER, Decor. W/Orig. Label On Base: "Made By Joseph Lehn In His 97th Year, March 3, 1890" ...$330.00

(A-PA '77)   *Pennypacker Auction Centre*
LEHN WOODEN SUGAR BUCKET, Orig. Colorful Decor., 9" $750.00

(A-OH '77)   *Garth's Auctions, Inc.*

◄ *To the left*

WALNUT LADDER BACK SIDE CHAIR, Woven Rush Seat $25.00
ONE DRAWER STAND, Turned Maple Legs, Curly Maple Drawer Front, Walnut Apron, Top Is Laminated Walnut & Hickory, Knob Replaced, Refinished, 21" x 23" x 30" H. $30.00
COOLER, Blue & White Spongeware, "4" On Side Over Hole For Spigot, Side Hairline, 11" H. $52.00
MIXING BOWL, Blue & White Spongeware, Crows Foot In Side, 12" Diam. $15.00
WROUGHT IRON PEEL, Ram's Horn Finial, 37½" L. $55.00
REVERSE PAINTING ON GLASS, Labeled "East Wiota Church, Wiota, Wisc. Built A.D. 1851, By F. H. Engebrevson", 19½" x 23¾" $80.00

(A-OH '77)   *Garth's Auctions, Inc.*

LOOP BACK WINDSOR CHAIR, Drk. Brown Finish $310.00
WOODEN HAND CRANKED MACHINE, For Compressing Rug Material, Old Red Paint, 33" H. $50.00
RYE STRAW BASKETS, (2), 15½" Diam. $20.00
CLOTHING BILLBOARD, "Hats and Caps From The Boston Clothing House, West Chester, Penna", Old Gilt Frame, 15" x 19" $15.00
WIRE EGG BASKET, 19" H. $80.00
TIN SCONCE, Tooled Back W/Rod For Hanging Betty Lamp, 15" H. $57.50

(A-OH '77)   *Garth's Auctions, Inc.*

COUNTRY HEPPLEWHITE TABLE, Dovetailed Drawers, Drk. Red Alligatored Paint, Minor Damage, 32" W., 16" D., 29" H. $65.00
POPLAR BOX, Dome Top, Drk. Brown Alligatored Paint W/Yellow Striping, Brass Bail Handle, 16" x 7¾" x 10" $47.50
ARROW BACK ROCKING CHAIR, Worn Green Paint & Yellow Striping $60.00
STONEWARE BATTER PITCHER, Reddish Slip, 9" H. $20.00
CARVED DUCK DECOY, Brown Varnish, 13¾" L. $37.50
SAMPLER, Homespun, "Rebecca Stone" & '183", Eagles, Dog, Tree & Adam & Eve, Framed, 9" x 18½" $55.00

(A-OH '77)   *Garth's Auctions, Inc.*

COUNTRY CARD TABLE, 1 Swing Leg, 1-Board Leaves W/Bread Board Ends, Old Red Paint, 36½" x 16" (32"-Open) $425.00
STONEWARE CROCK, 6-Gal., Incised Cow Highlighted In Blue, "Gardiner Stone Ware, Manufactory, Gardiner, Me.", 13" H. $55.00
ROCKER, Drk. Brownish-Red Ground W/ Striping & Stenciling In Green, Yellow & Orange $130.00
TIN CANDLESTICKS, Pr., Weighted Bases, Applied Floral Decor., 9½" H. $175.00
WOODEN STORAGE BOX, Pine, Sliding Lid, Polychrome Design On 5 Sides, 7" x 8¼" x 11" $320.00
OIL ON CANVAS PORTRAIT, Gentleman, Heavy Gilt Frame, 32" x 37" $190.00
CREWEL ON SILK, (The Male Macaw, 1804), Stitched At Bottom, Framed, 15" x 17" $290.00

◄ *To the left*

CRYPTO HIGH WHEEL CYCLE, Makd. Crypto Cycle Company, Geared Ordinary London, 53" H. $500.00

(A-VA. '77)   *Laws Auction & Antiques*

MICROSCOPE, Amer., Ca. 1800, Twin-Swivel Lens, Double Ratchet Adjustments, Tilt Base, Three Brass-Cased Lens Of Different Powers & Second Eye-Piece, Pieces Mkd. & In Orig. Fitted Case $150.00
HELIOGRAPH, Two Tripods, One Holding Mirror, One For Scope Contained In Separate Wooden Case, Leather Case W/Extra Mirrors & Spare Parts, Mkd. "Helio. 5" Mark V., London, 1940 . . . .$325.00

(A-VA '78)   *Laws*

(A-OH '77) Garth's Auctions, Inc.

STONEWARE JAR, Cobalt Signature "Lambright, Wenport", Base Hairlines, 6-Gal., 19" H. $37.50
PINE CHEST OF DRAWERS, Dovetailed W/Inlaid Ivory Escutcheons, Refinished, Replaced Wooden Knobs, 43" W., 18¾" D., 42½" H. $260.00
WOODEN CHURN, Stave Const., Metal Bands, Refinished W/Traces Of Red, 23" O.H. $115.00
STONEWARE JAR, Cobalt Leaf Design, Chipped Lid, 10¼" H. $27.50
STONEWARE BUTTER CROCK, 4-Gal., Impressed "A.O. Whittemore, Havana, N.Y.", Cobalt Blue Bird, Rim Chip, 13" Diam., 8¼" H. $200.00
STONEWARE JUG, 2-Gal., Impressed "J. & E. Norton, Bennington, Vt.", Cobalt Slip Design, Minor Lip Chip, 13½" H. $135.00
COPPER HORSE WEATHERVANE, Cast Directionals (1 Missing), Black, 20th C., 33" L $180.00

(A-OH '77) Garth's Auctions, Inc.

FIREMAN'S HAT, Aluminum W/Brass Trim, Label For "Cairns & Bros. N.J.", Repainted Red & Black, 14½" L. $20.00
CHERRY CRADLE, Dovetailed, Worn Red Paint, 42" L. $200.00
CAST IRON JOCKEY HITCHING POST, Worn Paint, 38" H. $145.00
PINE HANGING SHELVES, Refinished, 31" W., 6" D., 36" H. $85.00
SHEET IRON DOUBLE CRUSIE LAMP, 9" H. $20.00
PUNCHED TIN CANDLE SCONCES, (2), 9½" H. $52.50
TIN LANTERN, Glass Crown-Like Top, Incomplete Door, 9½" H. $10.00
TIN CANDLE SCONCE, Rod For Hanging Betty Lamps, One Candle Socket, 10" W., 12" H. $67.50
KELLOGG LITHOGRAPH SILHOUETTE, "Henry Alexander Wise", Frame 17" x 21" $10.00

To the left

SHERATON BANQUET TABLES, (Set of 3 Part), Flame Veneer Aprons, Replaced Cherry Tops, Minor Repairs, 43¾" W. (Extends to 130" L.), 30" H. $750.00
CHILD'S ROCKER, Orig. Brown Paint W/Yellow & White Striping & Fruit Stenciling On Crest & Seat $105.00
GAUDY LEEDS PITCHER, Blue, Green, Yellow & Yellow Ochre Decor., Base Of Handle Professionally Repaired, 10" H. $390.00
LEEDS CHARGER, Blue Feather Edge W/Pot Of Flowers, 5 Colors, 14½" Diam. $525.00
GAUDY STAFFORDSHIRE PITCHER, Blue, Green & Yellow Ochre Decor., Edge Flake & Hairlines, 9¼" H. $490.00
SAMPLER ON HOMESPUN, Alphabets, Pine Trees, Baskets Of Flowers, Poem & Strawberry Border, Modern Grained Frame, 15" x 17" $130.00
SAMPLER ON HOMESPUN, Alphabet & Genealogy, Old Gilt Frame, 16¾" Sq. $250.00

(A-OH '77) Garth's Auctions, Inc.

BOSTON ROCKER, Refinished .$110.00
WALNUT SCHOOL MASTER'S DESK, Dovetailed Cockbeaded Drawer, Embossed Brass & Iron Pull, Lift Lid W/Interior Compartment, Repairs, 31" W., 21½" D., 37" H. $220.00
BUTTOCKS BASKET, Woven Split Wood, Wooden Handle, 20" L. $50.00
SCHOOL BELL, Bell Metal, Wooden Handle, 9¾" H $27.50
SCHOOL BELL, Bell Metal, Wooden Handle, Metal Pitted, 9" H. $17.50
SCHOOL BELL, Bell Metal, Wooden Handle, 9" H. $20.00
SCHOOL BELL, Bell Metal, Wooden Handle, Brass Finial, 5¾" H. $12.50
N. CURRIER PRINT, "Surrender Of Cornwallis", Sm. Margin Tear, Trimmed, Pine Frame, 14¼" x 18" $85.00
BRASS HANGING TAPER HOLDERS, Pr., 20th C., 10½" H. $80.00
OIL ON BOARD PAINTING, Windmill, Gilt Frame, 19" x 23" $42.50

(A-OH '77) Garth's Auctions, Inc.

COPPER PAN, Dovetailed Const., Cast Iron Handle, Labeled "The J. Van Range Co. Manufacturer", 9" Diam. $65.00
PLANK SEAT BAMBOO WINDSOR SIDE CHAIR, Refinished $85.00
PINE CRADLE, Brown Grained Decor., 37" W., 20" D., 27" H. $95.00
TREEN COVERED JAR, Yellow, Repair In Lid, Age Crack In Base, 11" Diam., 10½" H. $155.00
BUGGY SEAT BACKBOARD, Old Green Paint W/Yellow & Black Striping & Yellow Horses' Heads, 15" x 42" $22.50

(A-OH '77) Garth's Auctions, Inc.

(A-OH '77)   *Garth's Auctions, Inc.*

LADDER BACK ARM CHAIR, Worn Black Paint W/Traces Gold Striping, New Woven Cane Seat $400.00
COUNTRY QUEEN ANNE TAVERN TABLE, Pine W/Poplar Legs, 1-Board Removable Top, Old Finish, 23½" x 34¾" x 30" H. $975.00
STONEWARE CROCK, 10-Gal., Cobalt Slip Drawing Of Woman, Albany Slip Interior, Base Hairlines, 13½" Diam., 17¼" H. $595.00
BIRDSEYE MAPLE BOWL, Hand Tool Marks, 22½" L. $165.00
CHINTZ SECTION, Red Frame, 13¼" x 14¼" $55.00
OIL ON CANVAS, Portrait Of Gentleman, Red Drapery Background, 1 Small Patch, Minor Restoration Necessary, Framed, 29" x 34" $600.00

(A-OH '77)   *Garth's Auctions, Inc.*

CHERRY COUNTRY FEDERAL STAND, Legs Repaired, Refinished, 18½" x 20" x 26" H. $190.00
ARROW BACK SIDE CHAIRS (Set of 6), Decor. W/Red & Black Graining W/White Striping & Hand Painted Rose Design On Crest, Seats Worn $600.00
ROCKINGHAM BOWL, 11½" Diam., 5" H. $40.00
OIL ON CANVAS PORTRAIT, Signed "F.E. Cohen, Painted", Gilded Gesso On Wood Frame, 33¾" x 37½" $220.00

(A-OH '77)   *Garth's Auctions, Inc.*

SHAKER LADDER BACK SIDE CHAIR, Faded Green Woven Tape Seat, New Lebannon, Front Posts — 18½" H. . .$235.00
SHAKER STANDING YARN SWIFT, Tyringham, No Finish, 39¼" H. . . .$95.00
PINE PIPE BOX, 18½" H. $100.00
SHAKER TOWEL BAR, Cherry Rod Mortised Into Pine Black Which Hinges To Wall Or Cupboard, Pewter Knobs Hold Towels In Place, 41" L. $195.00
HOMESPUN TOWEL, Enfield, Minor Wear, 26" x 30" $12.00
HOMESPUN TOWEL, 15½" x 49' $6.00

(A-OH '78)   *Garth's Auctions, Inc.*

BRASS BALL TOP ANDIRONS, Restored, 29" D., 18" H. $100.00
MAHOGANY QUEEN ANNE DROP LEAF TABLE, Restored, 19" x 46" W/18" Leaves, 28" H. $350.00
BRASS VICTORIAN CANDLESTICKS, Pr., Pushups, Mkd. "Solid English", 10½" H. $90.00
BOX W/Rose Malling Decor. W/Doors, Drawers & Hinged Lid. One Drawer A Replacement, Minor Wear, 7" x 7½" x 11" $135.00

(A-OH '77)   *Garth's Auctions, Inc.*

MINIATURE CHEST OF DRAWERS, Yellow Graining Over White Ground, 7" x 11" x 9¾" $75.00
MINIATURE PLANK SEAT CHAIRS, Pr., Putty W/Black & Gold Striping, Handmade, 8¾" H. $50.00
CANDLE DRYING RACK, Old Green Paint $95.00
ROCKING CHAIR, Worn Black Paint $95.00
OIL ON CANVAS PORTRAIT, Rebacked On Masonite, Restored Flaking, New Gilt Frame, 18" x 21" $35.00

(A-OH '77)   *Garth's Auctions, Inc.*

LADDER BACK ARM CHAIR, Repaired W/Replacement Of Back Post & Arm Post $180.00
SPINNING WHEEL, Stamped 1891, Wheel — 20½" Diam., 37" H. . . .$140.00
IRON CHOPPING KNIFE, Wooden Handle, 6" W. $10.00
WROUGHT IRON PEAL, Ram's Horn Handle, 51" L. $45.00
HANGING SALT BOX, Worn Grey-Green Paint, 9½" W., 9¾" H. $35.00
WROUGHT IRON BROILER, 22" L. $27.50
BRASS BED WARMER, Wooden Handle, 44" L. $160.00

(A-OH '77)   *Garth's Auctions, Inc.*

WALNUT COUNTRY HEPPLEWHITE WORK TABLE, Dovetailed Drawer, 2-Board Top, Refinished, 28½" x 42" x 27½" H. $110.00

LEATHER BUCKET, Seams W/Copper Rivets & Copper Rim W/Wire Rim Handles, 10½" Diam., 10½" H. $27.50

CAST IRON MAIL BOX, Worn Orig. Red Paint W/Black & White Striping, 12" x 6½" x 5¾" $35.00

WOODEN SMOOTHING BOARD, Carved Hearts, Hex Signs W/"1832", Handle Is 2-Headed Horse, Traces Red & Green Paint, 25" L. $205.00

WROUGHT IRON LADLE, 21" L. $27.50

IRON UTENSILS (2), Cast Fork, Wrought Spoon, 15" L. $25.00

WROUGHT IRON STRAINER, 18¾" L. $10.00

WROUGHT IRON UTENSIL RACK, Needs Minor Repair, Secured To Wall W/ Attached Spikes, 12¾" L. $35.00

SMOOTHING BOARD, Carved Compass Designs, Worn Painted Decor., 30½" L. $195.00

(A-OH '77)   *Garth's Auctions, Inc.*

TIN CAMPAIGN TORCH, Wooden Handle In Shape Of Rifle, 66" L. $90.00

SCHOOL MASTERS OR CLERKS DESK, Walnut, Dovetailed Gallery, 30" W., 21" D., 50" H. $210.00

DOME TOP BOX, Pine, Dovetailed, Drk. Green Sponged Decor. Over Yellow Ground, Replaced Leather Hinges, 18" x 9" x 7" $105.00

CORK HANGING BOX, 2-Compartment, Chip Carving, 9¼" W., 4¾" D., 10" H. $95.00

CARVED WOODEN SHORE BIRD, Inset Wooden Beak, 20th C., 12½" H. $175.00

WATERCOLOR, Rooster On Hill W/Tulips, Pine Frame, 6¾" x 9¼" $270.00

SILHOUETTE, Hollow Cut, Young Girl, Yellow Dress, Walnut Frame, 5½" x 7¼" $290.00

WATERCOLOR, Polka Dot Deer, Orange Clouds In Background, Pine Frame, 6¾" x 9¼" $295.00

(A-OH '77)   *Garth's Auctions, Inc.*

FOOT STOOL, Orig. Brown Sponge Painting Over Yellow Ground, Underside Signed, 16½" x 7¼" x 7½" H. $57.50

LADDER BACK ARM CHAIR ...$95.00

COUNTRY HEPPLEWHITE STAND, Cherry, Orig. Brass Embossed Knob, Pine 1-Board Top, Orig. Finish, Repaired Leg, 18" x 24¾" x 28" H. $185.00

REDWARE JAR, Applied Handles, Incised Lines, Brown Speckled Glaze, Interior W/ Yellowish-Green Slip, Lip Chipped, 12" H. $25.00

REDWARE BOWL, Red W/Green, Blue & Cream Slip Decor., Rim Flakes, 12¼" Diam., 3⅝" H. $115.00

SHIP ENGRAVING, Black & White, "L. Brall & Sons, London, 1871", "Off Portland", Walnut Shadow Box Frame, 34" x 42" $45.00

◄ *To the left*

(A-OH '77)   *Garth's Auctions, Inc.*

ARROW BACK SIDE CHAIRS, Pr., Refinished $110.00

HUTCH TABLE, 3-Board Pine Top, Birch, Maple & Pine Base, Traces Old Red, 48" Diam., 27½" H. $675.00

CARVED WOODEN DUCK DECOY, Orig. Paint, 14¼" L. $90.00

STONEWARE CROCK, 3-Gal., Cobalt Blue Quill Work Decor., 13½" H. ...$75.00

CARVED WOODEN DUCK DECOY, Orig. Paint, Balsa Body, 14½" L. .$120.00

PASTEL ON CANVAS PORTRAIT, Old Grained Frame, 15½" x 19¾" ...$320.00

(A-OH '77)   *Garth's Auctions, Inc.*

BRASS BALL TOP ANDIRONS, Pr., 24" D., 18" H. $130.00

BRASS FIREPLACE FENDER, 34" W., 10" D., 11" H. $85.00

EMPIRE LYRE FORM SOFA, Figured Mahogany Veneer, Damask Upholstery, 76" L. $1500.00

SILHOUETTES, Pr., Cut Full Figure Of Lady & Gentleman, Dated 1838, 7½" x 11¼" $270.00

EMPIRE MANTLE MIRROR, Gilded Gesso On Wood, 30" x 57" $155.00

(A-OH '77)   *Garth's Auctions, Inc.*
(ROW I, L to R)
POTTERY HUMMING BIRD FEEDER,
18th C., Red, Green & Black Decor., 5" H.
..........................$65.00
IRON SEWING BIRD, Red Pin Cushion,
5" H. $77.50
IRON PIN CUSHION, 6¼" H. ..$70.00
IRON SEWING BIRD, Red & Yellow
Decor., 5½" H. $75.00
COMPOSITION TIGER, Flocked Striped
Coat, 7½" L. $5.00
(ROW II, L to R)
BURL BOX, Inlay In Center Of Lid, 3¼"
Diam...........................$40.00
SCRIMSHAW IVORY CARVING, Lady,
Made In Form Of Neckerchief Slide, 1½" L.
.............................$75.00
MINIATURE SHOT FLASK, White Metal
W/Embossed Fan Ornament, Brass Spout
& Fittings, 4¼" H. $20.00
STAFFORDSHIRE CAT & KITTEN,
Pr., Red & White Coats W/Black Spots,
19th C., Mkd. W/Gilt Anchor, 2¾" H. ....
.............................$85.00
(ROW III, L to R)
SPATTERWARE CUP & SAUCER, Min-
iature, Brown, Saucer W/Old Hairline ....
.............................$85.00
STAFFORDSHIRE TUMBLER, Blk.
Transfer "Charity and Hope" W/Red, Green
& Yellow Enameling, 2¾" H. $40.00
CUP PLATE, Sprig Decor., 4¼" Diam. ..
.............................$5.00
(ROW IV, L to R)
CARVED WOODEN FABRIC STAMP,
1¾" x 3½" x 6" $7.00
COMPOSITION ELEPHANTS, (2), Grey
Flocking, 6" and 2½" L. $5.00

(D-CA '78)
KEEN-KUTTER POCKET KNIFE, Bone
Handle........................$65.00

(A-OH '77)   *Garth's Auctions, Inc.*
(ROW I, L to R)
BRASS BETTY LAMP, Wrought Iron
Hanger, 4½' L. $85.00
CAST IRON GREASE LAMP, 3-Legged
Base, Repaired Base, Cover Missing, 5¼"
Diam., 5½" H. $85.00
IRON BETTY LAMP, Thumb Screw, 6¼"
L. $110.00
WROUGHT IRON BETTY LAMP, Hang-
er & Pick, 5¼" L. $180.00
WROUGHT IRON BETTY LAMP, Hang-
er, Chicken Finial On Cover Latch, 4½" L.
.............................$115.00
(ROW II, L to R)
STONEWARE GREASE LAMP, Mottled
Brown Glaze, Saucer Base Chipped, Minor
Glaze Wear, 7" Diam., 7" H. $195.00
TASTER, Copper Bowl, Tooled Iron Han-
dle, 7" H. $80.00
IRON TASTER, 8¼" L. $35.00
STRAINER, Brass Bowl, Iron Handle, 8¾"
L. $140.00
TASTER, Brass Bowl, Iron Handle, 10" L.
.............................$80.00
STONEWARE GREASE LAMP, Greenish-
Grey Glaze, Old Hairlines In Base, 5¾"
Diam., 5½" H. $205.00

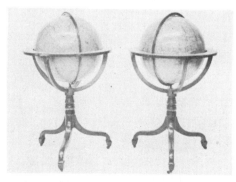

(A-MA '77)   *Richard A. Bourne Co., Inc.*
GLOBES ON STANDS, Pr., English, Late
18th-Early 19th C., Terrestial Globe By
C. F. Crunchley, London; Celestial Globe
By J. & W. Cary, London, March 1799,
20" Diam., 46" O.H. $3300.00

(A-OH '78)   *Garth's Auctions, Inc.*
WINDSOR ARM CHAIR, Bow Repair,
Worn Red Paint Shows Green Beneath ...
.............................$800.00
WOODEN DECOY, Bluebill Drake, Hol-
low Body, Worn Orig. Paint, Bill Chipped,
13¼" L. $105.00
CHERRY CANDLESTAND, 1-Board
Top, Replaced Legs, Worn Finish, 17" x
19" x 24½" H. $225.00
PINE TEA CADDY, Black Paint W/Gold
Stenciled Basket Of Fruit, Twin Pewter Fit-
ted Containers W/Lids, 11" L., 6¼" H. ...
.............................$215.00
OIL ON WOODEN PANEL PORTRAIT,
Woman, Unframed, 11¾" x 13" .$500.00
**CURLY MAPLE CHIPPENDALE
SCROLL MIRROR,** 1 Ear Repaired, 1 Ear
Old Replacement, Refinished, 13¾" x 24"
.............................$145.00

(A-OH '77)   *Garth's Auctions, Inc.*
PINE YARN WINDER, Mortised Con-
struction, 36" H. $50.00
ASH LARD PRESS, W/Galvanized Pan
W/Handle, 44" L. $50.00
COPPER PAN, Dovetailed Construction,
Iron Handle, 17" Diam. $55.00
INDIAN BASKET, Animal Figures, Prob.
Pima, 9½" Diam. $205.00
INDIAN RUG, Red & Black Border W/
Grey Ground, Animal Figures, Geometric
Designs, 45" x 70" $500.00

(A-OH '77)   *Garth's Auctions, Inc.*
WALNUT TILT TOP TABLE, Repaired Base Column, Refinished, 25½" Diam., 28" H. $200.00
MAHOGANY GENTLEMAN'S SLIPPER CHAIR, Mortised Constr., Minor Repair, 19th C. $95.00
BRASS CANDLESTICK, 8½" H. $145.00
BRASS CANDLESTICK, Sq. Base, 9" H. $70.00
LITHOGRAPHS (2), Hand Colored, "American Septemtrionale-Etat De New York", Terrytown & Sing Sing, Framed, 15" x 18" $40.00
BARTLETT ENGRAVINGS (2), Hand Colored "View Of New York From Wee-hawken" & "The Ferry At Brooklyn, New York", Framed, 12" x 15" $50.00

(A-OH '77)   *Garth's Auctions, Inc.*
PINE BLANKET CHEST, On Frame, Dovetailed Const., Bear Trap Lock, Key & Strap Hinges, Orig. Rose Mulled Decor. W/ Floral Work & Initials "S.H." & "1828", 59" W., 25¾" D., 33¾" H. $520.00
OVOID STONEWARE JUG, Blue Slip Decor., Date "1840", Chip On Lid, 16¾" H. $70.00
STONEWARE CROCK, 3-Gal., Blue Painted Feather, One Handle W/Chip, 10¼" H. $40.00
IRON TRADE SIGN, Cut Out Horse, 31" Diam. $400.00
DOUBLE CALIPERS, Wrought Iron, 13" L. $90.00
BRANDING IRON, Wrought Iron, "Extra", 25" L. $12.50

(A-OH '77)   *Garth's Auctions, Inc.*
PINE WORK TABLE, Dovetailed Drawer, 2-Board Top, Refinished, 30" x 47" x 30" H. $250.00
WROUGHT IRON GOOSE NECK ANDIRONS, Pr., Spit Rests, 17" D., 17½" H. $65.00
STONEWARE CHURN, Bird In Cobalt Blue, Wooden Lid, Dasher Missing, 14½" H. $170.00
SHAKER ARM CHAIR ROCKER, #7 Size, Refinished, Old Repair To Arm Support, Woven Reed Seat $65.00
WOODEN DECOY, Black Duck By Jim MacIlhinny, Rockwood, Mich., Orig. Paint, 17" L. $55.00
WOODEN CUPBOARD, Orig. Red W/ Yellow & Black Striping, Interior W/Shelves Painted Black, 11" W., 6½" D., 17¼" H. $70.00
WOODEN DECOY, Black Duck By John Peterson, Houghten Lake, Worn Paint, 1 Glass Eye Missing, 15½" L. $55.00

(A-PA '77)   *Pennypacker Auction Centre*
BRIDE'S BONNET BOX, Bottom W/ Tulip Decor., Lid Decor. W/Tulips, Drape & Man & Lady, Inscribed In German "I Give My Heart To You" $975.00

(A-OH '77)   *Garth's Auctions, Inc.*
LADDER BACK SIDE CHAIR, Woven Paper Seat $20.00
PINE SCHOOL MASTER'S DESK, Dovetailed Drawer, Lift Lid, Compartment W/6 Drawers, Refinished Light Color, 27" W., 24" D., 38½" H. $180.00
TOLE LAMP, Red & Gilt Paint, Clear Ribbed Glass, Electrified, 19½" H. .$60.00
BRASS VICTORIAN CANDLESTICKS, Pr., 6" H. $62.50
CAST IRON PLANTERS (2), Smallest Pictured, "Faure Revie", 13¾" x 5½" H. & 16" L., 6" H. $50.00
LITHOGRAPH, Handcolored, "Winter Morning" By Palmer, 18¾" x 22¼" $55.00

(A-OH '77)   *Garth's Auctions, Inc.*
WINDSOR SIDE CHAIR $120.00
OAK SAWBUCK TABLE, Old Finish, 17½" x 36" x 27" H. $180.00
STAFFORDSHIRE PLATTER W/Well, Med. Blue Transfer, "Rural Scenery", Chipped Table Ring, 21" L. $42.50
TIN DOUBLE SPOUT LAMP, 8" Diam., 8" H. $105.00
PEWTER PITCHER, Acorn Finial, Cast Handle, Mkd. "H. Homan, 8", Soldered Repair At Hinge, 12¾" H. $110.00
PEWTER WHALE OIL LAMP, Brass Collar & Brass & Tin Double Spout Burner, Filling Hole, Mkd. "R. Gleason", Dents In Font, 9¾" H. $150.00
PEWTER BURNING FLUID LAMP, Small Hole In Font & Rabbit Ear Burners Damaged, 6¾" H. $75.00

(A-OH '77)   *Garth's Auctions, Inc.*

DOME TOP BOX, Pine, Orig. Blue-Gray Paint W/2 Willow Trees, 3 Diamonds & Initials "S.C.P." In Red, 26¾" W., 10¾" D., 10¼" H. $115.00

COFFIN STANDS, Pr., Unpainted Pine, 19" L., 22½" H. $35.00

TABLE TOP DESK, Pine, 6 Interior Drawers, Each Drawer Front Attached To Sides W/1 Lge. Dovetail, Orig. Brass Drop Hardware (1 Incomplete, 1 Missing), Fold Down Lid Missing, Base Molding Replaced, 25½" W., 16" D., 12¼" H. $650.00

COUNTRY CORNER CHAIR, New Rush Seat, Replaced Rung In Base, Repaired Back Rest, Old Black Paint .$800.00

BRASS CANDLESTICK, Drum Base, 5" Diam., 4⅜" H. $170.00

CARVED WOODEN SHORE BIRD, Wooden Beak, Orig. Black & White Paint W/Spots, Modern Wooden Stand, 9½" W., 13" H. $230.00

REDWARE JUG, Interlocking Circles Of Yellow Slip, Greenish Clear Glaze, Glaze Wear On Base & Lip, 6" H. $115.00

(A-OH '77)   *Garth's Auctions, Inc.*

TAVERN TABLE, Maple Base, 1-Board Pine Top Has Age Split, Refinished, 20½" x 29" x 24" H. $1100.00

BOW BACK WINDSOR ARM CHAIR, Seat Splits, Green Over White Worn Paint $495.00

CORK SHORE BIRDS, (5), Driftwood Base, Long Island Sandpipers, 1 Beak Missing, 1 Replaced, 16½" L., Tallest Bird - 11" H. $155.00

WATERCOLOR PAINTING, Farmstead, Repaired Paper, Modern Frame & Matt, 23¼" x 31¼" $515.00

(A-OH '77)   *Garth's Auctions, Inc.*

COUNTRY WORK TABLE, Pine Breadboard Top, Worn Red Paint On Base, 31½" x 49½" x 28" H. $200.00

LARGE SPLIT WOOD BASKET W/ Handles, Minor Damage, 25" Diam., 15½" H. $72.50

OVOID STONEWARE JUG, Mkd., "N. White, Utica", Chip On Lip & Base, 11¼" H. $40.00

LARGE COVERED TREEN BOX, Orig. Decor. W/Brown Sponging Over Yellow Ground, 12" Diam., 8½" H. $1125.00

STONEWARE JAR, Stenciled Decor. W/ Label "E.B. Taylor, Richmond, Va." 11" H. $37.50

HANDCOLORED ENGRAVING, By "W.H. Bartlett, 1838", New York Bay, Framed, 12" x 14¾" $20.00

PINE HANGING SHELF W/2 Drawers, Scalloped Back, Old Red Paint, 15½" W., 5¾" D., 27½" H. $195.00

COVERED TREEN BOX (Second Shelf), Orig. Decor. W/Brown Sponging Over Yellow Ground, Age Crack In Side, 4" Diam., 3¾" H. $135.00

COVERED TREEN BOX, (Third Shelf), Broken & Repaired, 4¼" H. $70.00

COVERED ROBIN Mounted On Bark Block (First Shelf), 20th C., 8½" H. $17.50

HANDCOLORED ENGRAVING By W.H. Bartlett, 1838, "Peekskill Landing" (Hudson River) Framed, 12" x 14¾" $20.00

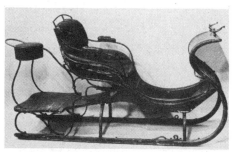

(A-OH '77)   *Garth's Auctions, Inc.*

CHILD'S PONY SLEIGH, Worn Black Lacquer Over Wood W/Brass Trim, Leather Tufted Upholstery Worn, 75" L. ..$300.00

(A-OH '77)   *Garth's Auctions, Inc.*

STONEWARE JUG, 2-Gal., Cobalt Slip Bird, Impressed "West Troy, N.Y. Pottery", Old Lip Flake, 14" H. $125.00

STONEWARE JAR, 3-Gal., 3 Cobalt Brushed Flowers In Cornucopia Container, Impressed "Edmands & Co.", Base Hairline, 13" H. $60.00

HUTCH TABLE, Mortised Stretcher Base, 3-Board Pine Top, Front Stretcher Broken & Reglued, Old But Not Orig. Red Paint, 44" x 53" x 28½" H. $750.00

STONEWARE JUG, 2-Gal., "2" In Brushed Cobalt, Impressed "West Troy, N.Y. Pottery", Hairlines & Chip On Lip, 14¼" H. $55.00

STONEWARE JAR, Brushed Cobalt Wild Flowers, Impressed "Ballard & Brothers, Burlington, Vt.", Rim & Handle Chip, 10½" H. $95.00

CHARCOAL & PASTEL DRAWING, Race Horse, "John Lackland, D.W. Smith", Minor Stains On Paper, Walnut Shadow Box Frame, 24" x 31" $160.00

(A-MA '77)   *Richard A. Bourne Co., Inc.*
(L to R)

EDISON STANDARD PHONOGRAPH, Oak Cabinet W/Horn & Arm For Holding Horn, 9 Edison Records, Crank Missing $150.00

EDISON PHONOGRAPH, "Amberola" Model, Quartered Oak Case, One Record, Working Condition $160.00

(A-OH '77)   *Garth's Auctions, Inc.*
DUMBWAITER, Mahogany, Revolving
Shelves, Repaired Splits In Bottom & Top
Tiers, Old Finish, 41" H. $350.00
HEPPLEWHITE SIDE CHAIRS, (1 of 4),
Mahogany, Triple Line Inlay On Top Rail,
Grey & Black Upholstery (worn on one
chair) $1700.00
SHEET BRASS CHAMBER STICK, In-
complete Push-Up, 6¼" x 6" x 4" .$20.00
TWO-PART MIRROR, Walnut & Mahog-
any, Reverse Painting Of Ship "Ariel", Re-
placed Reeded Corner Block, 11" x 23¼"
. . . .$105.00
OIL ON CANVAS PAINTING, Rebacked,
Unframed, 28¼" x 36¼" $300.00

To the right

(A-OH '77)   *Garth's Auctions, Inc.*
CAST IRON BOXER DOOR STOP, Orig.
Paint, 10" W., 9¾" H. $30.00
SIDE CHAIRS, Set Of 6, Orig. Brown
Paint W/Yellow Striping $450.00
PINE & POPLAR BEDSIDE STAND,
Orig. Graining In Imitation Of Curly Maple,
21½" x 22" x 31" H. $120.00
CARDBOARD BOX, Covered W/Floral
Wallpaper, Orig. Paper Label Inside Lid, 12"
Diam., 16" H. $40.00
CARVED WOODEN DECOY, Lesser
Scaup, Long Island, Glass Eyes, Orig. Paint,
11" L. $60.00
SEWER TILE LION, Hand Tooled, Initialed
"A.K.", 15" L., 9" H. $65.00
CHIP CARVED SPOON RACK, Wood
Very White, 16½" L. $65.00
PEWTER SPOONS, (2), 7¼" L. .$22.50
PEWTER SPOONS, (2), Continental
Touch Marks, 7" L. $24.50
PRINTED FRAKTUR, "Geburts un Tauf-
schein", 1841 Birth In Berks County Penn-
sylvania, Printed by "Peters", Harrisburg,
Pa., 16¾" x 19¾" $75.00

(A-OH '770   *Garth's Auctions, Inc.*
INDIAN COLLECTIBLES
(ROW I, L to R)
BASKET, So. Oregon Or Northern Calif.,
Tan, Brown & Black, 7" Diam., 5" H. . . . .
. . . .$145.00
GLASS BOTTLE, Indian Woven Cover,
Oregon, 12" H. $65.00
WOVEN HAT, Houpa Or Yarok, Sm.
Split In Rim, 7" Diam. $95.00
(ROW II, L to R)
POTTERY MUG, Black Designs On Red-
dish Clay, Chipped Base, 3¼" H. . .$17.50
BASKET, Woven Design Of Man & Ani-
mals, 8" Diam., 3" H. $35.00
COMB, Northwest Coast, Chip Carving,
Abalone Inlay, 9" H. $20.00
BASKET, Natural W/Green, Blue, Purple,
Yellow & Orange, Mikah, 4¾" Diam., 3" H.
. . . .$145.00
BASKET, Purple, Yellow & Drk. Blue,
Mikah, 4½" Diam. $55.00
(ROW III, L to R)
BASKET, Northern Calif. Or So. Oregon,
6¼" Diam., 4¼" H. $135.00
BASKET, Pima, 8" Diam., 2½" H. . . . . .
. . . .$125.00
BASKET, California Mission, 7½" Diam.,
4½" H. $150.00

(A-OH '77)   *Garth's Auctions, Inc.*
MAPLE TAVERN TABLE, Dovetailed
Drawer Has Curly Front & Orig. Iron Staple
Pull, 1-Board Pine Top, Refinished, 22" x
32½" x 27¼" H. $300.00
WROUGHT IRON ANDIRONS, Decora-
tive Scroll At Top, 17" D., 15½" H. $55.00
SHAKER LADDER BACK ROCKER,
Rush Seat, Side Rung W/Repaired Break .
. . . .$125.00
COPPER PITCHER, Wrought Copper
Handle, Dovetailed Const., 8½" H. . . . . . .
. . . .$55.00
PAUL REVERE TIN LANTERN, Punched
Design, Black, 15" H. $30.00
SAWTOOTH TRAMMEL, Wrought Iron,
Adjustable, 48" L. $40.00
SLAW CUTTER, Wooden, Old Red Stain,
Carved "1801", 19½" L. $95.00
INDIAN PRINT, Published By "Lehman
And Duval, 1854", Frame — 12½" x 16½"
. . . .$17.50
SAWTOOTH TRAMMEL, Wrought Iron,
Adjustable, 43" L. $32.50

(D-KY '78)
JOHN ROGERS GROUP, The Favored
Scholar $650.00

(A-OH '77)   *Garth's Acution, Inc.*
POPLAR DOME BOX, Green W/Black Edging & Yellow Striping Shows Red Beneath, Top W/Leaf Designs, Iron Lock & Hasp, 25" L., 13½" W., 13½" H. .$45.00
POPLAR JELLY CUPBOARD, 2 Dovetailed Drawers & Gallery, Orig. Graining In Red Over Yellow Ground, 44" W., 22" D., 52½" H. $245.00
NOAH'S ARK, Carved Wooden Animals (damaged), 22½" L., 9¼" H. $185.00
HOOKED RAG RUG, Black Dog W/ Red Ball & Collar, "Perky", Blue, White & Grey Background, 24" x 45" $150.00

(A-OH '77)   *Garth's Auctions, Inc.*
MAHOGANY CHIPPENDALE CHEST OF DRAWERS, English, 45½" W., 22" D., 36" H. $210.00
WOODEN DUCK DECOY, Old Paint, 12½" L. $52.50
WOODEN BOWL, 12½" Diam. ..$22.50
WOODEN DUCK DECOY, Feather Details, 13" L. $27.50
PEWTER CHARGERS, 16½" Diam. $310.00

(A-OH '77)   *Garth's Auctions, Inc.*
CHILD'S BENCH, Bootjack Ends, Pine W/Green Paint, 39½" W., 19½" H. $90.00
STONEWARE JAR, 3-Gal., "E.A. Montell, Olean, N.Y.", Cobalt Blue Decor, 10¾" H. $65.00
STONEWARE JAR, 3-Gal., "T. Reed", Cobalt Blue Decor., 11½" H. $195.00
STONEWARE JAR, 5-Gal., "5" In Cobalt Blue, 15½" H. $45.00
STONEWARE CANNING JAR, Cobalt Blue Decor., 9½" H. $70.00
STONEWARE BATTER PITCHER, 2-Gal., Cobalt Blue Decor., 13¾" H. $280.00
STONEWARE CANNING JAR, Cobalt Blue Shield, 9½" H. $50.00
OIL ON CANVAS, Indiana Farm, By Narcissa Lewis, 1882, Pine Frame, 27" x 34½" $220.00
PINE COOKIE BOARD, 15½" x 40" $70.00

(A-OH '77)   *Garth's Auctions, Inc.*
BLANKET CHEST, Poplar & Walnut W/ Drk. Orig. Grained Decor., Dovetailed Const., Back Of Lid Repaired At Hinge, 37" W., 18¼" D., 22" H. $110.00
STONEWARE BATTER PITCHER, 2-Gal., Impressed "E. Bishop, Near Burlington, Ohio", Blue Brushed Design At Spout, Chip & Hairlines At Top Edge, 13½" H. $75.00
CHILD'S WINDSOR CHAIR, Continuous Arm, Bar To Hold Child In Place, Pin Through Stretcher To Fasten In Hole In Floor, Worn Orig., Drk. Brown Paint, 19" H. $750.00
WOODEN BUCKET, Metal Bands, Stave Construction, Traces Of Paint, 8¼" Diam., 9½" H. $45.00
TALL POST BED, Pine W/Poplar Headboard, Orig. Rails, Refinished, 58½" x 80½" (outside measurements), 78" H. $950.00
THEOREM ON VELVET, Bird In Cage, Signed "Ellinger", 20th C., Framed, 21¼" x 23¼" $300.00

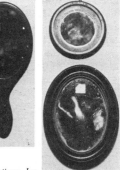

(A-OH '77)   *Garth's Auctions, Inc.*
COUNTRY CHEST, Pine W/Old Red Paint, Drawer In Cornice, Dovetailed Const., Back W/"March 23, Date 1789", & Name "_____ freman", Replaced Brasses, 35" W. At Case, 37½" W. At Cornice, 19" D., 46" H. $1500.00
WOODEN MORTAR & PESTLE, Burl Mortar, 7¼" D., 9" H. $185.00
BURL BOWL, 13½" Diam. $270.00
BURL BUTTER SCOOP, 8" L. .$205.00

(A-OH '77) *Garth Auctions, Inc.*
HAND MIRROR, Round Wooden Frame Cut From 1-Pc. Wood, Inset Mirror Each Side, Turned Handle, 5" Diam., 8¾" L. $62.50
HAND MIRROR, Molded Composition Frame, Patent Date "1878", 10¼" L. $10.00
ROUND HAND MIRROR, 1-Pc. Wood, 4½" Diam. $22.50
OVAL HAND MIRROR, Frame Cut From 1-Pc. Wood, 7¾" L. $27.50

(A-OH '77)   *Garth's Auctions, Inc.*
COUNTRY HEPPLEWHITE CANDLE-STAND, Cherry, Repaired Split On Top W/ Braces (Braces Missing), Leg Repaired, Refinished, 15" x 15¼" x 27½" H. .$250.00
ARROW BACK SIDE CHAIRS (Set of 6), Orig. Brown Paint W/Yellow Striping & Polychrome Floral Stenciled Crest, Minor Wear $570.00
ROCKINGHAM HOUND HANDLED PITCHER, Embossed Hunting Scenes, Spout Professionally Repaired, 11½" H. $150.00
SAMPLER ON HOMESPUN, Alphabets & Family Birth, Dated 1828 One Side; Rev: Family Death Record (None Listed) Poem & Scene Of Woman & Child In Garden, House & Flowers, Old Gilt Frame, 21½" x 27¼" $500.00

(A-OH '77)   *Garth's Auctions, Inc.*
PINE BENCH, Blue-Grey Paint, 58½" L., 14" W., 23" H. $105.00
STONEWARE JAR, 3-Gal., Ovoid, Chips & Crack, 13½" H. $20.00
TIN BAKING MOLD, Lamb, 13¼" L. $65.00
STONEWARE CROCK, 4-Gal., Brushed Cobalt Blue Design, Hairline & Repaired Hole, 14½" H. $105.00
TIN BAKING MOLD, Fish, 12¾" L. $25.00
BURL BOWL, 14" Diam., 6½" H. $175.00
STAVE CONSTRUCTED PAIL, Iron Bands, Wire Handle, Old Green Paint, 5½" Diam., 4½" H. $27.50
TIN FOOT WARMER, Slide Out Lamp, Single Spout Burner, 7¾" x 8½" x 3¾" H. $85.00
CIVIL WAR ENGRAVINGS, Pr., "Robert E. Lee", "Stonewall Jackson", 18' x 21" and 18½" x 21½" $85.00
LEAF SHAPE CUT-OUT, Gilt Frame, 8¾" x 10¾" $65.00

(D-MO '78)
WOODEN CORN SHUCKING PIN W/ Leather Thong, 5½" L. $12.00

 To the left

(A-OH '77)   *Garth's Auctions, Inc.*
HIGH BACK BED, W/Matching Stand, 2 Colors Graining In Imitation Of Burl W/ Tan & Yellow Striping & Free Hand Painted Roses & Other Flowers; Headboard W/Painting Of Sunset, Lake & Sail Boats, Orig. Decor. Rails, Bed Exterior Measurements: 56¾" x 76" x 85½" H.; Stand: 16" x 22" x 26½" H. $790.00
BRASS ANDIRONS, Pr., Polished, Repaired Spindles, Smaller Finials Replaced, 25" D., 25" H. $375.00
SHEET BRASS CANDLESTICKS, Pr., Insert Clamp, "Randell's Patent", 7¾" Diam...........................$95.00
CORN HUSK DOLL, Corn Silk Hair, Paper W/Doll's History To 1862, Glass Dome, 10½" H. $175.00

(A-OH '77)   *Garth's Auctions, Inc.*
CHILD'S WINDSOR ARM CHAIR, 2 Spindles Replaced On Back, Old Repair To Crest Rail, Refinished $90.00
PINE BLANKET CHEST, 6-Board, Old Green Paint, Till & 2 Drawers Under Till, Reset Hinges, 47½" W., 17½" D., 24¼" H. $115.00
WOVEN SPLIT WOOD BASKET, 11½" Diam., 3¾" H. $40.00
WOVEN SPLIT WOOD BASKET, 17" H. $30.00
WOODEN BASKET, Stave Const., 11" Diam., 10¾" H. $35.00
BIRD CAGE, Pine W/Wire Bars, Orig. Blue Paint, Minor Repair, 23½" W., 13" D., 21" H. $15.00
AMISH QUILT, Black W/Drk. Green, Blue, Purple & Lavender W/Pieced Baskets & 5 Kinds of Quilting, 69" x 95" $140.00

(A-VA '77)   *Laws Auction & Antiques*
ÉTAGÈRE, Resting On Brass Casters, 17" W., 17" D., 59" H. $600.00

(A-MA '77)   *Robert C. Eldred Co., Inc.*
CHINESE PORCELAIN AQUARIUM,
Enameled W/Jousting Scenes, Interior
Decor. W/Gold Fish, 12" H. $450.00
TEAKWOOD TABORET, Rouge Marble
Top, 32" H. $180.00
**CHINESE PORCELAIN GARDEN BAR-
RELS,** Pr., White Enameling On Blue
Ground, 12" H. $275.00

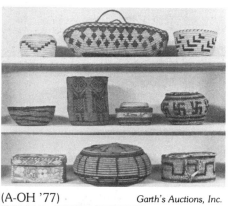

(A-OH '77)   *Garth's Auctions, Inc.*
INDIAN COLLECTIBLES
(ROW I, L to R)
COVERED BASKET, Hopi, Brown &
Ochre Geometric Design, 5½" Diam., 3½"
H. $20.00
BASKET, One Handle Reattached, 16" L.
................................$75.00
BASKET, Papago, Brown Geometric De-
sign, 6¼" Diam., 3½" H. $12.50
(ROW II, L to R)
WOVEN HAT, N.W. Coast, 6½" Diam. . .
................................$32.50
BASKET, N.W. Coast, Brown Figural Imag-
es, Edge Wear, 6" Diam., 7" H. . .$355.00
BASKET, W/Lid, Alaskan, Brown & Green
W/Image Of Boat, 5" L., 3" H. $35.00
BASKET, Grass Covered, Brown Swas-
tikas, 6¾" Diam., 4½" H. $37.50
(ROW III, L to R)
BIRCH BARK BOX, Decor. W/Poly-
chrome Quill Work, 3½" x 4¼" x 7½" . . .
................................$25.00
COVERED BASKET, Red, Black & Green
Design, 11½" Diam., 4½" H. $62.50
WOVEN BASKET, Grass Covered, Lid,
Handles Deteriorated, 8" L., 4" H. .$20.00

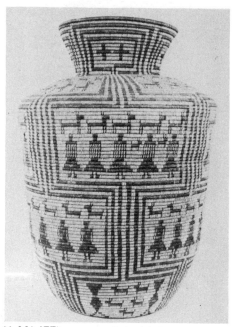

(A-MA '77)   *Richard A. Bourne Co., Inc.*
COILED BASKETRY VESSEL, Apache
Food Storage Basket, 18½" Diam., 26½"
H. $2400.00

A-OH '77)   *Garth's Auctions, Inc.*
INDIAN COLLECTIBLES
CONCHO BELT, 11 Pcs. Tooled Silver
Plus Buckle, Each Set W/Turquoise, 34" L.
................................$370.00
CLAM SHELL NECKLACE, 18" L. ....
................................$50.00
ARM BAND, Tooled Silver Set W/Tur-
quoise, 2½" x 3½" $55.00
SQUASH BLOSSOM NECKLACE, Sil-
ver Set W/Figured Turquoise $350.00
BRACELET, Silver W/Turquoise (Matches
Above Necklace) $85.00
SQUASH BLOSSOM NECKLACE, Sil-
ver Set W/Small Round Turquoise $375.00
SQUASH BLOSSOM NECKLACE, Sil-
ver, All Beads, Etc. Made From Liberty
Dimes $350.00
CONCHO BELT, 9 Pieces Tooled Silver
Plus Buckle, 36" L. $240.00
BEADED INDIAN LEATHER BELT,
Blue W/Red, Yellow & Black, 30½" L.
Plus Tying Straps $45.00

(A-MA '77)   *Richard A. Bourne Co., Inc.*
INDIAN DOLLS & RELATED ITEMS
(ROW I, L to R)
KACHINA DOLL, Hopi, Hand-Carved
Wooden Ceremonial Item Painted In Variety
Of Colors, Mkd. "Singer", Part Of Head-
dress Missing, 11" H. $110.00
KACHINA DOLL, Hopi, Hand-Carved
Wooden Ceremonial Item Painted In Variety
Of Colors, Foot Mkd. "Hair Dancer", 11" H.
................................$160.00
WOOD BLOCK, Made Into Kachina Doll,
10" H. $25.00
WOOD BLOCK, Made Into Kachina Doll,
8" H. $15.00
(ROW II, L to R)
AFRICAN BEADED FIGURE, Done
Over Bottle, Coils Of Red & White & Blue
Beads, 10" H. $5.00
PAPOOSE IN BABY BOARD, Deerskin
Covered Board Decor. W/Beads, Baby
W/Bead Features, Slightly Motheaten, 9" L.
................................$20.00
PAPOOSE IN CRADLE, Split Twigs Back-
board, Cloth, Baby W/Penciled-In Face,
Leather Motheaten, 10" L. $20.00
WOODEN ESKIMO FIGURE, Carved
Features & Painted Black Hair, Skin Jacket
& Hood, Arm Missing, Foot Broken Off,
7¼" H. $5.00

(A-OH '77)   *Garth's Auctions, Inc.*
WOODEN GRAIN CLEANER, Orig.
Red Paint W/Label "Eureka Mill, Pat'd
April 12, 1870, Cortrite, Norwalk, O.",
Incomplete, 60" W., 44" H. $40.00

(A-OH '77)   *Garth's Auctions, Inc.*

CANDLESTAND, Legs Repaired, 1 Foot Incomplete, Green Paint W/White Showing Wear, 11½" x 12" x 24" H. $130.00
CAST IRON GEORGE WASHINGTON ANDIRONS, Pr., Cast Initials "ESC DB VA", 15" H. $200.00
LADDER BACK SIDE CHAIR, Worn Split Wood Seat, Red Paint $35.00
REDWARE PLATE, 4-Line Yellow Slip Decor. W/Green, Clear Shiny Glaze, Coggled Edge, Unused, Minor Rim Flakes, 11½" Diam. $375.00
WOODEN COLLECTION BOX, Worn Green Velvet Lining, 5" x 9¼" x 22½" L. $40.00
KELLOGG PRINT, "George Washington" Paper Has Tears & Insect Damage, Flame Veneer Beveled Frame $15.00
PRINTED FRAKTUR, "Geburts and Taufschein", Printed By "Johann Sala Drider, Canton, Ohio", Never Colored Or Filled In, Modern Cherry Frame, 14" x 17". $10.00

(A-OH '77)   *Garth's Auctions, Inc.*

CURLY MAPLE SIDE CHAIRS, (1 of 4), Upholstered Seats $180.00
CHERRY BEDSIDE STAND, Cock-beaded Dovetailed Drawer, 1-Board Curly Maple Top Replaced & Drawer Bottom, 17" x 18" x 28½" H. $125.00
MAHOGANY HANGING BOX, Shaped Crest, Swivel Lid, 13½" H. $30.00
SILVER ON COPPER & BRASS COFFEE URN, Clambroth Glass Handles & Insert On Spigot Handle, Lid Marked "Burton Late Rippon & Burton, Oxford St.", Sm. Knob Missing From End Of Spigot, 18¾" H. $50.00
HANDCOLORED ENGRAVING, Paris, Published May 12, 1794 by Lauri & Whittle, No. 53 Fleet St. London, Frame: 17¾" x 25½" $35.00

(A-OH '77)   *Garth's Auctions, Inc.*

STONEWARE JUG, 3-Gal., Cobalt Blue "3" & Leaf, 16" H. $25.00
MAPLE CANDLESTAND, Feet Repaired, Refinished, 14" x 17" x 25¾" H. $165.00
WINDSOR SIDE CHAIR, Made Into Potty, Fold Down Door, Worn Red Paint $35.00
SHAVING MIRROR, Foot Broken & Re-glued, 12½" H., 7¾" W. $65.00
PENNSYLVANIA SHOW TOWEL, Red, Blue & Green W/Flowers, Birds, Deer & "Lidi Holi, 1814"; Cut Work Panel W/ Hearts, Birds & Stars, 16½" x 53" $110.00
PUNCHED TIN CANDLE SCONCES, 2 Similar, 10" x 10½" H. $50.00
FEDERAL MIRROR, Mahogany, Reverse Painting Of House, Old Mirror Glass, 16¼" x 31" $95.00

(A-MA '77)   *Julia's Auction Service*

TIN CANDLE MOLD, 48-Hole, One Tin Handle On Side Missing $135.00
TIN CANDLE MOLD, 36-Hole, Sq., Orig. & Complete $155.00
KNEEDING TROUGH TABLE, Amer., 17th-18th C., Dovetailed Drawer, 2-Board Top, Oak W/Pine Secondary, Top: 31" x 41½"; 32" H. $525.00

(A-PA '77)   *Brown Bros. Gallery*

CHIPPENDALE FRETWORK MIRROR, Mahogany, 19¾" H. $140.00
BRASS JELLY KETTLE, Signed "HB", 9" Diam. $40.00
STONEWARE CROCK, Grey, Blue Flowers & Leafage $55.00

(A-MA '77)   *Robert C. Eldred Co., Inc.*

IRON PARLOR STOVE, French, Ca. 1790-1800, Hoof-Foot Cabriole Legs, Brass Finials, 38" H. $350.00

(A-OH '78)   *Garth's Auctions, Inc.*
LADDERBACK ARM CHAIR ROCKER,
New Rush Seat, Minor Repairs, Refinished
. . . .$45.00
**WROUGHT IRON STATIONARY
BROILER,** Scrolled Iron Detail, 14" W. . .
. . . .$87.50
PINE BUCKET BENCH, Worn Red Paint,
38" W., 13½" D., 37½" H. $160.00
STONEWARE JUG, 3-Gal., Cobalt 3-
Headed Flower, Impressed Label "Leh-
man & Riedinger, Poughkeepsie, N.Y.",
Crows Foot In Base, 14" H. $60.00
STONEWARE CROCK, 3-Gal., Cobalt
Blue "3" & Quill Work, Rim Chip, 10¼"
H. $37.50
STONEWARE JUG, Impressed Label
"C.A.&E. Harrington, Druggist, Mass.',
14" H. $17.50
STONEWARE JUG, Impressed Label
"W.H. Jones & Co., 153 Blackstone St.,
Boston", Hairline, 11" H. $10.00
REDWARE JUG, Side Spout, Strap Han-
dle, Drk. Glaze, Chips, 10" H. $50.00
STONEWARE JUG, Cobalt Blue Flower,
Impressed "White's Utica", 12" H. .$25.00
STONEWARE BOTTLE, Hairline & Lip
Chip, 9½" H. $11.00
STONEWARE OVOID JUG, Mottled
Greenish-Brown Glaze, 9" H. $42.50
STONEWARE BOWL, Impressed Label
"A.L. Hyssong, Bloomsburg, Pa.", Hair-
lines, Repaired Rim Flakes, 11¼" Diam.,
5¾" H. $21.00
STONEWARE JUG, Stenciled Label
"Hyman Browarsky Wholesale Liquor
Dealer, No. 361, 5th Ave., Pittsburg, Pa.",
9" H. $27.50
STONEWARE BOTTLE, Paneled, 10" H.
. . . .$7.00
CURRIER & IVES PRINT, Small Folio,
"London From Kew Gardens", Framed,
12¼" x 15¼" $75.00

(D-NY '78)
YOST TYPEWRITER, 78 Keys, Made By
George Washington Newton Yost, Late
19th C. $250.00

(A-OH '78)   *Garth's Auctions, Inc.*
SIDE CHAIRS, (Set of 6), Plank Seats,
Refinished $570.00
STONEWARE JUG, 3-Gal., Impressed
" &L.P. Norton, Bennington, Vt.", Cobalt
Blue Hollyhock Flower, 15" H. $80.00
STONEWARE JUG, 2-Gal., Impressed
"J.E. Norton, Bennington, Vt.", Cobalt Slip
Flourish Design, Minor Lip Flakes .$105.00
POPLAR PIE SAFE, Tin In Doors & Sides
W/Stylized Flower Design, Punched W/
"1857", Replaced Hdwe., Refinished,
40½" W., 17½" D., 46¾" H. . . .$400.00
PIECED QUILT SQUARE, Green & Tan
Calico W/White, Modern Painted Frame,
15" x 15½" $7.50
STONEWARE FLASK, Minor Lip Rough-
ness, 6" H. $37.50
CURLY MAPLE BOWL, 19¼" Diam.,
6½" H. $275.00
IRON HOG SCRAPER CANDLESTICK,
W/Push Up, Thumbpiece Mkd. "Sargent
Birmm.", 7¼" H. $55.00

(A-OH '77)   *Garth's Auctions, Inc.*
COUNTRY SHERATON CUPBOARD,
Curly Maple, Birdseye Maple, Cherry &
Flame Grain Mahogany W/Pine Secondary
Wood, Dovetailed Drawers, Minor Veneer
Damage, 25" W., 24½" D., 36" H. . . . . . .
. . . .$375.00
GROTESQUE STONEWARE JUG,
Base Incised "Lanier Meaders", 20th C.
Folk Art, 8½" H. $85.00
HEPPLEWHITE CANDLESTAND, 1-
Board Top, Maple & Birch W/Drk. Varnish
Finish, Minor Repair, 15¾" x 18" $200.00
**DIAMOND MOLDED CHRISTMAS
LIGHTS** (6), Cranberry, Cobalt, Peacock
Blue (Edge Chips), Clear (Edge Chips),
Green & Drk. Amethyst (Edge Chips), 3¾"
H. $170.00
OIL ON CANVAS, Scene Of Castle By
Mountain Lake, Rebacked, Restored &
Cleaned, Gilt Frame, 22" x 28" . . .$35.00
N. CURRIER PRINT, Small Folio, "The
Fair Equestrian", Trimmed Margins, Pine
Frame, 12¼" x 16½" $85.00
CURRIER & IVES PRINT, Small Folio,
"A Home In The Wilderness", Trimmed
Margins, Pine Frame, 12½" x 16½" . . . . .
. . . .$185.00

◀ *To the left*

(A-OH '77)   *Stratford Auction Center*
BISQUE STATUE, W/3 Figures . .$55.00
GILDED TABLE $190.00
LAMP, Inverted Thumbprint Patt. .$80.00
FRAME $70.00
DRESDEN COMPOTE $180.00
CHERUB TORCHIERS, Brass & Copper
. . . .$300.00
MILK GLASS BANQUET LAMP, Enam-
eled, Embossed $90.00
SATIN GLASS BRIDE'S BASKET,
Cherub Base, Sandwich Wild Rose Bowl . .
. . . .$175.00
GONE WITH THE WIND LAMP, Em-
bossed & Gilded Rose Decor $120.00

(A-OH '77) · *Garth's Auctions, Inc.*

STONEWARE JUG, 4-Gal., Brushed Cobalt Blue Flowers, Impressed "Cowden & Wilcox, Harrisburg, Pa." $115.00
SPLIT WOOD BASKET, Woven W/ Wooden Handle, 22" Diam. $60.00
STONEWARE JAR, Ovoid, Incised Lines, Applied Handles, Brushed Cobalt Blue Decor., Impressed "J. Hamilton, Beaver", Rim & Handle Chips, 13½" H. ...$100.00
ROPE BED, Tall Posts, Orig. Side Rails, Old Red Paint, Minor Damage To Turnings, Outside Measurements: 53" x 75" $375.00
OIL ON BOARD PAINTING, Sleeping Baby W/Dog Drinking From Nursing Bottle, Framed, 19" x 22½" $195.00

(A-OH '77) *Garth's Auctions, Inc.*

TIN LANTERN, Removable Vent Finial, Wall Mounted, 2 Glass Panes Missing, Hinges Need Repair, Finial May Be Replacement, 28½" H. $90.00
PINE SETTLE BENCH, Mortised Corner Post Const., Storage Compartment Beneath Lid In Seat, Traces Red Stain, Refinished, 55" W., 19" D., 49½" H. $250.00
WROUGHT IRON REVOLVING BROILER, 22" L. $50.00
VICTORIAN CAST IRON FIRE BACK, 2 Hunting Dogs & Cattails In Relief, 21" x 27" $110.00
WROUGHT IRON BROILER, 19" L. ...
...............................$30.00

(A-OH '77) *Garth's Auctions, Inc.*

STONEWARE CROCK, 4-Gal., Impressed "Brady and Ryan,. Ellenville, N.Y.", Cobalt Bird On Stump, 11" H. $190.00
REDWARE COOLER, Tooled Rungs & Incised Horses Head, Hairline In Base, 14¼" H. $205.00
STONEWARE CROCK, 5-Gal., Incised Eagles W/Spear & Banner, Cobalt Blue Decor., 12" H. $85.00
WINDSOR SETTLE BENCH, Replaced Rocker, Refinished, 55½" L. $400.00
STONEWARE BUTTER CROCK, Covered, Brushed Blue Feather Designs, Chips Under Lid Flange, 8½" Diam. $165.00
STONEWARE CROCK, 3-Gal., Cobalt Decor., Minor Edge Chips, 10½" H
....................................$165.00
STONEWARE JUG, Impressed "Somerset Potters Works", Cobalt Slip Design, 11" H. $75.00
WOODEN FIREMAN'S AXES, Pr., Brownish-Red Paint W/Worn Striping & Gilt, 4" L. $105.00
CUT SILHOUETTE, Black & White Lithograph Background, Grained Frame, Signed "W.H. Brown", 12¼" x 16¼" ...$425.00

(D-MI '78)
EAGLE WATCH FOB, W/Clock Candy Container $45.00

(A-OH '77) *Garth's Auctions, Inc.*

CHILD'S SPINDLE BACK ARM CHAIR, Modern Black Paint, Woven Split Wood Seat $32.50
PINE SEAMAN'S CHEST, Dovetailed, Till, 3 Compartments, Strap Hinges, Old Red Paint Shows Black Beneath, 41" W., 15" D., 18" H..................$95.00
CAST IRON URN, 10½" H. $20.00
POPLAR BOX, Dovetailed, Orig. Brown Graining Over Light Colored Ground, Iron Lock & Hasp, Brass Escutcheon, 22" W., 10¾" D., 8½" H. $80.00
CAST IRON URN, 11¼" H. $25.00
MAHOGANY HANGING BOX, Replaced Hinges, Minor Lid Restoration, 8¾" W., 6" D., 14" H. $30.00
WROUGHT IRON BROILER, 21" L.
...............................$42.50
IRON CALIPERS, 31" L. $47.50
IRON MEASURING TOOL, 16" L. .....
...............................$40.00

(A-OH '77) *Garth's Auctions, Inc.*

EMPIRE CHEST OF DRAWERS, Paneled Cherry Ends & Top, Curly Maple Facade, Dovetailed Drawers, Knobs Replaced, Refinished, 46" W., 24" D., 46½" H.
...............................$460.00
CLEAR BLOWN JARS, (2), Patented "Aug. 14 & 30, 1886", Pontiled, Edge Chips, 12" H. $95.00
POPLAR DOME TOP TRUNK, Dovetailed, Iron Handles W/Lock W/Hasp, 24½" W., 13½" D., 11½" H. $65.00

(A-OH '77)   *Garth's Auctions, Inc.*
CHURN, Stave Constructed, Metal Bands, Lid & Dasher, Modern Green Paint, Churn 26½" H. $35.00
COUNTRY PINE CRADLE, Inset Rockers, Shaped Slats & Crest In Headboard, Worn Drk. Red Paint, 39" W., 20" D., 31½" H. $110.00
JACQUARD COVERLET, 2-Pc., Single Weave, Bird Border W/Signed Corner Blocks, "Packer, 1839", Blue, White, Mustard & 2 Shades Red, Fringe Replaced, 82" x 72" $95.00

(A-OH '77)   *Garth's Auctions, Inc.*
CAST IRON COFFEE GRINDER, Wooden Base, "Enterprise Mfg. Co., Philadelphia, Pa.", Tin Hopper, Red Alligatored Paint, Wheel: 24¾" Diam., 51¼" O.H. .$145.00
CAST IRON PARLOR STOVE, "Temple Parlor No. 4, Patented 1854, Vose & Co., Albany, New York", Top Ornament Incomplete, Base Cracked, 28" W., 19" D., 36" H. $335.00
SHEET METAL WEATHERVANE, Iron Standard, Bullet Holes, Aluminum Paint, 27" W., 55" O.H. $85.00

(A-OH '77)   *Garth's Auctions, Inc.*
BED NIGHT STAND, Dovetailed Drawer, Refinished Poplar & Birch, 19½" x 20" x 29" H. $85.00
TIN CANDLE MOLD, 12-Tube, 11" H. $115.00
BALLOON BACK SIDE CHAIRS, (1 of 4), Orig. Black Paint $180.00
ROCKINGHAM SEATED DOG, Minor Chips On Base, 11" H. $115.00
CURRIER & IVES PRINT, Small Folio, "My Little White Kittens Playing Domino", Trimmed Margins, Beveled Pine Frame, 12¼" x 16¼" $42.50
CURRIER & IVES PRINT, Small Folio, "My Little White Kitties Taking The Cake", Trimmed Margins, Beveled Pine Frame, 12" x 16" $40.00
OIL ON CANVAS PORTRAIT, Orig. Uncleaned Cond., 21½" x 25½" $180.00

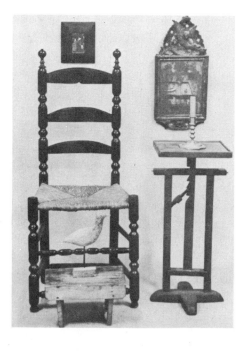

(A-OH '77)   *Garth's Auctions, Inc.*
COUNTRY SHERATON HUNT BOARD, Curly Maple & Pine, Dovetailed Drawers, Replaced Brasses, 45" W., 21" D., 36½" H. $2650.00
BURL BOWL, Rim Age Crack, 17" Diam., 7" H. $300.00
LIVERPOOL PITCHER, Blk. Transfer "Apotheosis" W/Washington Enthroned, Rev: Ship W/Amer. Flag; 9¾" H. $575.00
SAILOR'S DITTY BOX, Pine, Polychrome Flags & Shield, Blue Paint, 12¼" x 8½" x 7" $170.00
CARVED WOODEN RAM, 5½" H. $105.00
LIVERPOOL PITCHER, Blk. Transfer, "Commodore Preble", Rev: "Commodore Prebles Squadron Attacking City of Tripoli, Aug. 3, 1804", Base Chipped, 9¼" H. $550.00
TIN CANDLE SCONCES, Pr., Crimped Circle Top, 13" H. $165.00
BLUE & WHITE CHINTZ, "Andrew Jackson" & 6 Preceding Presidents, Unframed, 21¾" x 27½" $270.00

◄ *To the left*

(A-OH '77)   *Garth's Auctions, Inc.*
PINE FOOT STOOL, Blue Paint, One Leg Split, 7½" x 12¾" x 7" H. $15.00
SHORE BIRD, Redware, Beak Damaged, Incised "Hazel", 8" W., 11" H. . . .$60.00
LADDER BACK CHAIR, Old Black Paint $210.00
CANDLESTAND, Adjustable, Worn Red Paint, Adjusts to 28" H., Top-9¾" x 12" $985.00
BRASS CANDLESTICK, 5" H. . . .$57.00
PINE MIRROR, From 1-Pc. Wood, Black Paint, Glass Cracked, 6½" x 7½" $185.00
CAPE COD MIRROR, Crest Carved W/ Scrolls, Flowers, Fruit, & Bird, Orig. Polychrome & Gilt, Orig. Mirror, 10" x 22" $1350.00

(A-OH '77)   *Garth's Auctions, Inc.*
WROUGHT IRON ANDIRONS, Pr., 17" D., 19" H.................$45.00
CHERRY PIE SAFE, Dovetailed Drawers, 8 Punched Tin Panels - Pinwheel Design, Refinished, 40¾" W., 17¾" D., 46¼" H.
....$410.00
HITCHCOCK CHAIRS, Set of 7, 6 Sides & 1 Arm, Orig. Decor. Of Red & Black Graining W/Yellow Striping & Gold Stenciling, Rush Seats On 4, 3 W/Replaced Paper Rush........................$1190.00
DIVIDED KNIFE BOX, Exterior W/ Combed Graining In Brown & Yellow, Blue Interior, 12" x 9" x 4½" H.......$32.50
ZINC ROOSTER, Hollow Figure From Weathervane, Both Feet Missing, Damaged Leg, Worn Yellow Paint, Wooden Base, 19½" H.........................$250.00
WATERCOLOR ON PAPER, Opaque, Sailing Ship, Minor Paper Damage, Framed, 21½" x 22½"..................$55.00
PENCIL & WATERCOLOR DRAWING, Basket Of Flowers, Soft Colors, Old Gilt Frame, 13" x 16¼".............$95.00
WATERCOLOR ON PAPER THEOREM, Basket Of Flowers, Soft Colors, Paper Has Tears, Embossed Gilt Frame, 14" x 16"..
....$60.00

To the right ▶

(A-OH '77)   *Garth's Auctions, Inc.*
CURLY MAPLE DESK, Dovetailed Const., Interior W/8 Drawers, 8 Pigeon Holes, 2 Letter Drawers, Replaced Brasses & Hinges, Refinished 34¾" W., 18" D., 12½" Writing Ht., 40¾" H.................$2400.00
REDWARE DOG, Hollow, Clear Shiny Glaze W/Drk. Brown & Green, 6¾" H....
....$75.00
STONEWARE JAR, Impressed Decor. Of Stars, Braided Handles, Incised Lines, Rows Of Screw Heads & Hand Formed Bird Finial, Drk. Brown, Inside Lid Incised "Price 50 Cents", Minor Glaze Flakes, Beak Chipped, 9½" Diam., 11¼" H...$825.00
REDWARE DOG, Solid Moulded W/ Shiny Glaze, 7½" L.............$55.00

(A-OH '77)   *Garth's Auctions, Inc.*
CHERRY HEPPLEWHITE CHEST, Banded Inlay & Cockbeading On Frame, Dovetailed Drawers W/Line Inlay & Inlaid Ivory Shield Escutcheons, Replaced Brasses, Refinished, Minor Repair, 37" W., 19" D., 38" H.........................$925.00
BURL BOWL, 6" Diam., 2¼" H. $180.00
BURL BOWL, No Finish, 9½" Diam., 2½" H.......................$130.00
BURL BOWL, No Finish, 6¾" Diam., 2¾" H.......................$180.00
SMOOTHING BOARD, Carved "A.L." & Date "1711", 4¾" W., 26" L. .$290.00
OIL ON CANVAS PAINTING, Dr. Stephen Finch, Clyde, Ohio, Curly Maple Frame, 23½" x 28"...........$600.00

(A-OH '77)   *Garth's Auctions, Inc.*
CAST IRON DUCKS, Pr. (One Pictured), One W/Head Up, One Down, 6¾" H., & 11½" H.......................$180.00
PINE MULE CHEST, Lift Lid W/Till, Orig. Brown Graining Over Yellow Ground, 37" W., 17" D., 37¾" H............$525.00
WOODEN WHIRLYGIG, Dog Broken & Glued, Weathered Polychrome Paint, Figures 16½" H....................$20.00

(A-OH '77)   *Garth's Auctions, Inc.*
COUNTRY HEPPLEWHITE TEA TABLE, Cherry Base, Pine Top, 22" x 34½" x 27½".......................$775.00
STONEWARE CROCK, 3-Gal., Cobalt Blue Flowers, Impressed "J.E. Norton, Bennington, Vt.", 13¼" H.............$305.00
WINDSOR ARM CHAIR ROCKER, Iron Repair Holds One Arm In Seat, Refinished
....$300.00
BURL BOWL, Age Check In Side, Worn Finish, 9½" Diam., 3½" H......$155.00
IRON SQUIRREL WEATHERVANE, Worn Black Paint, Rusted Surface, Modern Metal Stand, 42" W., 35" H. $275.00
BURL BOWL, Refinished, 6¾" Diam., 3" H.........................$140.00

(A-OH '77)   *Garth's Auctions, Inc.*

STONEWARE OVOID JUG, 3-Gal., 2 Flowers In Brushed Cobalt Blue, Impressed "N. Clark & Co., Lyons", Base Chip $280.00

QUEEN ANNE DROP LEAF TABLE, Curly Maple, Swing Leg, Scrubbed Top, Minor Damage To Joint At End Of Leaves, 14" x 49" W/19" Leaves, 26½" H. $1850.00

STONEWARE CANNING JAR, Stenciled "Greensboro, Penn", Crack, 9½" H. $27.50

MINIATURE BLANKET CHEST, Orig. Graining In Curly Maple Imitation, 16½" W., 10" D., 11" H. $144.00

STONEWARE JUG, "J.W.Hoban, Waverly, N.Y." In Cobalt Slip, 11" H. . . .$60.00

HAND COLORED ENGRAVING, "My Little Pony, Published By B. Bramell, Philadelphia", Upper Edges Of Paper Deteriorated, Old Painted Frame, 8" x 9½" $25.00

FRAKTUR CERTIFICATE, Hand Drawn & Colored, Recording Birth In 1818 of Maria Mansz, Pine Frame W/Red Stripes, 11½" x 15¾" $700.00

HAND COLORED ENGRAVING, "My Little Pony, Published By B. Brammell, Philadelphia", Old Painted Frame, 8" x 9½" $40.00

(A-OH '77)   *Garth's Auctions, Inc.*

WOODEN STORAGE BOX, Orig. Red Paint W/Black Brushed Dots, 15" Diam. $30.00

STONEWARE BOWL, Impressed "Sipe, Nichols & Co., Williamsport, Pa.", Minor Damage, 10" Diam. $80.00

POPLAR DOUGH BOX, Breadboard Top, Traces Old Blue-Grey Paint, 20½" x 36" x 29" H. $115.00

WOODEN DECOY, Mallard Hen, Orig. Cond., Stamped "F.C." 19" L. . . .$110.00

WOODEN DECOY, Mallard Drake, Match To Hen, 18" L. $85.00

WROUGHT IRON PEEL, Ram's Horn Finial, 41" L. $55.00

WROUGHT IRON STATIONARY BROILER, 18" L. $50.00

WROUGHT IRON SPATULA, 18" L. $30.00

WROUGHT IRON FORK, Tooling, 20½" L. $20.00

WROUGHT IRON LADLE, 22" L. $20.00

WROUGHT IRON FIREPLACE TONGS, 28" L. $60.00

WROUGHT IRON PEEL, 41½" L. $35.00

(A-OH '77)   *Garth's Auctions, Inc.*

PINE COMMODE, 2 False Drawers, Top Lifts To Form Seat Back, Refinished, 25" W., 18" D., 29" H. $75.00

WALNUT TABLE, Drk. Varnish Finish, 15½" Diam., 10½" H. $27.50

TREEN COVERED BOX, Orig. Red Grained Decor., Yellow Ground, 11½" Diam., 12½" H. $900.00

HIDE COVERED TRUNK, Brass Studs, Iron Lock, Lined W/Polka Dot Wallpaper, Paper Label: "Robert Burr, Trunk Manufacturer, No. 9 Hanover Street, (nearly opposite the Shawnut House, Boston . . ."), Initialed "E.A.B." In Brass Studs, 12" x 7¾" x 5½" $20.00

HANGING PINE SHELVES, Refinished, Minor Repair, 21" W., 8½" D., 32" H. $85.00

BRASS MORTAR AND PESTLE, Polished, 4¾" Diam. $25.00

BRASS MORTAR AND PESTLE, Polished, 4¾" Diam. $40.00

FRAKTUR, Geburts & Taufschein, Decor. W/Tulips, Roses & Trumpeting Angels, Printed by "Johann Sala Druder, Canton, Ohio", Modern Cherry Frame, 14" x 17" $65.00

◄ *To the left*

(A-OH '77)   *Garth's Auctions, Inc.*

YARN WINDER, Wooden Strap Holding Reel Shaft Damaged, Reel: 26" Diam. $40.00

HUTCH TABLE, Birch & Pine, Drk. Finish, 40" Diam., 26" H. $750.00

STONEWARE CROCK, 2Gal., Impressed "West Troy Pottery", Cobalt Slip Bird, Painted Exterior, Cracks, 9½" H. . .$45.00

SHAKER BENTWOOD STORAGE BOX, Brown Varnish Finish, 13½" L. . . .$200.00

SHAKER BENTWOOD STORAGE BOX, Traces Old Red, 12" L. $275.00

SHAKER BENTWOOD STORAGE BOX, Worn Old Blue Paint, 9¾" L. $325.00

SHAKER BENTWOOD STORAGE BOX, Yellow Varnish, 9" L. $245.00

SHAKER BENTWOOD STORAGE BOX, Yellow Varnish, 7½" L. . . . .

(D-KS '78)   *Homestead Antiques*

OCTAGON SCREW CABINET, 72-Drawer, Sometimes Referred To As Hardware Store Nut & Bolt Cabinet . . .$650.00

(A-OH '77)   *Garth's Auctions, Inc.*
BIRCH HEPPLEWHITE STAND, Dovetailed Drawer, Legs & Drawer Striped W/Ink To Resemble Inlay, 18½" x 21" x 28" H. $190.00
HORSE PULL TOY, Wooden & Cloth Covered, 12½" L. $37.50
LADDER BACK ARM CHAIR, Woven Split Wood Seat, Old White Paint .$105.00
STONEWARE JAR, Impressed: "S. Bell & Son, Stras....", Chipped, 8¼" H. ..$22.50
WOVEN SPLIT WOOD BASKET, Hinged Lid, Wooden Handle, 12" H. 57.50
WALNUT BOOT JACK, 21" L. ..$15.00
WOODEN BOWL, Drk. Finish, 23" Diam. $75.00
TIN KEROSENE LAMP, Horizontal Font, Brass Burner, No Chimney, Worn Green Paint, 7" H. $22.50

(A-OH '77)   *Garth's Auctions, Inc.*
COUNTRY CHIPPENDALE RIBBON BACK SIDE CHAIRS, Pr., Old Red Paint, New Rush Seats $240.00
AMERICAN CANDLESTAND, Birch Base, Turned Ash Column, Pine Top, Refinished W/Traces Red Paint, Base Repaired Using Rose Head Nails, 18" Diam., 29½" H. $435.00
STONEWARE PITCHER, Brushed Blue Floral Designs, Rim Flake, 8" H. ..$195.00
MIRRORED TIN SCONCES, (4), Black Paint W/Minor Rust & Resoldering, Reflectors Are 7¾" Diam. $380.00
WATERCOLOR, Opaque On Brown Paper, Portrait Of Gentleman, Mounted On Masonite W/"Elder Henry C. Blinn, Canterbury, N.H. Shakers" On Back, Grained Frame, Minor Repairs To Background, 12½" x 28¾" $900.00

To the right
LADDER BACK SIDE CHAIR, New Rush Seat, Top Slat Replaced, Traced Old Red Paint $220.00
PINE FOOTSTOOL, Worn Green Paint, 7½" x 18" x 7¼" H. $60.00
WILLIAM & MARY BLANKET CHEST ON FRAME, Pine W/Orig. Red & Black Paint, Two Face Drawers W/Lift Top & Staple Hinges, Base Frame Restored, Replaced Drop Brasses & Escutcheons, 39½" W., 20½" D., 46½" H. $500.00
CARVED WOODEN SHORE BIRD, Orig. Black & White Paint W/Black Dots, Minor Repair, 10" W., 12¼" H. ...$85.00
PINE TABLE TOP WRITING BOX, Dovetailed, Staple Hinges, 2 Interior Drawers, Worn Red Paint W/Black Beneath, 20½" W., 12¾" D., 9¾" H. $425.00
CARVED WOODEN SHORE BIRD, Pale Green Paint W/Whittled Wooden Beak & Rod, 9" W., 16" H. $75.00
CARVED WOODEN SLEEPER DECOY, Drk. Color W/Traces Paint, 13¼" L. .....
..................................$165.00

OIL ON WOODEN PANEL PORTRAIT, Young Girl In Red, 15" x 18" $450.00

(A-OH '77)   *Garth's Auctions, Inc.*
BALLOON BACK SIDE CHAIRS (Set Of 6), Orig. Painted Decor. W/Yellow & Cream Colored Striping On Brown Ground, Hand Painted Flowers & Fruit On Crest, Splat & Seat Front, Signed "DeLong, Topton" $840.00
CORNER WASH STAND, Dovetailed Drawer & Gallery, Orig. Yellow Paint W/Tan & Black Striping, Vinegar Graining On Gallery & Top & Floral & Fruit Painting On Drawer Front, Drawer Knob Replaced, Top Replaced But Gallery Orig., 21½" W., 15" D., 39¾" H. $195.00
MOCHA PITCHER, Blue & Grey-Blue Bands W/Black Stripes, Minor Hairline Damage, 7¼" H. $85.00
WATERCOLOR, Urn Of Flowers, Paper Darkened /Age, Minor Damage Spots On Bottom Edge, Framed, 19" x 21" ..$35.00
THEOREM ON VELVET, Strawberries, Grapes & Peaches, Old Gilt Frame, 9¼" x 12" $95.00
THEOREM ON VELVET, Cherries, Plums, Pear & Peach, Old Gilt Frame, 9¼" x 11½" $100.00

(A-OH '77)   *Garth's Auctions, Inc.*
EMPIRE BUTLER'S DESK, Cherry W/Birdseye Maple Drawer Fronts, Cockbeaded Drawers W/Replaced Brasses, 46" W., 21½" D., 40" H. $400.00
BRASS VICTORIAN CANDLESTICKS, Pr., W/Pushups, 8¾" H. $65.00
CHERRY BOX, Dovetailed, Interior Locking Compartment, 11" x 19" x 7¼" .....
..................................$65.00

◄

(A-OH '77)   *Garth's Auctions, Inc.*

COUNTRY EMPIRE SIDE CHAIRS,
(4), Orig. Black Paint W/Yellow & Gold
Striping & Stenciled Foliage & Musical In-
struments W/Eagle, Worn Paint, Not Exact
Match $140.00
DRESSING TABLE, Dovetailed Drawers,
Orig. Yellow W/Striping In Black & Olive
Green, Stenciling, Orig. Embossed Brass
Knobs (1 Incomplete), 32½" W., 15¼" D.,
38½" H. $250.00
WOODEN DECOY, Canada Goose, Old
Working Repaint, 25½" L. $105.00
BRASS CANDLESTICKS, Pr., Bell-Like
Bases, Polished, 1 W/Repaired Lip, 9½" H.
.................................$95.00
WOODEN DECOY, Shorebird, Worn
Black Paint W/Yellow & White, 9" H. ....
.................................$65.00
OIL ON CANVAS PAINTING, "Coul-
ters Mill", Signed "M. Coulter", Masonite
Backing W/Minor Flaking, Walnut Frame,
17½" x 35½" $140.00

**MAHOGANY CHIPPENDALE CHEST
OF DRAWERS,** Dovetailed Drawers, Re-
placed Brasses $370.00
BRASS MID-DRIP CANDLESTICK,
9¾" H. $85.00
PINE DOME TOP BOX, Rose Head Nails,
Covered W/Worn Blue, Wallpaper, Lined
W/Mass. Newspaper Dated 1836, Staple
Hinges, 14" W., 7" D., 7¾" H. ...$55.00
**IRON & BRASS KETTLE GREASE
LAMP,** Wick Support, Base Is 5¾" D.,
8½" H. $215.00
OIL ON CANVAS PAINTING, Orig.
Cond., Back W/Inscription, "Painted For
Mrs. Lydia C. Bowher, Aged 24, By J. G.
Chandler, July 1846", Old Gilt Frame,
29½" x 34¾" $360.00

To the right

BOW BACK WINDSOR ARM CHAIR,
Minor Repairs, Old Mellow Finish ....
.................................$625.00
CHERRY CANDLESTAND, Alligatored
Varnish Finish, Repaired Split In Top & To
Base Where Legs Join, 16" Sq., 25" H. ..
.................................$400.00
BRASS CANDLESTICK, Small Hole In
Base, 6½" H. $95.00
**CLEAR RIBBED BURNING FLUID
LAMP,** Made In 3-Part Mold, Pewter Collar
& Double Spout Burner, Snuffers Missing,
5¼" H. $40.00
HOLLOW CUT SILHOUETTE, 'Rebec-
ca Jones, Drawn By Sarah Hustler At Under-
cliff From Her Shadow, 1787", Minor Dam-
age To Paper, Birdseye Frame, 14" x 19½"
.................................$190.00
WROUGHT IRON FORK, 29" L. ......
.................................$47.50
MAHOGANY CANDLE BOX, Dovetailed,
Sliding Raised Panel Lid, Old Finish, 23" H.
.................................$150.00
WROUGHT IRON WHATSIT, 18¼" L.
.................................$15.00

BOW BACK WINDSOR SIDE CHAIR,
Old Drk. Finish $220.00
HEPPLEWHITE BEDSIDE STAND,
Cherry $165.00
FOOTSTOOL, Traces Red Paint, 8½"
Diam. $12.50
WOODEN BOWL, 16" Diam. $32.50
BOW BACK WINDSOR SIDE CHAIR,
Worn, Alligatored Black Paint $100.00
OIL ON WOODEN PANEL, Dog, Signed
"W.A. Long", 8¼" x 11½" $27.50
SAMPLER, On Homespun, Alphabets &
"Ellen Clark, Age 12, Lehigh Co., 1826",
Framed, 11¼" x 16½" $185.00
WOODEN COMB BOX, Red, Gold &
Yellow Striping On Black Ground, 9" W., 7"
H. $17.50

PLANK SEAT SIDE CHAIRS, Set of 6,
Orig. Decor. Of Brown Feather Graining
W/White Striping & White & Tan Leaf-Like
Painting On Crests, Free Hand Painted Roses
In Red, White & Green $660.00
PINE STAND, 1-Drawer, Orig. Black
Decor. Over Red Ground, 25" x 24" x 29"
H. $250.00
BLOWN DEMIJOHN, Green, 21" H. ...
.................................$85.00
TOLE CANISTER, Black Ground, Fruit &
Flower Decor., 8½" H. $120.00
TOLE DOCUMENT BOX, Drk. Brown Ja-
panning W/Floral Front In Red, Yellow,
Green & White, Minor Wear, 9¾" x 7½" x
5¾" $500.00
THEOREM ON VELVET, Brown, Gold,
Blue & Green Flowers In Basket, Mahogany
On Pine Frame, Minor Repaired Veneer,
15¾" x 20¾' $160.00
WATERCOLOR ON PAPER, Basket Of
Flowers, Yellow, Blue, Brown & Green, Old
Gilt Frame, 13" x 16½" $220.00

(A-OH '77)   *Garth's Auctions, Inc.*

MAHOGANY HEPPLEWHITE CANDLESTAND, Tilt-Top, Grained Veneer & Cross Banding, Refinished, Base Repairs, 18" x 24½" x 28" H. $395.00
WINDSOR SIDE CHAIR, Extensive Restoration $110.00
PULL TOY HORSE, Wood & Composition, Replaced Ears, Tail & Mane, 7" L., 9" H. $27.50
ENGLISH TEA CADDY, Mahogany On Pine W/Ebony, Cross Banded Rosewood, 4½" x 5" x 8" $65.00
HANDCOLORED AUDUBON LITHOGRAPH, "Common American Shrew Mole", By "J.T. Bowen, Phila., 1843", Walnut Frame, 26¾" x 31¾" $120.00

(A-OH '77)   *Garth's Auctions, Inc.*

BANISTER BACK ARM CHAIR, Replaced Rush Seat, Worn Drk. Paint, Minor Repair $725.00
WOODEN DECOY, Scaup, Michigan, Paint Wear, 14½" H. $45.00
CANDLESTAND, Pine Top, Refinished, 14" x 16", 26½" H. $110.00
SHEET IRON ROOSTER WEATHERVANE, Tail W/Riveted Feathers, Barn Red W/Rust, Modern Stand, 37½" O.H. $350.00

(A-OH '77)   *Garth's Auctions, Inc.*

WINDSOR ARM CHAIR, Hole In Seat Plugged, Old Finish, Repaired Base $375.00
TOLE FOOT WARMER, Black Ground, Gold Stenciled Decor., Lid Has Wooden Frame, Int. Container For Charcoal, 7¾" Sq., 6" H. $75.00
BUCKET BENCH, Worn Green Paint, 13½" x 29" x 24¼" H. $90.00
SEWER TILE CHICKEN WATERER, Chipped, 12" Diam., 17" H. $20.00
STONEWARE BIRD FEEDER, Green Metallic Glaze, 8" H. $30.00
REDWARE COLANDER, 3 Feet & Handle, Tooled Lines & Zig-Zag, 8½" Diam. $85.00
STONEWARE BOTTLE, Impressed "J. Newton & Co., California Pop", Green Alligatored Glaze, 10" H. $35.00
FRAKTUR BIRTH CERTIFICATE, Rabel Haas In 1837, Berks County, Pennsylvania, Mahogany On Pine Frame, 10½" x 12½" $300.00
WATERCOLOR, Flowers, Frame: 6" x 7" $65.00
BLACK & WHITE CHARCOAL ON SANDPAPER, Ohio River, 17¼" x 22½" $35.00

(A-OH '77)   *Garth's Auctions, Inc.*

SIDE CHAIRS, (Set of 6), Orig. Drk. Brown Paint W/Yellow Striping & Free Hand Floral Decor., Minor Repair $510.00
CAST IRON HESSIAN SOLDIER AND-IRONS, Pr., 20th C., 20" H. $45.00
SPLIT WOOD BASKET, Wooden Handles, 23" L. $40.00
FIREPLACE MANTLE, Grained, Brown Over Yellow, Minor Wear, Wood Chipped, 46½" W., 7" D., 49½" H. $45.00
BLACK & WHITE ENGRAVING, "Rufus Putnam", Walnut Cross Corner Frame, 10" x 12" $20.00
WOODEN DECOY, Canvas Back Sleeper, Michigan, 16" L. $60.00
WOODEN BUGLE, Metal Repair, Peeling Red & Yellow Paint, 9½" H. $45.00
WOODEN DECOY, Bobtail Hen Redhead, Michigan, Paint Worn, 15" L. $50.00
N. CURRIER PRINT, "Married", Small Folio, Framed 13½" x 16¼" $45.00
OIL ON CANVAS PAINTING, Blacksmith, Unframed, New Stretcher, 21" x 45" $125.00

◄ *To the left*

(A-OH '77)   *Garth's Auctions, Inc.*

CHERRY CANDLESTAND, Varnish Finish, 17¼" Diam., 26" H. $400.00
WINDSOR ARM CHAIR, Seat W/Repaired Split, Green Paint $600.00
WOODEN DECOY, Bluebill Drake, C. 1890, Working Repaint, Neck Split, 13" L. $35.00
WOODEN DECOY, Old Squaw Drake, Maine, Wood Splits, 10" L. $45.00
POPLAR CANDLE BOX, Red Paint, 5¾" x 6" x 13" $70.00
HOOKED RAG RUG, Folk Art Scene, Red & Black Border W/Grey, Brown, Tan & White, Unused, 33" x 40" $255.00

(A-OH '77)   *Garth's Auctions, Inc.*
ROCKING CHAIR, Plank Seat, Refinished $135.00
CURLY MAPLE BEDSIDE STAND, Dovetailed Drawer, 1-Board Top, Refinished, 17½" x 19½" x 29" H. . . .$245.00
FOOT STOOL, Refinished, 8½" x 14" $17.50
STUDENT LAMP, Burners Mkd. "B.H. Duplex", Polished, Electrified, Canary Shades Cased In White, Replaced Brass Shade Supports, 20" O.H. $395.00
CURRIER & IVES PRINT, "No You Don't", Trimmed Margins, Pine Frame, 12½" x 16½" $35.00
CURRIER & IVES PRINT, "Paddy Murphy's Jantin Car", Trimmed Margins, Pine Frame, 13½" x 18" $65.00

(A-OH '77)   *Garth's Auctions, Inc.*
MAHOGANY HIGH CHAIR, Removable Base, Caned Back & Seat, Hole In Seat, Back Rail Has Break W/Piece Missing, Rail Is Dowel Replacement, 35½" H. .$110.00
COUNTRY BIRCH TILT TOP TABLE, Restored, 20" x 24" x 28" H. $130.00
MAHOGANY HIGH CHAIR, Orig., Retaining Rail, 36" H. $160.00
BOWL & PITCHER, Blue Transfer Of Boating Scenes, Impressed "Cauldon", 15¾" Diam., 11½" H. $125.00
OIL ON BOARD PAINTING, Wind-Swept Beach Scene, Signed "N.A. Knopf", Framed, 18" x 22" $185.00
OIL ON BOARD PAINTING, Rocky Maine Coast Scene, Signed "N.A. Knopf", 14¼" x 16¼" $55.00

(A-OH '78)   *Garth's Auctions, Inc.*
ARROW BACK SIDE CHAIR, Orig. Painted Yellow Decor. On Drk. Brown Ground, Free Hand Shell Painted On Crest, 1 Broken Arrow Slat $75.00
CHILD'S ARM CHAIR ROCKER, Woven Split Wood Seat $100.00
BIRCH COUNTRY HEPPLEWHITE PEMBROKE TABLE, Traces Red Paint, Minor Side Damage, 15½" x 42¼" W/10" Leaves, 28" H. $425.00
COMPOSITION PEACOCKS, Pr., Tin Tails, Wire Feet, White W/Green, Yellow & Black, Minor Damage, 9¼" H. $20.00
WOODEN MODEL, 3-Masted Sailing Vessel, Cloth Sails, Green, Black & White Paint, Signed "Built By Wm. J. Howard, Boston Light, Mass.", Minor Repair Needed, 35½" L., 27½" H. $310.00
DRAWING, Compote of Fruit, Pencil, Charcoal & Watercolor, Black Molded Frame, 14" x 17½" $65.00

To the right

(A-OH '77)   *Garth's Auctions, Inc.*
PINE DRESSING TABLE, Dovetailed Drawer, Orig. Yellow Paint W/Tan & Black Striping & Stenciled Fruit In Green & Black, 32¼" W., 15½" D., 37" H. $195.00
PINE FOOTSTOOL, Legs Mortised Through Top, Side Apron W/Edge Bead, Worn Grey Paint Shows Blue Beneath, 8¾" x 15¾" x 7¾" H. $45.00
WINDSOR ARM CHAIR ROCKER, Worn Black Paint Shows Yellow Beneath $140.00
COMPOTE, Clear, Flint, "Loop Pattern", 11¼" Diam., 7¼" H. $95.00
LITHOGRAPH, Hand Colored Indian Print By "Lehman & Duval, 1825", Minor Stains On Paper & Tear, 19" x 23½" $45.00
WATERCOLOR PORTRAIT, Full Length Of Young Woman In Turquoise & Black Dress Seated On Empire Sofa, Faded Colors, Rosewood On Mahogany Frame, 10" x 11½" $65.00

(A-OH '77)   *Garth's Auctions, Inc.*
(ROW I, L to R)
YELLOW WARE CANNING JAR, Hairline In Rim, 6¾" H. $27.50
SEWER TILE SHAVING MUG, Incised Intersecting Lines, 4" H. $35.00
ROCKINGHAM PITCHER, Embossed Flowers, Minor Chip On Spout, 8" H. $22.50
REDWARE JUG, Drk. Glaze, Chipped Handle, 7¼" H. $52.50
(ROW II, L to R)
TIN RABBIT CHOCOLATE MOLD, "Made In Germany", 8¼" H. $22.50
CAST IRON SEWING AID CLAMP, Dolphin Shape, 7" O.H. $70.00
CAST BRASS SEWING BIRD, Pin Cushion, 5" O.H. $45.00
CAST IRON DOOR KNOCKER, Wooden Base, 7" H. $20.00
TIN FISH BAKING MOLD, "Made In Germany", 10¾" L. $10.00
(ROW III, L to R)
CHICKEN PIP-SQUEAK, 6½" H. $30.00
WOODEN WHIMSEY TOY, No Finish, 11½" L. $17.50
CAST IRON DOOR STOP, Worn Polychrome, 4¾" H. $22.50

◄

(A-OH '77)   *Garth's Auctions, Inc.*
PLANK SEAT CHAIR, (Set of 4), Drk. Brown Varnish Finish $80.00
HUTCH TABLE, Base Compartment, Refinished, 28" x 45" x 28¾" H. ...$260.00
WOODEN DECOY, Canvas Back Hen, "Goulette", Michigan, 16¼" L. $20.00
WOODEN DECOY, Canvas Back Drake, Mate To Above, 16¼" L. $17.50
WOODEN DECOY, Redhead Drake, "Goulette" $30.00
WOODEN DECOY, Canvas Back Hen, Michigan, 15" L. $25.00
HANDCOLORED LITHOGRAPH, Lge. Folio, "New Bedford Fifty Years Ago", Grained Frame, Glued At Base Of Print, 21¾" x 28" $130.00
CURRIER & IVES LITHOGRAPH, Sm. Folio, "Rye and Rock", Trimmed Margins, Walnut Frame, 13" x 15½" $35.00

(A-OH '77)   *Garth's Auctions, Inc.*
STONEWARE JAR, Ovoid, Impressed "G. Brayton, Utica", Blue Design, 13¾" H. $85.00
BALLOON BACK CHAIRS, (1 of 6), Orange-Tan Ground W/Yellow Striping, 5 Orig. Cond., 1 Repainted $600.00
BIRCH CANDLESTAND, Repaired Base, Refinished, 15" x 16" x 27½" H. $210.00
CAST IRON MECHANICAL BANK, "Dark Town Battery", Orig. Paint W/ Minor Wear, Replaced Coin Compartment Cover, 10" L., 7" H. $360.00
WOVEN SPLIT WOOD CHEESE STRAINER, 16" Diam. $165.00
CARVED EAGLE CLOCK SHELF, Oak, 20½" W., 9½" D., 22" H. $125.00

(A-OH '78)   *Garth's Auctions, Inc.*
PINE COUNTRY HEPPLEWHITE TAVERN TABLE, Cut-Out Ovolo Corners On Top, Orig. Red Paint On Base, Old Green Paint On Top, Initialed "DN", Dated "1799", 19½" x 29½" x 25" H. .$475.00
CARVED WOODEN DECOY, Mallard, Worn Paint, 17" L. $135.00
WINDSOR SIDE CHAIRS, (Set of 4), Refinished $760.00
PINE DOLL CRADLE, 11" L. ...$35.00
TOLE TRAY, Drk. Brown Japanned Ground W/Yellow, Red, Green & White Floral Decor., Minor Wear, 2¾" x 7¾" x 12½" $160.00
PAPIER MACHE ROOSTER PIPSQUEAK, Orig. Ochre, Black, Red & White Paint, Repairs, 8" H. $40.00
NEEDLEWORK ON LINEN, Lady In Garden, Gold, Brown, Green, Tan & Cream Colors, Mkd. "Tuesday Morning May 31st, 18 __", Modern Frame, 17½" x 20" .....
........................$320.00
NEEDLEWORK ON SILK MEMORIAL, "Sacred To The Memory Of Sally Quincy Who Died 1821", Gilt Frame, Minor Wear, 14¼" x 19¼" $250.00

(A-OH '77)   *Garth's Auctions, Inc.*

(A-OH '77)   *Garth's Auctions, Inc.*
PINE FOOTSTOOL, Cut-Out Feet, Wide Side Aprons, Old Green Paint W/Drk. Red Beneath, Repaired Leg, 6½" x 13¼" x 7¼" H. $27.50
CARVED WOODEN SHORE BIRD, Tack Eyes, 1-Pc. Wood, Buckshot Holes, Black Paint, 10" W., 10½" H. $95.00
LADDER BACK ARM CHAIR, Woven Split Wood Seat W/Olive Linsey Woolsey Cushion, Several Layers Worn Paint - Predominantly Brown $475.00
CASKET SUPPORTS, Pr., 17" L., 15" H. $10.00
PINE BIBLE BOX, Rose Head Nails, Chip Carved Facade W/4 Houses W/Arched Doorways & Figure Of Man, Staple Hinges Replaced W/Iron Hinges, 17" x 11½" x 7½" $210.00
PINE BOX, Top Of Lid W/Chip Carved Hearts & Circles, Old Leather Hinges, 6¼" x 6½" x 12" $45.00
PRINTED FRAKTUR CERTIFICATE, House Blessing, Hand Colored, Paper Damaged, Old Frame W/Modern Painted Decor., 14¾" x 18½" $45.00

To the left
BANISTER BACK SIDE CHAIR, New Rush Seat, Worn Black Paint Shows Several Colors Beneath $160.00
MAPLE QUEEN ANNE LOWBOY, Dovetailed Drawers, Orig. Brasses, Refinished & Top Replaced, 19½" x 30½" x 27½" H. .
.............................$700.00
IRONSTONE PLATTER W/WELL, Black Transfer "Cleopatra" W/Polychrome Enamel, 21" L. $65.00
VICTORIAN BRASS CANDLESTICKS, Pr., Pushups, Polished, 9¾" H. ...$65.00
STAFFORDSHIRE BOWL, Black Transfer Seafaring Scenes, Polychrome Enamel, Hairlines, Minor Wear, Rim Repair, Impressed Mark W/Anchor, 12" Diam., 4½" H. $55.00
ORIENTAL REVERSE PAINTING ON GLASS, Tinsel Backing, Framed, 19" x 27" $55.00
ORIENTAL TABLE SCREEN, Carved Red Lacquer Landscape Scene & Seascape Scene, Damage To Lacquer, 25" W., 27" H. $75.00

(A-OH '78)   *Garth's Auctions, Inc.*
BIRCH WORK TABLE, Mortised Stretcher, Replaced Pine Top, 72" x 22½" W/10" Leaves, 28¾" H. $1075.00
WOVEN SPLIT WOOD & REED BASKET, Wooden Handles, 22" x 33" x 11" H.
. . . .$60.00
STONEWARE COOLER, Brown Bands & Cobalt Brushed Floral Designs, 21¼" H. . .
. . . .$145.00
WOODEN DECOY, Old Working Repaint, 18" L. $37.50
WOODEN DECOY, Swing Lead Weight Keel, Branded "L.F.B.", Worn Paint, 15½" L. $47.50
STONEWARE COOLER, Brown Bands & Cobalt Brushed Floral Designs, 21¼" H. . .
. . . .$190.00
PINE WALL POCKET, Repaired, 18" W., 15½" H. $50.00

(A-OH '77)   *Garth's Auctions, Inc.*
CHERRY DROP LEAF TABLE, Leaves & Top 1-Board, Refinished, Minor Repairs, 20¼" x 46" /20" Leaves, 30" H. . . . .
. . . .$250.00
STONEWARE SPITTOON, Floral Brush Cobalt Decor., Hairline Cracks & Chips, 7½" Diam. $37.50
CAST IRON & BRASS CANDLEHOLDER, From Calliope Pipes, 11" L., 8" H. . .
. . . .$27.50
COPPER TEA KETTLE, Dovetailed Seams, White Opaque Glass Handle, 9¾" H. . . . .
. . . .$80.00
CURRIER & IVES PRINT, "The Little Brothers", Pine Frame, 13½" x 17½" . . . . .
. . . .$55.00
CURRIER & IVES PRINT, "Little Brother & Sister", Pine & Maple Frame, 13" x 16¼" $35.00
CURRIER & IVES PRINT, "The Little Sisters", Pine Frame, 13½" x 17½" . . . . . .
. . . .$57.50

(A-OH '77)   *Garth's Auctions, Inc.*
ENGLISH MAHOGANY GEORGE II TEA TABLE, Swing Leg, 2 Swing Out Hinged Drawers In Apron, Refinished, Opens To 27½" Diam., 28" H. $1025.00
SATIN WOOD TEA CADDY, Inlaid Banding, 2 Lidded Lift Out Compartments, Minor Inlay Repair Necessary, Removable Splay Leg Stand, Box - 12" x 6" x 6½"; Stand - 18" H. $85.00
ROSE MEDALLION TEA SET, W/Wicker Cozy, Teapot & 3 Cups, Cozy Needs Repair, 9" x 6" x 6½" $145.00
NEEDLEPOINT PICTURE, Colorful, 3 Sm. Holes In Backing, 19" Sq. .$225.00

(A-OH '77)   *Garth's Auctions, Inc.*
ROPE DAY BED, Legs Have Old Red Paint, 25" x 79" x 13½" H. $450.00
WOODEN DECOY, Bluebill Drake, Wisconsin, 13½" L. $17.50
WOODEN DECOY, Coot, Michigan, Repainted, 12¾" L. $27.50
WOODEN DECOY, Mallard Drake, Balsa Body, Stamped "Ken Harris, Woodville, N.Y.", 17½" L. $25.00
WOODEN DECOY, Redhead Drake, Turned Head, 16¾" L. $35.00
WOODEN DECOY, Canvas Back Drake, Worn Paint, 16" L. $25.00
FIELD DECOY, Stick-Up, Canada Goose, Ohio, Painted Masonite, 26" H. . . .$10.00
HOOKED RAG RUG, House W/Black Border, Unused, 19½" x 28" $100.00
HOOKED RAG RUG, Rooster & Chick, Red, Black, Grey & Magenta, 20" x 29½"
. . . .$110.00

(D-AZ '78)
PACK SADDLE, Handmade, New Ends & Legs Added $90.00

(A-OH '77)   *Garth's Auctions, Inc.*
CHOPPING KNIFE, Iron, Twin Blades, One Blade W/Tooled Date "1833", Turned Wooden Handle, 26" L. $42.50
DROP LEAF TABLE, Birch, 19" x 42" W/ 11" Leaves, 29" H. $110.00
MUFFIN PAN, Cast Iron, 3 Legs & Handle, 7½" Diam. $5.00
WOODEN BOWL, 14" Diam. $10.00
PITCHER, Composition W/Metal Handle, Mkd. "United Indurated Fibre Co.", Pat. Date ;1885, 9½" H. $3.00
SAMPLER, Alphabets & Initials, Dated "1872", Framed, 14" x 14½" $25.00

SHERATON MAHOGANY KNIFE BOX,
Ca. 1780, Twisted Inlay, Exceptionally Fine
Example $275.00
ROSE MEDALLION COVERED DISH
W/Ornithological Decor. Panels & Floral
Int., Top Lip Roughage.........$170.00
**HEPPLEWHITE BOW-FRONT SIDE-
BOARD,** Mahogany, Unusual Inlaid Lip,
Double Tapered Legs W/Light Line & Cuff
Inlay, Boston Origin, 16½" L., 45" H. ....
.................................$1200.00
**TUBULAR SHAPED ORIENTAL VAS-
ES,** W/Red, Green & Gilded Decorated Foo
Dogs, "Ching Dynasty", Authenticated
Certificates, 11" H. $120.00

(A-OH '77)   *Garth's Auctions, Inc.*
DROP LEAF TABLE, Cherry W/Curly
Maple Legs, Refinished, 45" x 18" W/11"
Leaves, 27½" H. $625.00
BRASS BALL TOP ANDIRONS, Pr.,
18th C., 17" D., 12½" H. $135.00
BOW BACK WINDSOR ARM CHAIR,
Refinished W/Traces Black & Green Paint,
1 Arm Broken & Repaired $875.00
LEEDS MILK PITCHER, Gaudy Blue &
White, Rim Chips, 6" H. $105.00
LEEDS BOWL, Gaudy Blue, White &
Yellow Ochre, Rim Hairline, 11¼" Diam.,
3½" H. $250.00
LEEDS TEAPOT, Gaudy Blue & White,
Spout Chipped & Flake On Lid Edge, 12¼"
H. $165.00
OIL ON CANVAS PAINTING, Union
Army Encampment, Rebacked, Cleaned &
Repaired, Unframed, 24" x 28" ..$550.00
SAMPLER ON HOMESPUN, Alphabets,
House, Trees & Baskets Of Flowers W/
Floral Border; Pine Frame, 23" x 23½" ...
.................................$190.00

(A-OH '77)   *Garth's Auctions, Inc.*
(ROW I, L to R)
TIN LANTERN, Clear Hand Blown Globe,
Clear Pressed Paneled Font, Pewter Collar,
Dented Base, 14" O.H. $105.00
TIN KEROSENE LANTERN, "Made In
Germany Nier", Paper Label On Globe,
Unused, 15" H. $7.50
TIN KEROSENE LANTERN, "The
Adams & Westlake Co.", 1923 Patent Date,
Burner Missing From Font, 9" H. ..$10.00
(ROW II, L to R)
CHRONOMETER, Wooden Brass Fitted
Case, Face Mkd. "Parkinson & Frodsham,
Change Alley, London", Does Not Run, 6"
x 6"f x 6½" $335.00
TIN LANTERN, Brass Cap, Clear Globe,
Tin Font W/Brass Whale Oil Burner, Base
Catch Resoldered, Minor Rust, 11" H. ....
.................................$35.00
WOODEN CANTEEN, Stave Constr.,
Worn Orig. Blue-Green Paint, 7¾" L.,
6¼" W., 7½" H. $165.00
(ROW III, L to R)
IRON HOG SCRAPER CANDLESTICK,
Hanger & Pushup, 6½" H. $52.50
IRON HOG SCRAPER CANDLESTICK,
Hanger & Pushup, 6½" H. $55.00
LEATHER BOUND TRUNK, Brass Studs,
Iron Lock, Key & Hasp, Brass Bail Handle,
Wallpaper Lined, 4" x 6" x 10" ...$65.00
**IRON HOG SCRAPER CANDLE-
STICKS** (2), One Missing Pushup, One
Missing Hanger, 7" & 8" $30.00

To the right ▶

IRON LANTERN, Oil Burner, Red & Blue
Lenses, "The Adlake Non-Sweating Lamp,
Chicago", 16½" O.H. $40.00
STONEWARE JUG, 6-Gal., Cobalt Slip
Label: "Grant And Colfax 1868", 16½" H.
.................................$95.00
WOODEN SUGAR BUCKET, Stave
Const., Minor Lid & Band Damage, 9½"
Diam., 10" H. $30.00
ARROWBACK SETTEE, Reddish Brown
Paint, 55½" L. $260.00

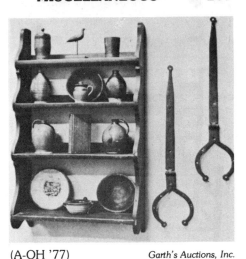

(A-OH '77)   *Garth's Auctions, Inc.*
HANGING SHELVES, Old, Drk. Paint,
25" W., 9½" D., 41¾" H. $225.00
(ROW I, L to R)
TREEN COVERED JAR, Turned Rings,
6½" H. $15.00
SHORE BIRD, Drk. Paint, Replaced Bill,
Modern Wooden Stand, 5" W., 6" H. ....
.................................$100.00
HORN TUMBLER, Wooden Bottom, 4"
H. $45.00
(ROW II, L to R)
REDWARE BOTTLE, Black Metallic
Glaze, Lip Glaze Wear, 6½" H. ..$40.00
REDWARE COVERED POT, Black
Brushed On Decor., Clear Glaze, Minor
Chips & Glaze Wear, 4¼" H. $50.00
TREEN BOWL, Red Interior, Green Ex-
terior, 7¼" Diam. $45.00
REDWARE BOTTLE, Black Shiny Metallic
Glaze, 6¼" H. $40.00
(ROW III, L to R)
REDWARE JUG, Greenish Clear Glaze,
Minor Chips & Hairline At Lip, 7" H. ....
.................................$25.00
WOODEN BOX, Book Shape, Lid Slides
Open, Red Paint, 2" x 4" x 7¾" ..$75.00
REDWARE JUG, Brown Splotches & Clear
Glaze, Incised Lines At Shoulder, Repaired
Lip Flake $65.00
(ROW IV, L to R)
TREEN BOWL, Worn White Painted In-
terior, Red Exterior, 8¾" Diam. ...$22.50
WHITE CLAY BOWL, 2 Applied Bands,
Interior W/Shiny Red Glaze, 5¼" L. .....
.................................$12.50
TREEN BOWL, Blue Exterior, Bottom
Branded "A.P.P.", 7¾" Diam. $50.00
WROUGHT IRON HINGES, Pr., 32" L.
.................................$45.00

(A-OH '77)   *Garth's Auctions, Inc.*

(A-OH '77)   *Garth's Auctions, Inc.*

ARROWBACK ARM CHAIR, Reinforced Back Supports, Refinished $95.00

POPLAR CHEST OF DRAWERS, White Porcelain Knobs, 35 Drawers, Minor Repair, Refinished, 26½'' W., 17'' D., 66½'' H. $375.00

CURRIER & IVES PRINT, Small Folio, "The Magnificent Steamship 'Teutonic' Of The White Star Line", Trimmed Margins, Pine Frame, 13'' x 19'' $130.00

CURRIER & IVES PRINT, Small Folio, "Cottage Life-Summer", Trimmed Margins, Pine Frame, 14¾'' x 18¾'' $85.00

(A-OH '77)   *Garth's Auctions, Inc.*

MINIATURE POPLAR BLANKET CHEST, 6-Board, Refinished, 15½'' x 9'' x 11'' $35.00

POPLAR DRY SINK, Dovetailed Drawer, Orig. Drk. Brown Graining, 42'' W., 18'' D., 36'' H. $300.00

STONEWARE JUG, 2-Gal., Cobalt Blue Brushed Design, 14'' H. $25.00

SPUN BRASS PAIL, Wrought Iron Handle, 13½'' Diam. $45.00

REDWARE MILK BOWL, Spotted Glaze, 15½'' Diam. $45.00

WROUGHT IRON ROTARY BROILER, Minor Damage, 10'' Diam. $45.00

PINE UTENSIL RACK, Wrought Iron Hooks, No Finish, 25'' W. $55.00

WROUGHT IRON TOASTER, 18'' L. $85.00

To the right

ENGLISH MAHOGANY TILT TOP TABLE, Dovetailed Birdcage, 2-Board Top, Refinished, 28¾'' Diam., 28½'' H. $250.00

CURLY MAPLE DESK, Slant Top, Fitted Interior, Pine Interior, Orig. Brasses, Replaced Feet, Sides Have Insect Damage, 18'' W., 16'' D., 39¼'' H. (28'' Writing Height) $1060.00

PEWTER TANKARD MEASURE, "½ Pint", Slightly Battered, 3¾'' H. . . . $35.00

PEWTER MEASURES (3), Tumbler Type, 2 Mkd. "5", 1 Mkd. "3"; 2'' to 2¼'' H. $27.50

PEWTER TANKARD MEASURE, "1 Pint B.L.", Minor Dents, 4¾'' H. . . $42.50

BRASS QUEEN ANNE CANDLESTICK, Scalloped Base, 7¼'' H. $230.00

BRASS SCISSOR WICK TRIMMERS, 6'' L. $55.00

OIL ON CANVAS PORTRAIT, Gentleman W/Beard, Signed "J. Wilson 1878", Unframed, Rebacked, Cleaned, 25'' x 30'' $115.00

OIL ON CARDBOARD PAINTING, Young Gentleman, Inscription On Back & "1915", Gold Frame, 11¼'' x 12¾'' $220.00

(A-OH '78)   *Garth's Auctions, Inc.*

BIRD-CAGE WINDSOR SIDE CHAIR, White Discolored Varnish, 16¼'' Seat Height $160.00

REDWARE FISH MOLD, Greenish Clear Glaze, Unglazed Back Has Surface Flaking, 12'' L. $67.50

TIN CANDLE HOLDER, Iron Handle, Worn Orange Paint, 5½'' H. $45.00

PINE CANDLESTAND, Plugged Holes In Top, One Foot W/Termite Damage, Refinished, 14¼'' Sq., 24'' H. . . . $65.00

BRASS BED WARMER, Ring Turned Handle, Engraved Pot W/Tulip On Lid, Polished, 47'' L. $175.00

COPPER PITCHER, Applied Handle & Bail, Air Hole In Center Of Lid, Tooled Decor., 8¾'' H. $15.00

INDIAN RUG, Geometric Patt. W/Drk. Brown, Red, White & Gray, Faded, 33'' x 60'' $70.00

(A-OH '78)   *Garth's Auctions, Inc.*

MAPLE & BIRCH QUEEN ANNE DROP LEAF TABLE, Swing Leg, Refinished, Replaced Leaves, Restored Feet, 16¾'' x 4½'' W/17½'' Leaves, 27½'' H. . . $725.00

BRASS DOUBLE STUDENT LAMP, Polished, Electrified, Replaced Yellow Enameled Milk Glass Shades $500.00

(A-OH '78)   *Garth's Auctions, Inc.*

(A-OH '77) *Garth's Auctions, Inc.*
PINE WATER BENCH, Stripped, 33" W., 11" D., 29½" H. $115.00
REDWARE JUG, Clear Shiny Glaze W/ Green, Minor Glaze Flakes, 11" H. .$95.00
PINE FOOT STOOL, 7½" x 12½" x 7½" H. $35.00
WOODEN DUCK DECOY, Black & White 14" L. $52.50
REDWARE JAR, Black Metallic Glaze, Base Hairline, 8" H. $22.50
REDWARE HANDLED DISH, White Slip W/Green Running Glaze, Covered W/ Clear Shiny Glaze, Shenandoah, 9" Diam. $210.00
REDWARE JUG, Drk. Green Shiny Glaze, Minor Glaze Flakes, 9¼" H. $55.00
REDWARE JUG, Drk. Green Shiny Glaze, Base Chipped, 8½" H. $32.50
REDWARE JUG, Drk. Brown Shiny Glaze, Base Chipped $15.00
REDWARE PORRINGER, Shiny Black Metallic Glaze, Repaired Rim Chip, 5½" Diam., 3" H. $70.00
REDWARE MUG, Tooled Lines Around Rim & Base, Shiny Black Metallic Glaze, Rim Glaze Wear, 5½" H. $87.50
LADDER BACK SIDE CHAIR, Woven Split Wood Seat Needs Repair $45.00
VORSCHRIFT FRAKTUR, Hearts & Vining Tulips Border, Alphabet & Date "1799", Hand Drawn & Colored In Yellow, Black & Red, Faded, Old Black Frame W/ Corner Blocks, 16½" x 19½" $485.00
TIN 3-BURNER TORCH, Cone Shaped Font, 7" Diam., 9" H. $155.00

(A-OH '77) *Garth's Auctions, Inc.*
STONEWARE JUG, 3-Gal., Cobalt Blue "3", 14½" H. $17.50
CHERRY STAND, Dovetailed Cockbeaded Drawers, Clear Lacy Knobs, Replaced 1-Board Top, 18½" x 20" x 28¾" H. $120.00
STONEWARE JAR, Incised "4", 13" H. $35.00
STONEWARE JUG, Impressed "I.M. Mead", Brushed Cobalt Blue Flower, 14" H. $105.00
MAHOGANY ON PINE BOX, Lid Inlay Damaged, Paper Lining Incomplete, 11" x 8" x 4" $15.00
CANNON BALL ROPE BED, Curly Maple Posts, Poplar Head & Foot Boards, Replaced Side Rails, Outside Measurements: 54" x 84" x 54" H. $350.00
N. CURRIER PRINT, "Susan", Pine Frame, 13" x 17" $45.00
HAND COLORED LITHOGRAPH, Fold Line Midway, Pine Frame, 12½" x 16¼" $25.00
N. CURRIER PRINT, "Mama's Pets", Pine Frame, 12½" x 16½" $45.00

 To the left

(A-OH '77) *Garth's Auctions, Inc.*
CHERRY PEMBROKE TABLE, Dovetailed Drawer, Refinished, Minor Repair, 35" x 18½" W/9½" Leaves, 26¾" H. $65.00
INDIAN DRUM, Bent Sapling Frame W/ Hide Covering, 16' Diam., 8" H. . .$85.00
TOLE COFFEEPOT, Black Ground W/ Red, Yellow, Green & Black, 8½" H. $100.00
PINE DOME TOP BOX, Orig. Red Paint W/Yellow Circles, Leather Hinges, 16¼" L., 7½" D., 7" H. $85.00
TOLE COFFEEPOT, Black Ground W/ Worn Floral Painting, 9¾" H. $355.00
OAK DRYING RACK, Mortised Pegged Constr., 48" W., 42" H. $110.00

(A-OH '78) *Garth's Auctions, Inc.*
CORNER CHAIR, Maple W/Old Black Painted Finish, Rope Seat W/Golden Rod Linsey Woolsey Cushion $250.00
CANDLESTAND, Maple & Birch, Hoof Feet, CT Origin, 26" H. $175.00
SHORE BIRD (L), Hand Carved, Turned Head, Tan & White W/Black, 13½" H. $190.00
SHORE BIRD (R), Hand Carved, Worn White, Brown & Black Paint, Head Repair, Beak Damaged, Buckshot Holes, 10" H. $115.00

(A-OH '77) *Garth's Auctions, Inc.*
POPLAR SCHOOLMASTER'S DESK, Interior Has Pigeon Holes & 2 Dovetailed Drawers, Replaced Gallery, Refinished, 30" W., 21" D., 41½" H. $160.00
CHILD'S CAPTAIN CHAIR, 18½" H. $50.00
CARVED WOODEN DECOY, Crow, Initialed "P", 9½" H. $30.00
CARVED WOODEN DECOY, Repainted As Redhead, 2 Sets Initials On Base, 13" L. $22.50
WATERCOLOR ON PAPER, Wooden Frame W/Built Up Floral Designs, 6¼" x 7¾" $55.00

(A-OH '77)   *Garth's Auctions, Inc.*
PINE BLANKET CHEST, Dovetailed, Till, Orig. Grained Decor. Reddish Brown Over Yellow Ground, 49" W., 21" D., 27½" H. $140.00
STONEWARE JUG, 2-Gal., Impressed Label: "Satterlee & Mory, Ft. Edwards, N.Y.", Leaf Design, 13¾" H. $55.00
STONEWARE JAR, 4-Gal., Impressed "T. Reed", Brushed Tulip Design, Cracked & Held With Wire At Rin, 13½" H. ..$20.00
STONEWARE JUG, 2-Gal., Impressed Label: "Whites Utica", Cobalt Single Flower, Base Chip, 14¼" H. $30.00
KELLOGG PRINT, "Household Pets", Margins Trimmed, Frame - 13" x 17" $30.00
WOODEN FOLK ART FIGURE, Worn Red & Green Paint, 21" H. $10.00
CURRIER & IVES PRINT, "Little Manly", Margins Trimmed, Frame W/Red Paint, 12¾" x 16½" $27.50

(A-OH '77)   *Garth's Auctions, Inc.*
YARN WINDER, 27" L. Arms, 40" O.H. $75.00
CAST IRON GYPSY KETTLE, Wrought Handle, 9" Diam. $17.50
WROUGHT IRON CANDLESTAND, Adjustable Fold Out Candle Arm, Heart Finial, 55" H. $85.00
WROUGHT IRON SAWTOOTH TRAMMEL, Adjustable, 30" L. $35.00
WOOL SPINNING WHEEL, Wheel is 49½" Diam. $135.00

(A-OH '77)   *Garth's Auctions, Inc.*
LADDER BACK ROCKERS (1 of 4), Rush Seat, 1 W/Broken & Repaired Top Slat, 1 Seat Needs Minor Repair ...$55.00
PINE BLANKET CHEST, Dovetailed Const., Yellow Striping & Tulip Trees W/ Red, Yellow & Green Flowers, Cream Ground, Signed "J. Weikal, West Salem, Ohio", 44½" W., 18" D., 24¾" H. ......
....$625.00
CAST IRON FIGURAL ANDIRONS, Pr., 12" D., 12½" H. $20.00
CARDBOARD BOX, Wallpaper Cover, Brown Floral Designs, Lid Needs Repair, Tears In Cardboard, 12½" W., 9" H. ....
....$30.00
TOLE BOWL & PITCHER SET, Crystalized Ground W/Red & Blue Stripes & Bands Of Color, Floral Decor., Worn, Hole In Bowl & Pitcher Base, 12¼" Diam., 11½" H. ..
....$55.00
CARDBOARD HAT BOX, Wallpaper Cover, Brown, Orange & Floral Patt., Lined W/Ohio Church Paper, Contains Gentleman's Beaver Hat, 12½" W., 9" H.$45.00
WATERCOLOR PAINTING, Jesus On Cross, Signed "Delin By F. Baun", German Inscription, Curly Maple Frame, 11" x 13"
....$45.00
TIN CANDLE SCONCES, Pr., Crimped Tops, 13½" H. $175.00
FRAKTUR BIRTH CERTIFICATE, Printed & Sold By Joseph Hartman, Lebanon, Framed, 14½" x 17" $95.00

(A-OH '77)   *Garth's Auctions, Inc.*
PINE BLANKET CHEST, 6-Board, Till, Staple Hinges, Old Red Paint, 49½" W., 18¼" D., 23" H. $225.00
BURL BOWL, Thin Burl At Handles, Riveted Copper Reinforcement, 15½" x 19" x 8½" H. $1025.00
HANGING SHELF, Paint Removed To Show Orig. Yellow, Crest Board Split, 13" W., 8" D., 23" H. $155.00
TREEN COVERED BOX, Red Sponging Over Yellow Ground Worn, 5" Diam., 5" H.
....$215.00
WOODEN BUTTER PRINT, Pineapple Design, 2½" Diam., 4" H. $12.50
REDWARE TURKS HEAD MOLD, Miniature, Greenish Exterior Glaze, Opaque White Interior Glaze, 4½" Diam., 2" H. ....
....$20.00
TREEN COVERED SAFFRON BOX, Walnut W/Old Varnish Finish, 7" H. ....
....$100.00
TREEN COVERED BOX, Old Drk. Brown Finish, Age Crack In Side, 3¼" Diam., 3½" H. $65.00
HANGING SPOON RACK, Reddish Brown Vinegar Painting W/Dashes On Racks, Old Break In Top, 15" x 25" ....
....$360.00
WATERCOLOR, 2 Couples In Cemetery, Colorful, 8¼" x 18½" $95.00

◄ *To the left*

(A-OH '77)   *Garth's Auctions, Inc.*
PINE BLANKET CHEST, Dovetailed Joints, Rose Head Nails, Compartment In One End, Repaired, Old Red Paint, 50½" W., 18½" D., 20½" H. $95.00
CHILD'S SLEIGH, Wooden Iron-Faced Runners, Orig. Worn Paint W/Lt. Blue Runners Striped In Black; Red & Blue Top W/ Yellow Striping, Sm. Painted Scene, Front Crest Incomplete, Interior Upholstered In Worn Brocade, 32½" L. $85.00
THEOREM ON VELVET, Fruit & Blue & White Dutch Plate, Stamped On Back - "Bill Rank Original", Modern Decorated Frame, 19¾" x 24¼" $75.00

(A-OH '77) *Garth's Auctions, Inc.*
COUNTRY QUEEN ANNE WORK TABLE, 1-Board Pine Top, Old Red Paint, Bottoms Of Feet Worn, 28½" x 42" x 26½" H. $625.00
BRASS ANDIRONS, Pr., 15¼" H. $155.00
STONEWARE CROCK, 4-Gal., Cobalt Blue Design, Impressed "N. Ballard, Burlington, Vt.", 11½" H. $60.00
CARVED WOODEN MODEL, Team of 2 Horses Pulling Maple Sugar Water Sled, Painted, Detailed W/Leather Harness, Mounting Board: 12¾" x 37½" . .$300.00
TIN TRAY W/Painting Of Mill, Gold Border, 21½" x 30¾" $27.50

(A-OH '77) *Garth's Auctions, Inc.*
WROUGHT IRON ANDIRONS, Pr., Ribbed Brass Stuart Crown Finials, Split Rests, 19" D., 22½" H. $260.00
QUEEN ANNE DROP LEAF TABLE, Walnut, 6-Leg, Top Has Patches & Repair To Rule Joints At Hinges, One Foot Broken & Repaired, Refinished, 50" x 17½" W/19" Leaves, 29½" H. $1600.00
TUREEN, 3-Pc., Med. Blue Transfer Scene of Florence, Mkd. "Spode", Old Chips On Lid, Tray Matches In Color, But Transfer Scenes & Borders Do Not Match, 14" L. $55.00
LITHOGRAPHS, Pr., Hand Colored, George & Martha Washington, Oval Gold Leaf Frames, Signed On Back, "E.C. Middleton, Cincinnati, Ohio, 1864", 19" x 22" $155.00

(A-OH '77) *Garth's Auctions, Inc.*
STONEWARE PITCHER, Leaf Decor., Cracked & Hairline In Handle, 11" H. $55.00
HANGING CHERRY CUPBOARD, Refinished, 18" W., 13" D., 35½" H. $100.00
LADDER BACK ARM CHAIR, Refinished, Woven Split Wood Seat $75.00
SEWER TILE HEAD, Hand-Molded, Nose Damaged, 11" H. $35.00
CARVED LIMESTONE DOG, 10¾" L. $65.00
CURLY MAPLE CUTTING BOARD, 14" x 24½" $102.50
OIL ON CANVAS PAINTING, Sunset Over Meadow Pond, Mkd. "Near Largs, A.K. Brown 1875", Gilt Frame, 20½" x 27½" $170.00

(A-OH '77) *Garth's Auctions, Inc.*
PINE BLANKET CHEST, Dovetailed Const., Iron Handles, Orig. Blue Paint W/ Polychrome Floral Designs, Iron Lock Missing, Initialed "F.B. No. 4", 55" W., 26" D., 21" H. $250.00
TIN DOUGH PAN, Iron Handles, 19½" Diam. $17.50
TIN COFFEE POT, 9½" H. $15.00
TIN CHURN, Wooden Dasher, 21½" H. $85.00
CRANBERRY PICKER, Wood W/Iron Rods & Galvanized Metal & Canvas Covering, Ends W/Worn Red Paint, 15" W. $40.00

(A-OH '77) *Garth's Auctions, Inc.*
STONEWARE CHURN, 8-Gal., "8" & 2 Flowers In Cobalt Slip, 19¼" H. . . .$55.00
BIRCH DROP LEAF TABLE, Refinished, Traces Old Red Paint, 17½" x 42" W/12" Leaves, 28½" H. $210.00
POTTERY JAR, Fox & Hounds Decor., Salt Glaze W/Amber Glaze Around Rim, 5¾" H. $60.00
REDWARE PLATE, Yellow Slip Decor., Coggled Edge, Edge Chips, 10" Diam. $80.00
WHITE CLAY JAR, Brown Glaze, Impressed "FE.&L.P. Norton, Bennington, Vt.", Chipped Handle, Rim Chips, 8½" Diam., 9" H. $65.00
HANDCOLORED FRENCH ENGRAVINGS, (3), 12¾" x 16"; 14" x 15"; 15½" x 19½" $155.00

(A-OH '77) *Garth's Auctions, Inc.*
PINE FOOT STOOL, Ends W/Cut-Out Hearts & Circles, Refinished, 7½" x 18½" x 14¾" H. $65.00
PINE BLANKET CHEST, Dovetailed Const., Till W/Compartment Beneath, Refinished, 43½" W., 23" D., 27½" H. $205.00
INDIAN RUG, White Ground W/Red & Drk. Brown, One Spot Needs Reweaving, 20" x 21" $5.00
CAST IRON RABBIT DOOR STOP, One Back Leg Broken, Worn White Paint, 12½" H. $40.00

(A-OH '77)   *Garth's Auctions, Inc.*

PINE WATER BENCH, Refinished, Replaced Bottom Shelf Rail, 41" W., 14" D., 47" H. $85.00
(ROW I, L to R)
REDWARE BATTER PITCHER, Pale Green Glaze, Minor Glaze Wear, 8¾" H. $37.50
STONEWARE PIE PLATE, Coggled Edge & Amber Glaze, 10" Diam. $35.00
STONEWARE JAR, Stenciled Label: "A. P. Donagho, Parkersburg, W. Va.", Minor Lip Chips, 10" H. $22.50
(ROW II, L to R)
STONEWARE JUG, 3-Gal., Cobalt Blue "3" & Brush Marks, 16" H. $32.50
STONEWARE JAR, Rim & Lid Chips, 11½" H. $10.00
STONEWARE JUG, 2-Gal., Impressed "White's Utica", Cobalt Blue Stylized Flower, Minor Chips, 14½" H. $52.00
(ROW III, L to R)
STONEWARE JAR, 2-Gal., Stenciled Label: "R.T. Williams, Manufacturer, New Geneva", Lip Chip, 12" H. $15.00
STONEWARE JAR, 3-Gal., Applied Handles, Tooled Neck, Cobalt Blue Brushed Floral Designs, Rim & Handle Chips, 14½" H. $70.00
STONEWARE JAR, 3-Gal., Stenciled Label: "Donaghho Co., Parkersburg, W. Va.", Cracked, 13¾" H. $22.50
WOODEN HAY FORK, Refinished, 69" H. $50.00

(A-OH '77)   *Garth's Auctions, Inc.*

◄ *To the left*

WOODEN HOBBY HORSE, Missing Base, Worn White Paint, 32½" L. $115.00
WOODEN HOBBY HORSE, Worn Orig. White W/Red Blanket & Yellow harness & Saddle, Wooden Frame, Iron Supports, Ears & 1 Glass Eye Missing, Base Mkd. "D.S. & Co. N.Y.", 42½" L., 42" H. $200.00
CHERRY CANNON BALL BED, Single Size, Orig. Rope Rails, 36½" x 78½" x 44½" H. $475.00
TALL POST CANOPY BED, Curly Maple & Pine, Orig. Rope Rails, Canopy Frame, 59" x 82½" x 84" H. $1850.00
EMPIRE TALL POST BED, American Walnut, Orig. Rope Rails, Canopy Frame, 66" x 84" x 97½" H. $1050.00
LITHOGRAPH, Reprint Of "N. Currier", Ca. 1920, "American Winter Scene, Evening", Framed, 23¾" x 30¾" $80.00

(A-OH '77)   *Garth's Auctions, Inc.*

◄ *To the left*

WINDSOR SIDE CHAIR, Old Black Paint. $95.00
WOODEN DECOY, Canvas Back Drake, Michigan, 15" L. $40.00
COUNTRY EMPIRE STAND, Poplar W/Orig. Reddish Graining, Dovetailed Drawers, 16½" x 21" x 31" H. . .$205.00
POPLAR BOX, Dovetailed, Orig. Brown Graining W/Gold Stenciled Label, "Co. Records, 6 MS Inf", Iron & Brass Lock & Hasp, 13½" x 8" x 7" $55.00
WOODEN DECOY, Black Duck Sleeper, Body Repair, 13" L. $50.00
PAPER CUT-OUT, Equestrian W/Bugle, Framed, 10½" x 12½" $200.00
HANDCOLORED LITHOGRAPH, "When The Flowing Tide Comes In", By S. Lipschuz, London, Framed & Matted, 17½" x 21½" $25.00

(D-AR. '78)

BOWL W/Blue Sponge Decoration On White Ground, 4½" H. $28.00

(A-MA '77)   *Richard A. Bourne Co., Inc.*

◄ *To the left*

ADJUSTABLE DOUBLE CANDLE-HOLDER, Hand-Wrought Iron, American, 18th C., Hole In Leg To Accomodate Electric Cord, 67" H. $1000.00
CARVED OAK BIBLE BOX, American or English 17th C., Refinished, 19½" L., 15¼" D., 6⅝" H. $350.00
PINE AND MAPLE TAVERN TABLE, American, 18th C., Repainted In Old-Style Red, 34" L., 18¼" W., 24" H. $600.00
PINE CONSOLE TABLE, American, 18th C., Worn Green Paint, 27" L., 17" D., 26½" H. $200.00

(A-OH '77) *Garth's Auctions, Inc.*

SHAKER LADDER BACK SIDE CHAIR, Woven Reed Seat Needs Repair, Enfield, One Post W/Split $230.00

COUNTRY HEPPLEWHITE PINE TABLE, 1 Drawer, 1-Board Top, Drawer Bottom Mkd. "Whitor", 17½" x 25½" x 28¼" H. $260.00

STONEWARE BATTER PITCHER, Cobalt Blue Slip Decor., 10½" H. $115.00

SHAKER LADDER BACK ROCKER, Old Rush Seat $230.00

WOODEN PEEL, Incomplete Blade, 63" L. $15.00

TIN COFFEEPOT, Punched Decor. W/Urn & Flowers, Brass Finial, Spout Tip Damaged, 11¾" H. $975.00

TIN SCONCE, Shelf For Candle, Hanger Tab, 13¼" H. $77.50

SHAKER BUTTER SCALES, Wooden Platforms & Bar W/Pencil Post Support, Repaired Split At Bar, 24½" H. . . $100.00

CARVED WOODEN HORSE'S HEAD, Grey Paint, Mounted In Chip Carved Frame, 6" x 7¾" $55.00

(A-OH' 77) *Garth's Auctions, Inc.*

SHERATON WING CHAIR, Tapestry Worn $650.00

WOODEN WHIRLIGIG, Carving Of Man W/Tin Visor On Hat, Weathered, 20th C., 12¾" H. $115.00

CHERRY STAND, Clear Glass Pulls, Old Finish, 20¼" x 20½" x 29" H. . . . $250.00

BURL BOWL, Rim W/Slight Depression, 9½" Diam., 4¾" H. $130.00

BRASS MID-DRIP CANDLESTICKS, Pr., Holes In 1 Drip Pan, 10" H. . $120.00

MOCHA COVERED JAR, Cream Colored Glaze W/Brown Earthworm Decor., Chips & Hairline In Base, 7½" Diam., 7¾" H. $130.00

ENGRAVING, "Gen. George Washington" W/Eagle & Laurel Wreath, "A. Doolittle, Sculp", Gilt Frame, 8½" x 10¼" $635.00

CHINTZ, Blue, White & Olive Brown, Washington, Flags & Eagel Banner W/ "E Pluribus Unim", Matted, No Frame, 19" x 28" $175.00

CURRIER & IVES PRINT, "An English Winter Scene", Walnut Frame, 12½" x 16½" $125.00

(A-OH '77) *Garth's Auctions, Inc.*

BANISTER BACK ARM CHAIR, Old Black Paint W/Yellow Striping & Floral Painting On Crest, Old Rush Seat, Feet Built Up 1¾" $550.00

COUNTRY QUEEN ANNE TAVERN TABLE, Maple Legs, Pine Aprons, Pine 2-Board Top, Refinished W/Traces Brown Paint, 25" x 36" x 25½" H. $775.00

STONEWARE JAR, Applied Handles, Brushed Blue Floral Band, Edge Chips, 13½" H. $95.00

HEXAGONAL RUG, Wool Felt Squares, Woven Backing, Colorful, Minor Wear, 39" $55.00

REDWARE JAR, Brown Splotches & Clear Shiny Glaze, Edge Wear & Hairlines In Base & Top, 8¾" H. $135.00

WOODEN BUCKET, Made From 1 Piece Wood W/Inset Bottom & Matching Lid, Old Red Paint, Metal Bands To Repair Age Crack, 17" Diam., 12" H. $65.00

SEWER TILE DOG, 7¼" H. . . $25.00

SAMPLER ON HOMESPUN, Alphabets & Poem, Floral Border W/Satin Stick In Blue, Green & Tan, Faded, Old Gilt Frame, 17¾" x 18¼" $85.00

SAMPLER ON HOMESPUN, Alphabets, Willow Trees, Strawberries In Basket, Floral Border, Good Colors, Framed, 17½" x 18¾" $95.00

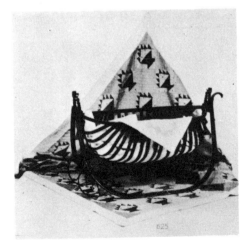

(A-VA. '77) *Laws Auction & Antiques*

SWINGING CRADLE, Ca. 1790, Orig. Paint & Stenciling Mkd. W. M. Snowden, Phila., Double Wheels One End, Curved Front Handle, Slatted Curved Cradle Pivots On Frame $450.00

(A-OH '77) *Garth's Auctions, Inc.*

PHAETON VICTORIAN BABY BUGGY, Miniature, Removable Front Handle, Wooden Carriage W/Orig. Brown Paint W/White & Yellow Striping, Missing Hand Hold On Handle, Wooden Foot Rest Broken & Repaired, Upholstered Seat, Velvet Lap Robe, 56" L. $390.00

(A-OH '77) *Garth's Auctions, Inc.*

VICTORIAN BABY CARRIAGE W/ Metal Banded Wooden Wheels, Orig. Black Paint W/Gold Striping & Decor., Adjustable Top Trimmed W/Gold Velvet & Fringe, Old Gold Velvet Upholstery, 52" L, 47" H. $225.00

(A-OH '78)   *Garth's Auctions, Inc.*

◄ *To the left*

DOUBLE BLADED WROUGHT IRON CHOPPING KNIFE, Mortised And Pinned Handle, 6¼" W. $40.00
EARLY WOODEN YARN WINDER, Mortised And Pinned Construction, Traces Of Old Red Paint, Wheel Is 26" Diam. $75.00
EARLY TIN STREET LIGHT, Clear Glass Globe And Brass Kerosene Burner, Embossed Label "No. 9 Globe Street, C.T. Ham, Mfg. Co's. Registered 1886", Worn Green Paint, 26½" H. $205.00
WROUGHT IRON TOASTER, Very Good Detail W/Tooled Handle And Twisted Back Support W/Tiny Shoe Shaped Foot, 17½" L. $270.00
WROUGHT IRON FLOOR STANDING LIGHTING DEVICE, Tripod Base W/ Adjustable Candle Socket And Rush Holder Finial W/Candle Socket Counterweight, 36" H. $725.00
EARLY TRESTLE BENCH, Turned Splayed Legs W/A Mortised Trestle Type Stretcher W/Turned Center Support. Molded Edge Top Has 2 Edge Repairs And Foot Of Center Leg Is Replaced. Refinished Walnut Is Very Light In Color, Top 9" W., 83" L. $575.00
STONEWARE JUG, 3 Gal., Impressed Label "E. Norton & Co. Bennington Vt.", Stylized Floral Spray In Cobalt Blue, Old Chip And Hairline In Base, 15½" H. .....
..................................95.00
WROUGHT IRON PEEL W/Nicely Formed Handle, 47½" L. $50.00
STONEWARE CROCK, 2 Gal., Impressed Label, "Riedinger & Caire, Poughkeepsie, N.Y." Bird In Cobalt Blue Slip, Inside Rim Chip, 9½" H. $125.00
OVOID STONEWARE JUG, Impressed Label "Gilson & Co., Reading, Pa.", Simple Plant Design In Cobalt ,15½" H. ..$80.00
HATCHEL W/Circular Arrangement Of Wrought Iron Nails, Shaped Beechboard W/ Heart Cut Outs, Initialed "M.S." and Dated "1825", 5½" x 21½" $135.00
ROOSTER WEATHERVANE, Copper, Embossed Hollow Body, Has Arrow, 28½" L., 25" H. $625.00
ROUND POPLAR COOKIE BOARD, Made From One Wide Board, 23" x 30¾" $65.00
WROUGHT IRON SAWTOOTH TRAMMEL, Gold Bold Detail, Adjusts From 36½" L. $85.00
LARGE IRON CALIPERS, 25½" L. ....
..............................$35.00

(A-OH '77)   *Garth's Auctions, Inc.*
COUNTRY HEPLEWHITE STAND, 1 Drawer W/Orig. Black Graining Over Unpainted Maple & Birch, 14" Sq., 27½" H.
..............................$175.00
STONEWARE JAR, 3-Gal., Covered, Impressed "Jordan", Cobalt Blue Designs, Hairlines In Handles, 13½" H. $60.00
COUNTRY QUEEN ANNE SIDE CHAIR, Piece Missing From Base Of Crest, Back Leg Split, Rush Seat, Drk. Brown Paint ....
..............................$220.00
CARVED WOODEN DECOY, Black W/ White Details, Keel & Lead Weight, 14¼" L.
..............................$15.00
CARVED WOODEN SHORE BIRD, Worn Paint, Beak Replaced W/Nail, Buckshot Holes, Metal Stand, 10¾" W., 13¼" H.
..............................$105.00

(continued next column)

CARVED WOODEN SHORE BIRD, Weathered, Traces Of Paint, Head Split, Modern Metal Stand, 8" W., 10½" H. ....
..............................$70.00
PRINTED FRAKTUR, "Taufschein" for "Johannes Gerberich", Hand Colored, Printed By "G. Baumann", Modern Frame, 16" x 19" $215.00
CAPE COD MIRROR, In Orig. Box, Carved Frame W/Open Work Crest W/Fruit, Flowers & Bird, Worn Gilt, Orig. Glass, 9" x 20"
..............................$350.00

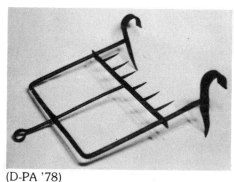

(D-PA '78)
WROUGHT IRON HEARTH BROILER, Adjustable $195.00

◄ *To the left*

(A-MA '78)   *Richard A. Bourne Co., Inc.*

U.S. CARTRIDGE BOX, Ca. 1808-39, Mkd. "Made By James Boyd, Boston", Cover Flap Embossed Around Edge W/ Floral Patterns, Center "E Pluribus Unum", & U.S. Eagle Holding Arrows & Olive Branches $550.00

(A-OH '78)   Garth's Auctions, Inc.

◀ *To the left*

STONEWARE OVOID JAR, 4 Gal., Simple Plant Design In Cobalt Blue, Small Flake On One Handle, 15¾" H. . . .$85.00
DECOY, Coot By Madison Mitchell, Original Paint Has Minor Wear, Painted Eyes, 12¼" L. $47.50
STONEWARE OVOID JAR, 4 Gal., Impressed Label "F.H. MERRILL" W/Splashes Of Cobalt Blue At Label & Handles, Glaze Crazing & Crows Foot, 14" H. . . . . .
. . . .$55.00
6 BOARD BLANKET CHEST, Pine W/ Double Arch Cut Out Feet & Chip Carving On The Side Edges Of Lid, Till & Lock Are Missing, Staple Hinges Are Reset, Original Red Paint, 49" W., 17½" D., 24½" H. . . .
. . . .$130.00
DECOY, Preening Brant W/Glass Eyes & Carved Tail, Branded "C.W." & Signed In Pencil "C. Pete Wilbur, Island Hts. N.J." Unused Condition, 16¾" L. $135.00
DECOY, Hollow Mason Premier Bluebill, Worn Old Paint & Tack Eyes (Eyes Do Not Match), Head Loose & Wear, 12¾" L. . . .
. . . .$75.00
LARGE POTTERY PITCHER, 3 Tooled Rings & 2 Tone Tan & Olive Amber Glaze, Minor Rim & Base Chips, 16" H. . .$47.50
DECOY, Brant W/Glass Eyes, Branded "C.W." & Signed In Pencil "C. Pete Wilbur, Isld. Hts. N.J." Unused Condition, 19½" L.
. . . .$95.00

◀ *To the left*

(D-MA '78)
BIRCH HEARTH BROOM, Ex. Cond, 49" L. $135.00

To the right

CYLINDRICAL COVERED INDIAN BASKET, Brown Geometric Designs, Probably Old Papago, 7¼" Diam., 8" H. . . . . .
. . . .$333.00
CAST IRON EAGLE W/Arrows In Talons, Very Worn Polychrome Paint, 50½" Wingspan $260.00
BOTTLE W/Finely Woven Basket Covering, Indian, Brown Geometric Design, Has Small Woven Cover, 12½" H. $135.00
ARROW BACK SETTEE, Cherry W/Poplar Seat, Turned Legs And Simple Shaped Arms, Old Refinishing, 90" L. $750.00
CAST IRON FIRE MARK, "U.F." W/ Early Fire Engine, Black Paint, (United Firemans Ins. Co.) 9" x 11¼" $95.00
CAST IRON FIRE MARK, Tree, (Mutual Assurance Co.-Phila.), Several Coats Of Paint, 7½" x 11¼" $95.00
ORIENTAL RUG, Kazak Prayer, 4 Borders W/Animals And Dated, 3'11" x 5'10" . . . .
. . . .$1000.00
CAPE COD MIRROR, Carved Wooden Crest Has Bird Reaching For Fruit With Flower On Very Top, Very Worn Polychrome Paint W/Traces Of Original Gilding, Completely original including Worn Mirror Glass, 10" x 21¾" $925.00

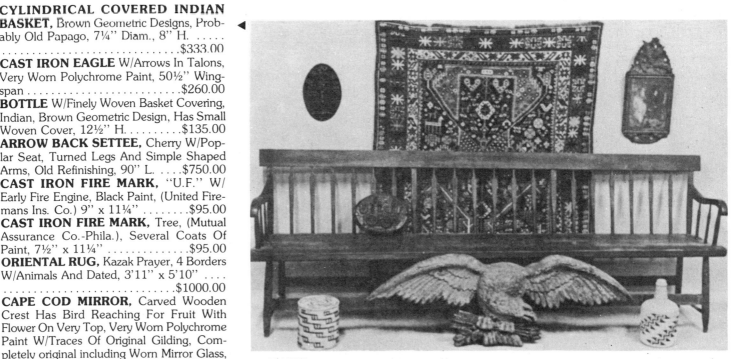

(A-OH '78)   Garth's Auctions, Inc.

(A-OH '78) . . . . *Garth's Auctions, Inc.*

(ROW I)

MINIATURE BASKET W/Lid, Green And Natural Split Wood W/Braided Grass Decor. 5" H. $12.50

MINIATURE CHINA TRADE BASKET W/Lid, Painted Floral Designs, Break In One Side, 3¼" H. $35.00

INDIAN BASKET, Woven Design In Concentric Squares, Minor Rim Damage, 7" Diam., 5" H. $75.00

MINIATURE BASKETS (2), Oval Split Wood W/Handle, 6¾" L., And Rectangular Reed And Braided Fiber, 4¼" L. . .$22.50

(ROW II)

MINIATURE WOVEN SPLIT WOOD BASKETS (2), Round W/Handle And Blue Strip, 5" H. and Covered 4" H. . . . . .
. . . .$30.00

OVAL BENTWOOD STORAGE BOX, Lid Has Scratch Carved Inscription "1809, Buq Rect. Box Boston", 6½" L. . . .$37.50

POPLAR BOX W/Till And Original Brown Graining, Replaced Leather Hinges, 3¾" x 4½" x 8" $52.50

NANTUCKET BASKET, Has Had Small Handles At One Time, 9" Diam., 4" H. . . .

OVAL BENTWOOD STORAGE BOX, 5½" L. $155.00

TWO PIECES, Small Pitcher Shaped Basket, Handle Has Damage, 5½" H., And A Pin Cushion In A Basket, Minor Damage, 2⅝" L. $32.50

(ROW III)

OVAL BENTWOOD STORAGE BOX, One Finger Of Box Is Incomplete, 9" L. . .
. . . .$20.00

MINIATURE SPLIT WOOD BUTTOCKS BASKET, 5¾" L. $40.00

INDIAN BASKET, Geometric Design, 8¾" Diam., 4½" H. $85.00

OVAL BENTWOOD STORAGE BOX, 4 Fingers, 9" L. $90.009

WOVEN SPLIT WOOD BASKET, Natural, Green And Purple, 5" Diam., 4¼" H. Plus Handle $30.00

To the right ▶

(D-NH '78)

TRAMP ART BOX W/Lift Top, Leather Hinges & Two Drawers, 8¼" W., 6¼" D., 8" H. $48.50

(A-OH '78) . . . . *Garth's Auctions, Inc.*

CAST IRON BOOT JACK, Good Cast Detail With Heart Cutout At One End, 11¼" L. $35.00

SEWER TILE PIG BANK, Made To Accept A Wooden Bottom, 10½" H. . . . .
. . . .$135.00

CAST IRON BOOT JACK, Attributed To The Shakers, 8½" L. $30.00

PINE DOVETAILED BLANKET CHEST W/Turned Feet And Till, Original Yellow Paint With Brown Wavy Lines And Black Trim. 43" W., 21" D., 24¼" H. . . .$370.00

NEW GENEVA FLOWER POT W/Attached Saucer Base, Old Chip On Saucer And One On Rim, 6½" H. $175.00

SEWER TILE MUG, 5¼" H. $37.50

ANIMATED BOER WAR TOY, Sliding Lid With Cut Out Handle Inscribed "If You Want To see Dewet, Open This Box", When Opened, Carved Wooden With Top Hat And Shouldered Rifle Pops Out, Man Has Fabric Costume With Ammunition Belt, Barrel Of Rifle Replaced, Exterior Marked "Boer P.O.W." 7¾" x 4¾" x 3¼" . . . .
. . . .$195.00

NEW GENEVA FLOWER POT W/Attached Base, 7" H. $160.00

NEEDLEPOINT PARROT IN TREE, Several Shades Varying From Lavender To Deep Purple, Framed So Side Fringe Shows, 12½" x 15¾" $17.50

FRAMED SECTION OF CHRISTIAN AND HEATHEN JACQUARD COVERLET, Red, White And Blue, 9" x 13" . . . .
. . . .$25.00

(A-OH '78)   *Garth's Auctions, Inc.*

WINDSOR ARM CHAIRS, Pr. W/Bamboo Turnings, Refinished, Feet Extended On One $585.00

COUNTRY HEPPLEWHITE DROP LEAF TABLE, Sq. Tapering Legs, Good Overhang, Completely Stripped & Unfinished, Replaced Hinges, 17" x 48" W/15" Leaves, 28¼" H. $375.00

STONEWARE JUG, 6 Gal., W/Pouring Spout, Cobalt Slip Bird, Wire Bail W/Wooden Handle, 19" H. $175.00

PATENT MODEL OF WASHING MACHINE, Wooden, Old Blue Paint, Partial Patent Papers W/Detailed Drawing "H. Cook Washing Machine, Pat. Apr. 26, 1870." Part Of Abrasive Surface Of Model Missing, 12¾" W., 8½" D., &½" H. . . . . .
. . . .$35.00

TRAMP ART FOOTED BOX W/Sliding Lid, 6½" x 6¾" x 5½" H. $17.50

TRAMP ART BOX, 5¾" x 6½" x 3¼" H.
. . . .$11.00

GRANITE WARE TEAPOT, Scalloped Rim Missing From One Scallop, 11" H. . . .
. . . .$27.50

REDWARE DIVIDED RECTANGULAR DISH, Yellow Slip Decor., Moravian, 10" x 13" x 2¾" H. $30.00

OVAL OIL PAINTINGS, Pr., Gentleman W/Chin Whiskers, Lady W/Lace Bonnet & Collar, Modern Frames, 30" x 36" . . . .
. . . .$125.00

(A-OH '78)   *Garth's Auctions, Inc.*

SET OF 8 MAHOGANY CHIPPENDALE STYLE CHAIRS, 6 Side & 2 Arm, Hand-carved W/Ball & Claw Feet, Carved Knees, Pierced, Ribbon & Tassel Carved Splat & Crest. Slip Seats Upholstered In Natural Linen, 19th C. $2080.00

GLOBE In Mahogany Floor Stand, Turned & Reeded Legs W/Brass Casters, Globe Marked "Manufactured & Sold By W.& T.M. Barton, 16 Salisbury Square, Fleet St. London", Repairs To Stand, Globe Shows Wear, 24" Diam., 45½" H. . . . .
. . . .$210.00

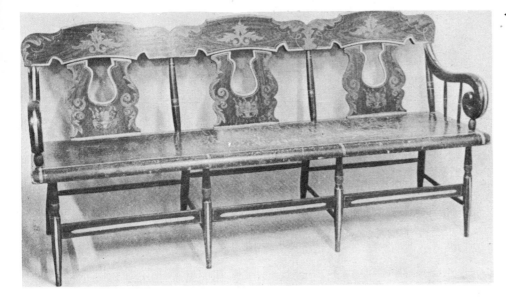

◀To the left

(A-OH '78) . . . .*Garth's Auctions, Inc.*
DECORATED SETTEE BENCH, Turned Legs, Wide Seat, Scrolled Arms, Boot Jack Splats And Shaped Crest, Orig. Brown Graining W/Yellow And Blue Striping, Stenciled Compotes Of Flowers And Fruit On The Splats, And Leafy Angel Wing Type Decor. On Crest In Red, Blue, Tan, and Brown, Seat Has Wear $775.00

(A-OH '77)   *Garth's Auctions, Inc.*
COUNTRY WORK TABLE, Curly Maple Legs, Dovetailed Drawer, Pine Top, Refinished W/Traces Old Red Paint, 24" x 48½", 10" Leaves, 27" H. $235.00
DOME TOP PINE BOX, Dovetailed, Grained W/Drk. Brown Paint, Yellow Ground, Worn Red Border Stripe, Iron Lock & Hasp Missing, Replaced Hinges, 24" W., 13½" D., 10½" H. $50.00
STONEWARE JAR, 2-Gal., Ovoid, Applied Handles, Impressed "S. Purdy, Portage Co.", Blue Splashes, Hairline, 11" H. $95.00
STONEWARE CROCK, 6-Gal., Cobalt Blue Floral Decor., Impressed "Whites Utica N.Y.", 13¼" H. $155.00
STONEWARE JAR, 1½-Gal., Bird In Cobalt Slip, 9½" H. $135.00
WROUGHT IRON TOASTER, 27" L. $75.00
RAILROAD LANTERN, Sheet Iron W/ Built-In Reflector, Chimney Mkd. "Acme Glass", Painted Aluminum, Burner & Font Cap Missing, 20½" H. $17.50
CAST IRON WAFER IRON, Outside W/Bust Of Man W/Goatee; Interior W/ Same Bust W/"Napoleon III, Empereur", 29" L. $100.00

(A-OH '77)   *Garth's Auctions, Inc.*
SIDE CHAIR, Orig. Painted Decor., Cream Ground W/Olive-Colored Graining, Red & Gold Striping, Back Slat W/Tulip Designs & Gold Floral Medallion, Old Rush Seat $15.00
DROP LEAF COUNTRY PEMBROKE TABLE, Pine Top, Ash Apron, Birch Legs, Refinished, 15¾" x 36" x 29½" H.; 10" Leaves $105.00
TOLE COFFEE POT, Yellow Sponged W/ Tan, Gold & Red Stripes, Lid W/Wooden Finial, 11½" H. $22.50
TOLE CONTAINER, Matching Lid, Colors Match Coffee Pot Above, 12" Diam., 10¾" H. $7.50
STONEWARE JAR, 2-Gal., Impressed Label: "S.T. Brewer, Havana", Cobalt Blue Double Flower, Minor Chips, 1" Rim Hairline, 11½" H. $105.00
WOODEN CANDLESTICK, Tin Socket, Refinished, 27½" H. $65.00
STONEWARE JUG, 2-Gal., Ovoid, Cobalt Blue "2" & Brush Work, Base Hairline, 13½" H. $45.00
FEDERAL MAHOGANY MIRROR, 2-Part, Feather Carved Ornament, Mirror & Reverse Painting Of Houses & Trees (Replacements), 10¼" x 23" $65.00

(A-OH '78)   *Garth's Auctions, Inc.*
CURLY MAPLE SABER LEG SIDE CHAIRS, Set of 7, Old Worn Varnish Finish, Some Repairs, ...$385.00
PINE FOOTSTOOL, Orig. Black And Red Graining W/Primitive Gold Stenciling Of Urn And Flowers, W/Yellow Striping, One Leg Old Replacement, 7½" x 11¼" x 6" H. $80.00
MAPLE CANDLESTAND W/Some Curl, Tripod Base W/Cut Out Cabriole Legs, Turned Column And Square One Board Top W/Cut Out Corners, Refinished, One Leg Old Replacement, 18¼" x 18¾" x 26¼" H. $220.00
BRASS OVAL TINDER BOX CANDLESTICK, Polished, 4" H. $170.00
ROCKINGHAM SEATED DOG W/ Free Standing Front Legs, 10" H. .$130.00
BIRTH CERTIFICATE FRAKTUR, Hand Drawn And Colored On Lined Paper W/ Vining Border, Tulips And Other Flowers, Records Birth of Elizabeth Tout, Paradise Township, Lancaster County, Pa., In 1854, Blue, Yellow, Green, Brown And Red, Framed, 11½" x 13½" $270.00
BIRTH CERTIFICATE FRAKTUR By Martin Brechall. Hand Drawn And Colored Stylized Floral Decoration In Typical Red, Yellow And Blue Watercolor. Records Birth In 1792 In Northampton Co. Pennsylvania, Old Walnut Frame, 18½" x 21¾" $1050.00

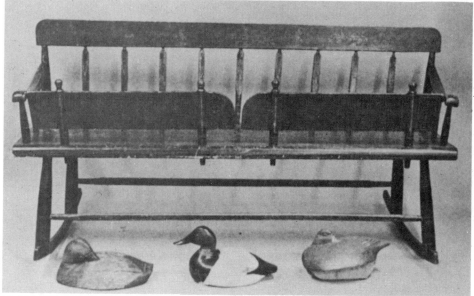

(A-OH '78)   *Garth Auctions, Inc.*

MINIATURE POPLAR CHEST, 6-Board, Till, Orig. Yellow Paint W/Red Brush Work, Hinges Reset, 28" W., 13" D., 15" H. . . . .
. . . .$220.00
CARVED WOODEN SWAN DECOY, Old White Paint, 34½" L., 18" H. $295.00
SHAKER DRYING RACK, Pine, Mortised & Pegged Const., 66" W., 48" H. . . . .
. . . .$50.00
WOODEN POSTS, Pr., White & Black Stripes W/Yellow, One Split, 69½" H. . . . .
. . . .$95.00

(A-OH '78)   *Garth's Auctions, Inc.*

DECOY, Sleeping Canvas Back Hen, Several Splits In Block & Working Repaint, 13" L. $45.00
DECOY, Canvas Back Drake, Old Paint In Good Condition, Tack Eyes, Wisconsin, 14" L. $47.50

DECOY, Sleeping Bluebill Hen, Glass Eyes, Michigan, 12½" L. $40.00
ARROW BACK MAMMIES BENCH, Unusual Double Baby Guards Are Removable, Original Black & Red Graining W/Yellow Striping, Gold Floral Stenciling Is Worn, 61¼" L. $495.00

◀ *To the left*

(A-OH '78) . . . .*Garth's Auctions, Inc.*

BOW-BACK WINDSOR ARM CHAIR, Old Repairs And Replacements Including One Arm And One Arm Support, Old Worn Brown Finish, Seat Is 17" H. $200.00
WROUGHT IRON ROTARY BROILER, Handle With Twisted Eye Hanger, 12" Diam., 22½" L. $95.00
CURLY MAPLE STAND, Well Turned Legs, One Dovetailed Drawer, Refinished To A Light Color, 21" Sq., 29" H.$310.00
WALNUT BOX W/Decor. Curly Maple And Mahogany Veneer, Inlaid Initials On Lid "A.L.S.", Interior Has Pull Out Tray And Lid Has Originally Held A Mirror. 11¼" W., 7¾" D., 6½" H. $67.00
REDWARE PLATE, 3 Line Yellow Slip Decoration And Coggled Edge, Old Hair-Line, 8½" Diam. $162.00
REDWARE FLOWER POT W/Brown Running Splotches, Saucer Not Original, 5¼" Diam., 5¾" H. $65.00
FOUR BIRD PRINTS (1 Illus.) By Audubon, Published By "J.T. Bowen, Phila." 3 Are Various Varieties Of Sandpipers, One Is A Plover, Unframed, 6½" x 10½" $110.00
WROUGHT IRON PEEL W/Rams Horn Handle, Corners Of Blade Are Damaged, 48½" L. $80.00

To the right ▶

(A-OH '78)   *Garth's Auctions, Inc.*
EARLY PINE HANGING SHELVES,
Scalloped Ends W/Continuous Molding,
Molded Cornice, Orig. Rosehead Nails Still
In Place, Ends Of Cornice Missing, Damage
To Some Molding, Old Red Stain, 62" W.,
5½" D., 50½" H. $295.00
(ROW I, L to R)
DECOY, Shoveler Drake, Glass Eyes And
Carved Details, Orig. Paint Has Minor Wear,
13½" L. $47.50
DECOY, Wisconsin Coot, Hollow And W/
Glass Eyes, Unused Condition, 11" L. . . . .
. . . .$27.50
DECOY, Blue Wing Teal Drake, Wisconsin,
Glass Eyes And Redwood Body W/Carved
Detail, Orig. Paint, 11" L. $40.00
DECOY, Mate To Above, 11½" L. . . . . .
. . . .$42.50
DECOY, Bluebill, Branded "C.K." For C.
Kluka, Carved Detail And Glass Eyes, Orig.
Paint W/Shot Scars, 12½" L. $37.50
(ROW II, L to R)
DECOY, Black Duck, Michigan, Hollow W/
Painted Eyes, Wear On Head Shows Differ-
ent Paint Beneath, 16" L. $22.50
DECOY, Green Wing Teal Drake, Wis-
consin, Glass Eyes And Orig. Paint, 10¾" L.
. . . .$25.00
DECOY, Ringneck Drake, Wisconsin, Glass
Eyes And Orig. Paint, 10¾" L. $32.50
DECOY, Bluebill, Tack Eyes And Worn
Working Repaint W/Repair At Neck, 13" L.
. . . .$22.50
DECOY, Coot By J. L. Smith, Balsa Body,
Glass Eyes And Minor Wear, 13¼" L. . . . .
. . . .$22.50

(ROW III, L to R)
DECOY, Blue Wing Teal Hen, Made By
Capt. Harry Jobes, Unused Gunning Decoy,
Glass Eyes, ½" L. $60.00
DECOY, Mate To Above, 13¼" L. . . . . .
. . . .$66.00
DECOY, Ringneck Drake By Gary Hall,
Unused Gunning Decoy, Glass Eyes, 15" L.
. . . .$40.00
DECOY, Goldeneye Drake By Dr. Miles
Pirnie, Branded "D.W.H.", Old Working
Repaint And Glass Eyes, 14½" L. .$35.00

(A-OH '78) . . . .*Garth's Auctions, Inc.*

———————————————

(A-OH '78) . . . .*Garth's Auctions, Inc.*

◀ *To the left*

DECOY, Bluebill by M. Smith, Unused
Condition, Glass Eyes, 14" L. $50.00
FOOT STOOL, Legs Mortised Through
Top, Old Mustard Paint Over Red, 8¼" x
20¼", 9" H. $37.50
DECOY, Canvas Back By Butch Schram,
Hollow And Glass Eyes, Old Paint, 18½" L.
. . . .$30.00
DECOY, Whistler By C. Kluka, Carved
Details, Glass Eyes, Bullet Scars, Branded
"C.K.", 14½" L. $52.50
CANNON BALL BED W/Bold Turnings,
Orig. Black And Red Graining W/Gold Sten-
ciled Fruit, Orig. Rope Rails, Exterior Mea-
surements, 51" x 80", 45" H. $350.00

◀ *To the left*

CORK DECOY, Black Duck With Tack
Eyes, Old Paint In Good Condition, 14½" L.
. . . .$17.50
DECOY, Seagull With Carved Tail, Glass
Eyes, Unused Condition, Signed In Pencil
"C. Pete Wilbur, Island Hts. N.J.", Also
Branded, "C.W.", 17¾" L. $65.00
DECOY, Blue Bill Drake, Hollow, With
Glass Eyes, Original Paint In Good Condi-
tion, Michigan, 15" L. $50.00
LOOP BACK WINDSOR SIDE CHAIR,
Bulbous Turnings In Base, Shaped Seat,
7 Spindle Back, Old But Not Original Red
Alligatored Paint With Yellow Striping, Old
Repair To Bow, Repaired Split In Seat, Seat
Height 16¼" $150.00
**PINE PIE SAFE ON HIGH SQUARE
LEGS,** Tin Panels Have Punched Decor-
ation, Stars And Leaves, End Panels Have
Gothic Arched Windows, Panels Are Rusted,
One End Panel Is Damaged From Rust,
Stripped Of Finish, 38¾" W., 17¼" D.,
44¾" H. $90.00
**STAVE CONSTRUCTED ALL WOOD-
EN SUGAR BUCKET** W/Lid And Handle,
Old Worn Green Paint, Rim Of Lid Has
Some Damage, 16" D., 14½" H. . . . . . .
. . . .$80.00
DECOY, Canvas Back Hen, Glass Eyes,
Worn Old Paint, Michigan, Head Has Age
Cracks, 15½" L. $25.00
DECOY, Glass Eyes (One Missing), Old
Paint, Split In Block, 16¼" L. $67.50
DECOY, Same As Above Including Con-
dition, 16¼" L. $67.50
TIN AND BRASS CANDLE LANTERN,
Spring Loaded Candle Holder Has Brass
Rim Stamped "Excelsior Pat. July 4, 1876",
10¾" H. $72.50

(A-OH '78)   *Garth's Auctions, Inc.*

QUEEN ANNE MAPLE HIGHBOY
W/Curly Maple Facade, Cabriole Legs
With Slipper Feet, Well Scalloped Skirt
And Overlapping Drawers With Wide Early
Dovetailing, Refinished And With Original
Brasses, (Several Pins Are Replaced), 2 Back
Boards Are Old Replacements, Rhode Is-
land, 39" W., 19½" D. At Cornice, 74¾" H.
...........................$9,500.00

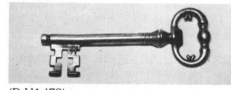

(D-VA '78)
BRASS CORK SCREW In Form Of Key,
6" L. $45.00

(A-OH '77)   *Garth's Auctions, Inc.*

PINE HUTCH TABLE, Compartment
W/Hinged Lid, 3-Board Top, Yellow Enamel
Paint, Top Covered W/Sheet Metal,
Turned Walnut Pins, 40" x 58" x 29" H. . .
...........................$350.00

(A-OH '78)   *Garth's Auctions, Inc.*

SHAKER LADDER BACK ROCKER,
#2, Orig. Finish And Label "Shaker's Trade
Mark, Mt. Lebanon, N.Y." Rush Seat, Re-
pair To One Back Leg Where Rocker Joins
...........................$310.00
STONEWARE JUG, 2 Gal., "2" and
Brush Splashes Of Cobalt Blue, 13¾" H. .
...........................$25.00
CHERRY STAND, Turned Legs And 2
Unusually Deep Dovetailed Drawers, Re-
finished, 19¾" x 20", 28½" H. . .$250.00
THREAD CADDY W/2 Tiers For Thread,
Turned Column And Pin Cushion Top, 8"
H. $67.50
**WALNUT DOVETAILED TWO SEC-
TION BOX,** Sliding Lid Has Primitive Chip
Carved Decoration, End Moulding Missing
From Top, 6⅝" x 5¼" x 13¼" . . .$57.50
"N. CURRIER" PRINT, "The Betrothed",
Top Margin Trimmed, Old Cherry Frame,
12¾' x 16¾" $40.00

◄ *To the left*   (continued)

CAMPAIGN TORCH, Tin W/Brass Burner
& Wooden Handle, 55" H. $80.00
PINE AND MAPLE SUGAR MOLD, 81
Scalloped Cut-Outs, 12"x39" $205.00
BENTWOOD STORAGE BOXES, (9),
Finger Constr. W/Iron & Copper Nails, No
Finish, Largest: 11" L., 4½" H. . .$430.00
SCOOP, Carved From 1 Piece Wood,
13½" L. $100.00
PINE SCOURING BOX, Hinged Com-
partment W/Abrasive Brick W/Orig. Paper
Wrapper, "Bath Brick", 9" W., 3¼" D.,
15" H. $50.00
WROUGHT IRON TASTER, Wooden
Hand Hold, 22½" L. $65.00
WROUGHT IRON TASTER, Cast Han-
dle, Mkd. "Horse Shoe Snuff" $17.50
WROUGHT IRON SCOOP, 11½" L. . . .
...........................$45.00
ASH FLAX WHEEL, No Belts, 29" H. . .
...........................$80.00

(A-OH '78)   *Garth's Auctions, Inc.*

**MAPLE COUNTRY CHIPPENDALE
DROP LEAF SWING LEG TABLE,** End
Aprons Are Curly, Top Has A Bit Of Curl,
Refinished, 13" x 42½" with 4" Leaves,
28½" H. $725.00

STONEWARE JUG W/Leaf Handle Supports, Wire Handle, And Amber Glaze,
Base Chips, 9½" H. $57.50

STONEWARE JAR, Three Gal., Brush
Floral Decor. In Cobalt Blue. 12" H. .....
...........................$90.00

REDWARE JAR, W/Interior Glaze, Impressed "Upton M. Bell, Waynesboro, Pa.",
Small Rim Flake, 8¼" H. $75.00

TOLE TEAPOT, Dark Brown Japanning
And Bright Polychromed Decor. In Yellow,
Red And Orange, Decoration On Back Side
Has Old Blistering, 9" H. $510.00

TOLE DEED BOX, Brown Japanning W/
Yellow, Red, Green & White Floral Decor.,
9" x 5¼" x 4¼" $425.00

PUNCHED TIN TEAPOT, Decor. On Both
Sides Of Pot Consisting Of Pot Of Stylized
Flowers With Date "1850" In Pot. Also
Punched Is Inscription "Manufactured By D.
Gilbert, Pottstown, (Pa.)" 10½" H........
...........................$2900.00

PIN PRICK FRAKTUR, Crown And Circle
With Star Flowers And Tulips In Red, Green,
Yellow And Black, Dated "1839", Framed,
9½" x 10¾" $575.00

FRAKTUR CERTIFICATE, Hand Drawn
And Colored Design, Boldly Drawn Tulips,
Other Flowers W/Urns On Pedestals, Wreath
And Bow, Etc., Good Bright Color, Red,
Blue, Green, Yellow And Black, Records
The Birth Of Lea Herold In 1824 In West-
moreland County, Pennsylvania, Framed,
15" x 18" $2350.00

HANDCOLORED CHILDREN'S PRINT,
"Girl And Cat", Modern Painted Frame,
6½" x 8¼" $65.00

(A-OH '77)   *Garth's Auctions, Inc.*

ARM CHAIR POTTY, Black & Red Graining W/White & Yellow Striping $35.00

CHERRY BEDSIDE STAND, 19½" x 20" x 29" H. $155.00

WOODEN DUCK DECOY, Inset Head, White & Black Paint, 12" L. $32.50

TOLE DEED BOX, Brown Japanning W/ Yellow, Red & White Floral Decor., Hasp Missing, 9" x 5½" x 4" $15.00

TOLE CANISTER, Black Ground W/Red & Yellow Decor., 8" H. $42.00

ARCHITECTURAL MIRROR, 2-Part, Reverse Gold Leaf Painting, 10" x 22" ...$30.00

(A-OH '77)   *Garth's Auctions, Inc.*

HORSE PULL TOY, Wooden Frame W/ Upholstered Body, Minor Wear, 25" H. $155.00

PINE CHEST OF DRAWERS, Dovetailed Feet & Cockbeaded Drawers, Reddish-Brown Graining, Late 19th C., 49¾" W., 21¼" D., 40½" H. $400.00

BRASS VICTORIAN CANDLESTICKS, Pr., Pushups, 11¾" H. $65.00

SILVER CANDLESTICKS, London Hallmarks, C. 1897, "H.W.", Wooden Inset Base Replaced On One..........$40.00

DOME TOP TEA CHEST, Mahogany on Pine, Minor Damage To Cross Banded Inlay, 3 Interior Compartments Lined W/ Metal Foil, Lid Interior Has Marbelized Paper, 15" W., 10" D., 10" H. $60.00

(A-OH '77)   *Garth's Auctions, Inc.*

(ROW I, L to R)

TIN COOKIE CUTTER, Man, 6" H..$5.00

MINIATURE CUP SAUCER, Blue Spatter Ware, Peafowl In Red, Yellow, Green & Black, Cup Cracked.............$77.50

CAST IRON MATCH BOX, Base W/ "E.G. Zimmermann, Verlag Bei, In Hanau", 3¾" H. $22.50

(continued top of next column)

(A-OH '77)   *Garth's Auctions, Inc.*

CURLY MAPLE EMPIRE CHEST OF DRAWERS, Dovetailed Cockbeaded Drawers, Figured Wood W/Birdseye & Curl, Refinished, 43½" W., 20½" D., 45½" H. $475.00

PINK LUSTRE BOWL, Black Transfer Scenes Of Ships & Sailors, Rim Hairline, Table Ring Chips & Rim Chips, 11¼" Diam., 4" H. $75.00

CAST IRON PULL TOY, Elephant W/ Bells, Worn Red Paint, 7¼" L. ...$55.00

GAUDY STICK SPATTER CHARGER, "Villeroy & Boch", 13" Diam.....$25.00

SAMPLER ON HOMESPUN, Alphabets W/Stripes & Stitches, Trees, Birds & Dogs; Green, Tan, White & Black, Framed, 13" x 21" $155.00

◄ *To the left* (continued)

(ROW II)

OPALESCENT MINIATURE CANDLESTICKS, Pr., 3½" H. $15.00

BENTWOOD STORAGE BOX, Red Sides W/White, Blue & Yellow Decor., Painted Family Scene On Top, 6" L. $27.50

(ROW III, L to R)

SOFT PASTE CUP PLATE, Yellow, Red, Green & Purple Lustre, 4½" Diam. ...$32.50

PURPLE LUSTRE CUP PLATE, Green, Red & Blue Enameling $35.00

STAFFORDSHIRE CUP PLATE, Black Transfer Of Man & Elk, Impressed 'Adams", 4" Diam. $7.50

STAFFORDSHIRE CUP PLATE, Purple Transfer Of "Canton Garden", 4" Diam. ...$5.00

(ROW IV, L to R)

MINIATURE STONEWARE JAR, Brown Glaze, 3" H. $10.00

TIN COOKIE CUTTER, Man, 3¼" H. ...$5.00

FOLK ART CARVED DOG (or fix), Red Paint, Limb Base, Damaged Tail, 4" L. ...$7.50

TIN BUCKET, "Napheys Leaf Lard, Philadelphia — 1776-1876", 2½" H. ...$17.50

MINIATURE STONEWARE JUG, Brown & White, 4¼" H. $7.50

(A-OH '77)   *Garth's Auctions, Inc.*

STUFFED DUCK, From Pieced Quilt, "P.B.", 11½" L. $3.00

STUFFED CAT, From Pieced Quilt, "P.B.", 15" H. $7.00

PINE & POPLAR BLANKET CHEST, Dovetailed, Blue Paint W/Yellow Striping & "J.B.V.Z.", Dated "1828, T. Spaun Bethlehem", 41" W., 16½" D., 21½" H. $310.00

LADDER BACK SIDE CHAIR, Rush Seat, Black Paint W/Yellow Striping, Restored Feet $30.00

ENGRAVED HORN, "T.H." W/Mermaids, Fish, Ships, Man In Rocker, Flags & Lady, 14" L. $125.00

WOOD & SHEET METAL MODEL, Tall Masted Ship, White & Red Paint, 55" L., 44" H. $100.00

PRINTED TEXTILE, Mythological Scene, Framed, 11" x 12¾" $10.00

(D-NY '78)   *Lee Vines Antiques*
BRONZE HEAD OF GIRL, "Harriet Freshmith", 5" H. $2000.00

(D-NY '78)   *Lee Vines Antiques*
BRONZE & IVORY FIGURE, Marble Base, Signed "Heber", 6" H. $750.00

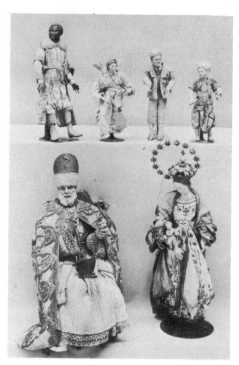

(A-MA '77)   *Richard A. Bourne Co., Inc.*
CRECHE FIGURES
(ROW I, L to R)
TERRA COTTA FIGURE, Moor, Inset Glass Eyes, Stuffed Fiber Body, Terra Cotta Legs & Arms, Elaborate Costume Worn, Paint Flaking On Head, 3 Fingers Chipped, 13" H. $400.00
ANGEL FIGURE, Carved Wood W/Inset Eyes, Paint Flaking, Costume Worn, 10" O.H. $250.00
TERRA COTTA FIGURE, Blind Italian Man, Blue Jacket Over Linen Trousers, Carved Wood Body, Thumb Missing, 10¼" H. $50.00
TERRA COTTA FIGURE, Boy, Inset Eyes, Terra Cotta Arms & Legs, Carved Wooden Body, North African Costume, 2 Fingers Missing, 9" H. $250.00
(ROW II, L to R)
TERRA COTTA FIGURE, Priest In Orig. Costume, Carries Simulated Leather-Bound Book, 19" H. $150.00
TERRA COTTA FIGURE, Madonna W/ Baby, Metal Crown W/Halo, Costume Worn, Minor Cracks On Baby, 20½" O.H. . . . . . .
. . . .$350.00

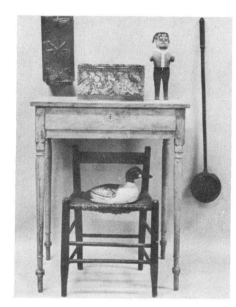

(A-OH '77)   *Garth's Auctions, Inc.*
PINE CLERK'S TABLE, Worn, Pale Cream Colored Paint, 20" x 28" x 34½" H.
. . . .$115.00
LADDER BACK SHAKER CHAIR, Old Drk. Paint, Rush Seat $280.00
PRIMITIVE WOODEN DECOY, White & Black Repaint, 14" L. $37.50
WALNUT COLLECTION BOX, Long Turned Handle, 7" Diam., 40" L. . .$67.50
WOODEN BOX, Covered W/Wallpaper, Floral Pattern, 12½" x 7" x 7½" . .$20.00
PAINTED WOODEN MAN, Horse Hair Coiffure, 20th C. Folk Art, 13" H. .$62.50
BLOCK TIN SCONCE, Tooled Star & Fans, 14" H. $135.00

(D-NY '78)   *Lee Vines Antiques*
FRENCH SILK FAN, Amber Colored Pierced & Gold Decor. Spokes, Sequen Outlined Scenes, Urns, Garlands, Etc., Signed "Van Santen", 7" W., Opens to 12¾" $85.00

(D-NY '78)   *Lee Vines Antiques*
BRONZE FIGURE, Football Player, By "J.S. Hartley, N.Y. 1898", 16" H. . . . .
. . . .$2000.00

(A-MA '77) *Richard A. Bourne Co., Inc.*
COPPER HORSE WEATHERVANE,
67¾" L. Arrow, 33½" O.H., Horse: 27" H.,
Approx. 34" L. $1600.00

(A-MA '77) *Richard A. Bourne Co., Inc.*
COPPER WEATHERVANE, 71½" L.
Arrow, Approx. 43½" H. $1500.00

(A-MA '77) *Richard A. Bourne Co., Inc.*
COPPER COW WEATHERVANE, Minor
Denting & Repairs, 68¾" L. Arrow, 28" H.,
Cow: 18" H., 32" L. $1250.00

(A-MA '77) *Richard A. Bourne Co., Inc.*
COPPER WEATHERVANE, Minor Bullet
Hole Repairs, 78¾" Arrow, Lead Horse
31" From Forefoot To Tip Of Tail, 24" O.H.
. . . .$3100.00

(A-OH '77) *Garth's Auctions, Inc.*
COPPER GOOSE WEATHERVANE,
W/Traces Of Gold Leaf, Cast Iron Directionals, 43" W., 81" O.H. $1550.00

(A-MA '77) *Richard A. Bourne Co., Inc.*
COPPER OSTRICH WEATHERVANE,
70" L. Arrow; 46" O.H. $1900.00

(D-NY '78) *Lee Vines Antiques*
BRONZE SCULPTURE, "The Fight", By
E. Deming, Mountain Lion Attacking Bear,
9½" H. $1500.00

(A-OH '77) *Garth's Auctions, Inc.*
EAGLE WEATHERVANE, Copper W/
Patina & Traces Of Yellow Ground Under
Gold Leaf, Sheet Metal Dial Faces, Wooden
Box, Eagle W/15" Wingspan, 40" O.H. . . .
. . . .$800.00

(D-NY '78) *Lee Vines Antiques*
TIFFANY BRONZE BULLDOG, Signed,
Tiffany Studios, N.Y., 2¼" L. $250.00

(D-NY '78) *Lee Vines Antiques*
BRONZE FIGURE, Self Caricature, Signed
In Script "Enrico Caruso 1909", Printed
Roman Bronze Works, N.Y., 6" H. . . . . . .
. . . .$1500.00